THE
COLUMBIA
HISTORY
OF
BRITISH
POETRY

THE
COLUMBIA
HISTORY
OF
BRITISH
POETRY

CARL WOODRING
EDITOR

JAMES SHAPIRO
ASSOCIATE EDITOR

Columbia University Press
New York

Columbia University Press
New York   Chichester, West Sussex
Copyright © 1994 Columbia University Press
All rights reserved

Library of Congress Cataloging-in-Publication Data

The Columbia history of British poetry / Carl Woodring, editor ;
associate editor, James Shapiro.
p. cm.
Includes bibliographical references (p.) and index.
ISBN 0-231-07838-2
1. English poetry—History and criticism.   I. Woodring, Carl,
1919– . II. Shapiro, James S., 1955— .
PR502.C62   1993 994
821.009—dc20   93-18226
                                                CIP

Printed in the United States of America

c 10 9 8 7 6 5 4 3 2 1

Contents

Introduction

Literature in the shapeless galaxy of Indo-European languages has no brighter constellation than that of British poetry. Its stars have over time been made of differing and changing stuff—fireflies, bonfires, and blazing suns. In the many years that have passed since a similar history has been attempted, critical views about this poetic heritage have changed significantly. One signal of these changes is to be found in the present volume's title, which describes a history of British, rather than English, poetry. Increasingly, scholars have come to appreciate the plurality of national voices that constitutes the poetry of the British Isles. The Columbia History of British Poetry is a testament to the power of the poetry written in England, Scotland, Wales, and Ireland, as well as to the recurrent impulse to retrace its history.

Within the collective history offered in the pages that follow are many overlapping, competing histories. The scholarly work of the last twenty years or so has exposed a disturbingly monolithic conception of the canon of English poets, replacing it with a less simple but far richer picture of the accomplishments of British poets over the course of twelve centuries. In the current volume, considerable effort has gone into making available voices long suppressed—from anonymous balladeers to women poets whose contributions have for too long been overlooked—while at the same time resituating some of the most celebrated poets within more sharply defined social and literary contexts, allowing us to measure their cultural and artistic contributions in a new light. One result is a livelier sense of the dialogue between poets within specific cultural moments as well as across the centuries, for the story of British poetry is one of conversations between poets, both the living and the dead.

In rethinking the boundaries of British poetry, the authors of the twenty-six chapters that follow have used a wide range of critical approaches. Some, like Elizabeth S. Donno in "Varieties of Sixteenth-Century Narrative" and Cary H. Plotkin in "Victorian Religious Poetry" have approached their subject in terms of genre or kind. Others, like George D. Economou in "Chaucer," have focused on single poets. For Carole Silver, in her chapter, "Pre-Raphaelite" poetry, a literary movement provides the organizing principle. For David Daiches, in his chapter, "Poetry in Scots," it is a national literature that proves central; for Edna Longley, it is that poets of Scotland, Wales, and Ireland celebrate powers inherited from Britons, rather than from Angles, Saxons, or Jutes. Many of the authors describe groupings of poets: Richard Feingold offers a venerable pairing in "Dryden and Pope," while Jerome H. Buckley, crossing the divide that usually isolates the Romantics from the Victorians, considers Wordsworth and Tennyson in tandem. And while some scholars have accepted more traditional chronological periods, they have chosen to do so in markedly untraditional ways; perhaps the most striking example of this is Margaret Anne Doody's revisionist "Poetry of the Eighteenth Century." The kind of critical dialogue to be found both within and between these chapters is made most explicit in Jerome McGann's chapter, "Poetry, 1785–1832," which consists of a conversation among three speakers. And the story of the material history of published poetry—wonderfully illuminated by David McKitterick in his chapter, "Printing and Distribution of Poetry"—is representative of the sustained interest throughout this volume in how poetry has circulated, and continues to circulate, among its readers. What Milton said of the fallen angels holds true of the contributors to this volume: "Thir Song was partial." Partial because any scholar's account of British poetry is necessarily biased, idiosyncratic, and characterized by theoretical independence; partial, too, in the sense that such narratives must be incomplete, fragmentary, and subject to change, even as conceptions of the traditions explored in this volume change in response to cultural and critical pressures.

One thing all these authors share is a deep sense of the social rootedness of poetry, of the reciprocal relationship between British poetry and British culture: they remind us that poetry is a social record of the kinds of events ordinarily excluded from the histories written of various nations and peoples. When we read Katherine Philips's "On the death of my first and dearest childe," William Wordsworth's sonnet on how "getting and spending" we "lay waste our powers," or Philip Larkin's lyrics on the banalities of contemporary life, we come into contact with the struggles that fill the lives the poets led, and the lives we now lead. Poems like these offer at least a glimpse of how to come to terms with the stuff of our lives, moments of suffering, of clarity, of hopelessness, of promise. This poetry bridges the centuries, and bridges the differences—racial, national, religious, sexual, economic—that potentially divide those of us who share a language.

We imagine many kinds of readers of this book. Students of British poetry, undergraduate and graduate, will find here a useful overview. Specialists in periods or poets will encounter new perspectives and new voices. But the book has also been designed for what both Samuel Johnson and Virginia Woolf have called "the common reader." For some readers, this volume may renew acquaintance with poets long forgotten; for others, it may offer an introduction to poems never before encountered. Brief biographies, suggestions for further readings, and a list of standard editions of the poets' works should make it easier for readers to investigate specific poets or poems independently. Above all, we hope that this volume offers a clearer sense of where British poetry has come from, and where it may be going.

Carl Woodring
James Shapiro

THE
COLUMBIA
HISTORY
OF
BRITISH
POETRY

Old English Poetry

THE OLD ENGLISH poems that have come down to us were composed over the course of four centuries (roughly 680–1100)—a span almost as long as that of the Roman Empire and about half that of all the succeeding periods of English poetry combined. Duration is distinction of a sort. So are great age and size. No current European literature can point to an extensive body of verse nearly so old. Some thirty thousand lines of Old English poetry have been preserved, occupying many hundreds of pages in the standard edition.

Anglo-Saxon vernacular culture was notably sophisticated, aristocratic, and mature. Gerard Manley Hopkins wrote to his fellow poet Robert Bridges: "I am learning Anglo-Saxon and it is a vastly superior thing to what we have now." (By recent convention, the term *Old English* is used for the language and vernacular texts of pre-Conquest England, *Anglo-Saxon*, for the people and culture.) W. H. Auden reported being "spellbound" by his first experience of Old English: "This poetry, I knew, was going to be my dish."

Scholarly tradition wants us to speak well of the works we study. There would be little point in talking about something that was not beautiful and truthful, not "interesting." Old English poetry has interest—almost too much interest—but its beauty is not in the usual places.

The verse is not in the usual places either. Thomas Warton's *History of English Poetry* (1774–1781)—the foundation of modern English literary history—begins at the close of the eleventh century, deliberately and self-consciously excluding Old English poetry: this verse, Warton argued, was different in kind from what followed. It did not provide a suitable infancy for the "rags to riches" story of English poetry that he was plotting.

Somehow people who study Old English poetry are still not deemed to be at the coal face, where the action is. E. D. Hirsch's list of "what literate Americans know" cites no Old English poem or poet, and never mentions the period (unless "Dark Ages" counts). Missing are *Beowulf, The Battle of Maldon*, Bede, Alfred, and the terms *Old English* and *Anglo-Saxon* (the list does include 1066, Norman Conquest, Battle of Hastings, King Arthur, and William the Conqueror).

Old English poetry, composed in a dead language and long unknown, unread, and untaught, exerted no influence on most of the names in the present volume. Nor does it obviously intrude on the concerns of the present. Tell a modern cultural historian that Old English poetry has something to say about alienation, and you get a shrug diluted by apathy.

For literary historians, the verse is an embarrassment, an enfant terrible resisting all attempts at interrogation. Not entirely oral in style, not entirely fixed in text, it remained strangely homogeneous and anonymous for at least twelve generations. To our ordinary modern questions about chronology, authorial styles, literary indebtedness, schools, genres, patronage, performance, transmission, theme and structure, even beginnings and ends, compositions of this sort give no intelligible or adequate answer. There is no agreement on the dates, absolute or relative, of the longer poems. Nor can we assume that the extant corpus of Old English poetry is representative of what once existed (just as we can never know the percentage of undiscovered murders). Confident statements about the "scop" or Anglo-Saxon oral poet are everywhere, enriching our lectures and enlivening our books: "[these] singers were honored and skilled performers for aristocratic patrons"; "the king's scop sat at the feet of the king"; "with a repertoire part memorized and part improvised, [the scop] accompanied his verses on the harp". But such descriptions are no more than hopeful speculations hallowed by repetition. King Alfred is the only known Anglo-Saxon to whom a quantity of Old English poetry is attributed.

No vernacular verse survives from the first Anglo-Saxon centuries, during which Roman Britannia was settled by Germanic speakers from the North Sea and Baltic littorals. Christianity and literacy reached the island in 597; the oldest Old English poetry extant, some thirty lines of manuscript verse, is roughly of the age of Bede (672/3–735); seventeen lines occur in two runic inscriptions, probably of the eighth century. Between 800 and 1066 Anglo-Saxon England experienced Viking raids and settlements, the reigns of Alfred (871–899) and his descendants down to Ethelred (978–1016), then renewed Viking attacks, a Danish king on the English throne (1016–1042), and finally the Norman Conquest (1066). Datable verse from this period includes eight poems commemorating historical events of the tenth and eleventh centuries; the latest, *Durham*, a twenty-one-line eulogy of that city and its saints, was composed around 1104.

With the exception of ten short inscriptions on stone, whalebone, gold, and silver, Old English poetry has come down to us in manuscripts, about one hundred of them. The verse is set out continuously, like prose, with only occasional metrical or syntactical punctuation. In about half these manuscripts the only vernacular poetry is either *Bede's Death Song* (five lines in thirty-five manuscripts) or *Cædmon's Hymn* (nine lines in twenty-one manuscripts), inserted in two Latin works respectively about or by Bede. People were not necessarily thirty-five times fonder of Bede's poem than of *Beowulf*, which like most Old English verse survives in a single manuscript; but little has come down to us from Anglo-Saxon England that was not copied by clerical scribes or saved in a church library, where the celebrated monk of Wearmouth-Jarrow had an edge over the monster slayer.

The earliest evidence for the existence of books of vernacular poetry is an anecdote told in 893 about the childhood of Alfred (849–899) at the royal court: his mother promised a "book of English poetry" to whichever of her sons learned it quickest (naturally Alfred won). We are subsequently told that Alfred was a great memorizer of "English poems" and that his two children educated at home "learned the Psalms and books in English, and especially English poems." Two extant manuscripts containing a quantity of vernacular poetry have Alfredian associations: a Paris codex in a mid-eleventh-century hand preserves the first fifty Psalms rendered into Old English prose by Alfred, and the remaining one hundred in verse; and a codex from the mid-tenth century, now only a collection of charred leaves, included a complete translation of Boethius's *Consolation of Philosophy* into Old English prose and verse, the former certainly by Alfred, the latter probably. It is conceivable that poetry known to Alfred was copied a century and a half later into one or more of the four so-called poetic codices. These were written in the period 975–1050 by a total of eight scribes and contain in all more than twenty thousand lines of Old English verse, the greater (in both senses of the word) part of the corpus.

Each of the four codices is a collection of works of different dates by different authors. In the contextless world of Old English poetry, these manuscripts are our chief evidence for how the poetry was read around the year 1000. The Junius manuscript—elaborately illustrated, imposing, and punctuated as if for recitation—contains scriptural poetry organized into two "books," the first based on Old Testament material, the second and shorter, on New. The Vercelli Book, copied in Canterbury toward the end of the tenth century and probably deposited in northern Italy by the end of the eleventh, preserves six poems interspersed in a collection of homiletic prose; far to the north, in present-day Scotland, a dozen lines from one of its poems, *The Dream of the Rood*, are carved on an eighth-century stone cross. The Exeter Book, a large and strictly poetic anthology, contains about 130 poems, moving from the great events of salvation history to a collection of sometimes obscene riddles. The last and least impressive in appearance of the codices preserves *Beowulf* and *Judith*, along with three prose works showing an interest, it has been argued, in the marvelous; the wonders described range from simple dragons and talking trees to huge, hirsute, polychromatic women fully accessorized with tusks, fangs, tails, and eleven feet apiece. A corpus of poetry "meagre in extent and eccentric in distribution" (this phrase taken from a description of Dark Age burials in England) must by its nature engender hypotheses and guesses rather than certainties.

The characteristic features of Old English poetry are hard to miss. John Milton found the style of *Brunanburh*, in comparison with the surrounding prose of the *Chronicle*, "over-chargd." At the turn of the eighteenth century, George Hickes described the relentless piling up of synonyms in the verse, the accumulation of weighty compounds, the loose appositions. At the turn of the nineteenth century Sharon Turner regretted the repetitiveness of Old English poetry, "the laboured metaphor, the endless periphrasis, the violent inversion, and the abrupt transition," warning readers against "confounding it with those delightful beauties which we now call poetry." At the beginning of this century, critics found it easy to believe that Old English verse was simpler, more innocent, less interesting to pry into than our own. "The audience for which the poet sang was different," wrote one scholar in 1907:

"Would not our estimate be greatly changed if we could bring to these poems, as men did then, the interest and curiosity of children?" "It was a childish country," observes Richard Wilbur in his poem "Beowulf."

Certainly Old English poetry is composed in a highly patterned, formulaic style, studded with vagueness, and working in this manner and medium does eliminate a number of fine possibilities: "a red wheel/barrow/glazed with rain/water" is out. But there are compensations: a single formulaic phrase, unremarkable, demanded by the meter, and exhausted by a chorus of previous poets, sometimes calls up a multitude of disparate and totally unexpected thoughts, the inferred unsaid, which in Old English poetry is often as important as the repeated just said.

Anglo-Saxon vernacular poets had a distinct lexicon at their disposal, a stock of about four hundred poetic words that never or very rarely occurred in prose (or, if they did, had a different meaning). These include many nouns for prince, man, woman, weapons, ships, battle, hall, mind, heart, and the like—commonplace things but expressed in charged language. Although the connotations of words within a single synonym group (e.g., *ruler, distributor, guide, leader, protector*) may have differed, their denotations (prince, lord) are indistinguishable. The compounds so frequent in the poetry work in a similar way: a "mead-hall" quickly metamorphoses into a "wine-hall" or "ale-house"; the queen, like an absentminded hostess, hands out "mead-cups" at the royal "beer-party" without raising eyebrows. Entire systems of interlocked compounds were constructed, all of which could be created and comprehended without reflection; they, like the poetic words, served a practical function, giving poets a wide choice of synonyms to satisfy alliterative requirements. The statistics recently drawn up for one late poem, *The Battle of Maldon*, are typical: out of a total of 535 lexical units (many occurring more than once), there are ninety-seven (18 percent) that never (or almost never, or not with the sense they have in the poem) occur in prose. Of these, forty-one are poetic words, and nine have a meaning they never have in prose. Forty-seven are compounds, of which only three also occur in prose. Of the sixteen compounds that are found only in *Maldon*, some (although we cannot tell which) may have been coined for the occasion.

The language of Old English verse was not particularizing like that of modern poetry, which cheerfully takes as its own the lexicon of finance, botany, or ornithology; nor is there any of that striving for intellectual specificity that we detect in Eliot's "piaculative pence" or Auden's "cerebrotonic Cato." Each Old English poetic word or compound is an archetypal node, an aggregate of meaning, that lumps rather than dissects. Characteristically, the poetry produced works as much by synecdoche as by amplification.

Longfellow was impressed by the lines in *Beowulf* in which a man mourns his son's death on the gallows (one of the few non-French terms to survive in common law). As the father looks upon his child's former dwelling, the sense of loss seems to be expressed on a more than individual scale:

> Gesyhð sorhcearig   on his suna bure,
> winsele westne,   windge reste,
> reote berofene—   ridend swefað ,
> hæleð in hoðman;   nis þær hearpan sweg,
> gomen in geardum,   swylce ðær iu wæron.
> Gewiteð þonne on sealman,   sorhleoð gæleð
> an æfter anum;   þuhte him eall to rum,
> wongas ond wicstede.   (2455–2462)

(He gazes, sorrow-grieving, on his son's chamber, the deserted wine-hall, the resting-place open to the wind, robbed of joy. Riders sleep, men in the grave; there is no music of the harp, joy in the courts, as there once were. He goes then to his couch, sings a sorrow-song, the lonely one for the lone one; it seemed all too spacious to him, the fields and the dwelling-place.)

Even with the verse stripped of its rhythm, the words muted and tired in paraphrase of translation, this is still recognizably poetry, touching the deep wellsprings of grief and loneliness, the temporality and finitude of an indifferent world. The father's (and poet's) eye moves from the corpse, the lifeless "bone-house" riding on the gallows, to a windswept hall, its horsemen vanished—an emptied world and the awful spaciousness of things. The meaning of some words is uncertain (e.g., *hoðman, reote, sealman*); the compression of *an æfter anum* untranslatable: 'the one for the other ' but also 'the lonely one for the only one ' (or vice versa); and the punctuation, modern and interpretive.

The poet's vagueness disturbs us. A recent translation turns "windswept resting-place" into "the draughty fire-place where the wind is chattering," a concrete, homey image that appeals to current taste. But the Anglo-Saxon poet's nonvisual and reticent "windswept resting-place" allowed his audience to recall other windy places: not only the "windswept walls" that form part of the "ruined hall" topos but also the wind-battered sea cliffs, the last defense of the land, and the "windy hall" beneath, in which Satan must endure eternity. The poet's sequence of images conveys with economy how, lacking one, the man bereft lacks the whole world. But why these unidentified "riders," why "harp-music"? The answer is that they, like hawk and mead-cup, are poetic shorthand, calling up a whole complex of ideas associated with the precariousness of earthly joy. Two hundred lines earlier, the *Beowulf* poet described another empty hall in terms of absence: "There is no delight of the harp, joy of the mirth-wood, no good hawk flies through the hall, nor does the swift horse pound the courtyard." The speaker of *The Wanderer* contemplates another ruined "wine-hall," buffeted by winds, and says: "Where has the horse gone? Where has the man gone? Where the treasure-giver? Where have the seats of banquets gone? Where are hall-joys?" The fact that any piece of Old English verse is likely to resemble others means that the individual poem could hold its punches, letting its resonant formulas make the connections. "Riders" and "harp" are loaded words, bearing traditional baggage that a poet had only to unpack, not invent.

A "*morning-cold* spear" in Old English poetry has little to do with degrees centigrade or time of day, and everything to do with misery, loneliness, and dread of attack, the emotional meaning of both terms in the compound. The poets paint vivid pictures of armies and arms on a battlefield where there is neither battle nor field, of violent storms at sea where there is nothing but sand and sunburnt desert. In the poem *Andreas* a tortured St. Andrew spends a night in prison. Outside winter rages:

> Snaw eorðan band
> wintergeworpum;   weder coledon
> heardum hægelscurum;   swylce hrim ond forst,
> hare hildstapan,   hæleða eðel
> lucon, leoda gesetu.   Land wæron freorig
> cealdum cylegicelum,   clang wæteres þrym,
> ofer eastreamas   is brycgade,
> blæce brimrade. Bliðheort wunode . . .
> (1255–1262)

(Snow bound the earth with winter-drifts; the air grew chill with fierce hail-storms; likewise rime and frost, hoary battle-stalkers, locked the homelands of men, the seats of nations. Lands were freezing with cold icicles, the might of the water congealed, ice bridged over the water-streams, the dark wave-road. Joyful in heart dwelt [Andrew] . . .)

There is no hint of this weather in the known Latin and Greek sources or in the Old English prose life of St. Andrew. It is winter in the poem because the saint, alone and locked in "cold fetters" beneath the earth, is enduring a night of "winter-cold" torments. The poet revives (or literalizes) a dead metaphor (snow binding the earth, ice fettering the sea); his "hoary battle-stalkers" (= rime and frost; a nonce compound playing on the formula-type *har hilderinc* 'hoary battle-warrior') with their "storm-hard" weapons imitate the saint's assailants. Even the syntax gets into the act: when rime and frost *lock* the homelands and seats of men, the verb (*lucon*) is placed so that it literally locks the two together; when ice *bridges* the seas, the verb (*brycgade*), in final position yet anticipating the alliteration of the next line, itself acts as a bridge, joining the sea terms on either side, syntax and sound mirroring the sense. In the final line a *blæc* 'dark ' sea alliterates with the strongly contrasting adjective (*blið* —'joyous '), from which it is separated by a full syntactic stop; this juxtaposition of opposites not only underlines the saint's constancy under duress, it also embodies a conviction, expressed throughout Old English poetry, that sudden reversals of fortune characterize life in this world. Formal sophistication and formulaic verse are not mutually exclusive.

The poetry of Anglo-Saxon England, both in Latin and the vernacular, reveals a pervasive fondness for riddles, for making the clear obscure, for elucidating by obfuscation. The much-praised "swan" riddle plays with the notion that the feathers of the swan, silent when the bird walks or swims, make beautiful music when it is in flight:

Hrægl min swigað   þonne ic hrusan trede,
oþþe þa wic buge,   oþþe wado drefe.
· ·
    Frætwe mine
swogað hlude   ond swinsiað ,
torhte singað,   þonne ic getenge ne beom
flode ond foldan,   ferende gæst.

(My garment is silent when I step on the earth, or rest in the dwelling, or ruffle the sea. . . . My trappings resound loudly and make melody, brightly sing, when I am not touching water and land, a traveling spirit.)

The parallel verbs *swigað* and *swogað*, so alike in sound, so contrary in meaning, outline the central paradox of the riddle: the existence of a creature, wrapped round by raiment, that is silent when earthbound and melodious when carried aloft. The poet sets his alliterating syllables free, to follow their nature or to divine some hidden truth, and uncovers a correspondence between name and essence, word and thing, a link more secure than he could have foreseen: a swan (*swan*) is destined to make melody (*swinsiað*), to soar aloft, because, as modern etymological science confirms, the two words are cognate, sharing the same Indo-European root. If the poet knew the traditional Latin etymology deriving *cygnus* 'swan' from *canendo* 'singing,' the more graceful convergence of *swan* and *swinsian* would have seemed to confirm the fitness of his native tongue to discover truths, to be an instrument of prophecy. A swan, the poet seems to be telling us, is most genuinely a swan when it is a "*traveling* spirit." Old English verse was constructed so that the "head-stave"—the alliterating word in the second half-line, here *ferende*—was not only a peak of metrical and rhetorical emphasis in the verse but also a key sense word.

A simple swan riddle introduces us to the visible world of nature, of impersonal order; a more complex riddle, something closer to the emblematic vision or poetic parable, would point to an area of experience not so accessible to the senses. Other Old English verse portrays a soul (*gæst*) slipping out of its fleshly raiment and journeying (*ferende*) to a city of perpetual song; Job, one poet says, composed a "song" depicting Christ as a "bird," whose flight up to heaven and down to earth represents the Ascension and Incarnation. The riddle poet does not explicitly say, with Yeats, "Soul clap its hands and sing"; but his swan, enfolded by formulaic half-lines, seems to be following a pattern long known to the imagination.

Our ignorance is great. A historical tour of Old English poetry is prohibited since no one can tell when, where, by whom, and under what circumstances the key texts were composed. Critics traditionally concentrate on a small group of poems regarded, for no good reason, as the heart of the literary canon: six short (*The Wanderer*, *The Seafarer*, *The Dream of the Rood*, *The Battle of Maldon*, *Cædmon's Hymn*, *Deor*) and one long (*Beowulf*). But Old English poetry, like some architecture, gains from being taken in large doses. This chapter groups the extant verse under three broad headings—mythological, heroic, and wisdom poetry—glancing at the remaining monuments from this vantage and that, rather like a guide in Rome trying, in the time allotted, to make a dead past mean something to the living.

Mythological Poetry

The vision of the world enshrined in the mythological poetry of the Anglo-Saxons is generally dark: stories of deceit, cruelty, captivity, war, disease, corruption; then, suddenly, momentarily, God's hand is revealed and the world is washed in light. The poets used their skill with words to depict this cosmic chiaroscuro, God's mighty acts illuminating human history from Creation to the Last Judgment. Although Adam, Noah, Abraham, and Moses are towering figures, the poets hint that they are still understudies, each performing the part of an unavoidably detained main actor; the climax, God's rescue of Israel (i.e., humankind), is reached with the arrival—in the Gospels—of the hero of the story.

The recorded beginning of Old English mythological poetry, Bede's famous story of Cædmon, the illiterate seventh-century laborer who lived near the monastery at Whitby, is also the only near-contemporary account of an Anglo-Saxon oral poet. Bede tells how Cædmon used to leave the feast when the harp was handed round for each reveler to sing to it in turn. One night, having bolted from the party and gone off to the cowshed, Cædmon received in a dream the gift of poetry. There was, of course, a catch: the award could be used only for devout purposes, for versifying the scriptural narratives read to him by the monks: Genesis, Exodus, and "many other stories of the Holy Scripture."

Cædmon is also an end: we shall never know what songs the feasters sang the night he left the banquet early. Perhaps the mythological poetry we have was composed to satisfy a felt need, an Anglo-Saxon audience's craving for what it once had. The *Beowulf* poet imagines what a pagan Danish minstrel around A.D. 500, singing of the origin of the world, would have sounded like: "He said that the almighty made the earth, the beauty-bright land, with water surrounding; he set, the glorious one, the sun and moon, lamps as light for land-dwellers, and he adorned the surfaces of the earth with branches and leaves; life too he created for each of the kinds that live and roam." Cædmon's nine-line *Hymn*, drawing on the opening of Genesis and envisaging God making heaven as a roof for mankind, then "middle-earth," shows a family resemblance.

More than a third of extant Old English poetry is based on the Bible, and more than three-quarters of this group narrate or meditate upon Old Testament books. The first of the four "poetic codices" to be published—MS Junius XI, named after the Dutch scholar who printed its contents in 1654—is sometimes referred to as the Cædmon manuscript, a title based on the now discredited belief that its verse was the work of Cædmon. The first poem in the codex, *Genesis* (2936 lines), is made up of at least two works, *Genesis A* and, incorporated into it at lines 235–851, *Genesis B*, an Old English rendition of an Old Saxon poem. The poems *Exodus* (590 lines), based on chapters 13–19 of the biblical book, and *Daniel* (764 lines), paraphrasing chapters 1–4 of its scriptural source, follow. Other Old Testament poems are, in the Exeter Book, *Azarias* (191 lines), an expanded and more explicitly Christian version of the songs of Azariah and the three children in *Daniel*; in the *Beowulf* manuscript, *Judith*, a 349-line fragment based on the Vulgate text of the Book of Judith (the equally apocryphal legends judged uncanonical by the Church are treated under "heroic poetry"); in the Vercelli Book, *Homiletic Fragment I* (47 lines), an expansion of part of Psalm 27; and in the Paris Psalter, poetic versions of Psalms 51–151 (5039 lines). Smaller Old Testament pieces include the riddling *Pharaoh* and *Lot's Daughters* in the Exeter Book; a versification of Psalm 50 in Cotton MS Vespasian D.vi (157 lines); and poetical fragments of psalms in MS Junius 121 and in Eadwine's Canterbury Psalter. In addition, allusions to Old Testament story occur in nonscriptural verse such as *Beowulf* and the so-called *Menologium*.

Old English poems on New Testament themes do not paraphrase the Gospels or recount stories such as the coming of the Magi or the marriage at Cana; they meditate instead on the five big "leaps": the Incarnation, Crucifixion, Harrowing of Hell, Ascension, and Last Judgment. This body of verse includes, in MS Junius XI, *Christ and Satan* (729 lines); in the Exeter Book, the three *Christ* poems (1664 lines), covering, respectively, the coming of Christ, his ascension, and judgment; and in the Vercelli Book, *The Dream of the Rood* (156 lines). A number of smaller pieces (e.g., *Lord's Prayer*, *Creed*, *Gloria*) also treat New Testament material.

The degree of dependence upon the scriptural text varies greatly, even within a single poem. *Genesis A*, regarded as a fairly faithful rendering, follows the sequence of the biblical book down to Abraham's attempted sacrifice of Isaac (the proper place to end, as the story was seen to foreshadow God's sacrifice of his only son in the New Testament). Episode by episode, sometimes in poetry of notable grandeur and luminosity, the audience is shown faith rewarded and disobedience punished, the world made and unmade again. Wordplay and other rhetorical devices highlight events of figural importance, especially those involving Noah and Abraham, the two pre-Mosaic beneficiaries of God's covenant with man. The wars of Abraham inspire some fine vernacular battle poetry. When the patriarch, trusting in God, achieves a great victory over the armies of the north, nine words of the Latin Bible ("with retainers he rushed upon the enemy by night and attacked them") are expanded into a full-scale conflict, attended by dark ravens, ring-adorned swords, noise of shields and shafts, and "sharp spears gripping unlovingly under the clothes of men." Old English poetic diction does not seem at home with scriptural sheep and mountains, bread and wine, cities and gardens, bride and bridegroom, cinnamon and honey. At the end of the biblical story of Judith, her rewards are the bedclothes and pots and pans of Holofernes; in the Old English *Judith*, she inherits his sword, armor, and helmet.

Anglo-Saxon "attitudes" are also operative on the losing side. The vengeful fallen angels in *Genesis B* demonstrate loyalty to their leader, defiance of the enemy, love of freedom, and hatred of servitude. Satan, the world's first rebel, is as heroic and unbowed as his counterpart in *Paradise Lost*. Because Milton's work appeared some twelve years after the publication of the Cædmon manuscript by Junius, whom Milton knew, critics still speculate whether he knew the Old English poem.

Exodus lingers in the mind as the alien, the oddly shaped and worded stranger haunting the halls of Old English poetry. Its diction seems more allusive and learned, its syntax more wrenched, its layering of meaning deeper than that in the other scriptural poems. The epic "plot" of *Exodus* is the myth of deliverance itself: the escape from Egypt, the crossing of the Red Sea (with two flashbacks to Noah and Abraham), and the destruction in its waters of the pursuing Egyptians. The final scene depicts the Israelites on the far shore, sharing out the spoils of war—Egyptian necklaces, ancient armor and shields, gold and precious cloth (a scene that serves as a model for the Christian appropriation of pagan literature).

Cycles of pride and downfall inform the narrative of *Daniel*, the last Old Testament poem in MS Junius XI. At the center of the Old English poem are the songs of Azarias and the three children in the fiery furnace; these canticles, asking God for deliverance and, in consonance with all creation, praising him, were used in the liturgy as set hymns of praise, comparable to the Psalms.

The metrical version of Psalms 51–150 in the Paris Psalter, the longest "poem" by far in Old English, is also the least read and admired. Yet the psalter was the biblical book most often copied and memorized in Anglo-Saxon England. The Old English poetic rendition uses heroic diction with noticeable reluctance, thereby distancing itself from the tradition embodied in the Junius XI paraphrases, and it is the only Old English poem provided with a facing Latin version in the same manuscript.

Like most poetry on New Testament themes, the verse collection that goes under the name of *Christ and Satan* follows no particular scriptural text; the gospel story is there, but the poet is forever abandoning narrative for exegesis and exhortation. Images of light and darkness play against each other; the laments of the fallen angels, the Harrowing of Hell, and the Last Judgment are featured; and hearers are urged to shake off the taint of evil and show themselves on the side of their rescuer.

The three Christ poems that open the Exeter Book all have learned sources, which they edit, embroider, and elucidate freely. *Christ I* (lines 1–439), densely metaphorical and allusive, is based on a series of antiphons sung on the days before Christmas. *Christ II* (lines 440–866) follows loosely the last part of an Ascension Day sermon by Gregory the Great. Christ, a triumphant war leader who has harrowed hell, is shown entering into his own city; to celebrate his victory, he distributes rewards to his followers: a catalogue of his "gifts" (the various spiritual and physical endowments of men) is then supplied. The poem concludes with a reference to the coming day of judgment, and the name Cynewulf spelled out in runes (probably the poet, perhaps the last reviser, or even a patron). *Christ III* (lines 867–1699), based on a sermon by Caesarius of Arles, is full of fire, blasts of wind, and startling noise, like the doomsday it portrays. After the sinful are swallowed by hell, the poet turns to the blessed enjoying the perfect weather of paradise, a garden painted by many poets since.

The Dream of the Rood is the earliest extant example in any European vernacular of a dream vision poem. It is also one of the most appreciated, studied, and anthologized of Old English poems, appealing to modern tastes in its emphasis, not on human guilt and pain, but on divine forgiveness and generosity. The poem has no definite source, and its relationship to the inscriptions on the Ruthwell and Brussels cross-es is unclear. It is usually seen as having a four-part structure: a riddle-like vision of a strange object that turns out to be a cross; the object speaks, describing its origin and how Christ willingly and heroically mounted it for the sake of mankind; it exhorts the dreamer to tell oth-ers what he has seen; finally, the dreamer talks about his weariness with the world and his longing for heaven. Experience is organized in terms of polarities, with images of an ideal world opposing those of a repul-sive one: the Cross as golden emblem of salvation, the Cross as bloody instrument of torture.

The extant mythological poems differ from one another in scale, focus, and degree of allusiveness, not in method or end. All the scrip-tural poems are concerned with the battle between good and evil, with the need to be faithful to one's lord; many have a strong figural or typo-logical dimension, revealing a deep familiarity with parts of the Bible beyond the sections narrated; and all hold out to their hearers a promise of release from the desert of daily existence, this dark world of danger and inexplicable events.

Heroic Poetry

Heroic values pervade Old English verse. The ranks of familiar but deeply held ideas are reviewed and marshalled by poet after poet: unfading glory as preferable to life itself; loyalty as the cement holding society together; the importance of courage, strength, honor, generosi-ty, self-control, and firmness of mind; a certain tolerance (from our per-spective) for boasting and bragging, for the brutishness of armed coher-ent packs. The Old English poems in this group resemble one another not only in being speech-filled martial narratives, but in their focus on the words and actions of a hero (or heroine), a human being of pas-sionate, unconquerable will, whose drive for glory on the field of battle raises him (or her) above the ordinary. The alternatives in this poetry are always starkly opposed to one another: the natural, instinctual, agreeable course (pay tribute rather than fight; let sleeping monsters lie; love your wife and forget about vengeance; marry that pagan and avoid martyrdom) brings disgrace; the learned, conditioned, disagreeable course brings praise. The hero exercises his individual free will and chooses the second. (And as Isaac Bashevis Singer said of free will: "We have to believe in it; we have no choice.")

Three of the five Old English poems based on Germanic legend, works rich in action and dialogue, belong here: *Beowulf* (3182 lines), the first great English national epic, which does not mention a single Englishman; *The Finnsburh Fragment* (47 lines), a single (now lost) leaf; and *Waldere* (about 60 lines), two separate leaves. (*Widsith* and *Deor*, lyrical monologues that allude, in a sometimes riddling way, to the world of epic, are treated under "wisdom poetry.") At least two works dealing with contemporary events belong here: *The Battle of Brunanburh* (73 lines), celebrating an English victory of 937; and *The Battle of Maldon* (325 lines), commemorating an English defeat of 991 and called by one of its many admirers "the only purely heroic poem extant in Old English."

The Anglo-Saxons acquired another heroic past in the lives of Christian apostles, martyrs, and saints. Here the vital relationship between loyal follower and gift-giving lord takes on new meaning. Heroic poems based on Christian legend include two in the Vercelli Book: *Andreas* (1772 lines), based on the apocryphal Deeds of St. Andrew and St. Matthew in the land of the cannibals; and *Elene* (1321 lines), signed by Cynewulf and rendering the Latin Deeds of St. Cyriacus; and three in the Exeter Book: *Juliana* (731 lines), also signed by Cynewulf and the only real saint's life of the group; *Guthlac A* (818 lines), a meditation on the life of this Mercian nobleman and native English saint; and *Guthlac B* (561 lines), based on the Latin life by Felix of Crowland (ca. 740) and relating the saint's final illness. The saint, no less than the secular hero, draws attention to a world in which bad fortune is better than good, and life is won by its loss; for the former it is heaven, for the latter, poetry, that makes going down to defeat worthwhile.

Woody Allen's warning to students in *Annie Hall* "not to take courses where they make you read *Beowulf*" is evidence at least that the poem is recognized by popular culture. (The name Gower would not work half so well.) We are, as usual, ignorant of the reception *Beowulf* had among the Anglo-Saxons, its date, its authorship, how widely it was known, or how highly it was regarded. The poem is a blend of folktale fantasy and epic gravity. Twice Beowulf (otherwise unknown) dispatches manlike, man-eating monsters; many years later, he kills a fire-breathing dragon and gets himself killed. The poet draws upon some twenty legends in constructing his northern heroic age; he presents such an internally consistent picture of Scandinavian society around A.D. 500 that his illusion of historical truth has been taken for the reality.

Beowulf says and does all the right heroic things: "Each of us must experience the end of life in the world," he tells the quaking Danes; "let him who is permitted achieve fame before death. That is for a slain warrior the best there is." Beowulf's victories over his opponents are praised by the narrator and also by other actors in the poem: he was "the strongest of warriors," "the strongest in might on that day of this life"; his loyalty, munificence, wisdom, and nobility are extolled, along with the formal speeches in which he makes his qualities known. "He held to his high destiny," says Wiglaf of the dead Beowulf, "of all men in the world he was the most glorious warrior." The last word in the poem is uttered by Beowulf's mourners, who commend their slain leader as "most intent on glory."

Heroic literature is temporarily out of fashion, at least in the West. We no longer assume that fighting is glorious or fun, or that *hero* and *warrior* are synonymous terms. If *Beowulf* is widely regarded today as the first great masterpiece of English poetry, it probably has less to do with its hero's might than its poet's melancholy. The poem's heroic fellowship is precarious, a bright hall stalked by menacing shadows. Scenes of rejoicing are swiftly undercut by forecasts of disaster; alliterative pairings like *æfter wiste . . . wop* 'after the feast . . . lamentation' and *gyrn æfter gomene* 'sorrow after joy' are dark, mocking refrains. The noble history related turns out to be the stuff that fantasies of younger brothers are made of: the fall of a leader, an underdog's defiant resistance, the automaticity of revenge (called by Auden the earth's only perpetual motion machine).

The Finnsburh Fragment deals in a vivid, close-up way with the same battle at Finn's stronghold sung of by the "scop" in *Beowulf*'s Heorot. The poet applauds the young warriors for repaying their lord's bright mead so abundantly in battle, just as a retainer in *Beowulf* urged his comrades to remember their vows at the mead-drinking, and a soldier in *The Battle of Maldon* reminded his companions of their hall-vows "over mead, on the bench." *Waldere*, treating the same legend that survives in the Latin verse epic *Waltharius*, provides examples of, among other things, the tension between heroic ideas and human affection, weapons with a legendary past, stolen treasure, the hero's headlong drive for everlasting glory, and the role of women in Old English poetry.

Brunanburh and *Maldon*, poems on actual tenth-century battles fought by contemporary kings and great magnates, adapt the heroic mode to patriotic ends. The first, one of the most familiar of all Old English poems through Tennyson's translation, sees no unresolvable contradiction between piety and the heroic life: its glory-filled battle, red with blood and illuminated by God's rising and setting sun, is viewed from a historical perspective reminiscent of Manifest Destiny. *Maldon* commemorates a bad day: the general fell, part of his army ran away, and the English lost. Nevertheless, some Anglo-Saxon poet turned this debacle into "the most heroic of poems," one famed for its "invincible profession of heroic faith." Byrhtnoth, the leader, chooses to fight rather than pay tribute, to bloody the Vikings rather than watch them sail off into the sunrise; after he falls, his loyal retainers choose to stay and die rather than flee and live. "Remember" is the first word spoken by a retainer in *Maldon*; one by one, those left on the field revive within themselves their lord's heroic song. The words uttered by one of them—"Spirit must be the firmer, heart the bolder, courage the greater, as our strength lessens"—are probably the most frequently quoted in all Old English poetry.

Not surprisingly, the Old English poems about the deeds of the "soldiers of Christ" are less well known, even though they tell highly dramatic, even rip-roaring stories. In *Andreas* St. Andrew embarks on an eventful sea journey to free his fellow apostle Matthew from the man-eating Mermedonians, undergoes torture, and by means of a miraculous flood converts his captors to Christianity. Most commentary on the poem is concerned with its possible verbal borrowings from *Beowulf* (or vice versa; the jury is still out). The differences between the two works, however, are just as striking. The action of *Beowulf* takes place in history, with eternity impinging only at moments; its tone is measured and full of regret. The action of *Andreas* is abstract and symbolic, performed on a cosmic stage; its tone, joyful and excited. Exaggerated violence and ecstasy are cultivated at every turn. Christ, as king, creates his *comitatus*, twelve companions serving as "thanes of the prince"; he determines their "lot." Andrew converting the heathen is the historical apostle but also a warrior in the cosmic battle between Christ and Satan. When the saint resolves to go alone to the land of the cannibals, his own retainers, protesting that if they did not accompany him they, lordless, would be welcome nowhere, make the right heroic choice. Yet in the dual vision of the poem, an act that occurs once is seen as having eternally occurred.

In the other poetic saints' lives, too, literal statements of loyalty, literal battles, literal conversions, somehow always end up portending moral, eternal, and spiritual archetypes. *Elene* tells of the search for the true Cross in Jerusalem by Helena, the mother of the emperor Constantine (who was granted a vision of the Cross as a sign of victory); it is also the story of Judas, the Jew who eventually assisted Helena in finding the Cross and became, as Cyriacus, bishop of Jerusalem. Both Constantine's opening battle with the Goths and his mother's excessively martial sea voyage are sometimes removed from their context and admired as set pieces; yet in *Elene*, the warfare of the emperor and the archaeological mission of his "war-queen" mother are much of the time indistinguishable from the Church Militant battling the unbelievers.

In *Juliana* a wicked governor seeks the saint in marriage; she, devoted to Christ, spurns him. The Old English Juliana is not the somewhat deceitful beauty of the Latin life but a fervent Christian; her fiancé, no longer the soul of sweet reasonableness, has become a follower of Satan; the war between the retainers of heaven and of hell gives structure and meaning to this most abstract of poems. A similar struggle between saint and devil is at the heart of *Guthlac A*, the first of two consecutive poems in the Exeter Book about this English ascetic (ca. 674–714). Having abandoned his former warrior life, Guthlac now spends a lot of time in the fens defending himself and his dwelling from demonic assailants. *Guthlac B* depicts death, a "slaughter-greedy warrior" and a "cruel loner," rushing upon the saint "with greedy grasps," unlocking his "treasure-hoard of life with treacherous keys," and finally, "stinging" the saint with "deadly arrows." Death's victory turns out to be Guthlac's— his soul goes forth, encased in light and melody, into heavenly glory, a reward from his Lord for heroic steadfastness and strength. It is different from Beowulf's end, but not very.

Wisdom Poetry

"A man must be firm in wisdom and measured, wise in heart, shrewd in thoughts, eager for wisdom, so he can get his share of happiness among men," observes a father to his son in the poem called *Precepts*. "I intend to teach people all the time," warns the narrator of *Judgment Day I*. "Learn this teaching," commands *The Order of the World*. These remarks are characteristic of the large and somewhat amorphous category of wisdom poetry. Its concerns are with the nature of the world, what life is, how it varies, how it works, its rules of conduct, how to succeed. The individual poems in this group are often hortatory and assertive, with a preference for the *deop, deorc, dimm, dierne,* and *diegol,* the 'deep,' 'dark,' 'obscure,' 'hidden,' and 'secret.' Anglo-Saxon wisdom comes in the form of poetic catalogues, charms, maxims and proverbs, riddles, allegories, dialogues, and—perhaps most distinctively—reflective, admonitory poems, sometimes spoken by an "I" who relates his or her life experience. These latter poems, which include such favorites as *The Wanderer, The Seafarer* (famously, if partially, translated by Ezra Pound), *The Ruin, Deor,* and *Widsith,* occupy the second half of the Exeter Book. One such poem might be a quirk; twenty or so suggest a taste.

The works just mentioned, along with *The Wife's Lament, Wulf and Eadwacer, The Husband's Message, The Riming Poem,* and *Resignation B,* are urgent, emotional compositions, each claiming to report the speaker's true experience. These "elegies," as they are sometimes called, review the brevity of human life and joy, the transience of the world—how time condemns itself, all man's endeavors, and all his edifices. The poets look back at a vanished world, at heroes who sought praise for their heroic deeds "until all departed, light and life together"; they tell us of loss, suffering, and mortality, and how the mind can steel itself against impermanence by not putting trust "where moth and rust doth corrupt." The poems tend to begin in vehement spontaneity, the outpouring of personal grief, and end in generalizations, as the speaker gradually converts raw experience into the perfect formality of wisdom. For some reason, the two poems that tell of longing and abandonment in a woman's voice do not offer the consolation of eternity, of a better, more enduring home. Three "elegies" are distinctive in form: *The Riming Poem* is, as its modern title suggests, the first English poem to use end rhyme consistently. The haunting *Wulf and Eadwacer* has a refrain; the only other Old English poem so equipped is *Deor,* whose repeated "That passed over; so can this" seems to turn every sorrow told into an exemplum of misery overcome. The consolation is transience itself.

Wisdom poetry circles repetitively around a core of related themes: the dangers of boasting, pride, and drink; man's ignorance, God's power; the devil's arrows and man's urgent need to fortify his mind. Most poems end with an admonishment to live well (i.e., righteously) in view of the eternal consequences of not doing so; some paint a cautionary picture of the terrors and stench of the wicked in the next world.

The didactic strategies of these poems are varied. They range from impersonal catalogues (*The Gifts of Men*, *The Fortunes of Men*) and poems spoken by a mostly undeveloped persona (*Precepts*, *Vainglory*, *Order of the World*, *The Phoenix*, *The Whale*) to full-blown monologues and dialogues (*The Soul and Body* poems, and *Solomon and Saturn*, which contains passages as powerful and memorable as anything in Old English verse). *Judgment Day I* and *The Fates of the Apostles* mix brief autobiographical notes with urgent doctrine; *Descent into Hell* merges the voice of the imagined prophet with that of the poet. Some poems resemble self-help guides on how to win eternity and influence the saints (*Instructions for Christians*, *An Exhortation to Christian Living* / *A Summons to Prayer*—now one poem); others present themselves as calendars (*Seasons for Fasting*, *Menologium*—misnamed) or mnemonics (*The Rune Poem*).

Wisdom can and should be competitive and demanding. The eight-line *Pharaoh* illustrates, in miniature, how this "outdoing" works. The questioner asks how many warriors there were in Pharoah's army when they pursued the Israelites. The answer: "I'm not sure, but there were six hundred chariots when they were drowned." The questioner must then "solve" the answer by recalling, first, that all who pursued died and, second, that there were three men in each chariot for a total of eighteen hundred casualties. Directness was not a virtue in Old English poetry.

Two compositions, *Maxims I* and *II* (the latter made up of three separate poems), consist of strings of commonplaces, generalized reflections on the properties and nature of things; their purpose remains a mystery. The poets provide a sequence of maxims tightly connected in form but disparate in meaning: the statement "a dragon must be in a barrow" is followed by "fish must spawn its kind in the water," "a king must distribute rings in the hall," and finally, "loyalty must be in a warrior, wisdom in a man." Part of our pleasure in these strands comes from their blend of the concrete and abstract, the physical and the moral, the banal and the profound.

A similar meditation on the multiformity of the world is provided by the nearly one hundred riddles preserved, in two large groups, in the Exeter Book. Among the everyday objects of sense experience transformed by the riddles are wrought instruments (rake and plow), domestic and church equipment (loom, churn, chalice), birds, animals, natural phenomena, weapons, and items of food and drink; there are runes, letters, cryptograms, and items connected with writing and books (recalling that *riddle* is the cognate object of *read*). Answers are not provided in the manuscript: the subject of riddle 4 has therefore been confidently identified as a bell, millstone, flail, lock, handmill, pen, phallus, and necromancy. But our inability to decide whether riddle 39, for example, is "about" day, moon, time, death, cloud, or dream, suggests that these disparate categories may have something important, and totally unexpected, in common. The copulating cock and hen (riddle 42), the metaphysical soul and body (riddle 43), and the double entendre key (riddle 44) are written on the same folio. Like the maxims, the riddles juxtapose the natural and the man-made, the corporeal and intellectual, the coarse and the sublime, dividing the world into exotic taxonomies far (we think) from our daily experience.

The Anglo-Saxon poets were masters of the word—in a culture in which words could still affect (and effect, as the twelve extant poetic *Charms* insist) events. Theirs was a supple and coherent use of the vernacular, the fitting together of alliterative and consonant syllables to prove or predict the mutual relevance of word and thing. Like their modern counterparts, composers of Old English verse were fascinated by linguistic detail, by the sounds and shapes of words and the sudden sparkle of meaning, but their reflection upon language went a step further, becoming a springboard to speculation about the nature of the world. Skill in this poetic art, developed by means of a pedagogy in which the Anglo-Saxons were the undisputed champions of medieval Europe, was used by its practitioners not only to express reality but to implement it.

This strong sense of the power adhering to words gives Old English poetry its distinctive character. There may be a persistence of Old English meter in the classic English pentameter line. And there may be phrases in our current language—"time and tide," "heaven and earth," "to have and to hold," "Guinness is good for you"—that are, distantly, "Old English." But although English lived on, the poetic art that startled and inspired Hopkins and Auden was among the casualties of the Battle of Hastings.

Roberta Frank

Further Reading

Bessinger, Jess B., and P. H. Smith. *A Concordance to the Anglo-Saxon Poetic Records.* Ithaca, N.Y.: Cornell University Press, 1978.

Bradley, S. A. J., trans. and ed. *Anglo-Saxon Poetry.* London: Dent (Everyman's Library), 1982. [Translations]

Campbell, James, ed. *The Anglo-Saxons.* Ithaca, N.Y.: Cornell University Press, 1982. [Historical and cultural background]

Gatch, Milton McC. *Loyalties and Traditions: Man and His World in Old English Literature.* New York: Pegasus, 1971.

Godden, Malcolm, and Michael Lapidge, eds. *The Cambridge Companion to Old English Literature.* Cambridge: Cambridge University Press, 1991.

Greenfield, Stanley B., and D. G. Calder. *A New Critical History of Old English Literature.* Rev. ed. New York: New York University Press, 1986.

Krapp, George P., and E. V. K. Dobbie, eds. *The Anglo-Saxon Poetic Records.* 6 vols. New York: Columbia University Press, 1931–1953. [Texts]

Shippey, T. A. *Old English Verse.* London: Hutchinson, 1972.

Stanley, Eric Gerald. *A Collection of Papers with Emphasis on Old English Literature.* Toronto: Pontifical Institute of Mediaeval Studies, 1987.

Stanley, Eric Gerald. *Continuations and Beginnings: Studies in Old English Literature.* London: Nelson, 1966.

Middle English Poetry

IDDLE ENGLISH is a relatively precise term to us. Hindsight and the usually artificial divisions of history enable us to fix on the conquest of England by the Normans in 1066 as a starting point: English disappears almost at a stroke in the written records, and when it reappears it has been transformed from Old English to Middle English. The end of Middle English is less easy to determine. We can look back to the great divide of the vowel shift that makes Chaucer's pronunciation so different from Shakespeare's or ours, or point to the introduction of the revolutionary new technology of printing to England in 1476. In literary terms the importing of the sonnet form marks a distinctive change in style and fashion; in religious terms Henry VIII's break with the medieval Church is crucial. All these events leave their marks in language and literature, but focusing on them blurs the essential continuities: spoken English evolved gradually; written English, simply by virtue of being written, provides us with fixed though fragmentary landmarks. Literacy itself would have given medieval writers a particular place within a social and linguistic structure. English, either spoken or written, was only one of the languages current in the British Isles, and English itself came in many varied forms.

There had been no one form of English even in the days of the first Anglo-Saxon settlers in the British Isles. The groups who came to England in the fifth and sixth centuries spoke a variety of related dialects: these took centuries to coalesce into today's standard written English. There is still an enormous variety of spoken dialects and non-standard variations within the English-speaking world in spite of the cohesive force of a standard printed language, but before printing even the idea of a standard exerted far less force. The dialects of Old English continued to develop throughout the Middle English period; Middle English might in some ways more properly be called "Middle Englishes."

We know about medieval English dialects because the language was written down more or less phonetically. Writing had come relatively late to the illiterate pagan Anglo-Saxon settlers of England. The Roman alphabet accompanied Christianity (which arrived in southeast England in 597); it was gradually and imperfectly adapted for the sounds of Old English chiefly for religious purposes. Eventually it was used for secular material, but literacy principally belonged with Latin, the language of the Church. Written English at first faithfully recorded the different dialects of Old English; but after King Alfred's reign (871–899) the dialect of the kingdom of Wessex gradually became a kind of standard literary medium. The violent impact of the conquest of England by French-speaking Normans in 1066 disrupted this orderly development; since all high office in the land and nearly all ecclesiastical positions were filled with French speakers, there was not much call for written English; the language was degraded to that of an underclass. The idle entertainments of a subject and still largely illiterate people did not seem worth writing down in any quantity—for almost no recorded English of the period immediately after the Conquest survives today. Latin was the language of the Church, and hence of education; the language of secular culture was French; English was spoken by the peasantry, and the verse in that language had, in any case in the earliest times, traditionally been oral. Manuscripts of Old English are lucky survivors; manuscripts of the very early Middle English period are almost nonexistent.

Written English does not emerge again in any bulk for over a hundred years. We can only guess at the kinds of English poetry composed during this lost century, when the whole language, as far as the records show, went underground. When the learned process of writing gradually extends its reach to English again the bulk of what appears is utilitarian religious material. Before the fourteenth century there is not much else: we have some lyrics, some romances, the *Owl and the Nightingale*—a mysterious dialogue in verse between two birds as to their respective merits, which has been variously interpreted—and the fascinating *Brut*, a vast and difficult history of the British, which seems to have been composed in an archaizing spirit in verse showing some strong similarities to Old English poetry. The *Brut* hints at the curious political relationships between the languages: an English poem about Celtic history drawn largely from a Norman French source, it contains almost no words derived from French. By the fourteenth century the English language was in the ascendant again, and by the end of that century there is a sizable body of recorded work; but the modern reader might feel that what emerges, although it looks much more like our language than Old English, is still distinctly unfamiliar. English had undergone vast changes—the loss of inflections and the enormous influx of vocabulary from Latin and French altered it almost beyond recognition—but it makes its multiform reappearance in writing in the descendants of the different dialects of its Old English days.

The Middle English in the surviving records reveals a startling variety of dialectal variants not only of pronunciation and vocabulary, but also of grammar and syntax. Since our written language is mainly inherited from the dialect of Chaucer, he seems familiar to us; but it was largely Chaucer's own work that placed London English at the center of the literary map. In Chaucer's day there were other ways of speaking and writing that did not carry the connotations that "dialect literature" has for us today: they are not necessarily the derisively recorded utterances of an underclass, or the evocations of a quaint nostalgic rusticity. Chaucer is the first writer in English to make jokes about other dialects of English (the Reeve's Tale)— perhaps in the literary circles of the royal court regional speech already sounded rustic and comic—but even in the fifteenth century regional writers themselves show little self-consciousness about their provincial speech. It is only by the end of the century with the emergence of printing that the descendant of Chaucer's London dialect becomes a definite standard, the Scots dialect of the neighboring kingdom its only rival for literary purposes. It is hard today to read "dialect literature" without the distraction of modern prejudices about standard English; but West Midland or Kentish speech was not quaint to its users, nor treated condescendingly by regional authors.

Poetry precedes literacy, and exists outside it, but nothing except speculation can tell us anything about unrecorded verse. What remains is only what was written down; and writing put English in the ambit of a very different culture. Literacy was bound up with a set of literary and cultural assumptions, sacred and profane texts written in Latin, and ideas about literature derived from Christian learning. When a man learned to read and write (women mostly did not), he learned not only in Latin, but within the scheme of the Latin learned establishment. English, in the world of written texts, was also necessarily inside the educational value system that went with literacy. Medieval schools existed to teach Latin to potential clerics; the development of the Latin word *ydiota* from its early sense of "uneducated, illiterate person," to the meaning "lay, not clerical," to its present sense of "idiot" reflects accurately a medieval sense of values.

Medieval learning, like medieval everything else, was profoundly hierarchical. The educational system was envisioned (and sometimes portrayed) as a vast pyramid or tower to which the key was Latin grammar. From grammar one ideally proceeded to the other liberal arts (logic, rhetoric, arithmetic, music, geometry, and astronomy) and eventually through philosophy to theology, the queen of all knowledge. It was, in some senses, a closed system; closed temporally, since human history was held to be finite, beginning in the garden of Eden and ending at Judgment Day. It was closed spatially too, since the earth was the center of the physical universe, and heaven lay outside the sphere of the fixed stars. Mankind's place at the material center was offset by being at the spiritual periphery. The ideal scheme of things had been radically altered by the original sin committed in the garden of Eden; Adam was held to have been created with a knowledge of all seven liberal arts as his own proper inheritance. Adam's Fall had ruined the arts (together with the human constitution, the animal kingdom, and the weather), but education could try to repair some of the damage; learning was seen as the first step in restoration. Man must be mindful that the perceptible world of the senses is only a stage in existence: his goal is the immaterial and spiritual world that he must learn to perceive in the chaos of earthly life.

Poetry fitted awkwardly inside this system of education. It was not per se a liberal art; nor was there any category for literature: both appeared bewilderingly in several different places. Grammar students might study prosody or comment on turns of expression, and they used Latin texts ranging from mnemonic verses to classical poetry. Poetry's use of figures of speech put it within the territory of rhetoric. One of the astronomical textbooks was written in verse. Boethius counted as a philosopher, but his *Consolation of Philosophy* contains many poems. Parts of the Bible were in some sense poetic, which put poetry within striking distance of theology. Definitions of poetry were confusing. The body of classical poetry embedded in the educational system differed from prose on the one hand by virtue of being written in meter; on the other it differed from more serious kinds of writing by virtue of its subject matter: it was full of fables, myths, impossible marvels, and monsters that seemed improbable even to the zoologically credulous Middle Ages. There was no necessary connection between metrics and fabulous subject matter, the two main features of poetry.

The encyclopedist Vincent of Beauvais (d. 1264) included both views in his *Speculum Doctrinale*; poetry is first "the art of adorning something with metre, according to the proportion of the words and the length and number of the metrical feet" (III.cix)—a pedestrian definition that is widespread. The fifteenth-century English translation of Palladius into rather painful verse and perhaps quite a lot of Lydgate suffer under the misapprehension that a poet's task is essentially one of versifying. It was a comfortingly utilitarian point of view: verse was easier to learn than prose, and the Bible contained lost Hebrew meters. There could be nothing essentially wrong with poetry seen simply as versification.

The other aspect of poetry—its fabulous subject matter—was much more difficult to deal with. Since medieval views of life did not suffer from our prevailing sense of the indeterminacy of things, God was a reality, and life on earth was a prologue to an eternity in hell or heaven; what we call "the real world" today was to be regarded as a temporary and seductive maze of illusions, through which each soul must find its way to truth. The way to heaven and hell was relatively clearly marked out by divine revelation (the Bible) and the authority of the Church, embodied in the clerical establishment, who were alone qualified to expound the Bible and the writings of the ecclesiastical authorities—or indeed any other writings. It is difficult to fit the subject matter of poetry into this scheme of things, unless the poetry is to be relentlessly didactic. Some poetic features—its figures of speech, for example—can be accommodated easily enough: they render the message more efficacious; but any subject matter that did not seem essentially Christian, moral, or useful was a source of unease.

The fables or fictions that were held by many to be the essence of poetry attracted much learned attention. The simplest solution was to dismiss the whole business of poetry as nonsense, or to relegate it to the periphery of learning: a solution adopted by the seventh-century authority Isidore of Seville (who puts poets amongst mysterious wisdom figures such as sibyls, pagans, and gentile gods), the later Hugh of St. Victor (who classifies poetry as an appendage to the liberal arts), and many other moralists past and present. But it was inconveniently apparent that the Bible on occasion makes use of fables (e.g., Jesus' parables or the story of the trees in Judges 9:8–15). St. Thomas Aquinas felt that Scripture needed to be excused for this: at the beginning of his *Summa Theologiae* he argued that the poetic aspects of Scripture were appropriate because they made it accessible even to the unlearned. He reveals the "establishment" wariness of poetry, which required it to prove its credentials for the purposes of salvation.

Not all authorities looked so gloomily on "fables." An important saying of the early Christian writer Lactantius was quoted by Vincent of Beauvais, and taken up enthusiastically by Petrarch and Boccaccio: "the poet's job lies in the very act of transforming true things into something else by means of an indirect and figurative mode of speaking, and adding a certain beauty." This recognition that there were different kinds of truth rather than a simple opposition between truth and lies was of enormous help to poetry lovers. They could deploy a wide range of options (all recorded by Vincent), from arguing that poetry contained scientific truths, e.g., that the fable of the lame god Vulcan taught the crooked nature of fire, to euhemerism, e.g., insisting that Hercules was only called a god because he was a great hero in prehistorical times. A development of this line of thought was the insistence that any story that taught something true was valuable: Aesop's fables instilled good moral qualities. And "truth," of course, meant something considered valid by the learned establishment: not truth to life or nature, but to invisible and eschatological reality.

Such defenses of poetry insist on its didactic value and encourage allegory: if a story could be read for its message, then a message could be embodied in a story, and the truth or value of the message would redeem the story from the charge of untruth. Petrarch and Boccaccio are most enthusiastic about this "hidden truth" theory of poetry and hand on a vocabulary of veils, mists, and kernels that was exceedingly popular in fifteenth-century England. Poetry was supposed to be written this way to hide holy truths from the eyes of the unlearned vulgar, and to give intellectual pleasure to the eyes of the discerning few. Such an unpleasant view of poetry can only be excused by the fact that it is itself an excuse: unless poetry could lay claim to some sort of truth, it could have no intellectual place at all in a world where heaven and hell were all-important realities (the world of Chaucer's Parson). Despite these attempts at sanitizing fiction, however, the whole matter of the poets left an uncomfortable mental residue. Poetry was still the "lowest amongst the arts" for Aquinas, and a glance at the dictionary shows that many of the collocations in English of such words as *poet*, *poesy*, and *poetry* are with *fables*, *lies*, and *feigning*. The fabulous images of poetry could only, the philosophers said, come from the suspect power of imagination or *phantasia* in the brain. We share imagination with the animals, and we should use it only in the service of cognition. Hence "falsehed and fantesye / And cursyd ymagynacyon" are often pejorative; they appear as villains in Skelton's *Magnyfycence* and in the morality play *Hyckescorner*.

The unsavory atmosphere surrounding poetry in the learned world is reflected in the attitudes of English writers, especially those who function within the orbit of learned, i.e., latinate, culture. The popularity of the dream vision, where the poet pretends to no more than telling us what he saw in an unverifiable dream, must owe something to this unease (dreams, although themselves the products of *phantasia* unsupervised by reason, were morally blameless). Chaucer, who of all medieval writers has something of the modern confidence in the "value" of literature (but see his Retractation), is therefore rather less typical than his contemporaries. Chaucer's followers lean heavily on his example to justify themselves as serious writers, but there is still a predominantly apologetic note in their work. They often claim to have nothing but their readers' good at heart, or, at the very least, they write to pass the time of day harmlessly lest the devil find something worse for them to do. It is impossible to escape the idea that in the medieval learned world poetry must be at heart didactic. Any entertainment value was at best dubious, and at worst, sinister.

Outside the learned world, it is safe to assume, songs and stories were taken less ponderously. Indeed, the anxiety of the educated about the value of poetry points to an unregenerate enjoyment of such things; moralists take it for granted that poems, whether seen as metrical devices or as beautiful fictions, are of themselves delightful, and hence morally suspect. But there was a class of people, largely independent of the learned world, to whom poems and verse were important: those who made their living by them. There must have been minstrels, singers, storytellers, and entertainers in great numbers, but they belong to a class whose unrecorded voices have not come down to us. It is apparent, even though what we have has been filtered through the literate, that there were some poets who treated their craft as a skill rather than an inferior art and who often seem more concerned with pleasing their audience than edifying it.

It is perhaps no accident that the poetry in which these characteristics are most evident is the alliterative verse that was written down in the North and West of England in the fourteenth and fifteenth centuries. It is perhaps too romantic to visualize a line of oral poets stretching back unbroken to pre-Conquest days entertaining the English-speaking population in their own tongue in the alehouse, while the "official" Latin and French culture of the governing classes pursued its parallel course in court, castle, and university. But alliterative verse does make use of Old English poetic techniques (although altered and developed); it does, like Old English, employ a highly specialized vocabulary, and the poet does present himself as a master of a difficult craft, a latter-day "scop." The pride in mastery and the sense of an important social role for the poet receive fresh impetus from the theorists of the Renaissance, whose altered priorities and exaltation of classical precedents prove to be enormously enriching, but the alliterative style itself goes out of fashion. Most alliterative poems survive in only one or two manuscript copies and owe their present fame to the scholars of the nineteenth century who rediscovered them.

The most famous of all alliterative poems are the four works contained in a single grubby fourteenth-century manuscript now in the British Library (MS Cotton Nero A, x). All four are written in a consistent West Midland dialect; we know nothing about the author or authors. The poems are technically highly skilled, learned, and full of sophisticated vocabulary wielded like a precision tool. A great many of the words are survivors of Old English, since lost, but many more are derived from French, Latin, and Old Norse, all deployed with the conscious expertise of a professional, not the self-deprecating irony of Chaucer.

Sir Gawain and the Green Knight is the most accessible of these poems. It is today the most nearly classifiable of all alliterative verse: more like a romance than anything else, it purports to be an adventure from the Arthurian cycle of stories. Framed by the legendary medieval history of Britain, the story tells how Sir Gawain accepted the challenge the Green Knight presented to the court of King Arthur at the New Year's feast to take part in a beheading contest. Gawain chops off the Green Knight's head, only to find that his blow is not at all final; the

Green Knight rides off insouciantly swinging his head by its hair, reminding Gawain to seek him out for the return blow a year later. Gawain keeps his word, but while searching for his adversary is hospitably received in a castle where he agrees to another game: to exchange his daily winnings with his host. While the host goes hunting, Gawain stays indoors, and on each of the three successive days his host's wife makes what appear to be attempts to seduce him. Quantities of slaughtered beasts are exchanged each evening for the kisses Gawain has received; but on the third day the lady gives Gawain a girdle that, she claims, will protect him against all blows. Gawain pays his host the kisses but not the girdle. When at last he confronts the Green Knight, the two games come together: Gawain is humiliated to realize that the Green Knight and his host are one and the same, and that at every point he has been in ignorance of the real dynamics behind the play.

The poet's extraordinary slant on chivalric adventure—his hero, a knight whose untraditional function is to stand still to be struck at and to reject a lady's advances, and the central part played by embarrassing, not heroic, situations—is set off by the virtuoso command of the knightly terminology of armory, courtship, and hunt. The elaborate description of Gawain's red-and-gold emblem, the symbolic pentangle, complemented by the lady's bright green girdle Gawain puts on over it, suggests a theory of signs far subtler than Petrarch's allegorical secret messages. The poet's cunning in interlacing the ideals of chivalry with the ethics of medieval Christianity and his skill in posing a moral conundrum so subtle that no two critics agree entirely on just where Gawain went wrong and how serious his sin was would put him on a level with Chaucer, if comparisons between two such different modes were not pointless.

The Gawain poet presents his subject as one who is fully in charge of it; he requests a hearing, "if ye wyl lysten this laye bot on littel quile," and promises a poem "with lel letteres loken" (linked with true staves) in proper alliterative style. The long lines with their four stresses linked by alliteration are divided into unequal clumps by a short rhyming "bob and wheel"; this device controls the narrative and descriptive units (thus averting the tendency of alliterative verse to run on shapelessly), and often provides a witty or surprising "cap" or turn to a stanza—as in the surprising mention of the greenness of the strange knight at the very end of the first description of him. The poet's control is asserted explicitly when he insists on the importance of his digression on the significance of the pentangle: "and quy the pentangel apendes to that prynce noble / I am intent yow to telle, thof tary hyt me schulde." The last lines are linked to the opening; the poem is presented as a finished artifact whose seeming completeness is belied by the ambiguity of its moral message.

The richness and subtlety of the alliterative style is even more fully displayed in another poem, now entitled *Pearl*, from the same manuscript. The speaker of the poem tells us he is a jeweler grieving for a lost pearl. He falls asleep on the flowery mound in a garden where he lost his jewel; his dream takes him into a marvelous landscape where he sees, across a stream, a beautiful maiden who is somehow the lost pearl. The main body of the poem is a dialogue between the uncomprehending dreamer and the wise maiden, who must explain the nature of heaven, the system of celestial rewards and the value of innocence. The poem analyzes brilliantly the strange blend of possessiveness and love in human grief: the dreamer never explains who his pearl is (although he hints that she is his baby daughter), but his love and longing for her are transmitted through his incredulous delight at her reappearance and his last gesture of throwing himself into the stream to rejoin her, only to awake again on the mound that is more clearly than ever a grave. The dreamer never really understands the nature of the heaven he is shown, but he is dimly comforted at the end. The poem is explicitly didactic, but the instruction is qualified by the reversal of roles: the maiden, an infant at her death, a female illiterate, is now the instructor, and the dreamer her slow pupil. Heaven is by definition beyond human comprehension, but here its paradoxes are dramatized; the last have become the first, and the dreamer is reduced to an appeal to affection alone because nothing else he hears seems to make sense to him:

> quen we departed we wern at on;
> God forbede we be now wrothe;
> We meten so selden by stok other ston.
> (378–380)

While the images of *Pearl* are the earthly analogies of light, jewels, and running water, the heart of the vision is a close borrowing from the book of Revelation, to which the poet appeals as the authority of guaranteed truth and which validates his own work as an individual revelation of the very same truth. The poem is an extraordinary blend of emotion and an intellectual analysis of that emotion; the dreamer feels intensely, and the maiden discounts his feelings as irrelevant to the real happiness he ought to be seeking. The poem can easily be summarized as a series of Christian truisms, but the poet demonstrates that those truisms conceal enormous complexities.

Pearl represents the most complex marriage of style and content in the whole body of alliterative poetry. The verse combines heavy alliteration with a complex rhyme scheme; the poem has an elaborate numerological structure; its 101 stanzas are linked throughout by concatenation, and the last line is almost the same as the first. It is, as has been remarked, like a highly wrought jewel box made for the pearl; the precision and detail of the frame contrast starkly with the numinous and unspeakable reality it contains. The whole poem suggests the complex unity of the single gem that is its main symbol. The detail and precision of the analysis—as in *Sir Gawain and the Green Knight*—still allow for diverse conclusions. Critics vary in their censure of the dreamer as they do on the precise nature of Gawain's sin: but in both poems the central medieval paradox, that man is a miserable sinner who is still promised a chance at perfection, is highlighted and not resolved. Both poems present an unattainable ideal, and both contrast it with inevitable human inadequacy, temporality, and grief: "the faut and the fayntyse of the flesche crabbed." The otherworldly ideal offered can only be expressed by images and implications and rereadings of the existing world—the reader must learn that jewels on earth are "really" fading roses, but that heaven can to some extent be apprehended in terms of actual roses and pearls, earthly light and human love. Paradoxically it is the jeweler's all-too-human love for his lost Pearl that enables him to "see" the New Jerusalem and understand an unimaginable bliss. *Pearl* implicitly asserts a much more profound view of poetry than any medieval theorist dared to present.

Many other writers in the alliterative style show the same authorial confidence in their skills and the same pride in their technical virtuosity. The poets write with a notable lack of apology, but often with a forthright acceptance of the didactic function of poetry. The other two poems in MS Cotton Nero A x both address themselves to moral virtues, and open with straightforward assertions: "Patience is a poynt, thagh hit displese oft," and "Clannesse, whoso kyndly cowthe comende / . . . Fayre formes myght he fynde in forthering his speche." Both poems go on to explore the meanings of the virtues of patience and cleanness (or purity) by focusing on their opposites: *Patience* defines its virtue by describing the impatience of Jonah, and *Cleanness* builds up a complex definition of a subtle virtue through a series of negative exempla. Their unabashed didacticism renders them less popular today than *Pearl* and *Sir Gawain*, but they would have satisfied medieval artistic canons the more successfully for being uncontaminated with any obvious fiction.

One of the suggestive peculiarities of alliterative poetry is that the vocabulary, and to a large extent the meter and style, are shared: that is, the same rare words, lines and half-lines turn up in different poems across the corpus of verse. The earliest critics tended to explain this by assigning several works to the same author or by proving indebtedness; more modern opinion makes use of such terminology as *the alliterative school* or *tradition*. It does suggest that in at least some parts of the country the most important thing about being a poet was to have the vocabulary and metrics to render one's subject matter—whatever it might be—into a recognizably "poetic" mold that strongly resembled existing compositions. The stress on vocabulary is important: the Latin learned views of poetry emphasized fictional content and metrics, but words and language were usually ignored. Practical handbooks (commentaries on classical poets, rhetorical textbooks) might approach vocabulary through the explanation of figures of speech, but this seems very different from the attitude of poets of the alliterative tradition. Such poets seem to have an unselfconscious veneration for something like the Old English poet's "wordhoard": a precise, detailed, technical control of a huge variety of words, synonyms, set phrases, archaic and poetic terms drawn in large part from non-Latinate vocabulary and secular culture. They transposed a variety of medieval works into the alliterative style: the Earl of Hereford had the absurd romance *William of Palerne* translated from French into English (before 1361) for the benefit of his household; there are other romances, plays, some delightful lyrics, quasi-historical works, stories from the Arthurian cycle (the stirring *Morte Arthure*), biblical legends and many religious works. Exceedingly intricate blends of alliteration and rhyme occur: the poems "Pater noster" and "De tribus regibus mortuis" printed with the works of John Audelay are particularly notable.

Among the best of alliterative poems are the three debate poems, *Winner and Waster*, *The Parliament of the Three Ages*, and *Death and Life*. They have barely survived in battered late manuscripts, and it is always assumed they belong to the same period, the mid-fourteenth century, though the evidence is slim. They are all dream visions. Each narrator

Middle English Poetry 35

goes out into a spring landscape, falls asleep, and witnesses a conflict or argument: in one case between the two economic principles of saving and spending; in the next, between the three ages of man, youth, maturity, and old age; and in the last, between Lady Life and Dame Death. The poet of *Winner and Waster* deploys his skills in virtuoso descriptions of birdsong, the heraldic accoutrements of his combatants, and the luxuries enjoyed by the profligate wasters:

> nysottes of the new gett so nysely attyred
> With syde slabbande sleves sleght to the grounde. . . .
>
> (410–411)

He has a keen satiric wit and characterizes his opposed principles very neatly (Waster says to Winner, "Thou schal birdes upbrayd of thaire bright wedis"); the poet presents an interesting (and still topical) argument on the interdependence of spending and saving; but he is less interested in sustained allegory, and the frame story of his debate does not really make sense (it does not help that the last few lines of the poem are lost). The satirist's discontent is apparent in the short prologue, where the poet makes the familiar complaint that the times are evil, lords no longer like to hear "makirs of myrthes that matirs couthe fynde" (line 20) but listen only to young fools ("a childe apon chere withowtten chyn-wedys") who repeat silly jokes. The true "maker of myrthes" composes his own "wyse wordes," and in the end the worth of the truly valuable poet will be apparent.

The resources of the alliterative style for creating an intricate and convincing surface are beautifully deployed in *The Parliament of the Three Ages*. The precision and detail of the description of the pleasures of life in Maytime, the narrator's successful hunt with all its proper terminology, the beauty and gusto of Youth, the parade of human glory and achievement described by Elde are all brought into sharp relief by the equally powerful awareness of transiency:

> And haves gud daye, for now I go; to grave moste me wende;
> Dethe dynges one my dore, I dare no lengare byde.
>
> (653–654)

Death and Life survives only in a corrupt seventeenth-century manuscript, but it seems to belong with the other alliterative debate poems. It differs from the *Parliament* in that the splendidly specific alliterative vocabulary is used more truly allegorically: Lady Life is not just life-on-earth, although the grass turns green at her feet; she stands for eternal life, offered to humanity through the Crucifixion. If the alliterative poets usually lavished their verbal skill on the material realities of this world, the author of *Death and Life*, like the author of *Pearl*, shows that it can also be used to present a movingly specific "fiction" of salvation.

The long poem known as *Piers Plowman* by William Langland (a contemporary of Chaucer about whom almost nothing is known) is an exception to the other works in the alliterative tradition in several ways. It is written in alliterating long lines, but it does not, in the main, employ the elaborate and obscure vocabulary of now-obsolete dialect terms used by the other authors. Langland's work, like theirs, escapes easy generic classification; it has been variously characterized as a dream vision poem, a prophecy, homily, quest, social satire, allegory, and something closely related to the drama of the period. All of these characterizations are in some sense true. Nor is Langland so comfortable with his role as poet or author as the other alliterative poets; the uncertainty of role and voice gives rise to a host of technical problems unparalleled in medieval literature. *Piers Plowman* exists in three or perhaps four versions; there are many manuscripts, but none of them is particularly authoritative. Langland, whoever he was, rewrote his work obsessively, often obliterating the bits that modern critics are most fond of; the whole work has more of the status of work-in-progress than anything else in medieval literature. Progress is the essence of the poem, and it must only have been stopped, not concluded, by the author's death. Generations of scholars have worked on establishing a text, but any discussion of the poem must reckon with the work's essential fluidity.

In main outline the "events" of the poem follow the same course in all versions: the narrator of the opening lines falls asleep and dreams, but his dream pitches him into waking life: he sees a "field full of folk" all busily alive and pursuing their various callings. A lady, Holy Church, tells him of heaven and hell, and bids him seek for truth; the dreamer, failing to understand, asks for Truth and is shown falsehood, the lady called "Meed." An extended allegory shows Meed (bribery, reward) corrupting society, but suggests that she can be controlled by the king and Reason. Reason then extends the message of reform to society: a sermon is preached to the crowd and the seven deadly sins come forward to make their confession; the whole crowd then rush off to seek for Truth. They meet Piers the Plowman—an exceedingly enigmatic guide, who offers to show them the way; the way somehow turns out to be the same thing as the plowing of the half-acre of land Piers owns. What seems like an initially hopeful scene degenerates: the agricultural cycle turns out to be too much for many of the pilgrims, and Piers's control slips. Truth sends a pardon; Piers and a priest argue about its meaning. In the earlier versions of the poem Piers tears up the pardon in a rage and departs on his own; the dreamer wakes up.

The second half of the poem shows the dreamer pursuing the quest alone: he now wants to find truth, or Piers, or the mysterious "Do wel" mentioned by the pardon; his search occupies a series of dreams, and dreams within dreams, populated by personifications of mental faculties and figures from history and Scripture. The text leads into a maze of knotty questions: Can man save his soul by intellect or learning? Can the institutions of the Church teach man how to love? After much incidental satire on contemporary affairs the dreamer is at last given another glimpse of Piers Plowman, who is now in some mysterious way identified with Christ. The problem is answered not in words, but in a vision of Christ's Crucifixion and the Harrowing of Hell. The dreamer wakens satisfied and goes to church to perform his Easter service; there he unexpectedly falls asleep again and witnesses the degeneration of religion from Christ's day to his own; the last vision is of the fortified barn Unity, besieged by all the forces of Hell and betrayed; the solitary figure of Conscience sets out, all over again, to find Piers Plowman.

The oddest thing about *Piers Plowman* is perhaps the stance of the narrator. His introduction of himself in the opening lines is full of ambiguities:

> In a somer seson, whan softe was the sonne,
> I shoop me into shroudes as I a sheep were,
> In habite as an heremite unholy of werkes,
> Went wide in this world wondres to here.
> (B.Prol.1–4)

Scholars disagree on whether the narrator is dressed like a sheep or a shepherd—a crucial distinction when imparting Christian doctrine. Hermits in the rest of the poem are presented as frauds; "unholy of werkes" sounds dubious, and wandering to hear wonders frivolous. An anxiety about the dreamer's role and a desperate urgency to find truth gradually take over the poem. The narrator in his waking moments grows ever more distrait: he is "witles nerehand" and "a fool" in between dreams; while asleep he at first merely observes, then becomes a stupid interlocutor of the dream authority, Holy Church, then when he finally joins the action—first tiptoeing up behind Piers Plowman and the Priest to find out what they are arguing about—he is by turns captious, cocky, obstinate, and bad-tempered. He is throughout very nervous about the role of poet as entertainer—minstrels are dubious characters in the poem—and about writing of sacred things. The minstrels in the Prologue who "geten gold with hire glee—giltless, I leeve" are at first carefully distinguished from a lower kind of entertainer, "japeres and jangeleres, Judas children" who "feynen hem fantasies" (B.Prol.34–36); in the later version they are all lumped together as those who "fyndeth out foule fantasyes and foles hem maketh / and hath wytt at wille to worche yf thei wolde" (C.Prol.35–37).

Langland's character Ymaginatif is definitely not a villain, and the human faculty of speech is described as "God's gleman, and a game of heven" (B.ix.102); but Ymaginatif rebukes the dreamer for writing poetry, "thow medlest thee with makynges—and myghtest go seye thi Sauter . . . for ther are bokes ynowe / To telle men what Dowel is" (B.xii.16–18), and professional storytellers who embark on religious themes "gnawen God with the gorge whanne hir guttes fullen" (B.x.57). Lords are exhorted to maintain at their tables the deserving poor instead of minstrels. Langland seems to reserve the word "poetes" for wise scholars who interpret the significance of the natural world; they, as magi, were honored at the nativity of Christ, "to pastours and to poetes appered the aungel" (B.xii.149), and they explain the moral symbolism of birds and beasts.

The narrator in *Piers Plowman* is learned, but not quite a priest; an entertainer, but not quite a minstrel. His quest is that of every Christian—the need to save his soul—but his religious learning and his poetic skills impose a complex social responsibility upon him. His reading of religious texts frequently causes him to clash with the official guardians of the texts, the clergy, and often lures him into diatribes against clerical inadequacy and hypocrisy. His own role of poet, set against the absolute dictates of Christianity, is a problem: an overpowering need to say what he believes with no easy aesthetic to justify it. Hence he readily destroys some of his most effective bits (such as the tearing of the pardon) in later versions because they do not get the meaning right. Langland perhaps has more in common with the attitude of mystical writers of his day: confronted by the absolute truth of God, all language was inadequate and figurative; hence the figurative-

ness of the poets could, by its very suggestiveness, take the audience far-
ther towards truth than direct statement.

Langland's work was far more widely read than that of the other
alliterative poets. He is much more approachable than any of them;
Piers Plowman is difficult in essence, but most of its lines are easy to
understand. Langland's desire to account for the whole state of man
manifests itself in a comprehensiveness not only of his sympathies but
also of his language: it encompasses the vivid and colloquial—voices off
calling "hot pies," the dead Emperor Trajan bursting in shouting "Ye,
baw for Bokes!," Holichurch's rebuke, "Thow doted daffe! . . . dulle are
thi wittes!" and Dame Studie's dismissal of anyone who attempts to pry
into divine secrets, "I wolde his eighe were in his ers and his fynger
after" (B.x.125). The language in which Christ's passion is recounted is
liturgical and celebratory, woven with Latin phrases and chivalric
imagery. There are a very few barren passages of medieval logic chop-
ping, but many vigorous and moving reinterpretations of biblical history, such as Moses' appearance as a scurrying scout spying out the land,
clutching his stone letters of promise that need only the seal to be
affixed. Characters traditional in medieval writing (such as the four
daughters of God) appear, speak, and act in ways that are unique to
Langland. Langland mixes modes: the opening scene of the field full of
folk features laborers behaving in a lifelike manner complete with vocal
effects; it is suddenly interrupted, in the B version, by an angel calling
out a message in Latin from heaven, followed by the sudden entrance
of a crowd of mice and rats, who conduct a lively debate on the problem of belling the cat.

Langland's allegorical figures, in defiance of their ontological status,
develop and change: the deadly sins burst into tears at the realization of
their wrongdoing, Scripture loses her temper, Holy Church is distinctly snappish, and the chief guide and key, Piers Plowman himself, is by
turns simple, baffled, authoritarian, and deceived, yet somehow turns
into Christ and is the only hope for humanity at the end. It is a poem
full of curious outbursts of bad temper, where characters insult each
other and storm off in fits of rage and bafflement. The poet, in the
happy words of one critic, has the habit of burning his narrative bridges
as soon as he has crossed them: it is all work-in-progress, and the
progress of the poem is never finished for either poet or dreamer. Modern as this sounds, the poet is yet convinced that there is such a thing as
revealed truth; what exercises him is the extreme difficulty of express-

ing it in human language. It is the opposite of cynical: whatever the poet's despair over the vices of his society, he still believes there is a truth to attain. The difficulty of expression compromises the poet's mission, and the lack of authority with which the poet speaks undermines his confidence. The crisis of the poem is reached in the Crucifixion scene (B.xviii), where we are shown what makes sense of Langland's world: the Christian paradoxes of death and life, sin and redemption, time and eternity all come together and enact (the scene is often compared to a medieval religious play) a drama that resolves the emotional issues of the poem without in any way solving its problems.

Piers Plowman is a highly personal, somewhat tormented poem, which uses the anguish of the half-mad narrator to ask radical questions about the nature of knowledge and the value of learning. Time and again, Langland confronts the problem that although medieval Christianity was a religion of learning, bookish and university-based, it also had to be acknowledged that salvation did not depend on learning or literacy, but on faith and love. At the very end of the poem, after all the dreamer's searching, he repeats his question:

> "Counseille me, Kynde," quod I, "what craft be best to lerne?"
> "Lerne to love," quod Kynde, "and leef alle othere."
>   (B.xx.207–208)

Neither learning nor poetry saves souls, which is what really matters in this world.

Langland's problem with learning is not felt so acutely in any other medieval author. Those in the Chaucerian tradition hold a more genial assessment of the value of books and writing, although they still downplay the role of the poet. It becomes a convention of authors to claim that they write their books to try to make something profitable instead of merely wasting time. Chaucer and Gower seem to have provided a psychological protection for them: if these could do such splendid and improving things in English, there could be no harm in trying to follow their tracks, showing due deference to their preeminence. The general didactic aim of literature could be interpreted loosely enough (if you were not too Platonist or austere) to make almost anything moderately worthwhile: Caxton asks his readers to approach Malory by taking "the good and honest actes in their remembraunce / and to folowe the same . . . for herein may be seen noble chivalrye / Curtoyse / Humanyte frendlynesse / hardynesse / love / frendshypp / Cowardyse / murdere /

hate / vertue and synne. Do after the good and leve the evyll and it shal brynge you to good fame and renommee." There were other authors besides Caxton who fell back upon St. Paul's statement, lifted right out of context, "for what things soever were written were written for our learning" (Rom. 15:4).

Chaucer's friend and contemporary, John Gower, distinguished by the epithet "moral" in the epilogue to *Troilus and Criseyde*, wrote large and overtly serious works in Latin, French and English. His English poem, *Confessio Amantis* (*The Lover's Confession*), was written at much the same time as *The Canterbury Tales*, and it is similarly a framed collection of stories. Gower's technical expertise in handling his smooth octosyllabic couplets is unobtrusively masterful, and his stories, taken from a variety of sources, are woven together with playfulness and wit. The tales are recounted in the course of a long confession made by the lover to Genius, priest of Venus; they are organized as telling examples to illustrate the seven deadly sins, at least insofar as the sins apply to the crimes and follies of lovers. The work displays an extraordinary ingenuity: a fundamentally serious religious ethic is consistently viewed aslant through the monomania of love, and encumbered with enormous and fascinating digressions that serve to delay the inevitable progression to the most interesting sin of all, lechery. Gower teases his audience with surprising turns and twists on the themes of love and virtue, before summoning Venus at the very end to dismiss the lover, disqualified from her service by his impotence and old age. But the poet frames the *Confessio* with a stern indictment of the contemporary world: the prologue evokes a golden time when men truly knew how to love, and contrasts it with the degeneration of corruption, violence and lust in the world of Richard II. It is hard to hold all the elements of the *Confessio* together: Gower offers it as a combination of profit and pleasure ("lore" and "lust"); but its analysis of human love in all its manifestations from comic to sublime, its playful wit, fierce denunciations of vice, earnest pleas for peace and charity, and splendid portrayal of a mutable and treacherous world in inevitable and irresistible decline almost pull it apart. If Chaucer offers us a world without comment, Gower offers us something more like an encyclopedia with a moral commentary; not as risqué as *The Canterbury Tales*, but not in need of apology or retraction either.

Chaucer's most famous follower was John Lydgate (d. ca. 1449), a long-lived monk whose enormous output has earned him much jocular abuse. Lydgate does not have any of the qualities which make Chaucer fresh for every generation that reads him; he is instead a much more typical product of his age, and was in consequence accorded an admiration even higher, in some cases, than that offered to Chaucer. Lydgate is above all a storyteller, and he undertakes to extend and enlarge the body of stories in English verse. He adds a tale to *The Canterbury Tales*, and embarks on some enormous translations: the *Troy Book* (from Guido della Colonna's Latin and a French translation) and the *Fall of Princes* (from Boccaccio's Latin and a French translation). These works show the medieval preoccupation with complete systems: the *Fall of Princes* is a giant catalogue of the downfall of notable people since the world began—the first story is that of Adam and Eve—showing the domination of Fortune over our world with the general didactic message not to trust to earthly things.

The *Troy Book* gives the whole complete story of Troy, which is far removed from Homer's partial (in all senses) account. The story of Troy for the Middle Ages began with Jason and ended with the death of Ulysses at the hand of his own unrecognized son by Circe. It provided a nostalgic paradigm for the downfall of civilization in the sacking of a great city: a reverberating image of loss. Lydgate ties his own translation to the English wars with France, but there must have been few times in the Middle Ages when this tale of hopeless valor, betrayal, and destruction was not all too appropriate. The story had grown steadily; minor characters like Troilus and Criseyde developed their own parts within it; the nations of Europe traced their origins back into it; it became everyone's history, combining the appeal of national epic and continuing soap opera. It is a mark of the distinction between Chaucer and Lydgate that Chaucer (like Homer before him) chose to focus on a tiny episode within the giant history, whereas Lydgate tried to encompass the whole thing systematically in serial style. Lydgate's verse is pedestrian but serviceable, and the story he tells has an undeniable power: the whole course of the war is traced from the initial insult offered to Jason and reaches its climax in the savage slaughter of the innocent Polyxena: a kind of moral sweep that judges even as it describes the course of events.

But Lydgate cannot let it rest there: he goes on patiently to provide accounts of the rest of the lives of all the participants; to him the whole story is more important than the literary climax. In the Troy legend the medieval blurring of the boundary between fiction and history is most apparent: "history" and "story" are after all the same word. We do not know if Lydgate thought of his work as translating, versifying, or embellishing, or a combination of all three:

> For in metring though ther be ignoraunce,
> Yet in the story ye may fynde plesaunce
> Touching substaunce of that myn auctour wryt.
> (TB.V.3491–3493)

But he is quite clear about the all-important purpose of it: in the tale one can recognize the instability of Fortune, murder, falsehood, treason, rape, adultery,

> As in this boke exaumple ye shal fynde . . .
> How al passeth and halt here no sojour,
> Wastyng away as doth a somer flour.
> (V.3565–3568)

The truth of the message, the moral, is what matters. One would be hard put to state the moral of *Troilus and Criseyde*. Lydgate articulates and illustrates the truisms admired in his age without the ability to embody them in memorable language. With the exception of his *Life of Our Lady*, where his verse rises to some beautiful ornate effects, the only line of Lydgate that stays in the memory is from a lyric, "All stant on chaunge like a midsommer roose"—and his editor suggests that this line is probably proverbial. Lydgate is, in a manner of speaking, the poet of the proverb, the earnest truism offered without Chaucerian irony or any exploration of complexity.

Thomas Hoccleve, a minor government official from 1387 until his death in 1426, grew up in the long shadow cast by Chaucer. His oeuvre is peculiar: some occasional and religious verse; a translation of Christine de Pisan's *L'Epistre au Dieu d'Amours* (1399); a semi-serious confessional poem, *La Male Règle*; a version of the *Speculum principis*; and a curious linked sequence of stories known today as the *Series*. Hoccleve is very insecure: he raises his voice in compliment and assent, rather than in Chaucer's tone of amused intimacy, and the occasions he celebrates are much more public. He seems to have aspired to join in the literary game of pretending to defend women, but where Chaucer is too wily to be nailed to a position, Hoccleve merely seems confused. The *Letter of Cupid* can only be seen as an attack on women by the exercise of giant ingenuity, and Hoccleve's pretended fear of women's angry response to it in the *Series* has the air of an all-male joke. In the *Series*, Hoccleve seems to have wanted to imitate Chaucer's first-person narrative frame and literary personality in a linked set of stories. He presents himself as the maligned and misunderstood friend of women who has to defend his innocence constantly (in the model of Chaucer in the Prologue to the *Legend of Good Women*), and as a penniless, mildly dissolute recovered lunatic who cannot persuade his acquaintances of his restored sanity. This persona is sufficiently bizarre to engage much of his modern interest: most of the critical industry has been devoted to diagnosing Hoccleve's mental condition.

Unlike Langland, whose waking madness signifies his alienated authorial status in a corrupt and confusing world and confers on him something of the aura of a holy fool, Hoccleve's real or artistic lapse from sanity is offered as a reason for adhering more closely to the religious and social norms of his day. He translates worthy works—such as Henry Suso's *How to Learn to Die*—in order to settle his wits, and provides careful moralizations for the other two stories in the *Series*. "Freend, I nat medle of matires grete," Hoccleve tells his interlocutor, and shrinks throughout from anything controversial. The rise of Lollardy since Chaucer's death led would-be official court poets into declarations of orthodoxy; it is significant that Hoccleve should explicitly reproach the Lollard Knight, Sir John Oldcastle, for reading Scripture instead of romances and the histories of Troy and Thebes. Hoccleve, like Lydgate, retreats to the moral platitude and safe didacticism. The inviting role of involved court poet needs authority: Hoccleve only wavers between the obscure personal confession and professions of solidarity and partisanship. His lengthiest and most popular work, the *Regement of Princes* (1411), shows him in full retreat into the part of poet as provider of wise truisms; a reminder that Chaucer's *Melibee* was one of his most copied works in the fifteenth century.

An incomplete, anonymous poem of the mid-fifteenth century, the *Court of Sapience*, belongs to the same tradition, though we know nothing at all about its author or setting. It looks back to Chaucer and Lydgate for its style, meter (rime royal) and inspiration, and provides a clear example of self-confident didactic allegory: but its serenity is achieved only by means of divorcing the action entirely from the actual world. Savagery and chaos are explicitly excluded; politics appears only as a learned abstraction. The framing allegory is minimal: the narrator seeks wisdom, falls asleep, dreams of a meeting with the lady Sapience, who then expounds to him all of the various subdepartments of wisdom available to man. The first and most effective book describes the crucial role of divine wisdom in the restoration of humanity through the Incarnation and redemption: it takes the form of a retelling of the traditional story of the daughters of God, Truth, Justice, Mercy, and Peace (from Psalm 85, Vulgate Psalm 84) who quarrel bitterly over the appropriateness of forgiving mankind for the original sin. Only the intervention of divine wisdom, Sapience herself, is able to solve the hopeless dilemma of the celestial relations between Justice and Mercy; and she recounts this tale as her greatest triumph. The poet has selected from a variety of Latin sources the fundamental units of his story, but he combines them with a moving and dramatic skill to produce an effect completely different from Langland.

The poet of the *Court* introduces the daughters at a different moment in sacred history, before the Incarnation, not after the Crucifixion; his rendering focuses on the arguments and the miraculous solution. The daughters first appear arguing their case before the throne of God: Mercy in bitter grief pleading for wretched man, Truth and Justice stating in measured terms the case for his continuing punishment, Peace insisting that she cannot live with discord, until Mercy collapses into a swoon at the impasse. Peace feels her "case" is lost; she delivers a magnificent valedictory speech to all the powers of heaven as she departs into exile. Then the three hierarchies of angels plead for the prisoner, mankind; Sapience offers to solve the dilemma by making the Son of God into man in order to restore his brethren to their former legal status; the angel delivers the message to Mary and the redemption follows. Jesus, on his triumphant return to heaven revives Mercy and restores Peace; the four sisters kiss each other. It is a careful and touching rendering of the bookish and legalistic side of medieval theology; since law was held to be universal, writers took great delight in demonstrating that even the actions of God could be seen as performed in accordance with the dictates of human law, although of course they would have put it the other way round: human law is an imperfect reflection of the law of God, and hence can be used analogically to help us understand the ways of God. The *Court*'s poet delights in playing variations on legal systems deployed as images: mankind is a traitor, Jesus wins by right of conquest as well as by purchase; he displays his legal title to man after his triumphant return. As theology, this was already very old-fashioned when the *Court* was written, but as a didactic vehicle, it is very effective. Allegory here fulfils its traditional function of explaining the abstract in terms of the concrete, without equating the two—and Sapience pauses in her narration to assure her audience that this is allegory, not history.

The same story in Langland is presented entirely differently: his daughters are mysterious figures who approach each other from the four corners of the earth in the darkness that follows the Crucifixion. What the *Court* author tries to express in terms of pathos and detailed argument, Langland presents as mystery and riddle. His Mercy, "a meke thyng with alle," is full of calm confidence and explains to Truth what the light before Hell means; Peace comes "pleyinge" bearing a letter from Love that explains the redemption. Truth and Justice respond with vernacular irritation and Langlandian bad temper, not courtly rhetoric: "Hold thi tonge, Mercy"; "What ravestow?" quod Rightwisnesse; "or thow art right dronke!" (B.xviii.187). All four sisters then join the audience of the poem to witness Christ's descent into Hell, and his own presentation of the arguments to a diabolic audience. The sisters' dance of reconciliation, the meeting of opposed extremes, is the heart of Langland's experience of God; the poem leads up to and away from precisely this point. In the *Court*, the story of redemption is instead the essential prologue to the rest of the poem which consists of a detailed and very old-fashioned account of the world of learning: first the dreamer is led by Sapience through the natural world where he sees an orderly array of precious stones, animals, trees, and plants, all characterized by their true properties and essential created natures, drawn from the best encyclopedias; then the dreamer arrives at the castle of Sapience, and is shown all human knowledge summed up in the courtyards of Science, Intelligence and Sapience herself, whose court contains the Seven Liberal Arts, the medieval academic curriculum. It is clear that the poet intended to go on to expound the seven major virtues (four cardinal and three theological) and possibly philosophy, but the poem breaks off abruptly. The poet presents all human knowledge and learning as flowing from a divine pattern; the "wyldernes" of this world conceals it, but a diligent seeker can recover it by proper study. The author even recommends suitable books and authors within the poem.

The *Court of Sapience* is the quintessential medieval learned poem. The poet works with assurance within an assured universe between the poles of an incomprehensible God, who may yet be glimpsed through revelation and his works, and the wilderness of sin, which may yet be escaped through diligence and contemplation. He is quite clear of the limitations of his work: allegory presents a certain truth, but is distanced from foolhardy assertion; redemption is like this, but this is only a story. The truth of fiction is here nicely indicated. When the poet gets to the virtue of faith, he repeats the creed for his readers, but points out that the higher mysteries of religion "in Englysshe ought not reherced be." Even the verse is assured beyond the usual competence of the fifteenth century: the *Court* is well written, with considerable metrical grace; it may only be a fragment, but it is an exceptionally well-built one.

Two other "learned poets," Stephen Hawes and John Skelton, were both members of the court of Henry VII. Skelton was probably the elder of the two and lived longer: he died in 1529. Although Hawes and Skelton are very different, they have some common preoccupations, especially in their concerns with the poet's function. They are both working after the invention of printing: a circumstance that is to have enormous consequences for a literary tradition. Both are learned poets, and both manifest slight signs of the advent of the Renaissance, chiefly with regard to what may be called the inspirational view of poetry.

Five works by Hawes survive, all only in printed copies. Three of them are allegories; the other two are a reproachful address by Christ to those who swear and a conventional celebration of the coronation of Henry VIII. The allegories look back explicitly to Chaucer and Lydgate, but owe an obvious debt to the *Court of Sapience*, which Hawes attributed to Lydgate.

In comparison with Skelton, Hawes is timid and modest. He declares that all he wants to do is to follow the steps of Lydgate, and he deplores any more frivolous view of poetry. His first known poem, *The Example of Vertu* (1503–1504), is a dream vision in which the narrator, Youth, is led by Lady Dyscrecyon to a ship; crosses the water of vainglory to an island ruled by Nature, Fortune, Hardynes, and Wysedom; witnesses a dispute amongst these ladies; courts Dame Clennes (Chastity) daughter of the King of Love; wins her by conquering the three-headed monster, the Devil, the World, and the Flesh; turns into Vertue; and has a sight of Hell before going to Heaven. Even this outline shows how Hawes espoused the didactic view of poetry: poets work "for the profyte of humanyte," and attempt to make their doctrine palatable by a transparent fiction, rhetorical devices, and a metrical vehicle.

Hawes's major work, his allegory *The Pastime of Pleasure* (1505–1506), repeats the plot of the *Example of Vertu* with many expansions and additions. The narrator, whose name we learn is Graunde Amoure, courts the lady La Belle Pucelle and wins her by conquering two giants and a dragon; he lives long, dies, and recites his own epitaph. Hawes claims again to be imitating Lydgate and does indeed produce a very medieval moral allegory, but there are some features in the *Pastime* that hint at the Renaissance, probably in spite of their author. The hero of the *Pastime* explicitly chooses a secular life, and is inspired on his way by the reports of the goddess Fame—a reliable lady quite different from Chaucer's capricious counterpart. The allegory throughout is uneasily secularized: the monsters are the traditional enemies of the lover, Slander, Delay, and Malice, but are conquered with St. Paul's armor of righteousness; Venus and Cupid are on Graunde Amoure's side, but the marriage is performed by Lex Ecclesie. To win his lady Graunde Amoure has to go through an extensive educational scheme, visiting the towers of the seven liberal arts for instruction; this is followed up by a visit to the Tower of Chivalry, where he learns to fight. Most interesting of all, in the tower of Rhetoric the instruction consists of a lengthy exposition of the processes of writing poetry; and this, clumsy as it is, is the first *ars poetica* in the English language. Graunde Amoure learns that poetry is produced by rhetoric, but with one important exception—one cannot draw the subject matter of poetry from the rhetorical rule books: poetry rises from the powers of the brain, and is then shaped by the rules of art. Hawes is maddeningly woolly in details: he uses "poet," "clerke," and "philosophe" as if they were all fully interchangeable, and he makes it clear only that he thinks the primary task of poets is "fables to fayne," and to pronounce "trouthe under cloudy fygures" (lines 717–720). The purpose of poetry is "to eschewe ydlenes," to improve knowledge, "to dysnull vyce and the vycyous to blame," and to preserve the fame of noble men (771–780). Although Hawes was himself a cautious experimenter in meter, he is fully medieval in his official indifference to any metrical component of poetry. When Hawes talks about poetry, he does so in terms of cloaked truth, misty fumes, feigned fables, and delightful rhetoric.

The end of *The Pastime* is noteworthy for the unexpected appearances, one after another, of the characters Death, Fame, Time, and Eternity (all described by the now-defunct narrator). These characters owe an obvious debt to Petrarch's *Trionfi*, probably mediated through a series of tapestries or paintings. They are iconographically very interesting, and make a surprisingly effective ending to the poem. But it must be admitted that however fascinating *The Pastime* sounds in description, it is wearisome to read. Henry Morley said Hawes "was held by the ears when he was dipped in Helicon"; he certainly had a tin ear for language and an unfortunate devotion to the Lydgatian metrical pattern known, damningly, as the "broken-backed line." His works were nonetheless very successful in the early years of the sixteenth century if we can judge by reprints and imitations; and any attempt to assess the literature of the period must come to terms with his popularity.

Hawes's last known work, *The Comfort of Lovers*, is an obscure personal appropriation of the characters of Amoure and Pucelle, who engage in a dialogue about their difficulties in love. The question of poetry arises again: the narrator explains that his only comfort in life comes from reading prophetic accounts of his own happiness with his lady in Chaucer, Gower, and Lydgate, and in finding letters written to them both on the walls of buildings. This sounds weird enough, especially when taken in conjunction with an image of the Holy Ghost later in the poem that carries the inscription: "I do enspyre oft causynge grete prophecy / Whyche is myscontrued whan some do enclyne / Thynkyng by theyr wytte to perceyve it lightly." The kindest way to assess this dark saying would be to consider it the first appearance in English of the Renaissance idea of poetry as "divine fury," closely related to prophecy and inspiration. Hawes's contemporary, Skelton, certainly espoused such a view; Hawes puts it forward only surreptitiously, in a poem full of mysterious emblems, hints, riddles, and private references. What is new in Hawes is his combination of theories of perception with traditional rhetoric to produce a theory of poetry, and his timid hints at a greater significance to poetry than medieval theory allowed.

Skelton, on the other hand, is the English answer to Rabelais: genuinely learned, arguably humanist, master of an astonishing range of vocabulary from the ornate to the crude, and a violent satirist, who spent his later years in attacking, with sporadic fervor, heretics, the introduction of Greek, and Cardinal Wolsey. He first appears as the tutor of the young Henry VIII, and is spoken of respectfully by Caxton as a scholar learned in Latin texts. Skelton's English work includes prose translations from Latin; his verse ranges from a conventional elegy in formal rhyme royal to hectic and shapeless diatribes in a meter of his own invention, and often includes many lines and tags in Latin. He refers to himself as "poet laureate" in most of his poems; this seems to mean that he had been awarded honorary degrees in rhetoric and was entitled to wear a special robe; he had an official position at court, although he was not the only poet laureate around. He eventually became a literary character in his own right: comic anecdotes and rude jokes that had collected around his name appeared in 1561 in a booklet, *The Merie Tales of Skelton.*

Skelton would have been a controversial figure in any period; in his own day the combination of scholarship, egotism, coarseness, and irreverence (he wrote parodies of the funeral service for two "knaves," his former parishioners, and another, "Philip Sparrow," for a pet bird) brought him under attack throughout his life. In his allegorical dream vision, *The Garland of Laurel,* Skelton provides a humorous self-defense. In a dream he sees Dame Fame asking Pallas if she may strike Skelton out of her register because he is so unproductive. Pallas summons Skelton to answer the charge; the trumpets blow to call all poets to judge, and Skelton is warmly welcomed by Chaucer, Gower, and Lydgate. He is given a tour of the castle and grounds; he sees crowds of inferior folk, entertainers and rogues, dispersed from the gates by a blast of cannon fire. He is then taken to a blissful garden featuring a phoenix and serious poetry, and finally meets the Countess of Surrey and all her ladies, who are busily making him a "cronell of lawrell" (a "garland" or crown of silk and gold embroidery work). He hastily composes eleven little lyrics in various meters to praise the ladies before returning to Fame, where an enormous, but, we are assured, selective list of his works is read out. The thunderous applause of the assembled poets wakes him up. Latin verses at the beginning and end of the work name Skelton as the English version of Homer, and more oddly, of Adonis.

This bizarre work is typical of Skelton in that it starts from the abstract, generalizing medieval allegory, complete with astrological setting and formal rhyme royal, which could be expected to work towards some sort of defense of the poet's learned academic role. The *Garland,* however, develops metrical and thematic variations that are highly personal and frequently desperately obscure—at one point Skelton descends into code to hide the real name of an enemy (deciphered in 1896 as Roger Statham; we are not much wiser), also known as Envyous Rancour. Skelton's sponsor at the court of Fame is Pallas, goddess of wisdom and learning, and the "poets" who turn up to hear his case include such learned authors as Cicero, Livy, and Vincent of Beauvais.

Clearly Skelton sees himself as a learned scholar rather than a versifier, and no mean one either: he makes the three great English poets greet him with veneration, and remarks with satisfaction that none of them is a poet laureate. But he does not consistently try to dazzle us with learning; among the verses offered to the ladies is a little poem that starts:

> By saynt Mary, my Lady
> Your mammy and your dady
> Brought forth a godely babi!

And he includes in the list of his works such titles as "The Balade of the Mustarde Tarte" and the "Gruntyng and the Grynninge of the Swyne" (unhappily now lost). Although the *Garland* pretends to be a charming occasional poem with a particular personal frame of reference—a visit to the Countess of Surrey and her ladies at Sherriff Hutton castle—it is now clear that the frame is largely a poetic fiction. Skelton may have composed this amalgam of conceit, insult, obscurity, and charm as his apologia, or it may be an elaborate joke: the portrayal of a sulky Fame being overwhelmed by the combined forces of Pallas, the notable writers of the known world, the Countess of Surrey, and Skelton's great list of works is very funny. Skelton suggests at the beginning that the whole dream might be the result of drinking too much. He hints at the old pose of the poet-who-has-annoyed-the-ladies, and offers the pretty lyrics in recompense. In all, it is an extraordinary blend of the personal and peculiar with the abstract and theoretical.

Although the role of public spokesman might seem appropriate for an official poet laureate, Skelton's work is most often dominated by his idiosyncratic voice and contentious personality. In the early *Bouge of Court* he is consistently allegorical and manages to keep personalities out; the villains are thoroughgoing allegorical abstractions. But where the opening of the poem has some resemblances to the *Court of Sapience*, the narrator's dilemma is not about putting the actual world into a divine perspective but with finding something suitably serious and allegorical to write about. Once asleep, the narrator finds not a world of abstract wisdom but a ship called Bouge of Court ("court rations") steered by Fortune and inhabited by a series of sinister characters, who so terrify the dreamer that he jumps overboard and wakes up. The rogues, traditional courtly bugbears such as Flattery, Riot, and Deceit, are characterized both by the dreamer (who calls himself Drede "Fear") and by their own speeches with a shrewd satirical eye: Skelton likes the idea of the learned poet, but he has little real use for the role of covert scientist or popularizing theologian or even general moralist. He does not use poetry to escape from the world or to put it in perspective: his work aggressively characterizes his own society, and asserts his place within it.

What Skelton really excels at is abuse and invective. His poem "The Tunnyng of Elinour Rummyng" consists of over six hundred lines of Skeltonics carefully divided into formal *passus*, complete with Latin epilogue, describing the appearance, ale brewing, and customers of Elinor Rumming:

> Some huswyves come unbrased,
> Wyth theyr naked pappes,
> That flyppes and flappes,
> It wygges and it wagges
> Lyke tawny saffron bagges;
> A sorte of foule drabbes
> All scurvy with scabbes . . .

The ale and its consumers sound equally disgusting, but are described with great verve and relish. Although the poem is signed "Skelton Laureat," it would be difficult to fit it into any medieval theory of poetry. In his epilogue Skelton pretends to invite dirty drunken women to listen to it, presumably for their castigation and reformation, but he can hardly be taken seriously since the invitation is in Latin. The poem is more properly a joke, a tour de force of low language and low life for the educated to laugh at.

The three poems Skelton wrote against Wolsey all use different speakers and modes: the parrot of "Speak Parrot" is a wise bird who makes oracular polyglot remarks in rhyme royal with baffling inconsequence. The politics of the day are filtered through the nonhuman, semidivine bird of paradise, whose snippets of talk are far more suggestive than informative. Scholarly industry has decoded a number of the parrot's darker remarks as allusions to Wolsey and his dominance over the young Henry VIII, but the poem is still largely a tantalizing riddle. Skelton has here perhaps taken up the old line about poetic obscurity for his own purposes: "Speak Parrot" is a poem that demands to be decoded: but the key, if there ever was one, is probably lost forever.

In "Colin Clout" the poet resorts to Skeltonics for a wide attack on religious and secular abuses, particularly Wolsey's luxury. The persona recalls the Langlandian figure of a simple rustic who can criticize society with greater truth than the rich and learned:

> For though my ryme be ragged,
> Tattered and jagged,
> Rudely rayne-beaten,
> Rusty and mothe-eaten,
> Yf ye take well therwith
> It hath in it some pyth.

But the persona is dropped entirely in the most vitriolic of Skelton's satires, "Why Come Ye Nat to Courte?" Wolsey, "the bochers dogge," "madde Amalecke," "Naman Sirus" is treated to accusations of all sorts, from treason to syphilis, in a linguistic register that ranges from a sneer at "the primordyall / of his wretched originall," to "The devyll kysse his arse!" Abuse was Skelton's speciality in his later life; he was invited by the King to engage in a flyting competition with Sir Christopher Garnesche, and he wrote several invectives against the Scots. When he wrote the poem "Against Venemous tongues," he knew what he was talking about.

The last known, and in some ways the nastiest, of Skelton's poems is his savage attack on two Cambridge students who were charged with heresy in 1527. It is interesting because Skelton added a postscript to it (as he did to many of his poems), in which he defends his right as a poet to embroil himself in theological and philosophical questions. After citing King David, a poet equal to any of the Greeks, Skelton makes an appeal to the "divine fury" view of poetry:

> With me ye must consent . . .
> How there is a spyrituall,
> And a mysteriall,
> And a mysticall
> Effecte energiall,
> As Grekes do it call,
> Of suche an industry . . .
> Of hevenly inspyracion
> In laureate creacyon,
> Of poetes commendacion,
> That of divyne myseracion
> God maketh his habytacion
> In poetes whiche excelles . . .

This is new in England. Diligent poets, earnest, improving (and sometimes guilt-ridden) poets of the Middle Ages give way to a more self-confident breed. They look to the newly discovered works of Plato for notions of divine inspiration and ally themselves with Renaissance artists in the reevaluation of the uniqueness and value of the artistic endeavor.

E. Ruth Harvey

Further Reading

Andrew, Malcolm, and Ronald Waldron, eds. *The Poems of the Pearl Manuscript.* Berkeley: University of California Press, 1982.

Burrow, John W. *Medieval Writers and Their Work: Middle English Literature and Its Background, 1100–1500.* Oxford: Oxford University Press, 1982.

Donatelli, Joseph M. P., ed. *Death and Liffe.* Speculum Anniversary Monographs 15. Cambridge, Mass.: Medieval Academy of America, 1989.

Harvey, E. Ruth, ed. *The Court of Sapience.* Toronto: University of Toronto Press, 1984.

Lawton, David. "Dullness and the 15th Century." *ELH* 54 (1987): 761–799.

Minnis, Alastair J., and A. B. Scott. *Medieval Literary Theory and Criticism, c. 1100–1375.* Oxford: Oxford University Press, 1988.

Offord, M. Y., ed. *The Parlement of the Thre Ages.* Early English Text Society 246. Oxford, 1959. Repr. 1967.

Pearsall, Derek. *Old English and Middle English Poetry.* London: Routledge, 1977.

Trigg, Stephanie, ed. *Wynnere and Wastoure.* Early English Text Society 297. Oxford, 1990.

Chaucer

W HILE greatly susceptible to the influence of his reading, Geoffrey Chaucer was a poet who rarely wrote without an experimental or innovative purpose or result. Chaucer's intellectual and literary curiosity and receptivity contributed an indispensable source of strength to his performance as a writer. The major achievements of his career, from such early dream visions as *The Book of the Duchess* (1368–1372) and *The Parliament of Fowls* (1380–1382) to the *Troilus* (1382–1386) and *The Canterbury Tales* (1388–1400), as well as unfinished works like *The House of Fame* (1378–1380) and *The Legend of Good Women* (1385–1386), which he appears to have abandoned for new projects of greater promise, all share qualities that reveal the unique nature of the Chaucerian enterprise. These qualities include a magisterial command of poetic line and literary form, a superb sense of mimesis and story telling, and an unrivaled gift for characterization and portraiture. His power as a narrative poet can be matched by a rare lyrical intensity, as in the artful introduction of several lyric passages in the *Troilus* at critical moments in its action. A keen ironist with a many-sided sense of humor, Chaucer explores the relationship between art and life as has no other poet before or after him.

Impressed by the energies and inquiries of his predecessor poets, both ancient and medieval, Chaucer moves along a path that at first glance looks familiar but which has actually never before been taken. Whatever may have fueled its beginnings, the Chaucerian poem, even when left unfinished, drives on its own course to its own destination. If the term *avant-garde* denotes the development of new and experimental concepts in art, then Chaucer was a kind of one-man avant-garde of fourteenth-century English poetry. What he learned from the poets who interested him gave him the kind of independence we may add to the qualities of variety and comprehensiveness John Dryden included among his reasons for calling Chaucer the "father of English poetry."

Recognized as a poet of stature in his own lifetime, Chaucer began to reach a truly national audience by the early decades of the fifteenth century, and with the first printed edition of *The Canterbury Tales* in 1476 by William Caxton, his reputation was well established and remained so through the sixteenth and early seventeenth centuries. Spenser, Sidney, Shakespeare, Milton, and their contemporaries had read him, but by Dryden's time Chaucer's work was relatively overlooked, accompanied by a corresponding hiatus in printed editions. It was Dryden who restored and critically defined his reputation. Chaucer has since enjoyed an increasingly important place in the literary canon of the English-speaking world; his poetry has been a regular subject of study at European and Asian universities, and critics as well as scholars have produced an impressive body of secondary literature concerning his poetry during this century.

An example of the highest level of critical debate stimulated by Chaucer's work can be seen in two responses to a single detail in the Wife of Bath's portrait. In the older historicist view of the Wife of Bath, informed more by group, moral rather than personal, artistic values, her deafness signifies the spiritual bankruptcy of her irredeemable, fallen nature, which does not hear the Gospel's message of charity, through the applicability of the scriptural admonition, "He that hath ears to hear, let him hear" (Matt. 11:15, 13:9, 43; Mark 4:9, 23; Luke 8:8, 14:35), and its patristic commentaries. A New Critical reading of the Wife, although it would not necessarily reject this signification of her deafness, would emphasize the complexity of her unique characterization, her sexual and marital history as developed in her portrait in the General Prologue, and the self-revelations of her prologue and tale. Chaucer's artful narration of the cause of the Wife's deafness, a blow to the ear by her latest late husband, rather than its religious and moral resonances, would make the stronger claim on the reader's attention.

Whatever the issues in critical debate about Chaucer's poetry, the foundations of its study lie in the great tasks of editing the manuscripts, understanding his language, identifying his literary sources and influences, and defining the canon of his authentic works. Chaucerian textual editing must deal with an unusually large number of manuscripts and early print editions that have been given manuscript status. *The Canterbury Tales* survive in six early print editions and eighty-three complete and fragmentary manuscripts. Second to this exceptionally large number are the sixteen manuscripts and three early print editions of *Troilus and Criseyde*.

While some important early poems like *The Book of the Duchess* and *The House of Fame* have each come down in only three manuscripts, and while it is likely that no extant manuscript of Chaucer's work was written during his lifetime, the sheer quantity of surviving manuscripts of his poetry attests to his early eminence. These manuscripts, however, vary greatly in character and completeness, which poses a major challenge to scholars to provide a reasonably reliable body of texts. The great editorial tradition of the last hundred years has classified in one place or another the entire body of extant Chaucer manuscripts and addressed problems raised by their differences. All manuscripts suffer some degree of corruption, and even the best of them, e.g., the base texts for important editions of *The Canterbury Tales* such as the Ellesmere for *The Riverside Chaucer* and the Hengwrt for *The Variorum Chaucer*, have had to be edited in light of variant readings from other manuscripts and early printings. Not surprisingly, the best efforts of textual scholarship to recuperate the "poem" are beset with uncertainties, just as Chaucer himself observed in his single-stanza poem *Chaucer's Wordes unto Adam, His Owne Scriveyn*, where the poet complains of having to rub and scrape the parchment in order to correct and rewrite the careless, hasty work of his personal scribe Adam.

If Chaucer and his editors have had to worry about scribal fallibility, the diversity and mutability of language itself have also given cause for concern. As Chaucer poignantly and prophetically remarks near the end of the *Troilus* in the passage that begins, "Go litel bok" (V.1786), the diversity of the English language and its writing in his time was so great he feared his poem might be miscopied or mismetered and, finally, misunderstood. To combat these effects, Chaucer scholars have paid and continue to pay serious attention to both his language and his versification. Concerning the latter, they have come to realize, through linguistic rather than manuscript evidence, that the pronunciation of certain light syllables, such as *-ed* and final *-e*, which belong to the inflectional and grammatical system of his language, enables a fairly regular iambic rhythm for his lines. The vexed question of the role of final *-e* in Chaucerian meter has been basically answered: it is generally pronounced at the ends of lines and wherever scansion requires it, but not when it is followed by a word that begins with a vowel or an *h-*, or when it appears in short unstressed words such as *hadde* and *hire*. Ironically, Chaucer's careful handling of sounded final *-e*, a practice uncommon among most fourteenth-century poets, was meaningless to the majority of scribes by the early 1400s. They wrote or suppressed it at will, in part because it gradually ceased to be sounded in Chaucer's Southeast Midland dialect, a silencing process that probably had started even earlier in the other Middle English dialects.

The Southeast Midland dialect, which included the London English of Chaucer's day, was one of five major dialects that developed in England after the Norman Conquest in 1066. Much closer to our own English, which descends directly from it, than to its West Saxon ancestor in Old English, Southeast Midland, by virtue of its currency in the seat of the national government, operated most prominently in the reestablishment of English throughout the country. Since the time of the Conquest, French had been the language of the aristocracy and much of the governmental administration; by the middle of the fourteenth century, English was being used more and more on every level of life. In courtly circles, in official documents, even in grammar schools, English replaced or enjoyed equal status with the Anglo-Norman French that had prevailed for over two centuries. Latin, of course, remained the language of learning, of the Church and university, and of some areas of government, but translations from it as well as from French became increasingly common. When English became once again the predominant vernacular language of the land, it was quite different from what it had been three hundred years earlier. Due partly to the influence of French and partly to the passage of time, Middle English dropped many of the inflected endings that denoted case and number in nouns, tense and person in verbs in Old English, and replaced them with prepositions, auxiliary verbs, and more highly structured syntax. This is not to say that Chaucer's English, notably more inflectional than modern English, did not rely on word endings for some of its meaning (as already indicated by the poet's use of final *-e*) or that its grammar did not preserve conventions that were normal in earlier English. For a useful summary treatment of these matters as well as of idiom, orthography, and pronunciation, one should consult the section

"Language and Versification" in the introduction to *The Riverside Chaucer*.

While it is tempting to think of English, French, and Latin as competing with each other in Chaucer's world, it is more productive to conceive of them as existing in a state of cultural fusion. It is not difficult to imagine that an individual like Chaucer, who grew up and spent his life speaking English and French and was literate in Latin (and who spoke very good Italian and some Flemish and Spanish as well), moved with unselfconscious ease from one language to the other. Still, Chaucer's decision in the early 1370s to begin his career as a courtly poet in English was clearly ahead of its time. Although both the steady reemergence of English as a language capable of meeting the needs of the populace and England's being at war with France intermittently since before Chaucer's birth strongly suggest that political and social conditions were right for his making this choice, there were other factors involved in the poet's determination to start and stay with English for his life's work.

These factors were primarily, if not purely, literary, and they reflect a book-loving nature of extensive dimensions and an intellect as keen on learning about the way poems work and enlighten as on understanding the ways of the world. "The lyf so short, the craft so long to lerne," Chaucer says in the first line of *The Parliament of Fowls*, writing of "Love," the force that fills both life and literature. From the earliest attempts to identify his sources to the appreciation of his literary appropriations and innovations, and on to the application of theories of intertextuality to his discourse, from antipodal positions that account for his literary production according to the cult of genius or to the cult of culture (and everything in between), almost all students of Chaucer, whatever their bias or desire, have agreed to place a high priority on defining the significance of his literary and intellectual relations.

Chaucer's Reading

There are no surviving records of Chaucer's formal education, but the traditional belief that as a boy he attended the almonry school of St. Paul's Cathedral and, in what was probably one of the most consequential events of his life, his documented appointment in 1357 as a page in the household of Elizabeth de Burgh, Countess of Ulster and wife of King Edward III's son Lionel, indicate two important sources of his "poet's education." At St. Paul's he would have been introduced to most of the Latin authors who appear in his poems. The move from the world of his prosperous London wine merchant family, comfortable and stimulating as it may have been, to the noble and courtly world of the royal family (in ten years he would become attached to the king's household), directly introduced him not only to the poetry and literary culture of France but also to some of the individuals who were foremost in its creation. In addition, many of his duties in the king's service, including diplomatic missions to the continent, provided him with opportunities to enlarge his literary awareness. Whatever and wherever his official assignments brought him, he seems always to have been searching for new poets and poems to read. To these sources of his poet's education he added a well-informed appreciation of the native English tradition and of several accomplished contemporaries and a remarkably wide familiarity with the Latin literature of the Middle Ages.

In the same intensely selfconscious passage near the end of the *Troilus* that begins "Go, litel book," where Chaucer expresses his apprehensions about the stability of language, he admonishes his poem to "kis the steppes where as thow seest pace / Virgile, Ovide, Omer, Lucan, and Stace" (V.1791–1792). Although he knew Homer only by reputation, Chaucer most likely got his first taste of Virgil, Ovid, Lucan, and Statius as a student at St. Paul's some three to four decades before he completed the poem that he trusted had earned him, an English "maker," a place among the great poets in Fame's temple. At school, he also would have been exposed to other Latin works such as the *Disticha Catonis*, a fourth-century A.D. collection of moral maxims erroneously attributed to Cato, to which Chaucer often refers as an educational staple, but it was the first reading of the poets of ancient Rome that was to act as one of the abiding and deep influences on his poetic thinking.

It is necessary to understand, however, that the medium in which Chaucer encountered this reading matter differed profoundly from the variety of text editions we take for granted. A bound medieval manuscript contained many works, sometimes unrelated to each other and sometimes specifically related, as in the assemblage of classical and medieval antifeminist works known as "Jankyn's Book of Wicked Wives" that Chaucer invented as the favorite reading of the Wife of Bath's fifth husband. Manuscript copies of works were sometimes incomplete and frequently contained errors; texts were often heavily glossed between the lines as an aid to translation; and many manuscripts contained titles mistakenly attributed to poets like Virgil and Ovid. Given this situation, and because much of a medieval person's contact with classical poetry came in the form of selected passages in anthologies known as *florilegia*, it is impossible to determine the extent and nature of Chaucer's knowledge of the Latin poets. How thorough, for example, was Chaucer's knowledge of the poetry of Statius, particularly the *Thebaid*? Although its darkly pessimistic, perversely tragic tale haunts Chaucer's descriptive and narrative imagination in several works, and Cassandra provides a twenty-five line account of its action in Book V of the *Troilus*, the ability of many medieval poets to make more of less or much of little challenges any absolute confidence we may have in our suppositions concerning Chaucer's complete familiarity with the *Thebaid*.

There is no hard evidence that Chaucer knew Virgil's *Georgics* or *Eclogues*. Nor can we assume he knew the *Aeneid* in its entirety, although the poem's preeminent reputation lends credence to Chaucer's full acquaintance with it, and Chaucer summarizes its action in a 220-line ecphrastic passage in the first book of *The House of Fame*. And when he relates the story of Aeneas's love affair with Dido, in a rather medievalized manner, in *The Legend of Good Women*, we must remember that the *Aeneid* was not the sole ancient source of this longest legend in the unfinished collection of stories about Love's female martyrs. Chaucer frequently drew upon more than one work in constructing his own version of a narrative, and in the Legend of Dido used her letter to Aeneas in Ovid's *Heroides* to close his poem. Even though Ovid was the poet of antiquity whom Chaucer knew best, there is a good chance that he never read the *Ars Amatoria*, the *Remedia Amoris*, or the *Amores*. He did borrow substantially from the *Heroides*, the *Fasti*, and the *Metamorphoses*, the last of which held Chaucer's interest throughout his life. Indeed, more than any other poem or poet with the possible exception of the French *Roman de la Rose*, it is Ovid's *Metamorphoses* that is demonstrably present through borrowing, reference, or allusion in the poems he wrote at every stage of his career. As a young, maturing poet, Chaucer may have learned something about style and tone from Ovid, but it was probably as a school boy in St. Paul's that he first encountered a major poem whose structure could contain many stories and whose narrative voice could contain a series of other narrative voices.

Chaucer's relationship with other medieval vernacular poets differed from his relationship with the poets of antiquity in at least one significant way. Whether predecessors or contemporaries, the French and Italian writers who interested him were also engaged in one way or another and in various degrees with the legacy of the ancients. Chaucer was an acute analyst of their appropriations from this literature—as he was of all of the elements of their writing—and his own stance towards the classics was in part directed by that of Jean de Meun and Dante, Guillaume de Machaut and Boccaccio. The influence of ancient poetry on Chaucer, in other words, is both direct and indirect, and from the time he entered royal service occupies an important although subordinate place in his participation, briefly as a follower and then as a pioneer, in the poetic project of his time and culture.

Chaucer's encounter with the courtly literature of France began in his youth, when he became a royal retainer, and continued as he matured and moved through the international aristocratic and governmental circles that introduced him to the new poetry and to some of its makers. In the course of his career, he met courtier poets like Jean Froissart, who, while at the English court during the 1360s with the young Chaucer, introduced him to the work of Guillaume de Machaut, the revered and highly influential poet-musician of the previous generation. The most distinguished follower of Guillaume de Lorris (the author of the first part of the *Roman de la Rose*), the prolific Machaut provided Chaucer with models of style, rhyme, and diction; of form, plot motif, and psychological situation; and with precedents by which to insinuate Ovidian and Boethian elements into the argument and substance of a poem, especially the dream visions. It is also possible that the narrative persona Machaut created for some of his works contributed to Chaucer's conception and development of his own narrator-character, one of the triumphs of his inventiveness.

There is, perhaps, no better epitome of Machaut's inspiration to elegance and musicality upon Chaucer than "Antigone's Song" in Book II of *Troilus and Criseyde*, which is based upon one of the older poet's lays: "O Love, to whom I have and shal / Ben humble subgit, trewe in myn entente, / As I best kan, to yow, lord, yeve ich al / For everemo myn hertes lust to rente" (827–830). It was for this and other transmissions from the French to English that another eminent poet of France composed a ballade in 1385 in praise of that "Grant translateur, noble Geffroy Chaucier." Eustache Deschamps was certainly familiar enough with Chaucer's work to witness his good repute in France. In that same ballade Deschamps praised Chaucer generally for his acts of carrying over the poetry of France to England and specifically for his translation of the *Roman de la Rose*, a poem that was of enormous influence upon Chaucer's writing throughout his life.

Begun in the mid-1230s by Guillaume de Lorris, the *Roman de la Rose* is an extraordinary narrative of over 22,000 lines about the subject of love on several levels. The originator, Guillaume, wrote the first 4,058 lines as an allegory of the psychology of love as it was understood in aristocratic and courtly culture. His treatment of *amour courtois* or "courtly love," a term invented in the nineteenth century, with its dream setting, its idealized springtime garden landscape, and its personifications of human faculties and qualities, established an archetype of "the love story" for the Middle Ages and the early Renaissance. Guillaume's narrative, which breaks off, possibly when he died, with the lover still far from successfully winning the favors of his beloved, was continued some four decades later by the scholar and translator become poet, Jean de Meun. Jean's continuation, which more than quadruples Guillaume's portion, ends with the lover's victory, but not before the stage for the quest has been expanded to include aspects of thirteenth-century society and its idea of the universe. Mythic and cosmic figures such as Venus, Nature, and Genius join personified characters drawn from Ovid and Boethius, among others, in a great debate about love that combines intellectual, humorous, and realistic modes.

The only extant version of the poem in English, *The Romaunt of the Rose*, containing all of Guillaume's part and nearly four thousand lines of Jean's, consists of three fragments by three different translators, only the first of which could have been by Chaucer. Whether Chaucer was responsible for this fragment or actually did his own, now lost, translation of the *Roman* is not nearly as important as Chaucer's lifelong engagement with the poem. The poem's fortuitous combination of the aristocratic-lyrical Guillaume and the earthy-intellectual Jean has provided a persuasive argument for the theory that one of the most crucial factors in Chaucer's achievement was his successful integration of literary courtliness and realism. The latter, also strongly affected by Chaucer's powerfully individualistic utilization of the French fabliau, reaches its high point in *The Canterbury Tales*. It is no accident that two of that work's greatest characters, the Wife of Bath and the Pardoner, were nurtured by their creator's skillful ability to embed in them two of

Jean's greatest figures, La Vieille, the old serving woman wise in the ways of love, and Faus Semblant, the hypocritical, self-confessing friar.

It may have been through certain French texts that Chaucer first became aware of the works of the three great writers of the Italian trecento, Dante, Petrarch, and Boccaccio. It may have been through his contacts with the Italian banking and merchant communities of London that he first heard of Dante's *Commedia*. Or it may not have been until the first of his two diplomatic trips to Italy in 1372–1373 and 1378 that he became aware of these authors' extraordinary blending of classical poetry and mythography with the international scholarly medieval Latin and vernacular lyric and romance traditions of Provence and France into an unmistakably original literature that elevated the status of the poet to a new height. Chaucer's involvement with this literature as an individual artist was clearly advanced both in terms of chronology and appreciation; he must have caught something from it about the dignity of the poet's calling.

Chaucer's major debt is to Boccaccio, of the three Italian writers, although he never mentions him by name; most important are Boccaccio's *Filostrato* (the source of the *Troilus*) and the *Teseida* (source of The Knight's Tale). What Chaucer did with his Boccaccian sources, both the literary works in Italian and the scholarly in Latin, has been much studied and has yielded many important insights into Chaucer's poetic originality as well as the nature of his literary obligations.

In addition to providing a Latin version of the Griselda story, Petrarch, the poet laureate who, in the Clerk's words, "Enlumyned al Ytaille of poetrie" (IV.33), supplied the words for Troilus's first lyric expression of the condition of being in love. The *Canticus Troili* of Book I, "If no love is, O God, what fele I so?" (400) is a translation into three stanzas of rime royal of Petrarch's Sonnet 88 (In Vita), number 132 in the *Canzoniere*, "S'amor non è." No one knows where Chaucer found this poem; it seems very unlikely that he could have known the *Canzoniere*, and if he did, would have limited his use of it to a single poem, and then even failed to recognize the poem's unique but repeated form.

If some Chaucerians suspect the character of Petrarch's influence may have exceeded these specific borrowings, many others have speculated about the nature and extent of Dante's influence on Chaucer. There are over one hundred and fifty passages in Chaucer's works that have been compared either verbally or contextually to passages in the *Commedia*, and about forty more to Dante's unfinished prose work the

Convivio, most of them to Tractate IV. Not every one of these comparisons needs to be conclusively proven to demonstrate that Dante had an effect on Chaucer. The passages of unarguable attribution in *The House of Fame*, *The Parliament of Fowls*, the *Troilus*, and *The Canterbury Tales* constitute adequate documentation of that, but the full extent of Dante's effect upon Chaucer remains an open question, from the proposition that *The Canterbury Tales* is an answer in the form of a "Human Comedy" to the challenge of Dante's "Divine Comedy" to the more recent proposition that Chaucer's first encounter with Dante destroyed the Anglo-Gallic poet's hard-earned self-confidence.

For the sake of convenience, the Chaucerian canon has long been divided into three periods, the French, the Italian, and the English. The division has never been accepted as completely adequate even by those who insist on observing it, for this perception of Chaucer's career reduces it to a sequence tied to his being inspired and dominated first by blocks of reading and then by a burgeoning of accumulated wisdom about human nature and English society. Just as the four hundred and ninety-three items in his life records, not one of which mentions his being a poet, tell a story about a civil servant, courtier, diplomat, and private citizen with his share of legal and financial problems, Chaucer's reading tells another. However difficult to determine its sway over his thinking and writing, the world of books within Chaucer's world of books was clearly one of the wellsprings of his creativity, perhaps the only one there is a chance of knowing. His recognition of Dante's greatness, for example, must have been accompanied by the recognition that they shared a number of favorite authors and poems like Virgil, Ovid, Statius, Boethius, and the *Roman de la Rose*. When Chaucer was writing the *Troilus* and most of *The Canterbury Tales*, if not earlier, his reaction to almost every poet was a reaction to several. Chaucer was especially interested in how poets managed other poets whose legacy they shared, not only because he understood that management to be one of the highest forms of the poetic enterprise but also because he became increasingly aware of his own ability to engage in it at their level.

Chaucer's Poems

There are three places in his poetry where Chaucer mentions his own works: *The Legend of Good Women* (F.329–334, 417–430; G.255–266, 405–420), the Introduction to the Man of Law's Tale (II.57–76), and the Retraction to *The Canterbury Tales*. In both versions of the Prologue to the *Legend*, the God of Love brands the Chaucerian persona as a traitor for having translated the *Roman de la Rose* and written of Crisyede's betrayal of Troilus. In his defense, Queen Alceste rejoins that Chaucer has written in praise of Love's name, listing specifically *The Book of the Duchess*, *The House of Fame*, *The Parliament of Fowls*, the story of "Palamon and Arcite of Thebes," and many shorter poems in his honor; that he has translated into prose the Boethius and (mentioned in version G only) the no longer extant *De miseria condicione humane* of Pope Innocent III; and that he has made a life of Saint Cecile and, long ago, "Origenes upon the Maudeleyne," a lost version of a pseudo-Origen sermon on Mary Magdalene. The Man of Law, apparently making no connection between Chaucer the pilgrim persona and Chaucer the poet, speaks slightingly of Chaucer's abilities, "he kan but lewedly / On metres and on ryming craftily" (47–48), and says without particular praise that Chaucer has told more stories about lovers than Ovid mentions in his *Heroides*. Still, the Man of Law seems to identify with the poet, who in his youth wrote about King Ceyx and his loyal wife Alcione (from Ovid's *Metamorphoses* XI in *The Book of the Duchess*) and later composed "the Seintes Legende of Cupide" (61), as he refers to *The Legend of Good Women*. About to narrate his own tale in a different hagiographic mode of the calumniated heroine, Custance, the Man of Law approves Chaucer's treatment of "wifhod" and his omission of tales about incest.

No doubt the Man of Law's story of Christian constancy in action was among the group of unnamed "bookes of legendes of seintes, and omelies, and moralitee, and devocioun" (X.1087) that Chaucer excepted from recantation in his much discussed Retraction at the end of *The Canterbury Tales*. In a canonical context, the Retraction is especially important because it provides, in what is apparently the poet's own voice, a catalogue of his authentic works. Chaucer specifically names only the translation of Boethius among the unrepudiated works, but in the Retraction proper he refers explicitly to the *Troilus*, *The Book of the Duchess*, *The House of Fame*, *The Parliament of Fowls*, *The Legend of Good Women*, to the "tales of Caunterbury, thilke that sownen into synne" (1085), and to the unidentified "Book of the Lion" (possibly a redaction of either or both poems titled "Dit du Lyon" by Machaut and Deschamps) before closing the list with the generalized categories of books no longer remembered and many a lecherous song and lay.

The translation of the *Roman de la Rose*, which was mentioned by Deschamps in his ballade to Chaucer and by the God of Love in *The Legend of Good Women*, is conspicuously absent from the Retraction. As the earliest work generally ascribed to him, *The Romaunt of the Rose* may belong with those forgotten poems of his youth that do not need specific reference. Even if the first fragment of the Middle English redaction, which covers most of the Guillaume de Lorris section, is all that Chaucer actually wrote, it is the appropriate point at which to begin consideration of the dream visions, a genre that Chaucer favored early in his career.

The opening section of Guillaume's poem established the prototypical pattern of the dream vision frame that Chaucer borrowed directly from Guillaume and from subsequent generations of French poets influenced by him. The major elements in this pattern were trust in the truthfulness of dreams, deference to an ancient authority like Macrobius on their nature, an entrance into the special world of love through the introduction of a first-person narrator who tells of his adventure in an enclosed garden during a perfect May, and a presentation of an exemplary story before the main action as one of its fundamental reference points. Chaucer, however, extended the narrative possibilities offered by these conventions so that each of his four dream visions enacts its own experiment with the form as it explores its unique subject.

The Book of the Duchess, *The House of Fame*, *The Parliament of Fowls*, and *The Legend of Good Women*, taken as a group, demonstrate not only that Chaucer was interested in pursuing the dream as a narrative structure but also that he was interested in the nature of the dream state itself. This interest, along with the psychological dexterity with which he handles dreamers and dreams, is apparent in many other works as well, especially the *Troilus* and several of the Tales. Except for the unfinished *House of Fame*, the dream poems conclude with the persona's commitment to writing them down, suggesting that the dream corresponds to the poetic process itself. For the persona, the dream precedes the poem's making, but for the reader, the dream is subsumed in its own poetic account. This account, in turn, is conditioned by Chaucer's claim that an old book is the source of the conventional exemplary story which launches and nurtures the poem. Thus we find Ovid's tale of Ceyx and Alcione in *The Book of the Duchess*; Virgil's *Aeneid* in *The House of Fame*; "Tullyus of the Drem of Scipioun" (Cicero's *Somnium Scipionis*) in *The Parliament of Fowls*; and the general praise for the authority of books expressed in the Prologue to *The Legend of Good Women*:

> And if that olde bokes were aweye,
> Yloren were of remembrance the keye.
> Wel oughte us thanne on olde bokes leve,
> There as there is non other assay by preve.
>
> (G.25–28)

Clearly, the old book, in Chaucer's hands, becomes an essential component of the genre.

In *The Book of the Duchess* the key book is Ovid's *Metamorphoses*, with its story of Alcione's confronting the death of her beloved husband, Ceyx. Chaucer's narrator retells a misread version of the tale of "Seys and Alcyone" before he falls asleep and dreams of the green wood, where he meets the friendly young hound that leads him deeper into the wood, where, in turn, he overhears a man in black lamenting the death of his lady. Chaucer's account of the Ovidian story contains many significant changes, including an ending in which Alcyone simply dies and the loving couple does not triumph over death through their metamorphosis into a pair of sea birds. This "misreading" not only implies that people read according to their needs, particularly poets who mine the works of their predecessors for ways of posing and resolving their own problems, it also invokes one of Chaucer's major themes, the relationship of poetry to grief.

Between the eight years of "sorwful ymagynacioun" (line 14) that afflict the narrator at the poem's beginning and his resolve at its conclusion "to put this sweven in ryme" (1332), there occurs a transformation of Ovid's story into the story of the Black Knight's inconsolable grief over the loss of his "goode faire White," which the Knight represents at one point as the loss of his Queen to Fortune in a game of chess. After a lengthy, complex dialogue in which the narrator maneuvers the bereft knight into confronting and accepting her death, he then offers him direct, simple consolation:

> "Allas sir, how? What may that be?"
> "She ys ded!" "Nay!" "Yis, be my trouthe!"
> "Is that youre los? Be God, hyt is routhe!"
>
> (1308–1310)

Both of them are changed in the process by which grief has been consoled through its metamorphosis into art, and the poet

Chaucer affirms that his use of reading is catalytic rather than emulative.

In writing *The Book of the Duchess*, Chaucer incorporated features from several French courtly poems; in *The House of Fame* he broadened his focus by calling upon elements from Ovid, Virgil, Boethius, and Dante. Different as they are in conception and outcome, these two dream visions are the only poems in which he used the staple verse of French poetry, the octosyllabic couplet. Abandoning this verse form with the last, mysterious line of the unfinished second dream poem, in which he refers to "A man of gret auctorite" (2158), Chaucer admits in the Invocation to Book III that "som vers fayle in a sillable" (1098), most likely an indication that he wanted his readers to understand he was concerned more with the number of syllables that were stressed than with the number of syllables themselves. Despite their shared verse form and classification as dream visions, *The Book of the Duchess* and *The House of Fame* are worlds apart. The former is a brilliant, one-of-a-kind success; the latter, ambitiously experimental and full of risk-taking innovations, fails in the end, but not until it makes a compelling display of Chaucer's gifts for dialogue, characterization, narrative control, and intertextual complexity.

Divided into three books, of which the unfinished third is as long as the first two combined, *The House of Fame* depicts a dream in which the narrator undertakes a haphazard journey to the goddess Fame's palace, which stands "Ryght even in myddes of the weye / Betwixen hevene and erthe and see" (714–715). Perhaps because the poet falls asleep on the tenth day of December, the expected springtime garden or forest green never materializes. Instead the dreamer finds himself immediately in a temple of glass that stands in the middle of a desert. The temple belongs to Venus, who is herself not present except in a portrait that shows her figure "Naked fletynge in a see" (133). Uncertainty is the dominant note of the narrative; even the Proem to Book I begins with an inconclusive account of the nature of dreams. This note is firmly struck in the ecphrastic passage describing the mural of Virgil's *Aeneid* in Venus's temple and is held through a variety of topics to the point where the poem breaks off. By underplaying the Virgilian roles of duty and destiny in Aeneas's departure from Carthage and by emphasizing Ovid's sympathetic treatment of Dido in the *Heroides* as an abandoned, wronged woman, Chaucer shows us that even a story as famous as that of Aeneas and Dido varies according to the versions of its successive tellers—Virgil's, Ovid's, the anonymous temple muralist's, as well as the narrator's—which we are left to sort out. Indeed, the story's "fame" subjects it to this condition. The Latin word itself, *fama*, is variable in its senses: it can denote rumor, news, and tidings as readily as desire for glory and earned good reputation. And Chaucer develops the theme of ambiguity in every kind of discourse by amalgamating different versions of Fame from Boethius, Virgil, and Ovid.

The work that most profoundly affected *The House of Fame* was Dante's *Commedia*. In the second and third books of Chaucer's comically unnerving vision of our doubt-filled world, there occur—almost run amok—a series of richly parodic parallels with Dante's vision of the otherworld. The most memorable of these, based on the eagle in Dante's dream in *Purgatorio* IX, is the pedantic, garrulous eagle who scoops up the narrator in his claws and carries him—the whole time chatting and lecturing irrepressibly—to the faraway domain of Fame's Temple. The deserted *House of Fame* may have been a victim of its own overwhelming representations of uncertainty, but there can be no doubt that, in creating its talking eagle, Chaucer discovered a gift for characterization that would be more fully realized before long in Pandarus, Harry Bailly, and Chauntecleer.

The Parliament of Fowls is also remarkable as a poetic vehicle for a multiplicity of voices in a variety of intellectual, literary, and colloquial registers, from the authoritative discourse of Africanus, both in the account of Cicero's *Somnium Scipionis*, which is the old book the narrator reads "a certyn thing to lerne" (line 20), and in the narrator's subsequent dream, in which Africanus appears as his guide; to the easy voice of Nature, who gently but firmly instructs her charges on this day of choosing their mates; to the humorous mimetic voicing of those charges themselves, reflecting in its full sweep of species in the kingdom of birds, from royal tercel down to lowliest seed fowl, a counterpart comprising all levels of human society.

Complementing this harmonious blend of various and sometime discordant voices, a narrative design to be fully orchestrated in the following decade's work on *The Canterbury Tales*, is a richly interwoven pattern of authors and texts, including Cicero's *Somnium Scipionis* (and Macrobius's commentary on it), Boethius, Claudian, Dante, Ovid's *Fasti*, Boccaccio's *Teseida*, the *Roman de la Rose*, and most important, Alan of Lille's *De planctu naturae*, on which Chaucer depended primarily for his portrait of Nature. Recent critical views of this pattern of wide-ranging dependencies suggest that it is indicative of authorial anxiety over its complexity, or of an extreme subjectivity, or of a subversive stance towards all forms of authority. The poem's narrator, it is true, closely ties his reading to an attempt to write something new concerning love, and he ends up, just before he falls asleep and dreams, with a lesson on the worth of common profit and morality in this world and the next he cannot help but value, even though it is not what he seeks: "For bothe I hadde thyng which that I nolde, / And ek I ne hadde that thyng that I wolde" (90–91).

Just as in *The House of Fame* the narrator was told by the eagle that he would be brought at Jove's behest to a source of tidings of Love's folk, so in *The Parliament of Fowls* he is told by Africanus that he will be shown matter to write about even though he is dull and not one of Love's servants: "I shal the shewe mater of to wryte" (168). The narrator's resolve to keep on reading at the end of his complex and ambiguous progress through this dream's garden of love suggests that he has still not found what he's looking for, yet may not be completely aware of the significance of what he has seen. Supporting the idea that the narrator does not fully appreciate what he has actually been granted in his vision is the accumulation of stronger, more frequent hints through the sequence of these dream visions that the narrative persona is less and less reliable. Also supporting this idea is the authority of the figure of Nature as opposed to Fortune and Fame, who are prominent in the two preceding visions. Like her prototype in Alan of Lille's *De planctu naturae*, Chaucer's Nature is the divinely appointed overseer of marriages and procreation. Unlike Nature and her priest, Genius, in Jean de Meun's *Roman de la Rose*, who press the case for sexual action with great urgency, she patiently guides most of her charges through their sometimes tumultuous mating rites to a successful conclusion, and even reassures some that it is all right to wait a year.

Possibly the poet-dreamer has served as a medium, albeit a not totally self-aware one, for the only trustworthy message available in his vision, a text generated by creatures directly under Nature's purview, the stately roundel the birds sing as they depart in praise of her ineluctable law of renewal:

> Now welcome, somer, with thy sonne softe,
> That hast thes wintres wedres overshake,
> And driven away the longe nyghtes blake!
>
> (680–682)

Like the lesson from Cicero's *Somnium Scipionis*, this cannot be easily dismissed, although it may not be what the narrator thought he was seeking at the start.

Some recent studies strongly suggest that our observation of Saint Valentine's Day as the major amatory holiday of the year originates in this third of Chaucer's love visions. More practically notable is the metrical form of the poem. Like the earlier, aborted *Anelida* and *Arcite* (late 1370s), an elaborate and complex experiment with epic and lyric forms based primarily on Statius and Boccaccio, *The Parliament of Fowls* is written in the rime royal stanza of seven decasyllabic lines rhyming *a b a b b c c*. Modeled on the ottava rima of Boccaccio, rime royal became Chaucer's favorite verse form, at least until he devised the decasyllabic couplet in *The Legend of Good Women*.

That both versions of the Prologue to *The Legend of Good Women* were written after the *Troilus* implies that Chaucer was still interested in the dream vision even after he had completed what was to be his only finished major poem. The shortest of the four dream visions in either the F (579 lines) or the G (545 lines) versions, the Prologue, as has already been noted, is a useful source of information about Chaucer's career. But it is also a poem of considerable accomplishments, and offers Chaucer's students a first-hand opportunity to consider his strategies of revision. The F version (ca. 1385), which survives in eleven manuscripts, has been accepted as earlier than G (ca. 1394), which survives in only one manuscript, although that manuscript is the earliest extant one of the work. Both follow the same general plan, with the narrator going out on a May morning to pay homage to his favorite flower, the daisy; with his falling asleep and dreaming that he is attacked by the God of Love for having translated the *Roman* and written the *Troilus*, but then defended by Alceste as one who has only translated what others have said and who has, in fact, written some acceptable works, even though he doesn't write particularly well. Ironically, some of the descriptions and dialogue are of especially high quality, showing just how well served his skills were by the new decasyllabic couplet. Particularly memorable is the inset "Balade" (actually three stanzas of rime royal), "Hyd, Absolon, thy gilte tresses clere," in honor of Alceste, who is about to appear as a transfigured daisy.

Queen Alceste, based on a woman in ancient myth who offers to die in place of her husband, Admetus, orders Chaucer to do penance for his trespass against the God of Love. She commands him to write, beginning with Cleopatra, only of good and true women who were betrayed by false men. That these prologues were intended to launch a large collection of stories implies that Chaucer was also thinking along the lines that finally led to the idea of the Canterbury pilgrimage as a frame of greater capacity and more dramatic possibilities than this unfinished series of nine tales of unvarying theme and action could offer. All nine of these "glorious" legends are drawn from classical legend and myth, and must have seemed very limited material for a poet who had already squarely met the challenge of exploring and testing against his own Christian and courtly world one of the greatest historical subjects antiquity had bequeathed it.

The story of the destruction of Troy, in which Chaucer and his immediate sources set their narration of the love of Troilus and Criseyde, was transmitted to medieval Europe by a number of works. Virgil's *Aeneid* and Ovid's *Metamorphoses* provided partial accounts of the first "great war" of the Western world, but the major sources were two Latin prose works of the fourth and sixth centuries A.D. There is no evidence Chaucer knew these two works directly, but he was familiar with the primary medieval intermediary based on them, the *Roman de Troie* (ca. 1160) of Benoît de Sainte-Maure and its late thirteenth-century translation into Latin prose by Guido delle Colonne. Benoît, the best candidate for inventor of the love affair, treated it in an incidental and minimal way in the course of his 30,000-line romance, but the true creator of the famous love story in the basic form in which it has been subsequently known was Giovanni Boccaccio. In 1338 he published *Il Filostrato*, a poem addressed to his own "nobilissima donna," Maria d'Aquino, in which he consolidated additional elements from Benoît with other sources to construct the tale of Troiolo and Criseida as a negative example of conduct in a love affair.

It is generally held that forty years later, in 1378, while on his second diplomatic mission to Italy, Chaucer acquired a copy of the *Filostrato*. If Boccaccio's version concentrates on shaping his source material into an account, with personal metaphorical implications and a transparently Italian fourteenth-century setting, of a love affair that ends in betrayal, Chaucer's adaptation attempts to restore the love affair to its historically significant setting in one of the foremost foundation myths of his world. This interest in a historical understanding of the events of the affair, along with several other artistic and intellectual concerns, provides an essential background for an explanation of the nature of

Chaucer's "translation" of Boccaccio's poem. The well-known statistical analysis of the relationship between the two poems shows that what Chaucer did with the *Filostrato* cannot be considered a translation in the conventional sense of the word. There are 5,704 lines in the Italian poem and 8,239 in Chaucer's, but only about one-third of Chaucer's poem, about 2,700 lines, can be traced directly to Boccaccio's. Why Chaucer, who often named his sources, never acknowledged Boccaccio may or may not be related to this fact. His reason for offering the name of "myn auctor called Lollius" (I.394) as his source for the entire work has never been definitively explained, even though a persuasive argument has been made that a mistranslation of a line in Horace led in Chaucer's time to a belief in a Roman authority on the Trojan War named Lollius.

Chaucer's adaptation recapitulates the action of the *Filostrato*, but *Troilus and Criseyde* differs from Boccaccio's poem in many respects. Chaucer deepened the characterization of the three principals, Troilus, Criseyde, and her older uncle, Pandarus (in Boccaccio, Pandaro is her cousin and of an age with the lovers), by making their emotions and motives more complicated. He expanded and added episodes to intensify the sense that the fate of the lovers is tied to that of their city, and that the fate of their city resembles the fate of Thebes, another city doomed in the period of human history that stood outside of the providential scheme of salvation.

But the most substantial contributions to the implications of the poem's action come from Boethius and Dante. Chaucer's translation into prose of Boethius's *De consolatione philosophiae* (early 1390s) was as significant to his artistic development as his earlier translation of the *Roman de la Rose*. Rendering into English the meaning of fortune, chance, destiny, providence, and free will as explained by the Lady Philosophy to the imprisoned Boethius, the author almost perfectly situated on the threshold of civilization's passage from the ancient into the medieval world, was probably the most demanding and rewarding intellectual exercise of Chaucer's life. The Boethian dimension pervades the *Troilus*, providing a pattern of understanding for the interaction of the operations of the internal world of the characters with those of the external, cosmic world. From Book I, in which the amatory expert Pandarus plays to the lovesick Troilus in a parody of Philosophy's instruction of Boethius, to Troilus's soliloquy in Book IV, in which Troilus attempts in vain to escape the conclusion with which he begins his reflections, "For al that comth, comth by necessitee: / Thus to be lorn, it is my destinee" (958–1082), Chaucer's appropriations from Boethius inform the narrative with philosophic and moral values, transforming Boccaccio's engaging narrative of a failed love affair with its personal, practical message to his most noble lady into a serious meditation upon the place of love in the world. In the words of the narrator's prologue to Book III, based on the eighth meter of Book II of Boethius, "God loveth, and to love wol nought werne, / And in this world no lyves creature / Withouten love is worth or may endure" (12–14).

Chaucer's use of Dante in the *Troilus*, while not as extensive as the Boethian adoptions, is of equal importance, for it reflects his intention to analyze on his own terms, just as Dante had done with his poetics of love in the *Commedia*, the significance of the courtly love tradition in the context of Christian doctrine. Different as they are, the trajectories of the lovers Dante and Troilus take much of their direction from the conventional wisdom of courtly love that the quality of the experience of love must be valued over its originating erotic desire and end. The ascent of Troilus's soul to the eighth sphere (a motif borrowed not from the *Filostrato* but from Boccaccio's *Teseida*) after Troilus's death at the hand of Achilles, both reported in the much debated "palinode" at the end of the poem, suggests that Chaucer did not want Troilus's experience as lover to be utterly dismissed. Despite its failure in this false world's brittleness, and its absolute supersession by the love of Christ, to which the "yonge, fresshe folkes, he or she" (V.1835) are recommended, it lingers, though forever lost, in the memories of the poets and their old books.

All of these Chaucerian literary interpolations, to which the narrator refers as things he has "in eched for the beste" (III.1329), enabled the poet to transform the Boccaccian story into his own complex masterwork. Not least among its complexities is its narrator himself, the sorrowful instrument who tells the double sorrow of Troilus, how he came "fro wo to wele, and after out of joie" (I.4). At times speaking, perhaps, as much for Chaucer the poet, who is his ultimate "auctor," as for himself, the narrator has license to expand the narrative record with ten lyric amplifications, but he finally must admit that he has no control over Criseyde's "trouthe" and the tragic outcome of the story. Like Pandarus, his surrogate within the poem, who seeks to bring about a love affair for his younger, at times maddeningly inept, friend, the narrator must finally give up on having things his own way, although, from the unique sympathy of his more distant perspective, he would never say, as does Pandarus (V.1732), that he hates Criseyde.

The artistic and emotional involvement of the *Troilus* narrator with the story helps to create a sense of distance between its action and its audience, an effect that critics have long admired. The move from this narrator to the narrator of *The Canterbury Tales* entailed one further step in Chaucer's development of this aspect of his art. Although reminiscent of the narrator of the dream visions, who awakens and reports all that he has dreamed, Chaucer's pilgrim also resembles Dante's pilgrim in that he professes to have have taken a journey, a recollective record of which he now shares. Pilgrim Chaucer, unlike Dante's pilgrim, is not the central character or protoganist, but he does occupy a place within the poem's narrative action. It is an ordinary place, in that he is but one of a group of pilgrim characters come together at the Tabard Inn on their way to the shrine of Saint Thomas à Becket in Canterbury, but it is also a central place because it is in his memory that the pilgrims, their tales, and their interactions along the way have been stored. Of the twenty-three pilgrims who tell tales, only the pilgrim Chaucer is a poet, and it is his memory that yields the account of their pilgrimage with its tale-telling contest.

The relationship between this pilgrim narrator and Chaucer the poet, and to some degree even Chaucer the man, has engrossed students of *The Canterbury Tales*, and indeed one's view of the relationship may have serious ramifications for how the entire work will be regarded. Arguments have been made in favor of keeping the three Chaucers strictly separated, with the pilgrim acting as a first-person fallible narrator; or of viewing them as indistinguishable from one another within a single figure who makes the necessary introductions of the social, moral, and authorial dimensions of his performance to the audience. Some readings stress Chaucer's literary pedigree, others his actual social status, as keys to understanding his significance as narrator of an extremely ambitious and complex, if unfinished, work. "Chaucer's plan" for *The Canterbury Tales*, whatever it may have been, has been identified, too closely perhaps, with the proposal made by the Host of the Tabard Inn, Harry Bailly, that each of the thirty pilgrims tell two tales on the way to Canterbury and two on their return. Like Pandarus, the Host acts as surrogate artist, attempting to order the story telling along the way. Just as Pandarus cannot save the love affair he has so carefully orchestrated, the Host cannot retain control over the sequence of the contest of tales he has arranged, in fact, loses it as soon as the first tale is told. After the Knight, who tells the first tale by virtue of drawing lots, completes his romance, the Host invites the Monk to match it, only to have the drunken Miller push himself into the sequence. The Knight's winning the draw as a serendipitous manifestation of hierarchy, allowing the pilgrim with the highest social rank to begin the game, and the Host's ability to manage the company are illusions of order.

The pilgrim narrator, for all of his alleged naïveté or simplicity, does not seem to share in these illusions. Twice he indicates, once near the end of the General Prologue and again in the Miller's Prologue, that he has subordinated his personal preferences and taste to the way things happened and the need to report them accurately and truthfully, which is to say, in their exact language. As narrator, he alone has, of course, the advantage of hindsight and already knows who said what, when and how. Unlike his distancing, sometimes disquieted, book-bound counterpart in the *Troilus*, this narrator conveys his experience of the event fully and without judgment or reservation, and leaves the burdens of discernment to his readers. Yet the transparency of much of his reportage has given rise to the recent debate over the attribution of certain passages that seem inappropriate to their tellers in the narration of some of the tales.

The relationship between the General Prologue (this title is a modern invention) and the various narrative links and tales, many of which have their own prologues, has been and remains a major concern for most Chaucerians. In one of the earlier, and for years most frequently taught, approaches to the structure of the entire work, the gallery of portraits was understood as a kind of program naming the dramatis personae of a fiction whose form was as dramatic as it was narrative. With each prologue and tale constituting a speech, or dramatic monologue, that invited analysis of character, a special emphasis could be given to the head links and end links as the sources of the poem's drama with all its conflicts and resolutions, the ultimate resolution being reserved for the traditionally allegorical representations of the way and end of the journey, in the words of the Parson, "Of thilke parfit glorious pilgrymage / That highte Jerusalem celestial" (X.50–51).

Another way of reading *The Canterbury Tales* has emphasized the realism of the pilgrims' characterizations and is heavily invested in the few topographical and internal references, e.g., to a tale just told or to one about to be told, made in the links as a way of ordering the sequence of tales according to geographic verisimiltide. No small amount of effort and ingenuity has gone into attempts to shift and reorganize the sequence of the fragments or groups of tales that are not explicitly connected to suit ideas of order suggested by scholars who harbor a deep desire and sense of prerogative to finish Chaucer's work for him. Since there is no objective way to eliminate the inconsistencies in the arrangement of tales in the best manuscripts, the Ellesmere order, with its discrepancies, is generally accepted as the closest we can get to Chaucer's intentions for the poem at the time of his death.

The dramatic and realistic approaches concentrate upon the question of the appropriateness of each tale to its teller, often based upon correlations between social class or type of teller with genre of tale, with the General Prologue portrait as the starting point. But recent views also propose that the tales just as easily, in fact more meaningfully, define and determine the portrait than the other way around; or that the real drama of the work lies not in the personality differences of its pilgrim tellers but in the stylistic individuality and variety of their tales. These critical mood swings between favoring the frame and favoring specific tales or groups of tales are inevitable. But one thing upon which almost all Chaucerians appear to agree is that whatever the poet took from the literary and oral traditions of his time as a starting point, be it Boccaccio's *Decameron* as a proposed model for the framed collection or an anonymous French fabliau as a source of one of the churls' tales, he makes it over into something completely his own.

If the postmodern critical notion that participation in genre inevitably means difference is correct, then the participation of a powerfully innovative imagination such as Chaucer's must mean unusually great difference. Almost every medieval type of narrative and mode of writing available to him, romance, fable, fabliau, saint's life, miracle tale, sermon, parody, satire, confession, appears in *The Canterbury Tales*, with a major and equal distribution of just over half of them into three major categories, the courtly, bourgeois, and religious: the Knight, the Wife of Bath, the Squire, and the Franklin tell romances; the Miller, the Reeve, the Summoner, and the Shipman tell fabliaux; and the Man of Law, Clerk, Physician, and Second Nun tell hagiographic tales. The Chaucerian handling of every one of them virtually destroys the possibility of their being used as effective models of imitation.

Most read of all of Chaucer's work, the General Prologue has elicited responses much like those to *The Canterbury Tales* as a whole. The incomparable gallery of portraits has gone through a process of study in which, at first, the focus was on identifying historical individuals as their bases, then on classifying and defining them as representatives of social types, and finally, on placing them within the literary tradition of medieval estates satire. None of these focuses works as well separately as they all do in concert, showing once again that it is the larger picture that enriches our study of Chaucer.

As the unforgettable opening lines of the General Prologue announce, behind their singular phrasing of the venerable poetic convention of the spring opening and all that follows in its wake, there stands an English maker, ready and able after the practice of a lifetime, to write the comedy to which he refers in his "Go, litel bok, go litel myn tragedye" stanza in the *Troilus*: "Ther God thi makere yet, er that he dye, / So sende myght to make in som comedye!" (V.1787–1788). Both Chaucer's tragedy and his comedy have taken their places with that highest standard of "alle poesye," to which every subsequent book is "subgit."

George D. Economou

Further Reading

Brewer, Derek, ed. *Geoffrey Chaucer: The Writer and His Background*. Cambridge: D. S. Brewer, 1990.

Dinshaw, Carolyn. *Chaucer's Sexual Poetics*. Madison: University of Wisconsin Press, 1989.

Donaldson, E. Talbot. *Speaking of Chaucer*. New York: Norton, 1972.

Howard, Donald R. *The Idea of the Canterbury Tales*. Berkeley: University of California Press, 1976.

Kiser, Lisa J. *Truth and Textuality in Chaucer's Poetry*. Hanover, N.H.: University Press of New England, 1991.

Leicester, H. Marshall, Jr. *The Disenchanted Self: Representing the Subject in the Canterbury Tales*. Berkeley: University of California Press, 1990.

Mann, Jill. *Chaucer and Medieval Estates Satire: The Literature of Social Class and the General Prologue to the Canterbury Tales*. Cambridge: Cambridge University Press, 1973.

Muscatine, Charles. *Chaucer and the French Tradition: A Study in Style and Meaning.* Berkeley: University of California Press, 1957.

Patterson, Lee. *Chaucer and the Subject of History.* Madison: University of Wisconsin Press, 1991.

Robertson, D. W., Jr. *A Preface to Chaucer: Studies in Medieval Perspectives.* Princeton: Princeton University Press, 1962.

Poetry in Scots: Barbour to Burns

THE language we call Scots has a common origin with English in that it is in large measure derived from the speech of the Anglian peoples who settled in northern Northumbria. In the seventh century Northumbrian kings established themselves and their language in southeast Scotland. However, the Gaelic-speaking Scots of the West pushed east and south to the Lowlands, and by the eleventh century Gaelic had become the dominant language of Scotland. Then came another change. From the twelfth century, kings of Scotland came under strong Norman influence. Though Norman French now became the language of the Court, northern English influence as well as Anglo-Norman immigration into Scotland altered the picture. When we add the Scandinavian influence from Viking settlers in northern England who moved north to Scotland, the product was a development of northern English or Anglian considerably influenced by Anglo-Danish (or Scandinavianized northern English). The result was the language we know as Scots.

Scots developed differently from English in many ways. It preserved certain Anglo-Saxon vowels that changed in English, or it developed them in a different way: it preserved a considerable vocabulary of Anglo-Saxon origin that was lost in English. Scots developed its own grammatical forms and its own ways of borrowing from other languages (e.g., verbs from the Latin infinitive instead, as in English, from the perfect participle passive: "dispone," "propone"; English: "dispose," "propose"). It retained or developed its own pronunciation. At the same time, English was close enough to Scots to be fully intelligible to educated Scots people and to provide Scottish writers an alternative in pronunciation and an enrichment of vocabulary where these might help to increase expressiveness. On the other hand, English writers could not use Scots as a source of enrichment: the language of the smaller and poorer country did not impinge on their consciousness in the way English did on that of Scots. The Scots had the advantage there: they were free of two kindred languages, and while the language they wrote was certainly Scots and not English, they could plunder English whenever it seemed advantageous.

In medieval and early Renaissance Scotland—apart from the Gaelic-speaking areas—people spoke Scots, and the poets built on that spoken language with borrowings from English, Latin, and French, with all kinds of rhetorical devices and "aureation," to construct a richly expressive literary medium capable of great range and subtlety. This was the language of the poets of Scotland from Barbour to Gavin Douglas and Sir David Lindsay, with Robert Henryson and William Dunbar at the center of the picture.

The earliest significant literary work in Scots to survive is *The Bruce* by John Barbour (d. 1395). Composed between 1375 and 1377, this long narrative poem tells the story of King Robert the Bruce, who fought successfully against great odds to prevent annexation by the English kings Edward I and Edward II. The poem is infused with high national feeling. The lines in the early part of the poem beginning, "A! Freedome is a noble thing," ring out as a remarkable affirmation of the significance of national independence for personal fulfillment. Indeed, "freedom" is here used to mean national independence probably for the first time anywhere.

The Bruce is written in octosyllabic couplets, a favorite verse form in early Scots poetry that remained so for centuries. *The Bruce* combines echoes of the Old French *chansons de geste* and certain formulaic devices with a tone, almost colloquial at times, of direct address to the reader. Barbour is recounting recent Scottish history and draws on oral rather than written tradition. Bruce's great victory at Bannockburn was won in 1314, a few years before Barbour's birth, but vivid memories of Bruce's struggle persisted in Barbour's day, and the poem has the flavor of a contemporary account, as well as some of the features of a folk narrative.

One of Barbour's motives was probably to inculcate lessons of kingship and patriotism. Barbour was writing his poem in the reign of Robert II, a king with none of Bruce's strong nationalist drive or charisma, and the poem may well have been a bid to arouse that earlier patriotic feeling. Bruce and his loyal helper, Sir James Douglas, appear as model heroic characters (although Bruce's guilt in slaying Comyn in church is admitted), and it is this sense of a mission carried through against all the odds that redeems *The Bruce* from the tedium of some of the detail. There are inevitably some dull moments in the nearly fourteen thousand lines, but the poem as a whole glows with a commitment to its subject in a way that distinguishes it from other heroic narrative poems of the age.

Barbour's narrative poem in octosyllabic couplets seems to have been a model for Scots poets and translators for over half a century. Andrew Wyntoun (1350?–1424?) wrote his *Orygynale Cronykil of Scotland* in this form. It starts with the Creation and attempts to set both the legendary and the more recent factual history of Scotland in the framework of Christian world history, but in spite of its ambitious scope the verse is pedestrian. Other works that show Barbour's influence include translations of *Legends of the Saints*, a *Troy Book* (of which only fragments survive), and a Scots version of parts of the *Roman d'Alexandre* cycle entitled *The Buik of the Most Noble and Valiant Conqueror Alexander the Grit*, completed in 1438.

The other hero of the Scottish Wars of Independence, Bruce's predecessor Sir William Wallace, is the subject of another long narrative poem, written some eighty years after *The Bruce*. Its full title is *The Actis and Deidis of the Illuster and Vailyeand Campioun, Schir William Wallace, Knicht of Ellerslie*, and it is traditionally attributed to "Blind Harry" or "Henry the Minstrel," who, according to John Major's *Historia Majoris Britanniae* (1521), was an itinerant minstrel who collected and recited legends about Wallace. It is in decasyllabic couplets, and has an appealing naïveté in its deployment of narrative and its admiration for the valor and fighting skill of the hero. *The Wallace* is much further removed in time from its subject than *The Bruce*. Although it uses traditions about Wallace that survived in the areas where he operated, it possesses many fewer elements of genuine history than the earlier poem. Its language has the sound of common speech, and the feeling that lies behind the story, as Harry tells it, is one of pride in his hero and his cause, not quite the high patriotism of Barbour, but what might be called a more popular version of that sentiment. The poem is in eleven books with a total of almost twelve thousand lines. It was turned into a modernized Scots by William Hamilton of Gilbertfield in 1722: this was the version read by Robert Burns which, as Burns wrote in his autobiographical letter to Dr John Moore, "poured a Scottish prejudice in my veins which will boil along there till the flood-gates of life shut in eternal rest."

There must have been many verse romances in Scots in the late Middle Ages, but few have survived. Sometimes it is difficult to distinguish a Scots poem from an English poem transcribed with simple orthographic changes into a work that looks like Scots. Some Arthurian romances come into this category. The liveliest of surviving Scots romances is *The Taill of Rauf Coilyear*, the story of Charlemagne, lost in a mountain storm, given shelter by a charcoal burner, and the socially interesting consequences. The poem is written not in Barbour's couplets but in an alliterative rhyming stanza of considerable artfulness—a notable example of the alliterative revival that was a feature of both English and Scottish poetry in the late fourteenth century.

The prestige and influence of Chaucer had an obvious effect on Scottish poetry from the beginning of the fifteenth century, although the title of "Scottish Chaucerians," which used to be given to fifteenth-century Scottish poets, has been discarded as inaccurate. It is difficult to pinpoint the influence of Chaucer (and also of Lydgate) on the Scottish poets. Middle Scots in the fifteenth century was a rich and flexible language, sufficiently akin to English to enable the Scottish poets to draw on English vocabulary to enrich and even decorate their Scots. There is no doubt that all the great Scottish "makars" (as the Middle Scots poets were called) regarded Chaucer as a master poet and rhetorician and learned from his craftsmanship. But they were all their own men, using their own language and having their own relationship with common European traditions.

Perhaps the most "Chaucerian" of all Middle Scots poems is *The Kingis Quair*, attributed to King James I of Scotland (1394–1437). King James was captured by the English in 1406 as a boy of eleven, and spent eighteen years in captivity in England. The poem describes the king's falling in love with the English Lady Jane Beaufort, whom he first saw from his prison window and eventually married, in a language that shows just the mixture of Middle Scots and literary and spoken Middle English we would expect from someone with King James's history. For all its Chaucerian qualities, *The Kingis Quair* is unique among both Scots and English poetry of the age for the freshness and individuality with which the poet's feelings are expressed (whether or not it is an autobiographical poem), even though this story of courtship is set within the medieval courtly love tradition.

The poem's verse form is the stanza of seven pentameter lines rhyming *a b a b b c c* known as "rime royal," probably first used in English in Chaucer's "Complaint unto Pity." The style and language owe something to both Chaucer and Lydgate (although the poet mentions only Chaucer and Gower as "my maisteris dere" in his concluding stanza), but the voice is very clearly the poet's own. The description of his emotion on seeing the lady from his prison window effectively combines stylization with spontaneity of feeling:

> And in my hede I drewe ryght hastily,
>   And eftsones I lent it forth ageyne
> And sawe hir walk, that verray womanly,
>   With no wight mo bot onely wommen tweyne.
>   Than gan I studye in myself and seyne:
> "A, swete, ar ye a warldly creature
> Or heavinly thing in likeness of nature?"

Throughout the poem the fluctuations of the poet's emotion are shown with a wry vigor. References to classical gods and goddesses have a certain sprightliness, and descriptions of natural objects are often both formulaic and vivid, as in this scene on a river bank:

> That full of lytill fischis by the brym,
>   Now here, now there, with bakkis blewe as lede,
> Lap and pleyit, and in a rout can swim
>   So prattily, and dressit tham to sprede
>   Thair curall fynnis, as the ruby rede,
> That in the sonne on thair scalis bryght
> As gesserant ay glitterit in my sight.

The animals observed, partly heraldic and partly natural, are listed in the other parts the poem, beginning (in a formula derived ultimately from Statius) with "There saw I" and going on to evoke the essence of each creature—as in "The lytill squerell, full of besyness." *The Kingis Quair*, with 1379 lines in 197 stanzas, lacks the sheer craftsmanship of the mature Chaucer—indeed, there is an amateurish tone about it. But if it has neither the brilliant virtuosity of Dunbar nor the subtlety and complexity of Henryson, it is nonetheless an accomplished poem and makes a worthy opening to the age of the makars.

The complicated thirteen-line stanza of *The Taill of Rauf Coilyear*, with its "tail" of four short lines, is used in *The Buke of the Howlat* by Richard Holland in the mid-fifteenth century. Holland, too, uses alliteration. *The Buke of the Howlat*, in seventy-seven stanzas, has an appealing Scottishness about it that differentiates it sharply from Chaucer's *Parliament of Fowls*, which clearly influenced it. The poem tells the story of an owl dissatisfied with its ugliness who persuades the Pope to ask Dame Nature to allow him to beautify himself with feathers donated by other birds. When she agrees, the owl becomes so offensively arrogant as a result that he is restored to his former state, and learns the lesson of humility. The skill and vigor of its alliterative verse, the wit and sprightliness of its description of the different birds with their human equivalents, and its unexpected but artfully managed introduction of a patriotic section praising the Douglas family, are memorable qualities of a striking and memorable poem. Holland's humor and irony—which go along with a high seriousness—are not Chaucer's humor and irony, and his language manages to combine artfulness with a vivid colloquial tone.

With Robert Henryson (d. ca. 1505) Scots poetry comes to its full maturity. Henryson is thought to have been a schoolmaster at the grammar school attached to the Benedictine Abbey of Dunfermline, in Fife, but little is known of his life. His most important poems are *Moral Fables of Esope* and *The Testament of Cresseid*. Henryson's *Fables* are in a well-established European tradition and include elements from the medieval beast epic, but the note of quizzical intimacy with the animals is all his own, and marks the beginning of a Scots tradition in animal poetry of which the best-known example is Burns's *To a Mouse*. In Henryson's fable of the town mouse and country mouse the colloquial ease of the presentation of the mouse world is something not seen in other European examples of fable. The country mouse is uneasy when she sees the luxury of the town mouse's dining facilities: "'Ye, dame,' quod scho, 'how lang will this lest?'" When the spencer comes in and finds them merrily at dinner, they escape promptly: "They taryit not to wesche, as I suppose." Although Henryson's work has a definite European dimension, his colloquial humanizing of the animals, conveyed in formal verse (rime royal) is very much a Scottish characteristic, parallel to but distinct from Chaucer's method in *The Nun's Priest's Tale*. The quietly matter-of-fact epitaph that Henryson's Troilus puts over Cresseid's grave is related to the quality we see in the *Fables*:

Lo, fair ladyis! Cresseid of Troyis toun,
Sumtyme countit the flour of womanheid
Under this stane, lait lipper, lyis deid.

Of the other poems attributed to Henryson none is certainly his. *Orpheus and Eurydice* tells the story, based on Boethius's *Consolations of Philosophy*, of Orpheus descending to the underworld in an attempt to bring back his dead wife, with a *moralitas* deriving from the English chronicler Nicholas Trivet. Of the short poems probably by Henryson *Robene and Makyne*, in the French *pastourelle* tradition, tells the story of a shepherd rejecting the love of a shepherdess only to discover too late that he loves her after all, and gives the moral: "The man that will not quhen he may / Sall haif not quhen he wald." The tale is told in sprightly eight-line stanzas with alternating rhyme; the pastoral setting is etched with sympathy, and the tone is both quizzical and matter-of-fact.

William Dunbar, the great virtuoso poet of the Scottish makars, stands alone—for metrical variety, for range of language (from "aureate" to brutally coarse) and of mood (devotional, celebratory, visionary, descriptive, moralizing, complaining, satirical), and for the skillful ways he brought his personality and circumstances into his poetry. Dunbar was the master craftsman of Middle Scots verse whom the modern Scots poet Hugh MacDiarmid looked back to (rather than to Burns) as a model. Active at the Court of James IV, he celebrated the wedding of the king and Princess Margaret of England in 1503 with a formal poem. We know that he survived Henryson, for Dunbar refers to him as dead in his great poem on death with the Latin refrain "timor mortis conturbat me"; that he seems to have taken priest's orders; and that he received a royal pension from 1500 to 1513. He tried to obtain a bishopric, but in spite of many appeals to the king he was unsuccessful. His relationship with the Court seems to have been intimate: he could address both the king and the queen in terms of remarkable frankness, complaining, asking, advising, celebrating, thanking, or simply joking.

Dunbar could write delicate love poems in the courtly love tradition, such as the one beginning: "Sweit rois of vertew and of gentilnes," in a rondeau stanza with the rhyme scheme *a a b b a*, as well as much more elaborate dream allegories, such as *The Golden Targe*, a triumph of rhetorical virtuosity in twenty-five richly sounding nine-line stanzas—the stanza used in Chaucer's "compleynt" of *Anelida and*

Arcite and by Henryson in "The Complaint of Cresseid." *The Thrissil and the Rose*, celebrating the royal marriage in twenty-seven rime royal stanzas, is another dream poem. Dunbar's use of what he calls "fresch anamalit terms celicall [heavenly]" is seen by himself as deriving from Chaucer—"O reverend Chaucer, rose of rethours all," as Dunbar hails him toward the end of the poem—but his "fresh enameling" is in a highly idiosyncratic style. In addition to Chaucer, Dunbar hails "morall Gower and Ludgate laureate" and refers to their "sugurit lippis and tongis aureate," indicating again the ideal he was aiming at in this and similar poems. The allegorical action in these dream poems, with characters from classical mythology and from *The Romance of the Rose* tradition, is in fact less interesting than the sheer virtuosity of the poetic performance.

Dunbar uses his "aureation" also in religious poems, notably in "Ane Ballat of Our Lady," with its chiming musical opening:

> Hele, sterne superne, hale, in eterne
>   In Godis sicht to schyne;
> Lucerne in derne [darkness] for to discerne
>   Be glory and grace devyne;
> Hodiern, modern, sempitern,
>   Angellicall regyne.

His poem on the Resurrection has a grave rhetorical force of a different kind, with its striking opening: "Done is a battell on the dragon black, / Our campioun Chryst confoundit hes his force. . . ."

The most intimate and perhaps to the modern reader the most appealing of Dunbar's poems are the shorter pieces about his own position and needs, often addressed to the king. His poem of new year's greeting to the king beginning, "My prince in God, gif the guid grace," moves from words of blessing and good wishes to the expression of the hope that the king will treat him with "hie liberal heart and handis not sweir [lazy]." He could address the king in a poem with the refrain "My panefull purse so prickis me," concluding with the remark that the only remedy for his painful purse was the king's generosity. He can attack abuses at Court in bitter poems of vituperation. He can write parodies of Latin religious offices, as in his use of the Office of the Dead in his poem "The Dregy [dirge] of Dunbar Maid to King James the Fourth being in Strivilling"; speaking from "hevins glory" (Edinburgh), he asks the king to come out from purgatory (Stirling) and join him "in paradise, / In Edinburcht." There are whole passages here in liturgical Latin: the spirit is that of the medieval Goliardic parody poems. Two poems to James Dog, Keeper of the Queen's Wardrobe, are in simple four-line *a a b b* stanzas. The first ends each stanza with the line "Madame, ye haff a dangerous dog"; the second, after Dunbar had received from James Dog the gift of clothing he sought, ends each stanza "He is na dog; he is a lam."

Dunbar can be irreverently bawdy in describing the king's sexual adventuring, as in the poem beginning, "This hinder nicht in Dumfermeling," where the king's behavior with his mistress is vividly and amusingly described in ten seven-line stanzas with a refrain expressing feigned surprise.

Dunbar produced one notable poem in the old Scots flyting tradition of mutual abuse, *The Flyting of Dunbar and Kennedie*, where Dunbar and his opponent Walter Kennedy rise to heights of fantastic insult in complex eight-line stanzas with both alliteration and rhyme. Dunbar used an older kind of alliterative line, unrhymed, in *The Tretis of the Twa Mariit Wemen and the Wedo*, which tells of the poet's lying concealed in a meadow on a midsummer night and overhearing a widow and two married women give totally frank accounts of how they cheated and abused their useless husbands and how they spread their sexual favors around. There is something of Chaucer's Wife of Bath and a variety of medieval antifeminist traditions in this poem, whose vocabulary is complex and sometimes violently bawdy, and whose 530 alliterative lines begin: "Apon the midsummer evin, murriest of nichtis, / I muvit forth allane in meid as midnicht wes past."

Dunbar's moralizing poems are some of his best. Besides the lament for the dead already referred to, there is the cheerful seven-stanza poem with the refrain "He hes aneuch that is content" and similar poems with stanzas concluding with similar advice, "For to be blyth me think it best" and "Without glaidnes avalis no tresure." Dunbar shows great versatility in his use of refrains.

He was capable of moods of real abandon, well illustrated in his poem describing a dance in the queen's chamber, which moves with enormous speed. The poet introduces himself in the fourth stanza:

Then cam in Dunbar the mackar,
On all the flure there was nane frackar
And thair he dancet the dirrye danton,
He hoppet like a pillie wanton

> For luve of Musgrave, men tellis me;
> He trippet quhill he tint his panton [lost his slipper]
> A mirrear dance mycht no man see.

One does not need to know that "dirrye danton" is a dance or that "pillie wanton" is unknown to scholars to relish the movement and indeed the abandon of this stanza.

One of Dunbar's liveliest poems gives a vivid and swift-moving account of a farcical fight between a tailor and a "soutar" (shoemaker) followed by a poem making amends, in which the poet dreams an angel comes down from heaven and cries, "Telyouris and soutaris blist be ye." This line, with its gravely ironic humor, concludes each of the ten four-line stanzas that compose the "amends."

Dunbar can also be gravely reproving, as in his poem addressed to the merchants of Edinburgh, attacking them for the dirt and disorder they allow in the city. He can paint vivid pictures of Edinburgh life of the day, whether in the "dirk and drublie dayis" of winter or at other seasons, and of the intrigues and squabbles of courtiers and clergy. And he can show naive joy at the arrival of the royal treasurer to bring him his pension in a poem with the refrain, "Welcom, my awin lord thesaurer!"

Dunbar's poetry displays with a vividness sometimes Breughelesque, sometimes Hogarthian, the life of late fifteenth-century Edinburgh—the Court of James IV and his queen at Holyrood, the jostling for benefices among the clergy, the behavior of merchants and lawyers, all the teeming activities of nobility, churchmen and citizenry. A sense of his own time and place is combined with a sure awareness of English, French, and Latin elements in medieval tradition, a relish of surface color and of the comic disarray of life in the world as it is. All this goes together with a sense of the transience of all earthly things and the ultimate relevance of everything to the Christian story. Dunbar may lack Henryson's gentleness and quietly ironic sympathy, but he has a range and virtuosity beyond Henryson's.

Dunbar's younger contemporary, Gavin Douglas (1476–1522), is best known for his pioneer translation of Virgil's *Aeneid* into Middle Scots rhyming couplets. This is not the sentimental Virgil of the Dido story or the plangent Virgil of *lacrimae rerum* so beloved of Tennyson: it is a vigorous epic Virgil rendered in terms of the late medieval and early Renaissance world that Douglas knew. And it is a Scottish Virgil, presented in a verse that, if it lacks the Latin poet's marvelous modulations of tone, achieves a quiet precision of diction impressive in its own way. A wholly original feature of the translation is the prologue to each of the books of the poem, the most impressive being those to Books VII, XII, and XIII, where Douglas paints pictures of winter, spring, and summer, respectively, not in traditional seasonal imagery but engaging vividly with the Scottish environment he knew. His description of winter is perhaps the most memorable of all such descriptions in Scottish poetry.

An earlier work by Douglas, *The Palice of Honour*, is an elaborate dream allegory written in a tricky nine-line stanza with an exuberance of decoration and an exhibitionist verbal dexterity that marks the poem as a showpiece. Douglas's "aureation" is not unlike Dunbar's, and his coined words help him in the difficult task of finding rhymes (restricted to two in each stanza). There are frequent changes of tone, marked by switches from highly Latinate terms to vigorous colloquial Scots. The poem concludes with a "ballad of honour" in three stanzas of richly chiming verse, in which the first has two internal rhymes to the line, the second three, and the third four—a piece of exhibitionist artifice. This learned and allusive poem with its frequent elaborate ornamentation is, surprisingly, not without humor, as in the self-portrait of the dreamer. *King Hart*, a much less elaborate allegory in a simpler eight-line stanza, was long attributed to Douglas, an attribution recently challenged.

Sir David Lindsay of the Mount was another Scottish poet who had a close relation with the Court, this time that of James V, whom Lindsay tutored as a child, eventually being appointed to the heraldic position of Lord Lyon King of Arms. *The Dreme of Schir David Lyndsay*, his first known poem, consists of about a hundred and fifty stanzas in rime royal. It opens with an "Epistil to the Kingis Grace," reminding the king how "Quhen thow wes young, I bure thee in myne arme," and how the poet sang to him and told him stories. We then proceed to the Prologue, where the poet describes his walking in a garden in winter, complaining of the cold, and then falling asleep as he sits wrapped in his cloak. The dream that follows is in the dream allegory tradition, but with a difference. It has an almost colloquial vividness. Dame Remembrance takes the poet down to Hell, where he sees all the corrupt leaders of the Church as well as unjust kings and lords. Then he is taken up through the seven planetary spheres (each described in detail) to see angels, Christ, and Mary before returning to Earth, whose divisions he describes according to the latest notions of cosmography. When he reaches Scotland he meets a man who speaks the "Complaynt of the Commonweill of Scotland," listing all the abuses of the time. The poem ends with "Ane Exhortatioun to the Kingis Grace" (in ten nine-line stanzas and a coda) exhorting the king to "considder thy vocatioun," remedy injustice, punish wrongdoing, and rule in fame and honor with the "counsell of thy prudent Lordis truew." The tone is quite different from that of Dunbar's poems to James IV. Lindsay is concerned with his country's problems and the plight of the people, not with himself and his own fortunes. The tone, sometimes even hectoring, is that of a teacher to a pupil.

The long *Dialog Betwix Experience and Ane Courteour*, in a variety of verse forms, is didactic to the point of tedium, but *The Testament and Complaynt of Our Soverane Lordis Papyngo* (parrot), mostly in rime royal, is vividly satirical with touches of lively humor. The *Complaynt*, addressed to the king in the octosyllabic couplets of Barbour's *Bruce*, also addresses the abuses of the time. Its tone is surprisingly familiar, very much that of a parent giving advice to a youngster, in spite of Lindsay's use of royal titles and his avowal in the final couplet of a "mynd full meik."

One of the most entertaining of Lindsay's poems is *The Historie of Squyer Meldrum*, in almost sixteen hundred octosyllabic couplets, very much in the tone of popular romance and reminding us sometimes, in its deadpan tone, of Chaucer's *Sir Thopas*. This is the story, told with a certain ironic gusto, of a real character of the time. It is followed by the *Testament* of Squire Meldrum, describing the happy musical celebration Meldrum wants at his funeral. A different kind of irony is shown in the spirited and colloquial *Complaint and Publict Confession of the Kingis Auld Hound, callit Bagshe, directit to Bawte, the Kingis best belovit Dog*, in which a former court dog confesses his misdeeds as an awful warning to the king's present canine favorite. This is in a tradition of animal poetry rather different from that of Henryson's *Fables*, a tradition that was to produce "The Last Dying Words of Bonny Heck" (a greyhound) by William Hamilton of Gilbertfield and Burns's animal poetry.

Sir David Lindsay's most memorable achievement was his long play *Ane Satyre of the Thrie Estaitis*, first performed in 1555. This work, mostly in rhymed couplets, is unique in Scottish literature, which has no other surviving play of the period. The Reformation Parliament of

1560 put an end to stage plays in Scotland at the very time when a dramatic literature seemed all set to emerge, so that there is nothing in Scotland comparable to the poetic drama of Tudor and Stuart England. Lindsay's is a long, undisciplined, self-indulgent play, but its brilliance in depicting vices and follies through the language and behavior of its characters, its vivid precision in locating contemporary problems in the actions of allegorical and symbolic figures are remarkable. Revivals of the play in recent years at the Edinburgh Festival have proved enormously successful. The story of King Humanitie led astray by Wantonness, Solace, Dame Sensualitie, Flatterie, Falset, and others, until reformed by Gude Counsall and others, and of the punishment of the Vices by Divine Correctioun and others may sound in summary like abstract allegory, but the figures have enormous vitality and humor. In addition to the personified virtues and vices there are real characters, such as the Soutar (shoemaker) and his wife, the Taylor with his wife and daughter, the Poor Man, the fraudulent Pardoner, who is a great comic character as well as a villain, and the eloquently moving figure of John the Common-weill. There is moral gravity, knockabout farce, and stirring eloquence in this great ramshackle play. In its attitude to religious abuses Lindsay comes close to the views of the Reformers, but it is behavior not doctrine that he is concerned with, and he never makes any statement that would be doctrinally suspect in Catholic eyes. Nevertheless, the play together with his satirical poems helped to place Sir David in the popular imagination as a great precursor of the Reformation in Scotland. As Allan Ramsay was to put it, Lindsay's satires helped "give the scarlet dame a box" sharper than "all the pelts of Knox."

A tradition of poetry of popular revelry, distinctively Scottish, begins with two poems *Peeblis to the Play* and *Christis Kirk on the Grene* (both doubtfully attributed to James V and also, even more doubtfully, to James I), written probably in the fifteenth century. These poems in ten-line stanza with a "bob and wheel" ending are genre portraits full of color and action. They remained popular until well into the eighteenth century and were imitated by both Fergusson and Burns. What they represented, however, was in stark contrast to the mood evoked when the Parliament of 1560 set its face against what an Edinburgh Town Council proclamation of 1587 called "all menstrallis, pyperis, fidleris, common sangsters, and specially of baldrie and filthy sangs. . . ." The reformed Church of Scotland, presbyterian in government and Calvinist in theology, looked to the Bible as the ultimate authority, and because there was no translation of the Bible into Scots, it was to English versions (first the Geneva Bible of 1560 and then the King James Bible of 1611) that the Church turned. A second, even stronger factor in weakening the authority of the Scots language for serious purposes was the removal of the royal Court from Scotland to England in 1603, when King James VI of Scotland inherited the throne of England to become James I of England, taking his court poets with him. Finally, the "incorporating union" of England and Scotland in 1707, making Scotland part of the larger political unit of Britain, further increased the prestige of the language of the richer and dominant part of the kingdom. English became the language of education and of "high" literature in Scotland, and the Scots language declined into a series of regional dialects used by jesters, antiquaries, writers of pastiche, depicters of urban low life or rustic peasant life, and nostalgic patriots. Exceptions will be discussed in due course, but in general the decline of Scots as a literary language can be traced quite clearly from 1560 through 1603 to 1707 and beyond.

There was, however, an impressive Indian summer of courtly literature in Scotland in the reigns of James V (1513–1542) and of James VI before he left for England in 1603. James V, who married the French Princess Madeleine in 1537, and after her death the following year married Marie de Lorraine, daughter of the Duc de Guise, brought a Franco-Scottish atmosphere to his Court, where poetry, music, and dance flourished together. The great court poet of this and the succeeding two reigns, and also a musician, was Alexander Scott (1515?–1583). Scott wrote in a consciously courtly tradition closely related to contemporary French poetry and music. How far that tradition survived after James V's death, when Marie's pro-Catholic faction was challenged by a pro-English Protestant faction, is difficult to say. We do know, however, that after her return from France in 1561 young Mary Queen of Scots encouraged poetry, song, and dance at the Court. Scott welcomed her back to Scotland with a courtly poem in Scots: "Welcum! oure lyone with the floure de lyce. . . ." The poem combines, in a manner we have seen in older Scottish poetry, admiration and admonition. Each of the eight-line stanzas ends with the same line, "God gif the grace aganes this guid new-yeir," in a manner reminiscent of Dunbar.

Scott was an accomplished and versatile lyricist whose most attractive achievement is his love poems, written as songs but with their own verbal music. Scott puts sonorous diction, well-crafted rhythm, and highly personal feeling at the service of the old courtly love tradition, to give it a new relevance and dimension, as well as a new relation to song and dance. At the Court of James V and, presumably, that of Mary, James's daughter, part-song for voices or instruments or both, known as "musik fyn," was an integral part of courtly entertainments that included various kinds of dance, spectacle, and ceremony.

Scott also wrote a poem in a very different style, more like the poems of popular revelry but also suggesting, in its burlesque of chivalric action, the parodic element of Chaucer's *Sir Thopas*: *The Justing and Debait up at the Drum* in twenty-one "bob and tail" stanzas. The tone can be judged from the opening stanza:

> The grit debait and turnement
> Of truth no toung can tell,
> Wes for a lusty lady gent
> Betwix twa freikis fell.
> For Mars the god omnipotent,
> Was nocht sa fers him sell,
> Nor Hercules, that aikkis uprent
> And dang the devill of hell
>   —With hornis—
> Up at the Drum that day.

Whatever the vicissitudes of Scott's career during the turbulent period that preceded young James VI's reestablishment of the royal Court at Holyrood in 1579, both Scott and the courtly tradition managed to hang on.

In 1581 the king's charismatic kinsman Esmé Stuart, Seigneur of Albany (Aubigny), arrived in Scotland from France to revive a court culture threatened by religious reformers. One of his company was Alexander Montgomerie, then thirty years of age and already an accomplished poet. Montgomerie established himself as King James's favorite poet (notably by a successful "flyting" with a rival, Hume of Polwarth) and was accepted by the king as his tutor in poetry. Although Montgomerie was to end his life in disgrace for his involvement in the murky political and religious intrigues of the time, in the 1580s he was the main force behind James VI's plan for a revival of poetry in Scots through the formation and encouragement of a "Castalian Band" of poets. Where James's grandfather, James V, had presided over a Court that encouraged the association of poetry, music, and dance in a Franco-Scottish courtly tradition, James VI's Castalian Band of poets was set a somewhat different program. Alhough they were encouraged to draw on the best of Continental poets, including French and Italian—Montgomerie himself was early influenced by Marot and Ronsard—James looked for a national poetry in Scots in a sophisticated rhetorical style. In his own work, *Reulis and Cautelis to be Observit and Eschewit in Scottish Poesie*, published in 1584, James remarked that works on the subject in English did not satisfy the differing rules of Scottish poetry. James wanted a characteristically Scottish poetry that was at the same time in the mainstream of European fashion; he also wanted a poetry more mannered and exhibitionist than suited Montgomerie, or indeed could suit any original poet. (James's own poetry is ingenious and self-consciously mannered.) In spite of Montgomerie's eventual disgrace, and the disturbing demands of politics on literature, there was a vigorous sense of Scottish poetic renaissance in the latter part of the sixteenth century, which disappeared when James left for England in 1603, removing at a blow the one effective source of patronage of the arts in Scotland—the royal Court.

Although Aubigny enjoyed the king's favor, his influence on the king was deplored by the Protestant lords, as a result of whose activity he had to flee back to France in 1583. Montgomerie was now chief cultural adviser to the king, who granted him a royal pension in August 1583, but his high standing at Court lasted barely three years. He continued, however, to write poetry, and if he was no longer the "Beloved Saunders, maistre of our art" that the king had called him in a poem addressed to Montgomerie in the early days of their relationship, he remained an active and an admired poet till his death, the greatest Scottish poet of his age.

Montgomerie's lyrics are in the courtly tradition of Dunbar, Lindsay, and Alexander Scott, and represent a conscious attempt to produce a poised and civilized poetry that would help restore cultural wholeness to a divided Scotland. A minor poet of the time, Sir Richard Maitland, had in his "Satire on the Age" expressed the sense of cultural loss produced by the civil and religious strife of the period: Where are "daunsing, singing, game and play" when "all mirrines is worne away"? Montgomerie sought to restore some of the lost merriness. Yet he was a fundamentally serious poet, who could write grave moral lyrics as well as poems of courtly compliment. The lyric beginning,

> Sweit hairt rejoiss in mynd
> With conforte day and nicht,

Ye have ane luif as kynd
As ever luifit weicht. . . .

has a charming courtly gravity, as have many of his love poems. The
combination of freshness and "enameling" can be seen in a lyric such as
that beginning,

Quhill as with whyt and nimble hand
My maistres gathring flours doth stand
Amidst the florisht meid. . . .

But the finest of Montgomerie's shorter poems is that on the solsequium (marigold), in four eighteen-line stanzas of varying line lengths
and marvelously complex, musical rhyming:

Lyk as the dum
Solsequium
With cair ou'rcum
And sorow when the sun goes out of sight
Hings down his head
And droups as dead
And will not spread
But louks [closes] his leaves throu langour of the nicht. . . .

This poem is also a part-song in the French style. Montgomerie's poetry, full of rich internal verbal music, is at the same time, remarkably,
often meant to be sung. His masterpiece, *The Cherrie and the Slae* (sloe),
a complex allegorical poem in 114 skillfully patterned fourteen-line
stanzas of richly musical language, was written to a dance tune known
as "The Banks of Helicon"; long considered to be a sophisticated philosophical work to be read and meditated in the study, it could have been
both danced and sung.

The allegorical devices employed in *The Cherrie and the Slae* go back
to the early Middle Ages, but the tone is original, and the stanza, with
its careful balancing of longer and shorter lines, was to become a Scottish tradition (used by Burns, for example, in his "Epistle to Davie" and
elsewhere). Much ink has been spilt on the precise meaning of the complex allegory. It certainly draws on the medieval tradition of dream
vision and love allegory and on the genre of the *psychomachia* or internal soul battle, but it also combines religious and philosophical discussion with extraordinary verbal dexterity and with subtle echoes of a
variety of elements in Renaissance thought. Critics who have examined

it carefully and submitted themselves to the spell of its language and rhythms agree at least on one point: there is nothing quite like this poem anywhere in European literature.

Montgomerie was also master of the sonnet, a pioneer of this form in Scotland. Many of his sonnets are full of wordplay, sometimes more ingenious than attractive. French models are preferred rather than the Italian preferred by English sonneteers. There are sonnets of compliment, of praise, of love, of complaint, and of satire, the complaints (often addressed to the king after he had withdrawn his favor and Montgomerie's pension) being on the whole the most vivid.

Other members of James VI's Castalian Band tried to put into effect some of the royal recipes for poetry, which the king summarized in a sonnet "painting out the perfect Poet" as involving ripe intelligence, wit, appropriateness, skill, "pithie wordes," appropriate tone, suitable figures of speech, and rhetorical sophistication. John Stewart of Baldynneis produced his "abbregement" of Ariosto's *Orlando Furioso* as his contribution to the king's program for rendering European poetic masterpieces into Scots. It is a remarkable performance, done with verve and skill and a conscious delight in poetic craftsmanship, cunningly reordering themes found in Ariosto's poem. It is in alternately rhyming decasyllabic lines that show a strain of high courtliness with self-conscious craftsmanship reflecting a Renaissance manner with roots in the courtly love tradition of the Middle Ages. Throughout the poem Stewart consciously strives to implement the precepts of his royal master, sometimes (as in the account of Roland's madness) with astonishing linguistic virtuosity that combines alliteration, onomatopoeia, and the use of parallel words in sequence known as "underwriting" in a bravura performance. Stewart's sonnet appealing to the king for help, beginning, "Dull dolor dalie dois delyt destroy / Will wantith wit wais worn with wickit wo," was calculated to please James with its high artifice. He asks the king to "grant grievous gronyng gratious guerdon guid" in the context of a courtly suppliant seeking royal "guerdon": a final moment of high courtliness in Scots poetry. After 1603 there was no one in Scotland to whom a poet could appeal for "gratious guerdon."

William Fowler (1560–1612) replaced Montgomerie as the king's favorite, and translated Petrarch's *Trionfi* at the king's request. He also arranged ceremonies for the Court and wrote sonnets under Italian influence. But after he left for England with the king to take up a position in the queen's household, his language became increasingly angli-cized. His best-known poem is a sonnet written during his stay in Orkney (before his departure for England), describing his position "upon the utmost corners of the world" and ending with a version of a well-known Horatian line: "So this I sie; quhaire ever I remove / I chainge bot sees, but can not change my love."

Another younger Castalian was Alexander Hume, who abandoned courtly Scots poetry not for poetry in English but (having become a Presbyterian minister) for religious poetry in Scots. Together with some indifferent "sacred verse" he wrote one fine poem combining quiet reli-gious feeling with perfect command of tone and language to evoke the course of a summer's day from dawn to dusk in a Scottish rural land-scape. Titled "Of the Day Estivall" (summer's day), it is written in sim-ple quatrains, beginning with an invocation to light:

> O perfite light, quhilk schaid away
> The darkenes from the light,
> And set a ruler ou'r the day,
> Ane uther ou'r the night.

The poem ends with a quiet benediction. The movement here is that of the Scottish metrical version of the Psalms, but the fifty-eight limpid stanzas are thoroughly domiciled in Scottish place and feeling. There is nothing like this poem in the work of the other Castalians or in earlier Scottish poetry.

One other memorable poem of this period—the only surviving poem in Scots by a poet whose other verse is in Latin—is a sonnet by Mark Alexander Boyd beginning, "Fra banc to banc, fra wod to wod, I rin," and ending,

> Unhappy is the man for evirmaire
> That teils the sand and sawis in the aire;
> Bot twyse unhappier is he, I lairn,
> That feidis in his hairt a mad desyre
> And follows on a woman throw the fyre,
> Led be a blind and teichit be a bairn.

This is a courtly love complaint with a difference, the powerful last line balancing the whole poem on the edge of despair. It is quite unlike King James's sonnets or those written to please him, and stands alone in the Scots poetry of James's reign.

The steady replacement of Scots by English as the literary language of Scottish writers is accompanied by a change of function for Scots still written. "The Life and Death of Habbie Simson the Piper of Kilbarchan," a nostalgic poem of the mid-seventeenth century by Robert Sempill of Beltrees laments, both sadly and humorously, the death of a famous piper and the loss of all the traditional tunes associated with his piping. Its stanza form, which Allan Ramsay called "Standart Habby" and which we know as the Burns stanza, became popular in eighteenth-century Scotland, and its mode, a half-humorous elegy, a common one. "Habbie Simson" was included in James Watson's *Choice Collection of Comic and Serious Scots Poems*, published in three volumes between 1706 and 1711 with the patriotic purpose of bringing together poems "in our own Native Scots Dialect," and so reminding Scottish readers of a literary heritage increasingly receding into the past. It is a very mixed collection and does not, in spite of the aim set out in the preface, confine itself to poems in Scots. But it does include "Christ's Kirk on the Green" (we give Watson's version of the titles), "The Cherry and the Slae," "The Solsequium," "The Flyting between Polwart and Montgomery," and Hamilton of Gilbertfield's "The Last Dying Words of Bonny Heck." Neither Henryson, Dunbar, nor (surprisingly) Lindsay is represented, but this jumble of what the editor found available is a symptom of the uneasiness felt in some quarters about what was happening to Scottish poetry.

Allan Ramsay (1686–1758) is a more interesting symptom. He combined a nostalgia for older Scottish poetry (which he both edited and imitated) with a desire to imitate the elegance and wit of the English poets of the Age of Queen Anne. Ramsay wrote English poems aiming at a Popian elegance, poems in Scots in the folk tradition, poems in Scots describing urban scenes of low life, genteel English versions of Scots folk songs, and his pastoral verse drama *The Gentle Shepherd*, which skillfully used a modified Scots in presenting Scottish rural life. Ramsay's collection of poems and songs entitled *The Tea-Table Miscellany* (1724–1737) contains some genuine old Scots folk material, some poems and songs of his own in a traditional Scots folk style, and some reworkings and "genteelizings" of Scots folk songs in an English neoclassic idiom.

In his preface to a volume of his poems published in 1721 Ramsay warmly defended the expressive capacities of Scots, yet he was on the defensive about his "Scotticisms." They may, he said, "offend some over-nice Ear," but they "give new life and grace to the Poetry, and become their Place as well as the *Doric* dialect of *Theocritus*, so much admired by the best judges." One cannot imagine Dunbar defending his Scots language in this way. Ramsay served Scottish poetry more unambiguously in editing *The Ever Green* (1724), a collection of older poetry in Scots largely taken from the Bannatyne Manuscript of 1568. The patriotic intention is made clear in his preface: "When these good old Bards wrote, we had not made Use of imported Trimming upon our Cloaths, nor of foreign Embroidery in our Writings." Ramsay is of course both right and wrong. The poetry of the older poets is anchored firmly in their own speech and country, yet it had a clearly European dimension.

The Ever Green introduced eighteenth-century Scottish readers to the poetry of Scotland's golden age, including a good selection from Dunbar, a less good one from Henryson, several poems by Alexander Scott, and the historical ballad "The Battle of Harlaw." Ramsay modified his texts as he saw fit, and even on occasion added stanzas of his own. But he did remind Scottish readers of at least a part of their lost Scottish heritage. In his own poetic practice, varied and sometimes confused as it was, he showed some uses for Scots in poetry of his own century—in vivid description of urban low life ("Elegy on Maggie Johnstoun"—she kept a pub just south of Edinburgh—"Elegy on Lucky Wood," "Lucky Spence's Last Advice"—she was "an Auld Bawd") and in songs of a folk flavor, such as "Up in the Air" and "The Young Laird and Edinburgh Katy." The role of the Scots language—or dialect, as it had become—seemed to be established.

It was the achievement of Robert Fergusson in his tragically brief life (1750–1774) to provide a new dimension to the use of Scots in poetry that, while it did not restore the rich comprehensive language of Dunbar and Gavin Douglas, nevertheless made Scots something more than a medium for nostalgia, pastiche, pastoral, and colorful pictures of low life. Fergusson, educated at Dundee Grammar School and St. Andrews University, had no need to be defensive about his lack of knowledge of the Latin classics in the original (as both Ramsay and Burns were), and in his Scots poems he was able to introduce a *gravitas* both of tone and of diction that poetry in Scots had lacked since the early seventeenth century. Using a Scots based on Edinburgh speech but enriched by his parents' Aberdeenshire and the dialects of Forfar and of Fife as well as by his reading of older Scots poets, he produced a Scots poetry of considerable resonance. While he wrote elegies in the Habbie Simson tradition and vivid accounts of Edinburgh life done with humor and gusto,

Fergusson also produced Scots poems that show him as a serious critic of his age who deplored many of the features of Scottish life that had developed since the Union of 1707. As a member of the socially mixed Cape Club, of which he was the official singer, "Sir Precentor," he mingled with a variety of Edinburgh characters, including musicians, painters, actors, and antiquaries, and felt himself part of a living community. At the same time he was deeply conservative; in such a poem as "The Ghaists, a Kirk-yard Eclogue" he showed his dislike of new economic and cultural developments.

Some of Fergusson's earliest poems were in standard English, but he soon established himself as a poet in Scots with regular poetic contributions to Ruddiman's *Weekly Magazine or Edinburgh Amusement*, beginning with "The Daft Days," a lively account of Edinburgh in the winter period between Christmas and early new year. The Scots here is assured, balanced, and confident, occasionally weighted with a Latinism that takes its place quietly in the run of the verse. His "Elegy on the Death of Scots Music" has as epigraph the lines from *Twelfth Night* beginning, "Mark it, Caesario, it is old and plain," thus setting the tone of elegiac stateliness not previously found in the "Standart Habby" stanza of this poem. "The King's Birth-Day in Edinburgh," also in "Standart Habby," has a mischievous assurance in its use of Scots and its handling of properties from classical mythology in a familiar Scottish context: "O Muse, be kind, and dinna fash us / To flee awa' beyont Parnassus." To rhyme the Scots phrase "dinna fash us" ("don't bother us") with "Parnassus," boldly claiming the right to use classical references in a rollicking Scots poem, indicates the influence on Fergusson of a Scots-Latin "vernacular humanism" developed early in the century by the editor Thomas Ruddiman and others. This movement had no future in a Scotland now so far from the Renaissance and the courtly tradition, but it left a brief legacy with Fergusson.

Fergusson's "Caller [fresh] Oysters" is another of his convivial poems; its opening shows him handling "Standart Habby" with a slowness and an openness not often found in this verse form:

Of a' the waters that can hobble
A fishin yale or salmon coble,
And can reward the fisher's trouble
    Or south or north,
There's nane sae spacious or sae noble
    As Firth o' Forth.

The poem "Braid Claith," again in "Standart Habby," is a pungent satire on the way in which clothes make the man. "Hallow Fair" celebrates an annual November market in the old Scots tradition of popular revelry, effortlessly combining vernacular raciness, local references, and classical allusions. "Caller Water," a poem of great charm in praise of fresh water, opens with a stanza about Adam in the Garden of Eden that taught Burns how to domicile scriptural characters in a familiar Scottish context: "When father *Adie* first pat spade in / The bonny yeard of antient Eden. . . ." "Mutual Complaint of Plainstanes and Causey" (sidewalk and street) is a dialogue in octosyllabic couplets that gave Burns the idea for "The Twa Dogs." The two companion poems "The Rising of the Session" and "The Sitting of the Session" give accounts of the life of Edinburgh when the Court of Session (Scotland's supreme court in civil cases) is and is not sitting.

Fergusson is perhaps best known for his grave descriptive poem in Spenserian stanzas, "The Farmer's Ingle," which gave Burns the idea for "The Cotter's Saturday Night." This is a deliberately conservative poem, describing with nostalgic affection a way of life that was changing rapidly. Like "The Ghaists" and other of his poems it reflects Fergusson's political and economic conservatism and that Scottish patriotism with which he associates it. Other significant poems of Fergusson are "Leith Races," in the same tradition and stanza as "Hallow Fair"— and the model for Burns's "Holy Fair"—and Fergusson's masterpiece "Auld Reikie" about his native city, in adroitly handled octosyllabic couplets derived from an English tradition developed by Butler, Swift, Prior, and Gay, among others. The couplets, shifting in tempo in accordance with the particular scene before the poet's eye, carry the expressive Scots forcefully to the ear, while the imagery, fixing the scene with its most significant component or appropriate symbol, builds up the city's sights, sounds, and smells. This is more than a Dickensian exploration of urban oddities or the search for a striking scene or incident: the whole poem is set in a framework of acceptance—acceptance of the whole of life, with its color, gaiety, debauchery, dreariness, pretentiousness, and weakness, companionship, loneliness, and sheer unadulterated humanity. Here Fergusson's often-indulged satirical impulses are subsumed in a wider humanist objective.

Fergusson in his short life left a handful of poems now recognized as some of the finest produced after the decline of the old court poetry. It was Burns's discovery of Fergusson's poems in Scots that, as Burns himself tells us, led him to realize what could be done in that idiom. Without Fergusson, "by far my elder brother in the Muse," as Burns called him, there would have been no Burns.

Robert Burns (1759–1796) has become so much of a Scottish national myth that the reality of his achievement is often obscured in the mists of sentimental rhetoric. Son of a tenant farmer in southwest Scotland, Burns shared during his early years the hard-working and materially ill-rewarded life of his class. Yet, with that zeal for education which distinguished the Scottish peasantry at that time, his father arranged with other farmers of the region to have his children taught from their early years by a well-educated young man, who drilled his pupils thoroughly in reading, writing, and English composition, and who introduced them to a wide selection of English literature from Shakespeare to contemporary English poets. It is a measure of the confused situation of Scottish culture that Burns, son of a Scottish peasant, received a formal education in English, learning by heart English poetry and learning to write an elegant Addisonian English prose. His letters, of which some seven hundred survive, are, except for a single one written to a close friend in racy Scots, composed in Augustan English of considerable formality. All around him Burns encountered Scots folk traditions in song and story, and he acquired some knowledge of older Scottish poetry from versions circulated in chapbooks and in collections such as Ramsay's *Ever Green*, but his formal education was an English education. The poet he quotes most in his letters and even sometimes paraphrases in his poetry is Pope.

Burns's earliest efforts had been influenced partly by the Scottish folk tradition and partly by his reading of English poetry. After his discovery of Fergusson's Scots poems he developed a poetic language of great variety, combining Scots and English in different ways. He showed remarkable skill in the verse letter, a form used earlier in the century by minor Scots versifiers, combining, as none of his predecessors had done, the formality of rhyme and meter, and of stanza forms derived from older Scots poetry, with the informality of tone suitable to letters to friends. These letters—the "Epistle to Davie," the "Epistle to J. Lapraik," "To James Smith," among many others—are written either in the "Standart Habby" stanza or in a modified form of the complex stanza of *The Cherrie and the Slae*, by Montgomerie. They generally begin by setting the scene, giving the season of the year in terms of the farmer's activities, then moving from the farmhouse, where he is writing, outward to Scotland and the world in general, to place at the cen-

ter of the poem some declaration of faith or generalization about life or
poetry or happiness.

> What's a' your jargon o' your Schools,
> Your Latin names for horns an' stools;
> If honest Nature made you fools,
>   What sairs your grammars?
> Ye'd better taen up spades and shools,
>   Or knappin-hammers.

> A set o' dull, conceited hashes,
> Confuse their brains in colledge-classes!
> They gang in stirks, and come out asses,
>   Plain truth to speak;
> An' syne they think to climb Parnassus
>   By dint o' Greek!

The poet then adroitly maneuvers the poem back to himself and his
correspondent before wittily signing off.

Burns also cultivated an old Scottish tradition of poetry about animals—"The Death and Dying Words of Poor Mailie" (a sheep), "To a
Mouse," "The Auld Farmer's New-Year-Morning Salutation to his
Auld Mare, Maggie"—in which he showed humor and sensitivity and
a farmer's feeling for the animals he encountered or worked with. But
most of all in his early poetry he developed a rich vein of satire. A passionate egalitarian from childhood—precociously aware that the
landowners' children he played with would, when they grew up, treat
him, son of a struggling tenant farmer, with condescension—he bitterly resented class divisions based on wealth and rank. "A Man's a Man
for a' That" is more than a piece of eloquent sloganizing: it is a passionately satirical expression of a central theme in Burns's thought.

Burns also resented the stern Calvinist creed of predestination that
flourished in his part of Scotland. He preached instead, as in the "Second Epistle to J. Lapraik," the doctrine that

> The social, friendly, honest man,
>   Whate'er he be,
> 'Tis he fulfils great Nature's plan,
>   And none but he.

"Holy Willie's Prayer" displays in a brilliant dramatic monologue the
creed of a devout Calvinist who, believing himself to be a predestined

member of the Elect, could be led into the most flagrant hypocrisy. The poem's opening sums up a central aspect of Scottish Calvinism as Burns heard it preached around him:

> O Thou that in the Heavens does dwell,
> Wha, as it pleases best thysel,
> Sends ane to Heaven an' ten to Hell
>   A' for thy glory,
> And no for onie guid or ill
>   They've done before Thee.

> I bless and praise thy matchless might,
> When thousands thou has left in night,
> That I am here before thy sight,
>   For gifts an' grace
> A burning and a shining light
>   To a' this place.

Satire of a less biting kind is found in "The Holy Fair," a description of the great outdoor communion service then common in the west of Scotland, at which preaching, drinking, and lovemaking went on simultaneously, and the claims of the spirit and of the flesh asserted themselves in ironic contiguity. Yet another kind of satire is found in the "Address to the Deil," where the Devil of folklore—a mischievous, Puck-like figure—replaces the evil tempter of the preachers and is reduced almost to a figure of fun.

A totally different kind of poetry is represented by the grave, slow-moving, lovingly etched picture of a farm laborer's family at home in "The Cotter's Saturday Night." In this poem, however, moments of sentimentality and even of posturing occur. These remind us of what might be called Burns's cultural vulnerability: he was susceptible to the cult of feeling typified by Henry Mackenzie's novel *The Man of Feeling*, and could on occasion assume the role of sentimental observer of the human scene. A peasant who had been made free of the world of polite literature, a Scot who was all too aware of the anglicizing forces among the arbiters of taste in Edinburgh, a fierce critic of social inequality with a deep sense of humanity, a remarkable capacity for friendship, and a passionate involvement in sexual love—this complex character walked a tightrope between the genteel world of the Scottish Enlightenment and the rough realities of peasant life. When in 1786 Burns decided to publish a book of his poems, he deliberately posed,

in his preface, as an uneducated peasant whose inspiration came solely from heaven. He was very well educated, but he shrewdly judged
that the "literati" of Edinburgh would be more favorably disposed
toward an unlettered farmer poet, a "phenomenon." He was right. His
poems were enthusiastically received both by simple country people
and by the sophisticated critics of the Scottish Enlightenment. In a
review of the poems by Henry Mackenzie, Burns was called a "Heav-
en-taught ploughman," and he was beckoned to Edinburgh as an
example of the genius of the natural man. He was glad to accept that
role—for a time and up to a point. Sometimes when he was conde-
scended to and patronized by people of wealth and position whose
intellects he knew to be inferior to his own, he let the pose drop, and
he was then accused of arrogance.

All this is reflected in Burns's poetry, which moves between conventional sentimental verse in Augustan English and lively Scots, with
varying mixtures. One might say that the complexities of Scottish culture in his day—with educated people still speaking Scots but writing
in standard English—forced a degree of role taking on Burns. At any
rate, he was adept at it. He could play the role of the complete anar-
chist—"a fig for those by law protected"—as in his "Cantata" *Love and
Liberty* (generally known as *The Jolly Beggars*). He could write songs
against the Union of 1707, belligerent patriotic pieces like "Scots Wha
Hae," he could play the sentimental Jacobite lamenting the lost Stuarts,
and he could also sound the note of loyal British patriotism. After being
lionized in Edinburgh, Burns felt unsettled and restless, and although
he returned to farming, he was not successful. He succeeded finally in
obtaining a position as an excise officer, which he held to the end of his
life in spite of getting into trouble politically over his sympathy with the
French Revolution.

Besides his satires, verse letters, animal poems, and poetry of popular celebration, Burns wrote one superb narrative poem, *Tam o' Shanter*,
based on an Ayrshire folk story. In octosyllabic couplets with cunningly varied diction, from vivid colloquial Scots to formal English, the
poem alters the speed of its narrative as it moves from description of a
cozy pub interior to the storm outside, then to the dance of the witches, then to the frenzied pursuit of Tam when he is discovered watching
them. A masterpiece of carefully patterned voices, the poem ends with
a mock moral, and this ironically pretentious moralizing note sounds
intermittently throughout.

To many, however, Burns's greatest achievement was his songs. The eighteenth century in Scotland was a great age of collecting and imitating ballad and folk song. The two collectors and publishers who asked for Burns's assistance unleashed in him a passionate activity of song writing and song collecting that lasted until his death. These pieces are in Scots tipped with English, or in English tipped with Scots, and show a remarkable gift for fitting new words to existing tunes. Burns took the crumbling and half-forgotten fragments of his country's folk songs and restored them, sometimes by complete rewriting, sometimes by supplying new verses to an old chorus, sometimes by filling out a mere suggestion he found in some half-remembered line or barely surviving refrain. He undertook to find words—old or refurbished or new—to all the existing Scottish airs that he thought worth preserving, whether they existed in his time as song tunes or as dance tunes. He traveled around Scotland picking up local traditions and local work songs. Many songs he never claimed as his own but presented as old songs he had discovered. "A Red, Red Rose" and "Auld Lang Syne," for example, are among those he never claimed as his: they clearly use traditional elements but also show his own craftsmanship at work. Burns could put his love songs into the mouth of either sex: some of the most popular are from the girl's point of view (e.g., "O Whistle and I'll Come to Ye, my Lad" and "O Wha my Babie Clouts Will Buy"). Burns could link love, sex, and parenthood in a way no other poet has done, rejoicing in all three. He could celebrate friendship as well as love, drink as well as sex, work as well as play, anger and indignation as well as happiness. In his best songs he speaks for life as it is actually lived, relishing the realized moment of experience. He has songs of posed sentimentality, too, but even these can break out into something true and haunting, as in his farewell song to Agnes McLehose, the "Clarinda" to Burns's "Sylvander" in a hothouse love affair that ended in disaster. The farewell poem he wrote for her, "Ae fond kiss and then we sever," is one of the world's great songs of parting. Burns the man is full of paradoxes and his poetry is full of contradictions. His whole career as a man and as a poet was a remarkable balancing act amid conflicting demands and loyalties. Burns was the last great poet to use Scots before the renaissance of Scottish poetry begun by Hugh MacDiarmid in the present century. There is something elegiac about his achievement, a sense sustained in the way his memory is cherished and celebrated.

David Daiches

Further Reading

Bawcutt, Priscilla, and Felicity Riddy, eds. *Selected Poems of Henryson and Dunbar.* Edinburgh: Scottish Academic Press, 1992.

Daiches, David. *The Paradox of Scottish Culture.* Oxford: Oxford University Press, 1964.

Daiches, David. *Robert Burns.* Rev. ed. London: Deutsch, 1966.

Jack, R. D. S. *Alexander Montgomerie.* Edinburgh: Scottish Academic Press, 1985.

Kinsley, James, ed. *Scottish Poetry: A Critical Survey.* London: Cassell, 1955.

Scottish Academic Press. *Longer Scottish Poems.* Vol. 1 (1375– 1650), edited by Priscilla Bawcutt and Felicity Riddy; vol. 2 (1650–1830), edited by Thomas Crawford, David Hewitt, and Alexander Law. Edinburgh, 1987.

Shire, Helena M. *Song, Dance and Poetry at the Court of Scotland under King James VI.* Cambridge: Cambridge University Press, 1969.

From Ballads to Betjeman

THROUGH the centuries English verse in a variety of forms has reached a large audience through broadsides, newspapers, magazines, and vocal performance. Only recently has popular verse received attention in classrooms and academic journals.

Among topics little taught in the classroom, the traditional ballad has been one of the most continuously researched. Although the word *ballad* initially referred to dance, the ballad of tradition is a story set to music, passed orally among the "folk" from generation to generation. Immemorial in origin and transmitted also by writing and printing, ballads were preserved at crucial stages, through singers unable to read, by memory. Francis James Child, for his *English and Scottish Popular Ballads* (1882–1896), found variants in manuscripts of the thirteenth through the nineteenth centuries. A large portion of the most continuously admired ballads appeared with various degrees of polish in Thomas Percy's *Reliques of Ancient English Poetry* (1765), which alerted Burns, Scott, Wordsworth, and Coleridge to the beguiling force of "folk" balladry. Before Child, sophisticated poets learned from balladry much as prominent twentieth-century artists were to learn from African sculpture. Ballads have exceeded every other source in pervasive influence on poetry of the last two centuries; the trail from the *Lyrical Ballads* of Wordsworth and Coleridge is unbroken.

Revered for their simplicity, traditional ballads show more often than tell; in telling, they usually avoid straightforward narrative. Often they convey a crucial detail only implicitly; the listener must be alert enough to supply the linchpin. Protagonist and speaker are often the same. As in other forms of popular song, refrain is common. In a large class of ballads details emerge by incremental repetition in a dialogue of questions and answers. In "Lord Randal" the son answers his mother's questions with a varied refrain ending, "I fain wad lie down," saying that he met his true love, that she fed him fried eels, that his hawks and hounds died, that he has been poisoned, that he is sick at heart, that he leaves property to his mother, sister, and brother, and finally that he leaves his true love "hell and fire."

A stanzaic form common enough to be known as the ballad stanza, printed in quatrains as here from "The Wife of Usher's Well," was probably in origin a pair of seven-beat couplets:

> Up then crew the red, red cock,
>   And up and crew the gray;
> The eldest to the youngest said,
>   'Tis time we were away.

This ballad in a dozen or so stanzas builds typically upon folklore, superstition, and sacred numbers: the three sons have returned after death. Ballad narratives often end, and sometimes begin, in catastrophe. In "Sir Patrick Spens" the sea captain knows, from the new moon with the old moon in her arm, that the king is sending him into a fatal storm. In "Edward" a son who in differing versions has murdered his brother, his father, or his bride answers his mother's final question by leaving her the "curse of hell" for counseling him to do it. In "Barbara Allen," thought to have passed across seas and into mountain communities with remarkably few variants (before and after Percy included two sophisticated versions in *Reliques*), the balladeer accounts for intertwined briars over two graves in his town by telling of the local girl who spurned sweet William on his deathbed because he had slighted her once in a tavern—only to die soon after from grief over her error. Bertrand Bronson began his fine book *The Ballad as Song* (1969) by calling into question all versions of "Edward" as too sophisticated for the simplicities of tradition. He warned that every ballad unrecorded before Percy, even as sung by unlettered mountaineers, might be contaminated by—and possibly have originated in—the Enlightenment. Like Joseph Hendren in 1936, Bronson endeavored to establish the primacy of tune over words.

Balladry saved most of its happy endings for episodes in the career of Robin Hood. Praise for later outlaws in later ballads tends to lament the offender's sorry end. For *Reliques*, Percy's friend James Grainger gave "Bryan and Pereene, A West-Indian Ballad" an ending as naively grim as he could make it—when a shark dyes the ocean red with Bryan's blood, Pereene collapses: "Soon her knell they ring." In an exception to the common woe of traditional ballads, the Turkish maiden in "Lord Bateman" freed the English lord from her father's prison, was promised the lord's half of Northumberland, remained true (one version says for 7 + 7 years = 33), crossed the sea (with her mother), and finally gained the promise of marriage to Lord Bateman in her own land.

Anonymous ballads, carols, songs, rhymed epigrams, and humorous epitaphs have been found in manuscripts and commonplace books of every period. *The Oxford Book of Light Verse*, "chosen" by W. H. Auden, includes an anonymous poem in Middle English with tumbling rhymes and alliteration for comic effect: to the Tournament of Tottenham came all the men of "Hyssylton, of Hygate, and of Hakenay"—"Of fele feyhting folk ferly we fynde." Of later verse the Oxford volume includes madrigals, "The Vicar of Bray," and songs by Thomas Campion and Thomas Moore, light perforce because designed to be heard as songs. Anonymous nursery rhymes, such as "Mary had a little lamb" and "Little Jack Horner," have been made an academic subject almost two-handedly by Iona and Peter Opie.

Broadside ballads, of the kind peddled by Autolycus in *The Winter's Tale*, were typically printed on one side of cheap paper and illustrated with crude woodcuts—reused regardless of their irrelevance to successive ballads. Hawked in the streets and at fairs, and ephemeral in popularity, they provided news of shocking events and freaks of nature for the less educated. The collection of such ballads by Samuel Pepys in the seventeenth century was edited by Hyder E. Rollins in eight volumes in 1929–1932, shortly after serious, unironic hawking of such ballads is thought to have ceased. Pepys divided his collection into ten categories, which include murder, love, cuckoldry, the state and the times, true and fabulous history, and bibulous fellowship. An eighteenth-century publisher in Seven Dials (London), James Catnach, made the gallows and final confessions a speciality. Ballads of the nineteenth-century industrial North uncovered by Martha Vicinus include protest, as in "Collier Lass" ("And our hearts are as white as your lords in fine places"), but Luddite objection pales when the new looms become sexual metaphors for seduction and consent. For most ballad scholars, "traditional" means superior; "broadside" indicates inferiority. Yet Pinto and Rodway, in the introduction to their anthology *The Common Muse*, could stress the influence of urban, "lowfaluting" ballads on Marvell, Swift, Prior, Gay, Blake, and Hardy. George Barker announced no abrupt change in his style when he entitled his last (posthumous) volume *Street Ballads*. Wordsworth and Coleridge had tried in *Lyrical Ballads* to incorporate the grit and grim humor of broadsides.

Satire in verse has been repeatedly popular. Dependably censorious against immorality and folly, with the unfailing characteristic of exaggeration, satire has enjoyed successive fashions in form. The tumbling verse of "beastly Skelton," recurrent in satire, has spilled into the nursery—as in Robert Southey's verses on the falls of Lodore: "Rising and leaping, / Sinking and creeping, / Swelling and sweeping . . . ." Nearly three centuries of octosyllabic couplets have claimed descent from Samuel Butler's *Hudibras* (1663–1678): "For Rhime the Rudder is of Verses, / With which like Ships they steer their courses." Polysyllabic rhymes for comic effect bore the name Hudibrastic until they found their master in Byron: "Juan"—"new one"; "Pompilius"—"born bilious"; "business"—"dizziness"; "pillar! He"—"artillery"; "intellectual"—"hen-peck'd you all."

Miscellanies published as *Poems on Affairs of State* during the last decade of the seventeenth century and the beginning of the next (and fully annotated in seven volumes by George deF. Lord et al. at Yale, 1963–1975), gathered major, minor, and anonymous poets, noblemen and hacks. One so gathered, belonging to almost all these categories, was John Wilmot, second earl of Rochester, a satirist of unalloyed wit but regarded for two centuries as debased by sexuality explicit and metaphorical, as in a debauchee's regret that age would force him "from the pleasing billows of debauch / On the dull shore of lazy temperance." Centuries that ignored the skill of Rochester's love lyrics remembered his "Impromptu" on Charles II, "Who never said a foolish thing, / Nor ever did a wise one."

Jonathan Swift, who practiced Hudibrastic rhyme in Butlerian couplets, could imitate if not rival his friend Pope—as in "A Satirical Elegy on the Death of a Late Famous General," celebrating the demise of the Duke of Marlborough: "Turn'd to that dirt from whence he sprung." It is satire that charges the duke with vice by replacing the expected "earth" with "dirt." In addition to exercising his delight in the language of servants, Swift derided romantic attempts to spiritualize female beauty, as in "Phyllis; or, The Progress of Love":

Or on the Mat devoutly kneeling
Would lift her Eyes up to the Ceiling,
And heave her Bosom unaware
For neighb'ring Beaux to see it bare.

In the literary circle of Pope and Swift satire could fade almost imperceptibly into lightly comic verse. William Walsh, mildly antiromantic, exposed in dimeter lines a rejected lover about to kill himself until he reflects that a new love is easier to come by than a new neck. John Gay, best known for depicting Prime Minister Walpole as a highwayman in *The Beggar's Opera* (adapted by Bertolt Brecht into *Der Dreigroschenoper*) and for his own epitaph in Westminster Abbey—"Life is a jest, and all things show it; / I thought so once and now I know it"—fused his talents for burlesque and the observation of low life in *Trivia; or, The Art of Walking the Streets of London.* There he made an occupational survey of the topography, with advice to gentlemen on dressing defensively and yielding the wall to maidens, laden porters, and the powdered fop, but never to bullies. Gay's success led a century of poets to scan London streets. Mary "Perdita" Robinson, who belongs more decisively to the history of royal misconduct than to that of poetry, was to make observations in verse, similar to Gay's, from her condition as a lamed woman of fashion. (Judith Pascoe gives details in the *Wordsworth Circle*, Summer 1992.) Rejection of London rakes and grime found its corollary in "The Deserted Village," where Goldsmith complained, like Hardy a century later, of desolation imposed by urban wealth and London ways.

Versifiers and publishers saw new possibilities in fables for illustrated volumes of satiric or comic verse. Gay's *Fables*, not memorable or distinctive in language, provided intellectual diversion through moralized tales of animals always above or below the human norm and usually intelligent enough to avoid coxcombs, college, and court. And the several editions provided work for the engraver.

Matthew Prior, who joined Swift's Tory party and was in consequence imprisoned for his successes as a diplomat and spy, could be coarser in jest than Swift, but he refined the love poetry of the Cavaliers into the elegance and decorum of *vers de société*. The understatement and tenderness to be perfected by Walter Savage Landor appear in a quatrain of Prior's poem "To a Child of Quality":

For, as our different ages move,
'Tis so ordain'd (would Fate but mend it),

That I shall be past making love
When she begins to comprehend it.

Such verse as Gay's and Prior's endures in libraries and anthologies, while doggerel dies and is reborn and transmitted in the streets and on lonely roads. By licensing plays and intimidating authors, Walpole suppressed virulent and guffawing political satire. One result was such poems as Goldsmith's on a Presbyterian minister who bound and hanged his cat for catching a mouse on Sunday, and similarly his verses on a mad dog that bit a godly, praying, comforting man—"The dog it was that died." These poems express a scorn absent from Thomas Gray's ironic and richly descriptive "Ode on the Death of a Favourite Cat, Drowned in a Tub of Gold Fishes." Under threat of censorship, poets also took the stance of imitating the satires of Juvenal with current particulars—as in *The Vanity of Human Wishes* by Samuel Johnson. In the 1760s ferocity returned with the rapidly fired missiles of Charles Churchill, represented in *The Faber Book of Comic Verse* by "The Pains of Education" on severe study and authorship rewarded in "vile submission."

Mark Akenside and the three Wartons (Thomas, father and son, and Joseph) were for poetry what Ann Radcliffe would become for the Gothic novel; by looking backward they account in considerable measure for the critics' now exploded category of "Pre-Romanticism." Gray made popular the legendary Welsh past, notably in "The Bard," from a base in Latin translations. In the same period James Macpherson with his Ossian and Thomas Chatterton with the Rowley poems achieved notoriety for dissimulation and earned fame for their timeliness in atavistic sensibility. Poets and artists, for at least a century, would express passionate identification with the fate of Chatterton.

As the eighteenth century approached its close, the Hudibrastic heritage allowed William Combe, greatly aided by Thomas Rowlandson's illustrations, to put "Doctor Syntax" on tour in a series of books ridiculing such fads as the picturesque. A new attention to the psychic well-being of children brought popularity to verses by women remembered and reprinted until the Great War of 1914. Even yet, adults who can no longer recite Jane Taylor's "Twinkle, twinkle, little star," and can no longer locate Mary Howitt's "'Will you walk into my parlour,' said the spider to the fly," have those verses deep in their consciousness as if from an oceanic source—regardless of help from Lewis Carroll's parodies.

Ironies abound here. The generation of Anna Seward, "the Swan of Lichfield," knew of the notorious Mary Wollstonecraft and "Perdita" Robinson, but they knew not of Aemilia Lanier, who had argued in verse in 1611 Eve's innocence and Adam's guilt in a world where women's beauty brings woe through faulty men: "If *Eve* did erre, it was for knowledge sake, / The fruit being faire perswaded him to fall:"— "Not *Eve*, whose fault was onely too much love," leading her to offer the fruit "whereby his knowledge might become more cleare." Nor did they know that Dorothy Wordsworth wrote verses unmentioned by her brother, but they would have thought it likely.

Although for genuine popularity verse must fulfill a condition described satirically in the century after Milton—"Rhyme is the poet's pride, and people's choice"—popularity comes in various forms. It might be a fad, like Ossian. It might, but need not, belong to what is called by D. B. Wyndham Lewis and Charles Lee in *The Stuffed Owl* "good Bad Verse." The better Good Verse can retain for centuries a large, devoted audience. Gray's Elegy, Goldsmith's "The Deserted Village," Cowper's "John Gilpin" (less, of course, than his "God moves in a mysterious way")—these earned early fame that continues yet in periodicals, anthologies, the textbooks of middle schools and colleges, and in family remembrance. The name of Ambrose Philips was early lost to his enduring nickname, "Namby Pamby" (for, among others, the line "Dimply damsel, sweetly smiling"); his contemporary John Philips, author of the rarity *The Splendid Shilling* (1701)—a successful parody (of Milton) in blank verse—won fame and influence for a century with his Virgilian georgic *Cyder*. The convention of satire in couplets, elevation in blank verse, Cowper overturned by defending Christian hope in heroic couplets against deist and priest, and by reducing his diction and tone in the blank verse of *The Task* to a conversational "divine chitchat." Sermon rather than satire, he argues there, is "the proper engine of reformation" and of "pleasure in poetic pains."

Robert Southey's popularity—except for "The Battle of Blenheim," the wit of Byron's attacks, and many parodies—has steadily faded almost from the moment he became poet laureate. James Hogg's verse tales of the supernatural in Scots left him, as a poet, always in the shadow of Burns; with paperback editions of individual poets replacing in colleges history-minded anthologies, Hogg sank out of sight until André Gide called attention to Hogg's best tale in prose. Catherine Maria Fanshawe lives through a delightful parody of Wordsworth and in casual references to her riddle "The Enigma on the Letter H." John Clare, who had his moment with the better-educated in London, owes his present high rank to college professors aided by psychiatrists.

College folk enjoy the witty letters of Edward FitzGerald; initially other poets, and then private and public presses, made his *Rubáiyát of Omar Khayyám* a staple. Prolific Walter Savage Landor, who boasted that he never sought an audience and never had one, composed several epigrammatic verses of permanent worth, but his presence in bulk on library shelves is a partnership of graduate study and publishers. To please his own day, Landor should have been a fiercer satirist.

Popian political satire continued to increase its progeny. While Shelley and Keats were gaining a few admirers for lyric ascent, partisan satire sold almost as widely as sermons. Pope's unquestioned stature served as excuse for the vituperative couplets and parodies of William Gifford, acknowledged by Byron as his most immediate model. John Wolcot ("Peter Pindar") vied with Gifford in nasty wit. He could, though, reproduce George III's stammering repetitions more convincingly—for his own time and after—than Tom Moore could make his vernacular Fudge family speak. For Gifford's *Anti-Jacobin*, the statesmen-to-be George Canning and John Hookham Frere joined in roasting young Wordsworth and Coleridge, Erasmus Darwin, and other friends of revolution.

The oppositional pamphlets of William Hone, with parodic verses like "The Political House that Jack Built," reached an astounding portion of the population, but the verse seldom approaches the power of the accompanying caricatures by George Cruikshank. Other contemporary satirists with many readers influenced Byron, but in Albert C. Baugh, *A Literary History of England*, 1948, Samuel C. Chew described T. J. Mathias—who altered his *Pursuits of Literature* through sixteen editions—in words that could be applied to all: "He smelt a rat in every corner and many of his corners were small and dark." That the special anxieties of an age create popularity for verse soon to lose readers by the thousands can be seen in the chapter of the present volume on Victorian religious poetry—where versifiers have created as well the way to Gerard Manley Hopkins.

Although apt parody can live if the poetry parodied lives, the *Rejected Addresses* of James and Horace Smith has lost the luster acclaimed on its occasion, the reopening of the Drury Lane Theatre in 1812, though some of the poems acutely parodied are still read and taught. Theodore

Hook, parodist, wag, and punster—"a *dyer* who by *dyeing* lives, a *dire* life maintains"—has continued to please, at least in anthologies, because he distorted language wittily. For Hook, each Whig rhymed with "*Ass*"—"*Ass*-serter," "*Ass*-ailer," "*Ass*-ured," "*Ass*-idious," "*Ass*-sumer," and eight other "*Ass*es"; and rhymed otherwise: "Grantham—"want'em"; "Granville—"anvil."

J. H. Frere found a second way to impress Byron's poetry, particularly *Beppo*, through his mock epic with a long title that came to be known as *Whistlecraft* and led other light-hearted and heavy-handed parodists into similar burlesques of the Arthurian revival. The most frequently reprinted volume in this succession was *The Ingoldsby Legends of Mirth and Marvels* by Richard Harris Barham. Despite a bit of Byronized Whistlecraft to buoy the language if not the matter of the verse (there was also prose), Barham specialized in gruesome narratives that sported with decapitation, witches, arrow-tailed devils, monks nearly (and sometimes decisively) drowned in ale, and characters who pronounce "Azores" as "Eye-sores"—bloody murder in flippant doggerel, with varying stanzaic forms frequently enriched by Gothic type, puns, and internal rhyme: "Oh! happy the slip from his Succubine grip!" "The Hand of Glory" (a "nurse's story") puts it for all the legends: "The prayer mutter'd backwards and said with a sneer!" Such comic verse and parody competed for the largest possible audience with Campbell, Hemans, and Scott, who, along with Longfellow and Poe, were to be taught to Betjeman at Highgate Junior School as they would continue to be in all English-speaking schools—except that Betjeman's teacher was T. S. Eliot.

Close behind *Ingoldsby*—in popularity and in other ways—came *The Bon Gaultier Ballads* by W. E. Aytoun and Sir Theodore Martin. Aytoun, with his burlesque *Firmilian* (1854), countered the popularity of the Spasmodic School, as Gifford had stanched the popularity of the Della Cruscans. *Gaultier* sets Victorian domesticity and commercial puffing of products against romanticized medievalism and the pseudo-oriental tales and lyrics of the gift-book annuals. "The Biter Bit" makes light of such unrequited love as Barbara Allen inflicted of yore; in "The Broken Pitcher" a Moorish maiden tips a brash Spaniard into a well. The lightly anti-Arthurian touch of Thomas Love Peacock is emulated in "The Massacre of the Macphersons"; the rhythm and very words of Kipling are anticipated in one anapest after another. "The Laureate's Tourney" of 1843 calls the roll of widely read poets:

"The lists of Love are mine," said Moore, "and not the lists of Mars;"
Said Hunt, "I seek the jars of wine, but shun the combat's jars!"
"I'm old," quoth Samuel Rogers.—"Faith, says Campbell, "so am I!"
"And I'm in holy orders, sir!" quoth Tom of Ingoldsby.

With glances toward the spitting and whittling Americans (for killing a ferocious snapping turtle, Cullen Bryant is paid in defaulted Pennsylvania bonds) there are parodies, not of Thomas Campbell's patriotic, popular "Hohenlinden" or Rogers's travelogues or Tom Moore's Ireland-rousing melodies, but of Moore's earliest erotic poems, of Leigh Hunt's squishy diction, of Tennyson, Lytton, Elizabeth Barrett, and both James and Robert Montgomery, who together flooded the bookstalls. Of Aytoun's serious *Lays of the Scottish Cavaliers, and Other Poems* the National Union Catalogue of the Library of Congress lists forty-three editions. "Edinburgh after Flodden," the opening ballad, sets the tone of Scottish patriotism:

But a rampart rose before them,
 Which the boldest dared not scale;
Every stone a Scottish body,
 Every step a corpse in mail!

Albert Friedman distinguishes from ballad-romances the ballad-lays of Aytoun and Macaulay, "rapid narratives full of gusto, heroic vaunts, and intrepidity," with an "adolescent zest for adventure." Such zest spills from serious into comic ballads.

Meanwhile, Prior rises again in the society verse of Winthrop Mackworth Praed: "A little glow, a little shiver, / A rose-bud and a pair of gloves." A critic in Alfred H. Miles's anthology *George Crabbe to Edmund B. V. Christian* called Barham's rhymes "the clatter of castanets", Praed's "a chime of silver bells." Jane Taylor adds to such verse, for example in "Recreation," a perspective no man could bring and sane thrusts no man did bring:

"Their upper servant told our *Jane*,
She'll not see twenty-nine again."
"Indeed, so old! I wonder why
She does not marry, then," says I;
"So many thousands to bestow,
And such a beauty, too, you know."
"A beauty! O, my dear Miss B.
You must be joking now," says she.

Lady Blessington's sardonic verses with a tail rhyme, "Your friend!," have survived in anthologies.

Although it is still possible to laugh with *Ingoldsby* and *Gaultier*, most such collections have been preserved in their "Seventeenth [etc.] Edition" largely because of illustrations by Richard Doyle and other fine caricaturists. Similarly, Rogers's *Italy* and *Poems* continued to flourish because he commissioned illustrations by Turner. *Ingoldsby* parodied serious poems by Thomas Hood ("I remember, I remember"; "I sing of a shirt that *never was* new!"), but Hood—in youth an imitator of Keats and later a castigator in *Punch* of social inequality—on his own comic ground was inimitable. Although he reveled equally with Barham and Aytoun in disaster and the physically grotesque, his transcendent puns took the sting out of dismemberment, as in the "pathetic ballad" of Faithless Nelly Gray, no longer enamored of a soldier, who had laid down his arms because he had lost his legs:

> "Why, then," said she, "you've lost the feet
>   Of legs in war's alarms,
> And now you cannot wear your shoes
>   Upon your feats of arms!"

One of Hood's longer narratives, "Miss Kilmansegg and Her Precious Leg," ends when the heroine, whose family was prosperous enough to replace her lost limb with a leg of gold but less haughty when she was murdered with it, is judged by a jury to be unburiable in sacred ground because it is suicidal to be done to death by your own leg. The thirty-four lines of "A Nocturnal Sketch" challenge other zanies to match its triple rhymes: "To go and see the Drury-Lane Dane slain,— / Or hear Othello's jealous doubt spout out,— / Or Macbeth raving at that shade-made-blade." In one of Hood's shortest squibs, "To Minerva," the punster has tired of poetry: "Then, Pallas, take away thine Owl, / And let us have a lark instead." Collective editions of Hood include caricatures that his readers—almost uniquely for comic verse—tend to ignore.

Hood gave an age of utility, industry, sexual squeamishness, and coercive corsets popular moments of caprice and whim. Three Victorians, Charles Lutwidge Dodgson, Edward Lear, and W. S. Gilbert lifted whim through the gates of propriety into sublime nonsense. Dodgson, under his pseudonym Lewis Carroll, composed the purest nonsense of the three, not as more nonsensical but as a more orderly reversal of logic. Lear, inclined toward an almost vapid purity as an ornithological and topographical draftsman, chose sloppier forms for violations of logic in verse. Gilbert added to his inheritance from *Ingoldsby*, *Gaultier*, and Hood superior twists of paradox.

All three borrowed from Victorian pantomime and burlesque the absurdities they invited us to call nonsense. As in Hood and *Ingoldsby*, the grotesque in Carroll, Lear, and Gilbert is a talisman for crowding one terror against another—and waiting in curbed anxiety for the terrors to suffocate. Hardly an unconscious device in these printed-out comics, the risible grotesque closely resembles the conscious cross-dressing of a transvestite.

Characteristically, Dodgson derived "Lewis Carroll" by idiosyncratically logical reverse translation from "Charles Lutwidge." The first verses in *Alice's Adventures in Wonderland* show how near to nonsense were poems with the utilitarian design of improving children morally. Isaac Watts's "How doth the little busy bee" becomes "How doth the little crocodile / Improve his shining tail . . ."! Awareness that "Improve" points toward improvement of estate and improvement by upward marriage reaches the reader either directly or through the hypocrisy of the welcome extended to little fishes by the crocodile's "gently smiling jaws." The tail improved is also a tale; in the next chapter a long tale becomes typographically a lengthy, diminishing tail. (Have parents explained this pun when reading aloud?) Few listeners in 1865 would need to be told that "You are old father William," "Will you walk a little faster?" and "Twinkle, twinkle, little bat" parodied commonly memorized poems by Southey, Howitt, and Taylor—with similarly disrespectful non sequiturs: "Do you think, at your age, it is right?" (All the originals parodied can be found in *The Annotated Alice* of Martin Gardner, and wholly or partially in Dwight Macdonald's *Parodies*.)

In the last chapter of *Alice* the White Rabbit reads to the jury an experiment to see if words arranged to make sense could mean nothing at all:

> I gave her one, they gave him two,
>   You gave us three or more;
> They all returned from him to you,
>   Though they were mine before.

And then, in the chess game of *Through the Looking Glass*, "Jabberwocky" tries out the proposition that nonwords in proper syntactic order can convey meaning:

'Twas brillig, and the slithy toves
  Did gyre and gimble in the wabe:
All mimsy were the borogoves,
  And the mome raths outgrabe.

After arguing that "slithy" is a portmanteau neologism, conflating "slimy" and "lithe," and with less conviction that "mimsy" conflates "miserable" and "flimsy." Humpty Dumpty (who had come to Alice from a nursery jingle) returns to the kind of nonsense recited by the White Rabbit: the speaker of the egg-on-a-wall's couplets sends messages to the fish to no avail, but when he fills the kettle at the pump, he finds that the door is locked. "That's all," said Humpty Dumpty, who, we remember, made each word mean "just what I choose it to mean." Tweedledee's song of "The Walrus and the Carpenter" begins in absurdity, with the moon accusing the sun of rudeness for shining at midnight, but more than logic is reversed when the cheerful breaking of commandments ends in reward for gluttony and hypocrisy.

Could the Dodgson who photographed little girls as naked as their mothers permitted have seen no intimation of sex in a croquet game wherein a hedgehog was to be hit on the head with a flamingo that "*would* twist" instead of keeping "its neck nicely straightened out," while the Queen of Hearts shouted "'Off with his head!' or 'Off with her head!'"? Yes, he could, and however wrong he may have been, history has nothing more important to teach us about ourselves, for Dodgson—confronted with a later audience taught to find in the croquet game sexual significance, conscious or unconscious, and taught other theories of language than his—would remain a Victorian able to declare that the episode is over all a game of antilogical nonsense created by a sufficiently conscious author. He might as author grant us the presence here, and throughout the Alice books, of war games, including wars of gender and generations.

Lewis Carroll's best longer poem, *The Hunting of the Snark* (1876), called by him "mock-heroic nonsense," pretends to be an epic of quest and trial. An early stanza becomes in later modification a refrain; bareness of diction makes the two pairs of rhyme chime louder:

They sought it with thimbles, they sought it with care;
  They pursued it with forks and hope;
They threatened its life with a railway-share;
  They charmed it with smiles and soap!

The names of all the crew begin with *B*—Bellman the captain, Baker, Butcher, Barrister, Billiard-maker, Beaver—except one, who could not remember names. "Jabberwocky" words recur, naturalized; nonsense goes in and out of logic and mathematics. Bellman announces early on, "What I tell you three times is true"; in Fit the Fifth a circular mathematical conundrum is proved true because crucial words were said not twice but thrice. The author's preface denies nonsense in the line, "Then the bowsprit got mixed with the rudder sometimes," by explaining that Bellman often had the bowsprit unshipped; nobody could remember which end of the ship it belonged to. One who accepts this explanation will understand that the world of spirits also may have an impenetrable logic.

Carroll's *Phantasmagoria*, communicating the author's genuine interest in Spiritualism, is long enough for every kind of ghost and ghoul, including an "*Inn-Spectre*," to float through it. It seems to have occurred to Barham and Hood no more than to Gay that phantoms might walk unseen in London, but in the era when the medium Daniel Dunglas Home convinced royalty and a few prominent scientists that the dead were speaking, Carroll's *Sylvie and Bruno* and its sequel traced in prose two children's encounters in the world posited by Spiritualists. Mastery of the game of nonsense continues in the song of the mad gardener:

> He thought he saw a Rattlesnake
>   That questioned him in Greek:
> He looked again, and found it was
>   The Middle of Next Week.

In 1869 and with a different illustrator in 1883 Carroll exploited in "The Lang Coortin'" an addiction to Scottish ballads:

> Aye louder screamed that ladye fair
>   To drown her doggie's bark;
> Ever the lover shouted mair
>   To make that ladye hark.

"Stolen Waters," reprinted in *Three Sunsets* (1898), engages sentimental ballads in serious rivalry. Even in double crostics Carroll remembered the relation of language to life: "A tooth-ache in each spoonful."

Next to Carroll's lawn, smooth enough for croquet and outdoor chess, Lear occupied a garden—part anhydrous, part bog. As an ornithological and landscape painter, Lear accepted placidly what his eye told him; his verse revels in what neither his eye nor any other eye had ever seen. Yet the landscape painter peeps through, as in the portmanteau "purpledicular crags." In 1846 Lear emerged as king of poetry's most intricately foolish form, the limerick. The verses and Lear's comic illustrations exaggerate human traits and situations into absurdity. For "There was an old man in a tree" he provides a self-portrait as Humpty-Dumpty with whiskers.

In each limerick, return "to go" in the last line assures success to the sense of going nowhere; the reader enjoys an expected frustration. Lear's one concession is the occasional introduction in the last line of a characterizing adjective, "placid," "judicious," "abstemious," "luminous," "expansive":

> There was a young lady of Firle,
> Whose hair was addicted to curl;
> It curled up a tree, and all over the sea,
> That expansive young lady of Firle.

The joke of aristocratic pronunciation echoes through the rhymes: "Moldavia"—"behaviour"; "Ischia"—"friskier"; "Janina"—"fanning her"; "beer"—"Columbia." Limericks before Lear—and most of those after—end in a third rhyme rather than in Lear's same word as above. Occasionally, Lear's joke is alliteration, as in "The New Vestments"— "all sorts of Beasticles, Birdlings, and Boys." Lear, like Carroll and Gilbert, delights in the grammatically and logically absurd: his pelicans sing in chorus, "We think so then, and we thought so still." Lear's drawings lend charm and credibility to unlikely rhymes: "She played on the harp, and caught several carp."

Cruelty, recurrent in early Lear as in nursery rhymes, meets reversal in some of his later poems. The Two Old Bachelors, who interpreted a recipe as requiring them to cut up an old sage, were banged on the head with a book and in consequence "were never heard of more." Like Dodgson, Lear was a bachelor who observed and courted other people's children. A favorite line in the nursery, "And the dish ran away with the spoon," had progeny in cavorting inanimate objects throughout Lear's verse, as later in Gilbert's magnet that loved a Silver Churn (in *Patience*). But Lear and his readers prefer objects, places, and creatures nonexistent outside his verse. An exception, though hardly so for Europeans, "The Akond of Swat," provides rhymes printed like headlines for joyous choral response by hearers: "SQUAT," "TROT," "BLOT," "YACHT," "SHALOTT."

The insanely happy wedding of "The Owl and the Pussy Cat," the Jumblies who went to sea in a sieve, the Nutcrackers and Sugar-Tongs that "never came back" (like all the yearned-for creatures in "Calicoe Pie"), and the several long and endless noses of the limericks—Lear brought all these triumphantly together in "The Dong with a Luminous Nose." Lear's biographers, Vivien Noakes and Angus Davidson, agree that irrecoverable losses in the late verses come from their author's deep despondency.

Supremacy of the absurd in Carroll and Lear left Gilbert to make the most of paradox. Gilbert's *Bab Ballads*, like a solo flute, tootles through eighty narratives the same purported disrespect for Victorian institutions as he tootles in libretti for the operas with Sullivan and other composers—and in the six "Lost Babs" not reprinted from the weekly *Fun*. The "Babs," not obviously a form of literary criticism, continue the comic vein of mocking romantic, sublime, and supernatural narrative.

When Gilbert's goblin opposes the Quaint Grotesque against the ghost's Grandly Awful, the competition ends—Scott could not have conceived such—in a draw. With airy dislocations of syntax to create stanzas incomparably fertile in obvious rhyme, the Babs ballads reverse the recognizable psychology of occupations and types—naval captains either serve wine and ices to the crew and provide as wives all their "sisters, cousins, aunts, and niece" (single to rhyme with Reece) or cruelly punish such misdemeanors as mutiny. Curates and vicars aspire to activities other than smoking, winking, and croquet. A duke, "mentally acuter," competes for the hand of a periwinkle seller, though "His boots are only silver, / And his underclothing pewter."

Paradox reigns, as in the revelation of *The Pirates of Penzance* that age advances at quarter speed for one born on February 29th. A bumboat woman, now seventy, called alternately Little Buttercup and Pineapple Poll, when young (at sixty) won Lieutenant Belaye though the rest of the crew were all young women in disguise. Bab cannot recommend the modesty of a couple married by telegraph "in two churches half-a-dozen miles apart." Victorian prejudices flourish in Gilbert's Christian, Anglican, imperial world—not always as crudely as in "King Borria Bungalee Boo":

> Four subjects, and all of them male,
>   To Borria doubled the knee,
> They were once on a far larger scale,

But he'd eaten the balance, you see
("Scale" and "balance" is punning, you see).

Gilbert's troubadours could no more succor a Jew than one of them could bring himself to win freedom for a maid behind bars for stealing a watch, although paradox fights on even terms with prejudice in "The Bishop and the 'Busman," where the lowly driver learns that he could win the bishop's daughter merely by losing his Jewish features. The puns of "The Yarn of the Nancy Bell" depend upon the vernacular: "'I'll be eat if you dines off me,' says Tom." Seeming satirically fierce when they appeared week by week in *Fun*, the Babs have been prized since as the chief source of Gilbert's Savoy operas.

Raising the spirits of a smaller audience than Gilbert's, C. S. Calverley built the firmest bridge between *Gaultier* and Betjeman. Rejecting the siren's call of absurdity, he praised and deplored beer, tobacco, the means and hazards of transportation, nursery tales, and ballads. Even the line "Bowers of flowers encounter showers," in "Lovers, and a Reflection," would be admired by Calverley's fans less for the ingenuity than for the burlesque of Jean Ingelow's Romantic sentiment. His "Ballad," a parody of Ingelow that takes in Gabriel Rossetti as well, italicizes a refrain to point up a lack of sense in the poetry parodied: "The farmer's daughter hath soft brown hair / (*Butter and eggs and a Pound of cheese*)."

Early on, Calverley was supreme at knocking the vertebrae out of doggerel while squeezing the air out of puppy love:

At my side she mashed the fragrant
  Strawberry; lashes soft as silk
Drooped o'er saddened eyes, when vagrant
  Gnats sought watery graves in milk:

but early and late his narratives of unrequited love—more subjective than comic—all end, poignantly or not, in anticlimax. The reader anticipates the ending when "The people said that she was blue: / But I was green, and loved her dearly."

Most of Calverley's parodies are light verse that would weigh nothing at all except that the reader recalls the originals. Exceptionally, his parody "The Cock and the Bull" devastated admirers of Browning:

You see this pebble-stone? It's a thing I bought
Of a chit of a boy i' the mid o' the day—
I like to dock the smaller parts-o'-speech,

As we curtail the already cur-tail'd cur
(You catch the paronomasia, play 'po' words?)

Even in travesty of Browning, Calverley maintains his own rhythm; in "The City of Dreadful Night" his contemporary James Thomson ("B. V.") displays ingenuity of structure, stanza, and rhyme, but the occasional fractures in rhythm would disqualify him almost as much as his persistent gloom from competition on Calverley's ground. A translator of Homer, Horace, and Theocritus, Calverley translated into Latin, eccentrically enough, verses of Tennyson, Keble, and Hemans.

Calverley's rival for pure talent in the manipulation of language, J. K. Stephen, produced such telling, durable parodies that they have eclipsed the other light verse in his *Lapsus Calami* (1891). E. C. Bentley gave his middle name, Clerihew, to biographies, designed to trivialize accomplishment, in four lines of unequal length:

Sir Christopher Wren
Said "I'm going to dine with some men,
"If anybody calls
"Say I'm designing St. Paul's."

Anticlimax usually begins in the second line, as here and in "Sir Humphry Davy / Abominated gravy." Bentley's "Ballade of Plain Common Sense" laments the inability of wise versifiers to awaken in a world of political and moral wreckage the "great, long, furry ears" of common sense.

G. K. Chesterton, Hilaire Belloc, and R. A. Knox, as Catholics, revived Dryden's vein of religious satire. Knox (brother of the parodist E. V. Knox) in "Absolute and Abitofhell" characteristically brought to heel the Canon of Hertford, who "Corrected 'I believe', to 'One does feel.'" Chesterton's verses go occasionally to the edge of nonsense, but return in praise of faith and stronger drink than ale. Belloc's *Cautionary Tales* (1907) created political portraits, "Godolphin Horne, Who Was Cursed with the Sin of Pride, and Became a Boot-black"; "Lord Lundy, Who Was Too Freely Moved to Tears, and Thereby Ruined His Political Career." In contrast with satiric aggression against the beliefs of others, May Kendall, in parodies and pellucid lyrics with a burden of thought, analyzed in *Dreams to Sell* (1887) the anxieties induced by discoveries in biology, astronomy, physics, and geology. When a trilobite reminds her of the human mix of Kant, Hegel, dynamite, and cannon, in her heart she cries:

"I wish our brains were not so good,
  I wish our skulls were thicker,
I wish that Evolution could
  Have stopped a little quicker;
For oh, it was a happy plight,
  Of liberty and ease,
To be a simple Trilobite
  In the Silurian seas.

Lord Lytton had gone before her in cosmic interests but without her refinement and radiance of language and thought. Keen cerebration distinguishes her verse from the durable epitaph and other verses of her near contemporary, Robert Louis Stevenson: "Home is the sailor, home from the sea, / And the hunter home from the hill."

Edith Sitwell, in the next generation, employed a modernist aesthetic to ascribe seriousness to rhythmic language apart from meaning; even after darkening portions of *Façade* (1923) in keeping with darkened times, she described the poems of that entertainment (in the preface to her *Collected Poems* of 1968) as "*abstract* poems—that is, they are patterns in sound." Erudition in her later poems could encompass ballad traits in ballad form, for example in a song written as if by Anne Boleyn, "At Cockcrow":

You'll hear my bone clack on your heart—
  Your heart clack on my bone.
That sound once seemed the first sunrise:
  Now I must sleep alone.

Stevie Smith, beginning later and from a lower rung, managed to make religious and social uncertainty much more personal than the cosmic anxiety of Kendall. With what Seamus Heaney describes as Smith's "disenchanted gentility" her buoyancy absorbed Cavaliers, Metaphysicals, Blake, and Dickinson. With condensation akin to parody she practiced nursery rhythms on the venerable subjects of love, faith, death, and housebroken dogs. For contrast with Kendall as well as with, say, the imagination-hungry Kathleen Raine ("I am the world, the world is mine"—"if only the god will come"), take Smith's early "Egocentric":

What care I if Skies are blue,
If God created Gnat and Gnu,
What care I if good God be,
If he be not good to me?

Balladry and *Christabel* meet in the haunted little poem beginning "He said no word of her to us / Nor we of her to him." Smith called subtly on the vernacular, as in rhyming "Whose best is only better" with "Forget him and forget her." She broke ballad rhythms for lines as prolonged as Ogden Nash's and for other considered reasons, as in her best-known poem, which ends, "I was much too far out all my life / Not waving but drowning."

Kendall, Sitwell, and Smith flirted with gravity. Elizabeth Jennings, the only woman represented in Robert Conquest's *New Lines* (1956), has spread gravity over a variety of tributes and a great range of subjects in (Margaret Willy's words) "lucid diction, use of traditional metres, and the keen and subtle intelligence in her exploration of ideas"—in other words, paying only unconscious tribute to the balladic and comic traditions of British poetry and instead reaching toward posterity. The popular and much-anthologized Thomas Kinsella is yet often academically ignored, perhaps because, though Irish, he follows Eliot's strand of modernism rather than Yeats's. Popularity of any sort is academically suspect.

Balladry as in Aytoun and Kipling, occasionally grotesque as in Barham and Hood, the social world of Praed, lighter verse as in Frederick Locker Lampson and Austin Dobson, religious and social satire as in Chesterton, self-communion like Smith's, the edge of jingle and the air of parody—all came together in the poems of John Betjeman. On occasion, as in "Diary of a Church Mouse," he verges on happy nonsense. Philip Larkin, in his introduction to the *Collected Poems* of 1971, enlarges the common view of Betjeman's subjects as "Victorian Gothic and sports girls and being afraid of death" into "poetry that embraces architecture" with "topography, religion, satire, death, love and sex, people and childhood" as subjects.

Heir to William Morris in fighting the desecration known as church restoration, Betjeman could combine in a single stanza the peal of bells, gaslight, tennis, and sex. His weakling protagonists recall Calverley as they sigh for athletic girls:

So happy, and so deep he loves the world,
Could worship God and rocks and stones and trees,

Be nicer to his mother, kill himself
If that would make him pure enough for her.

In Betjeman, though, the phrase "worship God" in a frivolous context
has satiric depth. In "Christmas," as a believer in Sacrament, he protests
the annual exchange of "inexpensive scent" and "hideous tie." An
Anglo-Catholic, he rejects the Calvinistic "godly usher" of every age:
"The dog lay panting at his godly feet." In "Exeter" the "doctor's intellectual wife" turned from the Church to Aldous Huxley until the doctor's Morris car was hit by a tram.

The titles of two gatherings tell the story: *Old Lights for New
Chancels* (1940) and *New Bats in Old Belfries*. But Betjeman reveled in
the particular too much to leave reformist enemies bloodied, and also
too much to sentimentalize his beloved parish churches, where "the
organ set them singing and the sermon let them nod." Grudges clear
enough in satiric titles soften in the curveting stanzas that follow. He
has sympathy for all who realize they must die.

In Betjeman's overpopulated England, the landscape and village of
Wordsworth and Crabbe crowd into one. He answers Crabbe as well as
Goldsmith in "The Dear Old Village": "Farmers have wired the public
rights-of-way / Should any wish to walk to church to pray," and woe to
the lesser farmer who crosses rich Farmer Whistle: "You'd never think
that in such honest beef / Lurk'd an adulterous braggart, liar and thief."
In the autobiographical *Summoned by Bells* (1960), Betjeman flattened
Wordsworth's blank verse into "slammed doors and waitings and a
sense of dread."

Everywhere the concrete and particular. In "A Subaltern's Love-
song" his Joan Hunter Dunn drives in her Hillman through "mush-
roomy, pine-woody, evergreen smells." Love of language colliding
with daily life reduces satire to innocence; going north in Oxford, the
poet passes "land-locked pools of jonquils by sunny garden fence"
before "a constant sound of flushing runneth from windows where /
The toothbrush too is airing in this new North Oxford air." "Love in
a Valley," taking its eight-line stanza from George Meredith's "Love
in the Valley," and making a challenge of concreteness even in the
reversal of "the" to "a," challenged also a poet who thought in
metaphors with the unmetaphoric detail characteristic of Betjeman.
Yet the speaker who begins her appeal with "Take me, Lieutenant, to
that Surrey homestead!" ends with a density of symbol: "So for us a

last time is bright light made." Unlike his obvious models in verse, from Praed to Belloc, from Charles Dibdin to George Grossmith, Betjeman must be read attentively; he crossed and recrossed continuously the border between verse and poetry. He took no step into modernism.

Betjeman's atavistic employment of the stanzaic patterns familiar from popular comic verse goes far to explain why John Murray could sell more than one hundred thousand copies of the *Collected Poems* of 1958. In "Preface to *High and Low*" (1966) Betjeman praised the English language for "such range, / Such rhymes and half-rhymes, rhythms strange, / And such variety of tone, / It is a music of its own." He offers in evidence Milton, Cowper, Wordsworth, Tennyson, and Dowson, but his practice caps, for now, the tradition of popular English balladry.

Carl Woodring

Further Reading

Friedman, Albert B. *The Ballad Revival: Studies in the Influence of Popular on Sophisticated Poetry*. Chicago: University of Chicago Press, 1961.

Gerould, Gordon Hall. *The Ballad of Tradition*. Oxford: Clarendon, 1932.

Noakes, Vivien. *Edward Lear: The Life of a Wanderer*. London: Collins, 1968.

Pinto, Vivian de Sola, and A. E. Rodway, eds. *The Common Muse: An Anthology of Popular British Ballad Poetry*. London: Chatto & Windus, 1957.

Sargent, Helen Child, and George Lyman Kittredge, eds. *English and Scottish Popular Ballads*. Boston: Houghton Mifflin, 1904.

Sewell, Elizabeth. *The Field of Nonsense*. London: Chatto & Windus, 1952.

Shepard, Leslie. *The Broadside Ballad: A Study in Origins and Meaning*. London: Jenkins, 1962.

Shepard, Leslie. *The History of Street Literature*. Detroit: Singing Tree Press, 1973.

Vicinus, Martha. *The Industrial Muse*. London: Croom Helm; New York: Barnes & Noble, 1974.

Printing and Distribution of Poetry

T O AN extent shared by few other kinds of literature, factual or imaginative, poetry is shaped both in its initial conception and in printing within the material form of a book. As, line by line, stanza by stanza, a poem is gradually formed into an ordered sequence, so the gathering of poems into a volume also demands choices of order and hierarchy, a sequence that by its various groupings will require balancing acts of compromise and tension among its various groupings. A volume of poems implies, and indeed presents in a formal physical shape to its readers, a series of works whose textual existence and nature is created anew by their placing and physical associations, page by page through a volume.

It will be obvious that this conjunction of literary inspiration and response to the means of publication is inescapable in collections of shorter poems—poems usually written over several years and often in different forms. Long poems such as *Paradise Lost*, Pope's *Dunciad*, and Byron's *Childe Harold's Pilgrimage*—each filling one or more volumes, with their own narrative or other structures—demand no decisions in their published sequence other than those developed by the pen on the paper in the process of composition. Similarly, sequences such as Shakespeare's sonnets or Tennyson's *In Memoriam* introduce their own order quite independently. But for all, whether poem or collection of poems, the conventions of the physical book and of book design dictate the essentials of the containing vessel.

From title page to final colophon the book is at once a constraint and a form to be exploited. Dedication, preface, and table of contents offer an introduction that can be balanced in the final pages by notes, index-es of titles and first lines, and, if appropriate, statement of limitation of the number of copies printed. In the eighteenth century, and less fre-quently in the nineteenth, lists of subscribers helped further to place both book and author in their social position among their readers.

Whether grouped by subject or by form, in chronological order of composition or (in the case of retrospective collections) of previous publication, each ordering was a result of the decision to assemble poems and their associated textual equipage in the fixed sequence of a book. In the last years of his life Tennyson insisted that his collected poems should always end with *Crossing the Bar*, written in 1889. And in 1851—the year he became poet laureate—he dedicated his poems with one addressed to Queen Victoria; this dedicatory poem stood at the beginning of subsequent collections. But while beginnings and ends could be thus established, the course between could be far from plain.

In 1796 Coleridge wrote of "poems on various subjects written at different times and prompted by very different feelings; but which will be read at one time and under the influence of one set of feelings—this is an heavy disadvantage. . . ." In believing that the poems would be read at a sitting, or at worst over quite a short space of time, Coleridge cer-tainly assumed too much; the linear organization imposed by the codex form of a book—of sheets printed, folded, and bound in a particular and final order—need not affect the manner, extent, or order of read-ing if the reader does not wish it. It will usually, however, affect the author's expectation of his *understanders*, to borrow a seventeenth-cen-tury term that was sometimes used synonymously with readers.

The inescapable editorial framing of what are rather loosely and (by convention) generally thought of as the contents of a book—those pages containing the words of the author named on the title page, rather than the pages that introduce and conclude them—provides the route toward reading. For although (since a book may be easily opened at any point) they may be readily avoided, they are by their nature both the proffered and the expected route toward understanding.

By way of reminder that these involved no idle decisions, the pub-lisher's address to the "understanders" of the first (posthumous) collec-tion of Donne's *Poems* (1633) was particular. It drew attention specifi-cally to the placing of the accompanying tributes, by Henry King and others, written shortly after Donne's death. And it explained that while the more usual place for encomia was at the beginning, "where perhaps there is need of it, to prepare men to digest such stuffe as follows after. . . . you shall finde them in the end, for whosoever reades the rest so farre, shall perceive that there is no occasion to use them to that purpose."

This ordering and framing of a printed book, although in several respects derived from manuscript practices, was different in one essential respect. Whereas each separate copy of a manuscript may be ordered, selected, and manipulated in the course of transcription so as to reflect the particular interests of copyist or commissioner, no such choice is available to the purchaser and reader of a normally printed book. The author, editor, publisher, and printer control presentation in a way that ensures uniformity, and hence, to a much greater degree, controls the act of reading and the means to understanding. But printing also offers both a defense and authority—qualities no less important than the often cited ones of wider dissemination and circulation of a particular work.

Another and very practical attitude, more positive to printing, was expressed by Michael Drayton in his *Polyolbion* (1612). Drayton seems to have entertained no doubts as to how his work should be published, replete with engraved maps (which would have been impossible to copy consistently in manuscript). He sought a large public—as befitted his subject, the history of Britain—and could not therefore countenance those restrictions of audience which circulation in manuscript implied: "Verses," as he put it, "wholly deduc't to Chambers, and nothing esteem'd in this lunatique Age, but what is kept in Cabinets, and must only passe by Transcription."

It is qualities such as these, of textual control and presentation, that vitalized the movement in the late sixteenth and seventeenth centuries away from the circulation of poetry in manuscript and toward its circulation in print. By the eighteenth century, circulation in print was normal. In the nineteenth and twentieth centuries printing has itself been used to control circulation (for example by very short print runs, feasible with the drastic reduction in the cost of printing during the nineteenth century—or by more or less private publication), while the application of unconventional techniques such as lithography (at least in the nineteenth century) and the use of the duplicating stencil and the photocopier have produced further means to economy or control. But, for most poetry the major transition from manuscript to print took place notably late in the history of printing—even two hundred years and more after Gutenberg's invention—when it was realized that printing frequently offered yet greater convenience than manuscript, new discipline, and an audience that could in any case, even in a manuscript culture, never be wholly controlled.

Moreover, the removal of poetry from a primarily manuscript culture to one that was by convention a printed one, was accompanied also by a new attention to the status and identity of the author as creator of a particular text, with a continuing interest in the accuracy of that text. In 1600 the preface to the anthology *England's Helicon* both drew attention to the attributions placed after each contribution and also sought to reassure reader and author alike that these names had been added in good faith.

The early seventeenth-century manuscript collection of poetry was most frequently an anthology or miscellany drawn from many authors according to taste, and frequently providing no attributions of authorship. Indeed, and much to the distress of many authors, where attributions were provided, they might be merely the result of hearsay or casual opinion, or even wishful thinking. Poem and author were not necessarily, in a manuscript tradition, to be regarded as inseparable and mutually supportive of the words on the page before the reader. By contrast, the printed book, with its own conventions of title-page authority, offered either anonymity or a clear statement claiming authorship. These new conventions were supported by, and dependent upon, stationers (or publishers) working within the constraints of the book trade and the conventions and legal particularities of copyright. Authorship and text were inseparable unless positive steps were taken to concealment. So, not surprisingly, printing became an act of self-identification as well as self-organization. "The Presse hath gathered into one, what fancie had scattered in many loose papers," wrote William Habington, on introducing his *Castara* in 1635. It was a grudging admission; and a similar reluctance to see one's poems put into print is evident in poets of the first half of the seventeenth century whose work was published only after their death; John Donne and George Herbert are but the best-known examples.

Printing, then, offered several advantages. Yet there were drawbacks as well. In particular, unauthorized printing posed a threat on a scale of a quite different order from the whims, wishes, and mistakes of manuscript transmission. Not only were mistakes multiplied a thousandfold with a printed edition. No less seriously, the temptations of reward by deliberate misattribution were also commensurately greater. In the "advertisement" to readers of his *Poems* (1645), Edmund Waller remarked that "this parcell of exquisit poems, have pass'd up and downe through many hands amongst persons of the best quallity, in loose imperfect Manuscripts, and there is lately obtruded to the world an adulterate Copy, surruptitiously and illegally imprinted, to the derogation of the Author, and the abuse of the Buyer."

The preface to later editions spoke of Waller's being "troubled to find his name in Print, but somewhat satisfied to see his Lines so ill rendered that he might justly disown them." From such a position it was easy to move to the business of promoting the edition now in hand, with assurance in 1645 from Waller himself: "in this booke they [the lines] appeare in their pure originalls and true genuine colours." Matthew Prior, writing in the preface to his great folio edition of his *Poems* in 1718, alluded to a collection of poems that "has lately appeared under my Name, tho' without my Knowledge, in which the Publisher has given me the Honor of some things that did not belong to Me; and has Transcribed others so imperfectly, that I hardly know them to be Mine. This has obliged Me, in my own Defence . . . to Publish an indifferent Collection of Poems, for fear of being thought the Author of a worse."

One of the most celebrated reflections on such dangers and misattributions (deliberate, malicious, or simply mistaken) was by Abraham Cowley in 1656. For the previous few years Cowley had been in France, keeping abroad following the execution of King Charles in 1649. Now, on his return, he found attributed to him a volume of verses, inspired by the civil war, in which he claimed he had had no hand: *The Four Ages of England* (1648). In the preface to his volume of *Poems* he not only disowned the 1648 volume. He also went on to reflect on the fortunes of other writers, especially poets, whose works were often not published until after their deaths. As a consequence, authorial control was absent, the opportunities for error abundant, and the temptation to take advantage of a reputation sometimes too much. Such collections, he complained, "we finde stuffed out, either with *counterfeit pieces*, like *false Money* put in to fill up the *Bag*, although it add nothing to the *sum*." This might be merely the indiscretion of friends, "who think a vast *heap* of Stones or Rubbish a better *Monument*, then a little *Tomb of Marble*; or by the unworthy avarice of some *Stationers*, who are content to diminish the value of the *Author*, so they may encrease the price of the

Book; and like *Vintners* with sophisticate mixtures, spoil the whole vessel of wine to make it yield more *profit*."

The greater the reputation, therefore, the greater the danger; Cowley named Shakespeare, John Fletcher and Ben Jonson as having suffered in this particular way. The 1656 volume was an act of self-defense in several ways. But for Cowley, as an author still living, it also seemed to require some justification—a justification that he could only find by appealing to the experiences of the dead. He announced that with this volume it was his intention to make himself "absolutely dead in a *Poetical* capacity." Publication of his verses was, again, self-defense—"not as a thing that I approved of in it self, but as a lesser evil, which I chose rather then to stay till it were done for me by some body else, either surreptitiously before, or avowedly after my death." The author, in other words, retained a measure of control over his own identity—in what he had written, what he chose to preserve, and the manner in which he chose to present it to the world.

As those involved in political or religious comment in the seventeenth century well knew, the circulating of work in manuscript avoided the need for licensing—legally an essential preliminary to publication for most of the century, though one enforced with widely varying rigor by the different authorities charged with the task. In the period between the restoration of the monarchy in 1660 and the flight of James II in 1688, under the Licensing Act of 1662 or its successors, political satire in verse was far more frequent in manuscript than in print, and its copying and circulation became a specialized and sophisticated business. As a result, many of these poems survive only in manuscript; others were printed for the first time only in 1689 or later, their popularity remaining until well into the eighteenth century.

But the act of printing and, following that, of publication brought also the necessity to translate the written into the mechanical word. Conventions in the manufacturing processes, the need to reconcile the requirements of a printing house with those of the author, the extent to which an author, rather than publisher, might be able to influence format, page layout, binding, quality of materials, and ultimately, cost—each required compromise. Not surprisingly, not all authors have taken a detailed interest in every stage, even when they have had the opportunity to do so. Setting aside those who have worked with private presses, there have been few poets of major stature who, like T. S. Eliot as director of Faber and Faber, have been able to supervise the translation of their work from manuscript to finished book at every stage. But even Eliot did not have the same immediate access to the means of printing as William Blake, working directly on his own etched plates, or William Morris, overseeing the design, illustration, and printing of his work at his own Kelmscott Press.

In Britain the first poets to see their work in print included John Skelton, in print by at least 1499, though most of his surviving editions date from somewhat later; Stephen Hawes, much printed by Wynkyn de Worde in the early years of the sixteenth century; and Alexander Barclay, whose eclogues were printed by Wynkyn de Worde and others from about 1518. In view of the rarity of most editions of these poets, it must be doubted whether examples of all printed editions have survived. But in some respects the procedures established at least by the late sixteenth century (the earliest period about which we have any detailed knowledge), remained much the same until the advent of machine printing in the early nineteenth century. Edition sizes in the sixteenth and seventeenth centuries usually remained quite small, certainly no more than about twelve hundred copies in the case of virtually all books other than Bibles, schoolbooks, and some official printing. Opportunities for proofreading were circumscribed by printers' needs to keep their equipment in constant use. In practice, for a small printing house with a barely adequate supply of type, this offered little time for proofreading.

We know considerably more about eighteenth-century edition sizes, thanks to the survival of major archival sources in manuscript from some London printers, most notably William Bowyer and William Strahan. Fifteen or sixteen hundred copies was the usual maximum for editions, and many books were printed in only about half that number. With machine printing and, still more important, the continuing growth of the reading and book-buying population, these figures increased dramatically. Poetry was to be found among the most popular books of all. Some ten thousand copies of Byron's *Corsair* (1814) were said to have been sold on the day of publication, and by the mid-century sales for some books soared. The first five editions of Tennyson's *In Memoriam*, all published in 1850, are thought to have numbered five thousand copies each. Nine years later, the first edition of Tennyson's *Idylls of the King* consisted of forty thousand copies, and *Enoch Arden* (1864) was first published in an edition of sixty thousand. One of the greatest long-term successes in the century was R. H.

Barham's *Ingoldsby Legends*, originally published in *Bentley's Miscellany* and the *New Monthly Magazine* from 1837. A new sixpenny People's edition in 1881 consisted of 100,000 copies.

In the twentieth century sales have been generally much smaller in relation to the size of the literate population. Eliot's *Selected Poems*, originally published in 1948, was reprinted in 1961—in a paperback edition of 26,120 copies. His *Collected Poems, 1909–1962* was published by Faber and Faber in an edition of 15,090; an additional eight thousand copies were published in the United States by Harcourt, Brace. Something of Philip Larkin's career may be followed in the gradual increase of edition sizes, from seven hundred copies for the first edition of *The Less Deceived*, published in 1955 by the Marvell Press, Yorkshire, to almost seven thousand copies for the first edition of *The Whitsun Weddings*, published in 1964 by Faber and Faber; in 1971–1973 paperback editions accounted for 18,500 copies. The effect of paperback publication on sales has led some firms to publish in this form from the outset, and to ignore the dwindling market for hardback copies.

The emergence of the literary journal in the eighteenth century—and perhaps above all the *Gentleman's Magazine* (1731–)—for the first time provided a suitable vehicle for the publication of poetry outside the ordinary confines of a book, yet without the overtones of the street broadside. Such publication did not need to imply that a book was envisaged. No less importantly, it had the advantage of immediacy—as in the celebrated case of Tennyson's "The Charge of the Light Brigade," first published in *The Examiner* in December 1854, less than a month after the event had been first reported in the newspapers.

Such publication also ensured a wider readership than could otherwise be expected. This was especially so in general periodicals such as (in the twentieth century) *The Listener*, *The New Statesman*, *Punch*, *The Times Literary Supplement*, or *Encounter*. Further, the appearance of periodicals primarily intended for the publication and discussion of poetry, such as *Poetry Review* (1912–), *Outposts* (1944–), and *Agenda* (1959–), has provided outlets on a more generous scale. The so-called little magazines, developed especially in the United States, have both provided an alternative to book publication and extended definitions of literary or social contexts. The idea of an alternative press has proved appealing in an environment dominated by Establishment houses. Since 1945 in particular, these little magazines have provided both a stimulus and their own distinctive voice to the publication of poetry, at the same time as edition sizes for books other than those by the most established authors have slipped further in relation to the size of the adult literate population.

For as long as the printing and publishing trades were undercapitalized and equipment barely adequate, errata were inevitable. They were the result of both poor management and obscure copy (poor handwriting and lax punctuation were constant complaints of printers), while the practice of correcting the forme, of type even in the midst of printing a run of copies meant that variant copies were the norm. Texts had a consequent fluidity about them that gainsays too extreme claims for the ability of printing to fix a text and provide a completely shared frame of reference.

Increasing investment in printing and publishing allowed more time in the schedule of production, and made it easier in the nineteenth century for authors to give more detailed consideration to their proofs. Tennyson was liable to rewrite heavily as well as to revise his texts from edition to edition. More recently, Sylvia Plath has recorded how Ted Hughes would, if allowed, rewrite a poem in print to the point where only another's intervention could halt the process. Such a procedure has found ample parallels among other authors—in prose as well as in poetry. To see a work in manuscript, in typescript, and then in print is, in effect, to see three different works, each prompting further revision, though the cost of alteration by typesetters has, especially since World War II, tended to discourage changes in proof on the scale once acceptable.

An author's manuscript, drafted and redrafted and copied out finally for the press, has several further stages through which it must pass before publication. Typography itself is an interpretation—the margins and the spaces between words, lines, stanzas, and separate poems each adding their own contributions to the way in which a poem and a volume will be viewed and read. The choice of typefaces will always be restricted, governed perhaps by publisher (perhaps also in consultation with the author), but subject always to the equipment available to the printer. Indeed, the poem itself to a great extent can determine the appropriate typographical form. Oliver Simon, a practicing printer at one of the most important presses in London, the Curwen Press, took a sane and straightforward view of this surprisingly neglected aspect of printing—in his *Introduction to Typography* (1945):

The choice of a good type face and its point size is governed by the importance of avoiding broken lines, therefore the types with a narrow set, and in relatively small sizes, are the most suitable, such as Bembo, Caslon, Ehrhardt, Fournier, Times and Walbaum. Type that is too large is a disadvantage because it means that the shape of the poem may be lost, and the shape of a poem is not only pleasing to the eye, but is a help to the mind in grasping the rhythmic character of the poem. This is important in much contemporary poetry when no traditional metrical scheme is followed.

Alertness to typographical form—as vehicle of the verbal text and therefore as a means toward its identity and interpretation—has been perceived by some as an essential, by others as a necessary chore, and by yet others scarcely at all. Coleridge was specific in his instructions to his publisher Joseph Cottle, when considering with Wordsworth the form of *Lyrical Ballads* in 1798: "18 lines in a page, the lines closely printed, certainly *more closely* than those of the Joan [Southey's *Joan of Arc*, 1796]—*equal ink, & Large margins*. That is *beauty*—it may even under your immediate care mingle the sublime!" Only a few months before, he had been similarly instructing Cottle on the appearance of his *Poems* (1797), with calculations respecting lines to a page, and thus sheets to a volume, with details of the setting of titles and page numbers: he was as much concerned with the price (and edition size) of the volume as with its layout. About a hundred years later, and by this time dealing with a much larger printing house and with machine printing rather than a hand press, W. B. Yeats took an even keener interest in the design of his books than had Coleridge.

In negotiating with T. Fisher Unwin for the production of his *Poems* (1895), Yeats required that he should be able to specify the height and breadth of his volume; that he should be able to specify the paper on which it was printed; that it should be printed by either Clarke or Constable, two large printing firms both notable for the quality of their bookwork; and that he should be consulted in choosing an artist for the title-page decoration ("good 'decorative' men are fairly plentiful just now & fairly cheap"). The volume was eventually printed as a crown octavo by T. and A. Constable, although after Yeats's first choice, Charles Shannon, had proved unobtainable to decorate the book, he had to accept a lesser figure, Herbert Granville Fell. Further, Yeats had specified the typography: "I like no headlines, the number of the page to be at the bottom, & single commas for quotation marks, & fairly large type but must leave type & the like to you

& the printer, as I have no books here [in Sligo] to consult and compare."

The details of typesetting required attention of a different kind, manifest in some degree to author and printer alike, and depending not least on the state of the author's manuscript. Page design usually depended on established conventions and on comparisons with existing models, as Yeats realized. Spelling, punctuation, italicization, and capitalization were all, in principle at least, under the more direct control of the manuscript copytext. "I have been engaged in Comma's, Semicolons, Italic and Capital, to make Nonsense more pompous and Fabbelow [furbelow, adorn with showy ornament] bad Poetry, with good Printing," wrote Prior to Swift in 1718. Swift himself was alert to the ways in which typography could be exploited:

> To Statesmen wou'd you give a wipe
> You print it in Italick type.
> When letters are in vulgar shapes,
> 'Tis ten to one the Wit escapes;
> But when in Capitals exprest,
> The dullest Reader smoaks the Jest:
> Or else perhaps he may invent
> A better than the Poet meant.

Swift's final admission, that the poet in fact may have less control over the reader than perhaps has been encouraged by careful articulation of words in their written and printed equivalents, does not deny the essential point—that printing is a compromise of two different processes, one personal and one mechanical, and as a compromise, it is open to different interpretations.

Furthermore, because Swift and his generation were writing at a time when the use of capitals and italics was undergoing a profound change, such typographical variety itself lent them ammunition more powerful than had been available hitherto or was to be available subsequently. Capitalization and spelling, for example, were critical to the appearance (and hence reading and meaning) of *Paradise Lost*—each is clearly marked on the surviving printer's copy, even though by this time in his life Milton himself was blind. Similarly, the distinction between roman, italic, and black-letter types had been exploited in *The Shepheardes Calender* by Edmund Spenser where the visual organization (including accompanying woodcuts) reflected the poetic and explanatory.

Distinctions between italic and roman types mark out proper names in dozens of sixteenth-and seventeenth-century poems. For a quite different part of the reading public, until well into the second half of the seventeenth century, stanzas and refrains in black-letter street ballads might be marked off by their typographical differences, with the refrains printed in roman type. One of the few extended examples of sixteenth-century printer's copy, Sir John Harington's verse translation of Ariosto's *Orlando Furioso* (printed 1591) clearly distinguishes—in its use of secretary and italic handwriting—between the different typefaces to be used in the printed version. Harington's spelling was normalized in the printing house, just as in the next century Milton's spelling in his autograph manuscript of *Comus* would be in the printed version.

But the changing typographical environment of the late seventeenth and early eighteenth centuries, with which Swift made such play, also created tensions between printer and author. Joseph Moxon, in his *Mechanick Exercises on the Whole Art of Printing* (1683–1684)—the first printer's manual to be published in England—explained in a celebrated passage that a compositor "is strictly to follow his *Copy*, viz. to observe and do just so much and no more than his *Copy* will bear him out for; so that his *Copy* is to be his Rule and Authority: but the carelesness of some good Authors, and the ignorance of other Authors, has forc'd *Printers* to introduce a Custom, which among them is look'd upon as a task and duty incumbent on the Compositer, viz. to discern and amend the bad *Spelling* and *Pointing* of his *Copy*."

Such instructions not only presupposed uniformity in the printing house—a uniformity that had been so noticeably absent as recently as sixty years before among compositors in William Jaggard's printing house working on the Shakespeare First Folio (1623)—but also suggested a more disciplined and uniform approach to the written language, in the shared practices of spelling, punctuation, and capitalization. "It behoves an Author," wrote Moxon in a separate passage, "to examine his *Copy* very well e're he deliver it to the *Printer*, and to Point it, and mark it so as the *Compositer* may know what Words to *Set* in *Italick, English, Capitals &c.*" In 1755, seventy years after Moxon, another author of a printer's grammar, John Smith, explained that these responsibilities had been inverted, the author now expecting the printer to contribute that discipline which his manuscript lacked.

There are many instances of authors taking the most extreme care over the reproduction of their text in print: Alexander Pope (d. 1744) is an outstanding example, while we have already seen Coleridge at work at the end of the century. That there is a division between poetry and prose—for both author and reader—seems reasonably clear. As Oliver Simon put it, when thinking of preparing texts for readers: "Poetry is more slowly and deliberately read than prose, which means that the reader is more than usually aware of typographical qualities."

Each generation has discovered its own conventions respecting the format and size of books—for all subjects, not just for poetry. To choose a larger or smaller volume is to make a statement even before the book's title can be seen, or the volume taken from the shelf. It is a statement that expresses relationships with similar literature; aspirations that may run counter to the expected; and above all, a statement of direction—toward particular readers and their particular cultural, social, and economic needs.

By far the most celebrated example—albeit posthumous, and therefore expressing the aspirations, standards and opinions not of the author, but of his editors and publisher—is the Shakespeare First Folio: a volume standing in stark contrast with the smaller quarto editions of individual plays and yet expressing at the same time, in its cramped typography, a compromise between literary status and economic practicalities. Among living authors of the time, Ben Jonson was ridiculed for presuming to call his plays *Works*, and to see them published in folio. In 1630 John Taylor, "the water-poet" and a versifier of some wit, much industry, and great tediousness, guyed such aspirations in his title to his own large folio, *All the Workes of John Taylor the Water-Poet. Being sixty and three in number*. To publish such volumes was to invite comparisons with classical authors, and in England especially with Chaucer, whose *Canterbury Tales* had been published in folio since 1477, and whose works had been most recently edited anew by Thomas Speght in 1598.

Indeed, in the pocket duodecimo format chosen for Herbert's *Temple* (1633) there are to be seen not only the reflection of a man as retiring and modest in his life as in his (posthumous) book, but also allusions to other books—in this case devotional works, published in the same format. Small type and narrow margins on a small crowded page make for economy; but they also serve the convenience of the reader and the circumstances of reading for which books such as *The Temple* were intended. Thus Humphrey Moseley, one of the most successful of all publishers of English poetry in the mid-seventeenth century, wrote of the small octavo edition of Cartwright's poems that he offered in

1651: "If you ask, why its crowded in so scant a Volume? 'tis for your own sakes; we see it is such weather that the most ingenious have least money; else the Lines are as long as in Folio, and would equall those of trebble its price." Both the format and the type size, Moseley later explained, had been chosen purposely so as to bring down the volume's bulk. Here the publisher was able, after Cartwright's death, to act as seemed most appropriate in a trade environment—no compromise with the author needed to be sought.

For readers, bulk and appearance were crucial, even if they did not always express this directly. Andrew Marvell, for example, responding to *Paradise Lost*—first published as a small quarto of 344 pages in 1667—wrote of Milton's unfolding his "vast design" in a "slender book." Tensions between Milton's concept and the material characteristics of the volume containing it were, for Marvell, an essential part of reading. His remarks in verse were thought sufficiently pertinent to be added to several later editions.

Inevitably, as in the case of Matthew Prior's great folio collected edition of 1718—issued with the encouragement of his friend and publisher, Jacob Tonson, and under the eye of Lord Harley, of whose household Prior was a part—it is the exception to convention that is most noticeable. In such projects as his collected Dryden (1701), in a series of large quarto editions of Latin poets, and most of all, in an ambitious large folio edition of Julius Caesar (1712), Tonson had already shown himself to be a publisher of imagination and enterprise. His edition of Prior, printed on three different sizes of paper so as to challenge or meet the aspirations of his readers, stood also as a statement of authorial authority—and was both a consummation of earlier editions in smaller formats and a corrective to them. But even as a folio, it was produced by Tonson on a scale—with typography to match the paper size—that set it apart from the quite recent habit of printing much poetry, on its first appearance, in folio. Dryden's *Absalom and Achitophel* (1681), a political piece, and *Alexander's Feast* (1697), composed for St. Cecilia's Day, were examples of this trend (especially noticeable in occasional poetry for royal or other occasions) which Prior and Tonson now took to extravagance.

Indeed, if one looks at the edition of Prior in the context of contemporary poetry publishing other than by Tonson, one of its closest challengers for magnificence is not a contemporary author, but a past: John Urry's edition of Chaucer, published by Bernard Lintot in 1721 on both large and ordinary sized paper, and likewise decorated with engravings. Although much poetry in the early eighteenth century was published in octavo or quarto for the first time, this was to change as, after these comparatively few years, folios fell out of fashion save where a brief or comparatively brief text could be matched with the cost of paper to produce a publication whose price seemed commensurate with a poem's probable market. David Foxon has linked this change in mood to the decision in 1715 to publish Pope's translation of the *Iliad* in quarto. The contrast of such a book with Nicholas Rowe's verse translation of Lucan in 1718, one of Tonson's most ambitious efforts, made the point at once. Quarto became more fashionable for collected editions, particularly in the classics and those English writers considered to have some claim to classic status. It has been suggested that this transition was especially encouraged by the publisher James Dodsley, who dominated publishing in poetry during the middle years of the eighteenth century. Publication of new poetry in folio was feasible not simply when it was fashionable or (as in the case of occasional pieces, whether celebratory or satirical) of current public interest. Its format also suggested a market that presupposed both the money to buy and the space to keep such books.

Not surprisingly, there were many exceptions to such trends. By first publishing *The Dunciad* as a duodecimo, Pope may have deliberately guyed, in bibliographical form, some of the same Grub Street assumptions and productions that he was attacking in his verse. An octavo edition followed quickly in the same year, 1728. Swift, no less ingeniously, exploited the broadside ballad tradition by having several of his poems published as broadsides, sometimes even with woodcuts. Both made a simple point in a bibliographical way, in alluding to an existing form so as to draw attention to their own critical voice.

Such exceptions, manipulating bibliographical expectations, serve simply to emphasize the otherwise widely established practice for poetry not intended for the casual hawker, of proceeding from larger to smaller formats and paper sizes as a poem's popularity was gradually proved. Although this pattern was perhaps at its most extreme in the first decades of the eighteenth century, its principles had been long established. They are still to be found, at the end of the twentieth century, in the relationship of first publication in hardback to secondary publication in paperback—a relationship that in recent years has been steadily whittled away for poetry and fiction alike. For poetry, it has become less well defined as the proportion of the reading public willing to buy relatively expensive hardback books (often of no great length) has declined. But in this the reading public has changed less than is sometimes supposed. "The bulk of readers are those who purchase octavos: the rich only can afford quartos, and they read nothing," commented the bookseller-publisher Joseph Johnson in 1793.

Such practices led to assumptions. The common practice of issuing serious poetry in quarto, a comparatively sumptuous and expensive format, also suggested claims to an audience limited by wealth, and thereby implied some claim to respectability. Southey, Thomas Campbell, and Thomas Moore were among those whose work appeared in quarto in the first decades of the nineteenth century, though this was the case for neither Wordsworth from 1793 to 1815 nor Coleridge after 1798—and never for Keats. Instead, octavo became more common and familiar thanks especially to the enormously popular works of Sir Walter Scott and of Byron. But with the first cantos of *Don Juan* (1819–1821), Byron's publisher John Murray, torn between admiration and disgust, deliberately varied his policy—first publishing them anonymously, in quarto, in order to restrict sales (initially at least) to those who could afford so expensive a work (the first volume cost £1.11.6, or about three weeks' wages for an agricultural worker of the time). Thus Murray ensured that the work could not be easily dismissed as vulgar or dangerous—for, in the words of one reviewer (possibly Southey), readers "who would have turned with disgust from its indecencies, and remembered only its poetry and its wit." Cheaper editions rapidly followed, and the poem was much pirated; but Murray's reputation had been protected and Byron's work could be safely published without further fear of prosecution.

The smaller octavo format established by the mid-nineteenth century, in which were published most of the works of Browning, Tennyson and Swinburne, was itself challenged by authors, and more generally by publishers seeking a fresh typographical voice. By adopting a somewhat squarer shape for volumes, or increasing their dimensions slightly, a new voice might be signaled by the book itself. Coventry Patmore's first major work, *The Angel in the House* (1854+), was published as a pott octavo, more than an inch shorter than his *The Unknown Eros* (1877), in the rather more unusual format of square octavo.

The later years of the nineteenth century witnessed many experiments, a trend made possible by developments in papermaking, type design, illustration, and bookbinding techniques. But the birth of these many changes is to be found in the middle years of the century. Fresh attention to earlier type designs—pioneered by the publisher and bookseller William Pickering and used in several of his editions of seventeenth-century poets—heralded a widespread fashion for older typefaces and allusive period design even for contemporary work. But parallel with this, and drawing on new techniques and skills in wood engraving, a taste for illustrated books arose: William Allingham's *The Music Master*, with designs by Arthur Hughes, D. G. Rossetti, and John Millais, appeared in 1855. This was published by George Routledge, whose sometimes lavishly illustrated books formed a substantial and important part of his business.

Edward Moxon, publisher of Tennyson since 1842, issued an illustrated edition of his poems in 1857 that rapidly became a byword for the successful illustration of poetry; Millais, Rossetti, and William Holman Hunt were among the artists who contributed. Bindings, too, offered the opportunity for originality in decoration as well as a means of attracting readers with an eye-catching exterior. The drab paper-covered boards that had characterized the first editions of Wordsworth, Coleridge, Southey, Keats, and Shelley had by the mid-nineteenth century given way to elaborately printed paper covers, or to cloth of various colors, frequently gilt, and for the more lavish books intended especially for presentation, sometimes printed with further color. The gaily decorated cloth gilt bindings of these newer editions were for display, particularly on the parlor or drawing room table. And although they were introduced for most kinds of general reading (with the notable exception of the majority of popular novels), poetry was particularly privileged in this manner.

The old distinction of the book trade—between the lightweight paper or cheap leather binding and the lavishly tooled binding in more expensive leather—gave way to a much greater diversity of materials and invention. Author and reader were thus brought into an even more closely defined relationship—not simply on the page, but even from the very binding. W. M. Rossetti and William Morris both designed the covers to their own poetry, while the last years of the century also saw the increasing use of well-known artists such as Beardsley, Charles Ricketts, Laurence Housman, and T. Sturge Moore to decorate both the pages and the covers of new publications. Thus, poetry was provided with yet a further frame of reference, which dust jackets and the cover decorations of paperbacks have since developed further.

Such developments made questions about the illustration of poetry seem the more urgent. Following a successful illustrated collection of Keats, Moxon prepared an ambitious series of illustrations for Tennyson's volume of 1857. Although both publisher and author benefitted from increased sales, Tennyson was reluctant to accept the illustrations. When in 1874 another publisher, Kegan Paul, suggested that the new collected edition be illustrated by pictures of the poet's homes and neighborhood—inspirations for Tennyson's poetry and a sop to his readers' curiosity as to the private life of the poet laureate—Tennyson was adamant in his opposition. Kegan Paul's idea was by no means new. In the early years of the nineteenth century there had been highly successful series of engraved views of the landscapes associated with Burns, Byron, William Cowper, and Robert Bloomfield. But the question was not simply one of intrusion. This difficult subject has been most clearly summed up—as a principle and not for Tennyson only—by Walter de la Mare in a lecture published in 1931: "The question of illustration is scarcely an issue at all, and if it be an issue it is a desperately controversial one. Mere pictorial representations, however admirable, in a volume devoted to poetry, seem to be a definite mistake." But then de la Mare went on to make exceptions of the book illustrations of the 1850s and 1860s, and to continue:

But every poem is everyman's poem, and any illustration of a poem is only the illustration of one man's conception of it. The two things therefore cannot but to some extent clash and overlap, except when the men of genius concerned are in such accord as were Carroll and Tenniel when gryphons and walruses were about.

The particularity implied in illustration, although it may indeed (as in the case of many eighteenth-century books) add a measure of luxury or (as in the case of Tennyson) encourage greater sales, intervenes as yet another intrusion between author and reader. The meeting of two imaginations—author's and reader's—is distracted by the intrusive insistence of illustration not inspired by, created by, or at least executed in the closest consultation with, the author. The enduring associative powers of a pictorial image, or a particular series of images, is well reflected in the continuing popularity, for example, of John Baptista Medina's engravings for *Paradise Lost*, first published in 1688 and followed or imitated many times thereafter—for long after the original engraved plates had been worn away. Such posthumous intrusion, however, is quite different from the kind of mutually supportive venture to be found, for example, in the collaboration between Ted Hughes and Leonard Baskin in this century, or the relationship between word and image in the emblem books by Francis Quarles and others in the seventeenth. Collaboration under more formal circumstances may be seen in the earlier work of T. S. Eliot. From his desk at Faber and Gwyer, Eliot exercised a degree of control over the appearance of his work, including illustration, greater than that accorded to most poets. Thus, his choice of McKnight Kauffer as illustrator for *Journey of the Magi* (1927) and *Song for Simeon* (1928), followed by Gertrude Hermes for *Animula* (1929) is directly relevant to understanding Eliot's own conception of these poems.

Among the poets who have been able to exercise a particularly close control over the design and manufacture of their books in printed form, two stand out: William Blake and William Morris. By the time he founded the Kelmscott Press in 1890, Morris was fifty-six. His first, typographically undistinguished volume of poetry had appeared as long ago as 1858. But in his abortive attempts at illustrated editions of *The Earthly Paradise* in 1865–1868 and of *Love Is Enough* in 1871–1872, Morris had signaled his interest in book design. Both *The House of the Wolfings* (1889) and *The Roots of the Mountains* (1890) were set in Basle Roman, a type unfamiliar to most readers of books at the time. With the Kelmscott Press, a press established originally not for Morris's own poems, but to publish medieval texts in an appropriate manner, and whose first book was intended to be *The Golden Legend*, he possessed himself of the means to control his own book production, as well as to be his own publisher. Specially designed type, scrupulously controlled collaboration in illustration and decoration, special paper and distinctive bindings combined to present not only Morris's version of a lost medieval world, but also the vehicle for his own poetry and for his view of others'—including works by Shakespeare, Keats, D. G. Rossetti, Tennyson and Swinburne.

Morris's outspoken attacks on the destructive effects of mechanization on personal skills have tended to distract attention away from the extent to which his distinctly personal return to earlier values in typography, design, and illustration was based on mechanical techniques developed only in his own century. The closest conjunction of author, artist, and manufacturer is epitomized in William Blake, a figure who assumed increasing significance during Morris's lifetime, especially between the publication of Gilchrist's *Life* in 1863 and the editing of his work by W. B. Yeats in 1893. Blake succeeded in reconciling author, illustrator, and means of production—as well as sale and circulation—by gathering each operation to himself. First, he designed each page for his work so that the words flowed into the pictorial or decorative elements—and the illustrations twined themselves around and among the words. Second, using his own technique of relief printing from etched copper plates he had prepared himself—linked either to color printing or to coloring by hand—he merged the imaginative and the reproductive within a single process.

In 1795, the year after he had completed *Songs of Experience* and in the midst of work on his illuminated books including *The Marriage of Heaven and Hell* (1793), *America* (1793), *Europe* (1794), *The Song of Los* (1795), and *The Book of Ahania* (1795), Blake wrote of "the pretended Philosophy which teaches that Execution is the power of One & Invention of Another—Locke says it is the same faculty that Invents Judges, & I say he who can Invent can Execute." Blake's techniques linked writer to artist to manufacturer, and ensured that each copy would have its individual characteristics—revision could continue even through production and publication, as each copy could be produced and colored separately. Copies were on occasion colored, and perhaps printed, several years apart.

But if in some ways Blake represented an ideal in the writer's control over his text, his work still remained to be read and interpreted in ways beyond his control. By material, typographical, and illustrative means, reading may be subject to management and manipulation; but it can never be wholly controlled. Censorship—political, religious, or moral—acknowledges this in a negative way. Most of those mentioned in the last pages have sought to exploit it in more fruitful dialogues, for example in leaving open (in however defined a manner) not only the opportunity for critical responses, but also questions of the performance and circumstances of reading. Although poetry is usually read as a part of a volume or as a contribution to a periodical, and usually in silence, such assumptions and attitudes have never universally applied.

Publication is most commonly taken to mean the reproduction of text on a page—manuscript or printed. But this is to ignore the equally powerful modes of oral delivery. Musical settings have added their own dimension, and not always to poems of obviously lyrical qualities. Lute songs and madrigals in the sixteenth and early seventeenth centuries; the introduction of music as an accompaniment to—and criticism of—the verbal texts of stage plays; the extraordinarily widespread developments of domestic music making in the nineteenth century, especially following the invention of the modern piano and the introduction of relatively cheap means of its mass production; and Benjamin Britten's use of George Crabbe's *The Borough* for *Peter Grimes* (1945) and of Wilfred Owen for the *War Requiem* (1961)—all are reminders that poetry is to be interpreted and redeveloped in ways that take it far beyond the individual reader in private silence.

Musical settings introduce a new series of elements into the publishing procedure, which may in some sense be termed a form of oral and aural typography, endlessly varied in the manner and circumstances of performance. By a combination of pitch, rhythm, and timbre of voice or accompanying instrument, composer and performer unite in interpretation, as new controls are offered to the pace and mood of reading. Parts of Tennyson's *Maud* are still remembered by some principally because of the setting by Arthur Somervell (1863–1937). In the case of William Blake, Sir Hubert Parry's setting of *Jerusalem* has not only made this the most widely known of Blake's poems. Both in musical style and in performance it has long since ceased to bear many of the meanings Blake might originally have intended: Parry composed his setting in the middle of the First World War, and it first made its way toward its present popularity when it was sung at one of the final gatherings in the votes for women campaign, in the Royal Albert Hall a few months later.

In a perhaps a more democratic tradition—insofar as it involves sections of the population not necessarily privy to such often private performances—the popular ballad, designed to be sung, represented for centuries most people's principal experience of poetry. Sir Walter Scott took up the Scottish tradition in his collected *Minstrelsy of the Scottish Border* (1802–1803), and was not afraid to amend the texts he was editing. But by the early nineteenth century the marriage of traditional Scottish and street ballads with what has been somewhat loosely called "high culture" had long since ended in divorce.

In sixteenth-century London, poems by Thomas Churchyard, Thomas Deloney, and John Heywood—crudely printed on single sheets—were all to be bought on the streets. But most such ballads were anonymous, their texts ceaselessly adapted in performance in a conjunction of oral and printed traditions. They were part of a trade far larger than the market for printed books, a trade that by its use of wood-cut illustrations, refrains and well-recognized characters (whether fictional or contemporary) appealed to a readership that was often no more than semiliterate. The ballad trade was still vigorous in the second half of the nineteenth century. Because the high volume of sales necessitated a well-defined and well-organized distribution network, its printing was concentrated until 1666 on London Bridge; in the nineteenth century two of the principal printers in London were James Catnach and John Pitts—both of Seven Dials, then a slum area (just to the east of the modern Charing Cross Road). Outside London, William Dicey in Northampton, and various printers in Newcastle upon Tyne dominated much of the country trade.

As a popular form of entertainment, the printed ballad, to be sung or recited, seems to have declined, in the last years of the nineteenth century, in the face of the cheap newspaper and then, after the First World War, of the radio. This migration from one form of communication to others was but a repetition of earlier transitions, just as the printed and manuscript record had once displaced oral delivery or (in the case of sermons or speeches, for example) been set beside it as another form of supposedly the same text.

To read poetry in silence, rather than to read or recite it out loud, is to approach it in a way that may perhaps be quite modern. The evidence of manuscripts of Middle English vernacular poetry suggests that it was more normal to hear it read aloud. Literature's spoken voice—a voice familiar in much more than ballads and song settings—is one that has been much obscured by the conventions of spelling, punctuation, and spacing that have proved to be some of the hallmarks of printing. A casual glance at an ordinary volume of poetry, offered to be read in private, carries no reference to performance other than the silent implication of its material form. In the last two centuries, Tennyson, Browning, and Walter de la Mare—and more recently, Seamus Heaney—have been among the many who have encouraged the reading of their poetry out loud, by personal example. In the nineteenth century, public readings and recitations became a familiar and cheap entertainment, an equivalent for verse—albeit on a somewhat smaller scale and (since they were not necessarily by the author) of a somewhat less personality-conscious kind—than Dickens's hugely successful public readings from his novels. Since then, some of the most notable developments in this respect have been on the radio. There, poetry found an eager advocate in Louis MacNeice, and a producer of sympathetic genius in Douglas Cleverdon. Dylan Thomas's own reading of his own and others' poetry on the radio (his radio play *Under Milk Wood* was first broadcast in 1954) was said to have influenced the style of his later work.

The radio producer D. G. Bridson in his memoirs *Prospero and Ariel* (1971) recalled Thomas as one who took full advantage of the voice— "often enough, it was an entirely new interpretation, for he could almost be guaranteed never to read any poem the same way twice. Different images were stressed, different contrasts heightened, different shades of meaning explored each time that he rolled the poem off his tongue." Likewise, Bridson also remembered in particular (among English poets) Basil Bunting's readings—the voice "a form of creativity in itself." Other poets may appear to read less dramatically, and more dully; but each adds to the silence of the printed page, where typographical conventions and publishing requirements inform the act of reading in the author's absence.

To move, as we have in these last pages, from manuscript to print and finally to the spoken voice, is to follow a formal—and modal—pattern for the sake of organizational convenience. In the twentieth century, the cheap and widespread availability of the voice, on radio or in recorded form, is a reminder of the origins of poetry in early antiquity. But it is also a reminder that, just as performance may be endlessly varied in its interpretation, so manuscripts and printing offer no more than a particular kind of beginning toward reading and exploration, a compromise— on ground that can never be neutral—between author and audience.

David McKitterick

Further Reading

Bennett, H. S. *English Books and Readers, 1475–1640.* 3 vols. Cambridge: Cambridge University Press, 1952–1970.

Foxon, David F. *Pope and the Eighteenth-Century Book Trade.* Rev. ed., edited by James McLaverty. Oxford: Oxford University Press, 1991.

Gaskell, Philip. *A New Introduction to Bibliography.* Oxford: Oxford University Press, 1972.

Gaskell, Philip. *From Writer to Reader: Studies in Editorial Method.* Oxford: Oxford University Press, 1978.

Griffiths, Eric. *The Printed Voice of Victorian Poetry*. Oxford: Oxford University Press, 1989.

Hagen, June Steffensen. *Tennyson and His Publishers*. London: Macmillan, 1979.

Lennard, John. *But I Digress: The Exploitation of Parentheses in English Printed Verse*. Oxford: Oxford University Press, 1991.

Love, Harold. *Scribal Publication in Seventeenth-Century England*. Oxford: Oxford University Press, 1993.

McGann, Jerome J. *The Beauty of Inflections: Literary Investigations in Historical Method and Theory*. Oxford: Oxford University Press, 1985.

McKenzie, D. F. *Bibliography and the Sociology of Texts*. London: The British Library, 1986.

Simpson, Percy. *Proof-reading in the Sixteenth, Seventeenth and Eighteenth Centuries*. Oxford: Oxford University Press, 1935.

Varieties of Sixteenth-Century Narrative Poetry

PPEARING the year following Queen Elizabeth's accession, the *Mirror for Magistrates*—a biographical compendium of English historical figures beginning with the reign of Richard II and extending to that of Henry VIII—was arguably the most influential publication of the sixteenth century, in large part because of its many literary derivatives. Designed to continue Boccaccio's *De casibus virorum illustrium* (translated by John Lydgate at the end of the fifteenth century as the *Fall of Princes*), the narratives were to exemplify the inconstancy of Fortune in human affairs. Thus nearly half of the "tragedies" included in the second edition (1563) were laid at the door of capricious Lady Fortuna; others were blamed on the evil nature of the individuals under review; and still others were attributed to the influence of the stars, or of the four humors, or of Providence and the ill will of man. Their import was largely admonitory—contemporaries might see in them, as in a looking glass, the appropriate punishment for evil deeds.

The scheme adopted for these versified narratives required the appearance of a ghost before an interlocutor to whom he related his story with its generally tragic conclusion. The various accounts were based on the contemporary chronicles of Robert Fabyan and Edward Hall and were linked by the prose exchanges among the several interlocutors; the major consequence of their publication in the *Mirror* was that history was now established as a suitable subject for poets to turn to.

Because the recitations of these historical ghosts were ex post facto, there was no dramatic tension in the accounts, but the narratives themselves nevertheless provided subject matter for writers in a number of other genres—complaints, tragic legends ("mirror" poems), chronicle history plays, and versified histories. Although the handling of verse in the *Mirror*—much of it in the seven-line rime-royal stanza of Chaucer's *Troilus and Criseyde*—was often less than effective, the metrical form established the general pattern for later writers of complaints.

Acknowledged as novel at the time, the "Induction" to Thomas Sackville's complaint of Henry, duke of Buckingham (written in 1561 and included in the 1563 edition of the *Mirror*) is of a different literary order from the other accounts. Sackville, too, uses rime royal, but—influenced by Virgil and Dante—he presents a dramatic setting with a descent into hell, where the poet encounters a range of figures, some of them abstractions, like Revenge, others worthies of history, like Alexander and Caesar, who once had been at the summit of Fortune's wheel. The figures are as sharply delineated as in a woodcut, and the verse is smoothly sustained. Also in 1561, Sackville (with Thomas Norton, later known as the "Rackmaster General" for his persecution of religious dissenters) applied the moral lessons of the *Mirror* in writing the first regular English tragedy, *Gorbuduc*; the two works signaled the end of his literary career at the age of twenty-five.

Another instance of a literary work stemming from the 1560s more notable for its literary influence than for its reputation is the long poem on Romeo and Juliet by the young Arthur Brooke, who drowned in 1563, the year of its publication. Brooke's narrative was derived from a French version, based in turn on an Italian source, but his own handling of matter, character, and language proved so suggestive that, it is generally acknowledged, Shakespeare recalled the work almost verbatim, or worked on his tragedy with a copy of the text at hand. Written in a popular verse form of the time, poulter's measure—rhymed couplets of alternating twelve-and fourteen-syllable lines broken by caesuras—Brooke's poem was also popular. A third edition appeared in 1587, the same year Christopher Marlowe was to mock the "jigging veins of riming mother wits" and introduce his mighty line with Part I of *Tamburlaine*.

In accord with a thematic emphasis drawn from the *Mirror* tradition, Brooke places his narrative in the context of Fortune's role—constant in nothing save inconstancy—alluding to her intervention some forty times. He also elaborates his characters, most memorably Juliet's nurse, and despite the heavy moralizing address to the reader, treats the lovers'

situation with sympathy as well as with a modicum of lubricity. Of
Romeo, about to ascend the balcony, the narrator comments:

> The seas are now appeased, and thou by happy star
> Art come in sight of quiet haven, and now the wrackful bar
> Is hid with swelling tide, boldly thou mayst resort
> Unto thy wedded lady's bed, thy long desired port.
> God grant no folly's mist so dim thy inward sight
> That thou do miss the channel that doth lead to thy delight.

In the early editions of the *Mirror* only two of the thirty-three figures treated were females, and of these only one was to have literary significance. This was the soldier-poet Thomas Churchyard's Jane Shore,
the wife of a London merchant who was said to have been the merriest
of King Edward IV's concubines. When the complaint form, particularly instances relating to fallen women, became popular in the 1590s,
the aged Churchyard re-dressed his earlier contribution to accord with
the new luxuriant style by adding stanzas on the fleeting nature of love
and beauty.

The initial impulse for such narratives came from the publication in
1592 of Samuel Daniel's *Complaint of Rosamond* together with his
Delia, a collection of sonnets, the conjunction of the two genres illustrating a new concern with the erotic. In these compositions the format
of the *Mirror* was retained if somewhat modified, but it was Ovid's narratives of deserted women, the *Heroides*, that provided their rhetorical
mode. The slender narratives are now laced with apostrophes to Time
and Fortune, with digressions relating to other historical or mythological accounts, and with their moralizing emphasis often concentrated
into aphorisms.

Daniel links the account of Rosamond—seduced by Henry II and
poisoned by his queen—to his sonnets, since her ghost can only reach
Elysium through the sighs of lovers like Delia. Enlisted to "register her
wrong," the poet thus gains a double benison: relief for Rosamond and
escape from his own grief. Brought from the safety of country life to the
dangers of the court (an anti-court motif that also appears in the developing genre of satire), Rosamond attracts the aged king by her youth
and beauty. At the urging of a "seeming matron," she is lodged in a solitary grange. There the king plies her with costly gifts—the "orators of
love"—among them a casket engraved with figures from classical myth
whose unhappy fate presages her own, and there he takes his "short

contenting." Motivated by both love and jealousy, he next secludes her in a palace set in a maze which he alone can enter by means of a clew of thread (like Theseus and Ariadne) and in which she becomes the "Minotaur of shame." His jealous queen manages to penetrate this labyrinth and compels Rosamond to take poison; the king then has her buried in state in a nunnery. Since even the marble of her tomb is subject to decay, only the poet's words can redeem her fame, but, in a unique inversion of the immortality topos, they, too, will be forgotten in later ages—a forecast that accords with the poet's own historical perspective.

Daniel's complaint was immediately popular with his contemporaries (and the story itself remained current as a literary topic through the eighteenth century). His verse conveys the pathos of her situation with a certain gravity of expression—"For tight cares speak, when mighty griefs are dumb"; his skillful use of submerged metaphors—"thy King, thy Jove, /. . . showers down gold and treasure from above"; and "the golden balls cast down before me"—subtly recalls to his readers the fates of Danae and Atalanta.

Shakespeare was among the contemporaries who reponded to Daniel's complaint, as is shown by echoes of the poem in *Romeo and Juliet* and by the publication in 1594 of Shakespeare's own example of the genre—*The Rape of Lucrece*. In *Lucrece*, however, Shakespeare departed from the post mortem evocation of the *Mirror* figures by focusing on their shifting psychological states. A short preamble drawing upon his two sources—Ovid and Livy—provides the necessary information about Tarquin's earlier visit to Lucrece in the company of her husband Collatine, at which time he was first "inflamed" by her beauty. The poem can now begin in media res, with Tarquin hastening on his second visit to Lucrece, spurred on by Collatine's unwise vaunting of her chastity. Having been hospitably received, Tarquin in the dead of night prepares to assault his hostess, though delaying long enough to weigh the issue of his "frozen" conscience against his "burning" desire—in what he terms a "disputation"—in this the first of many set passages. Despite Lucrece's prayers and persuasions, Tarquin remains unrelenting. Significantly, the poet allots only one stanza to the sexual act itself; his concern is depicting motivation and response.

Like other writers in the genre, Shakespeare fills out the poem with passages of rhetoric, employing a technique familiar to his readers and one designed to elicit their admiration—thus Lucrece's numerous apostrophes to and declamations on Night, Time, Opportunity, and her long excursus on the Fall of Troy. Recognizing at last that this "smoke of words" is a useless remedy, Lucrece resolves to die lest she produce a "bastard graff" (an explanation that escaped St. Augustine's attention when he asked why she should be praised if adulterous, why should she die if chaste). Revenge on Tarquin is part of her motive, concern for her good name is also part: "So of shame's ashes shall my fame be bred." Both were achieved to varying degrees—the first by the expulsion of the Tarquins from Rome; the second by the persistent appeal of her story through the centuries.

Written within a few years of the appearance of Shakespeare's complaint, although not published until 1600, the youthful Thomas Middleton's *Ghost of Lucrece* provided a sequel. Its moral derivation from the *Mirror* is indicated by a single line—"Call up the Ghost of gor'd Lucretia!"—while its passionate, often bombastic, language accords with the new turn-of-the-century style. A latent concern with dramatic form is shown in his use of a prologue, epilogue, and theatrical terms as with Lucretia's assertion at the outset: "The actor he, and I the tragedy; / The stage am I, and he the history."

Concurrent with the rise of the complaint form was that of the *epyllion*—a short epic presenting an erotic mythological narrative dressed in a lush Italianate style. It had been somewhat tentatively introduced in 1589 by Thomas Lodge with his *Scylla's Metamorphosis*—tentatively in that he needed to supplement his small volume with sonnets and a satire. Nonetheless, Lodge's epyllion introduces a number of elements that later writers were to exploit; thus on its publication there was a new genre in the making.

The kernel of the story is taken from Ovid's *Metamorphoses*, but Lodge shifts the locale to the river Isis, perhaps an indication that he had begun the poem while still a student at Oxford. The poet, grieving because of unrequited love, encounters the seagod Glaucus, who is grieving even more desperately for the same reason. Such personalizing and localizing of scene and situation became a common technique (which Daniel, for example, adapted to the complaint form in his *Rosamond*). For Glaucus, a wonder soon unfolds: a troop of nymphs appear, who, on hearing his complaint, recount a litany of other lovers—among them "the sweet Arcadian boy" and "Venus starting at her love-mate's cry." Thanks to the intervention of Cupid, Glaucus is freed of his infatuation and the disdainful Scylla is, in turn, compelled to become an unrequited lover. By introducing the echo motif, the poet intensifies Scylla's complaint (the retaliation perhaps of a suffering sonneteer). Scylla's fervid reaction to her plight results in her monstrous metamorphosis, which prompts the poet's concluding injunction to ladies to yield to faithful lovers.

In essaying this new form, Lodge exploits the element of *inventio*—the first of the five parts of rhetoric—which readers as well as writers learned in school and university and which late Elizabethans were to apply not only to the selection of a topic but also to its treatment. The use of verbal wit, fanciful ornamentation, and metrical virtuosity served to bring about the new poetic level of the 1590s. As late as 1589 nothing had been published quite as appealing to eye and ear as Lodge's verse in sixains—a form deemed most suitable for matters of love. This is his description of the arrival of Venus:

> Upon her head she bare that gorgeous crown
> Wherein the poor Amyntas is a star;
> Her lovely locks her bosom hung adown
> (Those nets that first insnar'd the god of war:)
>   Delicious lovely shine her pretty eyes,
>   And on her cheeks carnation clouds arise;
>
> The stately robe she ware upon her back
> Was lily white, wherein with coloured silk
> Her nymphs had blaz'd the young Adonis wrack
> And Leda's rape by swan as white as milk,
>   And on her lap her lovely son was placed,
>   Whose beauty all his mother's pomp defaced.

Poets were quick to follow Lodge's example and select other erotic figures for their narratives. Of these the most influential exemplars were the two sestiads of Christopher Marlowe's *Hero and Leander* (1593?; first extant edition, 1598) and Shakespeare's *Venus and Adonis*.

Although an account of Venus and Adonis appears in Ovid's *Metamorphoses*, Shakespeare exploits a Renaissance, not an Ovidian, element in focusing on the young hunter's reluctance to be wooed even by the goddess of love. This wooing she performs with élan, providing a catalogue of her many charms and the pragmatic argument (familiar from the sonnets) of his duty to reproduce in kind: "By law of nature thou art bound to breed." Despite her continued "arguments," a fainting spell, and a fallen embrace—"he on her belly . . . she on her back"—Adonis remains unmoved by her "idle over-handled theme," abruptly rejecting her argument that love is based on beauty: "You do it for increase: O strange excuse, / When reason is the bawd to lust's abuse!" Exclaiming then that love has fled the earth, Adonis unwittingly forecasts the end of the poem.

After Adonis leaves to hunt the boar, Venus sings a woeful ditty, "How love is wise in folly, foolish witty" (which Chapman may have recalled in Corynna's song in *The Banquet of Sense*) where "loving proves . . . our wisdom, folly." On discovering Adonis's gored body, Venus offers a lament prophesying the many ills that will henceforth attend on love. Plucking the checkered purple flower that has sprung up from his body and "weary of the world," she is conveyed through empty skies.

The poem exhibits its author's virtuosity in handling rhetorical techniques, ranging from hyperbole to aphorism to extravagant conceit; these are offset by realistic passages (such as the episode of the stallion pursuing the mare) and comic touches (even Adonis is moved to smile at Venus's fervency). Yet a serious note is struck in the emphasis on love as a means to arrest the evanescence of beauty—if love is dead, "black Chaos comes again."

While *Venus and Adonis* is also written in sixains, *Hero and Leander* is in couplets—frequently end-stopped but sometimes racing along for a half-dozen lines in a rapid narrative flow. By studding the poems with aphorisms, hyperbolic conceits, and witty oxymorons, Marlowe exploits the ironic situation of a novice lover wooing a "nun" sworn to the "priesthood" of Venus. The occasion is the feast of "rose-cheek'd" Adonis; the site a temple of Venus, which the poet describes in lavish detail—including a run-through of mythological figures who have also responded to the compulsion of love:

> The walls were of discoloured jasper stone,
> Wherein was Proteus carved, and o'rehead,
> A lively vine of green sea-agate spread;
> Where by one hand, light-headed Bacchus hung,
> And with the other, wine from grapes out-wrung,
> Of crystal shining fair, the pavement was,
> The town of Sestos call'd it Venus glass,
> There might you see the gods in sundry shapes,
> Committing heady riots, incest, rapes:
> For know, that underneath this radiant floor,
> Was Danae's statue in a brazen tower,

Jove slyly stealing from his sister's bed,
To dally with Idalian Ganymed,
And for his love Europa, bellowing loud,
And tumbling with the Rainbow in a cloud:
Blood-quaffing Mars, heaving the iron net,
Which limping Vulcan and his Cyclops set:
Love kindling fire, to burn such towns as Troy,
Sylvanus weeping for the lovely boy
That now is turn'd into a cypress tree,
Under whose shade the Wood-gods love to be.

The two protagonists are introduced in contrasting fashion. Hero is presented first in terms of her marvelous attire and second in terms of her effect on others—on gods, on nature, and on men who simply think on her and die—while Leander is presented in all his natural beauty. On seeing Hero, Leander is instantaneously enamored, and he sets out at once to woo her like a "bold sharp sophister," employing the rhetoric extolled by humanists but here in the cause of seduction: "Honour is purchased by the deeds we do." Having been won by his "deceptive" rhetoric, Hero awaits her lover, who arrives at her turret "feeble, faint and wan" from swimming the Hellespont, which separates the city of Sestos from Abydos. The initial responses of the two are described in slightly mocking fashion, but the consummation is set forth in cosmic terms: "this strife . . . (like that which made the world) another world begat / Of unknown joy."

The poet provides two analogous digressions—Neptune's attempt to woo Leander, now almost drowned, and Mercury's wooing of a country maid, an inverted *pastourelle* in that the god substitutes eloquence for "brutish force"; there are many etiological conceits explaining in short compass why, for example, the moon is pale or half the world is black. Throughout the two sestiads that make up Marlowe's contribution to the poem, his technique is to display his powers of invention as he ranges through the various arts for witty comparisons. It is a technique designed to compel admiration, and as the echoes and imitations of the poem indicate, it did so admirably. In 1598 George Chapman, impelled by a "strange instigation," added four more sestiads to complete the story, the long extension accounted for by his admitted reluctance to reach the tragic ending.

Within a year of the publication of *Venus and Adonis*, a conspicuous imitation was entered in the Stationers' Register—the official record maintained by London printers and publishers to ensure their rights to print or sell books. Entitled *Oenone and Paris*, the poem appeared in 1594 with the dedication announcing it as the "maidenhead" of the author's pen, paralleling Shakespeare's reference to Venus and Adonis as the "first heir of his invention." This is signed only with the initials *T. H.*, and the (apparently) single extant copy, now at the Folger Shakespeare Library, lacks a title page. Not until the twentieth century was its relation to *Venus and Adonis* noted and its attribution to the dramatist Thomas Heywood suggested.

T. H. turns not to Ovid's *Metamorphoses*, as Shakespeare had done for his material, but rather to the *Heroides* for the account of Oenone, a nymph on Mount Ida who had been wooed and won by Paris before his fatal judgment and his reward of Helen as the most beautiful woman in the world. The poem is largely dialogue—first the deserted Oenone's complaint and then Paris's jaunty response. Paris excuses himself on the grounds of the omnipotence of Cupid, which causes even the gods to take on "sundry shapes" for amorous ends—a passage showing that the poet knew Marlowe's epyllion as well as Shakespeare's, although he opts for the sixain form of *Venus and Adonis*.

During the 1590s poets began to look to their work in a quite professional way, relying still on patronage but also increasingly on publication. This development explains in part the rise to popularity of certain genres. Michael Drayton, almost an exact contemporary of Shakespeare and Marlowe, illustrates one such professional response to literary trends. Perhaps as early as 1593 and 1594 he produced two examples of the complaint form now fashionably imbued with the erotic, each carrying the title of its protagonist. The first of these offered the novelty of a male protagonist, Piers Gaveston—the favorite of Edward II—who had recently figured in Marlowe's history play on the romantically smitten sovereign. Although indebted to Marlowe's play both for language and interpretation, Drayton also used historical sources in what became his characteristic practice. In the second complaint the novel element was the selection not of a fallen but of a chaste heroine, Matilda the fair, who, resisting the blandishments of King John, is poisoned for her virtue.

Given his susceptibility to poetic fashions, Drayton also essayed his skill in the epyllion *Endymion and Phoebe*, published in 1595. A novel element here is the emphasis on the pastoral locale of Mount Latmus, a locale that is presented not in the naturalistic fashion of *Venus and*

Adonis but in the more typical Elizabethan manner of highlighting its artifice—it appears as a tapestried gallery trailing "clustered grapes" and "golden citrons," its silver sands strewed with pearl, and its birds tuning their "small recorders" to their loves. Here the chaste goddess, disguised as a nymph, woos the disdainful shepherd boy, disdainful because he is sworn servant to the goddess and to virginity. Given the unpredictable nature of love, Endymion in due course becomes the wooer; he is later transported to the sphere of the moon, where he learns of numerical mysteries which the poet, his muse now wearied, does not explain.

Drayton's best claim to a novel work—which also proved to be his most popular, with many editions during his lifetime—was *England's Heroical Epistles* (1597–1631). This, too, took its point of departure from the *Mirror for Magistrates* in that the aristocratic subjects are all British, but its form derives from the *Heroides*. Written in well-articulated couplets, which anticipate the later closed form with its abundant use of antitheses, Drayton's paired letters project both an immediate and a retrospective situation, with each pair of letters becoming, as it were, a miniature drama seen from the vantage point of the two protagonists. Thus in the exchange between Rosamond and King Henry the heroine admits her error and applies the image of her "strayed" youth to her present situation: "Only a clue doth guide me out and in / But yet still walk I circular in sin." The king, in contrast, recites a litany of ills attending his lofty state to excuse his action: "Is one beauty thought so great a thing / To mitigate the sorrows of a king?"

In terms of literary influence, Drayton's two *Epistles* between the earl of Surrey and the Lady Geraldine were the most important of the series, the first one appearing in 1598 and the second in 1599. Lacking historical verification, the romantic connection between one of Henry VIII's courtly makers and the youthful heroine was nonetheless to compel acceptance for two centuries. Surrey's poetic achievement as recorded in Tottel's *Miscellany* in 1557 had made him a significant figure to the Elizabethans, and although only one of his sonnets (which Drayton quotes in part in his annotations) links him directly to the lady, their relationship became widely established as fact. In 1594 it was buttressed by Thomas Nashe in his picaresque novel *The Unfortunate Traveller*, where Nashe offers a boisterous account of Surrey's (fictitious) Italian travels, including his defense of Geraldine at a tournament in Florence. Coupled with Surrey's sonnet and a reference in Holinshed's *Chronicles*,

Nashe's account led Drayton, like other of his contemporaries—and, it may be said, later readers—to accept the romance as true.

Drayton's interest in historical sources, attested by his Piers Gaveston, prompted him in 1596 to publish the *Mortimeriados*—a long narrative poem on the civil wars of Edward II. The poem incorporates a number of genre trends, among them the epic, including such devices as the invocation to the muses, battle scenes, and catalogues of the main contenders. Although the conventional intrusion of Fortune is acknowledged, Drayton emphasizes the heroic, even hubristic, nature of his titular figure: "To Mortimer all countries are his own." He is seen as a "mighty malcontent"—a character type, reflecting social tensions of the time, that became increasingly prominent in the literature of the 1590s. But Mortimer is also presented as the queen's lover, whose opposition to the king and daring escape from the Tower are shown in both a political and a romantic context. In 1603 Drayton revised the poem as *The Barons' Wars*, making it more historical and lessening the romantic aspects, with a consequent diminution of its most winning qualities.

Witness to his revisionist urge is Drayton's altering the verse from rime royal to ottava rima—a stanza form (*a b a b a b c c*) that he considered well proportioned, with the couplet providing a proper closure. This endorsement of the ottava form shows the impact perhaps of Daniel's *Civil Wars* but certainly of the two most popular Italian epics, Ariosto's *Orlando Furioso* and Tasso's *Jerusalem Delivered*, translated, respectively, by John Harington in 1591 and by Edward Fairfax in 1600.

Whether the epyllion seemed too focused on aesthetic and therefore pleasurable concerns, or whether it seemed altogether too frivolous for serious readers, by the mid-1590s discordant—or at least different—elements begin to intrude. This can be seen, for example, in Drayton's *Endymion and Phoebe*, where the poet makes a tentative approach to something mystical at the conclusion and then leaves off because of his wearied muse. That same year George Chapman, in his uniquely bizarre fashion, attempted to add intellectual depth to his epyllion *Ovid's Banquet of Sense*, selecting for his narrative not a mythological subject but the purported relationship of the Emperor Augustus's daughter, Julia (here called Corynna), with the most wanton of poets.

The slight narrative simply records Ovid's secret spying of Corynna as she is bathing, playing upon her lute, and singing; this permits him to register the responses of his senses, presented in no accepted hierarchial order but beginning with hearing and breaking off with touch (and an explanatory Latin gloss). One of Chapman's concerns is to render a verbal equivalent for each sensory response; a second is to elevate that response to a spiritual or intellectual level. Although elements of the erotic genre he has adopted jar at times with his serious approach, Chapman can introduce splendid images—as in his description of Corynna in a loose robe of tinsel: "The downward-burning flame, / Of her rich hair did threaten new access, / Of ven'trous Phaeton to scorch the fields." Each of these sensory responses is described in highly charged erotic language interwoven with Neoplatonic ideas, so that twentieth-century critics have diversely viewed the poem as a sensual debauch or a spiritual epiphany.

Another epyllion-related poem with a serious import, at least in the view of some twentieth-century interpreters, is John Davies's *Orchestra or a Poem of Dancing* (1596). Written by a young lawyer at the Middle Temple in the space of fifteen days, its sportive nature was acknowledged by two of his contemporaries, one of whom called it a "caper" and the other a "rhetorical trick." The description in each case is fitting, since the author's single technique throughout the poem's nearly one thousand lines is to exploit the device of amplification. The result is that the entire cosmos, as well as everything in it, is said to dance—the heavens, the elements, extending even to the laws of commonwealths and the affairs of men. The only exception to this, Davies says, is the Earth, but taking cognizance of the relatively recent heliocentric theory, he allows that some learned men would deny even that:

> Only the Earth doth stand for ever still,
>   Her rocks remove not, nor her mountains meet,
> (Although some wits enrich with learning's skill
>   Say heav'n stands firm, and that the Earth doth fleet
>   And swiftly turneth underneath their feet);
> Yet though the Earth is ever steadfast seen,
> On her broad breast hath Dancing ever been.

The intent of this amplification—the many analogies and their elaborations—as with other poets was to compel admiration, the dressing out of the poem's "fine invention" demonstrating its author's ingenuity and cleverness. One such instance is the account of the way rivers dance:

Of all their ways I love *Meander*'s path,
  Which to the tunes of dying swans doth dance,
Such winding sleights, such turns and tricks he hath,
  Such creeks, such wrenches, and such dalliance,
  That whether it be hap or heedless chance,
In this indented course and wriggling play
He seems to dance a perfect cunning hay.

Like Chapman's narrative, Davies's is slight. During Ulysses' long absence, Penelope is visited in her court by the Greek Antinous, who in the course of the evening asks her to dance. When she declines, not knowing the art, he responds with his discourse on the merits and universality of dancing. Davies uses a rime royal stanza, and the versification is dexterously handled; but unlike most examples of erotic mythological poems, he relies on the variations afforded by the topic rather than on its decorative treatment. The diction is markedly simple and direct (although the poem provides perhaps the first use of the term *courtly love*, which Antinous, a "fresh and jolly knight" employs in wooing Penelope to dance).

Several years later Davies directed his efforts to an expository treatise entitled *Nosce Teipsum* ("Know Thyself") taking his title from the well-known inscription on the temple at Delphi. By the end of the century he had composed nearly five hundred quatrains in the two "philosophic" essays that make up his treatise: the first dealing with human knowledge, the second with the soul and the issue of its immortality. Davies had judged well both in terms of matter and manner, since the poem was to go through at least fourteen editions before 1800.

Nosce Teipsum's appeal came from its Christian and humanistic basis. The first essay deals with man's desire for knowledge but with the Christian recognition of human culpability and, in accord with the Greek skepticism currently in vogue, the impossibility of achieving any certain truth. Davies handles this seemingly difficult matter with remarkable clarity and control, etching each quatrain with deft precision but never impeding the narrative flow. The first essay ends with the memorable stanza:

I *know* my life's a pain, and but a span.
I *know* my sense is mock'd with every thing;
And to conclude, I *know* myself a *Man*
Which is a *proud* and yet a *wretched* thing.

In the second essay he argues for the immortality of the soul, it has been said, like an attorney presenting a brief. This is an altogether apt description, for having been expelled from the Middle Temple in 1597/98 "never to return," Davies set about to redeem himself by writing this compendium of popular philosophy and theology and dedicating it to the queen, among others. Not only did he counter his earlier disgrace by this means, but he also provided a long-lasting epitome of Renaissance ideas.

From the mid-1590s on, Samuel Daniel, although not forgoing the patronage system, addressed himself more and more to the role of a professional poet. This is evidenced by the variety of genres he turned to following his initial success with the influential *Complaint of Rosamond*, and his sonnets to Delia. In the course of his long career—and in response to the literary tastes of the day—he essayed many other forms, including classical tragedy, versified history, verse epistle, literary criticism, philosophic poem, panegyric, pastoral drama, and court masque.

From this perspective it is not surprising that in 1595 Daniel published the first four books of his *Civil Wars Between the Two Houses of Lancaster and York*, a work that was to be revised, reissued, and enlarged up to 1609, by which time it had reached eight books and some seven thousand lines of ottava rima. This was set in the period that had been treated in the *Mirror for Magistrates* and had been or would shortly be treated by Shakespeare in his two tetralogies, first in the three parts of *Henry VI* and *Richard III* and then in *Richard II*, *Henry IV, 1* and *2*, and *Henry V*.

Daniel, like Drayton it seems, was assiduous in seeking out historical source material, leading, on the one hand, to his declaration in Book I that he does not poetize but rather versifies the truth; on the other hand, to the later charge that he was too much a "historian" in verse— this because his manner better suited prose. Yet in the beginning of the work he adopts epical trappings: the statement of purpose, the invocation to his sacred goddess (later "sacred Virtue"), and many epic similes. In following his sources for a period dominated by deposition, murder, and rebellion, what he lacked was a true epic hero, although he does provide Hotspur, for example, with a valiant speech before the Battle of Shrewsbury—one of the licensed inventions of historians since the time of Thucydides:

> This day (sayth he) my valiant trusty friends,
>   Whatever it doth give, shall glory give;

> This day, with honor, frees our State or ends
> Our misery with fame, that still shall live.
> And do but think how well the same he spends,
> Who spends his blood his country to relieve.
> What! Have we hands, and shall we servile be?
> Why were swords made? But to preserve men free.

Proceeding chronologically, although with a thematic emphasis on the horrors of civil dissension, Daniel intersperses a number of complaints, historically grounded like those in the *Mirror* but imaginatively reconstructed, for example, that of Richard II's queen when she mistakenly identifies the triumphant figure returning from the Irish wars as her lord rather than his deposer. He also places individual motivation within a universal scheme—thus the psychological realism of his comments about the murder and murderer of Richard:

> So foul a thing, Oh, thou *Injustice* art,
>   That tort'rest both the doer and distress'd,
> For when a man hath done a wicked part,
>   How doth he strive t' excuse, to make the best,
> To shift the fault, t' unburthen his charg'd heart,
>   And glad to find the least surmise of rest!
> And if he could make his seem others' sin,
> What great repose, what ease he finds therein!

Although in due course Daniel did write a history in prose extending to the time of Edward III—first published in 1612 and reprinted for some twenty years—he never gave up his passionate interest in poetry.

This is made clear with the publication in 1599 of *Musophilus*, containing a "general defense of learning," but which is, in point of fact, Daniel's personal manifesto, an intent clearly signaled in the dedicatory poem. Here he rejects the presentation of others' passions, rages, wounds, and factions—typical of the literary scene, and indeed the subjects of his own varied career—in order to set forth his personal views. In a period so persistently reliant on rhetorical and generic approaches, such an open assertion of self-expression is novel, suggesting an attitude more in accord with that of the Romantic period.

For the form Daniel chooses a dialogue in verse which takes place between Philocosmus (a lover of the world) and Musophilus (a lover of the muses), and their argument turns on the justifying or not of a literary career. In setting forth telling pragmatic points against such fruitless expenditure of wit and effort, Philocosmus is surely reflecting doubts that must have assailed Daniel himself over the years he endeavored to earn a living by his pen.

In providing Musophilus with answers to these doubts, Daniel offers two that are personally revelatory. Acknowledging that his age is negligent of learning, Philocosmus asks, How can a writer achieve fame when he inhabits a "scarce discernèd isle" and speaks a language that is unknown elsewhere? "How many thousands," he asks again, "never heard the name / Of *Sidney* or of *Spenser* or their books?" To this, Musophilus, although intending a thrust at continental arrogance, gives an answer that was to prove prophetic:

> And who in time knows whither we may vent
> The treasure of our tongue, to what strange shores
> This gain of our best glory shall be sent
> T' inrich unknowing nations with our stores?
> What worlds in th' yet unformèd occident
> May come refin'd with th' accents that are ours?

Musophilus's most revealing personal statement comes in responding to the charge of scant public recognition: "For the few that only lend their ear," he says, "that few is all the world . . .

> And for my part, if only one allow
> The care my laboring spirits take in this,
> He is to me a theatre large ynow,
> And his applause only sufficient is:
> All my respect is bent but to his brow,
> That is my all, and all I am is his.
> And if some worthy spirits be pleased too,
> It shall more comfort breed, but not more will;
> But what if none, it cannot undo
> The love I bear unto this holy skill:
> This is the thing that I was born to do,
> This is my scene, this part must I fulfill.

During the 1590s poets thus essayed a variety of narrative genres, with subject matter ranging from the mythological to the historical and philosophic to—at least with Daniel—the personal manifesto. Of these genres, which varied in response to the individual preference of a patron or the success of some recent publication, some were to have a wider and longer-lasting appeal than others.

One such was the epyllion. Invariably erotic in subject matter, it offered a range of possible treatments up to and including satire. But, on occasion, such elasticity of tone could raise questions about the author's intent. In 1598 John Marston's *Metamorphosis of Pygmalion's Image* seemed sufficiently lewd to some readers that he felt compelled to append verses indicating its satiric purpose. With Chapman the question has remained, Is his epyllion a spiritual epiphany or a sexual debauch? With Marston, Is it titillation, satire, or even parody? This flexibility, in consequence, allowed John Weever in 1600 to turn his epyllion *Faunus and Melliflora* into an account of the origin of satire. Like Shakespeare with the first heir of his invention, young poets could exploit the rhetorical tricks they had so recently learned at school or the university, and like Shakespeare, their choice of love as subject matter required a treatment that was, as Puttenham had pointed out in his *Art of English Poesy*, "variable, inconstant, affected, curious, and most witty."

Salmacis and Hermaphroditus, the most impressive of the several derivatives of Marlowe's epyllion, was published anonymously in 1602. Following its appearance in later collections (1618+), it was attributed to Francis Beaumont, who would have been about eighteen years of age at the time of initial publication. Based like most of the others on "sweet-lipped Ovid," it is the story of the lovely young offspring of Venus and Mercury and the equally lovely nymph Salmacis, who, having attracted the attention of Jove, is promised that she will become a star in exchange for the "amorous pleasures of her bed." Although content to yield, the nymph insists that Jove first get Astraea, the goddess of justice, to guarantee his word—a stipulation which elicits the narrator's comment: "Just times decline, and all good days are dead / When heavenly oaths had need be warranted."

There follows an account of Jove's visit to Astraea's palace, its description clearly modeled on the Elizabethan court—with its rout of doorkeepers and its aged porter who exacts his own fees. Venus obstructs the agreement by enticing Vulcan to withhold the thunderbolts from the king of the gods should he fulfill his promise to Salmacis. Jove complies, but in order to show his love, he makes Salmacis "twice as beauteous as before."

"Light-headed" Bacchus is the next to become enamored of Salmacis, and it is only by the intervention of Apollo that her maidenhead is preserved. This calls for an account of the hostility between

Apollo and the thievish Mercury and the sun god's promised reward to Salmacis that if she recovers his stolen chariot wheels, she shall have sight of the "most beauteous boy / That ever was." These several narratives move with great rapidity, but they are interlaced with gnomic couplets and witty conceits—the inventive element that the poet has picked up from Marlowe.

Since the beauteous Hermaphroditus, like Narcissus, becomes entranced by his own reflection in her eyes, Salmacis is forced to do the wooing, and she provides him with a recital of the proper technique:

> Fairer than love's queen, thus I would begin,
> Might not my over-boldness be a sin,
> I would intreat this favour, if I could,
> Thy roseate cheek a little to behold;
> Then would I beg a touch, and then a kiss,
> And then a lower, yet a higher bliss;
> Then would I ask what Jove and Leda did,
> When like a swan the crafty god was hid:
> What came he for? Why did he there abide?
> Surely I think he did not come to chide;
> He came to see her face, to talk, and chat,
> To touch, to kiss: came he nought for that?
> Yes, something else: what was it he would have?
> That which all men of maidens ought to crave.

Later, on seeing him naked on a river bank—"clapping his white sides with his hollow hands"—Salmacis is unable to resist. She follows him into the water, praying that they should never be separated; this the gods grant so that "neither and either might they well be deemed."

Another seventeenth-century publication, by Phineas Fletcher and recounting the love of Venus and Anchises, appeared in 1628 with the title *Britain's Ida*. Presumed to have been written much earlier, probably around 1605–1607, it was attributed by its publisher to Edmund Spenser, perhaps in an attempt to capitalize on the latter's acclaim, but with some reason, since Fletcher has subsequently been classified with the neo-Spenserians—in part because of his fondness for a long rhyming stanza and feminine rhymes. The discovery in this century of a manuscript containing the poem identifies its author and gives as its title the name of the two protagonists. A more likely form for it would be *Venus and Anchises: Britain's Ida*, paralleling Drayton's linking of his characters and locale in *Endymion and Phoebe: Idea's Latmus*. One pos-

sibility for the publisher's misattribution is that by the time of its publication Fletcher had long since become an ordained minister (1611), as
had John Marston two years earlier. Poets who responded to current literary fashions in their youth may well have wished to discount their
early efforts on assuming a soberer vocation.

Fletcher sets his epyllion, like the earliest exemplar, in a personal
framework. Sitting on the banks of the Cam, Thirsill reports the story
behind the scene in accord with his fair Eliza's wishes. It then begins,
"In Ida Vale (who knows not Ida Vale?")—a distinctive echo of
Spenser's "Who knows not Colin Clout?" There follows the account of
the youthful Anchises, who, like Adonis, finds his contentment in
hunting (including the tusked boar) until one day he has a glimpse of
Venus in a shaded wood. He next hears a voice singing of the delights
of love and Echo repeating the words: "Should thou live but once love's
sweets to prove / Thou wilt not love to live, unless thou live to love."

The sight of the goddess covered only with the "thinnest silken
veil"—she is elaborately described—causes him to swoon. Once recovered, he is instructed in the arts of love by Cupid himself. Having prof-
ited from this tutelage, Anchises in due course acts upon it; this Fletcher describes in a passage analogous to that in *Romeus and Juliet* written
more than forty years earlier:

> At length into the haven he arrives
> Where safe from storm the love-beat vessel rides,
> And as a ship that now the port achieves
> With sundry shot the angry Neptune chides
> And with a thousand joys, past fear derides.
> So th' happy boy in this fair haven blest
> Means here sometime his joyful bark to rest
> And mock those dangerous waves that late his boat opprest.

Some of the older critics of the twentieth century have caviled at (or
ignored) the sexual frankness of the Elizabethans; some have questioned the "low" diction they employed, objecting, for example, to
Shakespeare's description of Venus "smothering" Adonis with her kisses or to a poet's calling Helen of Troy the "foreign heifer of the Greeks."
One explanation for this is the debasing of specific terms over the centuries; another is the change in literary—and especially, pictorial—
tastes in successive periods. Fletcher provides a good instance of the latter in the description of his Rubenesque Venus (although to a twentieth-century reader it may suggest parody rather than the intended wit):

Her chin, like to a stone in gold inchased,
Seem'd a fair jewel wrought with cunning hand,
And being double, doubly the face it graced.
This goodly frame on her round neck did stand,
Such pillar well such curious work sustain'd.
  And on his top the heavenly sphere up-rearing
  Might well present, with daintier appearing
  A less but better Atlas, that fair heaven bearing.

A few writers in the seventeenth century turned to the more sensa-
tional myths, particularly those dealing with obsessions, in part because
traditional accounts had already been exploited and in part because of
the current trend to sensationalism exemplified in the drama. One such
was the actor William Barksted, whose *Myrrha, the Mother of Adonis or
Lust's Prodigies* appeared in 1607. Two years later he acted with the
Children of the Queen's Revels in Jonson's *Epicene.* Shoddily printed,
Myrrha shows that Barksted was familiar with the two most important
exemplars of the genre, especially in his adopting the Marlovian use of
aphorisms and etiological conceits. That he was also familiar with dramatic spectacle is shown by a fine image: "Night like a masque was
entered heavens' great hall / With thousand torches ushering the way."

Barksted expands on the Ovidian story of Myrrha's passion for her
father following on her two earlier experiences with Orpheus and then
with Cupid himself. The chaste reaction of the heroine in those two
instances serves to highlight the "infernal and unnamed desire" that
Cupid inspires in her—"his extrem'st love" now having turned to "direful
hate." With the connivance of her nurse, Myrrha sleeps with her father
for three nights before he discovers her identity. Fleeing his wrath, she
then wanders until the birth of the child—the beauteous Adonis—and
Myrrha's metamorphosis into the weeping tree that still preserves her
name. The poet devotes a few stanzas to Venus's later infatuation for the
disdainful youth, who in her view is "not flesh" but rather the "stubborn
issue of a tree," and then ends with a personal tribute to Shakespeare:

But stay, my Muse, in thine own confines keep
And wage not war with so dear-lov'd a neighbor,
But having sung thy day-song, rest and sleep,
Preserve thy small fame and his greater favor;
His song was worthy merit; Shakespeare, he
Sung the fair blossom, thou the withered tree.
Laurell is due to him; his art and wit
Hath purchased it; cypress thy brow will fit.

Six years later a second version of the tale appeared, carrying only the initials *H. A.*, now assumed to refer to Henry Austin, about whom nothing more is known. *The Scourge of Venus or the Wanton Lady with the Rare Birth of Adonis* was undertaken, according to the address to the reader, simply for its author's pleasure; nevertheless, there were two further issues in 1614 and 1620.

The subject continued to appeal, with one James Gresham in 1626 selecting from the vast reservoir of the *Metamorphoses* to translate (but not to elaborate) this particular story as *The Picture of Incest.* With additions and minor modifications the accounts of all three works remain the same, but the versification is different in each case—Barksted opting for a long rhyming stanza, Austen for sixains, and Gresham for couplets.

James Shirley's epyllion *Narcissus or the Self Lover* was entered in the Stationers' Register in 1618—when Shirley was in his early twenties—but not published until 1640, in a collection of his miscellaneous poems where the poet indicates its earlier composition with the epigraph "*Haec olim . . .*"

What little literary attention has been given to this epyllion, set in a pastoral context, stresses the Shakespearean influence. Echo's wooing of the young hunter parallels that of *Venus and Adonis* and, to some degree, that of Heywood's *Oenone and Paris*; the marked verbal echoes can, as in other cases, be considered the poet's tribute to another's achievement or—as some would have it—plagiarism. A conspicuous instance appears in the very first line with its unusual epithet for Echo as "sick-thoughted"—like Shakespeare's Venus. The pastoral ambience is similar to Drayton's *Endymion and Phoebe*, but doubtless development of pastoral drama in the first two decades of the seventeenth century also exerted its influence. The Italian text of Guarini's very popular *Pastor Fido* had been published in England in 1591, shortly after its initial appearance in Italy, and translated into English in 1602. As a future dramatist, Shirley was probably familiar with the play—either through the original or the translation; in any case he makes use of the echo motif that Guarini had employed in his drama and that Lodge had used even earlier.

In Shirley's epyllion Echo, the child of Sound and Air, has already lost the power of speech except to make a reply—a loss brought about because her chatter distracted Juno from noting Jove's amorous escapades. Her favored retreat now is one of hills with flowered passageways and trees "like Nature's arras." When Narcissus finds himself separated from his companions and exclaims, "Where am I?" the response comes, "Here am I"; to his "Will no man here?" comes the answer "O man hear."

On finding him asleep, Echo fervently kisses him and steals away, but, sensing her presence, Narcissus hails her, "Thou dost excell, and if a heaven, 'tis clear / That here it is, because thou are not there." Unable at first to answer his queries, she is finally given back her voice and becomes the wooer, offering him a catalogue of promised delights, including this enticement:

> Lovely Narcissus, prithee stay with me,
> If thou do thirst, from every spring shall rise
> Divinest nectar, and thy food shall be
> The glorious apples of Hesperides;
> A nymph shall be thy Hebe; if thou need,
> Shalt have another for thy Ganymede.

Narcissus flees nonetheless, stopping only at a goodly spring—the very one that served Salmacis and Hemaphroditus. Seeing his reflected beauty, he becomes his "own Idolater," but on recognizing his obsession, he dies, with only a saffron-colored flower to mark the spot.

With Shirley's poem the epyllion may be said to have run its course. It was a genre consonant with young poets writing in the first flush of literary achievement, but, as we have seen, during the 1590s and early 1600s many of these same writers essayed other varieties of narrative poetry. Their concern with historical matters, engendered by the *Mirror for Magistrates* and coupled with the stylistic flare of Ovid, produced the unique amalgam we know as Elizabethan.

Elizabeth Story Donno

Further Reading

Bullough, Geoffrey. *Narrative and Dramatic Sources of Shakespeare.* Vol. 1. New York: Columbia University Press, 1966. [Includes the text of Arthur Brooke's *Tragical Historie of Romeus and Juliet* and sources for Shakespeare's *Poems*.]

Bush, Douglas. *Mythology and the Renaissance Tradition in English Poetry.* Minneapolis: University of Minnesota Press, 1932; rev. ed., New York: Norton, 1963.

Campbell, Lily Bess, ed. *The Mirror for Magistrates.* Cambridge: Cambridge University Press, 1938.

Donaldson, Ian. *The Rapes of Lucretia*. Oxford: Clarendon, 1982.

Donno, Elizabeth Story, ed. *Elizabethan Minor Epics*. New York: Columbia University Press, 1963. [Includes texts of Lodge, Marlowe, Heywood, Drayton, Chapman, Marston, Beaumont, Fletcher, and Shirley.]

Donno, Elizabeth Story. "The Epyllion." In *English Poetry and Prose, 1540–1674*, edited by Christopher B. Ricks. London: Barrie & Jenkins, 1970.

Hulse, Clark. *Metamorphic Verse: The Elizabethan Minor Epic*. Princeton: Princeton University Press, 1981.

Keach, William. *Elizabethan Erotic Narratives*. New Brunswick, N.J.: Rutgers University Press, 1977.

Lerner, Laurence. "Ovid and the Elizabethans." In *Ovid Renewed*, edited by Charles Martindale. Cambridge: Cambridge University Press, 1988.

Miller, Paul William, ed. *Seven Minor Epics of the English Renaissance*. Gainsville, Fla.: Scholars' Facsimiles & Reprints, 1967. [Includes texts of Barksted and Henry Austin.]

Seronsy, Cecil. *Samuel Daniel*. New York: Twayne, 1967.

Sixteenth-Century Lyric Poetry

LYRIC POETRY has traditionally been regarded, along with the drama, as the greatest literary accomplishment of sixteenth-century England. Originally, the lyric consisted of verses to be sung and accompanied by an instrument—in ancient Greece, the lyre. This musical notion of the lyric persisted in both theory and practice throughout the Renaissance, inspiring a number of critical treatises on meter and harmony in English verse as well as a multitude of songs by musicians and poets such as Sir Thomas Wyatt, William Byrd, Edmund Campion, and William Shakespeare among others. While John Stevens has shown how complex and uncertain the relationship between music and poetry can be in this period, it is still evident that lyrics such as Wyatt's "Blame Not My Lute" were set to music and sung before a select, often courtly audience. At the same time, the circulation of these verses in manuscript and their subsequent publication in printed collections made the lyric into one of the period's most popular and durable forms of literature, combining the immediacy and charm of song with the cryptic pleasures of the text.

The lyric has perennially been given pride of place in both contemporary and modern anthologies of sixteenth-century poetry. *Tottel's Miscellany* (1557), a collection of songs and sonnets, went through nine editions in thirty years and inspired a flood of comparable publications such as *The Paradise of Dainty Devices* (1576), *The Phoenix Nest* (1593), and *England's Helicon* (1600). These, in turn, have been a source for later collections such as Francis Palgrave's *Golden Treasury of the Best Songs and Lyrical Poems in the English Language* (1861)—described by its most recent editor, Christopher Ricks, as the "best-known and the best-selling anthology of English poetry ever."

For Palgrave and many others, the lyric is the virtual spirit and supreme essence of poetry. Marked by brevity and intensity of emotion that Wordsworth called the "spontaneous overflow of powerful feelings," an acutely expressive subjectivity akin to the soliloquy, and an ineffably sensuous sweetness, the lyric speaks with a powerful immediacy. Moreover, it transcends the circumstances of its composition—proffering, in Palgrave's words, "treasures leading us in higher and healthier ways than those of the world." This exalted conception of the lyric, blending Romantic and Victorian sensibilities, has persisted into the twentieth century, influencing our conception of the canon in major works of scholarship such as E. K. Chambers's *Oxford Book of Sixteenth Century Verse* (1932).

Nevertheless, the preeminence of the lyric and the belief in its transcendent purity and simplicity has been challenged by recent editors and critics. In *The New Oxford Book of Sixteenth Century Verse*, Emrys Jones praises Chambers's scholarship while criticizing his predecessor's enthusiasm for "'dainty' pastorals and . . . pretty love songs." Recent scholarship and criticism have placed great emphasis on the historical circumstances of sixteenth-century poetic production, a tendency most evident in the approach called "New Historicism."

Nevertheless, modern readers of the Tudor lyric have been aware for some time of the complex historical and intellectual influences at work within this verse. One of the most powerful of these is the poetry of Francesco Petrarch, the fourteenth-century Italian humanist and poet whose *Rime Sparse* ("Scattered Rhymes") inspired hundreds of sonnet sequences and love lyrics throughout Europe over three centuries. Even as they adhere to Petrarchan conventions and conceits, many of these writers insist—as Sir Philip Sidney does in *Astrophil and Stella*—that they speak what they feel, while others slavishly imitate "poore Petrarch's long deceased woes," thus raising difficult questions about the lyric persona and its authenticity.

Another important influence is the Neoplatonic idealization of the beloved so eloquently articulated in Castiglione's *Book of the Courtier* (translated into English and published in 1561) in which love becomes a means of redemption. Thus Spenser makes of his lady a "sweet Saynt" and "goddesse" in the *Amoretti*, enshrining her "glorious ymage" in a "temple fayre . . . built within my mind." Such exalted sentiments repeatedly collide with an apparently heartfelt misogyny reinforced by puritanical guilt. These harsher feelings inspire several poetic "farewells to love," not all of which carry conviction. Shakespeare's sonnets evidently despair of ever making a clean break from the Dark Lady, despite their strong denunciation of "lust in action." Finally, the close connection of the lyric to a court repeatedly denounced as a snake pit of ambition and deceit undercuts a belief in the romantic golden world evoked by its verses. Wyatt's poetry bears the imprint of what he calls "the prease of courts," even as he proclaims his independence of the court's corrupting pressures.

The current picture of the sixteenth-century lyric is thus more pessimistic and complicated than the one evoked by the *Golden Treasury*—the lyric is no longer transcendent but historically situated and susceptible to various contradictory cultural influences. The emotions expressed are still intense but powerfully and even neurotically conflicted. The personality manifest is less attractive and more agonized, and the proclamations of love are often perversely hostile and misogynistic. Finally, the lyric can no longer attain "the higher and healthier ways" of a better, more poetic realm. Instead, it remains mired in the ulterior motives, bad faith, and imperfections of ordinary experience; there is no escape from the ways of the world. It is a view of lyric poetry that fits neatly with the late-twentieth-century view of life, as neatly as Palgrave's Victorian uplift fit his age. Our own darker view may not allow adequately for what Sir Philip Sidney describes as the power of "the erected wit" in his *Defence of Poesy*, but questions about wit's power to transform a "brazen" world to a "golden" one can be best addressed by reviewing the work of some of the poets of the period.

John Skelton fixed his gaze for the most part on the medieval past. His objections to the purist classicism of early English humanism, his praise for the old aristocracy and scorn for upstarts like Cardinal Wolsey, and his hostility to reformers all made him appear to later literary historians as a benighted, reactionary figure. His lively satires, coarse bawdry, and demotic vulgarity offended many later readers even as they proved immensely popular in his own time. Skelton is disparaged by George Puttenham in *The Art of English Poesy* (1589) for his earthy "rayling and scoffery," while Alexander Pope denounces him as "beastly Skelton."

Skelton's verses incorporate the popular voice, edged out of some of the more courtly collections of lyric poetry but never suppressed altogether. The first of the imitations of *Tottel's Miscellany*, entitled *A Handful of Pleasant Delights* (1566), consists entirely of ballads and "such pretty things / as women much desire." Moreover, Skelton's *Philip Sparrow* makes a reappearance in sonnet 83 of Sidney's *Astrophil and Stella* and other poems—nestled between the lady's breasts and as lecherously impertinent as ever—and even Sir Fulke Greville's high-minded *Caelica* echoes Skelton's bawdiness in its verses on Scroggins and his wife. In Skelton we confront a genuinely transitional figure poised between the achievements of Geoffrey Chaucer and the still loftier aspirations of Edmund Spenser.

Sir Thomas Wyatt was a prominent courtier and close associate of King Henry VIII who served him both in battle and in diplomatic missions to France and Italy. He was one of the earliest English translators of Petrarch as well as one of the first of Puttenham's "new company of courtly makers" arising near the end of Henry's reign to supplant the literary scribes, minstrels, and clerics of the late Middle Ages. Life could be dangerous for Henry's minions, especially for one who had been Anne Boleyn's lover, and Wyatt was arrested and imprisoned twice—first after charges of adultery were brought against Anne in 1536 and again in 1541 on charges of treason following the fall of his patron Thomas Cromwell—but each time he was released and pardoned having regained the king's favor.

Wyatt's poetry is marked by an intense inwardness and a mood of solitary introspection, in which the integrity of the speaker is asserted against the hypocrisy of the court and the fickleness of women. Yet, despite its private and personal quality, the poet's reactions to momentously public events are explicitly recorded. "Who list his wealth and ease retain" is thought to refer to the execution of Anne Boleyn, which Wyatt apparently witnessed from his prison window: "The bell tower showed me such sight / That in my head sticks day and night," and "In Mourning Wise" mourns for the men executed with her, a fate that might have befallen him.

The answer to the riddle in "What word is that changeth not" is the palindrome *Anna* embedded in a pun at the center of the poem; the "Brunet" (Boleyn had dark hair) described in "If Waker Care" was said to "set our country in a rore" in an earlier version; and "Whoso list to hunt" with its deer who wears Caesar's collar but remains "wild for to hold, though I seem tame" has always been taken as a grimly astute description of the ill-fated queen. These cryptic but provocative lyrics were performed at court and circulated in manuscript as part of an elaborately coded and dangerous game, in which intimate details of the poet's life—at once personal and state secrets—are elliptically publicized. It was a game Wyatt played, as Stephen Greenblatt has shown, with calculated recklessness and still somehow managed to survive.

The moral stance and tone of Wyatt's unnerving performances are accordingly inscrutable. He has traditionally been regarded as a paragon of the honest and straightforward plain style. Yvor Winters championed this style over what he calls the ornamental or Petrarchan style practiced by more imitative poets in his essay on "The 16th Century Lyric in England." Wyatt's simple, monosyllabic native diction, moralistic sententiousness, and insistent proclamation of his own "truth" or honesty and "troth" or steadfast fidelity certainly demonstrate his commitment to the plain style. Yet truth is of little avail against craftiness in many of these lyrics, and craft—in the sense of both art and deception—is inescapable in poetry, no matter how plain the style.

In Wyatt's verse there is ultimately a profoundly contradictory sense of the ineffability of truth combined with a doomed determination to put it into words. As Wyatt declares in his epigram 70, "But well to say and so to mean— / That sweet accord is seldom seen." The final impression of Wyatt's poetic persona is fundamentally ambiguous, for he is caught, as Greenblatt explains, in a perpetual conflict between factitious self-presentation and inscrutable inwardness. It is a conflict brilliantly captured in a poem attributed to Wyatt: "I am as I am and so will I be / But how that I am none knoweth truly."

Henry Howard, earl of Surrey, was a great admirer of Sir Thomas Wyatt and eulogized the older poet in his verse, but his own style is smoother and more polished with a more fluent and regular metrical scheme. The contrast can be seen by comparing their translations of Petrarch. Wyatt's "rougher" style is favored by most modern readers, but Surrey's was greatly admired in his own time. Certainly Surrey's was more influential, since he established the standard pattern for the sonnet in English—the so-called Shakespearean sonnet, with three quatrains and a final rhyming couplet—which required fewer repeated rhymes than the Italian or Petrarchan sonnet, with its octave and sestet. He also introduced unrhymed iambic pentameter or blank verse, the standard metrical form of English verse, in his translation of Virgil's *Aeneid*.

In translating Books II and IV of the *Aeneid*, Surrey combines a humanist commitment to the recovery of the great works of antiquity with a personal enthusiasm for epic heroism. In "An excellent epitaph of Sir Thomas Wyatt," Surrey praises the older man as the embodiment of classical *virtu* and national service, inspiring English youth to aspire to comparable fame. However, Wyatt's own assessment of service to king and country is more equivocal, as the profoundly ambiguous advice given to Sir Francis Brian in "A Spending Hand" indicates. Moreover, Wyatt chose to translate works of a more consolatory and Stoic cast—the Psalms and Plutarch's *Quiet Mind*—implying a turn away from worldly ambition.

As the oldest son of the duke of Norfolk and scion of a venerable aristocratic family, Surrey was consumed by a passion for worldly honor. He was raised as the companion of the king's illegitimate son, Henry Fitzroy, at Windsor. Shortly after his friend's death, Surrey was imprisoned at Windsor for striking a courtier—in the elegy "So cruel prison" he recalls their close bond as a kind of chivalric parity, "where each of us did plead the other's right." He is no more repentant in "London, has thou accused me" written after he was arrested for throwing rocks at the citizens and windows of London in 1543. An older counselor called him "the most foolish, proud boy that is in England," and his pride led inevitably to a fall.

As a cousin to Catherine Howard, Henry VIII's fifth queen, Surrey was also entangled in the dangerous sexual politics of Henry's final years. Unfortunately, he was much less adroit at surviving these entanglements than Wyatt, and after Catherine's execution for adultery he was accused of including the royal insignia on his own coat of arms and sent to the block not long before the king himself died.

The lyrics of Wyatt and Surrey were first published and prominently featured in *Tottel's Miscellany* (1557), the first in a series of poetical "miscellanies" or collections including verses by more than one author. This immensely popular and influential work contained forty poems by Surrey, ninety-seven by Wyatt, forty by the less-renowned Nicholas Grimald, and samplings of verse by other early Tudor authors including Lord Vaux, John Heywood, John Harington, Thomas Churchyard, and Thomas Norton. The collection presents an immense variety of metrical and poetic forms—poulter's measure, ottava rima, terza rima, heroic couplets, rime royal, and blank verse along with epigrams, satires, elegies, and an abundance of amorous lyrics. The aristocratic distinction of the contributors and the stateliness of their style were emphasized as selling points in the preface; most of the poems by Grimald, an obscure commoner, were dropped from subsequent editions.

By contrast, *A Handful of Pleasant Delights* (1566) lacked the prestigious pedigree and noble names of its more illustrious predecessor, consisting entirely of anonymous broadside ballads. Ballads were scorned as vulgar by many contemporaries, Ben Jonson insisting that a true "poet should detest a balladmaker," yet the courtly lyric never completely lost its connections to popular song, and the enthusiasm for both crossed class lines. In Shakespeare's *Hamlet* the well-born Ophelia sings snatches of ballads from a *Handful of Pleasant Delights* and elsewhere, while the grave digger sings verses by Lord Vaux from *Tottel's Miscellany.*

The effort to consolidate the authority of the "courtly makers" continued and intensified in later miscellanies such as *The Paradise of Dainty Devices* (1576), whose title page advertised the distinction of its poets, "sundry learned Gentlemen, both of honor, and woorshippe." The contents are marked by a didactic sobriety resembling the tone of *The Mirror for Magistrates* (1559). Similarly, *The Phoenix Nest* (1593), an elegiac tribute to the memory of Sir Philip Sidney, boasts that it contains the "rare and refined" work of "Noble men, worthy Knights, gallant gentlemen, Masters of Arts and brave Schollers." Nevertheless, snobbish claims for the lofty social status of lyric verse were not the sole concern of poetic miscellanies. *England's Helicon* (1600) unashamedly mingles the work of celebrated worthies with those previously unknown, insisting on a kind of equality in the republic of letters in which "the names of Poets . . . have been placed with the names of the greatest Princes of the world."

George Gascoigne is another genuinely transitional figure, writing in the early 1570s just before the real flowering of the Elizabethan lyric. A very talented and ambitious poet, Gascoigne saw himself as a worthy heir to Chaucer, England's greatest early poet, yet was ambivalent and uncertain about how to present himself and his work. Neither noblemen nor gentlemen were supposed to publish their work willingly because it was thought to be demeaning to seek fame or gain in print. Moreover, lyric verse was supposed to be the amateur pastime of a leisured elite, rather than the mercenary endeavor of professional writers. Wyatt and Surrey were published posthumously, but while they were alive, their work circulated in manuscript within a courtly coterie.

Gascoigne's solution was highly equivocal. He published a large collection of his verse and his prose entitled *A Hundreth Sundrie Flowres* (1573), describing it as a "notable volume" worthy of the poets of antiquity. Yet in his prefatory letters Gascoigne pretends that the collection is actually a miscellany of lyrics by a number of different nameless gentlemen-poets, even while assigning authorship of most for most of the poems to himself in the table of contents. Finally, he claims that the work was unauthorized, having been given to a printer without his permission. This was a common expedient at the time, also resorted to by Barnabe Googe, who claimed that his *Eglogs, Epytaphes, and Sonnettes* had been passed on to a printer by a friend in his absence.

There were certainly instances where the complaints were genuine— Samuel Daniel and Nicholas Breton actually had their work stolen and printed by unscrupulous publishers—but Gascoigne's complaints seem to be part of his fictional ruse. Aimed at titillating the initiated and mocking the obtuse, *A Hundreth Sundrie Flowres* is framed as an elaborate and somewhat defensive literary joke that also allows the poet to blow his own horn behind a subterfuge of irony and evasion. But Gascoigne's strategy was not entirely successful. The work was attacked and suppressed as slanderous and lascivious—especially the amusingly bawdy *Adventures of Master F. J.*—and a supposedly expurgated and more didactic revision was banned again in 1576.

Gascoigne has conventionally been seen as a paragon of the plain style, and his presentation of himself as a reformed prodigal near the end of his career—partially aimed at placating his critics—reinforces the moralistic interpretation of his poetry.

Gascoigne also wrote the didactic verse favored in the collections of his day: poems resembling Lord Vaux's "Aged Lover Renounceth Love" in *Tottel's Miscellany* or George Turberville's "The Lover Abused Renounceth Love" in *Epitaphs, Epigrams, Songs, and Sonnets* (1567). "Gascoigne's Goodnight" contemplates the poet's own mortality and anticipates the last judgement, and one of his final undertakings was a translation of Pope Innocent III's *De Contemptu Mundi*, which Gascoigne titled the *Droome of Doomesday*. However, in some instances, these moralistic verses are more a display of virtuosity than of conviction, and he warns his readers in another prefatory epistle not to mistake "in sad earnest" a renunciation of love written in jest.

Moreover, Gascoigne exults in his craft in every sense of the term— the intricate framing devices of *The Adventures of Master F. J.* that pro-

vide an ironic context for his amorous lyrics reveal his delight in the riddles, disguises, pseudonyms, and "dark speech" of courtly discourse. In
one of his best poems, "Gascoigne's Woodmanship," he prefers to interpret his failure to hit the mark figuratively—rather than "with plain
paraphrase"—because it allows him to excuse his shortcomings and
impress his reader with his ingenuity. Far from the orthodox "drab" poet
he is often taken to be, Gascoigne is instead a creative innovator whose
innovations were poorly received.

With Sir Philip Sidney we encounter the true flowering of Elizabethan poetry—a high point inaugurated by Spenser's *Shepheardes Calender* (1579), which was dedicated to Sidney—as well as Sidney's own
brilliant sonnet sequence *Astrophil and Stella* and his *Defence of Poesy*,
both works written in the early 1580s. With the reticence characteristic of the aristocracy Sidney published none of his work in his own lifetime, but interest in his work was assured by his exalted reputation as a
patron and statesman, not to mention his manifest skill as a poet. After
Sidney's death various printers sought to capitalize on his renown with
unauthorized editions of *Astrophil and Stella* in 1591. His family and
friends responded by publishing a canonical text of the poems in a folio
edition of his works (1598); two editions of the *Defence of Poesy* were
published in 1595, as were various versions of his *Arcadia* in 1590, 1593,
and 1598.

Sidney's renown as a poet has endured from his own day to ours, but
despite his literary success, his political career proved frustrating. The
nephew and heir to one of the most powerful men in England, Robert
Dudley, the earl of Leicester and a favorite and perennial suitor of
Queen Elizabeth, Sidney hoped to achieve great things. An idealistic
Protestant and internationalist, he pushed hard for a more active war
policy against Spain, but he evidently only succeeded in antagonizing
the queen. As a result, he spent much of his time at the edges of the
court or rusticated at his sister's estate in Wilton.

It was during these times of enforced inactivity that Sidney turned to
poetry, calling it his "unelected vocation" in the *Defence*. When Elizabeth reluctantly sent troops to the Netherlands under the command of
Leicester, things finally seemed to be going Sidney's way, and he
assumed a high military post under his uncle. Unfortunately, the campaign was poorly organized and eventually failed, and Sidney died of
injuries received in a minor skirmish. He was given a splendid funeral
and commemorated as a heroic martyr for the Protestant cause, but the

tributes never fully dispelled the aura of noble failure that still haunts his life.

That ambiguity suffuses his otherwise resonant affirmation of the ancient dignity of poetry and the power of the "erected wit" in his *Defence of Poesy*. Written as a response to Stephen Gosson's *School of Abuse* (1579)—a treatise attacking poetry as both deceptive and degenerate—Sidney's *Defence* ascribes tremendous moral authority and efficacy to verse. He argues that its power to move readers by appealing to their emotions as well as their reason makes it a great force for the good. By showing us the beauty of virtue, poetry can stir us both to know and do what is right. Sidney also draws upon a Neo-Platonic argument of Italian literary theorists to refute Plato, saying that poetry's imaginative vision allows us to see the transcendent ideal truths otherwise invisible to those bound by merely material realities. Nature's "world is brazen, the poets only deliver a golden" one, and by recovering a glimpse of perfection, we are inspired to strive to attain it. Finally, Sidney tries to brush aside Plato's attack upon poets as liars by frankly acknowledging the fictive nature of poetry and insisting that the poet—unlike the philosopher or historian—never seeks to pass off his creations as truths on a credulous audience. Such arguments arouse suspicions that Sidney is sophistically trying to have it both ways, and his humorous conclusion, in which he "conjures" his reader to believe every extravagant claim ever made for poetry's power, reinforces our sense of the ironies underlying his *Defence*.

Astrophil and Stella is also a profoundly ironic work of striking originality and considerable influence. Sidney's sonnets started a vogue that outlasted the decade inspiring similar sequences, such as Samuel Daniel's *Delia* (1592), Michael Drayton's *Idea's Mirror* (1594), and Edmund Spenser's *Amoretti*, as well as a number of lesser sonnet collections by Henry Constable, Thomas Lodge, Barnabe Barnes, and Giles Fletcher. The sonnet tradition in England was concluded—and, in a sense, deconstructed—by the belated publication of Shakespeare's *Sonnets* (1609), but many of the same unsettling ironies and ambiguities in Shakespeare's extraordinarily enigmatic sequence can be found in Sidney's.

Astrophil and Stella has as one of its most striking features a clearly delineated narrative—its stages described in Thomas Nashe's prefatory remarks to the unauthorized edition: "the argument cruel chastity, the prologue hope, the epilogue despair"—and various incidents are recorded, particularly in the songs included in the sequence, which function as turning points for the action. Astrophil steals a kiss, races on horseback to a furtive liaison, meets Stella in a grove only to part from her in sorrow, and is brusquely dismissed from beneath her window.

The plot is thickened and complicated by a series of explicit autobiographical references identifying Astrophil with Sidney (sonnet 30) and Stella with Penelope Devereux (sonnets 24, 35, 37), a well-born lady at court whom Sidney was once supposed to marry but who subsequently married Lord Rich, apparently leaving Sidney to pine for her. Nevertheless, the story presents with characteristic courtly evasion a deliberately confusing mixture of fact and elaborate role playing. When Stella is indifferent to Sidney's own plight but is moved to tears by a trite "fable . . . Of Lovers never knowne," Astrophil announces in sonnet 45's last line, "I am not I, pitie the tale of me."

In a sense, Sidney is simply revealing his artistic strategy, having turned the details of his life into a tale. However, his statement is an unnerving concession to Platonic suspicions of fiction's falsehood, and it coyly raises grave doubts about the authenticity of Sidney's persona and the sincerity of the feelings expressed. Questions are also raised regarding the claim advanced in the *Defence* that whoever "could see Virtue would be wonderfully ravished with the love of her beauty"—since in sonnets 71 and 76 virtue provokes lust rather than a contemplative revery, with beauty generating more heat than light and desire demanding food.

Finally, there is the larger question regarding the purpose of these sonnets. Are they part of a program of seduction aimed at charming the lady addressed and amusing other readers, or do they serve the higher didactic purpose prescribed for poetry in the *Defence*, with Astrophil's defeat and despair working as a cautionary tale? Or do they perhaps lead to a moral impasse and suspension of judgment comparable to the reaction prompted by the strange mistrial of the lovers in Sidney's *Old Arcadia*? Whatever the answer, it is clear that in Sidney's lyric verse we have reached a new level of poetic complexity and ambiguity.

Samuel Daniel was closely affiliated with the Sidney circle as a protégé of the Countess of Pembroke and tutor to her son, and he called her home at Wilton, where Sidney wrote his *Arcadia*, his "best school." Daniel's literary debut was inadvertently linked with Sidney's when twenty-eight of his sonnets were published in the 1591 pirated edition of Sidney's *Astrophil and Stella*. The authorized edition of Daniel's *Delia* was published the next year and dedicated to Mary Sidney, the Countess of Pembroke. "Care-charmer Sleep" (sonnet 49) is one of the more justly renowned of his sequence, but the next poem in which he criticizes other poets for indulging in the archaic accents and diction of chivalric romance (lines thought to be aimed at Spenser) and painting "shadows in imaginary lines, / Which well the reach of their high wits records" (sonnet 50) indicates one of Daniel's limitations as a poet. In one sense, this is a completely conventional jibe at poetic competitors and their mistresses, contending that the poet's beloved is truly beautiful while others perpetrate fictions; Shakespeare's claim that his love is "as rare / As any she belied with false compare" (sonnet 130) is a similar boast. Nevertheless, Daniel's fear that high wits may overreach themselves shows his fundamental lack of sympathy with Sidney's as well as Spenser's conception of poetry.

Daniel displays in his poetry a kind of determined literal-mindedness and an allegiance to fact that disqualified him as a poet in the eyes of Jonson and others. Lyric poetry held few charms for him, and he committed his energies to a vast and virtually endless verse history of England's *Civil Wars*, in which he proudly proclaimed "I versifie the truth; not poetize."

Michael Drayton was also directly inspired by *Astrophil and Stella*— a debt he archly acknowledges in his dedicatory verses to *Idea's Mirror* by quoting Sidney's sonnet 74 to declare his independence from Petrarchan convention: "Divine Sir Philip, I avouch they writ: / I am no pickpurse of another's wit." Drayton's irony exposes the pretense of such claims. Nevertheless, many of the poems in *Idea's Mirror* display a genuine originality and anticipate the immediacy and tension encountered in Donne's love poetry.

The most famous sonnet of the sequence (61) begins powerfully and memorably—"Since there's no help, come, let us kiss and part"—and proceeds to an urgent dramatic monologue aimed at a last-minute reversal of the direction set by the first line. The poet's disparagement of other lovers as "paltry, foolish, painted things, / That now in coaches trouble ev'ry street" evokes a London scene of urban energy far from the abstract idyllic landscapes of earlier love lyrics, and his assurance that his beloved shall "fly above the vulgar throng / Still to survive in my immortal song" reflects a more pronounced and aggressive tendency to hyperbole and self-aggrandizement (sonnet 6).

Edmund Spenser's sonnet sequence, the *Amoretti*, was published in one volume along with his *Epithalamion*, a long poem celebrating his marriage to Elizabeth Boyle in 1595. There is no necessary connection between the largely conventional Petrarchan mistress praised in the sonnets for her sovereign beauty (3) and reproached for her cruel tyranny (10) and the bride of the marriage song. Nevertheless, the song's happy anticipation of wedded bliss and the consummation of the couple's marriage casts its glow over the earlier lyrics. Unlike most other sequences, Spenser's *Amoretti* describes a love that is not inevitably unrequited or guilt-ridden. Despite the note of "pining anguish" in the collection's final line, sonnets 72 and 78, among many others, happily settle for contemplative contentment. Lustful desires are firmly exorcised, and the speaker commands himself to "Onely behold her rare perfection, / And bless your fortunes fayre election" (sonnet 84).

Maurice Evans notes the sharp contrast between Wyatt's and Spenser's treatment of Petrarch's vision of his beloved as a white doe: in Wyatt the hind flees from the hunter and proves too wild for any man, whereas in Spenser (sonnet 68 of *Amoretti*) the gentle deer submits to the speaker's touch as he "with her owne goodwill hir fyrmely tyde," and in sonnet 78 Spenser pursues the hind not as a hunter but a young fawn. A reconciliation of opposites is anticipated in the conceit of the spider and bee (sonnet 71), and the lovers achieve a deeply gratifying reciprocity (sonnet 82). In Spenser's love lyrics conflict is muted, transcendence is attained, and affections are returned, at least at some points in the sequence. The relative harmony of Spenser's love poetry sets it apart from most contemporary lyrics.

Spenser's ability to reconcile conflicts proves especially effective in his tributes to Queen Elizabeth. In sonnet 74 of *Amoretti*, Spenser compliments the three most important ladies in his life—all named Elizabeth—his mother, the queen, and his bride, "of all alive most worthy to be praysed." The poem is a delicate but precarious balancing act, gracefully harmonizing any conflict of emotional loyalties, even as it pays the highest compliment to his bride. Spenser, of course, wrote his great epic, *The Faerie Queene*, to honor Queen Elizabeth, making her the inspiration and end point for all its deeds of heroism, but even there, he preserves a separate space for his own, more personal attachments.

Near the end of the poem's final adventure (VI.x.25–28), the poet makes an appearance, speaking through his surrogate, Colin Clout, who sings the praises of his own mistress. Although she is a mere "countrey lasse," he places her above all other women and shows her waited upon by the Three Graces. This rustic beauty thus usurps the place given Elizabeth in the April eclogue of *The Shepheardes Calender*. The poet still feels obliged to apologize for this presumptuous tribute to another woman in a poem dedicated to the queen, and he asks "Great Gloriana" to pardon him for "making one minime [the very smallest amount] of thy poore handmayd." By his adroit combination of deference and audacity Spenser apparently manages to balance his personal and public allegiances in his love lyrics.

Other lyric poets, more highly placed and closer to the throne, were not so successful. One who had the most difficulty in this regard was Spenser's patron, to whom he dedicated *The Faerie Queene*, Sir Walter Ralegh. A courtier with few other connections, Ralegh depended entirely on the queen's favor, and for a time, that carried him quite far, securing him court monopolies and grants and, in 1587, the valuable post of Captain of the Queen's Guard—a post assuring him of constant proximity to the queen. In return, he paid fulsome tribute to her in verse, addressing her as "the true empress of my heart" in "Sir Walter Ralegh to the Queen."

Ralegh is the paragon of the Elizabethan courtly poet, adapting the compliments and conceits of Petrarchan poetry to the cult of Elizabeth—an elaborate system of ritualized praise and chivalric pageantry flourishing in the final decades of Elizabeth's reign. Elizabeth's chastity was the focal point for this devotion, especially after it became clear in the early 1580s that she was resolved never to marry. The cult included many other eminent worshipers, noble rivals competing to surpass one another in the eloquence and extravagance of their praise. Sir Henry Lee, the earl of Oxford, the earl of Cumberland, and the earl of Essex all wrote lyric proclamations of their love for the queen and joined in the annual tournaments held in her honor. For a time Ralegh's amorous professions proved effective, infuriating competitors for the queen's favor like Essex.

Unfortunately for Ralegh, Elizabeth found out that he had secretly married one of her maids of honor, Elizabeth Throckmorton, and she had them both imprisoned in the Tower in 1592. Spenser, a commoner far away in Ireland, could make room for more than one Elizabeth in his life, but such an accommodation proved more difficult for

Ralegh at court. Consequently, Ralegh is also a figure for whom the conventional courtly role of unrequited lover became painfully real. Resorting to one of the queen's favorite comparisons, the goddess of chastity, Ralegh had intoned "Praised be Diana's fair and harmless light," but now he saw Diana's less benign aspect—that of a cruel huntress.

In *Ocean to Cynthia* (another name for Diana) Ralegh takes note of the terrifying combination of "such fear in love, such love in majesty," and he depicts himself as "alone, forsaken, friendless, on the shore." The same note of anguished isolation resounds in his adaptation of the ballad "As you came from the holy land":

> She hath left me here all alone,
>   All alone as unknown,
> Who sometimes did me lead with herself,
>   And loved as her own.

Many of Ralegh's lyrics assume the jaded and skeptical tone encountered in Wyatt's verse. Christopher Marlowe's "Passionate Shepherd to his Love" proffers all the traditional pastoral allurements, including "beds of roses . . . A cap of flowers" and the songs of "shepherd swains," exulting in the precious artifice of these tropes. Ralegh's response, "The Nymph's Reply to the Shepherd," was coupled with Marlowe's poem in both *The Passionate Pilgrim* and *England's Helicon*, and rejects the seductive blandishments and ephemeral pleasures of Marlowe's verses, while raising doubts about the "truth in every shepherd's tongue." Similarly, "Farewell false love, the oracle of lies" laments that faith is repaid with ingratitude.

Like Wyatt, Ralegh also rebukes mistrust in love and deception at court, most defiantly in "The Lie." After instructing his soul to give the lie or challenge to a vast array of social institutions, he insists upon that soul's invulnerability to harm from this world. Similarly, in a poem addressed to Elizabeth—who responded with the condescending "Ah, silly pug, wert thou so sore afraid"—"Fortune hath taken thee away my love," he concludes his lament by insisting that, while "fortune conquers kings; / . . . No fortune base shall ever alter me."

Ralegh sought to maintain this pose of defiant equanimity at his execution on charges of treason in 1618, but despite his bravery in the face of death, the question remains whether Ralegh achieves the autonomy that he claimed or whether he is, in Gary Waller's words, the "quintessential court poet [whose] poems are determined by and finally silenced by, the power of the Court."

William Shakespeare's *Sonnets* have provoked more critical conjecture than any other collection of love lyrics, since most (1–126) are addressed to a beautiful young man and the remainder are aimed at the infamous Dark Lady. The first seventeen sonnets attempt a kind of vicarious seduction of the young man, urging him to marry and procreate, and sonnet 20 is a deliberately provocative male blazon—focusing attention at the end on the young man's genitals, even while professing indifference to them.

Shakespeare's promiscuous and fickle Dark Lady is the degraded opposite of the Petrarchan ideal, reduced in sonnet 137 to "the bay where all men ride, . . . the wide world's common place"—the latter pun highlighting the exhausted banality of the woman as romantic ideal. Despite her whorish vulgarity, the Dark Lady still proves irresistible. Her continuing attraction prompts feelings of disgust and revulsion, guilt and profound cynicism. The traditional farewell to love is especially vehement in sonnet 129, where lust's evil consequences are enumerated in lurid detail, but the poem concludes with an admission of defeat: "All this the world well knows, yet none knows well / To shun the heav'n that leads men to this hell."

Instead of breaking free of his tainted mistress, the speaker in sonnet 138 engages in a pact of self-conscious mutual deception: "Therefore I lie with her, and she with me, / And in our faults by lies we flattered be." Finally, there are hints of an affair between the young man and the Dark Lady, who seduces "his purity with her foul pride" (sonnet 144), and the poet responds to this betrayal with an eerie combination of mild reproach and bland acceptance.

At the same time, Shakespeare's sequence includes some of the most resonant affirmations of true love's—and poetry's—triumph over time: "Not marble nor the gilded monuments / Of princes shall outlive this pow'rful rime" (sonnet 55). And, while he doubts his own adequacy "as an unperfect actor" for the part, the speaker holds out the possibility of some "perfect ceremony of love's rite." Such a perfect, almost sacramental declaration of love can be seen as the principal aim of lyric verse (sonnet 23).

Finally, in the most popular and frequently cited of the sonnets, the poet seems to attain his goal, declaring the changeless durability of "the marriage of true minds" (sonnet 116). These articles of romantic faith are still undermined by the depravity of the objects of desire, both of whom prove false. Even more unsettling is the unreliability of a poetic persona whose "perjured eye" (sonnet 152) distorts everything, allowing "no correspondence with true sight" (sonnet 148). Shakespeare's final sonnets raise anew the doubts Sidney barely allayed in his *Defence* and revived in *Astrophil and Stella*. Poetry's links to emotion, which Sidney saw as a force for the good, here become a source of distortion and self-deception.

Many readers regard Shakespeare's *Sonnets* as the reflection of a terminal crisis of lyric poetry, and certainly that impression is reinforced by their arrival in print at the end of the sonnet vogue. Joel Fineman argues in *Shakespeare's Perjured Eye* that the *Sonnets* initiate a kind seismic shift in consciousness—from a visionary poetry of praise, transparency, and presence to a rhetorical poetry of disillusion, opacity, and irony. Fineman also sees them as the source of the modern conception of poetry, fashioning a self that is eccentric, alienated, inaccessibly inward, and hopelessly cut off from object relations. Like Hamlet, this new lyric protagonist proudly declares that "I have that within which passes show," while sadly admitting that "Man delights not me—nor woman neither." This is a persuasive and powerful argument, but the notion of a radical break in the lyric style is overstated.

A review of the development of the English lyric shows that Shakespeare's *Sonnets* simply intensify many of the conflicts inherent in the lyric mode. The beloved proves unworthy of devotion, but the Tudor lyric has incorporated such disappointments from its beginnings. The lover deceives himself and others, but complicity in deception and betrayal is again a familiar story. Finally, the slippery ironies of the lyric persona, which is usually a consciously assumed role, are often acknowledged in this poetry, and its paradoxical blend of passionate intensity and impersonality are constant and familiar features. The case for a dramatic departure from past traditions by Shakespeare or the Metaphysicals depends in part on the older view of the lyric as sweetly immediate and transparently simple.

Shakespeare's plays include a number of more traditional lyrics sung in performance, and these songs present an intriguing contrast to his sonnets—since many evoke the golden world conventionally associated with the lyric. His romantic comedies are, like John Lyly's plays for the choristers of the Chapel Royal, almost musical comedies in their combination of song and drama. *Twelfth Night* is suffused with music from the start—the duke asks the musicians presumably on stage to continue playing until his emotions surfeit on their own excess: "If music be the food of love, play on . . ." Feste, the most musical of Shakespeare's clowns, sings several pieces, including "O mistress mine"—a piece resembling airs by the contemporary composers Thomas Morley, William Byrd, and Thomas Campion.

The song's auditors are a drunken, aged playboy, Sir Toby Belch, and his feeble dupe, Sir Andrew Aguecheek, whose futile suit of the Countess Olivia is being encouraged by Sir Toby. Thus the song's poignant theme of carpe diem—"Then come kiss me sweet and twenty, / Youth's a stuff will not endure" (2.3.48–49)—is rendered somewhat ironic, if not ridiculous. Here as elsewhere in Shakespeare's plays the conventional sentiments of his lyric songs are profoundly complicated by the dramatic circumstances of their performance. Similarly, Feste's lament for unrequited love —"I am slain by a fair cruel maid"; (2.4.50–65)—mocks the extravagantly melancholy pose of Duke Orsino. Finally, the play ends with the duke's enigmatic song of the passage from childhood to "man's estate" and the old age of the world.

In *As You Like It* the singer Amiens welcomes anyone who wishes to escape the afflictions of the "working-day world" to join the banished duke and his merry company in the forest of Arden "under the greenwood tree," where each shall find "No enemy / But winter and rough weather" (2.5.1–8). The song is in turn mocked by Jaques, who "can suck melancholy out of a song, as a weasel sucks eggs" and whose own verses provide a tart counterpoint to the song's cheerful pastoral images. Amiens's next song draws a harsher distinction between the true companionship found in the greenwood and the hypocrisy that prevails at court and elsewhere:

> Most friendship is feigning, most loving mere folly
> > Then heigh-ho, the holly,
> > This life is most jolly.   (2.7.181–183)

Similarly, "It was a lover and his lass, / With a hey and a ho and a hey nonino"—with its nonsense syllables and trite rhyme words—can be seen as a kind of parody of conventional ballads, and it too is derided by the clown Touchstone (5.3.14–37). Nevertheless, this perennially popular song sets the stage for the marriage of the "country copulatives" and the happy ending of the last act. Both the play and its heroine, Rosalind, expose the banality of such sentiments, even as they acknowledge their truth and inevitability.

By altering the dramatic context, Shakespeare further complicates the significance of the lyric verse in his plays. The garden world of Belmont in *The Merchant of Venice* resembles the idyllic retreats of romantic comedy, and here too music features prominently. Nevertheless, the song preceding Bassanio's symbolic marriage choice, "Tell me where is Fancy bred" (3.2.65–72), inspires caution and calculation in this somewhat callow suitor, and Portia's description of herself as "the sum of something" blurs the distinctions between love and commerce that the play supposedly affirms.

In the even more harshly cynical "problem play" *Troilus and Cressida*, the double entendres and brittle cruelty of a seemingly light-hearted love lyric are accentuated by the context. The lewd go-between Pandarus sings of "love, love, nothing but love" to Helen and Paris, and his mirth at the injuries caused by "love's bow"—whose "shaft confounds not that it wounds, / But tickles still the sore"—dissolves at the song's conclusion into almost orgasmic gasps of laughter (3.1.116–125).

With *Hamlet* the idyllic innocence of pastoral and romantic ballads is utterly shattered. In a cryptic pastiche of his own Hamlet alludes to "the strucken deer" and calls his friend Horatio, Damon—but the golden world suggested by the name of a faithful shepherd has been irretrievably "dismantled" by his uncle (3.2.265–278). The ballad lyrics—such as "How should I your true love know" (4.5.23) and "For bonny sweet Robin is all my joy" (4.5.184)—sung by Ophelia with their conventional themes of love and death and fidelity and betrayal are made even more painful by her suicidal grief and madness.

The incongruous bawdiness of Ophelia's song of St. Valentine's Day, in which a maid courts a man, who then deflowers and abandons her, concludes on a note of helpless pathos and reproach:

> Young men will do't if they come to't —
> By Cock, they are to blame.
> Quoth she, "Before you tumbled me,
> You promis'd me to wed . . . "
> "So would I a done, by yonder sun,
> And thou hadst not come to my bed."
>   (4.5.60–66)

Ophelia's deranged singing "takes off the rose," as Hamlet says in another context, "from the fair forehead of an innocent love"

(3.4.43–44), while giving tragic expression to impulses which this play cannot accommodate.

In Shakespeare's late romances lyric song can express both innocence and experience as well as spontaneity and sophistication. The shift from the paranoia and misery of the first part of *The Winter's Tale* is marked by the entry of Autolycus singing, and the ballads hawked by this trickster and vagabond resemble him in their combination of ribaldry, cunning, and joie de vivre. "When daffodils begin to peer" celebrates spring as "the sweet o' the year"—a season beloved by Autolycus not only because "the red blood reigns in the winter's pale," but also because he can snatch the "white sheet bleaching on the hedge" while he and his "doxy" lie "tumbling in the hay" (4.3.1–12).

Perdita reigns as the queen of the sheep-shearing festival, distributing flowers and leading a dance of shepherds and shepherdesses, and afterwards one of Autolycus's admirers enthusiastically announces his arrival at the feast: "He has the prettiest love-songs for maids, so without bawdry (which is strange); with such delicate burdens of dildoes and fadings, jump her and thump her" (4.4.194–197). The terms repeated pointedly convey the bawdy meanings the rustic misses, and the scene's subsequent declarations of love and desire provoke a renewed outburst of paternal rage and repression, but this time it proves harmless. The natural appetites and vitality celebrated in the ballads are finally accommodated within the play through marriage and reunion.

Shakespeare's uses lyric verse in his plays as he does in his sonnets— to explore ambiguities inherent in the mode itself. Despite its apparent simplicity, the lyric is immensely sophisticated and flexible in its recognition of complexity, and this makes it an excellent counterpoint to a vast array of dramatic actions. The fools in both *Twelfth Night* and *King Lear* sing songs in which "the rain it raineth every day." Amiens in *As You Like It* agrees with Lear that human ingratitude is unkinder than bad weather. The songs in these plays provide a perspective on the joys and sorrows of all dramatic genres and occasions, one that is both movingly sympathetic and strikingly balanced.

The lyric tradition does not end with Shakespeare or Donne. While the enthusiasm for sonnet sequences certainly diminishes, the lyric continues to be a larger force in English poetry. In the seventeenth century it takes an increasingly religious direction—in the verses of Donne, Richard Crashaw, Henry Vaughan, and George Herbert. Herbert rejects the "fictions" and "false hair" of Petrarchan love poetry ("Jordan

I") in order to redeem the lyric from the disillusion and solipsistic impasse he finds inevitable in profane love, but this shift from praising the lady to praising God is hardly a departure from earlier trends in the sixteenth-century lyric.

The Jesuit martyr Robert Southwell wrote *St. Peter's Complaint* (1595) as an antidote to the languid eroticism of Shakespeare's *Venus and Adonis*, employing the standard paradoxes and sensuous conceits of Petrarchan verse to turn his readers away from desire. In "Look Home" Southwell says that "Man's mind a mirror is of heavenly sights, / A brief wherein all marvels summed lie," and his belief in human sufficiency and perspicacity is sustained by his belief in God. Claims for the mind's microcosmic autonomy are an article of faith and essential feature of lyric poetry—affirmed most famously in Sir Edward Dyer's "My mind to me a kingdom is" and reaffirmed in Andrew Marvell's "The Garden."

Poets who wrote philosophic and religious lyrics in the sixteenth century not only set a direction for those who followed, but they also reclaimed the possibility of a wholesome subjectivity, intellectual detachment, and virtue in love. This can be seen in three writers connected to Sir Philip Sidney—two writing near the end of the sixteenth century and the other in the first two decades of the seventeenth. Sir Fulke Greville was Sidney's closest friend and he devoted much of his life to preserving Sidney's memory, sharing responsibility with his sister, the Countess of Pembroke, for the authorized publication of the dead poet's works, and subsequently writing a biography of Sir Philip.

Greville also wrote a collection of sonnets entitled *Caelica*, never published in his lifetime. Although they have their origin in the sonnet vogue inspired by *Astrophil and Stella*, they strike out in a very different direction, praising a variety of somewhat shadowy mistresses, including Diana, Myra, and Caelica—the first apparently a traditional reference to Elizabeth. Greville's verse lacks the seductive urgency and purpose of Sidney's sonnets, and he announces at the start that "I have vowed in strangest fashion, / To love, and never seek compassion" (sonnet 4).

Initially, these various mistresses serve to embody unchanging virtue beyond the reach of world, but by the end of the sequence, they have dropped from sight. The fiction of courtship is abandoned, and the poems simply become intensely introspective reflections on human weakness, the vanity of the world, and death and the hope of redemption (sonnets 97–102), as well as occasional meditations on political corruption (sonnets 91, 95, 106–108). Greville demonstrates and develops the lyric's implicit capacity for contemplation. His profound *contemptus mundi* carries a conviction not always found in other poets, while displaying the lyric's ability to maintain one's distance from worldly concerns.

Mary Sidney, Sir Philip's sister and the Countess of Pembroke, presided over a select literary coterie at her Wilton estate and took responsibility for her brother's literary legacy. Although an intelligent and authoritative figure, she assumed in her own writing the somewhat subordinate role considered appropriate for women, overseeing editions of her brother's work and translating pious and edifying literature. Nevertheless, her translations display not only her talents as a lyric poet in her own right, but they also manage to establish a new independent direction. In continuing the translation of the Psalms she had begun with her brother, she embraced the sacred poetry Sidney praised but steered away from in the *Defence*—claiming that only those who had "no law but wit" were "right poets." The words of her translations thus acquire a truth and authority lacking in his.

Mary Sidney also translated Petrarch's *Trionfo della Morte* ("Triumph of Death"), which can be seen as Petrarch's palinode—in it the chaste Laura finally succeeds in winning her lover over to virtue and putting an end to the desire and vacillation of the *Rime Sparse*. In doing so, Sidney points to a resolution of the moral and emotional dilemmas besetting the lyrics of her brother and all his imitators. Moreover—as Margaret Hannay shows in *Philip's Phoenix*, a study of Mary Sidney—Laura is praised in this poem for her eloquence and wisdom as well as for her chastity and thus a previously passive mistress acquires greater authority and a more active role.

This resolution was taken up and pursued further by her niece, Mary Wroth, the daughter of Sir Robert Sidney and another talented woman of letters. Wroth wrote a sonnet sequence, *Pamphilia to Amphilanthus*, as well as a prose romance resembling her uncle's *Arcadia*, and both works were published together in 1621. She paid sorely for her violation of literary and sexual decorum:—one of her enemies attacked her as a hermaphrodite and urged her to "leave idle bookes alone / For wise and worthyer women have writte none." Her work was suspected of being a slanderous roman à clef, but the deeper scandal derived from a woman writer publishing her passions.

Indeed, Wroth seems determined to make a spectacle of herself—although she laments that "I should nott have bin made this stage of woe / Where sad disasters have theyr open show"—for she still demands that her audience "looke on mee; I ame to thes adrest / I, ame the soule that feeles the greatest smart" (sonnet 48). Her verse constitutes a stirring demonstration of her constancy in love and the redemptive power of suffering. By making her pain into a show of virtue, Wroth's lyric protagonist resembles both Pamela and Philoclea, the heroines of her uncle's sixteenth-century romance, and Pamela and Clarissa, the heroines in Samuel Richardson's eighteenth-century novels. Whether such heroism challenges or reinforces female stereotypes remains a serious question.

Nevertheless, this descendant of the Sidneys clearly made the most of her literary legacy, adapting the love lyric to a woman's voice. Like other writers before and since, Wroth realized the potential for introspective discovery inherent in the lyric, declaring in "A Crowne of Sonetts dedicated to Love" (sonnet 82) that "Itt doth inrich the witts, and make you see / That in your self, which you knew nott before."

Richard C. McCoy

Further Reading

Alpers, Paul, ed. *Elizabethan Poetry: Modern Essays in Criticism.* London: Oxford University Press, 1967.

Evans, Maurice. *English Poetry in the Sixteenth Century.* 2d rev. ed. London: Hutchinson, 1967.

Fineman, Joel. *Shakespeare's Perjured Eye: The Invention of Poetic Subjectivity in the Sonnets.* Berkeley: University of California Press, 1986.

Greenblatt, Stephen. *Renaissance Self-Fashioning: From More to Shakespeare.* Chicago: University of Chicago Press, 1980.

Jones, Emrys, ed. *The New Oxford Book of Sixteenth Century Verse.* Oxford: Oxford University Press, 1991.

Lewis, C. S. *English Literature in the Sixteenth Century, Excluding Drama.* Oxford: Clarendon, 1954.

Lever, Julius Walter. *The Elizabethan Love Sonnet.* London: Methuen, 1968.

Mazzaro, Jerome. *Transformations in the Renaissance English Lyric.* Ithaca, N.Y.: Cornell University Press, 1979.

Miller, Naomi J., and Gary Waller, eds. *Reading Mary Wroth: Representing Alternatives in Early Modern England.* Knoxville: University of Tennessee Press, 1991.

Norbrook, David. *Poetry and Politics in the English Renaissance.* London: Routledge, 1984.

Spearing, A. C.. *Medieval to Renaissance in English Poetry.* Cambridge: Cambridge University Press, 1985.

Waller, Gary F. *English Poetry of the Sixteenth Century.* London: Longmans, 1986.

Spenser, Sidney, Jonson

S PENSER, SIDNEY, AND JONSON stand out, among their Eliza
bethan and Jacobean peers, as poets of the English Renaissance.
They not only contributed to the body of writings that made
English poetry worthy of comparison with the Greek and Latin classics—the ambition common to the modern vernacular literatures that
partly constitute the Renaissance as a cultural movement—they consciously cultivated various ancient and modern genres that, once given a
local habitation, entitled English poetry to be considered part of European literature. Spenser, regularly compared by contemporaries to Virgil, emulated the Roman poet's career by writing an inaugural book of
eclogues (*The Shepheardes Calender*), which was the groundwork for a
national epic, *The Faerie Queene*. Sidney, although not the first to write
love sonnets in English, deserved to be called the "English Petrarch" as
author of the first true sonnet sequence, that is, a collection that continuously represents a single love situation and uses it to evaluate love as
emotional experience, social phenomenon, and cosmic reality. Jonson
domesticated the verse letters of Horace, claimed to write the first true
epigrams in English (in imitation of the Roman poet Martial), and cast
one of his greatest lyrics in the form of a Pindaric ode (another "first" in
English).

Exact contemporaries and well acquainted, although not social
equals, Spenser and Sidney must have regarded each other as collabo-
rators in establishing the authority of English poetry. But Jonson—
whose most famous remark about Spenser is that "in affecting the

ancients [he] writ no language"—has often been considered their antagonist. The generational difference between them corresponds to a difference in historical and cultural circumstances.

Whereas Sidney and Spenser were Elizabethans (in the fullest sense, since their careers in several ways involved the queen herself), Jonson was a Jacobean writer: he was the main writer of court masques for James I, and, more broadly, his works reflect the world, both city and court, of early seventeenth-century London. Moreover, he was a man of the theater, where his greatest and most distinctive achievements were comedies. These, unlike Shakespeare's, bore out the traditional idea of stage comedy as a realistic, urban form. Although, like Sidney and Spenser, Jonson modeled his poems on traditional types of European poetry, they were distinctly different types. Where Spenser and Sidney emulated the epic and pastoral, among ancient genres, and the grander forms of the Italian love lyric (canzones, hymns, sonnet sequences), Jonson eschewed the love-centered forms of modern lyric and imitated the ironic and realistic types of classical poetry, like epigrams and epistles.

How do these differences manifest themselves in actual poems? For a useful comparison, we do not want the extremes of, say, idealizing in Spenser or Sidney and satiric coarseness in Jonson. The following two short poems by Sidney and Jonson seem genuinely comparable. Each takes as its point of departure—what the Renaissance would call its "invention," or seed idea—the correction of a cliché about love.

> Not at first sight, nor with a dribbed shot
> Love gave the wound, which while I breathe will bleed:
> But known worth did in mine of time proceed,
> Till by degrees it had full conquest got.
> I saw and liked, I liked but loved not,
> I loved, but straight did not what Love decreed:
> At length to Love's decrees, I forced, agreed,
> Yet with repining at so partial lot.
> Now even that footstep of lost liberty
> Is gone, and now like slave-born Muscovite,
> I call it praise to suffer tyranny.
> And now employ the remnant of my wit,
>   To make my selfe believe that all is well,
>   While with a feeling skill I paint my hell.
> (Astrophel and Stella, 2)

I now think Love is rather deaf than blind,
 For else it could not be
  That she
Whom I adore so much should so slight me,
 And cast my love behind;
I'm sure my language to her was as sweet,
  And every close did meet
   In sentence of as subtle feet,
    As hath the youngest he
That sits in shadow of Apollo's tree.
Oh, but my conscious fears
 That fly my thoughts between,
 Tell me that she hath seen
 My hundreds of grey hairs,
 Told seven-and-forty years,
Read so much waste, as she cannot embrace
My mountain belly, and my rocky face;
And all these through her eyes have stopped her ears.
    ("My Picture Left in Scotland")

These poems have a good deal in common. In denying that he fell in love at first sight (as Petrarch had fallen in love with Laura), Sidney/Astrophel makes love a social experience, a matter of the powerful effect of knowing Stella in the world and circumstances of which *Astrophel and Stella* often gives a quite circumstantial account. This social anchoring of Petrarchan ideality underlies what the two poems share: each employs wit—in both our sense and the larger sense (reason, judgment) it had in early modern English—to understand the dilemmas and painfulness of love. Just as each poem begins with a denial of a love cliché, so each ends wittily, with a striking turn in the final line.

 Nevertheless, there is a fundamental difference between the poems, of which Jonson's reference to his physical appearance is only the most striking symptom. Despite his initial move Sidney's poetizing has the effect of recuperating the mythology of Petrarchan love. The brilliant handling, in the second quatrain, of the rhetorical figure known as *gradatio* not only plays out the idea of falling in love "by degrees," but with deeper wit recasts "what Love decreed," which may simply be a metaphor for the strength of one's feelings, as "at length to Love's decrees," where the emotion, fully personified, is reestablished as a deity. The revived figure of Love the tyrant underlies the concluding representation of the lover's dilemma, by contrast with Jonson's account of his "conscious fears"—every bit as realistic psychologically as "my mountain belly" is physically.

"Realism," of course, can be a tricky criterion. Although Sidney's rhetoric is more obviously artifical than Jonson's, it is the "feeling skill" of his poem that conveys the power of love as an emotion (for example, in the alliterated and half-rhymed phrase, "while I breathe will bleed," which makes the single wound of love the stuff of life). But one can see why two great moralist-critics of our time, F. R. Leavis and Yvor Winters, championed Jonson's verse for correcting and going beyond the decorativeness—both the frank rhetoricity and the dependence on poetic machinery—of Elizabethan verse. "My Picture Left in Scotland" well exemplifies Jonson's combination of "urbane grace," "native sinew," and "lively toughness" (Leavis's phrases, which adapt T. S. Eliot's definition of seventeenth-century wit as "a tough reasonableness beneath the slight lyric grace"). For Winters, Jonson was the culminating practitioner of an English "plain style," in which verbal skill is not displayed for its own sake, but is devoted to making language convey "an exact correlation between motive and feeling." Winters would connect the effect of truthful acknowledgment of feeling in Jonson's second stanza with the lucid relation of phrase to line of verse, the focused vividness of "fly," and the minimal personification of "tell me."

Jonson's difference from his Elizabethan predecessors strikes us most forcibly when we are reading individual poems. But if we develop our idea of these poets from their works taken as wholes, we shall see that their individual characteristics arise within a common endeavor. Our present notion of what counts as a poem obscures the degree to which Spenser, Sidney, and Jonson shared a single idea of poetry—one in which the epic is considered the definitive type of poem and is characterized by moral and political purposes. Spenser is the only one of the three who wrote what we would today call an epic poem. But Sidney made heroic poetry the centerpiece of his *Defence of Poesy*, and he revised his prose romance *Arcadia* to give it epic scope, stylistic dignity, and moral weight. Verse in the *Arcadia* consists solely of love complaints and pastoral eclogues, and these are all that will come under consideration in a modern "history of English poetry." But Sidney had declared in the *Defence* that "it is not rhyming and versing that maketh a poet" but "the feigning notable images of virtues, vices, and what else," and that two ancient prose works—Xenophon's idealized history *The Education of Cyrus* and Heliodorus's romance *The Aethiopian History*—were "absolute heroical poem[s]."

So if it is beyond the scope of this chapter to discuss the *New* (i.e., revised) *Arcadia*, we must keep in mind its centrality to Sidney's idea of writing poetry. Jonson's critical statements and works similarly display his commitment to the ideals of heroic poetry. In his early play *Poetaster*, as in *Timber*, his late compendium of "discoveries made upon men and manners," "the incomparable Virgil" is the king of poets. Similarly, even though *Timber* does not treat the epic as uniquely definitive of poetry, its ideology of the heroic statesman and of oratory as the foundation of writing is precisely what gave the epic its cultural authority in the Renaissance.

As for his works, Jonson wrote in none of the genres identified with Virgil, although he did write a short, rambunctious mock-epic, "The Famous Voyage." But the epic endeavor is evident throughout his works. One genre he made distinctly his own, the court masque, is founded on pagan mythologies and an ideology of royal and aristocratic heroism. Although Jonson was the English master of prose comedy, one of the plays he set most store by, *Sejanus*, is a tragedy (the one genre that rivaled epic for moral weight and literary dignity), and two of his greatest comedies, *Volpone* and *The Alchemist*, are in blank verse.

As with Sidney, to understand Jonson the poet we must be aware of writings that do not count as "poetry" in a volume like the present one. Beyond their exemplifying a larger idea of poetry than ours, his works can lay claim to the scope and adequacy to life that is associated with the epic. Just as Henry Fielding, trying to establish the dignity of the novel as a literary type, called it "a comic epic poem in prose," so we can say that Jonson's works, taken as a whole, are a comic epic poem in prose and verse.

Let us then turn to the great epic of Elizabethan England, *The Faerie Queene*, and ask how it defined poetry for its age. Like other Renaissance epics, it is a celebration of the nation and of the reigning monarch, who was literally thought to embody her realm. The poem is dedicated to Queen Elizabeth, who is represented by several figures. One, the Fairy Queen herself, never actually appears, although the knights who embody the virtues celebrated by the poem come from her court and are dedicated to her service. It is as if she represents an ideal realm, a kind of secularized heavenly court—the goal of action in this world but above its difficulties and doings. This dimension of her symbolism appears most fully in the story of Prince Arthur, who is said to have fallen in love with her in a dream and who seeks her in vain throughout the world—along the way serving as the arch-rescuer and associate of the poem's main figures and hence as a formal means of unifying its several books.

In addition to having an offstage presence, Queen Elizabeth is represented by two important figures within the poem. They are the demigoddess Belphebe, whose name suggests (in a commonplace of royal symbolism) the pagan goddess of chastity, and Britomart, whose name (recalling both her nation and the pagan god of war) indicates her role as the warrior maiden, who not only embodies the valor and political-sexual authority of the queen but is also said to be her historical ancestor. Beyond these characters, who are explicitly related to Elizabeth, *The Faerie Queene* is filled with female figures of authority, who rule a wide range of allegorical locales in the earlier books of the poem and various political realms and romance castles in the later books. If *The Faerie Queene* shares with other Renaissance epics the celebration of the poet's monarch, its particular character is largely determined by the fact that Spenser's monarch was a woman.

The rationale of the Renaissance epic was not only political, but also moral and allegorical. Sidney represents the *Aeneid* not as the epic narration of the founding of Rome, but as a series of moral exempla: "Only let Aeneas be worn in the tablet of your memory, how he governeth himself in the ruin of his country; in the preserving his old father, and carrying away his religous ceremonies; in obeying the god's commandment to leave Dido; . . . how in storms, how in sports, how in war, how in peace, how a fugitive, how victorious, . . . lastly, how in his inward self, and how in his outward government." In the explanatory Letter to Sir Walter Ralegh appended to the first edition of *The Faerie Queene* (Books I–III, 1590), Spenser said that "the general end of all the book is to fashion a gentleman or noble person in virtuous and gentle discipline." This could obviously include political virtues, to which—if we are to believe what Spenser says in the Letter—twelve concluding books (never written) were to be devoted.

But the books we have, the author says, present "the virtues of a private man," and their titles bear this out. They are, in order, the Books of Holiness, Temperance, Chastity, Friendship, Justice, and Courtesy;

only the next to last is an apparent exception. On its moral and allegorical side, Spenser's epic can seem quite removed from matters of royal authority and political control. What his great modern apologist, C. S. Lewis, called the poem's "allegorical cores" concern, in Books I–III, the experience of religious despair and recovery from it (I.ix–x); the temptations to the temperate soul of idleness (II.vi), avarice (II.vii), and sensuality (II.xii); the nature of sexuality as a power of nature (III.vi) and as a cause of emotional enslavement (III.xi–xii). In the second installment of the poem (Books IV–VI, published in 1596), the treatment is less allegorical—that is, it less seeks to represent the fundamental character of the human soul or psyche and the relation of that soul or psyche to the fundamental character of the cosmos itself. (One should add, even in the midst of these necessary simplifications, that *The Faerie Queene*, as opposed to *The Divine Comedy*, does not give a single view of these matters. Rather, Books I, II, and III consciously play out three different "fundamental" views: the Christian account of the errant soul and its salvation, the classical view of reason maintaining the balance among psychological forces, and the partly Neoplatonic, partly Petrarchan, and partly Christian sense of eros as the force that drives human affairs.)

In the last three books of the poem the dominant mode is romance, rather than allegory. In Book IV, which concerns the social virtue of friendship, there is sometimes a quite novelistic feeling, as characters multiply and are often rather mixed in their motives and behavior, less clearly identified than in Books I–III as "good" and "bad." Dwelling within their secular fictional worlds, these latter books come to engage more immediately the real world of their author and audience. Book VI, most explicitly in its famous pastoral episode (cantos ix and x), seems to recoil from the difficult actualities of the court and public affairs, as they emerge at the end of Book V. By the end of *The Faerie Queene*, the ideal of the courtier—that the cultivated individual is also the best public servant—is deeply troubled. The poem's final installment, "Two Cantos of Mutabilitie" (a fragment of an apparent seventh book, published posthumously in 1609), takes place in a spot withdrawn from human action and concerns not the world of human affairs but the structure of the cosmos itself.

The differing accounts of *The Faerie Queene* in the preceding paragraphs reflect Renaissance writers' double idea of the epic—political and nationalistic, on the one hand, and moral and allegorical, on the other. They also suggest the difference between mid-century critics and scholars, who reawakened interest in *The Faerie Queene* by accepting and defending its moral and allegorical purposes, and recent interpreters, who view the poem more critically as grounded in the power relations of Elizabethan politics, the unequal relations of men and women in sixteenth-century society, and England's colonial and imperial endeavors in Ireland and the New World. Without seeking to impose a misleading homogeneity, one can say that ideas of mastery and dominance are the common element in these motives and interests. They are clearly at the heart of political ideas and political reality in the sixteenth century, and equally central to imperialist and colonial endeavors. Among Spenser's "private" virtues they are most immediately evident in Temperance, in which the ideal mean between emotional extremes is conceived as reason's active control of the passions. Hence Guyon, the Knight of Temperance, must literally bind some of his foes and must exercise self-control in the presence of temptation; hence, too, the tendency to identify spiritual realms (allegorical castles, islands, territories) with the figures who rule them. Other titular virtues of *The Faerie Queene* are not directly defined by (self-) mastery or "governance." But right relation to a lord or master is central not only to Holiness, where the lord is God himself, but also to Chastity, even though the latter virtue, in Spenser's treatment, goes beyond virginity (represented by Belphebe, the imperious huntress) and centers on the monogamous desire experienced and represented by Britomart. It is not simply that in Book I "all the good is Gods, both power and eke will" (I.x.1) and that Britomart's falling in love is represented as the way

> in the gentlest harts
> Imperious Loue hath highest set his throne,
> And tyrannizeth in the bitter smarts
> Of them, that to him buxome are and prone.
> (III.i.23)

Just as importantly, the hero's right relation to these dominant powers is figured as the capacity to defeat foes, control others, or take decisive action—and negatively as imprisonment or inaction through dissipated energies. There is, in other words, a deep sense in which the virtues of *The Faerie Queene* are imagined as heroic. If an allegory represents the consonance of the human soul and the cosmos, a heroic allegory represents the soul as acting in consonance with the cosmos seen in terms of the powers that move and govern it. In Books IV–VI acts of valor in the world of romance are less securely consonant with the nature of things, and their significance becomes increasingly limited (e.g., to the political sphere in Book V) and problematic.

The Faerie Queene sometimes seems to depend on rather simple ideas of heroism and allegory. We may wonder what to make of a poem that begins with a knight, clad in "the armor of a Christian man" ("Letter to Ralegh"), encountering a dragon identified as Error and slaying her when his companion Una (i.e., One, representing Truth) tells him to "add faith unto your force" (I.i.19). But the point of the episode is not simply to convey the moral platitude that with faith the true Christian overcomes error. Nor is the knight immune from defeat. Spenser's heroes, like Homer's Achilles and all serious epic heroes, are vulnerable to and must define themselves in terms of the forces they seek to dominate. When the Red Cross Knight hears Una's cry

> in great perplexitie,
> His gall did grate for griefe and high disdaine,
> And knitting all his force got one hand free,
> Wherewith he grypt her gorge with so great paine,
> That soone to loose her wicked bands did her constraine.
> (I.i.19)

This is allegorical verse—far from Spenser's most remarkable, but instructive for just that reason—because it makes the physical action, the monster's wrapping her tail around the knight, represent a moral and psychological experience. Just as the preceding stanza concluded by referring to "the man so wrapt in *Errours* endlesse traine," where the two meanings of "traine" (tail and "deceipt") make represented action and metaphoric meaning interpenetrate, so here "perplexitie" not only names a state of mind but engages the physical action by its root meaning (Latin *plexus*, interwoven, entangled). The psychology in these lines can be called heroic, because the threatening entanglement is not made simply to disappear, but is translated into coherent action—"knitting all his force"—by human powers that explicitly answer to the enemy monster's summoning of strength in the previous stanza: "Yet kindling rage, her selfe she gathered round." (We can thus see that Una is not a magical *dea ex machina* but, as is typical with allegorical characters, represents an element of the hero's being.) Hence, in the final lines, "with so great paine" refers to both the utmost effort the knight can summon and what he inflicts on his enemy—that is, to both aspects of his "force." This kind of ambiguity is frequent, indeed ordinary, in Spenser's verse. Precisely for that reason it shows the strength of a style that can bring to life a commonplace like "spiritual struggle."

The sense of the hero's implication in the forces that threaten him underlies some of Spenser's most remarkable poetry. It is easy enough to see that Guyon must deal with Pyrochles, the embodiment of wrath, because anger was well recognized as an ambiguous motive, potentially destructive, but also to some extent necessary for effective action. More remarkable are passages that involve feelings at the opposite extreme from wrath. Pleasure and its settings provide some of the most distinctive poetry of *The Faerie Queene*. Spenser endowed English poetry with the rhetoric and rhythms of a passage like the following:

> And fast beside, there trickled softly downe
> A gentle streame, whose murmuring waue did play
> Emongs the pumy stones, and made a sowne,
> To lull him soft a sleepe, that by it lay.   (II.v.30)

For the Romantic poets, who were deeply influenced by Spenser, verse like this came from Fairyland itself, the realm of pure imagination. But for Spenser, it came from a more worldly sense of the problematics of human nature. The human center of the setting described by these lines is not a poet, but an arch-sensualist, spying on naked women:

> He, like an Adder, lurking in the weeds,
> His wandring thought in deepe desire does steepe,
> And his fraile eye with spoyle of beautie feedes.
>   (II.v.34)

With its image of steeping thought, the second line draws out the psychological dangers of the passivity induced by those trickling, murmuring streams, while in the next line, "spoyle of beauty" brings out the corruption of aggressive desires. The poisoning of the spirit suggested by the image of the adder (the proverbial "snake in the grass" brought brilliantly to moral life) is conveyed not by further imagery, but rather by the ambivalent "lurking" (is this creature waiting to strike or fearing to be discovered?) and by the unstable and displaced satisfactions suggested by the alliterated phrase "his fraile eye . . . feedes."

Despite what our discussion may have hitherto suggested, Spenser's allegorical representations are not confined to generalizing individual psychological experience. He is a master also of moral and spiritual debate—that is, of presenting plausible versions of human motives, values, and purposes that challenge ideas of heroic identity. The Red Cross Knight is almost seduced by Despair not only because of the famous lines evoking a desire for rest—"Sleepe after toyle, port after stormie seas, / Ease after warre, death after life does greatly please" (I.ix.40)—but also because old man Despair is an expert debater ("The knight much wondred at his suddeine wit"), who almost persuades Red Cross that if he judges himself by his own knightly standards, a just God must condemn him. (The theological idea of despair is not the world weariness that was all the Romantic tradition saw in this episode, but the believer's losing his or her hope of salvation by forgetting that the God of Justice is also the God of Mercy.) In Book II the expert debater (another aged cave dweller) is Mammon, who tries to make Guyon acknowledge his massive wealth as "the riches fit for an aduent'rous knight" (II.vii.10). But Guyon also has to deal with persuasions by the flirtatious Phaedria, who, in one of the wittiest passages in *The Faerie Queene*, sings a song of idleness that is based not on some obvious immorality, but on Christ's otherworldly recommendation to "consider the lilies of the field, how they grow; they toil not, neither do they spin" (Matthew 6:28).

Nor is moral confrontation in *The Faerie Queene* confined to episodes of explicit debate. In the climactic episode of Book III Britomart rescues Amoret—the virgin devoted to Venus, as her twin, Belphebe, is devoted to Diana—from the palace of the evil Busyrane, in order to restore her to her husband, Scudamour. The underlying idea is to free human sexuality to fulfill itself in faithful love—with Britomart's powers of penetrating the terrible wall of flame and staunchly enduring the sights of the palace being a heroic version of the fidelity the two lovers maintain to each other in their separateness and misery. In order to rescue Amoret, the Knight of Chastity must confront not arguments as such, but a series of tapestries and a masquelike procession that represent the power of Busyrane's lord Cupid and that challenge the knight (and the reader) to stand up against the ways in which they value sexual devotion.

The tapestries, in particular, contain some of Spenser's finest writing. They depict the pagan gods humbled by the power of love, but

made grand, even glamorous, by their erotic suffering. Yeats (who edited an anthology of Spenser's poetry and wrote a fine essay to introduce
it) certainly remembered the description of Leda and the Swan:

> O wondrous skill, and sweet wit of the man,
> That her in daffadillies sleeping made,
> From scorching heat her daintie limbes to shade:
> Whiles the proud Bird ruffing his fethers wyde,
> And brushing his faire brest, did her inuade.
>   (III.xi.32)

Here the god retains his power, but other scenes are compelling, even
when the god is humiliated. A powerful description of Neptune and his
sea chariot, riding the sparkling waves, his horses snorting the briny
waters, leads not to the god exerting his power over nature, but rather
suffering an all-too-human experience, whose own power is thereby
intimated:

> The God himselfe did pensiue seeme and sad,
> And hong adowne his head, as he did dreame:
> For priuy loue his brest empierced had.
>   (III.xi.41)

Even dehumanizing metamorphoses retain their fascination and thus
suggest the attractive powers of love. Neptune, in another scene, feeds
on fodder as a steer, but then "like a winged horse he tooke his flight"
and begets "faire *Pegasus*, that flitteth in the ayre" (III.xi.42). All these
representations are grounded in imaginings of humiliation and dominance. At the climax of the Busyrane cantos, the tyrant Cupid, riding on a lion, undoes his own blindfold in order to view, with sadistic
pleasure, the torment devised for Amoret—opening her breast and
displaying her heart, "quite through transfixed with a deadly dart"
(III.xii.21). This torture is nothing less than the traditional emblem
of being in love. This moment, one of those in which *The Faerie
Queene* most deeply engages the problematics of its culture, reveals a
fearsome possibility in being one of those whose hearts, as the poet
says at the beginning of Britomart's adventures, are "buxom" and
"prone" to "imperious Love." This is to say that the "bitter smarts" of
love are the signs and perils of being human, and they must be confronted and endured as Britomart does in undoing Busyrane's evil
charm.

The heroic mastery displayed, in various modalities, by Spenser's knights also underlies his culture's idea of the epic poet. The idea of imitating prestigious examples—as the Busyrane tapestries imitate the bravura performances in Ovid's *Metamorphoses*—involved the spirit of emulation, as if the writer were engaged in a rivalry or trial of strength with his models. We should follow the ancients, Ben Jonson said, "but as guides, not commanders." In a public exchange of letters (published in 1580), Spenser's mentor, Gabriel Harvey, spoke of the young poet's *Faerie Queene* project as an attempt to "emulate" and "overgo" Ariosto's *Orlando Furioso*.

When addressing the queen, the poet of *The Faerie Queene* represents himself as a humble suitor or dazzled admirer (as in the proems to Books I, III, and VI), but he is bolder when speaking of the poem itself. In the proem to Book II he rejects the accusation that Fairyland is an idle fancy by asking, rhetorically, who had heard of Peru or the Amazon or "fruitfullest Virginia" before the discoveries that resulted from the "hardy enterprize" of his age. In the proem to Book IV he defends his poem against the charge of wantonness by claiming, in words that align his own kind of endeavor with the adventures he depicts,

> that all the workes of those wise sages,
> And braue exploits which great Heroes wonne,
> In loue were either ended or begunne:
> Witnesse the father of Philosophie [Socrates], . . . etc.
> (IV.Proem.3)

These lines suggest one aspect of the poetic mastery implicit in *The Faerie Queene*, a claim to fundamental wisdom, both moral and "philosophical" (in the broad Renaissance sense, which included natural knowledge). This claim is explicit and intensive in a canto like that devoted to the Garden of Adonis (III.vi), where the poet represents the fundamental unions of form and matter in the natural universe and of body and soul in humans conceived as natural creatures. But the claim is also implicit in the encyclopedic range of *The Faerie Queene* and the ability of its poet to summon the wisdom of the ages and represent any aspect of human life.

In addition to exemplifying the idea that the poet, in Sidney's words, is "the monarch of all sciences," *The Faerie Queene* demonstrates the poet's technical mastery. This is most evident in the poem's distinctive style, interlaced with both "antique" words and neologisms, and in the nine-line stanza that Spenser devised for his epic—two pentameter quatrains, linked by a common rhyme, with a final hexameter ("alexandrine")—which has ever since been known to English poets as the Spenserian stanza.

Technical prowess had been conspicuous in Spenser's poetry from the beginning of his career. In the letters exchanged with Gabriel Harvey, he said, "a God's sake, may not we, as else the Greeks, have the kingdom of our own language?" This was said of a failed experiment (in which Sidney and other Elizabethans took part), to write English verse in the quantitative meters of Greek and Latin poetry, but the sense of having power over one's language underlies the immense expansion of the resources of English poetry—in verse forms, in metrical flexibility, in diction—that Spenser and his contemporaries achieved. Spenser's first major poem, *The Shepheardes Calender*, was among other things a technical showpiece. Its verse forms range from elaborate stanzas derived from continental models to the standard six-line (*a b a b c c*) stanza of earlier Tudor verse to balladlike meters suggestive of rustic naïveté and energy. There is a similar range in its diction (one aspect of which, the use of "auncient" English words, gets special attention in the prefatory epistle of E. K., the poem's unidentified editor), which is by turns adapted to the various purposes indicated by E. K. in categorizing the eclogues as "moral" (which includes some "satirical bitterness"), "plaintive," and "recreative."

Poetic fictions, Sidney says, are "but pictures what should be, and not stories what have been." To some extent, the preceding account has shared this idealizing bias by suggesting that the poetic heroes and the heroic poet of *The Faerie Queene* are adequate to engaging the forces they confront in themselves and in their world. This may indeed be the idea of the poem. But to many readers and critics, *The Faerie Queene* reveals a vulnerability to or complicity with the troubling realities it claims to master. The most notorious example, the Bower of Bliss canto (II.xii), is perhaps the most admired, imitated, influential, and controversial canto in the poem. From Milton's citing it (in *Areopagitica*) to show that Spenser was "a better teacher than Scotus or Aquinas," to Hazlitt's praise of its "voluptuous pathos and languid brilliancy of fancy," to Yeats's seeing a Spenser who is "a poet of the delighted senses," to C. S. Lewis's argument that the Bower's corrupt pleasures reveal "the exquisite health" of Spenser's own imagination, this canto has been a touchstone both of Spenser's poetry and its interpreters' poetics. But at the same time as it has been admired, it has also been viewed as deeply in conflict with itself. Its main action—Guyon's mission to destroy Acrasia's earthly paradise—is clearly intended to exemplify heroic temperance, both as self-control in the face of alluring pleasures and as a capacity for purposeful action. But the pleasures represented often seem more persuasive than the knight's resistance to them, and his concluding action, the destruction of the Bower (II.xii.83), is disturbingly violent, as if it were less a spiritual triumph than an act of vengeance, fueled by a deep ambivalence.

This is not the place to attempt to settle the question of the Bower of Bliss. The important point is that if Spenser's knights are heroes of epic—that is, if they are human in their strengths and achievements, not magically endowed in their natures or their accoutrements—then the forces they oppose are inherently part of their natures and situations, and a deep engagement with them, which is precisely what *The Faerie Queene* is to be praised for, can undo them or the poem that represents them.

Some such undoing seems to have been the fate of *The Faerie Queene* itself. There is a difference of views about the poem as a whole analogous to those about the Bower of Bliss. For some interpreters, the six completed books plus the "Mutability Cantos" are a unified whole—*The Faerie Queene* as it was meant to be—even though Spenser earlier projected a longer poem. For others, Spenser's project—fully to represent his world and the principles of action in it—comes apart in Books V and VI. The presumptive causes are Spenser's dilemmas (both conscious and unconscious) as an agent of English colonialism in Ireland and his resentment at failing to achieve favor at court.

The internal signs of the poem's disintegration are, first, the split between public and private, of which the climax is the withdrawal of Sir Calidore, the knight of Courtesy, to a pastoral world, where he and the poet question the value of courtly life and knightly endeavor; second, the poet's self-representations, both in his expressions of bitterness as an Elizabethan subject (implicit in his treatment of the Irish situation in Book V, explicit at the end of Book VI) and in his appearances in the role of poet. The first stanza of Book VI begins, "The waies, through which my weary steps I guyde, / In this delightfull land of Faery," and develops the contrast between the "sweet variety" of Fairyland and the poet's own "tedious trauell" (= both travel and travail) and "dulled spright." While this does not renounce his imaginative realm, it is far from representing his enterprise, as he did in the Proem to Book II, as like the voyages of discovery. In the pastoral cantos (ix and x) Sir Calidore climbs Mount Acidale, a semidivine rural precinct, and sees the three Graces dancing around a piping shepherd, who is identified as Colin Clout. "Who knows not Colin Clout?" the poet asks (x.16), aware that all his readers would recognize this as his own pastoral pseudonym in *The Shepheardes Calender* and in *Colin Clouts Come Home Againe*—a long poem written a year after the first installment of *The Faerie Queene*, in which criticism of the English court is balanced by an attempt to establish a domain of poetry and ideal love on the poet's home ground.

From Theocritus and Virgil, the founders of pastoral, poets have represented themselves as shepherds in order to acknowledge their limited powers in the real world and at the same time to claim a compensating authority in their powers of song. This doubleness is evident throughout *The Shepheardes Calender*, where the claim to be the "new poet," as E. K. calls him, capable of renewing English poetry, is held in check by a sense both of personal unfitness and of living in an unworthy age. Colin Clout's reappearance in *The Faerie Queene* has a similar double valency. On the one hand, his discourse on the Graces and his praise of his ideal beloved is one of the great set pieces of the poem, fulfilling for the last time its project of representing human virtue as a participation in the order of things. On the other hand, unlike the poem's other "allegorical cores," it is not a narration or the representation of a spiritual realm, but the speech of a single character—one who, moreover, is bound to the spot he inhabits as the condition of his vision and his song. There is thus an authorial self-division, at the end of Book VI, between Spenser's pastoral persona and the narrator who conducts Sir Calidore to the rather unsatisfactory conclusion of his adventures. If this indicates a certain loss of coherence in *The Faerie Queene*, it also helps us understand an important development in Spenser's writing in the last decade of his life.

After the publication of Books I–III of *The Faerie Queene* in 1590, Spenser wrote and published not only the last three books of the poem, but the most interesting and enduring of his so-called minor poems: *Colin Clouts Come Home Againe* (published in 1595), *Amoretti* (a sonnet sequence) *and Epithalamion* (a celebration of his own marriage; 1595), *Fowre Hymnes* (of Love, Beauty, Heavenly Love, and Heavenly Beauty; 1596), and *Prothalamion* (a "spousal verse" in honor of two aristocratic marriages; 1596). With the partial exception of *Colin Clout*, these poems are in genres in which Spenser had not written before. What is common to all of them is that they are large lyric forms—*Epithalamion* and *Prothalamion*, which adapt the long stanza of the Petrarchan canzone, are particularly remarkable formal accomplishments—and that, as opposed to the "minor poems" of the 1580s, collected and published as *Complaints* in 1591, they imitate and derive from the love poetry of the European Renaissance. Taken as a group, these poems represent an alternative body of major poetry to Spenser's epic. In a sense, however, they continue the project of *The Faerie Queene*. They contain much—mythological representations, issues of political and courtly service, love as both human experience and cosmic force—that could have found a place in *The Faerie Queene*. Formally, they are what we might call "public lyrics." The poet speaks in the first person, but on public occasions (the aristocratic double wedding celebrated in *Prothalamion*) or about public situations (the critique of the court in *Colin Clout*) or about love impersonally conceived as a cosmic reality (*Fowre Hymnes* and the end of *Colin Clout*). Even the epithalamion on the poet's own marriage, far from being merely private or personal, stages the event in nature, in country, town and church, and in the cosmos itself, and brings to bear on it a seemingly inexhaustible array of mythological personages.

These poems, in other words, can be seen as continuing the vein of Colin Clout's discourse on the Graces in Book VI. These late lyrics individually develop single aspects of *The Faerie Queene* and represent the poet's way of sustaining his commitment to the idea of heroic poetry in the face of the (apparent) untenability of his epic itself. If *The Faerie Queene* is threatened with disintegration in its later books, each of these public lyrics can be regarded as what the poem's final installment, the "Two Cantos of Mutabilitie," explicitly is—a coherent fragment of the original epic project.

The relation of Spenser's major lyrics to his epic indicates how Sidney's and Jonson's poems are related to their idea of poetry. In Sidney's case, this relationship is explicit in one of his two major bodies of poetry, the four series of "Eclogues" that separate the five books of *Arcadia*. In the prose romance itself, with its moral, political, and emotional entanglements, poetry is confined to brief lyric forms, predominantly expressing the isolation of desire and the dilemmas of love. The eclogues, by explicitly stepping back from the action, provide an opportunity for sustained poetic performance, on the part of both "native" Arcadians and courtly outsiders (including Philisides, Sidney himself in pastoral guise). The poems are impressive in their technical mastery, even though they are sometimes arid and relentlessly long. Sidney clearly set about to show that it was possible to "English" both classical quantitative verse and the various meters and verse forms of Italian poetry. Among the eclogues, there is one great poem—"Ye goatherd gods that love the grassy mountains," a sustained lament for an impossible ideal love, in the demanding form of a double sestina—and several highly interesting "public lyrics," including an epithalamion, a pastoral elegy, debates on the nature of love, a praise of solitariness, and a political discourse in the form of a beast fable.

As opposed to these poems, *Astrophel and Stella* has appeared to recent interpreters, who emphasize the social dynamics of Elizabethan courtiership and authorship, to be a coterie poem. There are numerous autobiographical elements in the sequence and a vein of playful wit that goes with the figure of the courtier, not the epic hero. Nevertheless, heroic ideas underlie the literary achievement of *Astrophel and Stella*— the rhetorical and representational power of individual sonnets, the ambition of the sequence as a whole, and its sense of consequential human issues. It is certainly significant that Astrophel plays out the conflict between the obligation to noble action in the world and the ambiguous imperatives of love that Spenser represents in Sir Calidore and that Sidney himself made the heroes' central conflict in *Arcadia*.

In *Astrophel and Stella* this conflict could be attributed to Sidney's actual situation in the world of Elizabethan and European politics. We know that there were times when he could have spoken the words that begin sonnet 21: "Your words, my friend, right healthful caustics, blame / My young mind marred." Nevertheless, the most remarkable sonnets in the sequence assimilate the courtier's and lover's conflict to the larger thematics that, for a Renaissance writer, derive from heroic poetry. Consider one of the most famous sonnets:

> Who will in fairest book of Nature know,
> How Virtue may best lodged in beauty be,
> Let him but learn of Love to read in thee,
> Stella, those fair lines, which true goodness show.
> There shall he find all vices' overthrow,
> Not by rude force, but sweetest sovereignty
> Of reason, from whose light those night-birds fly,

That inward sun in thine eyes shineth so.
And not content to be Perfection's heir
Thyself, dost strive all minds that way to move,
Who mark in thee what is in thee most fair.
So while thy beauty draws the heart to love,
 As fast thy Virtue bends that love to good:
 But ah, Desire still cries, give me some food.
(sonnet 71)

The Petrarchan sonnet (*Canzoniere* 248) from which Sidney takes his first line reveals the difference between the two poets' conception of human love. Petrarch's invitation, "Whoever wishes to see all that Nature and Heaven can do among us," is urgent, because all mortal things pass away: the sting in the tail of his sonnet is that he who does not come in time to see the union of virtue and beauty in one body (Laura's) "will have reason to weep forever." For Sidney, there is no hint of human transiency or of a "kingdom of the blessed" (Petrarch's phrase), which is the true home of virtuous mortals. All the urgency of his sonnet is in testing the claim that loving Stella is equivalent to loving Virtue itself. This is precisely what Sidney, in the *Defence*, claims about the effect of reading heroic poetry and admiring its heroes—hence the initial metaphor of reading in "the book of Nature" and the powerful double sense of the fourth line, which assimilates Stella's "fair lines" (i.e., the lineaments of her face) to the lines of verse, such as the one we are reading, in which the poet represents her goodness.

Sonnet 71 is notorious for the way its final line undoes the idealizing endeavor of the rest of the poem. But the point to observe is that the energy of the endeavor and hence the force of the revealed failure comes from the ideology of human heroism. What is at stake is the power of reason—"rude force" versus "sweetest sovereignty" (there are episodes in *The Faerie Queene* that play out these competing ideas)—and the force of the last line comes from the preceding vocabulary of striving and bending love to good.

It is perhaps natural for the modern reader to think that this sonnet sets up an opposition between a general human ideal, represented by the idealized mistress, and the individual first-person lyric speaker. This line of thought gets some support from one of the prominent emphases in *Astrophel and Stella*—the poet-lover's frequent scorn of literary conventions and his concomitant insistence that he utters what his own love prompts, rather than "poor Petrarch's long deceased woes" (sonnet 15). Similarly, in his brief remarks about love poetry in the *Apology*, Sidney says: "Many of such writings as come under the banner of unresistible love, if I were a mistress, would never persuade me they were in love; so coldly they apply fiery speeches, as men that had rather read lovers' writings . . . than that in truth they feel those passions, which easily (as I think) may be betrayed by that same forcibleness or *energia* (as the Greeks call it) of the writer" (pp. 138–139).

This may look like a call to express true feeling, but the central emphasis is on rhetoric, persuasive speech. Hence it is not surprising to find that the first-person speaker in *Astrophel and Stella* is generated and defined by—rather than merely set in opposition to—rhetorical and representational conventions. In sonnet 71 the "personal" outcry of the last line is attributed to the personification Desire. Moreover, the power of the line is due not simply to its surprise, but to the way it raises a genuinely allegorical question: Are we to understand this desire as one element in an internal conflict (like the "[de]bate between my will and wit" of sonnet 4) or—as the strong voicing suggests—has it taken possession of the poet's whole self?

Another famous final line also puts a supposed personal outcry in the mouth of an allegorical figure. The first sonnet of the sequence represents the poet "loving in truth and fain in verse my love to show," but frustrated by the inadequacy of the "inventions fine" he finds in "others' leaves." The sonnet concludes:

> Thus great with child to speak, and helpless in my throes,
> Biting my truant pen, beating my self for spite,
> Fool, said my Muse to me, look in thy heart and write.

Here the grammar of the sentence (the adjectives and participles that precede the main clause) make one expect that the subject will be "I." Displacing "I" to "my Muse" not only brilliantly suggests a moment of inspiration, but raises the kind of question we have just noticed in sonnet 71: What elements or forces constitute the lyric speaker and the poetic subject?

One could reasonably call Astrophel, the first-person speaker, the "hero" of *Astrophel and Stella*. The sequence concerns a developing situation, even if it does not present a full-fledged story, and some of the eleven "songs" that are interspersed among the 108 sonnets narrate specific episodes. But two other aspects of the sequence, already suggested by the poems we have discussed, bring out more distinct affiliations with heroic poetry. One is the claim to write with poetic authority. The conclusion of sonnet 45 shows that the "forcibleness or *energia*" of these poems turns persuasion of a mistress into an authoritative mode of self-presentation. The sonnet presents the irony, as Astrophel sees it, between Stella's failure to take pity on her woebegone lover and her shedding tears when she heard "a fable, which did show / Of lovers never known, a grievous case." The octave narrates the situation, and the sestet directly addresses Stella:

> Alas, if Fancy drawn by imaged things,
> Though false, yet with free scope more grace doth breed
> Than servant's wrack, where new doubts honor brings;
> Then think, my dear, that you in me do read
> Of lover's ruin some sad tragedy:
> I am not I, pity the tale of me.

There is more to this ending than the teasingly witty persuasion that the mistress can acknowledge her lover if she will pretend to ignore his actual social existence. The final line has a stronger force. With a definitively paradoxical formula, it is a self-declaration of alienation from self. In so presenting "the tale of me," Astrophel becomes not simply a courtly guise of Philip Sidney, but a representative lover. The very names Stella (Latin, star) and Astrophel (Greek, star-lover) suggest the potentialities of human nature that engage some of the most impressive sonnets (like 71, or 25, which tests a Platonic intuition that humans can view "those skies / Which inward sun to heroic mind displays"). In other poems Astrophel represents himself as not only similar to mythological demigods (Morpheus in sonnet 32 and, most remarkably, the moon, made masculine, in sonnet 31), but also as being, in his plight, the source of their meaning. A series of sonnets (38–40) on the lover's sleeplessness is distinguished from other poets' performances on this theme by the feeling of moral and psychological consequence that comes from representing humanly definitive conflicts played out in the lover's psyche. In the poems just alluded to, the speaker tends to be larger than (courtly) life, but even the courtly Astrophel is consistently defiant, setting himself against the world, as he claims to weigh all issues of human conduct and value in the balance of his love.

The lover's represented presence, combined with its poetic and rhetorical brilliance, gave *Astrophel and Stella* its literary authority. Its posthumous publication in 1591 set off a vogue of sonneteering to which in some sense we owe Shakespeare's sonnets and Donne's love poems, in both of which the love lyric takes on heroic dimensions—in the range of realities engaged and in the lyric speaker's claimed adequacy to them.

Ben Jonson's poems are English examples of classical genres in which Spenser and Sidney did not write—epigrams, epistles, odes, epodes, lyrics (in the strict sense of poems to be sung), and elegies (poems in couplets, usually worldly treatments of love). These poems are gathered in three collections. The 1616 folio *Works* contains a book of *Epigrams*, which the author called "the ripest of my studies," and fifteen poems called *The Forest*, because *silva* (woods), among Latin authors, denoted a poetic miscellany. The same metaphor appears in *Underwood* ("poems of later growth"), ninety poems published in the 1641 *Works*, which Jonson was preparing at the time of his death. The poems reflect the two sides of Jonson—the commitment to order and moral purity, on the one hand, and a fascination with appetite, physical turbulence, and performative virtuosity, on the other—that are evident in his plays and in the main structural device of his masques, where idealized representations of the monarch and his court are set against the coarse disorderliness of the antimasque. Jonson's songs established for English verse a vein of rhythmic fluency and chaste diction that is epitomized by the "Hymn to Diana" in *Cynthia's Revels*. At the other extreme, and equally Jonsonian, are the withering caricatures of his satiric epigrams and the vehement denunciations and inexhaustible comic catalogues of some of the longer poems.

It is not surprising that a turbulent spirit seeks out and affirms stability and order, but to write convincingly at both extremes is a major literary achievement. Equally impressive is the way Jonson's poetry, at its frequent best, avoids the moral rigidity and compulsive railing that one finds in a number of critic figures (clearly ironic self-portraits) in his plays.

One reason the poems are more flexibly alive than they can be made to seem is Jonson's sensitivity to what different genres call for and make possible. Epigrams and epistles give rise to satiric vehemence, songs call forth fluent loveliness. But the two elements can come together, as in the famous "Ode. To Himself," in which the brilliantly devised stanza—more elaborate than in songs, but still sustaining voice—accommodates satiric awareness of the state of poetry, the self-reproach that comes from it ("Where dost thou careless lie," it begins), and the moral and artistic quickening of the spirit that leads to the final resolve to "sing high and aloof, / Safe from the wolf's black jaw, and the dull ass's hoof." Convincing though they are in context, these lines may also suggest that the sense of life in Jonson's poetry depends on impulses to self-protection and rejection. But it is remarkable how responsive Jonson's verse is to its own conditions and those of the processes of judging one's self and the world.

If the relative fixity of an ode encourages celebrating sharp differences between "minds that are great and free" and the "chattering [mag]pies" of print and stage, the couplets of Jonson's epistles, elegies, and epigrams bring out the activity of discrimination. "To Penshurst" (the country house of Sidney's family) begins:

> Thou art not, Penshurst, built to envious show
>   Of touch or marble, nor canst boast a row
> Of polished pillars, or a roof of gold;
>   Thou hast no lantern whereof tales are told,
> Of stair, or courts; but stand'st an ancient pile,
>   And these grudged at, art reverenced the while.

As compared to the couplets of Dryden and Pope, the other great English neoclassical satirists, Jonson's are less closed and less given to neat symmetry. His sentences continue across line and couplet endings, to give the effect of a mind that notices details and imagines the motives of a situation. The sense of stable assertion in the last line quoted comes from a grammar that acknowledges the potential moral mobility of an observer and thus discriminates between two kinds of admiration and their objects.

Jonson's emphasis on moral discrimination and judgment follows from his refusal, despite impulses to remain "high and aloof," to consider himself exempt from the human condition. The satirist and his readers are to be esteemed precisely because, "living where the matter is bred," they have the strength to value poems about human frailties. (The quoted phrase is from epigram 94, "To Lucy, Countess of Bedford [Jonson's patron], with Mr. Donne's Satires.") Even a poem that is styled a farewell "To the World" (*Forest* 4), is firm about the conditions of its gesture:

> But what we are born for we must bear:
>   Our frail condition it is such
> That, what to all may happen here,
>   If 't chance to me, I must not grutch.

Else I my state should much mistake,
  To harbor a divided thought
From all my kind; that, for my sake,
  There should a miracle be wrought.

This humanism, however austere, underlies the continuity of Jonson's poetry with Spenser's and Sidney's. In writing his epigrams, a type of poem thought to be "bold, licentious, full of gall" (epigram 2), Jonson gave unprecedented prominence to poems praising noble (often in both senses) individuals. The characteristic vein is represented by his hailing William Roe as an embodiment of "that good Aeneas, passed through fire" (epigram 128) and his tribute to William Camden, the great scholar and Jonson's old teacher, as the one "to whom I owe / All that I am in arts, all that I know" (epigram 14). The *Epigrams* are thus not only a collection of satirical portraits (e.g., "On Court-Worm," "On Poet-Ape," "To Fine Lady Would-be") but equally importantly a gallery of contemporary heroes and heroines. The famous poem on Shakespeare, written for the First Folio edition of his plays (1623), is of a piece with these heroic epigrams. In all of them it is crucial to Jonson that the figures he praises are actual living persons. As he says in the great Pindaric ode, "To the Immortal Memory and Friendship of That Noble Pair, Sir Lucius Cary and Sir H. Morison":

You lived to be the great surnames
And titles by which all made claims
Unto the virtue. Nothing perfect done
But as a Cary, or a Morison.

Sharing the view that literary heroes are moral examples, Jonson inverts Sidney's argument that fictional figures are the more efficacious examples. Jonson's heroes are sustained not (like Spenser's) by the cosmos so much as by their human fellows—the circle of those who recognize and bear witness to nobility of spirit. Hence Jonson is a great poet both of the conditions of reading—the links of understanding between writer and audience—and of friendship, the like-mindedness that brings us together in shared trust and (as the food-and wine-laden epigram 101, "Inviting a Friend to Supper," shows) shared pleasures.

Jonson's idealizing realism, which led him to replace the fictional heroes of traditional epic with his living contemporaries, informs his self-presentation in poetry. Spenser's and Sidney's personae, Colin

Clout and Astrophel, are figures cast in specific literary roles; they thus gain representative force by a certain distancing from the writer's own person. Jonson, by contrast, claims literary and human authority in his own name. Hence of the two allied forms of discursive poetry practiced by his master Horace, he eschews satire—which, he must have felt, too much depends on casting the first-person speaker in a rigid literary role—and turns repeatedly to the epistle, of which the central idea is a relation, potentially wide-ranging and untrammeled, between speaker and addressee. The beginning of the epistle to his friend John Selden, the great antiquary, brings out the assumptions of the genre:

> I know to whom I write. Here, I am sure,
> Though I am short [i.e., brief], I cannot be obscure.

Just as the names of those he admired were of the essence of the stature attributed to them—since names both vouch for human actuality and serve to inscribe their bearers in discourse and print—so the poet's own name registers some of his deepest effects. His epitaph "On My First Son" (epigram 45) calls the dead child "Ben Jonson his best piece of poetry" (because "poet" means "maker"). At the close of the Cary and Morison ode, the poet addresses the surviving friend and says:

> think, nay know, thy Morison's not dead.
> He leaped the present age,
> Possessed with holy rage
> To see that bright eternal day,
> Of which we priests and poets say
> Such truths as we expect for happy men;
> And there he lives with memory, and Ben
>
> Jonson, who sung this of him, ere he went
> Himself to rest, . . . etc.

The sobriety and exactitude of statement here, the fact that memory is not in the least mythologized but exists solely in the minds of those who knew and valued Morison and who read and value this poem, shows why Jonson has been praised as a poet of the plain style. And yet the poem still "sings high and aloof." The division of the poet's name over the stanza break expresses the separation the poem addresses: the loss of a friend is as a loss of self. But the vocal energy that connects first and last names and thus bridges the stanzas suggests the power of poetry to restore the sense of human solidarity to which feelings of loss bear witness and which, if we are true to ourselves, they cannot erase. In this bold gesture—one of the most astonishing moments in English poetry—Jonson both affirms the poet's role as Sidney and Spenser had conceived it and enacts the terms on which he made it new.

Paul Alpers

Further Reading

Alpers, Paul. *The Poetry of "The Faerie Queene"*. Princeton: Princeton University Press, 1967.

Berger, Harry, Jr. *Revisionary Play: Studies in the Spenserian Dynamics*. Berkeley: University of California Press, 1988.

Fletcher, Angus. *The Prophetic Moment: An Essay on Spenser*. Chicago: University of Chicago Press, 1971.

Goldberg, Jonathan. *Endlesse Worke: Spenser and the Structures of Discourse*. Baltimore: Johns Hopkins University Press, 1981.

Hamilton, A. C., ed. *The Spenser Encyclopedia*. Toronto: University of Toronto Press, 1990.

Kalstone, David. *Sidney's Poetry: Contexts and Interpretations*. Cambridge: Harvard University Press, 1965.

McCoy, Richard. *Sir Philip Sidney: Rebellion in Arcadia*. New Brunswick, N.J.: Rutgers University Press, 1979.

Nelson, William. *The Poetry of Edmund Spenser*. New York: Columbia University Press, 1963.

Peterson, Richard S. *Imitation and Praise in the Poems of Ben Jonson*. New Haven: Yale University Press, 1981.

Trimpi, Wesley. *Ben Jonson's Poems: A Study of the Plain Style*. Stanford, Calif.: Stanford University Press, 1962.

Lyric Poetry from Donne to Philips

THE story of the English lyric in the seventeenth century is the story of the coming of age of a literary form. Our modern concept of the lyric, of the (relatively) short, primarily non-narrative poem, was invented in seventeenth-century England. We take the lyric to be the "normal" or normative form that poetry takes—it essentially defines our notion of poetry—but this is a relatively recent phenomenon. For the classical and medieval worlds, poetry meant something longer and primarily narrative— epic, brief epic, romance, or tale. If there was a hierarchy of genres, epic was at the top of it; lyric poetry was a "minor" form. In the Renaissance this hierarchy still obtained. Petrarch certainly thought his *Africa*, a Virgilian epic in Latin on Scipio Africanus, a more "important" work than his famous sonnets. Spenser certainly thought *The Faerie Queene* more definitive of his status as a "major" poet than the *Four Hymnes* or the *Amoretti*. There were "major" lyrics, like odes or canzones, but these could still not make a poet "major." And lyrics in the Renaissance were not primarily what we call lyric poems—they were songs (meant to be sung with accompaniment) or they were parts of sequences. Pastorals were often parts of sequences, and most of all, the sonnet, the most distinctive Renaissance lyric form, was typically composed in sequences or cycles.

The stand-alone lyric not meant to be sung and not part of a sequence is an invention of the seventeenth century—or perhaps, as with so many things, a reinvention of a Roman mode. The key new phenomenon is the title. This is truly new. Classical lyrics did not have titles; Renaissance sonnets do not have titles. Tottel's famous miscellany—*Songes and Sonnettes* (1557)—presented poems with titles, but these were editorial rather than authorial, and they were descriptions rather than titles: "The Lover Bewaileth the Absence of his Beloved," and so on. This feature of lyric poetry that we take for granted—that poems have titles (or are marked as "untitled" when they don't)—seems to have been invented in England in the first part of the seventeenth century. George Herbert's *The Temple* (1633) is the first modern collection of lyrics. Each poem has a title, not merely a description or designation, given to it by the author, often a title so witty or oblique that it could have been given to the poem only by the author.

And what do titles signify? First of all, they signify the full and final commitment of the lyric to print culture. Titles are part of the world of print. Second, they signify the sense of the lyric as a full and complete work in itself. Coincident with this—perhaps identical with it—they signify the lyric as a genre to which a major poet could be fully and exclusively committed. Again, Herbert is the clearest case, but his achievement would not have been possible without the powerful figures of John Donne and Ben Jonson behind him. These three figures—Donne, Jonson, and Herbert—dominate the field of the English lyric from the beginning of the seventeenth century to the restoration of the monarchy in 1660 after the triumphs and failures of the English revolution. These three poets were not only masters in themselves but were instantly recognized as such and proved to be fruitful and highly usable models for writers of the lyric in English for the next fifty years. The literary culture of England was ready for the emergence of the lyric in the different modes that these three poets represent.

Donne and the New Love Lyric

Perhaps the first thing to say about John Donne is that he was not a professional poet. He was, however, a professional intellectual. Writing poetry, for him, was not merely (as it might have been for Sir Philip Sidney) a gentlemanly accomplishment and recreation. It was a way for Donne to show his wit, his skill, his learning, his rhetorical command. It was a way of showing himself to be one of the brightest of the bright young lawyers at Lincoln's Inn seeking positions in the employ of one of the great councillors or noblemen. Donne did not publish his poems—that would have been vulgar and misleading (suggesting that he wanted to be an "author")—but his poems circulated very widely in manuscript.

Everyone who was anyone with an interest in literature in London in the 1590s knew that Donne was an accomplished writer of unusual and striking poems, a formidable "wit." Donne's poems were self-display and self-advertisement, but they were also more than that, and any account that does not attempt to suggest this "more" is as misleading as an account that overly idealizes the poems and treats Donne as an "author." Donne was a serious intellectual as well as a professional one. The pressure of intellection—of a complex, skeptical, probing, intelligence—is one of the most distinctive features of Donne's verse. This pressure penetrates the surface and is felt in the structure of even his lightest and slightest pieces.

Donne's earliest poetic endeavors included small "books" of satires and elegies as well as individual lyrics for friends to copy out. The choice of these forms, elegy and satire, is highly significant. It used to be said that Donne rejected models, but the truth is that he caused a revolution in poetry not by rejecting models but by changing them. He rejected Renaissance models, especially Petrarch, and imitated the Ovid of the elegies—urbane, detached, humorous, "low"—rather than the Ovid of the *Metamorphoses*—narrative, mythological, and "high."

From the beginning of his poetic career, Donne was writing a kind of antipoetry. When he began writing poetry in the 1590s, the sonnet boom (following the publication of *Astrophil and Stella*) was at its peak. Donne wrote satires. He may not be the first writer of Horatian verse satire in English (there is some dispute about this), but he is certainly among the first. His persona in the satires is probably much like his historical person—an intellectual struggling to maintain detachment from a compromised and engulfing political and social world. In the first of the satires, Donne addresses a "fondling motley humorist"—a foolish, unstable type—whom Donne follows, "against my conscience" into the street. The poem manifests Donne's characteristic techniques—bold, colloquial address, metrical roughness, striking phrases. Most of all, it manifests the complex drama of the Donnean lyric, where the speaker's attitudes as well as those of his interlocutor are being interrogated.

The greatest of the five satires is the third. This poem confronts the central concern of sixteenth-century Europe, the division of the Church into competing churches; it shows the seriousness of the witty young Donne, the man who was born into an intensely Roman

Catholic family but found himself impelled—not just pragmatically—to review his options. He knew about religious principles and religious resistance, but he had decided by the time of this poem (ca. 1595) that for him the key principle was the integrity of the individual conscience. It was in the name of this that he was willing to resist earthly authority, whether secular or "sacred." The major thrust of the poem is to defend religious/intellectual seeking—"To stand inquiring right, is not to stray," Donne insists. The only kind of obedience that one can give to an earthly power—"A Philip, or a Gregory, / A Harry, or a Martin"—is limited obedience: "That thou mayest rightly obey power, her bounds know." The writer of this poem, the young John Donne, is not about to accept anything on authority.

It would be surprising to find Donne taking a less probing and skeptical view of the erotic life than he does of power, or religion. He is equally unconventional in this realm, though he does not seek simply to shock the respectable and the "high-minded." The elegies are as formally and culturally daring as the satires—they are another form, unusual in English, adopted from Roman poetry—and they manifest an even wider range of tones than do the satires. A "mere" rhetorical exercise like "The Comparison" takes on real poetic power in its remarkably precise and detailed evocations of harsh versus tender lovemaking.

"The Bracelet" is a jeu d'esprit, a mock lament over "the losse of his Mistresses Chaine, for which he made satisfaction," but it is also something like a sustained defense of "worldliness." It is a meditation on gold—not only as a symbolic or physical or metaphysical substance, but as money. At its most interesting, the poem accepts a world in which gold "provides / All things," including friends and his mistress's love: "Thou wilt love me lesse when they are gone." Donne is trying to fully inhabit—with clear eyes but little bitterness—a nontranscendental world, a world fully defined by social realities.

Donne does this again in "Loves Progresse," the most "outrageous" of the elegies (not licensed for publication until 1669), in which he argues for a strongly genital focus in male heterosexual love. Gold returns. Donne distinguishes between abstractly "valuing" gold—"from rust, from soil, from fire ever free"—and loving it because "'tis made / By our new nature (Use) the soul of trade." Love exists in the realm of the social, the nontranscendental—"Although we see Celestial Bodies move / Above the earth, the earth we till and love." In his other great elegy about sex, "Going to Bed," Donne presents the physical as equivalent to, or a form of, the transcendental.

Ultimately, however, Donne's importance as a poet rests on the volume of lyric poems known (from the 1635, second edition) as the "Songs and Sonets." This is an odd title for the volume, since it suggests familiarity. The printer is harking back to Tottel's volume at the start of the Elizabethan period, but the Donne collection contains no sonnets and only two songs (one of them very peculiar). As one would expect from the satires and elegies, many of the "Songs and Sonets" are cynical about love and the erotic life, but, as one would also expect, this cynicism is often subjected to scrutiny.

"Communitie" is a consciously "libertine" poem. It argues—Donne as a young lawyer and rhetorician loves to argue—that all males may, indeed must, treat all women in the same way—as undifferentiated objects to be used. The key argument is that this is logically required; since women are "things indifferent," men must have a detached attitude toward them (this is very much a world of gendered "us" and "them")—"we may neither love, nor hate." The final stanza, however, unbalances the poem. Instead of praise of intelligent discrimination, we are told that "he that devours" and "he that leaves all" both proceed as properly as "he that but tastes." Abstinence and excess are suddenly possibilities. Libertine equilibrium seems hard to maintain. The final lines give up all pretense of equilibrium and become a defense of "devouring." The poem is fully aware of its instabilities, which become its subject. This happens repeatedly in the "libertine" and cynical "Songs and Sonets."

"The Indifferent" again dramatizes the difficulty of detachment as the speaker, who begins by parading his "indifference" progressively grows more vehement in his rejection of being emotionally "bound." His great fear is of making himself vulnerable. In "Womans constancy" the speaker avoids vulnerability through a preemptive strike against a betrayal he has no reason to expect. It is not clear which is greatest—the speaker's contempt for (and fear of) rhetoric, women, or himself. "Loves diet" shows the way in which misogyny functions as a defense. The speaker attains his much sought after indifference through devaluing everything he is tempted to cherish in the woman with whom he is involved.

These poems reveal cynicism as well as manifesting it; they show the pressures that shape it and that it fails to contain. The extraordinary thing, however, is not that Donne wrote these poems; one might have predicted their attitudes, maybe even their brilliance, from the Satires and Elegies. What is extraordinary is that Donne wrote a large handful of poems that magnificently represent what we normally mean by love—mutual, assured, exclusive, passionate, consummated, and committed. Donne was one of the creators of this conception. When he gave up the ideal of indifference and invulnerability, he came upon this other ideal. That this possibility could exist—and that he could experience it—struck him as little short of miraculous. His greatest love poems are filled with wonder and delight at the way in which shared and consummated love creates the experience of transcendence within the material world. "The good-morrow" seems to present this conception "dawning" on the speaker. Through contemplating the meaning of consummation, of mutuality, and of sincerity, a strange possibility occurs to Donne (or his "speaker"). He recalls a premise of Aristotelian physics—"Whatever dyes, was not mixt equally." Equality raises the possibility of permanence.

In another morning poem, "The Sunne Rising," Donne more militantly asserts the exemption of this one thing—mutually shared love—from the most basic rule that governs the universe, the rule of change: "Love, all alike, no season knows, nor clyme, / Nor howres, dayes, moneths, which are the rags of time." It is no accident that many years later in his life, after he had taken orders in the Church of England, Donne said of the mercy of God: "The names of first or last derogate from it, for first and last are but ragges of time."

Donne knew exactly what he was doing in these poems. Celebration, for him, did not require any suspension of his critical faculties or of the kinds of awareness embodied in the "cynical" poems. "The good-morrow" knows that the two lovers could be watching each other intently out of fear of betrayal. "The Sunne Rising" knows that its hyperboles are so outrageous as to call attention to their (literal) falsity. But capturing an emotional, not a literal, truth was the point. "A Lecture upon the Shadow" seems to bring cynicism right into the heart of the love experience. This poem uses noon rather than dawn as its moment. Noon becomes a metaphor of total candor—"a brave clearenesse" between the lovers. Any hint of falsity will create a shadow—or rather, it will bring on total darkness since, in the realm of love, "his first minute, after noone, is night." This sounds horribly pessimistic, but the point, as in "The good-morrow," is that love, unlike the sun and the earth, can continue "growing, or full constant."

"The Anniversarie" is even more startling in its double awareness. Love "keepes his first, last, everlasting day" in the face of full knowledge of death. This poem sees the lovers' finite lives on earth as more special than their anticipated lives in heaven (where *everyone* will be "blest"), and it acknowledges and then discounts, as ignoble, the thought of "treason in love." Fully enjoyed finitude seems better than eternity. "Loves growth" develops this perspective further and celebrates, non-cynically, the impurity and earthliness of human love.

"A valediction forbidding mourning" explores the outer limits of the nontranscendental absolute. Donne explains that among the prerogatives of lovers who are "Inter-assured of the mind" are the capacities to survive the pain of absence and to remain (somehow) connected through it. The famous image of the "stiff twin compasses" occurs in this context. The imagery in these poems—drawn from alchemy, astronomy, physics, and so on—led many critics, from the later seventeenth to the twentieth century, to speak of Donne as a "metaphysical" poet. This is an appropriate term only if it designates a favored frame of reference, not if it indicates a subject matter or intellectual ambition. The "metaphysics" in these poems explicates the emotion. Metaphysics and science were things that Donne was interested in, but he was mainly interested in them as ways of thinking about things that he was more interested in.

It is hard not to think that many of the celebratory love poems were written after Donne's marriage. This perhaps adds to their poignance. In 1601 Donne secretly married the niece of his employer, Sir Thomas Egerton, the Lord Keeper of the Great Seal. Probably to Donne's surprise, this marriage brought an abrupt end to his career as a rising courtier or civil servant. In the enforced retirement that followed, Donne had time to read and study. He returned to the questions that, along with sex and politics, dominated his life in the early 1590s, the questions on which the third satire meditated so boldly.

Turning his poetic focus (at least at times) from his erotic to his religious life, Donne proceeded, probably in the years 1607–1610, to do in this context what he never did in the erotic one, namely, to write sonnets. The sonnet, unlike the stanzaic lyric, did seem—in the terms of "The Triple Fool"—to "fetter" Donne. Or perhaps the choice of a form in which he was not fully comfortable unconsciously reflected a deeper discomfort. Donne had become a Protestant by this time, yet he had trouble fully inhabiting the Protestant devotional stance, the stance that

devalued agency and threw itself entirely on grace. This stance presented itself to Donne as a form of willed (and willful) submission to violence: "Burne me o Lord, with a fiery zeale"; "like Adamant draw mine
iron heart."

The most brilliant expression of this vision occurs in the sonnet that
begins, "Batter my heart," and ends with an eroticized version of this
prayer: "I / Except you'enthrall mee, never shall be free, / Nor ever
chaste, except you ravish mee." Yet even this poem does not maintain
the stance of the opening and closing prayers. Between these images
of regeneration through violence, Donne expresses a different vision,
that of the self or soul struggling "to'admit" God. Both visions are
coherent; to put them together is not. Yet this occurs repeatedly in the
Holy Sonnets. Donne often seems uncertain of his tone or stance. He
is best when he can make these instabilities his subject, as in "If poyso-
nous mineralls," in "O might those sighes and teares," and in the wonderfully baffled self-analysis of "Oh, to vex me, contraryes meete in
one."

When, a decade later, Donne turned from holy sonnets to stanzaic
religious lyrics, he was able to recapture some of the spontaneity and
range of his great love poems in three "hymns." Yet even these poems
have difficulty maintaining their affirmative stance. "A Hymne to God
the Father"—possibly Donne's last poem—is like "Oh, to vex me" in its
candid self-bafflement. Donne's lifelong self-scrutiny and self-fascina-
tion culminates in a brilliant, self-mocking refrain about the difficulty
of self-abandonment: "When thou hast done, thou hast not done, / For
I have more."

Ben Jonson and the New Social Lyric

Donne and Jonson were exact contemporaries. They were born within
a year of each other (around 1572) and both died in the 1630s. Many
literary histories contrast them, and there are, as we shall see, significant differences in their poetic modes. There are also significant similarities. It is important to start with the similarities—not only to set the
record straight but to understand the way in which the influences of
Donne and Jonson complemented each other in the later history of the
seventeenth-century lyric. To give full weight to Donne as satirist and
elegist is to understand his connections to Jonson. Neither of them
wanted to be either Shakespeare or Samuel Daniel in the 1590s. They

wanted to be more classical, more colloquial (these often go together), more "tough-minded," more worldly.

Jonson wrote three poems either to or about Donne. In the two addressing him Jonson praises Donne's poems as especially challenging—"longer a-knowing than most wits do live"—and praises Donne as an especially discriminating judge of poetry. In the third poem Jonson praises his addressee for desiring to see Donne's satires; her taste in literature attests to her human value: "Rare poems ask rare friends." Jonson was, not surprisingly, especially fond of Donne's earliest poetry, and he claimed to know "The Bracelet" by heart. Donne, for his part, contributed to the first edition of *Volpone* a Latin poem praising Jonson as equal, through both labor and genius, to the ancients. It is worth pondering, for our literary history, that one poem we have, a rather vigorous elegy, "The Expostulation," was ascribed to both Donne and Jonson in the seventeenth century. It may be by neither, but the significant point is the common attribution.

Unlike Donne, Jonson was a professional writer. He operated within both the patronage and the market systems of Elizabethan and Jacobean England. As a playwright, he wrote for the public theaters; as a masque writer, he wrote for the court; as a lyric poet, he wrote both for specific individuals and for the general reading public. In 1616 Jonson took the extraordinary step of arranging and overseeing the publication of *The Works of Benjamin Jonson*. This seems normal enough to us, but it was a surprising cultural event at the time. A contemporary poet was claiming that his writings in the vernacular were "works," including his plays ("What others call a play, you call a worke," as one contemporary wit put it). "Works" were the product of labor and art, were meant to last, and most of all, were what classical authors produced.

Jonson, in other words, was claiming that his writings were classics. They deserved the dignity (not stigma) of print and the careful editing that the classics received. Jonson's productions were Literature and he was an Author—categories that he was helping to invent. We can see some of the force of this if we compare Jonson's relation to his poems with Donne's (who published only his poems directly funded by a patron), and Jonson's relation to his plays with that of Shakespeare, who made no effort to publish his plays and clearly saw them as scripts for his production company. But Jonson wrote Literature. *The Works* is a magnificent folio.

This folio includes two volumes of poems, each volume bearing a classical title—*Epigrammes* and *The Forrest* (Latin: *Silva*). Jonson did not consider his epigrams ephemeral (as Donne almost certainly did his own); for Jonson, his epigrams were "the ripest of my studies." One of the things that Jonson was constantly doing—in the prologues to his plays and in many of his poems—was instructing his audience on how to appreciate Ben Jonson's "works" properly. "Rare poems ask rare friends" was actually a very deep principle for Jonson. The first of the epigrams is addressed "to the reader," and it is a typically brilliant, understated, and hectoring Jonsonian performance: "Pray thee, take care, that tak'st my booke in hand, / To reade it well; that is, to understand." Every word, every syllable, every accent, every punctuation mark here is fully meant.

The "care" that the reader is exhorted to "take" in taking up this book—the two kinds of "taking" are thereby equated—is to answer in kind the care that the author of this poem and "my booke" has already taken. Jonson imagines his reader in the world, "booke in hand." A single couplet must ring at the end, and Jonson has built this tiny poem to culminate in its final word. He professed to hate rhyme (a nonclassical feature) but made brilliant use of it—in "A Fit of Rime against Rime," in many of the poems, and here. He explains what he means by taking care and reading well—"that is, to understand." This final word is the only clear polysyllable in the poem; it takes up almost half of the second of the poem's two lines. The reader is not being enticed but challenged; he or she is being offered not delight, or pleasure, or escape but intellectual work. It is no accident that the printer of Donne's poems similarly addressed that volume not to the readers but "to the Understanders."

But what is it that we are supposed to "understand"? Jonson's poetry is not arcane in its conceits like Donne's "sullen Writ / Which just as much courts thee, as thou dost it." What we are to understand is precisely Jonson's art. We are to see that it takes art to write such straightforward-seeming poems, and we are to appreciate the "weight," not the difficulty, of his words. "Weight" was very important to Jonson. He was a very fat man, and he portrayed himself in his poetry as such. He did this for a number of reasons: to locate himself and his poems in an actual, historical world; to take advantage of the centrality of food in social life; to avoid involvement with the erotic (he has a poem about how his "mountain belly" interferes with a lady's reception of his excellent language); and perhaps most of all, to present himself as a figure with moral weight, that is, *gravitas*, a figure who understands "weighty" matters.

Jonson praises his teacher, the great historian William Camden, by exclaiming, "What sight in searching the most ancient springs! / What weight, and what authoritie in thy speech." Weight and authority in speech are what Jonson most covets. Praise is much more important in Jonson's epigrams (and his poems in general) than is blame. This may seem odd in an author of satirical plays, but Jonson seems to have used his poems primarily to articulate the positive ideals that are only implicit in the folly or vice-ridden world of the plays. He censures those who think his "way in *Epigrammes*" is new (not ancient), and also those who expect his epigrams to be merely satiric ("bold, licentious, full of gall"). Although he creates some fools in the *Epigrammes* (see "On Gut" and "On Court-worme"), the most ambitious of the epigrams—Jonson would have liked the paradox that small poems can be ambitious—are not satirical.

Jonson was as self-obsessed as Donne was, but where Donne's self-obsession was psychological and emotional, Jonson's was professional and ethical. Judging rightly, responding appropriately, speaking aptly— these were Jonson's great aims and obsessions. In "Inviting a Friend to Supper," a classically based epigram, Jonson's stress is on imagining an occasion that will perfectly balance food, wine, and learned exchange. In mourning the death of his first son, Jonson is haunted by a sense of having made, as in his classical source, an inappropriate emotional investment. The poem is oddly moving in its sense of guilt and inability to attain the detachment that it seeks—"O, could I loose all father now." He cedes the dead boy highest honor by calling him (his namesake) "Ben. Jonson his best piece of poetrie." Pride in authorship is both used and rejected here.

The fact that Jonson repeatedly put his name into his poems is part of the relentlessly social focus of his world. The speaker of "The goodmorrow" has no name; the speaker of Jonson's poem to his son is identified with the historical author. The longer poems that compose most of *The Forrest* continue the ethical and social themes of the *Epigrammes* in other forms—the verse epistle ("which," Jonson says, "as yet / Had not their forme touch'd by an English wit"), the ode, the epode, and the "country house poem." Jonson may not have invented this latter form in English (it existed in classical Latin)—the honor of origination may go to a woman poet, Aemilia Lanier—but his two poems of this kind established the mode in English. These poems are among his greatest "works." The first and better known of them, "To Penshurst," is a remarkable evocation of a self-sufficient manor in which nature, culture, and economic activity are all in benign and happy harmony. Partridges willingly sacrifice themselves; eels "leap on land"; the tenant farmers on the estate bring produce that is not in fact needed and they are welcomed as guests. Social differences disappear (or fail to signify) in the face of abundance. Jonson's role is to "remind" the owners of these places of the value of what they have. Since the object of the hyperboles here is not an individual but an imagined form of life, the result is not flattery but the creation of a social myth.

Donne was a skeptic and a revolutionary in the love tradition; Jonson barely participated in it. Yet Jonson, too, made some contributions to love poetry in English. First, he added a new range of sentiment—not erotic love but *philia*, friendship and rational affection. Jonson said that he loved Shakespeare "this side idolatry," and the poem that he wrote for the 1623 Folio that attempted to make Shakespeare's plays Literature (though not Works) bears out Jonson's claim. It is a work of measured love and of literary criticism in verse. It is the tribute of a classicist to a poet who had "small Latine and lesse Greeke," and it finds a way of praising Shakespeare that does not "give Nature all." Jonson's second contribution to English love poetry is in his songs. These mostly occur in the plays and masques, but they define a mode of elegant, classicizing, consciously artful eroticism.

Finally, Jonson wrote some remarkable poems to potential love objects. It is a tribute to the power of Jonson's influence that the best of these (beginning "Faire Friend, 'tis true") is ascribed in one manuscript not to Jonson but to one of his followers. The stance of the poem verges on impertinence ("I neither love, not yet am free"); its tone is that of a benevolent lecturer. The central stanza is pure Jonson—whether he wrote it or not. The speaker's feeling for the addressee "is like Love to Truth reduc'd, / All the false values gone, / Which were created, and induced / By fond imagination." Love without mythology is the idea. The speaker offers a nonhyperbolic response—"you may collect, / Th' intrinsique value of your face, / Safely from my respect." "Respect" is the name that this poem ultimately gives to its stance, but the possibility of unhyperbolic love will be of as much interest to poets later in the century as Donne's extraordinary hyperboles.

George Herbert and the New Divine Lyric

Herbert situated his poetic project at the center of Reformation theology, at the doctrine that Donne found so difficult: salvation by faith. Faith, in this view, is a gift, not an achievement. To trust in God—to believe in one's salvation by God—can only be bestowed by God. The human will can only go wrong because it is fundamentally self-asserting; ultimately, it wants to trust not God but itself. This would seem to be a very bleak and negative doctrine—no role for will at all; no agency; no merit—but to see it as bleak is entirely to misunderstand its fundamental psychological dynamic.

The essential idea was that the conception of contributing to one's salvation was both blasphemous—how could one do something worthy of such a reward?—and terrifying—how did one know one had done enough, had done whatever was required properly—hard enough, fully enough, long enough, consistently enough, wholeheartedly enough? The aim of the doctrine was freedom from anxiety and self-concern. Everything that could have been done has already been done by another (Christ); grace consists of God counting ("imputing") Christ's sacrificial act as yours. And to guarantee the stability of the system—its freedom from human tampering, responsibility, and worry—it must be impossible to lose God's grace once one has it. Otherwise, we are back to anxiety.

The doctrine of predestination existed to explain salvation and to make clear its independence from human behavior. It was not needed to explain damnation, since sin (human nature) did that well enough. One can only make sense of the success of the Reformation by seeing its central assertion as, in the words of the Church of England Articles of Religion, "a most wholesome Doctrine, and very full of comfort" (Article XI, "Of the Justification of Man"). "Comfort" is the key word. Article XVII presents predestination as "full of sweet, pleasant, and unspeakable comfort."

Herbert constantly dramatized the psychological structure and impact of this doctrine. He devised and mastered a new kind of lyric, the comic religious poem. In "The Holdfast" Herbert uses every structural pause in the "Shakespearean" sonnet form to trace out the shape of a human encounter with the absoluteness and strangeness of "faith alone." The poem is a comic narrative of what was, at the "moment" narrated, a puzzling experience. The speaker pokes fun at himself, seeing his resolution to be perfect in the religious life as a form of aggression—"I threatned to observe the strict decree / Of my deare God with all my power and might." Through dialogue with an unnamed "one," the speaker is then brought to a moment of puzzlement. He can do nothing, not even bravely concede that he can do nothing—"to have nought is ours, not to confesse / That we have nought." The poem ends, however, not on the speaker's puzzlement, but on his illumination. He realizes through the words of "a friend" (previously "one") that "all things are more ours" by being held fast by someone else, "who cannot fail or fall."

Herbert loves to make fun of "common sense." In "Redemption," another extraordinary sonnet, a speaker seeking "redemption" from a lease seeks his Lord in all the obvious places—"in heaven at his manour" and on earth "in great resorts"—but is distracted by "a ragged noise / Of theeves and murderers." There he sees his Lord, who "straight, *Your suit is granted*, said, and died." The mysteriousness of grace is the point, its distance from normal assumptions (a great Lord will be in great places, and so on). In "Artillerie" Herbert creates another commonsensical speaker, who when "a star shot in [his] lap" reacted normally—"I rose, and shook my clothes." He is rebuked for this, for rejecting pain that might have helped him. He attempts to set up a treaty with God—"I have also starres and shooters too. . . . Then we are shooters both." Suddenly, however, he comes to a realization borrowed from "Loves Exchange," one of Donne's love poems: "There is no articling with thee."

Perhaps the deepest and most subtle of the comic poems in *The Temple* is the third poem entitled "Love," the final lyric of the volume through all Herbert's revisions. This poem is comedy of manners, and the human speaker in it is not mocked. His problem is excessive humility, but Herbert is shrewd enough to see that the assertion of humility can itself be a form of aggression. The framework is the host-guest one so dear to Jonson. As the poem proceeds, increasingly in dialogue, the guest is finally forced to accept his role—"You must sit down," says the Host, "and taste my meat." The human speaker does "sit and eat," allowing us to see what irresistible grace is for a poet who sees God as a person rather than, as in Donne's Holy Sonnets, a force.

The Reformation critique of "works" and of egotism made the writing of poetry problematic. Herbert dealt with this problem by dramatizing it. He wrote as many poems about poetry as Jonson did, but where Jonson was always sure of the value of poetry, Herbert was always suspicious of it. In the second of the two poems entitled "Jordan"—the stream which, for Herbert, replaces the Helicon—Herbert dramatizes (as he does in "Sinnes Round") the process of creation: "My thoughts began to burnish, sprout, and swell, / Curling with metaphors a plain intention." As the poem became more elaborate, the creator found himself more invested in it, it became more his—"So did I weave my self into the sense." The poet found himself again rebuked by "a friend" for all this unnecessary and misguided "expense." Art is ultimately not the point. The God that Herbert worshipped values sincerity over art, even inarticulate sincerity—"All Solomons sea of brasse and world of stone / Is not so deare to thee as one good grone." So why did Herbert polish and improve his poems? Clearly he saw them as rebuking their own pride and dramatizing that rebuke. It is obvious why he did not publish his volume, but why arrange and revise it so meticulously?

His seventeenth-century biographer provides a useful story: the dying Herbert sent the volume to a friend who was only to publish it if he thought that any "dejected poor Soul" might find comfort in it. This reminds us that the volume contains anguish as well as comedy. There are five poems entitled "Affliction" (making it the most-used title), and the first of these is filled with very raw anguish. A "dejected poor soul" could see from poems like those and like "Longing" and "The Crosse" that sufferings, lapses, and conflicts were part of the life of the regenerate. Moreover, Protestant introspection—like "imitating the ancients"—was something that had to be learned. In a poem like "The Flower" Herbert provided a model for simultaneously evoking and interrogating emotion that was comparable to that which Donne provided in his greatest love poems, and that was perhaps even more culturally significant.

Carew, Herrick, and the "Cavaliers"

Thomas Carew and Robert Herrick were exact contemporaries of George Herbert, although Herrick alone lived past 1640. Carew and Herrick are the best of the so-called Cavaliers—the group of poets associated with the court or the ideology of Charles I, the King who was ultimately executed by Parliament in 1649 in the name of the laws and "the people" of England. Carew died just before civil war broke out, but he was very much a figure of the Caroline court—although not necessarily an uncritical admirer. Many of his lyrics combine Donnean wit and impudence with Jonsonian polish (and impudence).

In "Ingratefull beauty threatned" Carew uses Donnean candor and Jonsonian awareness of the power of poetry to chastise a woman who has been (in the fiction) taking seriously the hyperbolical praise that the poet has previously bestowed on her. This tone of undeceived negotiation—with poetic hyperbole as one counter in the bargain—is new to English poetry. Carew's love lyrics show how easily the influence of the two masters can blend, though the nature of the blend remains his own. Neither Donne nor Jonson could have written to a woman that in her beauty departed flowers "as in their causes, sleep"—though Carew could not have written so without them.

At times, Carew fully adopts the Jonsonian mode. He wrote two fine country house poems, one of which, "To my friend G. N. from Wrest," truly bears comparison with "To Penshurst"—not just as an intelligent adaptation (like Carew's "To Saxham") but as a poem of equal "weight." Just as "A Rapture"—Carew's version of Donne's "Going to Bed" elegy—develops an ideology of pleasure, "To G. N." develops an ideology of use. It secularizes and then resacramentalizes religious language. The biblical and Protestant contrast between idols and life becomes: "In stead of Statues to adorne their wall / They throng with living men, their merry Hall." Bacchus and Ceres are present—offered not to the eye (as statues) but "to the taste": "We presse the juycie God, and quaff his blood, / And grinde the Yeallow Goddesse into food." This the Real Presence indeed. This poem alerts us, as does the elegy for Donne, which is devoted to the preacher as well as the poet, that Carew, though a "Cavalier," is concerned about religion. Carew's poem to George Sandys "on his translation of the Psalmes" ends on a powerful vision of substituting "the dry leavelesse trunk on Golgotha" for the classical poet's "verdant Bay."

Robert Herrick does not seem to have felt much tension between the paganism of his secular lyrics (*Hesperides*) and his religious *Noble Numbers*. This is due partly to his own sensibility and partly to his politics—these reinforced each other nicely. Herrick's constitutional anti-Puritanism becomes a genuine political position in a world in which traditional village holidays—"Maypoles, hock-carts, wassails, wakes," as Herrick puts it in "The Argument of his Book"—were matters of intense cultural, political, and religious conflict. The king (Charles I) and his most prominent bishops supported the traditional "sports," while the "Puritans," of course, did not. This helps us see why Herrick, a minister in the Church of England, could sing of Maypoles and of "cleanly wantonness," and yet say of heaven, at the end of "The Argument," that he "hope[s] to have it after all." Herrick is a pure Jonsonian. Donne does not exist for him. Where Carew saw Donne as "worth all that went before," Herrick says of Jonson (in one of the many poems that he wrote to and about the master), "Here lies Jonson with the rest / Of the poets; but the best."

One can see in these short lines much of what Herrick "worshipped" in "Saint Ben"—absolute prosodic skill combined with a mastery of tone and stance. Herrick developed the Jonson of some of the songs ("Still to be neat" and "Come my Celia") into a large gathering of consciously artful erotic poems—poems that play at various erotic speech acts and that celebrate beauty (including their own) but have no specifically sexual urgency. Herrick's "many dainty mistresses" are ideas of mortal beauty in the poetry; they are in many ways equivalent to his daffodils and blossoms.

"Corinna's Going a-Maying," Herrick's greatest poem on the "carpe diem" theme ("seize the day"—Horace, *Odes* I.xi), encompasses much of his special range. "Corinna," whose name is from Ovid's elegies, is enjoined to rise and put on her "foliage" for May Day. It is "profanation" to disobey "the Proclamation made for May" by nature (and the King in the reissued *Book of Sports*). Corinna is urged to "take the harmless follie of the time." Sex is not an issue, but transitoriness is—"Our life is short; and our days run / As fast away as do's the sun" (Ptolemaic astronomy helps the conceit here). It is crucial for Herrick that the "follie of the time" be "harmlesse."

As one would expect from this moral concern, there are continuities as well as discontinuities between *Hesperides* and *His Noble Numbers*. One of the finest of the "pious pieces," "The white Island: or the place of the Blest," blends Herrick's worlds beautifully without confusing them. The pagan idea of sleeping in the grave—"calm and cooling sleep"—gives way (with some resistance) to "Pleasures, such as shall pursue / Me immortaliz'd, and you." Jonsonian craftsmanship makes this triumph possible.

Many other wonderful lyrics were written by the "Cavalier" poets under the separate aegis of Jonson or under the combined aegis of Donne and Jonson. Two kinds of poems may be singled out and taken to represent the achievements of this group. The first is the "Against

Fruition" lyric, a poem in which the poet warns either another lover or his own mistress against sexual consummation. This would seem to be an odd ploy in a world where "beauties" are constantly being demystified (as in Sir John Suckling's songs); where "Platonic" love is constantly mocked (see William Cartwright on "this thin love" in "No Platonic Love"); and where a woman's scruples (conscience or honor) are constantly seen as monstrous, misguided, or unnatural (see, for instance, Thomas Randolph's "Upon Love Fondly Refused for Conscience's Sake"). But the attack on consummation follows from all this. Donne's "Farewell to Love" and "Love's Alchymie" are the foundation texts. Since consummated sex is paltry and plebeian ("my man," as Donne puts it, "Can be as happy as I can"), the answer must be, as Suckling advises a "fond youth," to "ask no more" than the opportunity for courtship since "fruition's dull" and "while it pleases much the palate, cloys." Abraham Cowley, in his "Against Fruition," explains that knowledge kills worship—"a learn'd age is always least devout."

The other type of "Cavalier" poem that should be mentioned is the Epicurean political poem. These are often modeled on Anacreon, the great Greek poet of the drinking song, or on Horace. Herrick's "The Bad Season Makes the Poet Sad" is a piece of this sort—imagining how wonderful things would be if the "golden age" before Parliament's triumph over the king were to return. The greatest poem of this sort is "The Grasshopper" by Richard Lovelace. Lovelace transforms Anacreon's happy grasshopper—"Voluptuous, and wise withal, / Epicurean animal," as Cowley puts it—into an emblem of poignant ignorance of future sorrow: "But ah, the sickle!" The poem turns from the emblem of ignorant summer to a wintry celebration of private friendship, in which festivity, the "crown" of winter, Saturnalia and Christmas (banned by Parliament in 1644), can be restored.

"Cavaliers" turned Divine: Crashaw and Vaughan

Crashaw's editor proclaimed the poet "Herbert's second but equal" in 1646; Vaughan attributed his conversion (before 1650) to "the blessed man, Mr. George Herbert." By the mid-seventeenth century Herbert was as powerful a cultural presence as Donne or Jonson, but his influence worked in different ways on his two major "followers." Both Crashaw and Vaughan began as "Cavalier" poets, both turned to divine poetry, but Crashaw retained a deep continuity with his "Cavalier" self, while Vaughan became—poetically (though not politically)—almost a "new man." Crashaw's *The Delights of the Muses* was published together with *Steps to the Temple* in 1646. His editor, finding this conjunction something of an embarrassment, insisted that *The Delights*, "though of a more humane mixture" are "as sweet as they are innocent." He need not have worried. There is as little sense of actual sexuality in this volume as in *Hesperides*.

In an epigram in *The Delights* Crashaw writes that he "would be married" but "have no wife"; he would be "married to a single life." This seems (as "mere" wit often does) profoundly true. Crashaw wanted warmth, intimacy, and above all, passion, but not in any ordinary sexual or social sense. Crashaw wanted ecstasy—it is his great note—but ecstasy of a sensual-intellectual not physical-sexual sort. "Music's Duel," Crashaw's translation of a neo-Latin poem by an Italian Jesuit, opens *The Delights* in both the 1646 and the 1648 editions. It is a paean to the ecstatic power of music; both the nightingale and the human musician are "ravisht" by the sounds they produce.

In Christianity Crashaw sought this same experience (or imagination) of sensual, spiritual, and largely noncognitive ravishment. He found Protestantism too negative. He wanted a religion of love, and love conceived as eros rather than agape. He found what he sought in the Church of Rome, to which he became a convert, and especially in the writings of the greatest female saint and mystic of the Counter-Reformation, Teresa of Avila. Crashaw's poems to Saint Teresa are among his most distinctive achievements. There is almost nothing else like them in English (except perhaps Keats at his most "embarrassing" or Shelley). Crashaw celebrates the experience that Saint Teresa recounts; he imagines "sweet and subtle pain," delicious mystical wounds. For Crashaw (who is ambivalent about Teresa's actual status as a woman), the saint is a spiritual Anacreon, celebrating the "strong wine of love" which we can drink "till we prove more, not lesse, then men."

Vaughan remains very much within the Protestant fold, but he, too, celebrates and personally claims extraordinary religious experiences. Vaughan was a more than competent (and quite upright) "Cavalier" and classical poet, but his decisive experience with Herbert's poetry in the late 1640s produced a situation unique in English poetry. Herbert's poetry became the material of Vaughan's. In his best poems, however, Vaughan establishes a distinctive vision. What makes this vision distinctive is his engagement not only with Herbert, the Bible, and Protestant theology but also with the rich and sometimes contradictory traditions of Platonism in the West.

Platonism could work either to value or to devalue the physical world. The material could be valued as the means for spiritual ascent, or it could be devalued as merely the (initially) necessary and disposable means. Vaughan wrote great and distinctive poems expressing each pole of this dichotomy as well as great poems that shift between them. The world of white light is the world of harsh, world-rejecting Platonism. One of Vaughan's poems of this kind, "The World," famously opens, "I saw Eternity the other night / Like a great Ring of pure and endless light." The "world" is harshly devalued—although this means primarily the social world—and the poem ends on a moment of Herbertian revelation when an authoritative "one" wittily converts the opening "great Ring" into a Calvinist sign of election. At the opposite pole is what might be called "the green world," the world of nature conceived of as benign and, most of all, as filled with, even participating in, the Spirit. Mornings seem to have had a sacramental quality for Vaughan— "the quick world / Awakes and sings" ("The Morning-watch").

"They Are All Gone into the World of Light," perhaps Vaughan's greatest poem, exists somewhere between the poles. Its primary thrust is longing for the soul's freedom—"They are all gone into the world of light! / And I alone sit lingring here"—but the world "here," sunset on a hill (probably in Wales), is rather tenderly evoked. Unlike Herbert, Vaughan is not regularly at his best—one of T. S. Eliot's criteria for a lyric poet truly being "major"—but when Vaughan is at his best, he is quite a remarkable poet.

Women Lyric Poets from Lanier to Philips

Women are constantly, of course, talked to and about in seventeenth-century lyrics, but we also have a significant body of lyric poems produced by women in the period, much of it of high quality. It was, as we have seen, a very good period for the lyric. Much but by no means all of the better poetry by women is, not surprisingly, religious. "Souls no Sexes have," a poem very late in our period strongly asserts, but in practice this does not seem to have been a widely held view. Jonson ascribed "a learned and a manly soul" to his female ideal, and, perhaps even more troublingly, the "effeminate" and gynophilic Crashaw worried that in the picture of Saint Teresa with a seraph that normally accompanied the

Vida, Teresa might be taken to be "some weak, inferiour, woman saint," rather than a mighty (potent and masculine) seraph herself.

In general, seventeenth-century women who write poetry are quite self-conscious about doing so. They are constantly—and understandably—on the defensive. They almost always identify themselves as women. A related effect is that the familiar topos of the poem as a child to which the writer has given birth is used with special force and frequency by writers who can invoke their status as actual or potential biological mothers (we have seen Jonson, as father and poem maker of his son, appropriating this.)

Aemilia Lanier grew up in the Elizabethan court (she was the daughter and the wife of court musicians), and was an exact contemporary of Donne and Jonson. Her book of poems *Salve Deus Rex Judaeorum*, published in 1611, was an attempt—like so many other volumes—to win patronage. Her opening poem to Queen Anne speaks of "that which is seldom seene, / A woman writing of divinest things." She speaks of her verse as "rude unpolisht lines," although she was in fact quite an accomplished metrist. She disclaims "that I Learning to my selfe assume, / Or that I would compare with any man." She appeals to Nature and, in another poem, to God's power which "hath given me powre to write." She sees virtuous women as having a special relation to the Muses, whom (with a fine enjambment) she sees as "living alwaies free / From sword, from violence, and from ill-report." The best of the dedicatory poems is "To the Ladie Anne, Countess of Dorset," a stanzaic poem that is rather like a Jonsonian epistle in developing a moral theme—"God makes both even, the Cottage with the Throne"—and insisting that the gentry must "for all the poore provide." *Salve Deus*, a seminarrative poem on the events surrounding the Passion, contains a remarkable defense of Eve and of women by Herod's wife, culminating in the plea: "Then let us have our Libertie againe, / And challenge to your selves no Sov'raigntie. . . . Your faults being greater, why should you disdaine / Our beeing your equals, free from tyranny?" Lanier ends her volume with the country-house poem that may precede "To Penshurst," a "Description of Cookeham," which especially emphasizes a private, pastoral, female society of learned friendship—a theme we will see developed very fully by a later woman poet.

Lady Mary Wroth, whose father was the owner of Penshurst, is the only known female author of a sonnet sequence in the England of our period. The sonnets of *Pamphilia to Amphilanthus* are smooth and competent in their versification. They give us a Petrarchism without irony, without comedy, and without visionary release. They are a poetry of pure loss and constancy—"wittness I could love, who soe could greeve." It is an interesting question whether these poems can be seen to represent a distinctively female interiority. Wroth did not stand entirely alone as a Jacobean woman poet. There is a lucid dream vision defending women's learning prefixed to Rachel Speght's *Mortalities Memorandum* (1621), and a superb and politically shrewd historical poem on the first part of Queen Elizabeth's reign by Diana Primrose (*A Chaine of Pearle*) published in 1630, but the great burst of published (and unpublished?) woman's poetry before the Restoration takes place in the interregnum. Bradstreet's *The Tenth Muse* appears in 1650; *Eliza's Babes* in 1652; Ann Collins's *Divine Songs and Meditacions* and Margaret Cavendish's *Poems and Fancies* in 1653. Many of Mary Carey's unpublished "Meditations and Poems" must have been written in this period, as were many of Katherine Philips's poems (published in 1664).

Anne Bradstreet, by virtue of being an American émigrée, has received a good deal of critical attention. She is not primarily a lyric poet. Her most ambitious and best poems—like those of Margaret Cavendish—are expository and encyclopedic in design. The learning and ambition of these poems are more impressive than her better-known personal lyrics, which are moving and dignified in their plainness, but rarely striking in language or thought. "Eliza," Ann Collins, and Mary Carey are all more impressive as lyric poets. The author of *Eliza's Babes: or the Virgins-Offering* is a very accomplished mock-"Cavalier" religious poet. In "The Dart" she uses the title image as effectively as Crashaw does, and with Herrick-like succinctness: "Shoot from above / Thou God of Love, / And with heav'ns dart / Wound my blest heart." "To a Friend for her Naked Breasts" is tonally a very complex poem combining admiration for audacity with an intense awareness of sin.

Ann Collins does not show the direct influence of Herbert, but his volume is clearly prominent among the cultural preconditions for hers. Collins brings a powerful intellectual grasp of Calvinist theology to bear on the details of her own psychological experience. In a "Song" beginning "The Winter of my infancy being over-past" Collins uses winter and spring imagery in as sophisticated and striking a way as

Vaughan does in "Regeneration." The "fruit most rare" ("That is not common with every woman") of her "garden . . . enclosed" is that "Which Grace doth nourish and cause to flourish." Syntactic elegance and theological precision come together here.

Mary Carey's meditations and poems exist only in manuscript. She is a witty and audacious religious poet. In a poem on the death of her fourth (and, until then, only surviving) child she "commands" God: "Change with me; doe, as I have done / Give me Thy all; Even thy deare sonne." In a remarkable poem, "Upon ye Sight of my abortive Birth" Carey both keeps the actual "little Embrio, voyd of life, and feature" in mind and transforms it into a metaphor that helps her come to terms with her experience. The culminating prayer is "Lett not my hart (as doth my wombe) miscarrie." This is one of the most convincingly triumphant "affliction" poems of the seventeenth century.

Katherine Philips was the most celebrated woman poet of the century; she deserves a prominent place among the "Cavaliers." Like Carew, Suckling, Cartwright, and others, she easily assimilates the influences of both Donne and Jonson. She is very fond of both the couplet style of the Jonsonian epistle and the short quatrains of Donne's "Exstasie." She has a gift for phrasing, for cadence, and for poetic design—for creating whole poems with an intelligible movement and a genuine conclusion. Along with Lovelace—to whom she is perhaps most poetically kin—Philips ranks as one of the great poets of the "Cavalier winter," and especially, of friendship. She makes "coterie poetry" into an ideology; she is probably to be believed when she expresses horror at the fact that her poems have been (and therefore must be) printed. She applies Donnean metaphysics to the theme of friendship—"Souls are grown, / By an incomparable mixture, One." Her sense of the social nature of identity is profound—"We are ourselves but by rebound." For "Friendship in Embleme," Philips adopts Donne's famous compasses (from "A valediction forbidding mourning"). She sees friendship as both better than marriage—purer and freer from constraint—and necessary to marriage, which must either "turn to Friendship or to Misery." "Sympathy" is the virtue or quality that she primarily celebrates. That "Souls no sexes have" (see "A Friend") is fundamental to her conception of friendship. No wonder the elegists praising Philips had problems with traditional gender distinctions. Cowley solved the problem by upping the ante: "'Tis solid, and 'tis manly all, / Or rather, 'tis Angelical."

Epilogue: Marvell and the Restoration

If Andrew Marvell had not existed, a survey like this might have had to invent him. Marvell wrote at least one major lyric in each of the major modes of the English lyric from Donne to the Restoration. "On a Drop of Dew" is an emblematic nature poem that gracefully balances immanence and transcendence—between which poles, as we have seen, Vaughan's poetry shuttled. "The Garden" continues and deepens the philosophical theme, but adds to it the theme of retirement so important to the "Cavalier" tradition (though Marvell was never a royalist). Again, Donne and Jonson are both strongly in evidence. "The Definition of Love" uses Donnean quatrains and Donnean imagery (drawn from mathematics, mapmaking, and astronomy) to "define" a rather un-Donnean state of mind, "Magnanimous Despair." "To his Coy Mistress" develops one of the great Jonsonian and "Cavalier" themes, carpe diem, in a most un-"Cavalier" way, so that the "persuasion to enjoy" turns into a mutual suicide pact.

Marvell inhabited poetic traditions with remarkable completeness. He even, in one poem, "The Coronet," adopted the mode of Herbertian self-mocking narrative, and—following "Jordan" (II), but in his own terms—confronted the essential impurity of his own poetic piety. But Marvell did not remain a lyric poet. Just as we see Donne moving from satire to lyric at the beginning of our period, we watch Marvell moving from lyric to satire at the end of it. Marvell continued to write after the Restoration, but his modes became satire and prose.

After the much-desired Restoration, Vaughan noted somewhat bemusedly (in a poem celebrating Katherine Philips as a pre-Restoration poet): "since the thunder left our air / [The] laurels look not half so fair." Not until the first half of the twentieth century did the lyric regain the position that it had in the first half of the seventeenth.

Richard Strier

Further Reading

Carey, John. *John Donne: Life, Mind and Art.* New York: Oxford University Press, 1981.

Greer, Germaine, Susan Hastings, Jeslyn Medoff, and Melinda Sansone, eds. *Kissing the Rod: An Anthology of Seventeenth-Century Women's Verse.* New York: Farrar, Strauss, 1988.

Hammond, Gerald. *Fleeting Things: English Poets and Poems, 1616–1660.* Cambridge: Harvard University Press, 1990.

Lewalski, Barbara. *Protestant Poetics and the Seventeenth-Century Religious Lyric.* Princeton: Princeton University Press, 1979.

Marcus, Leah. *Childhood and Cultural Despair: A Theme and Variations in Seventeenth-Century Literature.* Pittsburgh: University of Pittsburgh Press, 1978.

Sanders, Wilbur. *John Donne's Poetry.* Cambridge: Cambridge University Press, 1971.

Schoenfeldt, Michael C. *Prayer and Power: George Herbert and Renaissance Courtiership.* Chicago: University of Chicago Press, 1991.

Sharpe, Kevin. *Criticism and Compliment: The Politics of Literature in the England of Charles I.* Cambridge: Cambridge University Press, 1987.

Strier, Richard. *Love Known: Theology and Experience in George Herbert's Poetry.* Chicago: University of Chicago Press, 1983.

Summers, Joseph. *The Heirs of Donne and Jonson.* New York: Oxford University Press, 1970.

Milton

K NOWN in his own day more as a political polemicist than as a
poet, Milton's poetic renown grew soon after his death in the
last part of the seventeenth century. From the end of the
eighteenth century his reputation, built mainly on *Paradise Lost*, reached
monumental status because of the enormous significance assigned variously to three dimensions of his work: his philosophical and theological
ideas, his artistic genius, and his revolutionary politics; it has waxed and
waned depending on how decisively the prestige accorded him in any
one of these dimensions outweighed distaste for the other two.

It is one of the ironies of Milton's reception that, as the poet who did
most to legitimate the literary artist's quest for fame, he never quite saw
his own poetic fame realized in his lifetime. And yet Milton was to
achieve posthumous celebrity in a manner that helped shape the cultural ideal and personality type that we have come to know as the
Author. We now take for granted a literary culture dominated by
authors, full-time writers who claim an authority based on a superior
ability to perceive a higher truth. In Milton's day it was still more likely that a writer of poetry was a cultivated amateur whose full-time occupation was more typically that of courtier or statesman and who wrote
poetry often as a form of sophisticated recreation. The fits and starts of
Milton's attempt to establish literary authority for himself reveal the
uneasiness that accompanied authorship in its early stages.

Among seventeenth-century English poets, Milton stands out in his
immensely self-conscious, self-constructed, single-minded drive to gain
fame through the religious, moral, and political authority of poetic pro-

nouncements that find their most complete expression in epic. In a literary tradition already begun by Edmund Spenser and Ben Jonson, Milton came to see the entire political and religious nation as the subjects of that authority. And from early on he associated the vehicle of this authority with some combination of Christian doctrine and classical form. Even more than his forerunners Spenser and Jonson, Milton constructed a continually changing self-image of his developing authorship in an interlaced narrative of both professional vocation and personal identity—a poetic career manifested in a continually self-commenting and self-revising oeuvre that, with a combination of anxiety, defensiveness, and self-confidence, projects its own fulfillment in the epic.

Early Poems

Milton's first full-scale publication under his own name, *The Poems of Mr. John Milton*, appeared in 1645. The volume includes most of his early poetry, offered as a kind of pledge of the great epic yet to come; each poem is accompanied by a note indicating (or misindicating) Milton's age at the time of its composition, suggesting that he regarded the volume as a record of his early poetic development. Included in the volume are his Latin elegies, written between 1616 and 1620, when he was eighteen to twenty-two years old. In these poems one can observe the youthful Milton experimenting with two models as the basis of his poetic persona. In themselves more showy than good, these elegies reveal Milton's early vacillation between religious lyric and—astonishing in retrospect—erotic lyric.

The erotic elegies (I, V, and VII) are particularly interesting because they represent a path not taken. Imitating Ovid in these poems, Milton associates poetic and sexual power.

At times he sees the ideal expression of this sexual/poetic potency in pastoral lyric melody, at times in an ecstatic epic elevation to the seat of the Muses, where he is privy to the secret of the gods; these two poles—pastoral and epic—are to be defining points for Milton throughout his work. Many of the elegies reveal what was to become a pattern in Milton's early work, a fixation with beginnings—with suitable smaller poetic forms that would project a suitably grand ending in a major poem. This pattern is already apparent in elegy VI as well, where Milton experiments with the poetic persona he was ultimately to claim as his own, that of the Christian poet. Milton here uses the pastoral metaphor of the shepherd for specifically biblical themes to define the epic poet as a priest in touch with divine secrets, now because of his ascetic life and sexual abstention; by the end of the poem he announces he is writing a pastoral Nativity poem, as if to commence a personal narrative that will fulfill itself in epic.

Above all, the Latin elegies show that for Milton poetry is a vocation; it is successfully practiced only as part of the total design of one's life. And while the imperative to settle on a vocation most certainly stems from Milton's urban, Protestant, middle-class background, the poet-priestly vocation unfolds for Milton according to the pattern that was believed to describe Virgil's poetic development, beginning with an apprenticeship in pastoral lyric and ending in a heroic poem.

Significantly, all of Milton's models for the Christian poet in the Latin elegies are classical pagans, including Pythagoras, Tiresias, Orpheus, Homer, and Virgil. The Latin elegies are a vivid example of a fundamental ambivalence in much of Milton's work—the Greco-Roman tradition as both an antithesis to, and a historical foreshadowing of, Christian revelation. But if Milton's early poems reveal his need to construct a poetic voice by identifying with one or another strand of an entire culture, his choice of persona is also related to an intensely personal issue as well: Milton aspired to be a poet against the wishes of his father, who wanted him to be a priest in the Anglican Church. In his early career, Milton experimented with a wide variety of poetic forms, in several languages, both ancient and modern, but the poems in which Milton both establishes and tests his vocation as poet-priest are three: the Nativity Ode, *Comus*, and *Lycidas*.

"On the Morning of Christ's Nativity" (1629), commonly known as the Nativity Ode, is Milton's first ambitious poem. The design of the poem indicates Milton's understanding of his priestly role. The poem explicates a central icon in Milton's culture, the birth of Christ, by showing its relationship to the larger narrative of Christian salvation. But in addition to this doctrinal function, the poem also has a performative dimension: it integrates present time into sacred time by poetically reenacting salvational moments in biblical history in the manner of a liturgical performance. Through the manipulation of tenses it treats events in the life of Christ as if they were ongoing, and thus Milton inserts "us" into the history of redemption.

The poem achieves both its explicative and performative function by recreating passages of biblical narrative understood typologically, that is, as prophetic prefigurations or foreshadowings of the ultimate redemptive fulfillment. But the poem has also to be read as a celebration of Milton's own nativity, his poetic birth. It begins by attributing itself to the "heavenly Muse" and ends by naming itself "our . . . song," as if its audience had become a congregation led by the poet through the complexities of worship. That the Nativity Ode was written in the month of Milton's nativity—and his majority—may not be accidental. Milton's boldness in staging his poetic ambition in a religious lyric contrasts sharply with other religious poets, like George Herbert and Andrew Marvell, who were troubled by the conflicting interests of divine praise, on the one hand, and self-projection inherent in the very act of writing poetry, on the other.

However, almost as soon as Milton triumphantly stepped into the role of poet with the Nativity Ode, he ceased to write more poetry of the same caliber. Throughout the early 1630s he did not sustain the momentum of his first attempt to embody his sense of vocation in another ambitious poem. In the early 1630s he further pursued the theme of redemptive time only in short lyrics such as "On Time," "Upon the Circumcision," and "The Passion," this last left unfinished, and as he noted in 1645 *Poems*, "above the years he had." During this time Milton also wrote "L'Allegro" and "Il Penseroso," about the contrasting moods of poetic inspiration.

Milton himself was painfully aware of the discrepancy between his avowed poetic vocation and his meager poetic output. In a letter written at age twenty-three to an unknown friend, who had apparently chided him for spending too much time studying to be a poet instead of actually writing poems, Milton defends his belated poetic production as the result of a God-given desire to write well rather than early. Included in the letter was his seventh sonnet, "How soon hath time," which recounts just how profoundly the crisis of poetic output threatened his sense of vocation. Lamenting the passing of his youth without the fulfillment of his poetic promise, he concludes that he cannot, solely on his own, control the unfolding of his poetic development, which can evolve only within God's time.

The poet-priest thus turns in upon himself, applying the notion of redemptive time to his own career and vocation. Milton makes it clear that poetry is for him, not only a profession, but also a religious vocation as understood in Protestant thought as a religious calling to a particular form of work. And indeed, by 1637 Milton seems to have sustained enough of the assurance expressed at the end of sonnet VII to promise his father, in "Ad Patrem," that he will repay his support with the fame he will accrue from his future priestly epic and that will guarantee his poetic immortality.

To this point in his life Milton's notion of poetic vocation was an almost entirely private fantasy, known mainly to his father and his classmates. *Comus* (1634) is a court masque that represents Milton's first foray into the world of professional poetry. The masque, a genre given literary prominence by Ben Jonson, was a lavish dramatic entertainment produced at court and at aristocratic houses usually to celebrate its patron, an ironic beginning for the professional career of a future revolutionary. After *Arcades* (an earlier and less important entertainment) *Comus* is Milton's first attempt to exercise his vocation publicly and professionally by writing for a courtly patron, presumably for material compensation. Both works were produced by the court musician and friend of Milton's father, Henry Lawes, who asked Milton to write the text for each. The specific occasion of *Comus* was the inauguration of John Egerton, Earl of Bridgewater, as Lord President of Wales.

The narrative begins as the Lady and her two brothers (played by the Egerton children themselves) get lost in a dark wood; Comus, a wild satyrlike figure representing sensual excess, attempts to seduce the Lady, who represents reason and sexual restraint. Struck paralyzed by Comus, she is finally rescued by the river goddess Sabrina; the Attendant Spirit, the masque's internal narrator played by Lawes himself, then presents the children to their father and mother, Lord and Lady Egerton; dramatic and real time and place converge. The masque is a ritual initiation of the children, who, upon successful testing of their virtue, are ceremoniously presented to their parents, the rightness of whose rule is signaled by the purity of their heirs and issue. Milton thus uses the Platonic doctrine of chastity to legitimate Egerton's dominion.

Not surprisingly, Milton once again marks the relation of sexual restraint to poetic vocation and epic power in a complex series of associations linking Sabrina to Aeneas, his nephew Brutus (the legendary founder of Britain) and Spenser. The glance towards epic in this pastoral masque places it on a trajectory guided towards a British heroic poem. However, the primary poet figure in the work is not Milton, but the Attendant Spirit, uniquely identified with Lawes, the shepherd-singer, the unveiler of truth through fictional fabrication. Lawes the musician rather than Milton the poet is associated with Spenser when, disguised as the Thyrsis, Lawes invokes the example of Meliboeus—Spenser's pastoral name—to call upon Sabrina to save the Lady. Ironically, as the writer of the text of *Comus*, Milton is unable to identify authorially with the epic aspirations implied in its pastoral mode.

This displacement from authority over his own text, willing or unwilling, in a kind of aborted authorship is apparent even in the 1637 publication of *Comus* as *A Maske Presented at Ludlow Castle*, the title by which the work was known in Milton's day. The publication of *A Maske* does not become the occasion for Milton to make an authorial claim, in contrast to the epic aspirations hinted at in the poem's text. Referring namelessly to the writer of the text, Lawes signs only his name to the dedication on the title page of *A Maske*. Not until the 1645 *Poems* does Milton overcome this displacement of authorship and authority by claiming the masque for himself when he includes it in his collected *Poems* under his own name. Not until then does *A Maske* unequivocally authorize the association of Meliboeus with Milton as the progeny of the pastoral Spenser on his way to epic. For unknown reasons, Milton was not commissioned to write any more masques.

Anxiety over unfulfilled authorial vocation reached crisis proportions yet one more time in *Lycidas*, in which the literary connection between pastoral and epic becomes inextricably linked with Milton's sense of his own personal history. *Lycidas* is Milton's third ambitious poetic attempt, and certainly his most successful so far. Milton represents the internal crisis of vocation this time as a response to an external catastrophe, the death of Edward King, a Cambridge schoolmate who died when his ship foundered on his way home to Ireland. King's Cambridge classmates put together a volume of memorial verse, a volume to which Milton contributed, presumably because of his reputation as an aspiring poet rather than any close tie to King. *Lycidas*, a pastoral elegy, is the last poem in the volume and is signed simply "J. M."

In a highly self-conscious gesture, the speaker appears in his persona as a poet to announce that he is unprepared to deal with the momentous subject of mortality. The conventions of the pastoral elegy, the conventions in which the subject of mortality has been traditionally contained, form an obstacle that the poet feels compelled to overcome in order to legitimate his poetic mastery, but once those conventions are mastered, he experiences a breakthrough to new and abundant poetic output.

Representing his student relationship with King—in accordance with pastoral convention—as that of two shepherds, Milton explores the traditional metaphor of the shepherd as both poet and priest. (King was in fact studying for the ministry, and he wrote verses, however undistinguished.) The death of the young poet provokes a set of existential questions: Why give up the pleasures of life (he refers to specifically sexual pleasures) to devote oneself to poetic fame if one can be so arbitrarily cut down? Why (the question is asked in the voice of St. Peter) do corrupt priests thrive while a good priest perishes so young? The poet is answered by voices that Milton identifies as breaking out of the pastoral genre to supply an otherworldly perspective: Apollo instructs the poet to consider fame from the viewpoint of celestial rather than earthly reward; and St. Peter himself answers by asserting that retribution is meted out only in heaven.

After each explanation the pastoral mood returns, but only with the admission that the genre on its own could not contain its own subject—could not provide an adequate explanation for the death of Lycidas. And so when the poet returns to the conventional pastoral funeral procession in which all of nature mourns the death of a shepherd by strewing flowers on the hearse of Lycidas, he reminds himself that the body of Lycidas lies not in any sarcophagus, but beneath the sea. The poet finds himself on the verge of despair to discover once again that a pastoral convention—poetry itself—has failed.

However, the poem takes a sudden turn when the poet himself supplies a heavenly perspective: he announces that although Lycidas may be physically under the sea, his soul has been resurrected in heaven, where he inhabits a celestial pastoral world. Milton has rehabilitated his chosen genre by spiritualizing it—by Christianizing the classical—thus rendering it capable of containing what it was meant to make intelligible—death. In mastering death, he has mastered the genre that initiates the vocation of poetry. The poem, which begins with doubts about the poet's readiness and ability, ends by establishing the authority of the poet's own voice. Strangely introducing a new voice by switching to the third person in its final section, the poem now steps back from the experience it has described to portray the poet preparing to sing new pastoral songs with eagerness, tranquility, and ease. Milton has finally completed his own poetic initiation. *Lycidas* represents one of the rare moments in which Milton's sense of past promise, present achievement, and future hope come together with confidence. *Lycidas* is Milton's last, but most successful, endeavor to construct a beginning.

Although the text of *Lycidas* resolves poetic doubt by enacting poetic mastery, that resolution, again, does not become an occasion for a public authorial claim; the poem appeared in an obscure miscellany, obscurely signed by the poet only with his initials. The poem's occasion and its textual self-assertion are at odds. As in the case of *Comus*, Milton was to claim the poem in the fullest sense only when he published it in his 1645 *Poems*. The Latin inscription on the book's title page suggests that Milton considered the volume as a whole to be his pastoral beginning, implying a promise of more ambitious poetry yet to come. Indeed, in minor Latin poems written soon after *Lycidas*, Milton proclaims himself the model English poet who will write a new epic based on British history, an epic in which King Arthur will figure significantly. Ironically, Milton was not to publish another major poem until *Paradise Lost* in 1667, over twenty years later. In fact, by 1645 Milton had already decided to leave poetry for political writing.

Prose

In 1642 the civil war between the monarchy and Parliament broke out. Both a religious and political revolution, it began as a struggle between the established Anglican Church and radical Protestants (commonly known as the Puritans), who demanded a reformed Church closer to continental Protestantism and less like Catholicism. Milton interrupted his poetic career to write political prose supporting the radical Protestants (especially the Presbyterians) in the name of religious liberty against the enforced conformity of the Anglican Church, which was meting out harsh punishment against outspoken nonconformists. Milton reveals his need to maintain the integrity of his own personal narrative by treating this detour as if it in fact really was part of his plan all along: he is now working for the Church, "to whose service by the intentions of my parents . . . I was destined as a child, and *in my own resolutions*" (emphasis added).

At the same time, autobiographical passages in his first works in the cause of the Church, *The Reason of Church Government against Prelaty* and *Apology for Smectymnuus* (both written in 1642), reflect on his poetic calling; having suspended, if only temporarily, his drive toward a poetic career, Milton now unequivocally considers poetry his natural element, and attributes to himself a poetic authority that could easily be thought overblown, considering he had by this time written only three substantial poems, two of them fairly short. But Milton is still obsessed with preparedness. He now worries whether he is prepared to write effective political prose—the labor of his left hand he calls it—as he once worried about his readiness and ability to write poetry.

During this period Milton further adds to his poetic persona a record of scholarly preparation already defended in his letter justifying his poetic belatedness; he constructs for himself a narrative of personal intellectual development, a narrative that reenacts a literary history beginning with the Latin elegists, and continuing on to Dante and Petrarch, the chivalric epic, and finally to Socrates and Plato, the philosophers who epitomize chastity as the enabling virtue of epic. In fact, in the 1645 *Poems*, Milton adds a retraction to his Latin elegies, declaring that the study of Socrates has taught him to encase his breast with ice for protection against erotic impulse so that he can gain epic strength.

Milton deepens this connection between his personal and literary narrative when he considers his current political activity as the final preparation for a heroic poem. As he puts it in the *Apology*, "he who would . . . write well hereafter in laudable things, ought himself to be a true poem," presumably, in his case, by involvement in a just cause. In the *Reason of Church Government* Milton specifically pledges, after more study and experience of the world, a major work—a national, military, religious poem, either a long or short epic, but possibly a tragic drama, whichever is most "doctrinal and exemplary to a nation." This poem will do for the English what ancient classical and biblical poets (as well as modern Italian poets) did for their countries. Based on ancient models, the poem will project the "pattern of a Christian hero," drawn on a king or knight from British history.

During his prose period Milton composed the vast majority of his works, the works for which he was primarily known among his contemporaries—prose pamphlets promoting personal, religious, and civic liberty, including liberal divorce laws and limited freedom of the press. His defense of the execution of Charles I brought him to the attention of Cromwell, the parliamentary general and Puritan head of state, who ultimately appointed him Secretary for Foreign Tongues, a position in which he was responsible for state correspondence and the defense of Puritan policies to a European audience. In the process he went blind.

In 1654 Milton undertook to celebrate the leaders of the English revolution in his *Second Defense of the English People*, in which he arrives at the threshold of achieving the voice that will speak *Paradise Lost*. Milton celebrates the parliamentary heroes of the Civil War, but he also distinctly reveals his faltering faith that the new order will be able to sustain itself. He concludes by insisting that he has done his part by providing counsel, especially in his written works; he compares the *Second Defense* itself to an epic, almost as if he had with this prose work fulfilled his long-standing promise to write an epic. If that is so, Milton has revised his self-narrative by declaring his prose not an interruption, but the very fulfillment of his epic claim, both in his writing and in his person.

Most significant, Milton here takes one of several occasions (including sonnet XIX: "When I consider how my light is spent") to defend himself against charges that his blindness was a divine punishment for supporting regicide. He declares his blindness a divine gift—a substitution of spiritual for physical sight—which renders him "almost too holy to attack." He has uncannily become the blind seer, the very image of the epic poet—like Homer—that he idealized in his youthful elegies.

It is impossible to tell whether Milton would have felt his epic ambition fulfilled in the *Second Defense* had the revolution not failed and had the Stuart monarchy not been restored in 1660 with the return of Charles II, the son of the beheaded king whose execution Milton defended in his prose tract *Eikonoklastes* (1649). But it is clear that after the failure of the political institution that provided a framework for his sense of himself as a person and a poet, Milton's notion of both epic and poetic authority likewise dramatically changed.

Paradise Lost

When Milton returned to poetry to fulfill his "covenant with any knowing reader," a covenant made in *The Reason of Church Government* to write a great epic, he did in fact write in all three genres he considered in that prose work: a long epic (*Paradise Lost*), a short epic (*Paradise Regained*), and a tragic drama (*Samson Agonistes*). Milton further develops themes that appeared in earlier works, such as temptation and the inverse relationship between the epic and sexuality. (In two of the three last works failed action results from a dysfunctional relation with a woman.) However, none of his heroic poems is quite the work he projected in 1642. Perhaps the most obvious indication of his changed notion of epic is his choice of subject for *Paradise Lost*: a cautionary tale about committing the wrong action. Milton probably began writing *Paradise Lost* in the mid–to late 1650s, roughly about the same time that he completed the *Second Defense*, whose incipient disillusion it reflects and intensifies. That is, Milton's great epic appeared, and much of it was written, after the collapse of the political and religious ideals to which he had devoted much of his life. A questioning attitude toward action pervades Milton's three last and major poems. Although Milton considered writing a tragic drama about the Fall as early as the 1640s, his choice of that biblical event as the subject of *Paradise Lost* must be seen in light of the failed revolution. The work stands in startling contrast to most epics, which typically celebrate a great action.

Although encyclopedic in scope, broad in its learning, and bold in its poetry—encompassing the battle in heaven between God and Satan, the story of Creation, and angelic dialogues on the major intellectual and scientific issues of the day, and concluding with a vision of universal history—*Paradise Lost* is after all about being wrong. Its central action, the Fall, is about transgressing the boundaries of proper action—a transgression at times uncomfortably close to Milton's own participation in rebellion. *Paradise Lost*, like *Paradise Regained* and *Samson Agonistes*, is riddled with questions about the very nature of a right action, in stark contrast to his confident assertion at the beginning of the revolution that true wisdom is knowledge of "what is infallibly good and happy in the state of man's life" (*The Reason of Church Government*).

The problem of action in *Paradise Lost* is translated into its problematic generic form. Milton's prefatory note on his use of unrhymed verse makes it clear that he conceives of *Paradise Lost* in the mold of Homer and Virgil. But the reader is immediately struck by all the inversions of classical epic conventions. The heroic ethos of epic is strangely embodied in the villain of the work, Satan. Instead of the council of the gods, we are presented with a council of devils. More broadly, the plot pivots around a peripeteia, or fall, more characteristic of tragedy than epic, and a tragic rather than epic hero—Adam—dominates the work. Moreover, *Paradise Lost* is an epic whose central action occurs in a garden, a place usually depicted in epic as a counterfoil to epic action.

This genre slippage betrays a deep-seated fear of loss of control. To narrate the work Milton must cross a formidable epistemological divide—he must discern secrets of prelapsarian existence while in the state of postlapsarian exile from Eden. Milton distances himself from the potential presumption of this move by claiming divine inspiration, projecting the same prophetic voice he assumed when he defended his blindness in the *Second Defense*. In four extended invocations to his muse (at the beginning of Books I, III, VII, and IX) he either asks for or explains the inspiration that allows him to go forward with the epic enterprise. In Book III he claims inspiration from the same source that inspired Moses and that supervised Creation itself. His blindness, he insists, is the very mark of his spiritual insight, his divine authority. In Book IX he climactically proclaims that, "unimplored," he is nightly visited by his celestial muse, who inspires his "unpremeditated Verse."

But Milton rarely makes this claim without raising the possibility of error, like the Puritan theologians who cautioned that belief in possession by the Holy Spirit may really be a Satanic delusion. In fact, Milton's call for divine aid at the very opening of *Paradise Lost* is uncannily echoed by Satan's demonic aspirations. Milton's opening prayer to be raised by divine inspiration above all other epic poets—raised high enough to "justify the ways of God to men"—is directly followed by a description of Satan's rebellion, a description suffused with metaphors of rising, "aspiring / To set himself in Glory above his Peers" (just as Eve is "heightened" when she eats the forbidden fruit). The troubling parallel between Satan and the poet is deepened by Satan's association with perversions of poetic faculties, such as his "proud imaginations," his conjuring use of fancy and illusion to begin his seduction of Eve. Milton leaves open the possibility that, like Satan, he too may be "self-raised."

In the invocation to Book III he addresses the divine light he cannot see, and asks, "May I express thee unblamed?" In the invocation to Book VII, having just related the battle in heaven between God and Satan, he ponders whether "I have presumed" to narrate matters heavenly, and asks that his muse bring him down safely lest he fall on earth "erroneous . . . and forlorn." At the end of the invocation to Book IX he raises the possibility that he has waited too long to write *Paradise Lost*; he wonders whether the poem may actually be not inspired, that it may in fact "all be mine, / Not Hers, who brings it nightly to my Ear." Three-quarters into the work, he thus raises the possibility of its fundamentally mistaken claim; almost a century after his model Spenser had established the authority of an English epic voice, Milton is still insecure in his own epic role.

Milton's counterpointed assertion and questioning of his authority to undertake "things unattempted yet in Prose or Rhyme" (I.16) reflects a more widespread trepidation about action in the world in general, as is exemplified in the metaphor in Book I of a ship seeking refuge at sea by anchoring onto an island, which turns out to be a sea monster. The difficulty in distinguishing succor from danger pervades *Paradise Lost*; all Milton's post–Restoration works ponder the uneven and puzzling relationship between knowledge and action. In *Paradise Lost* the relationship between the two centers on Milton's insistence that Adam and Eve have free choice to obey or disobey the injunction against eating, appropriately, from the tree of knowledge, a free choice unaffected by God's foreknowledge that they will disobey.

Milton's notion of freedom is such, however, that it exists only in dialectical relation to disobedience; choice is meaningless without the possibility of choosing wrongly—an idea extensively developed in his best-known prose work, *Areopagitica* (1644), which argues against pre-publication censorship. For Milton, there is no time in human history when one could avoid the possibility of a wrong choice with potentially disastrous consequences. And the difficulty of choosing correctly is further suggested by Adam's warning in Book IV that the "Tree / Of Knowledge [is] planted by the Tree of Life, / So near grows Death to Life." This fundamental ambiguity complicates the relationship between knowledge and choice throughout the epic.

Underlying the easy existence of Adam and Eve in Eden is an intellectual conundrum that defines both the condition of their personal relationship and the possibility of its collapse in their fall—the paradoxical correlation between unity and differentiation, similarity and dissimilarity, oneness and hierarchy. Milton conceives of similitude as a fundamental metaphysical principle of Creation: Christ and Adam are similitudes of God, Eve a similitude of Adam. In many ways, understanding this principle is the most important intellectual, emotional, and moral challenge of living in Eden, a challenge that manifests itself in the very nature of moral choice. It is precisely this paradoxical relationship between unity and hierarchy that Lucifer could not accept when God begot the Son, in Milton's heterodox Christology, by elevating one angel to be Head of the other angels, his Body, in order to better unite them as one; Lucifer's reaction against this paradox is the cause of the first rebellion—the rebellion of the fallen angels in heaven and their consequent fall.

The challenge Satan faced in the elevation of the Son resurfaces in the very first moments of Eve's consciousness. Directly after her creation, as she recounts it in Book IV, Eve was attracted to her own reflection in a pool of water. Adam instructs her that in fact she is *his* true image. He persuades her to follow him rather than her watery reflection, imploring, "whom thou fliest, of him thou art / His flesh, his bone." "Part of my Soul I seek thee," he pleads, "and thee claim / My other half." Eve finally responds to this last appeal to oneness with a recognition of Adam's superiority as her head and guide. Throughout their relation Milton plays upon their resemblance as the shifting combination of parity and subordination, equality and hierarchy, symmetry and asymmetry; Adam and Eve thus remain within the proper parameters of resemblance in a way that Lucifer did not. Eve's mistake at the pool highlights Eden as a place of intellectual labor, where difficult moral and perceptual discriminations must be made.

As the relationship between Adam and Eve develops, discrimination between parity and hierarchy is increasingly invested with emotional charge, as in the debate in Book IX about working separately in the garden in order to work more efficiently. Eve creates the enabling condition of the Fall when she suggests that she and Adam separate "to divide our labors." At the core of Milton's epic is a domestic quarrel about the proper order of what Adam calls "household good." The quarrel resonates with parallels from Milton's first marriage while it connects the entire epic to the emerging structure of the middle-class family in the seventeenth century. Among Adam's arguments against separating is his insistence that it would be better to face Satan together. He appeals alternately to his hegemony over her as well as their complementarity. Adam asserts that he would be stronger than she to resist Satan, but only because of her presence, adding that Eve, too, would receive strength from his presence were Satan to approach her first. The logical movement of his speech typically maintains their relationship as both symmetrical and asymmetrical, as also suggested by Adam's address to Eve as "Sole *Eve*, Associate sole," implying both her dependence and independence.

Eve contends that true happiness can only result from "integrity," the unitary strength of the individual. Adam replies that free will can be directed well only within the social unit of the family, the real context of moral judgment; to withstand temptation, they must "mind" each other. However, in apparent frustration, Adam loses the balance between hegemony and complementarity: first, he commands Eve to prove her "constancy" by obeying him, and then he abruptly relents, resigned to her desire go her own separate way, but apprehending trouble for a "much deceived, much failing, hapless *Eve*."

It is through Eve that *Paradise Lost* meditates on what it is like to be wrong. Convinced by Satan she will be intellectually raised to a "divine Similitude" if she eats the forbidden fruit, Eve first puzzles over whether she can now be "more equal" to Adam, but finally decides to share "equal Lot" with him by inviting him to eat as well. Adam immediately recognizes she is lost, but instinctively decides to follow her, drawn by "the Link of nature." "Our State cannot be severed, we are one, / One Flesh; to lose thee were to lose myself," he declares. Adam and Eve ultimately cannot sustain the emotional and intellectual conditions of the earthly Paradise, the difficult, delicate balance between complementarity and hierarchy.

Even Adam's mistake is difficult to evaluate morally. The explicit censure of his decision to follow Eve does not enervate the heightened beauty of their *Liebestod*, emotionally charged by Adam's offer to sacrifice himself for love of Eve. The very wrongness of his action is the typological prefiguration—and therefore the historical inauguration—of the redemptive death of the second Adam, Christ. The coincidence of sin and its opposite in the Fall intimates a moral complexity that makes ethical judgment almost unfathomable. At the historical and personal moment in which Milton writes *Paradise Lost*, typological foreshadowing is no longer the key to understand how to usher in the Kingdom of Heaven on earth, as Milton and his political peers believed on the eve of the revolution. Typological fulfillment in and through the second Adam may ultimately lead to personal redemption, a "paradise within," but in the meantime, prophecy renders the divine will in history endlessly complex for time-bound human beings. Typological foreshadowing, once the mark of the poet-priestly voice, has become instead the mark of bewildering ethical choice, a fall into history as much as redemption out of it.

Paradise Regained and *Samson Agonistes*

If in his early career Milton felt anxiety over finding just the proper poetic beginning in pastoral, it is evident by the time of *Paradise Regained* (1671) that he felt the same uneasiness about ending in epic. Echoing Spenser and Virgil, the first line of *Paradise Regained* astonishingly identifies Milton as the epic poet by referring to the much longer, more ambitious *Paradise Lost* as his garden poem, his pastoral apprenticeship. *Paradise Regained* and *Samson Agonistes* were published together in 1671, and though there is some question about whether *Samson Agonistes* was actually written before or after the Restoration, most scholars choose the post-Restoration period of composition. Both works are about redeemers coming to understand their redemptive actions; they meditate on history to fathom the oxymoronic, passive nature of redemptive action.

Paradise Regained is about Satan's temptations of Christ when Christ is just about to enter into manhood—when he is about to realize his vocation as redeemer; the work opens with Christ pondering just how he will perform the act of redemption. Through a series of tempta-tions—the main subject of the work—Satan seeks both to confirm that Christ is the Messiah and to forestall his own destruction. Satan tries to incite Christ with a desire for public recognition and power. He chal-lenges him to make himself known: he tempts him to perform a mira-cle, to turn stone to bread in the wilderness; he tempts him to have his name spread through wealth in the first of several vast worldly specta-cles he presents to Christ. He further tempts Christ with the worldly knowledge of Greece and Rome, which Christ stingingly rejects in favor of the completeness of biblical knowledge—perhaps the most troubling attitude readers of the classical Milton have had to digest. As symbol of wealth, power, and political empire, Rome plays an especial-ly important role for both Christ and Satan: Satan tempts Christ with the conquest of Rome not only for fame and worldly riches, but also as the occasion of redemptive action—Rome is the oppressor of Israel; to conquer Rome is to deliver Israel, and thus inherit David's throne and fulfill the prophecies of redemption.

Behind this temptation is the problem that gnaws at Milton in his last two works—regret over the attempt to second-guess divine "pre-diction," to act as if one could be a step ahead in the redemptive narra-tive. From the start, Christ's response to this temptation is simply patience, passivity. Through adversity with Satan he stops trying to know what he must do to save mankind, accepting that he will realize his redemptive nature only if God works through him in God's own time. As he says in Book III, "who best / Can suffer, best can do," where *suffering* retains the sense of passivity and patience derived from its Latin equivalent, *patiens*.

In effect, Christ's response to Satan's frustrated demand, "What dost thou in this World?" is simply *nothing*. In the final temptation Satan transports Christ to the top of the Jerusalem Temple and challenges him to fall so that he can fulfill the prophecy of being lifted up to safety by angels; only by standing still, however, is Christ rescued. His inaction is the confirmation that he "may now begin to save mankind." Christ represents the ideal (perhaps a fantasy) of action without agency.

The title character of *Samson Agonistes* learns the lesson of *Paradise Regained* only by first succumbing to the temptation that Christ resisted—second-guessing the redemptive narrative. In this regard *Samson Agonistes* is Milton's most overtly autobiographical statement in poetry, his most explicit and extensive exploration of the nature of vocation. There are numerous parallels between Samson and Milton's personal life, including his blindness, his first marriage, and his views on divorce recorded earlier in his four divorce tracts (1643–1645).

Samson Agonistes has especially conspicuous parallels with Milton's personal and political situation after the failure of the Puritan Commonwealth. The Philistine courtly reveling of lords and priests during the festival of the god Dagon reflects Milton's view of the Stuart court. The tragedy is set after Samson's betrayal by Dalila, when Samson's promise to deliver the Israelites from Philistine conquest appears to have failed, leaving Samson blind, in disgrace, a slave and prisoner of the Philistines. Harapha taunts Samson with the accusation that he is a usurper, "a Murderer, a Revolter, and a Robber", a "League-breaker"— terms that recall Stuart accusations of regicide against the rebels, including Milton himself.

Similarly, at the beginning of the drama at least, Samson deals with the same kind of situation that Milton had to after the collapse of the Commonwealth: he ponders the limits of conformity to civil power in order to survive in a society with whose norms he was fundamentally at odds, although by the drama's end (if not by Milton's) any such conformity will be insupportable. It is tempting to read the work as Milton's final, wrenching attempt to find a biblical narrative of political fall and spiritual regeneration with which to identify.

Like *Paradise Lost*, *Samson Agonistes* presents the problem of action as a problem of knowledge, particularly knowledge of how salvation will be achieved in the historical narrative of Israel and the personal narrative of Samson himself. The work opens with Samson defeated, a blind captive slave, meditating on the nature of what he thought was his calling to deliver Israel—an issue he painfully wrestles with as he encounters each of the work's characters who come to confront him, including his father Manoa, his betrayer Dalila, and his warrior counterpart Harapha. The question of vocation begins when Samson is baffled by his election as a Nazarite, "a person separate to God, / Designed for great exploits," assuring himself that when he fought the Philistines, he acted not out of delusion as a private individual in "Single rebellion," but on divine command.

Samson concedes he was wrong when he thought he understood "Divine Prediction," believing now—wrongly, it will turn out—that he has been severed from the providential plan. He cannot understand the divine narrative from within the narrative. The difficulty of reading that narrative is underscored when he has to explain why he married outside his tribe: he married his first wife, the woman of Timna, because of a divine command he felt from "From intimate impulse" to be the first step in his mission to deliver Israel. The divine plan, Samson is prophetically given to understand, is achieved by transgression of the Law. When the woman of Timna proved false, he anticipated "Divine Prediction" on his own by marrying a Philistine woman, Dalila, as a logical deduction from his first divinely ordained marriage.

The encounter with Dalila further probes salvific action within the context of the middle-class domestic relationship at the heart of the drama, as emphasized by Milton's most significant change in the biblical story—he makes Dalila Samson's wife. She insists she gave him up to the Philistines to protect him from "perilous enterprises," while she "at home sat full of cares and fears." Proposing to relieve him of all public vocation, Dalila now offers him "domestic ease." She further explains that by trapping him, she sacrificed her private happiness to the public good of her people. Completing the role reversal, Dalila finally flaunts her fame and honor as the woman who delivered *her* nation—she has become the renowned public actor, attempting to reduce Samson to a private person confined to the home. A theme largely ignored in *Paradise Regained*, right action is enmeshed with issues of sexual identity, in this case assigning epic action and fame to a woman.

However, Dalila's victory is vitiated by Samson's realization that liberty may be found in passive suffering rather than active performance. Similarly, Harapha, the Philistine hero who appears in the garb of a chivalric knight, rightly perceives Samson's contempt for all his "gorgeous arms" as a further disparagement of the epic ideal. Conventional epic action has been displaced onto both feminine and masculine representations of the ungodly: Samson now reaffirms his faith in the Hebrew God as sole source of his strength.

A messenger soon arrives to command Samson to entertain the Philistine lords as a stage fool or jester in Dagon's temple, described as a theater. He eventually agrees to go because he feels some dimly understood "rousing motions" that dispose him to believe he will perform some remarkable act this day. He becomes the Pauline wise fool, allowing himself to be led, degraded, by interior illumination to the Philistine temple. Indeed, a messenger relates that after he performed feats of strength, Samson was brought to rest between two pillars. There he inclined his head in prayer or contemplation, the messenger uncertainly reports, whereupon he brought the temple down upon the Philistines and himself. In the drama's final irony blindness and captivity turn out to be the very condition of Samson's redemptive act. Echoing Milton's defenses of his own blindness, the Chorus affirms that Samson acted "with inward eyes illuminated," in contrast to the Philistine's "blindness internal." In his ultimate regeneration Samson hangs ambiguously between being an actor in the full sense of the word and a passive vessel of divine action without human agency, like a Phoenix, which is "vigorous most / When most unactive."

The paradox is complicated by two contrasting readings the drama offers of itself. On the one hand, Samson's father proclaims that Samson has acted heroically as an epic figure who will inspire Israelite youth to comparable feats of redemptive action in a kind of prophecy—or fantasy—of the ultimate collapse of the Stuart Restoration. On the other hand, Samson's position with his head inclined, his hands outstretched between the pillars, bringing redemption through self-immolation, mirrors Christ on the Cross, only one of many prophetic parallels between Samson and Christ. The prefiguration of Christ reminds us that no earthly action can bring about full redemption, which can only come in the fullness of time with the Second Coming; Samson's redemption of the Israelites, after all, lasted only a generation.

In the spirit of these two perspectives on Samson's final action, the final words of *Samson Agonistes*, "all Passion spent," likewise reveal a double perspective: the phrase may refer to the completion of tragic action marked by catharsis, or, in contrast, it may refer to the incompleteness of Samson's action until indeed all passion is spent on the

Cross. *Samson Agonistes* may be Milton's final troubled contemplation of his youthful belief in his own action in the Civil War, a contemplation whose finality complicates the authority he once eagerly sought and once confidently felt he possessed.

Martin Elsky

Further Reading

Fish, Stanley Eugene. *Surprised by Sin: The Reader in Paradise Lost*. Berkeley: University of California Press, 1971.

Grossman, Marshall. *Authors to Themselves: Milton and the Revelation of History*. Cambridge: Cambridge University Press, 1987.

Hill, Christopher. *Milton and the English Revolution*. New York: Viking, 1978.

Kerrigan, William. *The Sacred Complex: On the Psychogenesis of Paradise Lost*. Cambridge: Harvard University Press, 1983.

Nyquist, Mary, and Margaret W. Ferguson, eds. *Re-Membering Milton: Essays on the Texts and Traditions*. New York: Methuen, 1988.

Parker, William Riley. *Milton: A Biography*. 2 vols. Oxford: Clarendon, 1988.

Radzinowicz, Mary Ann. *Toward Samson Agonistes: The Growth of Milton's Mind*. Princeton: Princeton University Press, 1978.

Riggs, William G. *The Christian Poet in Paradise Lost*. Berkeley: University of California Press, 1979.

Tayler, E. W. *Milton's Poetry: Its Development in Time*. Pittsburgh: Duquesne University Press, 1979.

Wittreich, Joseph Anthony. *Feminist Milton*. Ithaca, N.Y.: Cornell University Press, 1987.

Dryden and Pope

HE most original poetry written after Milton and before Blake was the work of John Dryden (1631–1700) and Alexander Pope (1688–1744). In the vigor of their engagement with the public life of their age—the intellectual, political, religious, and literary controversies in which the culture of the Enlightenment was revealing and creating itself—Dryden and Pope articulated the modern sound of that culture; and in the almost ninety years spanned by their two careers, theirs were the voices in which others either found or lost their own.

Their modern sound is a complex creation; its local features include, as in this couplet from Pope's *The Rape of the Lock*, a colloquial ease that we might associate with urban savvy:

> *Snuff*, or the *Fan*, supply each Pause of Chat,
> With singing, laughing, ogling, and all that.

But urban savvy can be sounded in many registers:

> Echoes from *Pissing-Alley*, *Sh*[adwell] call,
> And *Sh*[adwell] they resound from *A*[ston] Hall.
> About thy boat the little Fishes throng,
> As at the Morning Toast [i.e., excrement]
>   that Floats along.

These lines from *MacFlecknoe*, both obscene and polite, could be uttered only by one entirely intimate with the city, yet their urbanity also declares a plain disapproval of the urban, a disapproval rooted in realms of imagined experience utterly beyond the bounds of the squalor Dryden's poem fantasizes, exposes, revels in, and mocks. Certainly one aspect of the modernity of such writing is its very disdain for a present moment whose chief recommendation is only the energy by which it generates its filth.

The colloquial ease is a local sign of what we more generally recognize as the major characteristic of Dryden's and Pope's verse—its sociability. This is something more than their occasional celebrations of "the feast of reason and the flow of soul," something of wider import obvious in the eagerness of their interest in the secular record of human accomplishment and human failure—in politics, in church government, in business, in the arts. It can be an aggressive interest, often tied to a readiness for controversy, and therefore the sociability revealed in Dryden's and Pope's writing is never merely amiable and is very often harsh. It everywhere reflects the worldliness of an age tagged by its chief wits as "knowing and judicious," a phrase sometimes intended as praise, sometimes as sneering. It is the tag that marks the sophistication of the Enlightenment—its growing awareness that what has happened before on earth was merely human history, that what is to come is also to be constructed only by human minds and hands, and that what happens above the planet—other than physical motion—is unknowable, although not yet to be dismissed as a matter of concern.

This secular savvy is immediately apparent to us in the amused and conversational ease with which Pope begins his *Epistle to Burlington*, a poem on how to use your money well, a poem he thinks of as a "moral essay":

> 'Tis strange the Miser should his Cares employ
> To gain those Riches he can ne'er enjoy.

But Pope cannot end the poem without directing a long moment of withering abuse at one whose bad taste in landscaping and interior decoration and kitchen staff would exclude him not only from good society, but might also keep him from heaven—that is, if there were sufficient authority in the poet's curse upon his bad company:

> Treated, caress'd, and tir'd, I take my leave,
> Sick of his civil Pride from Morn to Eve,
> I curse such lavish Cost, and little Skill,
> And swear, no Day was ever past so ill.

Here social and aesthetic judgments are supported by suggestions of religious ones: not only the poet's cursing and swearing, but also his pain and discomfort, declare the ideal proximity of his host's residence to Hell itself. Pope supports this declaration by echoing a reminder of the fall of Milton's Mulciber, the architect of Hell's palace in *Paradise Lost*. As Milton had put it, "from morn / To noon he fell, from noon to dewy eve, / A summer's day." And, indeed, if Milton's Satan was damned for the pride that set him against God, so Pope's Timon is damned for the civil version of that deadly sin. That Pope should want us to hear this sudden resonance of his "moral essay" with Milton's Christian epic tells us that, as between the civil and the deadly sin, even a secular age sometimes found less difference than we might have supposed.

Moreover, if we had any doubt that the good taste, the sociability, and the modernity of the Enlightenment could sometimes find accord with its religious past, we might consider what Timon's library, in its own gesture of mistaken sociability, excludes: "His *Study!* with what Authors is it stor'd? / In Books, not Authors, curious is my Lord . . . / For *Locke* or *Milton* 'tis in vain to look, / These shelves admit not any Modern book." Locke is the great philosopher of empiricism, Milton the great epic and prophetic poet—but Pope strikingly links them together as modern authors. Their union in Pope's line of verse (and presumably on the shelves of the libraries inside the fine houses to which Timon would receive no welcome) tells of the ideal accord some sought for between secular and religious habits of mind.

Perhaps the most profound sign of Dryden's and Pope's originality was in their invention and re-creation of imaginative structures in which that difficult accord could be attempted and scrutinized: the verse essay, the epistle, the imagined dialogue, the mock-heroic, the imitation, the sublime but still polite "great ode" (examples of which are Dryden's *Alexander's Feast*, his *Ode to the Pious Memory of Anne Killigrew*, and Pope's *Ode for St. Cecilia's Day*)—these were the forms in which they worked, along with others harder to classify, like the polemical, heroical, satirical, journalistic, and philosophical composition of Dryden's *Absalom and Achitophel*. But common to all these kinds of poems is the opportunity they open for the voice of a modern sensibility. This was a critical sensibility, alert to the discoveries and engaged with the controvertists of the time; it revealed itself in a voice that might approve of or excoriate them, but that still spoke conversably in the sophisticated idiom of the new intellectual world, and, at its most remarkable moments, spoke even with heroic and vatic accent.

Of the forms and devices of Dryden's and Pope's poetry, the heroic couplet is the most characteristic. Virtually everything they wrote, they wrote in couplets—including in Dryden's case, many plays. The versatility of their handling of this instrument revealed in it a capacity for suppleness hardly to be guessed at from the apparent rigidities of the form itself. These are not merely a matter of the inevitable rhyme—although it is important to note that in their practice, Dryden and Pope for the most part emphasize the rhymes and insist upon strong pauses at the line's end. At their best, they do so without loss of fluid movement and without blunting dramatic and discursive energy.

Of all the devices that distinguish poetry from discursive writing, likeness of sound has perhaps the least to do with thought itself; yet as Dryden and Pope manage it, the rhyming couplet will emphasize grammar and syntax, and through grammar and syntax it will suggest the operations of thought. It is a fine instrument for displaying discrimination, as Dryden does here in assessing his Achitophel: "Yet, Fame deserv'd, no Enemy can grudge; / The Statesman we abhor, but praise the Judge." It works brilliantly in defining the paradoxes of human character; again, Dryden's Zimri: "So over Violent, or over Civil, / That every man, with him, was God or Devil." And for the elegant brutality of realistic assessment, the couplet is unsurpassed:

See how the World its Veterans rewards!
A Youth of Frolicks, an old Age of Cards,
Fair to no purpose, artful to no end,
Young without Lovers, old without a Friend,
A Fop their Passion, but their Prize a Sot,
Alive, ridiculous, and dead, forgot!

The preceding passage, taken from Pope's *Epistle to a Lady* (once again, a poem he thought of as a "moral essay"), describes the behavior of middle-aged unmarried women, and explains how they came to their condition. What is striking in this satire of social and moral failure is the almost entire absence of figurative language—of image, of metaphor, of simile. Submerged in "Veteran" is a metaphor, perhaps, suggesting combat as well as age, and this suggestion tells us something about the "World" within which these women move—the social existence that, when vitiated, is a warfare upon earth, dealing out rewards and punishment with relentless attention to what Freud would call the reality principle. Yet that reality principle is itself contemplated within this passage not through image or metaphor, but entirely through the medium of grammar, of syntax.

Here syntactical parallels and oppositions have obviously discursive force, from which they develop their emotional energy and moral point. We are forced to think of "Passion" in terms of its consequent "Prize," this moral-logical parallelism encompasses the similar set that links "Fop" and "Sot." In these "cause and effect" parallels drawn between youth and age, between frolic and cards, between behavior meriting ridicule and the living body overwhelmed in oblivion, the unforgiving logic of social and moral ruin is revealed.

The strong force of the recognitions emerging from these parallels is certainly an effect of poetry, but the poetry here is virtually devoid of characteristics we might call "poetic." Now this spareness, this pretense that grammar and syntax outlined by rhyme can do the work of image and metaphor, is itself a gesture of the poet's in the direction of the critical preferences and habits of the Enlightenment. In the major philosophical documents of the time—certainly in Hobbes's and in Locke's—how language constructs (and threatens) meaning is a central topic. Almost always associated with this inquiry, we find a disdain for the abuses of jargonish, imprecise, and fanciful writing. To be modern is to prefer *things* over *words*, to scorn the professional and "gothick" jargon of the scholastic philosophers, and to excoriate the eloquence of the rhetoricians and the poets—"this vicious abundance of *Phrase*, this trick of *Metaphor*, this volubility of *Tongue*, which makes so great a noise in the World . . . this beautiful deceipt," as Thomas Sprat puts it in his *History of the Royal Society*.

Fully imagined and eloquently expressed writing was understood to be the product of what the philosophers called "wit" (and what the Romantic poets and theorists came to call "imagination"), but the spare writing that was true to thought, was made by the faculty of "judgment." For the critical philosopher of language, wit joined the unjoinable and made metaphors—unicorns; judgment analyzed and took apart these lovely but cognitively useless constructions—giving us back goats and horses.

To write poetry in a modern way, then, was to declare oneself not entirely uncomfortable with the philosopher's suspicion of sound and of wit; and it was to set oneself the task of making sounds the critical intelligence could comfortably hear, discovering the illusions by which poetry could pretend to be discourse—and still be poetry. To succeed at this task was not quite trickery—or if it was, it was the trickery in which the poet and his work became sociable to their age. A large element in the original genius of both Dryden and Pope was precisely their invention of this modern, this sociable, this discursive, and still, this *imaginative* voice. For wit in all its energy pervades their writing. In the very passages surrounding that explosion of grammar narrating the doomed transformation of society girls into solitary women, Pope says what he wants to say in powerfully figurative language of the most obvious kind; in fact, it is the figurative language that prepares us for the discursive. Here are the lines that just precede the passage cited above:

> As Hags hold *Sabbaths*, less for joy than spight,
> So these, their merry, miserable Night;
> Still round and round the Ghosts of Beauty glide,
> And haunt the Places where their Honour died.

These doomed women may be the object of discursive admonitions, but they are also, subtly, the stuff of poetry and imagination, and in this ambiguity the figurative language suggests unexpected sympathies with the victims of the discourse.

Writing as a moralist, Pope may assert a link between the idea of the witch and the idea of the old maid, the idea of the witches' sabbath and the idea of the society ball—but at the same time, and in metaphor of unusual complexity, he is entirely true to the distinction between the ugliness of the hag and the gliding loveliness of the "the ghosts of beauty." That the "ghosts of beauty" are still alive, that simply to be present in society in their situation is to haunt it—these notions drive the metaphor toward a complexity of feeling and thought no less than what we might find in moments of great intensity in Shakespeare or Donne.

This play of wit against discourse within the heroic couplet is more generally evident in the decisions Dryden and Pope made about the larger forms they would work in. Most notably, under the cover of the satirical sophistication of the mock-heroic poem—and within the feigned conversational judiciousness of the verse satire and epistle—they were able to acknowledge the urbane modernity of Enlightenment culture, and in behalf of that modernity, to debunk the grand myth-making, the extended narratives, the heroic posturing of the great epic poem.

But the great epic poem—its classical models and even more awe-somely, Milton's almost contemporary achievement in *Paradise Lost*—was for Dryden and Pope, as it was for the age in general, still an object of veneration, the sign of the powers of the imagination working in their highest union with the powers of the judgment. So that as Dryden and Pope deploy the urbane ironies of the mock-heroic, the epistle, and the satire, their joking does not quite undo the mythic, the grand, and the heroic; nor, conversely, do they simply diminish the urbane and skeptical with reference to the earlier and larger world of the imaginative and mythmaking mind. Instead, in the new urbanity of their making, the heroic world of the mind is itself reclaimed for the modern age, in a modern form. It is, perhaps, a ghostly and oblique presence in its modern and ironic version. But as such it gives structure to the world of modern experience, it makes it observable, it makes it intelligible, and it opens it to evaluation.

Indeed, the newer versions of heroic style imagined and invented by Dryden and Pope and made conformable by them to the authentic tastes of a knowing and judicious age are emblems for poetry itself in such an age. In it the presence of the heroic and the poetic may be likened to the presence of the sylphs in *The Rape of the Lock*. These sylphs are the small gods ruling over the beau monde, whose gorgeous and shallow lives it is in part the poem's discursive task to laugh at. Just about as much of the divine as the world of fashion can contain, the sylphs are, of course, precisely Nothing. And yet, were it not for them, nothing at all of pleasure and delight could be seen, felt, or tasted.

> Loose to the Wind their airy Garment flew,
> Thin, glitt'ring Textures of the filmy Dew;
> Dipt in the richest Tincture of the Skies,
> Where Light disports in ever-mingling Dies,
> While ev'ry Beam new transient Colours flings,
> Colours that change whene'er they wave their Wings.

These etherial, these entirely insubstantial, entirely fictive beings, are yet the agents of the senses: around the outlines of their transparent forms, the light gathers and is shaped, and by the waving of their wings, colors are made visible, mingled, incessantly transformed, and the sky comes alive in disport.

But if we owe to these airy sylphs whatever it is we come to see of our familiar world in its most charmed moments, it is also true that the poet's irony saves us from the embarrassment of abandoning ourselves to belief in them. The sylphs delight us precisely because other components of the poetry allow us to limit our commitment to them. Those other components include irony, tonal variety, allusion, argument, conversation, topicality—all that would make its initial appeal to our education, our intelligence, and our knowledge of the world.

Samuel Johnson praised Dryden for inventing a language by which "we were taught . . . to think naturally and speak forcibly." If this means that in Dryden's language discourse and imagination are embodied in each other, then Johnson's praise describes the great satirical poems of Dryden's later career—*Absalom and Achitophel, The Medal, MacFlecknoe, Religio Laici, The Hind and the Panther.* Dryden was almost fifty when he wrote the earliest of these, and had for many years been primarily at work writing and producing plays which enjoyed considerable contemporary favor but which have had no life in the English theater since.

Yet the continuities between the stages of Dryden's career are real ones: his interest in contemporary philosophical controversy and scientific discovery, his engagement in political argument both theoretical and polemical, his corresponding interest in religious dispute, again both theological and polemical—these characteristic concerns are evident in the early poems celebrating the Restoration of Charles II and proposing a heroic version of England's new commercial and military enterprises; they are evident again in the heroic plays, which stage and debate the conflicts generated by vainglorious beings asserting the absolute freedom of their political and erotic wills. And they are evident finally in their most stylish and complex articulation in the great satires and discursive poems of Dryden's later career, poems in which he responded to the political crises that threatened the restored monarchy and generated constitutional debate of the first importance.

To a twentieth-century reader, perhaps the least familiar of the attitudes embodied in Dryden's work is his celebration of monarchical and aristocratic institutions against the challenges to those institutions inherent in the secularizing and commercializing tendencies of Enlightenment culture. Dryden's defense of the monarchy in the so-called Exclusion Crisis of the early 1680s gives us *Absalom and Achitophel,* a poem whose modernity is obvious in its attention to character and psychology, in its journalistic contemporaneity, in the high informality of its familiar address. Yet this claim for its stylistic modernity must be made in the face of Dryden's endorsement of the old-fashioned political theory of Sir Robert Filmer, who discovered the origins of political legitimacy in the transactions binding the fallen Adam to his unfortunate posterity. It is interesting that John Locke began to think through his arguments for an entirely secular basis for political legitimacy at about the time Dryden was defending the monarchy in traditional, and partly mystic, ways.

In fact, the clash of modern voice and traditional attitudes is apparent in all Dryden wrote. Early poems, like "To my honor'd friend, Dr. Charlton," "Astraea Redux," and "Annus Mirabilis," are marked by a genuine interest in contemporary scientific discovery, a sense that the work of men like Boyle and Gilbert and Harvey was worthy of celebration and could come to be part of the matter and the language of poetry. Indeed, there is a celebratory punctiliousness in Dryden's introduction of apparently scientific terminology from time to time into his verse—and even a few footnotes to explain the new language, as in "Annus Mirabilis." But at the same time as he gestures in this way towards the modern moment, he can reveal his fondness for magical and mysterious assertion.

This is particularly obvious when he writes about the restoration to England's throne of Charles Stuart. This event Dryden could never think about in simply naturalistic terms, though he certainly understood the character of that kind of thinking. His political poetry becomes, therefore, problematical—and very interesting—in its insistence that the monarchy is not to be entirely understood by the habits of mind either political or physical science requires, that the links between the king's doings and the actual world may sometimes be magical ones, and that they can be told about in the ways that myths are told.

It is not surprising, then, that Dryden's critics have often focused on the character of his skepticism, and have sought to understand whether or how he succeeded in resolving his skeptical inclinations with his mind's other essential characteristic, its preference for traditional forms of political and religious authority. In fact, Dryden's poetry is shaped at its very core by the dualities of his mind, and the strength of his writing is rooted precisely in his refusal to resolve intellectual and imaginative contradictions whose terms appealed to him with equal and opposing force. In this refusal his poems invite the contemplative attention of the reader and offer, as poetry, opportunities for a free-mindedness not to be anticipated in the initial, and very real, polemical intentions of the writer. Perhaps it is the surprising presence of the contemplative opportunity within the polemical occasion that is the distinguishing mark of Dryden's most original and imaginative writing.

In substance and intention Dryden's greatest poems are certainly warring documents, commissioned players on the king's side in the controversies of Restoration politics, informed by the terms of those controversies, and rhetorically shaped to the king's needs. The intricacies of argument and tone in the poems give evidence of the intricacies of Restoration politics, a few highlights of which may be schematized as follows. Within a contentious, postrevolutionary environment in which Englishmen understood their religious and political interests to be indistinguishable, a nominally Protestant but privately Catholic Stuart monarch, Charles II, had been restored to England's throne in 1660 on the invitation of a firmly Protestant Parliament. This Parliament had ten years earlier beheaded the restored king's father but had then been unable to sustain its experiment in republican government; Parliament's welcome to the new king was therefore much tempered by the sense of its own constitutional legitimacy as a sovereign arm of the English government. The new king, whose sexual generosity perhaps matched his political sophistication—or cynicism—had fathered some children but no legitimate ones, and so a succession crisis was inevitable; what the king *did* have was a brother—a brother perhaps less cynical, but also less politically intelligent and certainly less willing to keep his Catholicism private. This brother would become the next king—much to the displeasure of the Protestant Parliament, some elements of which would, in the so-called Exclusion Crisis, unsuccessfully resist his claim to the throne.

The Parliament, always unhappy about the Catholic private preferences of Charles, would become downright hostile to the Catholic outspokenness of his brother James and would finally oust him in 1688. More, into this brewpot we also introduce continuous and raucous conflict among the English Protestant sects themselves, most of them radically in opposition to the episcopal establishment restored and empowered by Parliament and king; add also a pervasive fear among Englishmen of Catholic plotting against "internal security"; add McCarthy-like mountebanks inflaming those fears; add, quite possibly, some actual Catholic international intrigue lending some credibility to these mountebanks.

These were some of the controversies out of which Restoration politics were formed. Now, if Dryden's verse contributions to them were entirely the polemical documents their first appearance indicates them to be, they might adequately be summarized as supporting the king's political position—*Absalom and Achitophel*, for example, propagandizes for the king and against the cabal seeking to exclude his brother. And Dryden's support for the king in this Exclusion Crisis was entirely consistent with his support—in *Religio Laici*—for the king's leniency toward the dissenting Protestant sects, a leniency displeasing to the king's harsher Anglican supporters in Parliament during the Exclusion crisis, as Steven Zwicker has shown. But leniency towards these sects in both *Absalom* and *Religio Laici* was not inconsistent with distaste for them, and Dryden's support for the king's politics conforms with his favoring an aristocratic ethos over what he imagines to be the new way of the Puritan, the revolutionary, the inner-light Protestant individualist, the businessman, the parliament man.

We see Dryden's aristocratic preferences in his approving portrait of the sexually vigorous, cavalier-like David/Charles in *Absalom and Achitophel*, in the corresponding disdain for the sexually monstrous Shaftesbury/Achitophel, and the pinched commercial puritanism of Shaftesbury's henchmen—we think of Shimei, his "cool kitchen" and his "hot brains." And we see this preference also in the outright social contempt Dryden expresses in *Religio Laici* for the "mechanick" classes and their inner-light protestant individualism: "The Book thus put in every vulgar hand, / Which each presum'd he best cou'd understand, / The *Common Rule* was made the *common* Prey; / And at the mercy of the *Rabble* lay." And in perhaps the most subtle moment in all of Dryden's polemical writing, the opening to *Absalom and Achitophel*, with its suave and outrageous defense of the king's promiscuity—outrageous precisely because it wittily asserts a biblical legitimacy for the libertine behavior condemned by Charles' Puritan antagonists—this opening to *Absalom* in its sophisticated irony, its humor both reverential and irreverent, in its flaunting the king's very vulnerability as his prime strength, is Dryden's most characteristic expression of favor for an aristocratic ethos.

Indeed, John Traugott has pointed out the high libertine humor of Charles/David's resemblance to the rake of Restoration comedy ("The Rake's Progress from Court to Comedy: a Study in Comic Form," *Studies in English Literature*, 1967). Ripe with a sense of royal and aristocratic entitlement, the lines describe a patriarchal fantasy simultaneously Edenic, erotic, political—and entirely sanctioned by the highest of authorities:

In pious times, e'er Priest-craft did begin,
Before *Polygamy* was made a sin;
When man, on many, multiply'd his kind,
E'r one to one was, cursedly, confin'd:
When Nature prompted, and no law deny'd
Promiscuous use of Concubine and Bride;
When, *Israel's* Monarch, after Heaven's own heart,
His vigorous warmth did, variously, impart
To Wives and Slaves: And, wide as his Command,
Scatter'd his Maker's Image through the Land.

But, of course, Dryden's great poems are not only polemical documents. Their engagement in controversy is vigorous indeed, but they display a linguistic complexity taking them well beyond their plain argumentative intention. In their tonal variety alone, ranging as they do among the discursive, the conversational, the ironic, the vituperative, the elegiac and the lyrical, they display a range of attitudes far richer than the service of a political passion requires. For, in fact, in their linguistic richness, Dryden's political and religious satires participate in the central activity of the Enlightenment, the contemplative and critical examination of all claims of all authority.

Nor is this critical activity an effect merely of some "intellectual spirit"; it is impossible to disentangle that critical spirit from the extraordinary events of the age. In the civil wars, in the regicide, in the republican interlude, even in the fact of the "restoration," events themselves enforced challenges to all the old notions about the supernatural sanctioning of political and religious institutions, events alone would stimulate in the thoughtful and the imaginative nervous intimations of the contingency of our institutions, political and religious—intimations of their origins in human desires and deeds within a history that did not answer to the great idea announced in the shaping words of a divinity. Dryden's most interesting writing shadows forth this recognition even as it mounts a conservative defense of the king and his lords and the Church. Doing so, his polemic becomes his poetry.

Absalom and Achitophel, for example, despite its easy and aristocratic dismissal of the king's Puritan enemies, despite the ironic ease of its opening joke, and despite its invocation of the biblical text itself in sup-

port of the legitimacy of the succession of James—*Absalom* itself is alert
to all that is problematic in the very notion of political legitimacy, and
its alertness complicates the poem's polemical intention. Its polemical
position is based on the notion that divine sanction is the source of
"right"; all opposition to sanctioned authority is therefore easily
mythologized as a version of Satan's original rebellion against the highest of authorities—hence the resonances of Milton's *Paradise Lost* that
Dryden archly admits into his poem. But nowhere in Dryden's poem do
its biblical and mythic resonances infuse its narrative as they infuse Milton's; biblical allusion functions merely to make of the poem a kind of
roman à clef, a witty guide to the main players in the Exclusion Crisis,
not authentic evidence of the intersection of eternity and time, of the
sacred and the historical.

Indeed, the Exclusion Crisis spawned a host of polemical narratives
based upon the irresistibly scandalous resemblance of the sexual careers
of God's David and England's Charles, and you could make use of the
analogy whether you were for or against the king. This polemical flexibility of the Bible story would of course tend to undermine its authority as a guide to God's sanctioning will, as Michael McKeon implies in
an important discussion ("Historicizing *Absalom and Achitophel*," in *The
New Eighteenth Century*, 1987). This is why it is possible to see in Dryden's use of the sacred mythology in *Absalom and Achitophel* more than
a suggestion of a keen, libertine wit. We immediately turn our attention
to the secular components of the poem, and these finally consume our
interest: the portrayal of character; the willing consideration of prudential as well as providential styles of argument in support of the king's
right; the conflicting portraits of the king, vigorous and weary, merciful
and ruthless; the strangely elegiac presentation of the king's aristocratic supporters, which seems to acknowledge the unrestored losses many
of them incurred in their loyalty throughout the Interregnum.

Certainly Dryden prefers the older alternatives: the organic polity
whose king and lords and commons are bound to each other in ties as
old and authoritative as those binding Adam's issue to the consequences
of Adam's sin. But the poem's imaginative life is in its oblique representation of those preferences. We notice how the confident wit of the
poem's opening is alert to the idea that man in history and not God in
heaven declares and defines what is then taken to be sacred ethics: is not
polygamy *made* a sin at some point in time, that point at which priest-
craft begins? And priestcraft, plainly, is *begun*—we would now say "con-

structed"—here on earth. After all, what priests here construed to be sinful in David's lust was precisely what earlier warmed the very heart of Heaven. With good reason Ruth Salvaggio (in her *Dryden's Dualities*) has seen in these witty lines an inspired doubletalk.

To be sure, at the end of his poem Dryden has his sovereign assert his authority with a magically victorious raising of his arm, as if the royal gesture were itself a political act. As he threatens to unleash "the fury of a patient man," Charles/David raises his arm, the insurrection ends, the Almighty nods in consent, thunder rolls, a new series of Time begins, and "willing Nations [know] their Lawfull Lord." But, of course, Charles prevailed by power and policy, not by magic; the raising of the arm that ends the poem is only his entirely legal proroguing of Parliament in 1682, and the "Series of New Time" it initiated was abruptly curtailed six years later when James II fled for France to engender a line of "pretenders" to the throne.

Dryden's penchant for the magical and mythological certification of his political preferences, the deep connection between those modes of imagining and his conservative preference for king and cavalier—these are obvious. But accompanying these habits, subjecting them to a contemplative irony, enriching them into thought, are the brave invitations to free speculation that Dryden issues to his ideal audience. For the most part, this audience does not yet wear its old devotions merely as the masks that cover smiles of contempt (as Gibbon quipped about the philosophical sophisticates of the late Republic), but among Dryden's readers were those who possessed the libertine awareness that a set of masks might be all we have to defend, and that in their defense we discover, construct, and scrutinize our beings. Dryden is not uninterested in pleasing such readers.

Dryden gave to his other great poem on political and religious controversy the title *Religio Laici*—an adequate translation of which, in the light of what the poem actually does, would be "the character of a pious Christian, born into the Anglican communion, educated in classical philosophy, grounded in Christian theology and in Church history, alert to and free-minded about contemporary theological controversy, but holding decided opinions on the political implications of one's religious choices." All readers of this poem notice its extraordinary tonal sweep, its corresponding range of feeling, and the continuo of reasoning upon which its rhetorical and affective structure is founded.

The poem's opening reveals the profound piety of its author, evident in his hymnlike consideration of reason's limitations against revelation's power. But his is no "inner-light" fanaticism, dismissing reason's claims; instead, in language of exquisite logical and figural precision, he demonstrates what Martin Price in *To the Palace of Wisdom* has called "the precarious but valuable function of reason."

> Dim, as the borrow'd beams of Moon and Stars
> To *lonely*, *weary*, wandring *Travellers*,
> Is *Reason* to the *Soul*: And as on high,
> Those rowling Fires *discover* but the Sky
> Not light us *here*, So *Reason*'s glimmering Ray
> Was lent, not to *assure* our *doubtfull* way,
> But *guide* us upward to a *better Day*.
> And as those nightly Tapers disappear
> When Day's bright Lord ascends our Hemisphere;
> So pale grows *Reason* at *Religions* sight;
> So *dyes*, and so *dissolves* in *Supernatural Light*.

To say that the starlight of Reason is extinguished by the daylight of Revelation was a common way of speech in Dryden's day but the idea is deliberated here in such poised argument, its poetry structured by such careful sequencing of the most ordinary of logical pointers—"And as," "so," "not to," "but to," "And as," "so," "so," "so"—that the common trope astonishes both with its discursive aptness and what seems to be its original visual force. And yet, if the reasonableness of Dryden's lay speaker is as obvious as his eloquence (so that we can imagine Locke, the empiricist, at ease with his conversation), we still cannot miss this speaker's readiness for religious and political brawling.

Recall his social contempt for those "horny fists" he saw mauling the pages of the sacred texts, and listen to the bite of the poem's close. Defending his choice of a "plain style" for his poem, he notes that "while from *Sacred Truth* I do not swerve, / *Tom Sternhold*'s or *Tom Shadwell*'s *Rhimes* will serve." This swipe at Sternhold's popular versions of the Psalms and at Shadwell's bad plays obviously contrasts with the dignified piety of the poem's opening and reminds us that in Dryden's day one's religious experience can never be dissociated from one's social being, that engaging in controversy is inevitable and responsible, and that controversy properly calls upon one's passions and preferences as well as one's reason and piety.

The poem inquires into the implications of the biblical criticism of the great French Catholic scholar Father Simon, who showed that the sacred texts themselves are imperfect "editions." What, for example, might this mean for the Protestant insistence upon one's private encounter with the biblical text? Does it, indeed, strengthen the Catholic insistence upon the authority of "traditions" and upon the pope's infallibility? And can the Anglican Church have anything useful to say to Simon's challenge, given its own project of being both Protestant and institutionally authoritative—if not infallible? Dryden's answers to these questions are not easy to pin down, but what emerges finally in the poetry is a portrait of the man asking them—an intellectual and social being, both adroit and engaged; cosmopolitan but rooted in his own culture; in framing his opinions, independent of Church and State, but counting it important to seek accord with their institutions.

The urbane voice in which these contraries are apparently resolved is, perhaps, itself the grand fantasy of the poem, its central poetic creation. But, after all, the resolutions are only apparent ones, and the speaker settles the central issues only by dismissing them—by saying that he speaks for himself, but also submits to his Mother Church; that the Bible itself is clear enough on all important matters; that you don't even need to be able read it in order to be saved ("Th'unletter'd *Christian* who believes in *gross* / Plods on to Heaven; and ne'er is at a loss"), and that those few who want a more precise guide to its meanings are essentially engaged in nothing more than literary criticism.

Were *Religio Laici* entirely the discursive inquiry it pretends to be, these concessions would seem to undermine the poem's whole project. But, in fact, they are the poem's major statement. For they say that between religion's heavenly and its earthly manifestations, there is a great divide; that claims to authority are very difficult to authenticate; and that even very high authorities, like the patristic writer, and later saint, Athanasius—whom Dryden, in rejecting his insistence upon the damnation of even virtuous heathens, historicizes as Arius's overzealous antagonist and personalizes as "th'Egyptian bishop," "the good, old Man"—were also particular people, inhabiting particular places at particular times, working out their ideas in relation to particular tasks and particular situations. Dryden's life gives no clearer evidence of this understanding than in his own conversion in 1685 to Roman Catholicism upon the accession to the throne of the unfortunate—and Catholic—King James II.

In his *Epistle to Doctor Arbuthnot* Alexander Pope honors Dryden, reminds us that two generations separate them, and in a telling parenthesis, still establishes a link with his great predecessor:

> But why then publish? *Granville* the polite,
> And knowing *Walsh*, would tell me I could write;
> Well-natur'd *Garth* inflam'd with early praise,
> And *Congreve* lov'd, and *Swift* endur'd my Lays;
> The Courtly *Talbot*, *Somers*, *Sheffield* read,
> Ev'n mitred *Rochester* would nod the head,
> And *St. John's* self (great *Dryden's* friends before)
> With open arms receiv'd one Poet more.

As he reveals his link to Dryden to be somehow constituted in their friendships (he himself was twelve years old at Dryden's death, and it is only in legend that the two were said to have met), Pope seems to envision the literary life as an ideal unity of society and mind. But we are struck also by a harshness that accompanies this vision of the sociable imagination: "Why then publish?" is the exasperated question Pope puts to his own career, nor is it a question he comes to answer in *Arbuthnot* in terms that accord with the high positives implied in the poem's vision of the literary life as conducted within his circle of good readers, good writers and good friends. *They* ought to have been audience enough, Pope says, for certainly their approval and their love embody the discrimination and the generosity that, as Pope would have it, privilege the life of the imagination.

In fact, Pope's own career becomes a central topic of the great satirical poems of his last decade and a half; in them, attack directed outward and scrutiny of himself are joined together to clarify and vindicate his career's deviations from the path suggested by these grand fantasies of humanism. In dramatizing, in the satires, epistles, "moral essays"— and in the ongoing project of *The Dunciad*—why he publishes, Pope will show us a literary life that is a warfare upon earth, a devotion to satire not in easy accord with the geniality of mind he professes to admire, and finally a reinvention of satire and sociability in which the meanest of the traditional genres attains the grandeur of epic, and the most pleasant of the virtues reveals the power of the heroic.

The remarkable achievement of Pope's later career was to write poems which fused the positive energies of the old epic, the anger of satire, and the skepticism and subjectivity we expect in the writing of a "knowing and judicious age." The Roman poet Horace had emphasized his own disinclination for the epic and for the martial doings central to it. And certainly Pope's imitations of Horace, the important work of his later career, give us an excellent rendition of Horace's civilian voice. But Pope's Horatian poems are also his most original, personal, and agitated writing; in their own versions of high civility, Pope imitates but also measures his distance from Horace and, in a manner one could not have predicted, goes on to create a link between the heroic and the sociable in the career of the writer of satire.

In his most accomplished poems, Pope will cause us to imagine some version of himself undergoing some significant development in the very act of writing the poem at hand. Like Dryden, he focuses on public affairs, but in his engagement with them, it is his tendency to foreground the poet's person. What connection there is between the "real" Pope and his imagined, often theatrical, versions of himself is, of course, an important question, but not different from what we might ask about any autobiographer. It would not, however, be irresponsible to assert that Pope's ideal versions of himself make better use of craftiness, deviousness, and anger than did their fleshly counterpart, who, as Johnson quipped, could not drink tea without stratagem. Physically misshapen, usually in pain, almost never without a professional quarrel, devious in his literary dealings even with his friends, this "actual" Pope displayed himself in his poems as a being whose anger was a gift of the gods, whose writings were heroic acts, and whose passion itself could be a mode of civility. Although his poems, like all satire, are public writings deeply implicated in contemporary events, they are also major documents in the history of self-portrayal, not to say self-fashioning.

Pope aims his later satire at the modern, commercial society coming into being after the collapse of the Stuart monarchy. His targets might have been Dryden's: the Hanoverian kings invited to the throne by a Whig parliament; the financial machinery invented by a society intent on growing rich and powerful—a national bank, a national debt, stock and bond markets; the standing army financed by these instruments; the political style governing such a society—deal making, influence, bribery; and the larger consequences, as Pope saw them, of this political and commercial energy: a culture in shreds, a cheapened literary marketplace in which obscure beings hacked out a living by turning out "products" pleasing to a debased and newly rich readership, or by writing propaganda in support of an illiterate king and a corrupt ministry.

These writers and publishers, readers and politicians, scientists and hobbyists, are magnified in Pope's most exuberant and intense satire into the agents of cultural and moral collapse; they are the fabled "dunces"—the zanies who creep up from the enormous documenting apparatus below the text of *The Dunciad* to swarm and cavort within it as they join in the crazy carnival that Pope, with some solemnity and much hilarity, envisions as the end of the classical-Christian culture he took to be the foundation of his own imaginative and moral life. Taken together, the targets of Pope's satire constitute a caricature version of a modern society—energetic, vulgar, incoherent, and rich. And Pope's positives amount to an opposing caricature—a vision of a monarchical and aristocratic society, magically incorporating the organic order of a feudal paternalism, the sophisticated skepticism of the Enlightenment, the civic virtue of classical republicanism, and the material pleasures made available by capitalism.

Pope's satire is deeply implicated in the actual history of his own time, but Pope's reader should be aware that the world he shows us, like the image of his own being, is a powerfully imagined one, seen through anger, distorted, intense, and very exuberant. It constitutes the first great criticism we have of our modern culture, even as it participates fully in it. These comments apply particularly to Pope's later poems, which are related to the early ones as by a revisiting and a revision.

In the youthful *Windsor Forest* and *Essay on Criticism*, Pope fashions an almost entirely positive vision of the integration of imaginative mind, political virtue, and social pleasure. In *Windsor Forest* the imperial energies of Queen Anne's Tory England, represented as eager with health and restrained by virtue, are the objects of an astonishingly precocious but stylistically old-fashioned display of talent: in the poem's ornate and conventional mythologies wood nymphs give their names to England's honored geography, tutelary spirits rise from their riverbeds, grasp emblematic urns, utter positive prophecies.

Pope's *Essay on Criticism*, ostensibly a treatise on literary theory published when Pope was not yet twenty-three, is actually an elegant celebration of literary culture, a positive vision of imaginative mind generously integrated with social being, of the individual talent growing into its tradition, of reader joined with text, of critic with poet, of artistry with nature, of part with whole, of society with cosmos. Articulated in the modern idiom of the Enlightenment, these ideas link Pope's poem to some central notions of the humanist Renaissance.

And these are the ideas that are tested even as they guide the impassioned satiric poems of Pope's later career. Between them and the early writings was the decade and more that he devoted to his translations from Homer. From these translations Pope grew rich, in part because the same literary marketplace he lashes in *The Dunciad* and elsewhere was composed of publishers and readers eager for his work. It may be that his project to deliver Homer in a manner pleasing to a modern age helped to form the wonderful blend of the heroic and the civil that we hear in the voice of the Horatian poems to come.

More certain is it that the voice of those imitations of Horace is a grand and original artifact, made in Pope's supple manipulation of the couplet to accommodate an astonishing range of tonalities, and in his crafting, from its discrete and epigrammatic mechanism, of whole verse paragraphs coherent as larger units of sound, thought, and feeling. In managing the transitions from verse paragraph to verse paragraph, Pope develops the line of feeling, the emotional curve that unifies his "epistle" or "satire." Certainly one way to read his later poetry is to ask how the sounds of speech at the poem's end developed from those it began with—to ask this question with the sense that its answer is one of the poem's meanings.

And finally, Pope's art in his later poems reveals his capacity to naturalize the conventional mythology and generic apparatus he inherits from Homer and Virgil. He does not reject this rhetoric, but he submerges it, all in order to bring it to the surface again in versions appropriate to the epistle, the verse essay, the satire—the literary kinds constituting authentic matter for Pope's urbane readers. But in making the old rhetoric of genre and myth familiar in modern terms, Pope does not lessen his demands upon his imagination, he intensifies them.

In the fantasy "bits" of the first of his two moral essays on the use of riches, as an instance, a visionary hilarity is produced precisely by Pope's witty superimposition of the dress and manners and financial instruments of his modern moment upon the ways of older and simpler times. Here, for example, is how the art of bribery has been improved by the invention of the money markets:

Blest paper-credit! last and best supply!
That lends Corruption lighter wings to fly!
. . . .
A single leaf shall waft an Army o'er,
Or ship off Senates to a distant Shore;
A leaf, like Sibyl's, scatter to and fro
Our fates and fortunes, as the winds shall blow. . . .

A witty collision of old myths and modern ways produces this grand and jocular fantasy attributing magical power of enormous and corrupting consequence to the stealthiness and abundance of paper money. Bills of credit are the sibyl's leaves of capitalism, and if their end result is disaster, Pope's exuberant fantasizing nevertheless reveals his understanding of the imaginative intensity that capitalism answers to, as, in a moment of great poetic interest, he colors its financial instruments with the charm of old fables even as he tells a tale of modern ruin. Such imaginative play is a sign of the entirely positive use Pope makes of his "belatedness."

These naturalizing tendencies are most interestingly apparent in *Moral Essay 4*—also known as the *Epistle to Burlington*. Here, without any of the shepherds and nymphs and singing contests and mythological narrative that marked the earlier *Pastorals* and *Windsor Forest*, the essential work of pastoral and georgic is incorporated within the conversational manner of a letter. In that manner Pope articulates an ideal vision of pleasure reconciled with work, of nature commanding (as in pastoral) reconciled with nature commanded (as in georgic), all accomplished in the imagined projects of a busy and virtuous nation. I have shown in *Nature and Society* that as the conventions and mechanisms of pastoral and georgic are here submerged and then brought forth in versions suitable to conversation, they are the more strongly realized as shaping myth.

Notice in these lines how the reference to a "laughing Ceres" envisions as an historical, not a magical, process the conversion of the inauthentic ostentation of bad ownership into the projects of pleasured profit.

Another age shall see the golden Ear
Imbrown the Slope, and nod on the Parterre,
Deep Harvests bury all his pride has plann'd,
And laughing Ceres re-assume the land.

Notice also how the reference to Ceres contains within it the memory—but not the mention—of her daughter's abduction by the god of miserable wealth, and Proserpine's cyclical release from Pluto's bonds. Our memory of the myth is given to us here to guide our judgment of the ruin of bad wealth, given to us precisely in Pope's brilliantly reticent refusal to insist upon the myth's more literal, old-fashioned, form. In just this way does Pope's sophistication make a world of fine fabling authentically and poetically present to his modern-minded reader. It is an act of high imagination.

Along with this adroitness in its re-creation of classical genre, *To Burlington* reveals a supple tonal movement from which we derive our sense that the poem is uttered by a dramatically active speaker, a speaker whose own presentation of himself evolves in the course of his speaking his poem, or writing his letter. The curve of feeling shaping *To Burlington* is traced in Pope's movement from a voice chatty and intimate, then aggressive and irritated, to the high, authoritative, and visionary speech of the poem's close. Pope comes to this voice as he comes to the vision of the virtuous polity a grand architect might design, a good king might build, and a poet/prophet might celebrate, and the meaning of the poem is very much entailed in the poet's discovery of that high voice. It is precisely the discovery that vatic and heroic authority can be asserted in a modern voice and directed to an urbane audience: what he begins as an apparently informal letter to a respected and accomplished friend, a set of musings on the use and misuse of wealth, Pope transforms into nothing less than a visionary representation of the conditions under which a poet will stand at the political center as spokesman and celebrant, as the epic writer of what Milton called "a poem doctrinal to a nation"—for a nation that deserves it. Such a notion about poetry's high purpose has its sources in the humanist Renaissance.

But this heroic sense of career is as much a subject for scrutiny as for celebration in the major poems of Pope's last decade: *The Epistle to Doctor Arbuthnot*, the several imitations of Horace's epistles and satires, the two dialogues known as *The Epilogue to the Satires*, and the revisions of *The Dunciad*. In these poems, taken together, Pope explores his career in poetry as it developed, not in the terms envisioned in *An Essay on Criticism* and *To Burlington*, but in response to a public world falling far short of the ideal envisioned there—and in response perhaps to personal impulses as aggressive as they were generous, as congenial to satire as they were to celebration. In satire, Leopold Damrosch observes, the rebellious and anarchic impulses in Pope "could define themselves as custodians of moral order." And certainly, there is much in these later poems that exists in oblique relation to their high humanist ideal of ethical and imaginative equilibrium in the person of the poet capable of epic. It is Pope's achievement to have managed, in the aggressive, the angry, and the *modern* voice of the satirist, a scrutiny of self and career that both preserves and questions the humanist stance implied in his epic vision of the connection possible between poet and polity.

Nor is it possible to distinguish the ethical from the stylistic project here. If indeed Pope was interested in "placing" his individual talent within the humanist tradition he goes so far to redefine, then this undertaking was shaped by a skill in writing couplet verse unmatched by any other. It is this skill that constructs, for example, the rapid rhythms of animated conversation that permit Pope to dramatize and scrutinize what distinguishes him—now from his admired friends, now from his detested enemies:

> Let *Sporus* tremble—"What? that Thing of silk,
> "*Sporus*, that mere white Curd of Ass's milk?
> "Satire or Sense alas! can *Sporus* feel?
> "Who breaks a Butterfly upon a Wheel?"
> Yet let me flap this Bug with gilded wings,
> This painted Child of Dirt that stinks and stings. . . .

Here, at a critical moment in the *Epistle to Arbuthnot*, the interchange marks the difference between Pope's own fury at the "enemy," Lord Hervey ("Sporus"), and the bemused contempt of his friend, Arbuthnot. Against Arbuthnot's fine, dismissive, ridiculing wit—"who breaks a butterfly upon a wheel"—Pope's passion can seem excessive, itself somewhat ridiculous, even an embarrassment. All this he acknowledges in the drama of the exchange, and then goes on triumphantly to vindicate his fury in the grander, darker vision of the enemy he suddenly constructs from his friend's milder, merely dismissive wit: a butterfly to you, an insect to me; beautiful, but also painful, also insidious—he stinks, he stings, he buzzes, he annoys. More, it is the "witty and the fair" he annoys. And more, when looked at directly—that is, poetically—this insect enemy of mind and beauty is no less than another version of Satan—for to possess the social arts and then to trivialize them as "Sporus" does, is to be damned in small talk: to transform wit to gossip, puns, politics and lies, so to impose on the grand innocence of civility, and so to re-create in society the first sin of the first garden.

> *Eve's* Tempter thus the Rabbins have exprest,
> A Cherub's Face, a Reptile all the rest. . . .

There is perhaps no more powerful an instance of Pope's familiarizing an ancient myth than in this reenvisioning of Satan in the contemporary figure of a well-known and sometimes sparkling presence at court, and there is no more powerful an assertion of Pope's imagination than in this definition of civility as heroism against its trivialized—or merely decent—embodiments.

The triumphant note of that assertion is heard throughout Pope's Horatian poems, and in various keys—sometimes a grand declaration of self-sufficiency, sometimes a statement of resignation felt as victory, sometimes as heroic boast delivered as satiric wit:

> Yes, I am proud; I must be proud to see
> Men not afraid of God, afraid of me. . . .

And, in perhaps Pope's most dazzling moment, he links this triumphant claim for satire not only to the heroic, but also to the holy:

> O sacred Weapon! left for Truth's defence,
> Sole Dread of Folly, Vice, and Insolence!
> To all but Heav'n-directed hands deny'd,
> The Muse may give thee, but the Gods must guide.

Such a grand assertion, in which Pope promotes satire into epic and prophecy, gains its authority from the daring virtuosity of the couplet rhetoric that sets up its moment. The rapture of this instance is cannily prepared for in Pope's play against the conventional notion that satire is a "low" genre, that it works by demeaning its subject, unlike the "high" genres of epic and tragedy which were said to heighten and ennoble their material. But here Pope daringly conceives a rapturous and heroic close for his satirical poem by first insisting upon the obscenity that satire licenses, as—in a moment of outrageous scatological wit—he attacks the joint literary projects of some members of the House of Commons:

> Let Courtly Wits to Wits afford supply,
> As Hog to Hog in Huts of *Westphaly*;
> If one, thro' Nature's Bounty or his Lord's,
> Has what the frugal, dirty soil affords,
> From him the next receives it, thick or thin,
> As pure a Mess almost as it came in;
> . . . .
> From tail to mouth, they feed, and they carouse. . . .

Yet, from this "low" rhetoric, Pope, in hardly fifty lines, will build the rhythms and the sentiments making possible the heightened and rapturous claims for satire immediately to follow. This is an act he manages by constructing an agon with his interlocutor, whose sense of decorum, literary and social, is offended by the impassioned satirist's obscenity, and whose brand of civility is defined entirely by his insistence on the "decorums":

> This filthy Simile, this beastly Line,
> Quite turns my Stomach—

But his case is hopeless against the satirist's lightning riposte:

> So does Flatt'ry mine;
> And all your Courtly Civet-Cats can vent,
> Perfume to you, to me is Excrement.

And then the attack will quicken to the moment of its rapture, in which the person of the satirist, just now capable of a stinging obscenity, will be represented as sacred to the gods themselves. It is an act rivalling Milton's in *The Second Defense of the English People*.

From such rhetorical virtuosity and daring, Pope's definition of the heroic emerges; it is embodied in the wide range of role, of tone, of diction he commands to produce an image of a being both free and generously bound to others. But the heroic claims of these poems are authenticated also by the scrutiny Pope imposes upon those claims. His speaker is always aware of an alternative to the stance he chooses, always aware that his literary heroism has had its costs, and that its sources in his personality are perhaps less admirable than the poet's crafted image of himself would suggest. This self-questioning is apparent in the irony the endings of Pope's poems can generate when considered against their major statements. How, for example, are we to evaluate the satirist's grand assertion of his generous link to "all mankind" in the poem just cited, as against his closing statement not many lines later of his isolation—after all, his is the last pen for freedom? And how is his defense of civility in *Arbuthnot* to be weighed against his blessing at poem's end, which so precisely distinguishes between the poet's inwardness and his friend's sociability?

> O Friend! may each Domestick Bliss be thine!
> Be no unpleasing Melancholy mine. . . .

And what of Pope's decision to write these poems as dialogues—dialogues which, as in *Arbuthnot*, acknowledge the obsessive energies that drive the satirist and distinguish him from the friend he admires, the parents he celebrates; or which, as in *The Epilogues*, dramatize his more than faintly ridiculous ineffectuality in the eyes of the merely bemused interlocutor he detests? In fact, the characteristic development of Pope's Horatian poems is toward a concluding moment in which the social activity of the poem's body—conversation, argument, homily—comes to an end and the poet speaks for himself and as if to himself—to affirm a self-possession not to be communicated, not even to his intimates. But along with what is affirmed, there is also much that is questioned. Our final impression of these poems is that they are the instruments of Pope's self-scrutiny as well as self-celebration; that in them his various perceptions of himself—as free, and as possessed; as grand, and as mean; as linked to others, and isolated from them—are allowed their fullest play against each other. Certainly the writer of Pope's Horatian poems owes much of his ideal conception of himself to literary history, but nothing from within its web of words could have assured the appearance of one who would, in the contemplation of that ideal being, communicate a realistic self-awareness all the while he was demonstrating that satire could be epic, that such epic could be written in the three hundred or so lines that normally go into an epistle, and who would then insist that the writer of such sophisticated and heroic conversation pieces was not only like Homer and Virgil—he was also fit to join the company of Achilles and Aeneas!

And if Pope's career is significantly linked to literary history, then surely his construction of an epic voice for a modern age survives through Wordsworth, through Tennyson, through Yeats—all of whom clearly hold that important matters require for their exploration a grand public voice, and that for this voice there can be no more insistent a subject than the private being.

Richard Feingold

Further Reading

Bredvold, Louis. *The Intellectual Milieu of John Dryden*. Ann Arbor: University of Michigan Press, 1934. Reprinted 1956, 1966.

Brower, Reuben. *Alexander Pope: The Poetry of Allusion*. Oxford: Clarendon, 1959.

Damrosch, Leopold. *The Imaginative World of Alexander Pope*. Berkeley: University of California Press, 1987.

Feingold, Richard. *Moralized Song: The Character of Augustan Lyricism*. New Brunswick, N.J.: Rutgers University Press, 1989.

Ferry, Anne. *Milton and the Miltonic Dryden*. Cambridge: Harvard University Press, 1968.

Harth, Phillip. *Contexts of Dryden's Thought*. Chicago: University of Chicago Press, 1968.

Mack, Maynard. *Alexander Pope: A Life*. New Haven: Yale University Press, 1985.

Mack, Maynard. "The Muse of Satire." *Yale Review* 41 (1951): 80–92.

Stack, Frank. *Pope and Horace: Studies in Imitation*. Cambridge: Cambridge University Press, 1985.

Willey, Basil. *The Seventeenth-Century Background*. New York, Doubleday Anchor, n.d.

Williams, Aubrey. *Pope's "Dunciad": A Study of Its Meaning*. Hamden, Conn.: Archon, 1968.

Winn, James A. *John Dryden and His World*. New Haven: Yale University Press, 1987.

Zwicker, Steven. *Politics and Language in Dryden's Poetry: The Arts of Disguise*. Princeton: Princeton University Press, 1984.

Poetry in the Eighteenth Century

E VEN when we avoid the two great branches of emotive historical narrative, the Decline and the Progress, we are still ham-
pered by the inevitable version of the eighteenth century as a
placid period—a period dominated by a desire for order. A rage for
order need not in itself of course issue in calm, but until very recently
the order was posited as a calm. That is a tribute to the success of Whig
propaganda in the eighteenth century (and later), for it was most certainly to the political and economic interests of the powerful group of
Whigs in politics and commerce to make out that English life had a
natural and inevitable balanced order, which they had discovered and
now represented.

But relatively few people, even Whigs, really bought that for breakfast, dinner, and supper. In the arts in England, and especially in the art
of poetry, wherever we encounter order, we can see an experiment—or
a set of experiments. And one kind of order in a poem may allow the
poet to produce certain favored kinds of disorder and dissonance. In
histories the "sun of Enlightenment" has too often hidden the private
night.

A better key to the period than the opposition between order and
disorder can be found in the problems set up by a strongly felt need to
make literature—and especially poetry—*public* in all its manifestations.
That literature at its best, its most effective, deals with public matters
in public language had been generally felt, and widely demonstrated,
during the Restoration. Dryden was the great exemplar of the public
poetry, not because he was a public poet, a one-time poet laureate, but

because all his best poems deal with public concerns. Dryden could give an official semipersonal or personified personal reaction to a public event. He could keep the private man divorced from his office. For Pope, that was not going to be possible. Pope knew that he was not only to live the public life himself, but that his poetry would have to be expressively public and constantly publicizing.

The eighteenth century knew very well that the private is the political—and that the public is the political. The advent of "Enlightenment" meant the desire to shed light on all aspects of human life, and to make them public. The number of things "not fit to be mentioned" was perceptibly diminishing. The *Old Bailey Session Papers* and the *Ordinary's Account* rapidly gave the public details that before it had not been thought proper or interesting to observe or record. The condition of sexually molested babies, the stains of menstrual blood on the clothing of an accused murderess—these things found room for statement. Such detailed presentation of small things or dirty things or dull things must have seemed strange to those contemporary readers still not used to the new "scientific" measurement. The New Science, according to which things were to be observed, measured, described aptly and recorded, was able to move from the laboratories and the gentlemanly Royal Society and go out into the world, where light was largely the light of the press.

The scientific doctrines of weighing and measuring suited a mercantile cast of mind, and were part and parcel of the Whig ideology. Yet the purer Whig ideology often soared beyond the interests of actual Whigs, and brought a countermovement of demand for the public communal life, for record of behaviors, moneys and events. Public life after 1700, or at the very latest after 1715, had become more insistent, and more taken for granted. A new generation had absorbed the implications of Locke's essay *Concerning Human Understanding* as well as his *Treatises on Government*. The mind and its working, the inner recesses of what we know as "person" seemed visible in a way they would not have done to a writer or reader of 1670. No tiny crevice of the personality seemed beyond scrutiny. Laurence Sterne's *Tristram Shandy* (1760–1767) is a paradoxical assertion that the private life—however eccentric or masturbatory—can be made public; at the same time, it is a defiance of this view.

Eighteenth-century literature has from time to time been accused of being "obscene." What disconcerts modern readers is not the mentioning of things not in accord with some social code, nor the lubricity, but, presumably, the touch of coyness and experimentation—the various reflections of a desire not to be offensive—with which the English of the period refer to sexual or scatological matters, while reminding us that we are bearers ourselves of large, unclean, smelly bodies with all their parts and secretions and discharges. The lightest hint sophisticates. The eighteenth-century writers want to play with our embarrassment, make us know that we are known. That knowingness, that introduction of the public gaze in works of sexuality, would not seem so very surprising if women alone were the objects. But men are included as well as women. We know that women are objects of the male "gaze," but eighteenth-century literature makes *everyone* the object of the public gaze. And the sense of public gaze is present whether or not the subject or object is erotic.

In works as diverse as the poetry of Pope and the fiction of Samuel Richardson—novelist and printer—the image of the Enlightenment is naturally enough the sun, which in the eighteenth century gets a different meaning from its Platonic one. The Enlightenment sun is busy glaring, ferreting out, strongly lighting up, putting into print. A certain testiness about the sun becomes evident in later Augustan poetry. When Milton's Satan grimly protests against the sun, in *Paradise Lost* IV, he just seems splendidly perverse. But moments of doubt, tones of doubt about the sun and its beams, are scattered throughout eighteenth century literature. There is a sense of the oppressiveness, the too-muchness of the great waves of light that come rolling irresistibly over one, that make everything visible until the tired eyes lose the power of seeing or discerning, as in James Thomson's "Summer":

> 'Tis raging Noon; and, vertical, the Sun
> Darts on the Head direct his forceful Rays
> O'er Heaven and Earth, far as the ranging Eye
> Can sweep, a dazling Deluge reigns; and all
> From Pole to Pole is undistinguish'd Blaze.
> In vain the Sight, dejected to the Ground,
> Stoops for Relief; thence hot ascending Steams
> And keen Reflection pain.

Thomson, one of the chief Whig propagandists of the time, was one of the most enthusiastic exponents of Newtonian physics, of the commercial globe and maps, of the measurable world, and he also has a steady poetic topic in the relation of the eye to the light. He is a poet of visibility, of sober sanity in Enlightenment. Yet Thomson here, remarkably, announces a point at which light becomes overwhelming. The "ranging Eye" must stop its free movement, oppressed by the oppressive Sun, which seems to shoot at the head, and the entire visible environment is transformed painfully into the flood of light that hurts the eye. Subjected to the "undistinguish'd Blaze," and losing the capacity to distinguish objects, sight has lost itself.

Phrases from Ovid on man walking erect and facing upward stand behind Milton's and Blake's human form sublime. Thomson, in "Spring," draws upon the Ovidian passage: "Man superior walks / Amid the glad Creation." But Thomson knows that man cannot always live up to the sublime posture. In the heat of summer he acknowledges the tentative and circumstantial nature of our superior gaze; we droop. Even looking down provides no retreat, because the rays reflected from the ground still have power to pain. This excellent passage wonderfully captures the entrapment of the seeing eye and the powerful mind in even more powerful light. The wonderful eye—that masterful organ—and the powerful mind alike prove capable of weariness; they exhibit incapacity. For all his love of light, the poet finds a limit to endurance of light. Thomson, like Pope in the *Second Pastoral*, in talking about the sun's "blaze" captures the dubiousness of enlightenment, the negative side of being enlightened, that is, of being always in the glare of public light, the eye of the public in an arid, public space, dried and burned by the ceaseless hot waves of attention and attentiveness.

We find in the eighteenth-century poets, major and minor, male and female, a tendency to write about twilight and night. The attention given to night pieces might seem to represent a reaction against the surplus of ceaseless public light, a search for "Relief." In a punning allusion to *Hamlet* (I.iv.54) Pope had said James Ralph "makes Night hideous," referring to Ralph's poem *Night* (1728). In Pope's lines Night may be assumed to be hideous; making her more so is a sort of gilding of hell's lily, an offense against the day world. Ralph's poem on a subject increasingly fashionable was probably an influence on Collins's later "Ode to Evening." Ralph certainly praises Night as a source of relief and a benign influence:

Lo! sable night ascends the dusky air,
And spends her deep'ning shadows all around;
Her silent influence stills the noisy world,
And wakes the studious soul to solemn thought.
. . . .
  O thou, whose secret haunt is far remov'd
From all the restless, glaring scenes of day,
Sweet contemplation, daughter of the night!
O deign thy favour to th'adventrous muse. . . .
(I.1–15)

Ralph is less "hideous" than Pope leads us to expect, and he is certainly in the line that leads from Thomson to Young, Collins, and Cowper—but his prefatory argument for the utter superiority of blank verse to rhyme alone would have sufficed to damn him with Pope.

That there is a paradox in writing about Night (a time that, if properly respected, deprives one of the use of books and writing) did not discourage Augustan poets. Arguably the most successful of their nocturnes is the "Nocturnal Reverie" by Anne Finch, Countess of Winchilsea. Finch's poem (1713) exhibits a delight in the beauty of a quiet freedom offering new and refreshing relations of objects to each other and to the human present, replacing the order and understandings of day.

When in some River, overhung with Green,
The Waving Moon and trembling Leaves are seen;
When freshen'd Grass now bears it self upright,
And makes cool Banks to pleasing Rest invite,
Whence springs the *Woodbind*, and the *Bramble*-Rose,
And where the sleepy *Cowslip* shelter'd grows:
Whilst now a paler Hue the *Foxglove* takes,
Yet checquers still with Red the dusky brakes.

Everywhere there are images of restoration and refreshment, mingled with the idea of transformation. Metamorphosed by night and moonlight, natural objects are refreshed and revived. The grass is "freshen'd"; the Cowslip, "shelter'd," can fall asleep. Finch's poem is an evidently deliberate proof that images of obscurity can be soothing rather than sublime. The poem as it moves tugs delicately at hierarchies, shifts regular orderings of things, so that even the senses lose their rankings, and the sense of smell is restored, as well as the sense of hearing. Sight loses its capacity to measure, to judge dimension or distance. "And swelling Haycocks thicken up the Vale." Haycocks loom large and indeterminately bulky; as the sight cannot engage in judgment, vision becomes tactile. The loss of the day's judgment or rationality, its measurement, order, and hierarchy, is felt as a great and continuous relief, expressed openly toward the end of the poem:

> Their shortliv'd Jubilee the Creatures keep,
> Which but endures, whilst Tyrant-*Man* do's sleep:
> When a sedate Content the Spirit feels.
> And no fierce Light disturbs, whilst it reveals.

Finch brings off a concealed pun here in her compound "Tyrant-*Man*." It can seem for a moment that she means "Man" in general, but we can sense beneath that a protest that the real "Tyrant" is the masculine human. She herself does not disturb the landscape, nor does Lady Salisbury, to whom a compliment was paid in an earlier line. The two women seem to be roaming, fantastically free, over this night world, and they are in harmony with it—a freedom that can only be found "whilst Tyrant-*Man* do's sleep."

For woman, as for the animals, the Jubilee is shortlived. "In such a *Night* let Me abroad remain, / Till Morning breaks, and All's confus'd again." Audaciously, Finch reverses the expected or "natural" order whereby Night is thought of as a time of confusion and Day as a time of openness and regularity. Morning "breaks" the tranquility so briefly restored, and a new and pleasing order of things is to be fragmented again by the strong confusions of the daylight world. The rules, hierarchies, and rationalizations that characterize the daylight world are here felt to be chaotic, the ruin of another way of being that was nearly within our grasp.

It seems not uncommon to associate morning with a certain loss or discomfort—and without any primary engagement in the aubade tradition of the lover's lament at dawn. Finch has some odd company in Swift, whose short mock georgic "A Description of the Morning" (1709) recreates the urban morning as an increasing outburst of noise and sordid activity:

> The Smallcoal-Man was heard with Cadence deep,
> Till drown'd in Shriller Notes of *Chimney-Sweep*.
> Duns at his Lordships Gate began to meet,
> And Brickdust *Moll* had Scream'd through half a Street.

Finch in her poem does not go into the details of the confusions of morning, while Swift delights in rendering them. For both poets, the advance of day means the replacement of the natural by the man-made, and the loss of silence. Finch's emphasis on change of vision, on the conversion of visual images to auditory or tactile ones, and on the pleasure of communing in solitude with a landscape that has given up its allegiances to day will be captured in William Collins's famous unrhymed "Ode to Evening" (1747), truly a marvel of rhythm and sound. Collins emphasizes more than Finch the steady progress of transformation in observing the personified Evening at work in various seasons, and marking when and how the changes happen:

> be mine the Hut,
> That from the Mountain's Side,
> Views Wilds, and swelling Floods,
> And Hamlets brown, and dim-discover'd Spires,
> And hears their simple Bell, and marks o'er all
> Thy Dewy Fingers draw
> The gradual dusky Veil.

Collins still gives spectatorship and the control of the eye more authority than Finch does (a masculine prepossession?); his "Hut" must have a superior view. Yet he too collapses sight into touch, as the visible darkness, the dusk, becomes both "Dewy Fingers" and "Veil" or a pile of whirling dead leaves temporarily at stop: "While sallow *Autumn* fills thy Lap with Leaves." Hearing gains perceptibly over sight, from the simple bell heard in spring to the shrieking dominant winds of winter. Collins's poem offers an escape, a relief from day; we may read it at noon and imagine the pleasures of evening with its promises of softness, pleasure, and cool restorations.

Finch's poem deliberately represents an escape from the institutional; but from the institutions of the time, from the Anglican Church and the Universities, came other invocations of the night. The most famous of these in its time (aside from Gray's *Elegy*) was the very popular and often-printed *Night Thoughts* by the clergyman Edward Young. Young's first major success was in a series of satires entitled *Love of Fame, the Universal Passion* (1725), and some thought him a better satirist than Pope. Often quoted in his century, Young has not been much regarded in our own, and what was thought of as his masterpiece, *The Complaint, or Night Thoughts on Life, Death, and Immortality* (1742–1746), has been little read since the mid-nineteenth century. In its own age, Young's nine "Nights" were tremendously popular, both in England and on the Continent, translated not only into French and German but into languages more remote, such as Hungarian. It went through over thirty editions during the century.

Young's poem struggles, sometimes in interestingly complicated ways, both against the night and with it. Night is definitely objectified and personified (as not in Finch, for instance). A sable goddess, Night in "rayless Majesty, now stretches forth / Her leaden Sceptre o'er a slumb'ring world." It is easy to see that Young's Night is not only derived from traditional iconographical and poetic sources, such as Spenser, but that it or rather *she* is an immediate reflection and in some ways counterpart of Pope's goddess of Dulness (herself, "With Night Primeval," restoring "the great Anarch's ancient reign," strongly related to the iconographic and poetic traditions of personified Night, especially in Spenser). Pope's goddess is a power to be condemned and resisted. The day world of ceaseless striving, clarity of vision, order, hierarchy, and regulation must be asserted—and this is a remorselessly masculine world. The power of seeing is the power of control; the night world brings on terrible blindness. Young's poem takes issue, implicitly, with Pope. Not least does it do so in the choice of blank verse, which by this time seems in itself a rejection of the world of day, of authority, reason, and social order. These things, like socially based moralizing, are best left to the daylight operations of rhyme, the satirist's tool.

As the century progresses, blank verse steadily becomes, not what it was in Milton, the vehicle for high heroic thought and action, but the means of expressing personal sensibility. It is thus associated with what John Sitter calls "Literary Loneliness." Blank verse is often the medium for carrying out what Sitter defines as "feminizing and internalizing" the poetic impulse itself, in the personification of imaginative entities as feminine. Johnson in his poems and Goldsmith in *The Deserted Village* evidently wish to maintain the serious import of rhyme, and to sustain the habit of moral and social observation. But the tendency of what their age called "the age" was against them, leading toward the explosion out of regular form signified by Macpherson's Ossian and all of Blake's later writings, as well as toward the calmer inwardness of Cowper's blank verse in *The Task*. Cowper owes a serious debt to his mid-century predecessor Young, who so importantly called upon the relief of night and darkness, and the personal consciousness. Young's

powerfully feminized night is admittedly given many negative attributes, and the stoppage of day's activities prefigures not only personal
death but the annihilation of the world. Yet Young is urged to pursue
the images of silence and death because he is in mourning—or rather,
Young's personal mourning for his wife ostensibly contributes to the
tone of mourning of the speaker of the poem. To pursue the Night
world is to find not leaden cessation, but the possibility of a refreshment
of spiritual power, and the power of thought.

> *Silence* and *Darkness*! solemn Sisters! Twins
> From ancient *Night*, who nurse the tender Thought
> To *Reason*, and on *Reason* build *Resolve*
> (That column of true Majesty in man).
>
> (*Night* I.28–31)

Night in its night world of dark and quiet, in a reversal of Pope's image
of Dulness nursing Cibber, assists and nourishes reason.

Young hastens to rectify the balance; after the infantile pleasures of
being nursed, of acquiring a feminized receptivity, the mind acquiring
reason must assert its masculinity—"*Resolve*" is masculine, a male "column." Authority, hierarchy, control are reassumed. The poem is full of
such slippages and compromises (one of the reasons why Barbara Pym
finds it so apt for fun in her novels). But we may be struck by the recurrent theme in *Night Thoughts* of the spiritual nourishing power of Night
and the night world. In the eighteenth century, there are memorable
moments when it is not the Sun that is the Platonic illuminator, but the
Night. This exchange can be seen developing in Milton's "L'Allegro"
and "Il Penseroso," although denied in *Comus* and *Paradise Lost*.
"L'Allegro" and "Il Penseroso" were of great importance to poets near
the mid-century, and were to be set to music by Handel. The Sun during the century is increasingly felt to be utilitarian. It becomes associated with the regulating and controlling eye that ensures the social control of others. Night is the time for inner communing, for spiritual
apprehension and development for growth, change, and inspiration. It
is also a time for understanding death and overcoming the fear of death
that the day world too much encourages.

In endeavoring to represent the heroic effort to become attuned to
the inward self and to the life beyond the social and intellectual, Young
chooses to employ blank verse. The influence of Milton—the Milton
of *Paradise Lost*—is most apparent. Milton had made blank verse the

suitable verse of high, solemn, spiritual subjects. The practice of Pope primarily had made the heroic couplet—the use of an iambic pentameter line in paragraphs of rhyming paired lines—seem a poetic form almost inevitably social, practical (in the sense of moral), and satiric. It can be argued that no such clear division is to be felt in the poems of Dryden or other poets of the Restoration.

It is perhaps a peculiarity of Restoration imagination that on all sides (not just that of the King-and-Church men) deep personal experience could be associated with institutions imaginatively conceived. Young is an Anglican churchman, but his meditations cannot point at last triumphantly to a Church Triumphant (as Dryden wanted to do); what happens, the event of the poem, must be personal meditation, zigzags of thought, and the endeavor in the darkness to convert his friend Lorenzo, a private turning along a personal thought line.

The poets of the early mid-century—the era roughly from the first publication of Young's satires in 1725 to the death of William Collins in 1759—turned back to the Jacobeans for poetic forms, images, and turns of language. We have had some trouble in focusing on this relationship of the "Augustans" to the "Jacobeans" because our histories of "the Gothic" have really been dealing with developments of the novel toward the end of the century. There is a tendency to think of graves, ghosts, darkness, etc. as the accessories and prerequisites of the Gothic novelists, and with them of Romantic poets. A group of poets, including Gray and Collins, used to be referred to as "Pre-Romantic"—a nicely question-begging term that tended to confuse students about chronology. It was hard to remember that Thomson wrote in the 1730s and Blair in the 1740s, or that Gray wrote most of his work in the 1740s and Collins likewise.

We had wanted so much to say that there was a neoclassical period which lasted right up to the midpoint of the century, and that the other interests, wet and sloppy as they appeared to some historians and teachers, had come along later, with the dissolution of everything dry and manly and the outbursting of "the Gothic" and the French Revolution. But that is not at all the picture. In the first half of the century writers who had learned from the Restoration writers that there are no set models for literature were busy altering the inheritance from the Restoration writers themselves, and looking over the heads, as it were, of the Restoration crowd to other English poets. It is certainly true that the Metaphysical strain did not die out, but was transformed. It is also

true that the strains so specific to the "Jacobean" writers—the characteristic morbid taste for bones conveyed in deliberately strained connections and jarring similitudes that leave a shudder in their wake—had
never disappeared, especially in drama.

We find a new desire on the part of many eighteenth-century poets,
especially those writing in the 1740s and early 1750s, to dwell on death,
to speak in accents mimicking the Jacobean of worms and graves and
epitaphs. We are to be startled and amazed within the night world that
withdraws us from the public world of society, reason, and social order.
We are to meditate on death, and to see even our social connections in
another aspect. "From human Mould we reap our daily Bread. / . . . O'er
devastation we blind Revels keep; / While bury'd Towns support the
Dancer's Heel" (*Night* IX). This is a thought about death we are urged
to feel imaginatively—what the eighteenth century called a "sentiment," meaning a thought that can be felt, or a feeling that can be articulated.

We don't hear anything like it again until Edward FitzGerald translated the *Rubáiyát of Omar Khayyám*; there are some similarities in
Hopkins's "Margaret are you grieving?" We cannot avoid loss, we are
surrounded by loss and decay; indeed, we live upon them. Gruesomely,
not just the rose (as in Omar) but our daily bread is derived from the
mouldering dead. That which is gone, past, dead is in fact very immediately present. The dead do not seem to be quiet in their graves here,
as the dead are at least quiet in Thomas Gray's *Elegy in a Country
Churchyard* (1750). Their hollow ceiling, our earthen floor, seems to
shake at their subdued activity. Throughout the passage, Young recreates the return of the repressed. The night world will not allow us to
contemplate only the clean, dry, tidy world of order and action and the
rules, for the "night thoughts" bring in the ideas that the day tries
earnestly to forget.

So fascinated did the poets of the 1740s become with death and the
grave that recent criticism posited a "Graveyard School" of poets.
Robert Blair, a Scotsman and the Anglican clergyman of a parish in
East Lothian, achieved fame with one signal poem, *The Grave* (1743).
Like others of this kind (including Gray's *Elegy*) *The Grave* exhibits a
referential fondness for *Hamlet*: "Where are the Jesters now? the men
of Health / Complexionally pleasant?" The rapid development of *Hamlet*'s popularity in this period may perhaps be explained in part by the
poetic preference for what might be called "works of the Night World,"

works that question reason, order, life's shallower cheer (Polonius), institutional confidence (the King), and the quick patter of rational wit (Yorick). Here in Blair's poem we catch flickers of the Metaphysical wit, tamed a little, but turned again to Jacobean purposes, marveling at disintegration: "Sorry Pre-eminence of high Descent, / Above the vulgar born, to rot in State!" (154–155); "'Tis but a Night, a long and moonless Night; / We make the *Grave* our Bed, and then are gone" (762–763).

The characteristics of such contemporary poetry did not go unremarked or uncriticized at the time. William Whitehead made fun of Young's poem in "New Night Thoughts on Death: A Parody" (1747):

O Night! dark Night! wrapt round with *Stygian* gloom!
Thy *riding-hood* opaque, wrought by the hands
Of *Clotho* and of *Atropos* . . .
. . . .
Death's a dark lanthorn, life a candle's end
Stuck on a save-all, soon to end in stink.
The grave's a privy; life the alley green
Directing there—where 'chance on either side
A sweet-briar hedge, or shrubs of brighter hue,
Amuse us, and their treach'rous sweets dispense.

Whitehead captures the tinny grandeur of the flourishes inherited from the baroque, including the large personifications, but he also sees that these can become extremely awkward when combined with the revived taste for the Metaphysical homely image in an unexpected context. Comparisons are ridden out beyond the bounds of suitability and interest, as in the dogged determination to compare life to a journey to the outhouse every step of the way. The private world of night and self-communing is jocularly turned by Whitehead's daylight satire into the *privy* world. The parodic attack on poetic meditations on the grave was certainly timely. The neo-Jacobean touches that Whitehead picks on and comically imitates can be found in poets other than Young.

A marked difference between poems of this period and the nondramatic lyric or meditative poems of the seventeenth century is the strong, new respect for copiousness. A Jacobean or Metaphysical poet would not *go on* the way poets do in the 1720s–1740s. In many cases, there seems no particular reason ever to stop. It is noticeable that when the most eminent poets of the period—including not only Thomson, but also Pope—reissued a work, they repeatedly lengthened it. The effect of plenitude militates against the sense of restriction in the imagery of loss or death; there is a luxury about the expression of decay largely foreign to the more laconic seventeenth century. Johnson says of Thomson's diction that it is "florid and luxuriant," even "too exuberant"; he praises the "wide display of original poetry" in Young's *Night Thoughts*:

The wild diffusion of the sentiments, and the digressive sallies of imagination, would have been compressed and restrained by confinement to rhyme. The excellence of this work is not exactness but copiousness . . . in the whole there is a magnificence like that ascribed to Chinese plantation, the magnificence of vast extent and endless diversity.

In the *Lives of the Poets* (1770–1781), looking back with particular attention to the earlier part of the century, Johnson is able to see distinctly and to sum up forcefully some of the creative or aesthetic principles at work in that earlier period. To display originality had become a desideratum by Young's time; Young wrote one of the first texts about "originality" in his *Conjectures on Original Composition* (1759). The duty of the poet is to exhibit originality with energy, to display vigor of mind in digression, to disdain confinement. There is in author and reader a love of ornament and display, a decided taste for the jolt of the unexpected. We see in Johnson's paragraph a Rococo acknowledgment of art and artifacts of exotic (non-European) culture; unexpectedly Young's large poem becomes a Chinese garden.

Copiousness may be taken as a key word in relation to the poetics of the period. Poems wish to display copiousness, and unstoppability. It is a point of great importance to eighteenth-century writers (not just the poets) to give the impression of unstoppable flow, sweeping like Denham's celebrated Thames in *Cooper's Hill* (1655): "Though deep, yet clear, though gentle, yet not dull, / Strong without rage, without oreflowing full." The early eighteenth-century poets wished to incorporate some degree of "rage" in the flow, some principle of energy and inevitable forward movement. The image of life as a river perpetually appears in verse and prose of the entire period. "Think we, or think we not, *Time* hurries on / With a resistless unremitting stream" says Blair (*The Grave*, 479–480). Blair's thought had been more pungently expressed by Isaac Watts in *The Psalms of David Imitated*, "Man Frail and God Eternal" (1719): "Time like an ever rolling Stream / Bears all its Sons away." Poets and prose writers alike borrow the inevitable forward energy of time itself, and the reader is caught in the stream of unstoppable flow. Copiousness, unstoppability—and to these we must add "diversity" as in Johnson's striking, almost oxymoronic, phrase "endless diversity."

The poet must be able to surprise and please us by producing unexpected things, moment by moment. The best way to achieve all of these effects and to create the impression of sincere originality is to produce a poem spoken by a personal voice. Pope does this of course in the *Moral Essays* and the *Imitations of Horace*, and Young in *Night Thoughts*—but we find the same first-person point of view in short poems as well as long, as a look at either of Roger Lonsdale's two anthologies will tell us. Personal experience is the stuff of the new poetry. Even nonexperience or negative experience will suffice, as in "Verse Epistle" by Jane Brereton (1685–1740):

> I seldom go to Park or Play,
> And once a Fortnight drink my Tea
> Needle, or Book 'twixt Thumb and Finger
> Till tuneful voice of Ballad-singer
> Will, sometimes, make me throw it by,
> And to the Window swiftly fly;
> From thence I hear the tatter'd Dame,
> To dirty Mob, extol the Fame
> 'Of glorious *Charles* of *Swedeland*'!
> ("To Mr. Thomas Griffith," 36–43)

This poem (written in 1720 but not published until 1744) exhibits a light and ambiguous compliment paid to the old oral culture by one who is well ensconced in the new print culture—to whom new experience comes largely by reading. The clean, modern, middle-class woman sits upstairs reading, but will cast a glance below at the bedraggled oral muse, the "tatter'd Dame."

Copiousness—unstoppability—diversity. These three words would do very well to describe the new Grub Street world of perpetual publication. The later seventeenth century was the first period to cope with the fact of constant publication affecting common life, but the eighteenth century saw such an expansion of the products and use of the printing press that the people who lived at the time were in many ways justified in speaking of it as an unprecedented phenomenon. In the throes of a similar change now ourselves, we can sympathize better than we used to do with the sense of fear or estrangement that often accompanied this great change. Pope and Swift both famously found fault with the new state of the world that allowed equal access to the printed page— to the authorship of the printed page—to persons who should have been under authority, ready to accept the revelations of their betters.

Authority underwent a metamorphosis. There was no authority in Church or State in the sense there had been before, there was only opinion and then another opinion, blast and counterblast. Of course that had been the case in the Reformation, a movement powerfully aided by the printing press, but the clerical agents of Reform had not really seen prophetically the degree to which their own authority would be upset. Writings by the uneducated, by cranks, by women tumbled off the press. As long as the public would buy, a bookseller would print, with no regard to decorum, no deference to duly constituted leaders. Of course this was not perfectly true, and the government, especially under Walpole in the 1720s, meddled much more than the Church was able to do. Yet even when censorship and downright suppression are taken into account, the press offered a vision of the contemporary world that had never been seen before. It was a self-reflective world. In a way, writings on religion and politics offered less of a challenge to the ideal of authority than did the variety of miscellaneous writings on every subject under the sun. People were being encouraged to have opinions, to express themselves. It must have seemed as though the world were full of writers as well as readers.

We have only recently been taught to regard the demographic factors of English life in the eighteenth century as important to our understanding of the period. But as soon as we consider that the population of England and Wales doubled (or nearly) during that century, we can see that by the end of the first third of the century a great proportion of the population must have been young, and that the proportion of the young would only increase as the century proceeded. Is not the strange fashion of wearing powdered hair and then powdered wigs that came up at this time in western Europe—and most noticeably in France and England—a fashion strongly related to age groups? Wigs appear at other times in history, but the assumption of white or gray hair is unique to the eighteenth century. It may well be that the young people of the governing classes felt an unconscious need to assert their right to do things, while reassuring others, both their elders and their own generation, that they were perfectly capable—the fashion is an illustration, an emblem, of the saying "old heads on young shoulders." The white and gray powder cannot long disguise from us the youthfulness and energy of those who most fully participated in the century's activities and changes—and among both activities and changes must be counted the writing and reading of the new poetry.

The new kind of reading public included boys born in the lower, the working, classes, like John Gay, Samuel Richardson, and William Hogarth, as well as women of both upper and middle classes. If we look at the poetry of the eighteenth century, we must acknowledge the enormous output. One of the steadily proliferating areas was poetry. Poems were popular and salable in a way not easy to imagine nowadays, and the logic of the marketplace meant, for instance, that women could buy each other's works, and supply audiences sufficient to support a volume. No writer had to depend on an imprimatur.

The new magazines were also arenas of publication—most important the *Gentleman's Magazine* (founded 1731). Edward Cave, its editor, included in the poetry columns a number of poems by women, from the very beginning. Jane Brereton contributed to it regularly under the pseudonym "Melissa." The regular poetry section of the *Gentleman's Magazine* was reserved for correspondents, unpaid, like writers of Letters to the Editor. The experience of appearing in print was stimulating to provincial ladies as well as to provincial gentlemen—and to women and men of ranks below. In an earlier period, the women bold enough to be known to be writers of poetry were generally ladies of the highest birth, such as Katharine Philips ("Orinda"), Anne Killigrew, or the Countess of Winchilsea. In the new period it becomes increasingly common for middle-class women to write and even to appear in print. Some were not even of the middle class.

One of the best artists in the shorter kind of poems of this period is Mary Leapor, who was not entitled to call herself a lady or a gentlewoman. She was the daughter of a gardener, and worked for some time as a cook-maid. In her short life she produced a number of poems, as well as a play that did not succeed in getting produced. Leapor's dying wish was that her poems (which already had an appreciative audience) should be published, and they were published by subscription in April 1748. Subscribers included the Countess of Hertford and Stephen Duck, "the thresher poet," another spectacular success, in contemporary view, exhibiting the poetic capacities possibly to be found in the lower orders. Such a miscellany of supporters would not have been imagined in 1670, or even 1700. Mary Leapor arrived posthumously in Parnassus—or in Grub Street.

This proliferation of writers is just what Pope is complaining of in the *Dunciad*. The divine calling of poet, the Virgilian vocation, ought not to be claimed by all and sundry, the ragtag and bobtail. Pope had to squint his eyes to prevent himself from seeing that it was precisely that print culture, that chaotic Grub Street republic of exchange and proliferation of the word, which had enabled him, the socially and physically disadvantaged son of a Roman Catholic draper, to make a stir in the world and win not only the fame of posterity but the more solid blessings of (rented) house and garden, medical attention, books, travel—all the things so lacking in the life of, for instance, Mary Leapor.

In the *Dunciad* Pope constantly and with emphasis equates Dulness with femininity and the female principle, and with Night. Dulness also causes (or spawns) the terrible maggotlike mass of pullulating writers and their writings; she presides over the copiousness and diversity of those who have new access to the print world. But the tyranny of Church and King that Pope officiously despises in Book III (of both the 1728 and 1744 versions), the various padlocks on the mind, are going to be opposed only in such a tumult and controversy and noise, such a clattering morning as Grub Street offers. Without the publicity of this very public, impertinent, daylight world, Pope could not have survived.

Pope was dead and in his chest before Mary Leapor died and her poems were published. Judging by Pope's reaction in the *Dunciad* to other lower-class writers such as Defoe, or to female writers such as Eliza Haywood, Mary Leapor might have figured in a new *Dunciad*, had Pope lived long enough. Mary Leapor's own poems exhibit the longing of the lonely and deprived person to join the exchange of current poetry and thought, as well as a refreshing and witty skepticism about these exchanges and their forms and formulae of expression. Her mode is sensuous and comic, if ostensibly self-deprecatory.

> 'Tis twenty Winters, if it is no more,
> To speak the Truth it may be Twenty four:
> As many Springs their 'pointed Space have run,
> Since *Mira*'s eyes first open'd on the Sun.
> 'Twas when the Flocks on slabby Hillocks lye,
> And the cold Fishes rule the watry Sky:
> . . . .

You see I'm learned, and I show't the more,
That none may wonder when they find me poor.
Yet *Mira* dreams, as slumb'ring Poets may,
And rolls in Treasures till the breaking Day:
While Books and Pictures in bright Order rise,
And painted Parlours swim before her Eyes;
Till the shrill Clock impertinently rings,
And the soft Visions move their shining Wings:
Then *Mira* wakes—her Pictures are no more,
And through her Fingers slides the vanish'd Ore.
Convinc'd too soon, her Eye unwilling falls
On the blue Curtains and the dusty Walls:
She wakes, alas! to Business and to Woes,
To sweep her Kitchen, and to mend her Clothes.
("An Epistle to a Lady," 6–32)

The poet, as "Mira," mocks her poetic position, defining herself in the favored, bardic category ("as slumb'ring Poets may"), while steadily undercutting not only her own position (she is a houseworker) but the imagined position of "Poet." She is redefining the idea of "Poet," and her redefinition works because of her arresting sensuousness, the aptness with which she can reassemble images of the lived-in world. Her world is a world of odd and sordid things—"slabby Hillocks," "dusty Walls." The deglamorization of everything is an important part of her procedure. Yet such deglamorization is a common activity among poets of the period, certainly not excluding Pope himself. Homely images, things of a startling ordinariness, even ugliness, may all get included in poetry: "Yet eat, in dreams, the custard of the day"; "On once a flock-bed, but repair'd with straw."

Mira's day world, which she confronts with such rueful vigor, is not a place of comfort or reassurance. She, too, points to the need for the night world, for the pleasure of escape, retreat, relief. In her case, the reality is in dreams, and the dreams are pointedly nonspiritual, indeed materialistic dreams of things that to others (such as most of her readers) would be commonplace possessions. She destabilizes our middle upper-class vision by making us realize that what is ordinary pleasure to us is fantastic luxury to others.

Leapor, however she too may wish for the relief of night, is one of the Enlightenment investigators, determined to bring all the elements of common life—seen and unseen, unconscious as well as conscious—

to our attention. In one of her longest poems, "Crumble-hall," she takes us through the house and grounds of gentlefolk in a startling and subtly humorous variant on the country-house poem so well established since Ben Jonson wrote on Penshurst. Donna Landry has written a fine and searching analysis of this poem which sufficiently shows that the powerful innovation of this piece arises from "a diffusion of the servant's perspective throughout the text" and points to the fact that Mira's unawed vision not only includes the workers on the estate, the servants' lives and their rooms, but also takes in "incongruous disclosures that undermine Crumble-hall's pretensions to awesome gentility." Landry makes us fully aware of the extent to which Leapor's poem is a satire, even a parody, of Pope's *Epistle to Burlington*.

I wish to stress the extent to which Leapor in her original and playful—aggressively playful—description exhibits diversity in her copiousness and unstoppability. Variousness and copiousness emerge through the very persistence with which the heroine digs into odd nooks and quarters (such as but not only the servants' quarters) and finds what is kept hidden from view (including of course the fact that the servants have a life). She looks through lumber rooms and indulges in one of the favorite conventions of the period, the catalogue:

> Old Shoes, and Sheep-ticks bred in Stacks of Wool;
> Grey *Dobbin*'s Gears, and Drenching-Horns enow:
> Wheel-spokes—the Irons of a tatter'd Plough.
>   (99–101)

The italicizing of Dobbin's name gives the old horse briefly and comically the status of a person, and the now unusable "Plough" in being "tatter'd" turns from hard to soft—from iron to something very like cloth. Wool breeds ticks, and horses get sick and need drenching-horns to force medicine down their throats. Nature is not only prosaic but in conflict with itself, productive of discomforts.

Leapor, here as elsewhere, remorselessly lets light in upon the disregarded, the discarded, and the disguised. Both male and female poets of the period, Grub Streeters or countryfolk, gentles or ungentles, are constantly engaged in this activity, letting in the light. Yet the strain of the light tells on women as well as men. "A regular contributor to the *Gentleman's Magazine* from the 1730s when she first met Johnson"—so Lonsdale describes her—Elizabeth Carter wrote a number of poems, as well as her famed scholarly translation of Epictetus. Her best known poem is the "Ode to Wisdom," which Samuel Richardson in effect stole in 1747 to print in his *Clarissa*. This "Ode to Wisdom" is really an Ode to Evening or to Night:

> The solitary bird of night
> Thro' the pale shades now wings his flight,
>   And quits the time-shook tow'r,
> Where shelter'd from the blaze of day,
> In philosophic gloom he lay,
>   Beneath his ivy bower.
>
> With joy, I hear the solemn sound,
> Which midnight echoes waft around,
>   And sighing gales repeat.
> Fav'rite of *Pallas*! I attend,
> And, faithful to thy summons, bend
>   At Wisdom's awful seat.
>
> She loves the cool, the silent eve,
> Where no false shows of life deceive,
>   Beneath the lunar ray.
> Here *Folly* quits each vain disguise
> Nor sport her gayly-colour'd dyes,
>   As in the beam of day.

The images at the outset are similar to those in parts of Gray's Elegy, and both Gray and Carter look back to Shakespeare and to Milton without ever truly imitating either. Both are interested in expressing the value of the individual, of the personal self in undictated imagination and meditation. For Carter, as for Young and others, the nighttime is to be identified as the time of contact with the deeper self who cannot appear in the daylight's social regime. It is interesting to see how Carter subverts Milton here. There is a strong echo of the tempting words of Satan to Eve in her vicious dream:

> Why sleepst thou *Eve*? now is the pleasant time,
> The cool, the silent, save where silence yields
> To the night-warbling Bird . . .
>   . . . now reigns
> Full Orb'd the Moon, and with more pleasing light
> Shadowie sets off the face of things.   (V.38–43)

Eve is very wrong (even if just in dream, she seems already to have fall-en) to listen to the glowing voice praising the Night, and then to get up and wander about in the night world. Carter, like Ann Finch before her, picks up some of Milton's sensuous, appealing images and turns them to another use. The Night World becomes the good place, the good time. Folly, sin, and error are to be associated with the day. The "blaze of day" is too much—more glaring than useful. Woman does not err, but becomes more truly wise and virtuous by the freedom given her (herself a "solitary bird") to commune with nature herself and divine wisdom in the shade and stillness.

Divine Wisdom in Carter's piece is figured in pagan wise as a goddess, as Pallas Athena, but the tone and images surrounding this goddess subtly conflate her with Diana, the chaste goddess of the moon, a more feminine principle than Athenian Pallas. Pallas is, indeed, metamorphosed yet again into a kind of hearth goddess: "Thine are Retirement's silent joys, / And all the sweet, engaging tyes / Of still, domestic life." The hearth is not, however, a conventionalized hearth—there are no references to husband, children, family, but merely to peace. It must be admitted that the poem is interesting rather for what it attempts than for what it achieves: it is a stiff little piece with effective moments that merit it a place in any anthology of "retirement poetry" of the eighteenth century. And there is a good deal of what may be called "retirement poetry"—poetry that primarily emphasizes the "Relief" from glaring day, from the wearing blaze of the social and the public life.

Perhaps no taste produced more minor poems in the period than this taste for poems of retirement. One of the best known was *The Choice* (1700), by John Pomfret, a clergyman in Bedfordshire, who anticipated the taste of the age to come in his detailed, self-centered, and specifically materialistic view of the ideal life, as well as in his proclaimed taste for retreat from the hurly-burly. If heaven gave him a choice of "Method how to live," he would spend his hours in "blessed Ease and Satisfaction."

> Near some fair Town I'd have a private Seat,
> Built Uniform, not little, not too great:
> Better, if on a rising Ground it stood,
> Fields on this side, on that a Neighb'ring Wood.
> It shou'd within no other Things contain,
> But what are Useful, Necessary, Plain:
> Methinks, 'tis Nauseous, and I'd ne'er endure
> The needless Pomp of gawdy Furniture.   (1–12)

Pomfret's ideal, like many such retirement ideals, harks back to Horace and his self-representation both in the *Odes* and the *Satires* (we can catch here, among other things, thin echoes of the *Persicos odi*). This one poem won Pomfret a (small) place in Johnson's *Lives of the Poets*, and it is Johnson who tells us that Pomfret was once denied preferment in the Church because of "a malicious interpretation of some passages in his Choice; from which it was inferred, that he considered happiness as more likely to be found in the company of a mistress than of a wife." So difficult it is for a Bedfordshire clergyman to live according to—or even to imagine himself in—the Horatian ideal. Johnson adds that the objection was easily obliterated: "for it had happened to Pomfret as to all other men who plan schemes of life; he had departed from his purpose, and was then married." If it seems odd that Johnson should take the jocular ideas of the speaker in a poem as representing a serious scheme of life of the actual poet himself, we can see the extent to which the eighteenth-century readers preferred their poems to have a decided and believable autobiographical content, a preference markedly emphasized during the literary period covered roughly in historical terms by the reign of George II (1727–1760).

Matthew Green in *The Spleen* (1737) turns some of the retirement tropes into a recipe to cure melancholy. The same poet had already endorsed the "L'Allegro" view in a slightly earlier poem repudiating the philosophic and spiritual retirement prescribed by the Quakers. Green rehearses the view that "The world can't hear the small still voice, / Such is its bustle and its noise," but only to deny in the end, if not all value to *contemptus mundi*, at least the possibility of ever living in that manner. William Cowper offers what might be called the apotheosis of the busy retirement poem in *The Task*. He speaks of himself impressively as fated to loneliness, "the stricken deer that left the herd / Long since"; even though Christ withdrew the nearly fatal arrows, the suffering solitary retires from the world: "in remote / And silent woods I wander, far from those / My former partners of the peopled scene" (III.108–119). Yet the lonely retirement becomes almost as cosy and crowded as that imagined by Matthew Green in *The Spleen*, a poem in which "Contentment" modulates into multiplying possessiveness.

Cowper as the stricken deer once fled "to seek a tranquil death in distant shades" but now his distant shades are lively and organized, a piece of day work:

> Friends, books, a garden, and perhaps his pen,
> Delightful industry enjoyed at home,
> And nature in her cultivated trim
> Dressed to his taste, inviting him abroad—
> Can he want occupation who has these?
> (III.355–359)

Cowper's object in *The Task* might be said to be the sane reunion of day world and night world—but he avoids any of the horror of deep night. The phrase he uses to describe the winter garden of the green-house is a telling oxymoron: the flowers, he says, "form one social shade" (586). Diversity becomes unity, even as the oxymoron's order claims *society* for *shade*, and rescues "shade" from loneliness or dangerously intense self-communing.

When real retirement approaches, many poets express a fear of being too much alone, and begin to repopulate their imagined solitude with friends and to vary it with activities. As soon as retirement during the day is imagined, it becomes, apparently, almost impossible to imagine it as truly retired. Only the Night World allows the serene leisure of solitude, the freedom from demands. This was an era in which the idea of the personal self, the "subject," was undergoing tremendous emphasis and change, as shown in Felicity Nussbaum's *The Autobiographical Subject* (1989). The idea of the personal self, of subjectivity, of individuality was gaining new significances, even new identity. The individual self was a matter of great importance in politics and economic ideology (among other things). Yet at the same time as the idea of the strong individual with a sentient if often inarticulate inner self is created, recreated, and emphasized, there is an increase in tension between the pulls of the public and the private. For is not the "self" molded by society?—or should it not be? To escape from society might be to transgress against the self, to elude one's proper molding and useful formation. That way madness lies. "Be not solitary; be not idle," Johnson warns. At the same time, satirists, divines, philosophers, and poets were all concerned with the vacuous follies of social life, the impediments placed in the way of individual thought, self-recreation, and spiritual refreshment and growth.

If not all comic authors of the period were as ready as Sterne to pursue the *private* to the *privates*—Uncle Toby posted home from the bowling green "to enjoy this self-same thing in private;—I say in private"—the best writers were acutely aware of the conflict between private and public, including the tendency of the private to become public as soon as it is looked at. Comic poets create speakers who show that they know that any speaking out of private desires entails the creation of a persona for public use.

Lady Mary Wortley Montagu in a light poem entitled "The Lover: A Ballad" (written 1721–1725, published 1747) creates an intelligent and witty persona, a highly sexed but fastidious young woman who describes the ideal lover she is looking for. He must be neither pedant, rake, nor fop, he must have good sense and good nature (those constant prescriptions for *women*), and he must understand the difference between private and public. He must not give their relationship away by any signs in company:

> In public, preserve the Decorums are just,
> And shew in his Eyes he is true to his trust;
> Then rarely approach, and respectfully Bow,
> Yet not fulsomely pert, nor yet foppishly low.

> But when the long hours of Public are past,
> And we meet with champaign and a Chicken at last,
> May every fond Pleasure that hour endear;
> Be banish'd afar both Discretion and Fear.
> Forgetting or scorning the Airs of the Croud,
> He may cease to be formal and I to be proud.

This kind of poem could probably be written only by a member of the aristocracy, like Lady Mary, for the aristocracy understands, and has long understood, the necessary public affectations and restraints which make court life possible and give rise to an etiquette that must govern the conduct of any affair, including a sexual affair. Lady Mary dares to assert the assumption of a public personality—at a time when most of her fellow-poets, male and female are assuming "sincerity" as well as "originality." She knows that the social self must be all surface. There is even a pleasure in the masquerade, the secretion of the hidden truth during "the long hours of Public." She makes *Public* a substantive, an entity rather than a modifying adjective. What characterizes "public" as a section of life is spectatorship—the eye of lovers and watchers is central, and no signals must be given to the enemy. Even the heroine herself is a watcher, busy scrutinizing her beloved's behavior for any dangerous veering from decorum. The private life—what happens after "the long hours of Public are past"—is characterized by nonvisual senses, by the pleasures of taste (champagne and chicken) and the implied pleasures of touch in sex, which also becomes gustatory pleasure.

Most eighteenth-century writers, including poets, could not make the distinction between public self and private self so airily. Lady Mary indeed fosters the fears of private life in some of her readers, who will see the dangers of allowing women any license to be private. Only by making women always public personages, entities always looked at and scrutinized, can husbands and fathers be sure of themselves. Yet that is a paradox, too—the paradox of *The Country Wife*—for to take a woman into public life is to teach her the copiousness and diversity of men and manners which apprise her of new wants.

The eighteenth century had no answer to its conundrums, no release from its paradoxes. The Day World, with all its bustle, noise, and blaze, was essential to the new Enlightenment and would not go away. The Night World might be looked to longingly, as the reciprocal image, the objective correlative of that private self which the Day World also needed to exist (or to imagine existing, as in new capitalist theory).

Yet to describe Night is to illuminate it—to turn Night into Day. Poetry offers little relief, refreshment, retirement, or escape because the very description of the twilight escape, the nocturnal refreshment, the private communing must turn these things into public activities, and render all the dark landscapes as places on the measurable map. Milton's paradox, describing the flames of Hell as "darkness visible," becomes paradoxically realized. Darkness does become "visible" once we describe it, and Night Thoughts, once uttered, become the property of Day.

Margaret Anne Doody

Further Reading

Davie, Donald. A Gathered Church: *The Literature of the English Dissenting Interest, 1700–1930*. London: Oxford University Press, 1978.

Doody, Margaret Anne. *The Daring Muse: Augustan Poetry Reconsidered*. Cambridge: Cambridge University Press, 1985.

Hunter, J. Paul. *Before Novels: The Cultural Contexts of Eighteenth-Century English Fiction*. New York: Norton, 1990.

Landry, Donna. *The Muses of Resistance: Laboring-Class Women's Poetry in Britain 1739–1796*. Cambridge: Cambridge University Press, 1990.

Lonsdale, Roger, ed. *Eighteenth Century Women Poets*: An Oxford Anthology. Oxford: Oxford University Press, 1989.

Lonsdale, Roger, ed. *The New Oxford Book of Eighteenth-Century Verse*. Oxford: Oxford University Press, 1984.

Nussbaum, Felicity. *The Autobiographical Subject: Gender and Ideology in Eighteenth-Century England*. Baltimore: Johns Hopkins University Press, 1989.

Price, Martin. *To the Palace of Wisdom: Studies in Order and Energy from Dryden to Blake*. New York: Doubleday, 1964.

Sitter, John. *Literary Loneliness in Mid-Eighteenth-Century England*. Ithaca, N.Y.: Cornell University Press, 1982.

Trickett, Rachel. *The Honest Muse: A Study in Augustan Verse*. Oxford: Oxford University Press, 1967.

Blake

IN 1783 a book called *Poetical Sketches by W. B.* was privately printed. The friend responsible adverted readers that its contents
"were the production of untutored youth, commenced in his
twelfth, and occasionally resumed by the author till his twentieth year;
since which time, his talents having been wholly directed to the attainment of excellence in his profession, he has been deprived of the leisure
requisite to such a revisal of these sheets, as might have rendered them
less unfit to meet the public eye." With such an introduction, readers
may have been expecting something like Stephen Duck, the Thresher
Poet. If so, they must have been surprised to encounter a book of considerable sophistication, its poems reflecting an unusual range of the literary interests of the later eighteenth century: the Elizabethan lyric,
Spenser's *Hymnes*, the Shakespearean history play, the ballads of Percy's
Reliques, the Ossianic prose poem, and Gothic charnel house poetry.
Yet these poems are by no means merely imitative. The opening
addresses to the four seasons, perhaps the finest achievements in the
volume, handle their central, Age-of-Sensibility personifications in
such a way as to make them border on myth:

> O thou, with dewy locks, who lookest down
> Thro' the clear windows of the morning; turn
> Thine angel eyes upon our western isle,
> Which in full choir hails thy approach, O Spring!

An "untutored youth" who could so delicately combine the abstract and
the sensuous was clearly headed for a remarkable poetic career. The

particular nature of that career was to be deeply affected by his "attainment of excellence in his profession."

William Blake was an engraver's apprentice for seven years, and then studied drawing at the Royal Academy of Arts. Gifted visually as well as verbally, he taught himself to combine word and image in a new form—illuminated printing. After *Poetical Sketches* his books were not issued in letterpress (although a single set of printed proofs, dated 1791, exists for a poem called *The French Revolution*). Blake was himself the author, designer, and publisher of his works. Typically, he drew his designs and wrote his text (in mirror writing) on copper plates, etched the plates, inked them, printed them in relief, and painted the sheets in water colors. However, some of his illuminated books were color-printed in the 1790s, and a few were printed in intaglio. In the resulting work, design could be as important as text. We should therefore be aware that in discussing Blake's poetry out of its illuminated visual context, we are leaving out one dimension of his composite art. Nevertheless, his poetry has a rich textual existence, whether in the lyricism of the *Songs of Innocence* or in the "strong heroic Verse" of *The Four Zoas*. Those who have come to appreciate Blake's poetry have usually come to it through typographic texts, and even Blake scholars read Blake's calligraphic hand only for their own special purposes.

Blake's first illuminated book of poetry was *Songs of Innocence*, issued in 1789 and then combined with *Songs of Experience* in 1794 to make a dual volume subtitled *Shewing the Two Contrary States of the Human Soul*. The Contrary States sometimes appear overtly, as in poems paired by the same title or by obviously contrasting figures, sometimes by implication. What is common to both States is incompleteness, despite the apparent attractiveness of Innocence and the apparent wisdom of Experience. This can be seen, for example, in the two poems entitled "The Chimney Sweeper." In *Innocence* we have a poem with a beautiful surface and some disturbing moral assumptions. The speaker's attempt to console Tom Dacre "when his head / That curl'd like a lamb's back, was shaved" seems close to a sick joke—"for when your head's bare / You know that the soot cannot spoil your white hair" (5–8). Similarly off-putting is the Angel's injunction to Tom that "if he'd be a good boy, / He'd have God for his father & never want joy" (19–20). There is something smarmy about this Angel's endorsement of a God of good boys, and the conclusion would be appalling if taken at face value: "Tho' the morning was cold, Tom was happy & warm, / So if all do their duty, they need not fear harm" (23–24). This seems to enjoin the sort of contentment the child is made to promise at Confirmation in the Book of Common Prayer:

To honor and obey the king and his ministers. To submit myself to all my governors, teachers, spiritual pastors and masters. To order myself lowly and reverently to all my betters. Not to covet nor desire other men's goods. But learn and labor truly to get my own living, and do my duty in that state of life, unto which it shall please God to call me.   *(The Book of Common Prayer, 1559)*

Blake knew that such carrion comfort the mind appalls, as does the Chimney Sweeper of *Experience*. This child has been reduced to a mere object, "a little black thing," but he is precociously aware of his condition. Cued by a presumably adult interrogator, he bitterly remarks that his father and mother have gone up to Church "to praise God & His Priest & King / Who make up a heaven of our misery" (11–12). In the reverberations of such a powerful statement, it is tempting to disregard the vision of the first Chimney Sweeper altogether. Yet Blake wasn't an innocent child in 1789; he was in his thirty-second year, and it's hard to believe that he was an exceptionally late bloomer who only heard the voice of Experience three or four years later. (It's true that earlier versions of three *Songs of Innocence* were included ca. 1784 in the manuscript satire *An Island in the Moon*, but even then Blake was a mature adult and presented a very Experienced portrait of himself as Quid the Cynic). The first Sweeper's vision of boys "leaping laughing" down a green plain is succeeded but not obliterated by the direct statement of things-as-they-are of the second speaker. Each version of reality is incomplete.

The oppositions and disjunctions of the two Contrary states appear throughout *Innocence* and *Experience*—in other pairs like the two "Holy Thursday" poems, in contrastive figures like the Lamb and the Tyger, the Piper and the Bard, and in counterstatements like "The Divine Image" and "the Human Abstract." Another kind of disjunction is found in "The Little Girl Lost" and "The Little Girl Found." This pair—originally part of *Innocence* but moved into *Experience* in later copies of the combined *Songs*—may anticipate a resolution of contraries, but the resolution they present is a false one. Little Lyca, only seven summers old, wanders into the desert, where she falls asleep and is viewed by a "kingly lion" and other beasts of prey. These gambol around her and then convey her "naked" to their "caves" (51–52).

Here we can recognize the Swedenborgian doctrine of correspondences, according to which different animals represent different affections. The wild beasts have to do with the child's sexuality, something of which Blake was explicitly aware (as in *Visions of the Daughters of Albion* 6:4, where he calls infancy "lustful"). The parents in the second Lyca poem search for their child, but the child "Starv'd in desart wild" is only a "fancied image" (12, 14). The reader knows that Lyca is in good hands (or paws), and therefore the parents' anxiety projects their own fear of sexuality. The irony deepens when the mother collapses into a virtual personification, carried by the father "arm'd with sorrow sore" (22); more effectual arms are borne by the lion, "a spirit arm'd in gold," who shows them "their sleeping child / Among tygers wild" (36, 47–48). Yet this is not a true solution. The "lonely dell" they all dwell in "To this day" (50, 49) anticipates "th' untrodden ways" among which Wordsworth's Lucy lived, but even with "very few to love" her, Lucy was better off than Lyca. Lyca's sexuality has been accepted, but what is she going to do with it if she lives only with her parents and with beasts who may become spirits but not human beings? The persistent theme of the *Songs* is the disjunction of the Contraries, not their resolution.

The interplay of Innocence and Experience is also the subject of two longer works concerning, on one level at least, the descent of the soul and its vicissitudes in the lower world. These are *The Book of Thel* (1789, but with a final plate that may have been etched in 1791 or later) and *Visions of the Daughters of Albion* (1793). *Thel* begins in a pastoral landscape in which the heroine experiences intimations of mortality. She is reassured of the unity of all life by the Lilly of the valley, the Cloud, the Worm, and, finally, allowed to enter the world of Experience vicariously through the house of "the matron Clay." Thel sees nothing but sexual strife, sorrows and tears in the lower world, and she flies back to her cloistered and neglected virtue.

Visions takes up the theme of what happens to a woman brave enough not to retreat. Oothoon, an incarnation of female desire, is on her way to make a gift of her virginity ("the bright Marygold of Leutha's vale," 1:5) to Theotormon, the man she loves. She is attacked and raped by Bromion who then, in a reenactment of the story of Amnon and Tamar in 2 Samuel 13, blames it all on her. Theotormon, truly the god-tormented man, laments, despite Oothoon's insistence that "I am pure" (2:28).

Although Oothoon, like Mary Wollstonecraft in *A Vindication of the Rights of Woman*, condemns "this hypocrite modesty" (6:16), *Visions* is far from an unambiguous endorsement of feminism. Blake's ambivalence can be seen in Oothoon's masochistic "calling Theotormons Eagles to prey upon her flesh" (2:13) and in her offer to catch other girls for Theotormon to enjoy while she watches their love play. The Daughters of Albion, the women of England, passively "hear her woes, & eccho back her sighs" (7:13). The poem brilliantly presents the problematization of the female libido but offers no solution.

Another work that combines the elements of Innocence and Experience is *The Marriage of Heaven and Hell* (1790–1793?). Written in part as a satire on the Swedenborgians with whom Blake had associated not long before, this prose poem ironically undermines all forms of dualism. "The voice of the Devil" proclaims that "Man has no Body distinct from his Soul," and Milton is shown to be "a true Poet and of the devils party without knowing it." Swedenborg's error lay in conversing with Angels and not with Devils, for in the world of *The Marriage* Angels are self-righteous, priggish, and life-denying, while Devils inhabit the flames of Energy. The Contraries of the *Songs* are necessary to human existence, for "Without Contraries is no progression" (3). All the same, these Contraries occupy positive and negative poles: one would rather be among what Blake called the "Prolific" than what he called the "Devouring," just as the narrator of *The Marriage* prefers the ambience of Milton's Hell to the "Vacuum" of his Holy Ghost. The statements made in *The Marriage* must be referred to their satirical framework; they are not necessarily aphorisms that can be wrenched out of place and turned into good advice. Blake probably would have preferred that we not take too literally Proverbs like "Sooner murder an infant in its cradle than nurse unacted desires" (10).

Visions and *The Marriage* are among the books Blake produced while living at Lambeth, south of the Thames, from autumn 1790. The other "Lambeth books," as they have come to be called, are six works comprising "the Bible of Hell" that Blake promised his readers in *The Marriage* (24). The first two of these, *America* (dated 1793 on its title page) and *Europe* (1794), are the only poems that Blake himself subtitled *A Prophecy*. With Unitarian radicals like Joseph Priestley and the young Samuel Taylor Coleridge, Blake viewed the history of his own times, the times following the American and French Revolutions, as fulfillments of the writings of the Old Testament prophets; his Prophecies are not predictions of the future but expositions of forms and forces underlying historical events. "A Prophet is a Seer," as Blake once noted, "not an Arbitrary Dictator."

America begins with a "Preludium," in which Orc, the "hairy youth" who incarnates Energy, is in chains, tended by the shadowy female figure who will be called Vala in Blake's later works. She is an earth goddess who is speechless until Orc's "fierce embrace" shocks her into recognition: "Thou art the image of God who dwells in darkness of Africa" (2:8). In the Prophecy itself, "warlike men" appear on America's shore to confront the forces of "Albions Angel," England's ruler. In the conflict that follows, Orc proclaims freedom in terms combining the millennial prophecies of Isaiah with the Resurrection in the Gospels (plate 6). However, Orc already has both human and serpent forms, suggesting the dual possibilities of revolution as they appeared to Blake in the mid-1790s: it might humanize the world, or it might become bound into the cyclical recurrence of history. With the defeat of Albion's Angel, Britain itself is threatened by the revolutionary flames of Orc; but at a crucial moment the father god Urizen comes to the aid of his viceroy, freezing the situation with his "stored snows" (16:9). The ensuing respite for "Angels & weak men" is only temporary, for "their end should come, when France reciev'd the Demons light" (6:14–15).

Europe has its own "Preludium," in which the shadowy female laments the "all devouring fiery kings" to whom she must give birth, "Devouring & devoured" (1:4–5); but she is relieved by a vision of the birth of a divine child. Then the Prophecy itself moves from an imitation of Milton's ode "On the Morning of Christ's Nativity" through "the night of Nature" (9:3)—eighteen centuries of history—to the point at which *America* ended, with Albion's Angel and his councillors lying defeated. The poem ends with the apocalyptic manifestation of Orc in "the vineyards of red France" (15:1) and "the strife of blood" (15:10) that begins the wars of the allied powers against the French Revolution.

With *The Book of Urizen* (1794), Blake turned to the cosmogonic aspect of his myth. *Urizen* presents itself as a parody of Genesis, playing on the idea of a biblical text with its double columns and its division into chapters and verses. Its God is a patriarch who combines the most repressive aspects of reason and religion. His withdrawal from a harmonious union of Eternals in something like the Neoplatonist Pleroma precipitates the creation of the material world. Los, the Eternal Prophet, keeps Urizen from falling further by chaining him, but this activity has a deleterious effect on Los himself, making him divide into male and female. In a version of the ironical myth assigned to Aristophanes in *The Symposium*, Los pursues his female counterpart, Enitharmon. As a result of their union, Orc is born, then chained to a mountaintop by his jealous father, bringing the situation round to that of the "Preludium" to *America*. However, the general tone of events has become darker, and the primordial creation myth, expanded in *The Book of Los* (1795), approaches the dualism that Blake had satirized in *The Marriage of Heaven and Hell*.

If matter is so far removed from Eternity, how could even the most energetic human efforts create a millennial society? The answer is not to be found among the Lambeth books. In *The Song of Los* (1795) "the darkness of Asia was startled / At the thick-flaming, thought-creating fires of Orc" (6:5); but the poem concludes with a premature, grisly resurrection in which "The Grave shrieks with delight, & shakes / Her hollow womb" (7:35–6). *The Book of Ahania* (1795), a sequel to *Urizen*, presents a new rebel, Fuzon, who maims Urizen only to be killed by him, as Blake sees the France of Robespierre's Terror becoming what it beheld. The Lambeth period, as we can see, had been a fertile time for Blake. Then, after 1795, Blake published no new illuminated books until he issued *Milton* in 1808 or later. Part of the reason was a temporary redirection of his energies, for in 1795 he was commissioned to illustrate Young's *Night Thoughts*, which led him to execute the astonishing number of 537 water color designs and 43 engravings. However, the *Night Thoughts* edition was published in 1797, and still no new illuminated works appeared. Blake may have been intimidated by increased government repression, and the arrest of Richard Brothers, the self-styled "Prince of the Hebrews," may have been a cautionary example. Brothers, too, had written books of prophecies, and he, too, had denounced war and empire. In March 1795 Brothers was arrested under an Elizabethan act "against fond and fantastical prophecies"; after being examined by the Privy Council, he was confined in a madhouse. The example can hardly have been lost upon Blake, who later wrote on the title page of Bishop Richard Watson's *Apology for the Bible* "To defend the Bible in this year 1798 would cost a man his life" (p. 611).

By 1798 Blake was certainly writing, if not publishing, prophetic verse. 1797 is the date on the title page of the manuscript he at first called *Vala*, but work on the poem continued, amid many other projects, for perhaps a decade. The original plan called for a combination of the cosmogonic subject matter of the Books of *Urizen* and *Los* with the political mythology of *America* and *Europe*, all embodied in a fourfold structure that would avoid the dualism implied by his earlier creation myth. It centers upon four androgynous beings, whom Blake at some point began calling "Zoas" (from the Greek for "living creature," the "four beasts" of Revelation 4:6).

These are the component physical/psychic forces of the Eternal Man, Albion. Their separations into male and female and their wars against one another precipitate a series of falls of which humanity is the passive victim. Tharmas, the "Parent power" (3:6) of perception and sensation, is at the beginning already separate from the earth mother, Enion. She gives birth to Los and Enitharmon, whose fierce contentions are modeled upon those of William and Catherine Blake. Luvah, incarnating human desire, and Vala, the world of nature that is its object, engage in a Romantic agony that further reduces the human condition. Urizen casts out Ahania, who, a rejected Wisdom figure, falls far into Non Entity. These conflicts are at the same time a *psychomachia* taking place within Albion and an allegorization of the wars of Europe in Blake's time.

Orc is born in Night the Fifth very much as in *Urizen*, and then bound with the Chain of Jealousy. Blake could hardly carry over the political myth of *America* at this point, as he may originally have expected to do, since France must have been well on the road to Empire by the time he got to this point of composition. Therefore in Night the Seventh he made Orc, instructed by his old enemy Urizen, abandon his human form entirely and become a serpent, rising in power among the stars of Urizen. No longer offering a possibility of millennial peace, Orc himself is consumed by the flames of the final conflagration in Night the Ninth.

This would have left the work without a redemptive center of gravity had Blake not introduced new poetic conceptions and changed others in the later written parts and in additions to earlier Nights. The role of Los was deepened so that he would not be merely one of four Zoas but the agent of Albion's regeneration, and the resolution of the conflict among Los, his reasoning Spectre, and his Emanation became a major theme. A body called the Council of God was introduced to observe and occasionally direct events, and the Lamb of God was made to descend wearing Luvah's robes of blood. This new material is related to a series of visionary experiences Blake had in the very early 1800s. While they provide the poem, finally called *The Four Zoas*, with some of its most memorable passages, these elements do not jibe very well with the structure Blake had developed for *Vala*, and reading the palimpsest manuscript, one has the sense of a series of desperate rescue attempts being made by the author. Perhaps it was his own recognition of this situation that led Blake to abandon the manuscript at last and to concentrate upon the ambitious but realizable projects of *Milton* and *Jerusalem*.

The background of *Milton* lies in what Blake later called his three years' slumber on the banks of the Ocean. In 1800 the world was suddenly changed for William and Catherine, for in September of that year they moved to the village of Felpham in Sussex. The occasion was what seemed a major professional opportunity provided by a very minor poet. William Hayley, author of *The Triumphs of Temper*, was writing the biography of William Cowper, a poet whom Blake also admired. He engaged Blake to engrave the illustrations, and he also set about finding other ways to help Blake earn money by illustrating Hayley's own ballads and by painting miniature portraits. At the same time, Blake thought he could carry out his own projects in painting and poetry. The problem was that the two agendas were incompatible. Blake increasingly felt that Hayley was condescending to him and was reducing him to mechanical drudgery out of envy of his creative talents. His growing personal unhappiness at Felpham was compensated for by a series of visionary experiences that confirmed his sense of identity as a poet-artist.

On April 25, 1803, he informed his friend and patron Thomas Butts, "That I can alone carry on my visionary studies in London unannoyed. . . ." Before he could put this decision into practice, however, Blake quarreled with a drunken soldier whom he ejected from his cottage garden, and he consequently found himself charged with damning the King and other seditious utterances. Although he was acquitted (with the help of Hayley, who provided a lawyer), Blake was deeply shaken by this experience. His accusers, judges, and Hayley himself all found their way into his two most ambitious illuminated books.

Milton is "a Poem in 2 [originally 12] Books," but this does not indicate the true divisions of the work. It begins with a single-page "Preface" in prose and verse and then, after a brief epic invocation and thematic statement, goes on with the "Bards prophetic Song"—2:23 to 13 [14]:

44—that provides a background myth for the descent of Milton into the world of Generation and his investing Blake with prophetic/poetic power. At 27 [28]: 66 a new movement begins, describing regenerate Nature as a vision of the creator-God Elohim; this section straddles the "2 Books," merging with the next great movement, the descent of Milton's sixfold Emanation Ololon, which begins at 31 [34] and culminates in her union with Milton in Blake's garden at Felpham in 42 [49]. This apocalyptic event is preceded by the manifestation of Satan as Antichrist and followed at the close of the poem by the "Human Harvest" that begins the Last Judgment. While these events must necessarily seem diachronic as here described, Blake means us to imagine them synchronically, as he indicates by having episodes like Milton's struggle with Urizen and Milton's entering Blake's left foot occur at several points, as if everything in the poem were happening at once.

The "Preface" is an expression of the new confidence Blake felt as a result of his recent visions. "The Sublime of the Bible" is set above (and behind) all classical models, and "Young Men of the New Age"—Blake's hoped-for audience—are exhorted to renew the arts and to reject war. In verses reminiscent of one of Charles Wesley's hymns, Blake transplants the life of Jesus to England, figuratively reversing Richard Brothers's Anglo-Israelite theory—rather than settling in the historical Jerusalem, Britons are to build the city of hope in their own green and pleasant land. The Bard's Prophetic Song then recounts in coded terms Blake's view of his years at Felpham.

This is a roman à clef whose key only partially fits its lock, for Blake took such care lest the prototype characters recognize themselves that some of their identities remain conjectural. Still, the broad outline is clear. Mild-mannered Satan is William Hayley trying to do the work of the true poet-artist, Palamabron-Blake. When they exhange roles at Satan's instigation, the result is threatened chaos. The ensuing controversy reaches up to the Halls of the Sons of Albion and threatens to cause disruption there as well. Then Milton, already "Unhappy tho in heav'n" (2:18) is moved to significant action. Milton wishes to redeem his past error of having driven his sixfold emanation, comprising his wives and daughters, into Ulro, the subbasement of reality, exiling the female part of his identity. He had also, in the eyes of the Blake of the 1800s, contributed to the division of humanity in taking part in the international politics of his era. To redeem these errors, he voluntarily descends into the lower world.

An archetypal hero, Milton must encounter the perils of the way. First he must pass through the Vortex of nature in order to enter space-time. Then the repressive reason of the "Demon Urizen" threatens him. Milton refuses to engage in destructive battle but instead molds Urizen with "the red clay of Succoth" (which Hiram used for the Temple ornaments). Like Bunyan's Pilgrim and Apollyon, "The man and Demon strove many periods" (19 [21]: 27). Though offered earthly power by Rahab and Tirzah, Milton ignores this temptation (as Jesus in *Paradise Regained* rejects Satan's offer of the kingdoms of the world) and so sets into motion the redemptive action of the poem. Entering William Blake's left foot, Milton empowers Blake to see the "Vegetable" world from the perspective of Eternity. Los as the spirit of Prophecy embraces him, "And so I became one Man with him arising in my strength" (22 [24]: 12–14).

Despite the miscomprehension of Los's two ungenerated sons, who see only the old Milton and fear he will reinforce the political and religious divisions of Europe, Los urges the eschatological significance of Blake/Milton: "He is the Signal that the Last Vintage now approaches . . ." (24 [26]: 42). Paradoxically, this impending event leads to a vision of the created world at its most glorious, with its constellations, gorgeous clothed Flies, flowers and herbs, and songs of the Nightingale and the Lark. These images are set in the matrix of a myth of the descent of the pre-existing soul into its material body, now seen not as oppressively restrictive as in *Urizen* but as benevolently protective, "the beautiful House for the piteous sufferer" (28 [30]: 7).

In the last half dozen plates, the apocalypse takes place in Blake's garden. Satan now manifests himself as a parody of the Christ of the Parousia, "Coming in a cloud, with trumpets & flaming fire" (38 [43]: 50). Milton refuses to annihilate Satan, as he previously refused to annihilate Urizen, but instead calls upon the sleeping Albion to subdue his Reasoning Spectre and cast him into the Lake (as is done to the beast and the false Prophet in Revelation 19:20). With this, the sleeping body of humanity begins to stir, though he cannot yet rise. Rahab/Babylon, Moral Virtue, now appears in her true form as dragon and harlot; the Virgin Ololon combines with Milton to produce a new, composite being; Jesus is seen clad in the writing of Divine Revelation; and William Blake falls outstretched upon his garden path to undergo a Last Judgment in his own living body. End time is thus realized for an individual, though not yet for the human race.

As Northrop Frye remarks in *Fearful Symmetry*, "*Milton* describes the attainment by the poet of the vision that *Jerusalem* expounds in terms of all humanity." It does so, as do the Gospels according to tradition, by addressing each of its four chapters to a particular audience: "The Public," "The Jews," "The Deists," and "The Christians." In its universality, however, *Jerusalem* still has a great deal of particularity concerning its creator. A quatrain of plate 27 evokes places on those semi-rural outskirts of London that the child Blake must have explored:

> The Jews-harp house and the Green Man;
> The Ponds where Boys to bathe delight:
> The fields of Cows by Willans farm:
> Shine in Jerusalems pleasant sight.
>   (13–16)

The extended lyric of which these lines are part shows that Blake had lost none of the melodic gift that marked his earliest songs.

In contrast, the struggle of Blake's creative self with his apprehensions and fears is appropriately expressed in powerful rhetoric that describes the conflict between Los and his Spectre. Why should Blake continue to address a public that ignores him, asks the Spectre—"Wilt thou still go on to destruction? / Till thy life is all taken away by this deceitful friendship?" (7:9– 10). When Los subdues the Spectre "on his Anvil" (91:43), it is in terms metaphorically describing Blake's work at his chosen profession of engraving. Sometimes Blake speaks out in his own person, as in 34 [38]: 41–43, where he sketches his career as a poet-prophet:

> I heard in Lambeth's shades:
> In Felpham I heard and saw the Visions of Albion
> I write in South Molton Street, what I both see and hear
> In regions of Humanity, in Londons opening streets.

Elsewhere Blake's seven-footed lines can express the ranting of the enemies of humanity or the suffering and lamentations of their victims, but here they convey his own poetic voice with memorable clarity. Indeed, more than any of his other works, *Jerusalem* displays Blake's range and versatility as a practitioner of verse.

In *Jerusalem* Albion once more represents the body of humanity, and throughout most of the poem, he is threatened with destruction by his terrible Sons and Daughters. The Sons are for the most part named after figures associated with Blake's trial, most notably Scofield his accuser. Hayley is represented as Hyle (also, ironically, the Greek word for matter). Another aspect of the destructive forces that Blake saw attacking the divine humanity is embodied in Hand, whose name derives from the pointing hand used by the Hunt brothers as their signature in *The Examiner*. It was over this editorial siglum that Blake saw his exhibition of pictures condemned in September 1809 and himself called "an unfortunate lunatic." The Daughters, who are named after females in the mythological history of Britain, are, if anything, more bloodthirsty than the Sons; because of their allure, Los, Albion's "strong Guard" (19:38) does not dare approach them but sends his Spectre after them. Through much of the work, Albion lies asleep, separated from his emanation, Jerusalem, who is a city yet a woman as in Revelation. Cast out and condemned as a harlot, like Oothoon in *Visions*, Jerusalem's role is largely one of uttering pleas for divine love, mercy, and brotherhood; the wickedly seductive Vala has the more active role. In the postapocalyptic world, however, "Sexes must vanish and cease / To be" (92:13–14): Vala and Enitharmon disappear from the text, which ends by naming the emanations of all human forms Jerusalem.

When Albion awakens, he seizes his bow "firm between the Male & Female Loves" (97:15), suggesting an existence beyond genital sexuality, and with one fourfold Arrow of Love annihilitates the Druid Spectre. Plate 98 then presents a breathless rush of activity, with Blake pushing to their limit the "terrific numbers" that he reserved for "the terrific parts" (plate 3), crowding the line to its breaking point to suggest the forces of the apocalypse:

> And they conversed together in Visionary Forms dramatic which bright
> Redounded from their Tongues in thunderous majesty, in Visions
> In new Expanses, creating exemplars of Memory and Intellect
> Creating Space, Creating Time according to the wonders Divine
> Of Human Imagination . . .   (28–32)

Existence continues to be an interplay of forces, with "the great city of Golgonooza" still existing in "the Shadowy Generation" (98:55) and earthly forms being recycled to and from their "Planetary lives" (99:3).

Readers have come a long way from the dismissal of *Jerusalem* as the "perfectly mad poem" that Robert Southey found it to be (see *Blake Records*, p. 229). Blake's mode of "Allegory addressd to the Intellectual powers," as he called it in a letter, makes great demands but offers great rewards. Blake's apt figure for the reader's experience in *Jerusalem* is a version of following Ariadne's thread—the golden string that, if wound into a ball, "will lead you in at Heavens gate, / Built in Jerusalems wall" (plate 77). The difference is that, like the Human Forms of the end of the poem, having found our way out, we will want to find our way in again.

Morton D. Paley

Textual Note: Blake's writings are quoted from *The Complete Poetry and Prose of William Blake*, rev. ed., ed. by David V. Erdman (New York: Doubleday, 1988). The texts of lyrics are referred to by line number, of longer poems by plate or page number followed by a colon and then the line number(s). Prose is cited by page number.

Further Reading

Adams, Hazard. *William Blake: A Reading of the Shorter Poems*. Seattle: University of Washington Press, 1963.

Bentley, G. E., Jr., ed. *Blake Records*. Oxford: Clarendon, 1969.

Beer, John. B*lake's Visionary Universe*. Manchester: University of Manchester Press, 1969.

Damon, S. Foster. *A Blake Dictionary*. Rev. ed. Hanover, N.H.: University Press of New England, 1988.

Damrosch, Leopold. *Symbol and Truth in Blake's Myth*. Princeton: Princeton University Press, 1980.

De Luca, Vincent Arthur. *Words of Eternity*. Princeton: Princeton University Press, 1991.

Erdman, David V. *Blake: Prophet Against Empire*. 3d ed. Princeton: Princeton University Press, 1977.

Essick, Robert N. *William Blake and the Language of Adam*. Oxford: Clarendon, 1989.

Frye, Northrop. *Fearful Symmetry*. Princeton: Princeton University Press, 1947.

Gilchrist, Alexander. *Life of William Blake*. Edited by Ruthven Todd. 2d ed. London: Dent, 1945.

Gleckner, Robert F. *The Piper and the Bard*. Detroit: Wayne State University Press, 1959.

Hilton, Nelson. *Liberal Imagination: Blake's Vision of Words*. Berkeley: University of California Press, 1983.

Mellor, Anne K. *Blake's Human Form Divine*. Berkeley: University of California Press, 1974.

Paley, Morton D. *The Continuing City: William Blake's "Jerusalem."* Oxford: Clarendon, 1983.

Coleridge

C OLERIDGE once divided his poems into those written chiefly
from the age of seventeen to twenty-five, those written from
twenty-five to thirty-three, and those written afterwards.
Coleridge was twenty-five in 1797, the year in which the second edition of his *Poems on Various Subjects* was published, and in that same year
he became involved with William Wordsworth in the great experiment
of the *Lyrical Ballads*. Most of the material from the two editions of
Poems he later classified as as "Juvenile Poems," while he regarded his
Lyrical Ballads contributions as poems of his maturity. The three great
poems of the marvelous, by which Coleridge is known to almost every
reader of English literature, were composed from 1797 to 1800; the
three mature "conversation poems" in 1797–1798; and "Dejection: An
Ode," in which Coleridge declared the failure of his creative powers, in
1802. Seldom has a great poet's best work been produced in so short a
period, even if we include (as we should) "To William Wordsworth,"
written in the winter of Coleridge's thirty-third year. Most of the poetry that he produced after that was deliberately in a minor key, though
some of it is of great interest, as are some of the very early works.

If we consider the *Poems* of 1796 and 1797, together with the work
later entitled "The Destiny of Nations," which was intended for the
1797 volume but not published until 1817, we seem to be considering
a young poet, strongly influenced by the blank verse of Milton and the
odes of Thomas Gray, preparing for a career as a writer of religious and
political works. "Religious Musings," upon which Coleridge was then
prepared to stake his reputation, is the most ambitious of these. Look-

ing upon the state of society from a cosmic perspective, "Religious Musings" presents the French Revolution as an apocalypse to be followed by the millennium of a just society and the descent of the throne of God. When he began this poem in December 1794, Coleridge had already written the greater part of "The Destiny of Nations" as a contribution to Southey's epic *Joan of Arc* (1796), projecting allegorical visions of the American and French Revolutions as proleptic of universal peace. In shorter poems Coleridge expressed his responses to events in Revolutionary France and in his own country. "To a Young Lady with a Poem on the French Revolution" presents the poet as imaginatively participating in the bloody defense of the Revolution but, significantly, closes with his turning to domestic life.

The "Ode on the Departing Year" views the events of 1796 as a series of nightmare visions of war and empire, prophesizes the imminent destruction of Albion, and concludes with the isolated poet, "unpartaking of the evil thing," in religious contemplation. Sonnets lament the apostasy of Edmund Burke from the cause of Freedom, sympathize with Joseph Priestley as driven to America by the Birmingham mob, and praise libertarian figures like Erskine, Sheridan, Koskiusko, and LaFayette. Although there are also some poems of personal sentiment like the beautiful "Lines Written at Shurton Bars," the emphasis is on the public realm.

Coleridge did not immediately abandon this subject matter after 1797, but as he self-critically put it, he "pruned" his style and "used my best efforts to tame the swell and glitter of both thought and diction." In "France: An Ode," originally published as "The Recantation," Coleridge reviewed his past Revolutionary sympathies from the perspective of 1798 and faced the collapse of his former millennial hopes. Now he declared that Liberty could be found only among clouds, sea, and woods, "The guide of homeless winds, and playmate of the waves!" In "Fears in Solitude," that same year, he voiced his feelings of anxiety and isolation at the prospect of a French invasion, yet blamed his countrymen for having offended God by their cupidity and corruption. It would no doubt have been difficult to go on writing meditative political poetry without finding a center of value somewhere, but satire was still possible. In "Fire, Famine, and Slaughter," Coleridge excoriated William Pitt for the blood shed in the Vendée and in Ireland; and in "The Devil's Thoughts," written in collaboration with Southey, the institutions of British society are inspected by the Devil to provide a model for hell. These two apocalyptic-grotesque poems, first published anonymously in 1798 and 1799, were enormously popular, but by the time they were written Coleridge's poetic career was taking a much different course.

In a famous account in the *Biographia Literaria* Coleridge recalls the walks and talks with Wordsworth in the Quantock Hills that led to the genesis of *Lyrical Ballads*, and describes the division of labor that took place between Wordworth and himself. Wordworth's subjects "were to be drawn from ordinary life," while in Coleridge's share "the incidents and agents were to be, in part at least, supernatural; and the excellence aimed at was to consist in the interesting of the affections by the dramatic truth of such emotions, as would naturally accompany such situations, supposing them real." The reader who expected "The Rime of the Ancient Mariner" to be a poem of supernatural horror like Bürger's "Lenore" would be at first gratified but finally disappointed, for the ultimate interest would be (in a word dear to Coleridge) psychological. Nor would the poem be morally satisfying in the end. In response to the criticism that it did not have enough moral, Coleridge declared: "It ought to have had no more moral than the *Arabian Nights'* tale of the merchant's sitting down to eat dates by the side of a well and throwing the shells aside, and lo! a genie starts up and says he *must* kill aforesaid merchant *because* one of the date shells had, it seems, put out the eye of the genie's son." The "Rime" had its own logic, its own laws.

One aspect of those laws is the motive for the killing of the albatross. Deliberately left motiveless, this deed is a forerunner of the *acte gratuite* to be so prized by French existentialism. It demonstrates free will, and in the case of the Mariner, the debasement of the will. He then becomes Other, combining aspects of Cain and the Wandering Jew into a single figure who also anticipates the *poète maudit* of Rimbaud. Robert Penn Warren in "A Poem of Pure Imagination" equates the deed itself with the Crucifixion, and although not all readers will accept Warren's consistent bifurcation of Understanding and Imagination in the poem, his interpretation remains a powerful influence on many later ones. The sailors, by approving the deed once the fog lifts, put themselves in the place of the community acquiescing in the death of Christ.

The Mariner's weapon is a crossbow, and "cross" as verb and noun reinforces the identification of the albatross with Jesus; associated with the moon glimmering through fog, the bird is an example of

Coleridge's characteristic imagery of the Imagination. It also displays the characteristic "translucence" of a symbol as Coleridge would memorably define it in *The Statesman's Manual* (1816)—"a translucence of the special in the individual or of the universal in the general" and "above all . . . the translucence of the eternal through and in the temporal." Although these words were written as late as 1816, we should remember that the nature of symbolism was a lifelong preoccupation of Coleridge's—years before *Lyrical Ballads* he wrote, in the poem that became "The Destiny of Nations,"

> For all that meets the bodily sense I deem
> Symbolical, one mighty alphabet
> For infant minds . . .

As for the Mariner, he has gone through a regenerative experience—at the same time expressed in and resulting from his blessing of the water snakes—restoring the Coleridgean principle of "the one life within us and abroad" ("The Eolian Harp"). Yet his confession to the Hermit brings only a temporary catharsis, and he must continue to tell his story. In his desire to transfer his guilty self-awareness to others, he uses the power of his "glittering eye"—a form of hypnotism known in the later eighteenth century as "animal magnetism." So the Wedding Guest never gets to participate in the communal joys of the bridal feast but goes home to rise "sadder" (meaning more serious) and wiser, while the Mariner continues to pass like night from land to land with the "strange power of speech" that is poetry itself.

When Coleridge prepared the text of the poem for publication in *Sibylline Leaves* (1817), he made two major changes. He ruthlessly pruned the diction of the *Lyrical Ballads* version, sometimes eliminating single archaisms, sometimes whole passages of charnel-house verse. The scene remains medieval, with the Mariner's references to saints and to "Mary Queen," but it is no longer eighteenth-century Gothic. Coleridge also added the brilliant invention of the marginal gloss, introducing a learned, sometimes pedantic editorial persona, a commentator often not averse to stating the obvious, yet at times surprisingly eloquent—"No twilight within the courts of the sun." The marginal gloss, somewhat archaic itself, makes the poem seem even more so, and contributes a perspective different from that of hypothetical author, narrator, or hypothetical reader. It is rightly in this later form that Coleridge's masterwork has become best known.

Another great poem of the marvelous written in the *Lyrical Ballads* period, but one never intended for the joint publication, is "Kubla Khan." Not published until 1816, it was then accompanied by a long prose preface, the purpose of which was to set it off from most other poetry and to make it more of a psychological curiosity or, in the words of its subtitle, "A Vision in a Dream." According to Coleridge's account, the poem was a "fragment" of a longer one he had composed in drug-induced sleep after reading about Kubla Khan's garden and palace in Samuel Purchas's seventeenth-century *Pilgrimage*. While writing down the words, "he was unfortunately called out by a person on business from Porlock," and the rest of the "two to three hundred lines" was lost. Today there is little doubt that the interruption came from the same person who persuaded Coleridge not to write his crucial chapter on the Imagination for the *Biographia Literaria*—Samuel Taylor Coleridge. The prefatory matter works to disarm criticism, at the same time claiming for "Kubla Khan" the privileged Romantic genre of the fragment and the equally privileged status of the dream. The doubts cast upon Coleridge's account of the poem's production have by no means diminished the interest of readers—indeed, we are now free to experience "Kubla Khan" as poetry rather than as a substitute for it.

The opening lines locate Kubla Khan's pleasure dome in a landscape of the mind. The river Alph, suggesting the first letters of the Greek and Hebrew alphabets, is an image of what Coleridge in the *Biographia* would call "the living Power and prime Agent of all human Perception"—the primary Imagination. Nature and art, ancient forests and pleasure dome, are held in a tension mediated by walled gardens partaking of both. The pleasure dome itself, its reflection floating "midway on the waves," is stationed between the closely related though seemingly opposite realities of the conscious and unconscious mind—"a sunny pleasure-dome with caves of ice!" The poet's role is to re-create its architectonics in a poem, forestalling the threat of "Ancestral voices prophesying war," a message all too appropriate in the wartime 1790s. A new muse is the source of his vision—not the Greek Euterpe or Milton's Urania, but "an Abyssian maid" nearer the ancient earthly Paradise. As the poet longs to "revive within me / Her symphony and song," his poem becomes the first of a long line, culminating in Valéry's *Le cimetière marin*, to have as a theme its own coming into existence. In its closing lines the poet is transformed into a mantic being whom the community fears. Yet what we are left with is not the attempt to contain him by primitive ritual but the Edenic origin that is a guarantee of his poetic truth: "For he on honey-dew hath fed / And drank the milk of Paradise."

If "Kubla Khan" is a whole poem masquerading as a fragment, "Christabel," Coleridge's third major poem of the marvelous, is strongly directed toward a completion it never attained. Part I was written in Somerset in 1797, Part II, which reflects the topography of the Lake District, at Keswick in 1800. The two parts were to be published in the second edition of *Lyrical Ballads*, and Wordsworth's decision to exclude them may have contributed to a blockage that became insurmountable. By the time Coleridge published "Christabel" in 1816, he had to appeal in a preface to the reader's faith in his originality, for by then Scott's *Bridal of Triermain* and Byron's "Siege of Corinth," both influenced by Coleridge's poem, had appeared. Blaming his inability to finish on the "state of suspended imagination in which his poetic powers had been," Coleridge now thought he could go on with the work. Although this was not to be, he did confide in his friend James Gillman about his plan for the poem, while a shorter and different précis was given to his son, Derwent, and these summaries suggest that the completion of the poem had been plotted in detail.

"Christabel" is a poem of surprising revelations, transmutations, and changes of situation having to do with the intimate connection between the Christlike heroine and her mysterious visitor, Geraldine. Geraldine, the poem suggests, is both lover and mother—on the night that they couch together she "Seems to slumber still and mild, / As a mother with her child." That night only Christabel sees the deformity of Geraldine's bosom, and on the next day she alone perceives Geraldine's serpentine transformation—but in the "dizzying trance" she falls into, it is Christabel herself who appears reptile as she "shuddered aloud with a hissing sound." Consequently, she must watch in dreamlike passivity as her father leads Geraldine forth in her place. If Gillman's scenario is correct, the themes of sexual propinquity and exchanged natures would have continued with Geraldine's transformation into a semblance of Christabel's faraway lover. At the crucial moment of the marriage ceremony, the real lover would have entered, bearing the ring of their betrothal; and Geraldine, like her immediate descendant, Keats's Lamia, would have disappeared. It is sometimes said, on the basis of a statement by Coleridge himself linking "Christabel" to Crashaw's hymn to Saint Teresa, that Christabel experiences vicarious suffering to redeem her absent lover. Only in the context of a fully worked-out poem, however, could such a meaning be fully established. An association with Saint Teresa would also have an intensely erotic element, as Bernini and George Eliot understood.

Almost as important as these poems of the marvelous in Coleridge's oeuvre are those in a subgenre of his own making: the conversation poems, following Coleridge's own term for "The Nightingale," which first appeared in *Lyrical Ballads*. An emblem of these monologues in blank verse could be "that film, which fluttered on the grate," the "*stranger*" of "Frost at Midnight" (1798):

> a companionable form,
> Whose puny flaps and freaks the idling Spirit
> By its own mood interprets, every where
> Echo or mirror seeking of itself . . .

The mode is associative, or rather an artfully shaped fiction of association, one image leading to another, seeming to follow the processes of thought itself. The discourse is not imagined as meditation, but rather as an address to an intimate of the speaker's. This listener may be identified immediately (Sara Coleridge in first line of "The Eolian Harp," Charles Lamb in the original subtitle of "This Lime-Tree Bower My Prison") or may be the subject of a dramatic turn in the poem, as in the "Dear Babe" Hartley in "Frost at Midnight" and "my friends!" William and Dorothy Wordsworth in "The Nightingale." Typically, these poems explore their worlds by the use of significant images like "the nigh thatch / Smokes in the sun-thaw," embodying a transformative natural process in "Frost at Midnight." The rook crossing the sun in "This Lime-Tree Bower" and the baby's eyes "that swam with undropped tears" in "The Nightingale" are also images delicately poised on the threshold of symbolism. One doesn't know how far to take them, and that is of course part of Coleridge's artistry.

Two other works of major importance have affinities with the conversation poems: "Dejection: An Ode" and "To William Wordsworth." The former began as a long verse letter to Sara Hutchinson, Wordsworth's sister-in-law, with whom Coleridge had fallen hopelessly in love. A confessional poem of personal misery, it makes contact at several points with the first four stanzas, then in manuscript, of Wordsworth's "Ode: Intimations of Immortality." There Wordsworth raised the question of how the intensity of perception and feeling falls off between childhood and maturity. Coleridge attempts to answer for himself, blaming his condition on the joyless-ness of his "coarse domestic Life" and on his escape into "abstruse research," resulting in the suspension of his "shaping Spirit of Imagi-nation." In contrast to the harmony of self and nature in "The Aeolian Harp," addressed in a happier time to another Sara, there appears and reappears the image of an Aeolian lute, driven by the strong wind to "A Scream / Of agony by torture lengthen'd out." As Coleridge believes the soul creates the metaphorical garment that is the reality according to which nature is perceived, his is a "shroud," Wordsworth's is a "Wedding Garment." After considerable shortening, revision, and rearrangement, "Dejection: An Ode, Written April 4, 1802" was pub-lished on Wordsworth's wedding day—at once a commemoration and a bitterly ironical self-comparison.

In its further revised, final form "Dejection" is not merely less imme-diately personal. The disappearance of much of the confessional con-tent gives other parts of the "Ode" greater prominence, making its theme a secularized version of the failure of millennial hope. The image of the wedding-garment recalls the new Jerusalem of Revelation 21:2, "prepared as a bride adorned for her husband," and "a new Earth and new Heaven" adapts the language of Revelation 21:1 for a state now regarded as unattainable by the poet. The Joy of the Lady is as absolute and as inexplicable as the "grief without a pang" of the speaker. She exists as a *schöne Seele* in her separate sphere, while he in his desiccated apartness is like one of Blake's Spectres. Yet, paradoxically, from his state of accidie a memorable poem emerges.

Coleridge's true farewell to poetry of an ambitious order is not "Dejection" but the poem he addressed to Wordsworth after hearing the whole of *The Prelude* read by its author over several evenings during the Christmas season of 1806. Like "Dejection," this poem establishes a strong connection with Wordsworth while at the same time dismally contrasting Coleridge's situation, and like "Dejection," it moves along the interface of the secular and the sacred. Coleridge casts his past self in the role of a John the Baptist figure "Who came a welcomer in Her-ald's Guise, / Singing of Glory, and Futurity." As well as "guide," Wordsworth is "comforter," recalling the fourth Gospel's word for the Holy Ghost: "And I will pray to the Father, and he shall give you anoth-er Comforter, that he may abide with you for ever" (John 14:16; see also 14:26 and 16:7).

Panegyrized as the author of "that Lay / More than historic, that prophetic Lay," Wordsworth is one of "The truly Great / [Who] Have all one age, and from one visible space / Shed influence!" For himself, Coleridge amplifies the theme of relative inferiority he had sounded since their first meetings, but this time in a way that he knew would disturb the "beloved faces"—Sara, Mary, Dorothy, and William, all of whom had been present at the reading. Coleridge himself is represented as dead, the products of both his own thought and of his joint labor with Wordsworth as "but Flowers / Strewed on my corse, and borne upon my Bier, / In the same Coffin, for the self-same Grave!" With this funerary image, Coleridge removes his poetic self from any further comparisons with the subject of his panegyric.

In the decade or so following 1806 Coleridge wrote little poetry. In these years his separation from his wife was confirmed, his friendship with Wordsworth ruptured and only imperfectly reestablished, and his dependence upon opium increased. Occasionally his imagination flashed out—as in a Notebook poem of 1811, part of which was was later published as "Limbo," where "that great ancestral flea" of John Donne's poem crosses the rivers of Hades and "frightens Ghosts as Ghosts here frighten men." Full of Joycean linguistic play and strange resonances, the poem conveys a terrible sense of vacuity that explains why Coleridge at this time had not much poetry in him. Nevertheless, during this period he managed to deliver several series of literary lectures in London and Bristol, to publish the twenty-seven numbers of *The Friend* (1809–1810), and to revise his play *Osorio* as *Remorse* for a successful production at Drury Lane Theatre.

There was productivity even in his indolence, and from 1815 his energies began to revive. He wrote another play, *Zapolya*, in 1815, began the dictation of the *Biographia Literaria*, and arranged his *Sibylline Leaves* for publication. In 1816, with Byron's encouragement and assistance, the *Christabel* volume appeared, also containing (at last) "Kubla Khan" and the anguished "Pains of Sleep." *Sibylline Leaves* and the *Biographia* were published in 1817, and Coleridge was stimulated to think of himself as a poet again. The poems he went on to produce in his later years were works in a minor key, but some of them are works of very great accomplishment, deserving far more attention than they have been given.

Coleridge's later poems are typically written in slack couplets sometimes intermingled with other verse forms. When he published them in his *Poetical Works*, he grouped them as "Prose in Rhyme, or Epigrams, Moralities, &c." However, this is the sort of strategy that Charles Lamb had identified long before as "your ingenious anticipation of ridicule." These poems have serious themes but convey them in a way different from the poems of the marvelous. They feature personification, abstraction, and allegory—all of which the Preface to *Lyrical Ballads* had seemed to banish, but which remained part of Coleridge's poetic sensibility.

Equally important is the persona of the aged poet, devoid of hope yet possessing a sensibility that delicately expresses the pathos of his situation. Typical is the verse of "The Improvisatore" (1827). After a long prose conversation about the nature of love and marital happiness, the Improvisatore descants on how, although Hope is dead for him, he has found contentment. However, the accommodation to life is not always so successful. In "Work without Hope" the amaranth, mythologically an eternal flower but also another name for love-lies-bleeding, represents the failure of the poet's life: "Bloom, O ye Amaranths! bloom for whom ye may, / For me ye bloom not!" This significantly recalls the delicious vision of Paradise in "Religious Musings," with "odours snatched from beds of Amaranth." Paradise is no longer seen as attainable in this life; it was this very passage that Coleridge chose to quote in making fun of his youthful self in chapter 10 of the *Biographia Literaria*.

The most terrible visions of Coleridge's later poetry occur in what have been called his "Asra" poems, after the anagram he created for Sara Hutchinson's first name in earlier lyrics like "A Day-Dream." Although not named in "Love's Apparition and Evanishment" or "Constancy to an Ideal Object," Sara/Asra is a major theme in her absence. In "Love's Apparition and Evanishment" Coleridge tropes himself into a blind Arab who turns his face to Heaven in the desert. With his inner eye he beholds Hope dressed as a bridesmaid but "lifeless." At a kiss from "Love, a sylph in bridal trim," Hope revives; but the kiss "Woke just enough of life in death / To make Hope die anew." The poem thus links with the imagery of "The Rime of the Ancient Mariner" (the exclusion from the wedding feast, the allegorical figure of Life-in-Death) and of "Dejection" (the wedding garment) to project the emotional desolation of the poet. Another significant linkage occurs in "Constancy to an Ideal Object." Here the poet addresses the "yearning Thought" of the beloved that haunts him despite his recognition that this is the image, not the reality, of the beloved. "She is not thou, and thou art only she" seems to echo Donne's Tenth Elegy, "The Dream," which begins "Image of her whom I love more than she . . ."

Unlike Donne, whose persona jauntily resolves to make the best of it, Coleridge regards his quest as a pursuit of "nothing," like a woodman's pursuit of the Brocken specter. In lines 22–24 his life becomes that of his own earlier creation:

> a becalmed bark,
> Whose Helmsman on an ocean waste and wide
> Sits mute and pale his mouldering helm beside.

Yet the same poem provides Coleridge with a more positive allusion when, in the short verse epitaph he wrote for himself in 1833, the poet expresses his faith in a life to come: "That he who many a year with toil of breath / Found death in life, may here find life in death!" Such interplay with earlier poems reminds us of the richness and variety of Coleridge's poetic career.

No discussion of Coleridge as a poet should omit his lifelong engagement with the sounds of words in prosodic experiments. Sometimes, as in in the mnemonic "Metrical Feet: Lesson for a Boy," this takes a completely external form. In a poem like the "Hexameters," addressed to William and Dorothy Wordsworth, the rhythmic pattern seems to be the motive for a virtuosic display: "All my hexameters fly, like stags, pursued by the stag-hounds, / Breathless and panting, and ready to drop, yet flying still onwards . . ." In "Christabel" the experiment is an integral part of Coleridge's imaginative creation.

> Is the night chilly and dark?
> The night is chilly, but not dark.

The lines of "Christabel" ordinarily have four stresses among seven to twelve syllables, a method that anticipates the sprung rhythm of Gerard Manley Hopkins. In the technique of his verse, as in so many other aspects of his work, Coleridge was both a great traditionalist and a prophetic experimenter.

Morton D. Paley

Textual Note: At the time of writing, there is no modern scholarly edition of Coleridge's complete poems. (Two are in preparation: one by J. C. C. Mays for the *Collected Coleridge*, another by Fran Carlock Stephens for Oxford University Press). Most of the quotations are taken from *The Poetical Works of S. T. Coleridge*, 3 vols. (London: William Pickering, 1829). Quotations of poems not in that collection are taken from *The Poetical Works of Samuel Taylor Coleridge*, ed. E. H. Coleridge, 2 vols. (Oxford: Oxford University Press, 1912), and quotations from the "Letter to Sara Hutchinson" (not in the 1829 or 1912 editions) are taken from the Everyman's Library *Poems*, ed. John Beer (London: E. P. Dutton, 1991).

Further Reading

Abrams, M. H. *The Correspondent Breeze*. New York: Norton, 1984.

Beer, John. *Coleridge the Visionary*. London: Chatto, 1959.

Everest, Kelvin. *Coleridge's Secret Ministry*. Hassocks: Harvester, 1979.

Fruman, Norman. *Coleridge: The Damaged Archangel*. New York: Braziller, 1971.

Holmes, Richard. *Coleridge: Early Visions*. London: Hodder, 1989.

House, Humphry. *Coleridge*. London: Hart-Davis, 1953.

Lowes, John Livingston. *The Road to Xanadu*. 2d ed. Boston: Houghton, Mifflin, 1930.

McFarland, Thomas. *Coleridge and the Pantheist Tradition*. Oxford: Clarendon, 1969.

Parker, Reeve. *Coleridge's Meditative Art*. Ithaca, N.Y.: Cornell University Press, 1975.

Schaffer, Eleanor. *"Kubla Khan" and "The Fall of Jerusalem."* Cambridge: Cambridge University Press, 1975.

Warren, Robert Penn. "A Poem of Pure Imagination," *The Rime of the Ancient Mariner*. New York: Reynal, 1946.

Woodring, Carl. *Politics in the Poetry of Coleridge*. Madison: University of Wisconsin Press, 1961.

Poetry, 1785–1832

AA, XX and NN gather to talk.

AA. According to the official guides, our best view of the Romantic ranges extending across the great divide of 1800 will be found in 1798, or perhaps the immediately adjacent 1800: from that splendid overlook called *Lyrical Ballads*. It's a picturesque and (historically) important locale.

Equally arresting, however, is that more remote point known as *Songs of Innocence and of Experience* (1794). A favorite now of many, this vantage was scarcely known or frequented until the Pre-Raphaelites popularized it in their late-nineteenth-century aesthetic adventures.

Neither of these now famous spots of time will lose its hold upon the imagination. We may start a long, an interesting, and a reasonably thorough exploration of Romanticism and its majestic adjacencies from both places, as many have already shown.

> "spots of time": A key Romantic concept, formulated by Wordsworth in his *Prelude* project. Wordsworth's idea is that experience yields certain sacred moments that preserve a restorative power through one's later life. Such moments often come without one's realizing their importance at the time of their occurrence. Memory clarifies their significance. These moments testify to the invisible but permanent presence of a benevolent Spirit in the universe. See *Prelude* (1850) Book II.208–286.

Traditional and favorite routes are, however, just that—traditional and favored. This particular world of the sublime and the beautiful is so extensive and complex that we may enter it, or move about its regions, in an endless variety of ways.

For instance, on the way to *Lyrical Ballads* we will inevitably skirt another spot that provides, in its fashion, an even more magnificent view of the territory. I mean the once–famous but now somewhat neglected outcropping called *Poems, chiefly in the Scottish dialect* (Kilmarnock, 1786). From the latter the way leads directly on to both Blake's *Songs* and Wordsworth and Coleridge's *Lyrical Ballads*. The route from Burns's 1786 *Poems* to *Lyrical Ballads* is well known if no longer so well frequented. But the rigs o' Burns run into the range of Blake. We trace this route very clearly by following certain of their shared territorial features: their critiques of moralized religion, their sympathy with the ideals of the French Revolution, and their commitment to what Blake called "exuberance" and "energy" (and Wordsworth, later, the "spontaneous overflow of powerful feelings").

Blake found his way by various paths, it is true, but one of them followed the trail of Burns. Indeed, Blake marked the route he took in one of his greatest early works, "The Tyger," although later travellers have failed to note the signs he left:

> When the stars threw down their spears,
> And water'd heaven with their tears:
> Did he smile his work to see?
> Did he who made the Lamb make thee?

Blake's starry spears of 1794 broke across the earlier sky of 1786 in another satanic text, Burns's great "Address to the Deil." The second line of Blake's verse is an English translation of Burns's Scots:

> Ae dreary, windy, winter night,
> The stars shot down wi' sklentan light,
> Wi' you, *mysel*, I gat a fright. . . .

Blake's "smile"—like the high-spirited comedy of that associated text *The Marriage of Heaven and Hell* (1793)—is a memorial tribute to Burns, who also liked to treat his gods and demons with familiarity. Like Blake, he knew that all deities reside in the human breast, as the very next lines of his address to the "deil" show:

>   Ayont the lough;
> Ye, like a *rash-buss*, stood in sight,
>   Wi' waving sugh.
>
> The cudgel in my neive did shake,
> Each bristl'd hair stood like a stake,
> When wi' an eldritch, stoor *quaick, quaick,*

> Amang the springs,
> Awa ye squatter'd like a *drake*,
>   On whistling wings.

From Blake back to Burns; and from Burns on to Wordsworth, who learns to take spiritual instruction from the quotidian orders of nature out of texts like Burns's:

> O'er rough and smooth she trips along,
> And never looks behind;
> And sings a solitary song
> And whistles in the wind.
>   ("Lucy Gray," 1800)

XX. Where did Keats take his lessons, from Burns or from Wordsworth?

> Mortal, that thou may'st understand aright,
> I humanize my sayings to thine ear,
> Making comparisons of earthly things;
> Or thou might'st better listen to the wind,
> Whose language is to thee a barren noise,
> Though it blows legend-laden through the trees.
>   ("The Fall of Hyperion," written in 1819)

AA. From both and from neither. What we see here is a way of writing, a way of imagining the world, that was characteristic of Romanticism. The sensibility is broadly dispersed, translated, transmuted. A legend-laden wind blows across the whole stretch of these everlasting hills. Although it has no beginning, we will not encounter it in the nearby range of the Augustans.

"legend laden": Keats here touches on the strong ethno-mythological impulse apparent throughout Romantic art. The ballad revival fed into Romantic primitivism; early cultural documents were recovered and imitated because they were read as "legend laden." Romantic art made one of its objects the recovery of unconscious, innocent, and naive powers.

xx. I'm not so sure about that. James Macpherson's Ossianic texts often exhibit the same kind of weather. In the first of his *Fragments of Ancient Poetry* (1760), for instance, the warrior Shilric returns to his home in the Scottish highlands to discover that his beloved Vinvela has died in his absence. The fragment records a conversation between the parted lovers, but Macpherson's text makes it clear that we are not overhearing a human conversation, we are observing a sensibility conversant with legend-laden winds.

> By the mossy fountain I will sit; on the top of the hill of winds. When midday is silent around, converse, O my love, with me! come on the wings of the gale! on the blast of the mountain, come! Let me hear thy voice, as thou passest, when mid-day is silent around. (I.ii)

The superstitions of Burns, the local tales memorialized by Wordsworth, the mythologies of Keats—all follow the same structural pattern we see here in Macpherson.

Note the date of this, 1760.

AA. And we can find similar things even earlier—for example, in the work of Gray and Collins from the 1740s and 1750s. The cultural fault lines along which the geography of Romanticism was formed will not be mapped on the grids of Cartesian geometries—what Blake called "the mill [of] Aristotle's Analytics." We need topological measures for discontinuous phenomena of these kinds, non-Euclidean mathematics of the type first pursued (for example, by Gauss and Bolyai) in—the Romantic Period itself! What we've been looking at here, in this view across the range that includes Burns, Blake, Wordsworth, Keats, and Ossian . . .

XX. . . . and they don't exhaust this landscape by any means.

AA. . . . no, of course not; but what we've been looking at is a kind of topological basin where sets of "attractors" (as the mathematicians say) hold dispersing phenomena in random patterns. Patterns, because the phenomena exhibit recursive forms (a few of which we have noticed); random, because the possibilities for other patternings are endless. We may come at these scenes and experiences from many directions. Patterning dissolves and other patterning appears; some of these patternings will recur in mutated forms, some will not. The locale is (like its own natural light) "incoherent"; but it is also a dynamic and self-integrated whole.

How do we get to know it, then? people sometimes ask. And I want to say, simply by looking at it. "If the doors of perception were cleansed . . ."—you know the rest. Even when we think we're following that great romantic star, the imagination, we often close ourselves up and see only through the narrow chinks of our caverned brains. Take Blake and his *Songs* and "The Tyger," for instance. Turn your view away from Burns for a moment and observe the *Songs* from the vantage of children's literature, or against the background of that related and overlapping phenomenon, the tradition of emblematic writing. A whole new world of realities suddenly rises to your sight. And it is endlessly interesting, we could wander in this new world for a long time.

It is a world inhabited, for example, by that famous and highly influential family, the Taylors of Ongar. The highfalutin imaginations of Coleridge and Southey and Wordsworth shook their heads in melancholy dismay at what they saw as the failed and mad magnificence of Blake's writings. Jane Taylor had no such problems. Just as Blake incorporated (and thereby reinterpreted) Burns's "Address to the Deil" in "The Tyger," Jane Taylor (1783–1824) did the same to Blake's poem. She answered the famous theological questions of "The Tyger" with the augury of an innocence we have all but forgotten, so serious do we often get, so far do we wander from the pleasure principles laid down in the fields of childhood:

> Twinkle, twinkle, little star,
> How I wonder what you are!
> Up above the world so high,
> Like a diamond in the sky.
>
> When the blazing sun is gone,
> When he nothing shines upon,
> Then you show your little light,
> Twinkle, twinkle, all the night.
> ("The Star," 1806)

In effect, Taylor is reading Blake's "Tyger" through Blake's "Dream," another text recollected in Taylor's "Star." It is a crucial literary-historical move— whether we are passing through remote areas of our histories or through nearby (and perhaps academic) regions. When Blake added the *Songs of Experience* (in 1794) to the *Songs of Innocence* (1789), he established a critical

"Romantic dialectics": Blake's diad "Innocence" and "Experience" is a version of the dialectic more famously set out in Schiller's "On Naive and Sentimental Poetry" (1795–1796), and in Wordsworth's distinction between the "spontaneous overflow of powerful feelings" and "emotion recollected in tranquillity" ("Preface," *Lyrical Ballads*, 1800). According to these two (subsequently normative) views, contemporary poetry— that is, Romantic poetry—"takes its origin from" the "sentimental" or "recollective" element—from the self-consciousness that permits a modern poet to recreate "in the mind" "an emotion, similar to" the original "naive" and "spontaneous . . . feelings." That *self-consciousness*, later denominated "Romantic model for Romantic dialectics that would proliferate and endure. Taylor's poem is important because it reminds us that the dialectic is reversible, that

> irony" (in Germany) and secondary imagination (by Coleridge, *Biographia Literaria*, 1817), is the critical term which for these thinkers generates the reciprocal concepts of the "naive," the "spontaneous," and the "primary imagination."

the world of experience might be undone by entering it through Blake's "Lamb" or Taylor's "Star" or as it would later continue to be by works like Christina Rossetti's "Goblin Market" (1862). For this is a long and complex history that has been adopted by both parties to the dialectic.

XX. And as Blake said, the parties are and should be enemies. Wordsdworthian recollection, the determinative model for Romantic memory, stands forever opposed to the primary energies celebrated by Burns and Blake. . .

AA. . . .and to the simplicities pursued by Taylor. It is crucial to be clear about the differential shining out in poems like "The Star"—a work that stands far closer, in ethos and history if not in time and style, to Burns's and Blake's poems and songs than to

> "secondary imaginations": No idea is more fundamental to Romantic art than the idea of "imagination." On the other hand, no idea is more protean. In general, Romantic imagination designates the power—usually associated with a poetical sensibility—to perceive nonordinary reality, or the nonordinary aspects of the everyday world; and to create and project to others one's perception of such things.

the secondary imaginations of Wordsworth and Coleridge. Certain of Wordsworth's most splendid poems, so hateful to Blake, define the difference with great exactness. A guiding and protective star presides over the landscape of Wordsworth's "Michael" (1800), for instance, but the history that Wordsworth sees throws it into eclipse:

> The Cottage which was nam'd The Evening Star
> Is gone, the ploughshare has been through the ground
> On which it stood; great changes have been wrought
> In all the neighborhood. . . .

The cottage and its symbolic name have "slip[ped] in a moment out of life" into the care of a memorializing imagination ("To H. C. Six Years Old"). As in "The Solitary Reaper," Wordsworth accepts—triumphs in—the imaginative displacement of primary experience: "The music in my heart I bore / Long after it was heard no more." That displacement is unnatural to Burns, for example, whose song voice is inseparable from the voice of the girl known to Wordsworth only at two removes. So in Blake and Burns and Taylor, "the melancholy slackening" so characteristic of one strain of Romanticism does not (typically) "ensue" (*Prelude* VI, 1850). Sorrow and happiness do not run in alternating currents, their relations are direct and immediate. All is "naive." The Wordsworthian model:

> We Poets in our youth begin in gladness;
> But thereof come i' th' end despondency and madness
> ("Resolution and Independence," 1807)

is applied to this other Romantic strain only with difficulty because the logic of Wordsworth's "thereof" is refused. This happens because the dialectic of gladness and despondency, pleasure and pain, is not imagined as a conceptual relation but as an existential one. We see the situation clearly in much of Burns's work, not least of all in his masterpiece "Love and Liberty—A Cantata" (commonly called "The Jolly Beggars," 1799).

> The Caird prevail'd—th' unblushing fair
>   In his embraces sunk;
> Partly wi' LOVE o'ercome sae sair,
>   And partly she was drunk:
> Sir VIOLINO with an air,
>   That show'd a man o' spunk,
> Wish'd UNISON between the PAIR,
>   An' made the bottle clunk
>   To their health that night.

XX. Yet how difficult this resort to the wisdom of the body, even in an age self-devoted to Nature! Burns's lines expose the kinds of contradiction most writers could only engage through various forms of displacement. It violates decorum (social as well as literary) to make such a witty rhyme of the excessively correct (and English) "unblushing fair" ("unblushing"!) with the low dialect (and Scots) "sae sair," or to "pair" in this way all the other incongruities raised up by the passage. The inhuman treatment of women in traditional love poetry is here overthrown.

"self-devoted to nature": Many Romantic writers—not all—gave a special privilege to the idea of nature. Wordsworthian Romanticism tends to a kind of pantheism. Nature was generally regarded as a kind of spiritual resort, a refuge from the conflicts and divisions of life in society.

NN. Yes, but it is a reckless—ultimately a masculine—overthrowing, is it not? Splendid as Burns's love poetry is—including his more genteel love poems—he cannot deliver the complex truths exposed in the sentimental styles developed (mainly) by women writers in the late eighteenth and early nineteenth centuries.

"sentimental styles": Other than the ballad revival of the eighteenth century, no pre-Romantic movement was more important for Romanticism than sentimentalism. The aesthetics of sentimentalism are defined early in Mark Akenside's *Pleasures of Imagination* (1744). The Della Cruscan movement of the 1780s and 1790s provided the crucial immediate stimulus for the development of Romantic forms of the sentimental.

Ridiculed as "unsex'd females" by reactionaries like Gifford, Matthias, and Polwhele, writers like Hannah Cowley turned female experience in the male world to a test of that world's hidden truths. In Cowley's "Departed Youth" (1797), for example, we see the birth of a new Venus from the wreck of her sixty-four-year-old body. The thefts of time are taken back in the poem's imperative to "Break the slim form that was adored / By him so loved, my wedded lord." The metaphysics of a Sternian sentimentality lead Cowley to exchange the body of her first nature—adorable, married, passive—for a *vita nuova*:

> But leave me, whilst all these you steal,
> The mind to taste, the nerve to feel.

As in the rest of the poem, Cowley here breaks the slim forms of her earliest language. As generous as Burns ("my loved lord") and, if less vigorous, just as determined, her behavior preserves her inherited proprieties. "Departed Youth" invokes a whole series of favorite eighteenth-century terms and phrases from the lexicon of sensibility ("lively sense," "sentiment refined," "taste," "nerve," "feel") only to reembody them through a series of syntactic and lexical wordplays. If the poetic style is different, the poetic demand is exactly like the one Yeats would make famous, in the poetry of *his* old age, a century and more later.

Readers, especially twentieth-century readers, often miss what is happening in texts like these because they forget the conventions of a poetry written under the sign of what Shelley called "Intellectual Beauty." It is a sophisticated, an artificial sign—like that fanciful nature you two have been playing with in your conversation. But Romantic nature, as you know, is an allegorical construct of urbane minds. In the late eighteenth century, the allegory tended to assume picturesque forms because of the authority of sentimentalism. Cowley's verse and the entire Della Cruscan movement operate under that authority.

Although commonly understood to involve mental as opposed to sensuous phenomena, intellectual beauty is precisely the sign for a determination to undermine the body/soul distinction altogether. When Robert Merry ("Della Crusca") publishes his intention to quit poetry, Cowley ("Anna Matilda") writes to dissuade him:

> O! seize again thy golden quill,
> And with its point my bosom thrill;

The self-consciousness of such eroticism—it is nothing less than the Metaphysical verse of sentimentalism—is exactly the "point." Cowley calls for a "blended fire" of poetry and sexuality:

> The *one*, poetic language give,
> The *other* bid thy passion live;

Later Romantic writers become preoccupied with Paolo and Francesca, Launcelot and Guenevere, Tristan and Isolde, in order to explore what D. G. Rossetti would call "the difficult deeps of love." The kiss is the earliest figure of those deeps, and it focuses a great deal of Della Cruscan writing:

> The greatest bliss
> Is in a kiss—
> A kiss by love refin'd,
> When springs the soul
> Without controul,
> And blends the bliss with mind.
> (Charlotte Dacre ["Rosa Matilda"], "The Kiss")

The fact that we cannot tell whether it is the kiss or the soul that "blends the bliss with mind" underscores the radical confusions being sought in texts like these. They execute the drama that Mark Akenside called the "pleasures of imagination" (1744). Coleridge's measured "balance and reconciliation of opposite and discordant qualities" here "springs . . . without controul" because Dacre's theory of imagination stands closer to a "Prolific" Blakean "Energy" than to Coleridge's more famous conceptual approach to the subject.

XX. Yes, and when Thomas Moore, in one of his many kissing lyrics, celebrates the same kind of "sweet abandonment" ("The Kiss," 1801), he marks the close relation between eros and madness that Romanticism perceives and pursues. A great theme of Romantic culture, madness is the index of thwarted desire. Writers of the period fashion a poetry of madness in order to gain (paradoxically but precisely) the "controlless core" (Byron, *Don Juan* I, stanza 116) of imaginative abandonment. Demon lovers and desperate brains: both are familiar Romantic tropes, and while the one descends into the culture largely through the propagators of the ballad revival, the other is the offspring of those sentimentalist projects and writers you seem to favor.

In each case, a grammar of the fantastical is deployed in order to express what would be difficult or impossible to say otherwise. A pair of this period's early and influential writers, M. G. Lewis and Charlotte Smith, exemplify these two grammars very well, as we can see in this sonnet by Smith (1797):

> *Sonnet. On being Cautioned against Walking*
> *on an Headland Overlooking the Sea, because*
> *it was Frequented by a Lunatic*
>
> Is there a solitary wretch who hies
>   To the tall cliff, with starting pace or slow,
> And, measuring, views with wild and hollow eyes
>   Its distance from the waves that chide below;
> Who, as the sea-borne gale with frequent sighs
>   Chills his cold bed upon the mountain turf,
> With hoarse, half-uttered lamentation, lies
>   Murmuring responses to the dashing surf?
> In moody sadness, on the giddy brink,
>   I see him more with envy than with fear;
> *He* has no *nice felicities* that shrink
>   From giant horrors; wildly wandering here,
> He seems (uncursed with reason) not to know
> The depth or the duration of his woe.

A machinery of transferred epithets, Smith's sonnet gradually measures a series of figural reflections between the seascape, the lunatic, and Smith herself. But even as these identifications culminate in the ambiguous grammar opening the sestet, Smith unfolds a glimpse of a far more wildered mental landscape. The self-consciousness of Smith's art—her "*nice felicities*"—produce the poem's final, disastrous revelation: that the delicate workings of the sonnet execute an awareness of the "giant horrors" one constructs by raising illusory (i.e., rational) defenses against them.

There is an imagination in Smith's sonnet at war with its cursed artifice and its limited, shrinking consciousness. Warned (reasonably) against a direct encounter with the lunatic, Smith goes to meet him in imagination because her own "moody sadness"—her feelings—possess a deeper knowledge than her defensive, civilized understanding. In 1812 Byron would make the drama of "Consciousness awaking to her woes" world-famous in the story of Childe Harold (Canto I, stanza 92). This story, however, began to be told in the late eighteenth century's literature of sensibility, as Smith's sonnet shows. It is the story of the sleep of reason, its illusory dreams, and its "awaking" to that complex Romantic understanding that "Sorrow is knowledge" (*Manfred* I.1).

A crucial feature of Smith's sonnet is its style of sincerity—a style that would come to characterize so much Romantic poetry. The purpose of the style is to make the immediate experience of "the poet" the dramatic focus of the text—as if "the poet" were herself the poem's central subject, as if she were subject to the revelatory power of the poem she herself decides to write. Romantic melancholy is one affective consequence of the deployment of such a style: *mon coeur mis à nu*, and at one's own hand.

"style of sincerity": Although Romantic art tends to represent itself as spontaneous and unstudied, these qualities are aesthetic effects of rhetorical strategies. Two key devices are (1) a detailed presentation of a concrete immediate context for the poetical text (epitomized in the famous subtitle of Wordsworth's "Tintern Abbey"); (2) the construction of a poetic revery, as if the reader were "overhearing" the poet musing—in several senses—aloud.

Much Romantic poetry will devote itself to a search for ways to defend itself against the dangerous self-divisions fostered by this style of sincerity. The most famous of these defenses was raised by Wordsworth, whose journeys into his *selva oscura* brought, his poetry argued, an "abundant recompense" for psychic wounding and suffered loss.

> For I have learned
> To look on nature, not as in the hour
> Of thoughtless youth; but hearing oftentimes
> The still, sad music of humanity,

> Nor harsh nor grating, though of ample power
> To chasten and subdue.
>
> ("Tintern Abbey," 1798)

That lesson would guide and trouble a great deal of subsequent poetry. Accepting—indeed, undergoing—such loss, Wordsworth discovered "That in this moment there is life and food / For future years," discovered (literally) a new spiritual life:

> a sense sublime
> Of something far more deeply interfused,
> Whose dwelling is the light of setting suns,
> And the round ocean and the living air,
> And the blue sky, and in the mind of man:
>
> ("Tintern Abbey")

Smith's sonnet does not romanticize her suffering in this way. For Smith, the recompense lies simply in the text's having broken through the curse and sleep of reason to discover the holiness of the heart's affections, however disordered. Indeed, the unstable character of feeling generated by her sonnet is the exact sign that a breakthrough has occurred.

AA. But Romanticism had other ways for exploring unknown worlds. The impersonal character of Blake's *Songs* would succeed to the age's greatest representation of psychic and social derangement in that epic of "the torments of love and jealousy," *The Four Zoas*. Madness in this work, however, appears an objective state of general spiritual existence rather than the subjective experience of a particular person. Consequently, the poem creates a textual environment where readers are thrown back wholly on their own resources. To read *The Four Zoas* is extremely disorienting because one must traverse the work with no guidance or protection—as if Dante were to have made his journey to hell without Virgil.

In the Romantic poetry of sincerity readers are spectators of the worlds and experiences that appear to be undergone by the poets. In this respect the Romantic poet serves at once as topic and guide for the reader, whose function is to observe and learn lessons of sympathy—to "overhear" the poetry, as J. S. Mill later said. Blake's poetry, by contrast, calls the reader to acts of final (self-)judgment. The great question posed by all of Blake's poetry is simple but devastating: How much reality can you bear to know? "If the doors of perception were cleansed every thing would appear to man as it is, infinite" (*The Marriage of Heaven and Hell*, plate 14): but the world of the infinite will not be reconnoitered as if one were going a casual journey. It is a world of ultimate things, a world where one may expect only to be weighed and found wanting.

XX. Blake was interested in the poetry of Ossian and the ballad revival because such work appeared to deliver one into completely alien worlds: not the worlds of dreaming or the dreamer, but the worlds of dreams-as-such—those orders existing independently of the (un)conscious mechanisms that can sometimes establish contact with them.

Some of Coleridge's greatest poetry is essentially an argument that such ideal orders do in fact exist, "Kubla Khan" being the most famous and perhaps successful of these works. When he finally published the poem, Coleridge cased it in an elaborate prose framework that called attention to the dreamed character of the text and experience. Paradoxically, this personal rhetoric heightens the impersonal quality of the vision, as if the poetical text were the residue of a concrete world subsisting beyond mortal ken, a prelapsarian world where words rise up as things, a world occasionally glimpsed (perhaps in dream) by time–and space-bound creatures.

In "Kubla Khan" the act of dreaming is a trivial event when set beside the ideal world that appears to have suddenly and transiently arisen to view. It is as if the appearance were recorded to measure the distance between mortal dreamer and immortal dream. We observe the same kind of rhetoric in, for example, a poem like Byron's "Darkness." Beginning with a perfunctory gesture from the dreamer ("I had a dream, which was not all a dream"), the poem unfolds a detailed catalogue of Armageddon, which assumes an independent substantiality like Coleridge's vision of the world of Kubla Khan.

Byron's rhetorical procedure is put into relief when we set it beside the literary example that spurred him to his poem—Thomas Campbell's "Last Man." Although most of Campbell's poem is a first person report of a dream of apocalypse, the dreamer is carefully defined at the outset as an imaginary "last man." Consequently, the fictional status of the poem is always clear. Coleridge and Byron, on the other hand, represent their texts through a rhetoric of immediacy. As a result, when their texts discard the psychological supports for their visionary representations, we appear to have entered worlds of dream rather than the dreaming experiences of particular persons.

The uncanny effect of Byron's poem is most disorienting not because the apocalypse we enter is a negative one, but because the otherworld of the text appears an independently authorized existence. As in the texts of the evangelists, the mediator of such an existence is not the focus of attention. (Because Byron was so famous, perhaps especially at the moment of this poem—1816—the subjection of dreamer to dream is all the more arresting.)

Keats's dream poetry is quite different, as one can see by looking at his great sonnet "A Dream, after Reading Dante's Episode of Paolo and Francesca" (1820):

> As Hermes once took to his feathers light,
>   When lulled Argus, baffled, swoon'd and slept,
> So on a Delphic reed, my idle spright
>   So play'd, so charm'd, so conquer'd, so bereft
> The dragon-world of all its hundred eyes;
>   And, seeing it asleep, so fled away—
> Not unto Ida with its snow-cold skies,
>   Nor unto Tempe, where Jove griev'd a day,
> But to that second circle of sad hell,
>   Where 'mid the gust, the world-wind, and the flaw
> Of rain and hail-stones, lovers need not tell
>   Their sorrows. Pale were the sweet lips I saw,
> Pale were the lips I kiss'd, and fair the form
> I floated with about that melancholy storm.

As in "The Fall of Hyperion," this poem gives not the dream as such but Keats's experience of entering the uncanny world of dream. The event is typically Keatsian, as one sees in early poems like "Sleep and Poetry" and "On First Looking Into Chapman's Homer." Although not literally a dream poem, the latter is, like "The Fall of Hyperion," the record of the discovery of the power of imaginative vision. The difference separating Keats's work, in this respect, from Blake's and Coleridge's and Byron's measures the close affinity of Keats to Wordsworth. Keats's dream poetry follows the form of, for example, the Arab-Quixote dream sequence detailed in the *Prelude* Book V—in this kind of work we behold the dreamer first; the dream itself is mediated as an experience of discovery.

In the Wordsworthian model, the discovery is then self-consciously meditated and read by the poet. In all such work the contrast with Byron's "Darkness" could not be more complete. As with *Manfred*, "Darkness" records a process of (as it were) *un*discovering the powers of the human mind. The epigraph to *Manfred* is telling: "There are more things in heaven and earth, Horatio, / Than are dreamt of in your philosophy." The special perversity of Byron's work would be picked up later by Poe, Baudelaire, and Nietzsche.

NN. Mediated or unmediated, Romantic dream poetry traces itself to the strange materials made available by late eighteenth-century philologists and ethnographers: ballad editors like Bishop Percy and Joseph Ritson, translators like Sir William Jones and Charles Wilkins. Jones's influential translations of Sanscrit originals are explicit testimonies to the reality of originary existences. The Vedic hymns reveal utterly strange worlds:

> Hail, self-existent, in celestial speech
> NARAYEN, from thy watry cradle, nam'd;
> Or VENAMELY may I sing unblam'd,
> With flow'ry braids that to thy sandals reach,
> Whose beauties, who can teach?
> ("A Hymn to Na'ra'yena," 1785)

The strangeness of these pieces of "celestial speech" measures something besides the distance between Orient and Occident. Indeed, the cultural differences between these two great worlds are not what drives Jones's interest in the Vedic hymns. On the contrary, the universalist eighteenth-century style of Jones's texts fashions a verse argument about secret congruences between East and West.

Through Jones's translations the Sanscrit texts reveal the vision of an originary and transcendant unity of being. The Vedic hymns are important for Jones's imperial intellect because they carry an "attestation strong, / That, loftier than thy [poetry's] sphere, th' Eternal Mind, / Unmov'd, unrival'd, undefil'd, / Reigns. . ." ("Hymn to Su'rya," 1789).

AA. Well, important as Jones was, Western writers found their favorite unknown worlds much closer to home, in the folk literature of European culture. The poetry of the period is dominated by those sophisticated appropriations of original song and ballad materials, the literary ballads: texts like William Taylor's "Ellenore" (translated from an already sophisticated German text), Coleridge's "Rime of the Ancient Mariner" and "Christabel," Keats's "Belle Dame Sans Merci," Baillie's "Ghost of Fadon." Taylor's "Ellenore," for example, opens under a traumatic sign ("At break of day from frightful dreams / Upstarted Ellenore"), but the story means to deliver us over to strange realities all the more "frightful" just because they appear conscious and undreamt.

xx. Which is why the work of M. G. Lewis calls for special attention, as I said before. It not only represents a vigorous contemporary literary tradition, it was a tradition denounced by Wordsworth, who anticipated

The Monk (1796): This book signals the importance of "the Gothic," and in particular the Gothic novel, for Romantic writers. "Tales of Terror" and "Tales of Wonder" appear throughout the period and they testify to Romanticism's preoccupation with conditions of social and psychological dislocation, on the one hand, and with mythic and primitive materials on the other.

later criticism's retrospective view of the issues involved. When Wordsworth refers (in his 1800 Preface to *Lyrical Ballads*) to "frantic novels, sickly and stupid German Tragedies, and deluges of idle and extravagant stories in verse," he is reflecting on literary work of the 1790s that Lewis epitomized and fostered. No text illustrates better what Wordsworth disapproves than *The Monk* (1796), that wonderful "frantic novel" imbedded with several "extravagant stories in verse."

Wordsworth's phrase "idle and extravagant" points to what is most distinctive and peculiar about Lewis's work—its marriage of the comic and the ludicrous with the horrible and the terrifying. Rent by internal contradictions, the work appears to have little interest in bringing them under control—as if pure effect (and affect) were the sole resource and only plan of the writing. In this respect *The Monk*'s imbedded poems reflect the novel as a whole—and none more so than the famous ballad (much parodied, much imitated) "Alonzo the Brave and the Fair Imogine."

A tale of betrayed love, revenge, and damnation, the poem's most disturbing effects develop from the "idle and extravagant" way it handles its materials. When Alonzo returns from the dead to claim his false beloved at her wedding feast, he comes helmeted, his identity concealed. Faced with this strange wedding guest, Imogine barely manages to keep her composure:

> At length spoke the bride, while she trembled—"I pray,
> Sir Knight, that your helmet aside you would lay,
>   And deign to partake of our chear."

The lady is silent: the stranger complies,
  His vizor he slowly unclosed:
Oh God! what a sight met Fair Imogine's eyes!
  What words can express her dismay and surprise,
When a skeleton's head was exposed!

All present then uttered a terrified shout:
  All turned with disgust from the scene.
The worms they crept in, and the worms they crept out,
And sported his eyes and his temples about,
  While the spectre addressed Imogine:

Although marked with the sign of comedy, the text's extreme civility ("partake of our chear," "dismay and surprise," "turned with disgust," "sported," and the like) is finally far more deeply disturbing than the poem's stock figural horrors. Lewis has introduced disorder into the most primitive levels of his work by upsetting the poem's aesthetic base. The text is anarchic—"idle and extravagant"—precisely because, as Wordsworth saw, it has made itself the primary instance of its im/moral subjects. A lord of misrule presides over this ballad—over the way the ballad materials are rhetorically managed. The poem exhibits a reckless and cosmopolitan savagery resembling nothing so much as the fiction of the Marquis de Sade.

AA. According to Wordsworth, these landscapes of savage places and demon lovers figure a natural world corrupted by men—specifically, by men (and poets) like Lewis and, later, Byron.

XX. But the devil's account is that the messiah fell and formed a heaven of what he stole from the abyss. According to this view of things, Lewis's work exhibits the eternal delight of its own idle and extravagant energies. How did Keats put it later? "might half slumbering on its own right arm" ("Sleep and Poetry"). Corruption and sin are problems according to the still sad music of humanity, not according to the mighty working of the universal order of things, the music of the spheres.

Henry Boyd's academic treatment of Dante is misguided, Blake says, because the critic brings ethical touchstones to Dante's work. But poetry for Blake is committed to the splendid struggles of Good and Evil. "The grandest Poetry is Immoral," according to Blake's view ("Annotations to Boyd's *Dante*"). And his further thought is also very much to the historical point. The Byronic and the Wordsworthian, the city and the country, the aristocrat and the bourgeois: "These two classes of men are always upon earth, & they should be enemies" (*The Marriage of Heaven and Hell*, plate 16).

NN. No doubt. But those two classes of men are not the only citizens of these worlds.

XX. True. Wordsworth and those who sympathized with his work—Coleridge and Hazlitt, for example—found as little to praise in the work of George Crabbe as in the work of Lewis, although Crabbe could hardly be seen as an idle or extravagant versifier. His representations of madness, for example, so detailed and methodical, empty themselves of all their Romantic possibilities. With "Peter Grimes" (1810) he writes a kind of case report of a deranged mind:

> "'All Days alike! for ever!' did they say,
> 'And unremitted Torments every Day.'—
> Yes, so they said:" but here he ceas'd and gaz'd
> On all around, affrighten'd and amaz'd . . .
> Then with an inward, broken voice he cried,
> "Again they come," and mutter'd as he died.

One has only to compare Grimes's imaginary visitations with those of Byron's Giaour. Both apparitions rise up from watery graves, but while Byron's hero lives in a charged erotic world—his despair is sublime and finally transcendent—Grimes has no access even to the negative dialectics of Romanticism. For Crabbe's work is a dismissal of eros, the world he sees and represents is survivalist at best. The grimmest reading of the culture of the period that we have, Crabbe's poetry is, for that very reason, an indispensable limiting case for criticism.

NN. But very much a special case. I was recollecting another differential. We customarily think of Byron's spectacular arrival on the cultural scene in 1812 as a turning point in the history of Romanticism . . .

XX. . . .as it surely was. His work distinctly sharpened the Romantic critique of culture. Byron's importance was to have (fore)seen that Romanticism itself would become a cultural norm. For this reason his work became the bar sinister across what he called the "wrong revolutionary poetical system" of Romanticism (letter to Murray, September 15, 1817).

The movement's systematic inertias deflected its revolutionary potential, turning the poets into schoolmasters, imagination into pedagogy. As Wordsworth, addressing Coleridge, declared:

> Prophets of Nature, we to them will speak
> A lasting inspiration, sanctified
> By reason, blest by faith: what we have loved,
> Others will love, and we will teach them how;
> *(Prelude* XIV)

The Byronic resistance to this potential in Romanticism recalls the exuberant independence of Burns and Blake. But later Romantics, paradigmatically Byron and Shelley, developed the sorrow that came with twenty and more years of dark knowledge:

> But all the bubbles on an eddying flood
> Fell into the same track at last, and were
> Borne onward.
> ("The Triumph of Life," 1822)

NN. Byron's and Shelley's knowledge comes from deeper roots. Look at the cultural scene through Mrs. Barbauld's *Eighteen Hundred and Eleven* (1812), published the same year as Byron's *Childe Harold. A Romaunt.* As dark a vision as Byron's, Barbauld's poem imagines a world at war with itself. The torments of contemporary civilization are not tares among the new spring wheat; they are a function of the presiding "Genius" of the European world in general:

"a world at war with itself": Barbauld's poem is a late reflection on the dominant political event of the Romantic age—the French Revolution and its aftermath, the Napoleonic wars.

> There walks a Spirit o'er the peopled earth,
> Secret his progress is, unknown his birth;
> Moody and viewless as the changing wind,
> No force arrests his foot, no chain can bind;

Seen from a contemporary vantage point, this is the spirit of what Mary Shelley would call "The New Prometheus," here imagined raising up "the human brute" from ignorance and darkness. Like Shelley's Frankenstein, Barbauld's Prometheus is a figure of severest contradiction—as one sees in the startling conjunction of "moody" with the Miltonic poeticism "viewless." A spirit of grandeur, beauty, and great power, he is a "destroyer and preserver" in a sense far more darkly imagined than Percy Shelley's West Wind. According to Barbauld, "arts, arms, and wealth destroy the fruits they bring."

Barbauld's is a root-and-branch critique of a systemic malaise. The most disturbing thought of all is that a demonic force can be traced as easily in the "Arts" as in any other feature of civilization. The (Romantic) imagination that art is not among the ideologies is dismissed in Barbauld's text—as it was not in Byron's famous poem of the same year, and as it typically would not be in most Romantic texts.

Whereas Byron's despair held out a secret Romantic (i.e., personal) hope, Barbauld's final hope—the poem ends with a vision of freedom for America—can only suggest an unnerving question: If spring comes, can winter be far behind?

Comparable to *Childe Harold. A Romaunt* in so many ways, Barbauld's poem differs from Byron's in one crucial respect— it genders the issues. The "capricious" Promethean Genius is gendered male; the knowledge of suffering, female. To note this

"an alienated imagination": Romanticism feeds off various experiences of alienation and is preoccupied with marginal writers and localized sensibilities. The idea is that alienation (as well as various congruent forms of experience, like historical backwardness) give privileged insight precisely by standing apart from normal experience. In this context, women's writing of the period possesses a singular importance.

is not to suggest the poem is arguing a moral equation of men with evil and women with good. It *is* to suggest, however, that a new way of seeing may emerge when an alienated imagination comes to consciousness. The fact that Barbauld's poem—unlike Byron's—was denounced and then forgotten as soon as it appeared is telling, particularly given the respect and fame that Barbauld's work enjoyed. Barbauld's poem seemed grotesque and anomalous from a writer who had come to define the proprieties of the feminine imagination for almost fifty years.

In this respect her poem would prove a song before the dark sunrise of the poetry of the 1820s and 30s. Literary history has all but forgotten this interregnum because its work is marked with the sign of a bourgeois Cain. With the emergence of Gift Books and literary Annuals as the dominant outlets for poetry, the arts appeared to have indeed destroyed their own best fruits and scattered the high altars of the imagination. It is a fast world dominated by a self-conscious trade in art and a studious pursuit of cultural fashion in every sense.

In face of it twentieth-century readers have learned to avert their eyes and await the coming of the reliable seriousness of Tennyson and Browning.

Two women—they both wrote for money, to support themselves and their families—preside over the poetry scene that developed with the deaths of Keats, Shelley, and Byron. One was Felicia Hemans, who would prove the most published English poet of the nineteenth century. The other was Laetitia Elizabeth Landon, the famous L. E. L., whose death in 1838 turned her life and career into one of the foundational cultural myths of the period.

In certain respects the two writers could not be more different: Hemans's work focuses on domestic issues and a Wordsworthian ideology of "the country," whereas Landon, distinctly an urban writer, explores the treacherous crosscurrents of love. Because each moves within a clearly defined female imagination of the world, however, their work independently establishes new possibilities for poetry.

XX. But what's so special about these two women? Literary historians have had no trouble characterizing the immediate aftermath of high Romanticism in relation to writers like Beddoes, Darley, Hood, and Clare.

AA. All interesting and important writers. But have they been read to deepen our understanding of Romanticism? Not even Clare has made much of a difference in this respect, although his work might easily have served. Neither his class position nor his madness has been taken seriously enough by critics or literary historians. Hemans and Landon are important because their feminized imaginations establish clear new differentials. Their work gives us a surer grasp of what was happening in those forgotten decades of the 1820s and 30s.

Take Hemans for instance. The draining melancholy of her poetry carries special force exactly because of its domesticity. What is most unstable, most threatened, is what she most values—the child and its immediate world, the family unit (centered in the mother). Hemans's central myth represents a home where the father is (for various reasons) absent. This loss turns the home to a precarious scene dominated by the mother. As in Wordsworth, one of Hemans's most important precursors, the mother's protective and conserving imagination presides over a scene of loss (see "The Homes of England," for instance, or "The Graves of a Household"). But whereas

Wordsworth's (male) myth of (feminine) nature licenses what he called a "strength in what remains behind," Hemans's is an imagination of disaster because (unlike Wordsworth's nature) Hemans's mothers are so conscious of their fragile quotidian state.

The disaster is clearly displayed in poems like "The Image in Lava" and "Casabianca." Theatrical by modernist conventions, these lyrics deploy Byronic extravagance as a vehicle for measuring social catastrophe and domestic loss. "The Image in Lava" studies the epic destruction of Pompeii in a bizarre silhouette of a mother cradling her child. The artist of the end of the world is here imagined not on a grand scale—as a Blakean "history painter"—but rather as a miniaturist. For Hemans, catastrophe is finally what Byron famously called "home desolation," and world-historical events are important only because they help to recall that fact.

> Babe! wert thou brightly slumbering
> Upon thy mother's breast,
> When suddenly the fiery tomb
> Shut round each gentle guest?

Hemans's poem is imagining a new burning babe and a new sacred heart. The events at Pompeii comprise a mere figure for the "impassioned grasp" that bonds child to mother. Burning in the fire of their relationship—setting their fires against "the cities of reknown / Wherein the mighty trust"—mother and child transcend the Pompeiian world. As Blake might have said, they "go to Eternal Death" (*Jerusalem*), which now reveals itself in and as the poem Hemans is writing, what she calls a "print upon the dust."

In "Casabianca," another poem of fiery immolation, Hemans emphasizes the psycho-political basis of destruction in "the cities of reknown." Explicitly set in a modern context (the Battle of the Nile, August 1798), the poem anatomizes the ideology of glory in the death of the thirteen-year-old "son of the admiral of the Orient," Commodore Casabianca. Standing to his duty in a secular fiery furnace, the boy is the central figure of a complex iconograph of the violence society exacts of itself as payment for its pursuit of power and glory. The sentimentalism of the scene is a feminizing textual move. The boy pleads for a word from his "unconscious" father that would release him from "the burning deck," but the language of the father is defined as a fearful symmetry of heroic silence and awful noise.

The upshot is a poem of violent death brooded over by a beautiful but ineffectual angel of (maternal) love.

It is crucial to understand that Hemans's feminine imagination does not solve the problems it exposes. Her sentimentalism is revelatory. Readers cannot forget that "Casabianca" recollects one of Nelson's mythic victories over the French, and a turning point in the Napoleonic wars. But Hemans's poem deliberately forgets to remember that saint of English imperialism. Nelson and England's sea power supply the poem with its obscure and problematic scene.

Standing with the young Casabianca on the burning French flagship, Hemans puts the war and its champions in a better perspective: in worlds where power measures value, imaginative truth seeks to find itself in powerlessness. The young Casabianca's moral and emotional position, what the poem calls his "still, yet brave despair," defines the complete equivocalness of what he represents. That he stands as the *figura* of "Casabianca"—of Hemans's own poetry in general—is finally a central argument of the work.

Landon's writing devotes itself to similar pursuits, as a text like "Lines of Life" or her many poems for pictures show. "The Enchanted Island," for instance (after Francis Danby's painting of the same title), implodes upon its own "dream of surpassing beauty." Itself enchanted by that equivocal (and double-meaning) fantasy, Landon's poem initiates a severely antithetical reading of certain proverbial Romantic ideas, like "A thing of beauty is a joy for ever" and "Beauty is Truth, Truth Beauty." The truth that Landon repeatedly discovers in beauty—including the beauty of art—is death.

Keats of course had begun to make similar discoveries, but Landon's more intimate (female) knowledge of the institutions and machineries of beauty gave a special privilege to her work. Whereas Keats (like Byron) imagined a transcendent power coming from sorrow's knowledge, Landon's knowledge is like Eve's original (cursed) discovery of the cruel fantasy grounding the ideal of transcendent power.

Landon's imaginative authority rests in what she is able to fashion from her experience of passivity. The dynamic of love and courtship—Landon's great subject—supplies the (female) object of the enchanted (male) gaze with a special self-consciousness. The women in Landon's poems are shrewd observers of their spectacular society—cold spectators of a colder spectacle repeatedly masked in the warm colors of dissimulating love. In such a world the distinction between a woman and a thing of beauty is continually collapsing, as one sees in Landon's wonderful lines "Lady, thy face is very beautiful," where we are never sure if the text is addressing a mirror, a painting, or a woman.

A poet of *dis*enchantments, Landon works by putting the vagueries of imagination on full display:

> Ay, gaze upon her rose-wreath'd hair,
>   And gaze upon her smile:
> Seem as you drank the very air
>   Her breath perfumed the while:
>   ("Revenge," 1829)

The enchanted i(s)land is equally under the spell of the assenting "Ay" and the gazing eye. The relation between the "Ay" and the eye is a recurrent preoccupation:

> Ay, moralize,—is it not thus
>   We've mourn'd our hope and love?
> Alas! there's tears for every eye,
>   A hawk for every dove.
>   ("A Child Screening a Dove from a Hawk, 1825)

Here Landon muses on a painting by Thomas Stewardson, which is triangulated by two fearful eyes (dove, child) and one cold eye (hawk). Studying the aesthetics of the painter's moralizing and sympathetic eye, the poem succeeds through its ironic and self-conscious appropriation of the hawk's point of view.

The cruelty of the poem—not to be separated from its sentimental sympathies—anticipates the equally cruel drama displayed in "Revenge," which retraces Blake's "torments of love and jealousy":

> But this is fitting punishment
>   To live and love in vain,—
> O my wrung heart, be thou content,
>   And feed upon his pain.

In this world, love's "yes" is joined to the spectacular eye ("Ay, gaze . . .") and the coupling proves disastrous. Landon's speaker succeeds by entering fully into the terms of the relationship. Identifying with both her rival and her false lover, the speaker overgoes Keats's *voluptas* of pain by an act of incorporation. The poem thus inverts Keats's "Ode to Melancholy," a work Landon seems to be specifically recalling. Her speaker "feeds" not on a fantasy lady's "peerless eyes" but on the "pain" masked by such a relationship. Landon's speaker becomes a "cloudy trophy" hung in the atrocity exhibition of her own poem.

Tennyson's early poetry is an effort to put a more benevolent construction on the hollow and mordant writing that filled his world. Although deeply influenced by Byron and Landon, he never even mentions the latter, and he struggles to exorcise his Byronic melancholy throughout his life. "The Palace of Art" comes forward under the famous injunction of Tennyson's early friend R. C. Trench: "we cannot live in art."

This thought locates what would become a key nexus of Victorian ideology—the preoccupation with social improvement and the commitment to the ameliorative power of public institutions and culture. Tennyson's poem imagines the "art" that "we cannot live in"—a specifically Romantic art—as unlivably self-critical, desperate, voluptuous. Arnold's normative critique of Romanticism, first defined in the preface to his 1853 *Poems*, is already articulated by the early Tennyson.

NN. Well, Baudelaire read Tennyson quite differently, as I recall—as the third in his dark triumvirate of Byron, Poe, Tennyson. Trench's remark carries a deeper critique of art and the worthwhileness of living in what Wordsworth called "the very world which is the world / Of all of us" (*Prelude* XI). Baudelaire's work is written under that deeper, more atrocious sign: "Anywhere out of the world." He reads Tennyson as a kindred spirit.

Trench spoke to Tennyson as a well-fed wit of the bourgeois world that Baudelaire, like Byron and Poe before him, refused. Trench's distinction between art and the world poses a practical decision and assumes the absolute value of a quotidian life in society. Tennyson is a thoroughly Victorian writer partly because his life's work unfolds under the challenge laid down by his friend. Everywhere assuming the validity of that thought, Tennyson's work puts it to the test of his poetic imagination:

That he who will not defend Truth may be compelled to Defend a Lie,
that he may be snared & caught & taken   (Blake, *Milton*, plate 8)

Because Tennyson (like the Lady of Shalott) is an artist and not (like Trench) a knight or burgher, his work comes to its Baudelaire-an positions by agreeing to defend the untruths of his corporeal friend Trench.

XX. So Tennyson is just another late Romantic.

NN. Not at all—anymore than Baudelaire is a late Romantic. Of course Tennyson and Baudelaire don't abandon the inheritance of Romanticism: one traces many connections to their immediate forebears, as one does in Browning, or Arnold. Tennyson is Victorian because the dominant context for his work is social and institutional. In the Romantics the context is subjective and interpersonal.

Even when Tennyson writes a poem of self-exploration and expression—*In Memoriam*, for example—the work is organized to move beyond the personal: the poem is, after all, framed on one end by an address to Queen Victoria and on the other by a celebration of the marriage of Tennyson's sister. Byron's *Don Juan* is every bit as socially conscious as *In Memoriam*, but its egotistical sublimity is overwhelming. The contrast with Tennyson couldn't be sharper.

AA. Yes, and the development of that paradigm Victorian form—the dramatic monologue—helps to define the differences. Putting a frame around its subjects, the monologue drops the appearance of a mediating consciousness. Byron's "dramatic monologues"—poems like *The Lament of Tasso* and *The Prophecy of Dante*—are clear vehicles of self-expression. "Ulysses" (1832) and *Pauline* (1833) are not, partly because they could not be: unlike Tennyson and Browning, Byron's "dramatic monologues" come from an author already famous as a poetic ventriloquist.

"dramatic monologue": Although formal equivalents of this mode can be found throughout the Romantic period, the sub-genre is distinctly Victorian. Paradoxically, its Romantic foreshadowing appears not so much in poems like *The Lament of Tasso* as in "The Solitary Reaper" or *Childe Harold* or any other highly subjective Romantic work. In Romantic writing, the "monologue" is a "dramatic" presentation of the poet *in propria persona*.

XX. Perhaps Tennyson and Browning are just more guarded and circumspect in their dramatic monologues—as if the formulas of Romanticism, and especially late Romanticism, bore too much reality for Byron's shocking public displays. That, at any rate, appears to be what Clare believed, as his late acts of Byronic imitation show. That they are "madhouse" poems—poems of an incarcerated self—

defines the point of such work exactly. As his work began to be culturally appropriated, Clare's madhouses began to frame his work—the way his class status was used to frame his other work.

In this sense the Northampton madhouse should be seen as the formal equivalent of the Victorian dramatic monologue. Northampton allows readers to turn Clare into a social and cultural subject even in his own writings. The event is quintessentially Victorian. It even defines the High Victorian way with Romantic writing in general:—culture over anarchy, the triumph of art as sweetness and light.

AA. Is that a Victorian or a Romantic way? The cult of the primitive and uneducated genius, the ethnographic reading of art—are these not preoccupations of the "Romantic period"?

XX. The history of cultural forms appears always to move in opposite directions, doesn't it?

Jerome McGann

Further Reading

Abrams, M. H. *Natural Supernaturalism: Tradition and Revolution in Romantic Literature*. New York: Norton, 1971.

Bloom, Harold, ed. *Romanticism and Consciousness: Essays in Criticism*. New York: Norton, 1970.

Butler, Marilyn. *Romantics, Rebels, and Reactionaries: English Literature and Its Background, 1760–1830*. Oxford: Oxford University Press, 1981.

Hayden, John O. *The Romantic Reviewers, 1802–1824*. Chicago: University of Chicago Press, 1968 [1969].

Jordan, Frank, ed. *The English Romantic Poets: A Review of Research*. New York: Modern Language Association, 1985.

Klancher, Jon. *The Making of English Reading Audiences, 1790–1832*. Madison: University of Wisconsin Press, 1987.

McGann, Jerome. "Rethinking Romanticism," *New Literary History* 59 (1992): 735–754.

McGann, Jerome. *The Romantic Ideology*. Chicago: University of Chicago Press, 1983.

Manning, Peter J. *Reading Romantics: Texts and Contexts*. New York: Oxford University Press, 1990.

Mellor, Anne K., ed. *Romanticism and Feminism*. Bloomington: Indiana University Press, 1988.

Rajan, Tilottama. *The Supplement of Reading: Figures of Understanding in Romantic Theory and Practice*. Ithaca, N.Y.: Cornell University Press, 1990.

Rosso, G. A., and Daniel P. Watkins, eds. *Spirits of Fire: English Romantic Writers and Contemporary Historical Methods*. London and Toronto: Associated University Presses, 1990.

Siskin, Clifford. *The Historicity of Romantic Discourse*. New York: Oxford University Press, 1988.

Byron, Shelley, and Keats

"The web of our Life is of mingled Yarn"
Keats in a letter of 1817 after meeting
—Shelley and other writers

SAILING home from a visit with Byron, Percy Bysshe Shelley drowned when his schooner, the *Don Juan*, capsized. A volume of Keats's poems found in his pocket helped identify his body. In *Adonais*, his elegy on Keats's own death, Shelley counts himself ("one frail Form, / A phantom among men,") and Byron ("The Pilgrim of Eternity") among those who weep. The three men engaged one another often during their brief lives, as they suggested poetic projects for one another and argued about the methods and materials of poetry.

Keats's plea in his first long poem, "Sleep and Poetry," was not granted—"O for ten years, that I may overwhelm / Myself in poesy; so I may do the deed / That my own soul has to itself decreed." But in the seven years he had as a poet, he published forty-five of his one hundred forty-eight poems in three volumes: *Poems* (1817), *Endymion* (1818), and *Lamia, Isabella, The Eve of St. Agnes, and Other Poems* (1820). The couplets of "Sleep and Poetry," the myth making of *Endymion* and *Hyperion*, and the narratives of "Isabella" and "The Eve of St. Agnes" preceded seven remarkable months in the history of English poetry—March to September 1819—when Keats conceived and composed his six major odes: "Ode to Psyche," "Ode to a Nightingale," "Ode on a Grecian Urn," "Ode on Melancholy," "Ode on Indolence," and "To Autumn."

In a letter of 1821, musing on Shelley's claim that the hostility of reviewers helped put Keats in his grave, Byron recalls his own reaction when the *Edinburgh Review* excoriated his first poems: "It was rage, and resistance, and redress—but not despondency nor despair." Two years after taking revenge for reviews of his *Hours of Idleness*—by writing *English Bards and Scotch Reviewers*—Byron describes how in 1812 he "awoke one morning and found myself famous" with the publication of Cantos I and II of *Childe Harold's Pilgrimage*. His Turkish tales were as popular. *The Corsair* sold ten thousand copies on publication day to a reading public of approximately two hundred twenty thousand.

While visiting Shelley on Lake Geneva, Byron further developed the figure of Childe Harold and the heroes of the tales. Cantos III and IV of *Childe Harold*, *The Prisoner of Chillon*, *The Siege of Corinth*, and *Manfred* continue the evolution of the Byronic hero. These cantos of *Childe Harold* also reflect what Byron refers to as Shelley's "dosing" him with Wordsworth "even to nausea." Poetic dramas such as *Marino Faliero*, *Cain*, *Sardanapalus*, *The Two Foscari*, and *Heaven and Earth* raise issues of heroism, politics, and poetry. His some two hundred and fifty poems range in length from four-line epigrams to the more than two thousand stanzas of *Don Juan*. That comic epic portrays the nominal hero in love and war, continuing into seventeen cantos, until Byron's own death in the war between Greece and Turkey.

Shelley received previews of *Don Juan*. A letter of 1821 to his wife, Mary (the author of *Frankenstein*), describes a typical day in Ravenna with Byron. Shelley gets up at noon and writes letters until Byron awakes at two and has breakfast. They talk and read until six when they ride through the pine forests. After dinner at eight, they talk until five or six in the morning. Shelley then writes that Byron "has read to me one of the unpublished cantos of Don Juan, which is astonishingly fine. It sets him not above but far above all the poets of the day: every word is stamped with immortality. I despair of rivalling Lord Byron, as well I may, and there is no other with whom it is worth contending."

Shelley's notion of a group of poets who contend with one another suggests the competitive energies that stimulate them as artists. Shelley's *Julian and Maddalo* (1818) reflects one debate with Byron. Julian, Shelley remarks in the preface to the poem, remains "passionately attached to those philosophical notions which assert the power of man over his own mind," a power that allows "good" to be made superior to "the evil in the world." Count Maddalo, on the other hand, asserts, "How vain are such aspiring theories."

From 1813, when he published *Queen Mab*, until 1822, when his work on "The Triumph of Life" was cut short, Shelley remained preoccupied with "such aspiring theories," writing of the possibilities for social and moral reform. The poet, he insists in *A Defence of Poetry*, is the one with power to transform and reform men and women and their institutions. The poet changes man's perception of the real. The reconciliation of "good and the means of good," as he phrases it in "The Triumph of Life," is a crucial problem addressed in his poetry.

Shelley's early portrayal of the poet in *Alastor* presents a man who refuses any compromise in the reconciliation of vision and reality; he is consumed by his quest. Two other major poems of 1816, "Hymn to Intellectual Beauty" and "Mont Blanc," describe hidden forces of nature and the individual mind's relationship to them. The "Love, Hope, and Self-esteem" brought by visitations of Intellectual Beauty become the forces of political and social revolution in *The Revolt of Islam*, *Prometheus Unbound*, and *Hellas*. The poet of "Ode to the West Wind," through whose lips trumpets a prophecy of resurrection and regeneration, seeks to sing like the lark in "To a Sky-Lark." "The Witch of Atlas" shapes the power of poetic imagination. "The Sensitive-Plant," *Epipsychidion*, "To Jane," and a number of other lyrics composed in the last two years of his career explore love, morality, and the significance of poetry. In his short life, Shelley wrote some four hundred and fifty poems.

In a letter of 1821 Shelley urged Byron to "subdue yourself to the great task of building up a poem containing within itself the germs of a permanent relation to the present, and to all succeeding ages!" This exhortation precedes by a month Shelley's critical insight, in his *Defence*, that persons and ages create ever "new relations" with great poetry.

The energy and beauty of his powers seem to dispersethe narrow and wretched taste in which (most unfortunately for the real beauty which they hide) he has clothed his writings.

Shelley, writing of Keats's *Hyperion*, in a letter of 1821 to Byron.

Byron, Shelley, and Keats were historically conscious writers aware of the cultural debates that mold literary traditions. The issue of "taste" becomes paramount as they debate exactly whose literature they should link themselves to. In writing to Byron about Keats, Shelley observes how significant the figure of Alexander Pope has become: "Pope, it seems, has been selected as the pivot of a dispute in taste. . . ." Byron solidified the grounds for this debate when he responded, in a pamphlet, to attacks on Pope initiated in *Strictures on the Life and Writings of Pope* by the poet and critic Reverend William Lisle Bowles. "Indeed," Byron wrote in a letter of 1821, "I look upon a proper appreciation of Pope as a touchstone of taste—."

For Byron, Pope is like the Parthenon, fixed against the failure of contemporary writing to show quality or of criticism to occupy the "Throne of Taste." "Ode! Epic! Elegy!—have at you all!" Jeering at the indiscriminate English bards on the scene in 1808—the laureate Pye, Southey, Wordsworth, Bowles, Coleridge, and Scott—in *English Bards and Scotch Reviewers*, Byron satirizes the degeneration of English poetry. "Scotch" reviewers, especially Francis Jeffrey and George Lamb of the powerful *Edinburgh Review*, help shape the sad literary scene in which "MILTON, DRYDEN, POPE, alike forgot, / Resign their hallow'd Bays to WALTER SCOTT."

The people no longer rise with the poet, who is now rapt only by himself rather than being the voice of a whole "polished" nation. "Time was," Byron's critical myth continues, when poetry allied sense and wit, when an "English audience felt" nature in common. Now Wordsworth is his own hero, and Coleridge is "tumid" and obscure. To work with common language and subjects, to demonstrate, as Wordsworth phrases it in the Preface to the second edition of *Lyrical Ballads*, that there can be no "*essential* difference between the language of prose and metrical composition," is an unacceptable poetic enterprise. As he tells "the tale of Betty Foy, / The idiot mother of an 'idiot Boy'," Wordsworth participates in the degeneration of English verse, and becomes a bard "Who, both by precept and example, shows / That prose is verse, and verse is merely prose. . . ."

In later apologizing to Coleridge for these charges, Byron regretted the "generality" that blunted his young attempt at older satire. But a specific Byronic interest remains in the poem—its mix of personal display with nostalgia for a unified reason and taste, just before the poet's own epochal trip in 1809 to "classic lands." When it is most unlike Pope, as when Byron worries the connection of the public weal to his own passion and pleasure, *English Bards* signals Byron's writing to come, which will mix conflicted self and society in ways that really "have at" received modes.

While maintaining his disagreement with Keats's "principles of poetry" and "abuse of Pope," Byron in a letter of 1821 also apologizes to the memory of John Keats. The evolution of poetic power Keats describes in "Sleep and Poetry" and *Endymion* connects itself to the tradition of genius tragically cut short—as exemplified by Thomas Chatterton, who lived from 1752 to 1770 and to whom *Endymion* is dedicated. Keats differentiates the couplets he writes in "Sleep and Poetry" from those of Pope and eighteenth-century neoclassicists who "sway'd about upon a rocking horse, / And thought it Pegasus."

In "Sleep and Poetry" an Apollo-like charioteer, having evolved from an erotic, pastoral setting, "with wond'rous gesture" animates the natural world. This imaginative perception cannot be maintained but—in a typical Keatsian process—deliquesces, and "a sense of real things comes doubly strong." Reality seeks to overcome this vision, rising "like a muddy stream." The poetic imagination, which defines itself in the rest of the poem, enables "the great end / Of poesy, that it should be a friend / To sooth the cares, and lift the thoughts of man."

Poetry brings pleasure and joy. The narrator, who with "full happiness" will "trace the story of Endymion," begins by insisting, "A thing of beauty is a joy forever." Keats revises the myth of Endymion—a prince made immortal and put into an endless sleep, during which the moon goddess visits him—into a story of a young man's quest. A passionate encounter with an inconstant female presence—the moon, Diana—drives Keats's Endymion to the depths of the earth and sea. He comes to "a jasmine bower, all bestrown / With golden moss. His every sense had grown / Ethereal for pleasure."

A vision of sexual consummation allows poetic description, the presence of a poet, who "sang the story up into the air, / Giving it universal freedom." Endymion, however, awakes alone and "most forlorn upon that widow'd bed. . . ." While the light of the moon always finds him, under the ocean Glaucus, who has been entranced by the nymph Sylla, warns him about involvement with such an "arbitrary queen of sense." Able to reunite Glaucus, Sylla, and a procession of other lovers, Endymion's own vision of love for Diana is set against the reality of a physical relationship with an Indian maid. Ready to renounce "cloudy phantasms," "the air of visions," the "daintiest Dream," Endymion contemplates telling his children, "There never liv'd a mortal man, who

bent / His appetite beyond his natural sphere, / But starv'd and died."
Then the Indian maid becomes Diana, and the lovers "vanish'd far
away."

The last line of the poem describes Endymion's sister, Peona, who,
having witnessed the transformation, returns "home through the
gloomy wood in wonderment." Gloom and wonder typically characterize the Keatsian experience of moving from passion to its aftermath,
from dream to reality. To infuse the gloomy wood with wonderment is
the poet's power.

Keats offers the poem with trepidation more as a statement of his
own poetic potential than as a finished work. The anxieties expressed in
his preface to *Endymion* were well founded, for "Scotch Reviewers" and
other literary critics savaged the poem and its author. In a letter of 1820,
which he may never have actually sent, an outraged Shelley berated
William Gifford, the editor of the *Quarterly Review*: "Why it should
have been reviewed at all, excepting for the purpose of bringing its
excellences into notice I cannot conceive, for it was very little read, and
there was no danger that it should become a model to the age of that
false taste, with which I confess that it is replenished." In another letter
of 1820 Shelley touches on "false taste" when, in discussing Keats, he
refers to "the bad sort of style which is becoming fashionable among
those who fancy that they are imitating Hunt and Wordsworth."

Despite his own purposeful echoes of Wordsworth in such poems as
Alastor and "Hymn to Intellectual Beauty," Shelley makes the problematic nature of influence or imitation central to his discussion of Keats and
poetic taste in a letter of 1821 to Byron: "I certainly do not think Pope, or
any writer, a fit model for any succeeding writer." In his early work Keats
favors the characteristics of Leigh Hunt's poetry that break with eighteenth-century modes. His sonnet "Written on the Day That Mr. Leigh
Hunt Left Prison" portrays Hunt—the poet-essayist who had been
imprisoned for attacking the Prince Regent in the pages of the
Examiner—as stepping back to before the eighteenth century in order to
take flight with Spenser and Milton "to regions of his own his genius true."
This poetic sphere encompasses an exaggerated idiom, an erotic figuration
that employs participial adverbs—"pantingly," "droopingly," "beaming-
ly,"—and adjectives ending in *y*—"lawny mantle," "downy rest."

Shelley comments on a certain overabundance in the verse in a letter
to Keats of 1820. "I have lately read your 'Endymion' again and ever
with a new sense of the treasures of poetry it contains, though treasures

poured forth with indistinct profusion." Such work, he tells Keats, will simply not sell. He goes on to emphasize his own attempts "to avoid system and mannerism."

Although wary of emulating others, Shelley insists in the preface to *Prometheus Unbound* that every poet is to some extent the creation of his age, the reflection of contemporary artists. He, too, writes in couplets of Endymion and the moon. *Epipsychidion* narrates a quest for passion and love and for the language to describe it. The poem may be read as a positioning of Shelley's own sexual relationships. In this cosmology he is the earth and Mary Shelley the moon. Claire Claremont, Mary's stepsister and one of Byron's lovers, is the comet. Nineteen-year-old Emilia Viviani, to whom the poem is addressed (the "noble and unfortunate Lady Emilia V———, now imprisoned in the convent of ———"), is the sun.

The poem begins by suggesting possible descriptions of Emily, but none are adequate. Images in language simply cannot fix her reality. Shelley then sets the restraints of marriage against the speaker's passion for Emily and the impossibility of maintaining human passion—the confining morality of being "chained" to one person against the exuberance of uninhibited love. In allegorizing these multiple loves, the poem celebrates its ability to create what the psyche does not have and then to move towards it.

This particular power and freedom of imagination, vitally important to Shelley, Keats, and Byron, define a significant interconnection among them. Despite their obvious differences, Shelley writes of the common ground of their work in a letter of 1819—a "certain similarity all the best writers of any particular age inevitably are marked with, from the spirit of that age acting on all." Shelley notes a "similar tone of sentiment, imagery, and expression"; and in the preface to *Prometheus Unbound* he writes that a "peculiar style of intense and comprehensive imagery . . . distinguishes the modern literature of England."

From the late eighteenth century on, writers sensed their activity in a common literary field and were aware of the interconnections among themselves. From the late eighteenth century, literary historians have characterized these similarities as *Romanticism*. Friedrich and August Wilhelm Schlegel used the term in Germany to discuss the poetry of Goethe and Schiller. Blake, Wordsworth, and Coleridge have usually been grouped together as first generation Romantics, Byron, Shelley, and Keats as the second. Numerous definitions of their similarities exist, from Walter Pater's "the addition of strangeness to beauty," to Watts-Dunton's "the renaissance of wonder" to Stendhal's proclamation: "All good art is romantic." By the early twentieth century, Arthur O. Lovejoy announced that the term *romantic* meant so many different things "that, by itself, it means nothing. It has ceased to perform the function of a verbal sign." In his essay "On the Discrimination of Romanticisms" Lovejoy proclaims this multiplicity of meanings to be a "scandal of literary history and criticism." Twenty-five years later, however, René Wellek argued in "The Concept of 'Romanticism' in Literary History" that reading in the context of certain categories—Imagination, Nature, and Symbol—allows us to characterize writers as "Romantic."

In the late twentieth century the whole possibility of discussing Romanticism as a viable literary, historical category (along with the possibility of writing literary history) has been called into question. Drawing on Nietzsche and Foucault, it is possible to see history as a fiction produced by certain powerful, self-promoting Western ideologies. The traditional periodization of history in Western culture is then made suspect.

For early-nineteenth-century poets, however, literary associations with contemporaries as well as the concept of literary history become vital issues. When Keats discusses Wordsworth and Milton, he is also debating his own poetic path. Grousing about a review of *The Revolt of Islam*, Shelley in a letter of 1819 writes that the only remark worth commenting on is that he imitates Wordsworth—"It may as well be said that Lord Byron imitates Wordsworth, or that Wordsworth imitates Lord Byron. . . ." For Shelley, great writers are necessarily connected to their contemporaries because their works commonly derive "from the new springs of thought and feeling, which the great events of our age have exposed to view."

I recommend the Revolution of France as a theme involving pictures of all that is best qualified to interest and to instruct mankind.

       Shelley in a letter of 1816 to Byron discussing Byron's poetic future.

As sources of poetic inspiration, "the great events of our age" begin for Shelley, Byron, and Keats with the French Revolution. Frequently associated with revolution, Romantic verse often focuses on the French Revolution and its aftermath, on the reorganization of Europe under Napoleon, and on his defeat by Wellington in 1815, which eventuated in the political restructurings that the victorious Allied powers imposed. "This is the age of the war of the oppressed against the oppressors," Shelley proclaims in his preface to *Hellas*. Oppressions of nations and of classes are at issue. The Greek rebellion against Turkey, the struggles of the northern Italian republics against the Austrians, the wars and revolts in Spain, Irish Catholic rebellion, and attempts by British laborers to improve their working conditions are bases for the intensely political nature of the poetry of Byron, Shelley, and, to a lesser but still important extent, of Keats.

In two early poems, *Queen Mab* and *The Revolt of Islam*, Shelley considers the possibilities for revolution and reform. Queen Mab—"the fairies' midwife" in *Romeo and Juliet* and a figure commonly associated with eighteenth-century children's stories—takes the soul of the sleeping Ianthe on a journey in her magic car. Showing Ianthe the "desolate sight" of the world's past and present, Queen Mab provides commentary that outlines Shelley's views on the political, religious, and cultural systems of Europe in the nineteenth century. "'Palmyra's ruined palaces,'" the pyramids of Egypt, the temple at Jerusalem, and the "'moral desart'" where "'Athens, Rome, and Sparta stood'" evidence the transitoriness of empires and human power. "Kings, priests, and statesmen, blast the human flower." Ahasuerus, the wandering Jew, is summoned. His centuries of punishment make him well qualified to deride Christian justice and the horrors religious systems impose. The fairy queen speaks of how man also violates the world by eating animal flesh and by imposing the restraints of marriage.

While falsehood, madness, and misery may be everywhere, "the eternal world / Contains at once the evil and the cure." An image Shelley also used in *The Cenci*, that of evil as a scorpion bound "with a wreath / Of ever-living flame," suggests that evil must destroy itself. Understanding the "Spirit of Nature" as the "all-sufficing Power, / Necessity" offers some hope for the future. Shelley draws on Baron d'Holbach to assert that every molecule acts only as it must. In accepting the doctrines of religions that see man as fallen and that depend on the omnipotence of an illusory, supreme being, humans create the chaos that supports the oppression of their rulers. When reason, which necessarily must assert itself, allows man to understand the workings of the world, reform must occur. The future promises glory "When man, with changeless Nature coalescing, / Will undertake regeneration's work."

The Revolt of Islam presents what Shelley in a letter of 1817 describes as "the *beau ideal*" of the French Revolution. Raising the possibility of nonviolent revolution, the poem considers the struggle as one of teaching and persuading more than of fighting. Such a revolution, Shelley continues in his letter, is "produced by the influence of individual genius and not out of general knowledge."

In *The Revolt of Islam* Shelley connects the power of revolution with the power of love. Two lovers, Laon and Cythna, rebel against the oppression of women—"Can man be free if woman be a slave?"—and against the tyranny of Othman the Turk. In keeping with persistent attempts to avoid and reverse violence, Laon finally surrenders himself to be burned alive—a punishment called for by a Spanish priest. Laon has negotiated Cythna's freedom, but she joins him in death. The spirits of the two are liberated to tell the story of what revolution can be. Originally, Laon and Cythna were brother and sister, but the element of incest in addition to the condemnation of religion was so objectionable to his publishers that they forced him to make substantial revisions. Keats observes in a letter of 1817, "Shelley's poem is out & there are words about its being objected too, as much as Queen Mab was. Poor Shelley I think he has his Quota of good qualities, in sooth la!!"

Despite constant public censure and continuing unpopularity, Shelley persisted in responding in verse to the political events of his age. "Ode to Liberty" commemorates the uprising of Spanish liberals that occurred in the spring of 1820. Popular revolts in Italy inspired "Sonnet: To the Republic of Benevento" and "Ode to Naples." In England, near Manchester at St. Peter's Field, mounted soldiers (some of whom were drunk), fired on a group of men, women, and children peacefully rallying for parliamentary reform. Derisively dubbed Peterloo in a jibe at Tory pride over Waterloo, the event enraged Shelley, who then composed "The Mask of Anarchy, Written on the Occasion of the Massacre at Manchester."

"The Mask of Anarchy"—which has become the classic Romantic example of how great political poetry survives its local origin—is about resisting not just murderous state power, but also the way that power forces itself to be understood. It shows how poetry can be most political by focusing on what is most poetical—the force of images in the world. In crisp three–and four-beat ballad lines and traditional allegorical tropes, Shelley broadcasts an ideal, linking metaphor and political action. The single meanings tyranny imposes cannot ultimately withstand the multiple meanings of liberty: "'Ye are many—they are few.'"

Murder, Fraud, and Hypocrisy appear in front of Anarchy, the state that lets Peterloo happen. They wear the faces of individual ministers, while the comprehensive emblem on anarchy's brow is a numbing unified code: "I AM GOD AND KING, AND LAW!" The "adoring multitude" frees itself from this code when a plural order of meanings resists the single faces and meanings of the dominant, repressive order. Hope, looking like Despair, awaits destruction "with patient eye." Then a "Shape arrayed in mail" and associated with England's maternal earth rises from mist to light to image—a manifestation of the spirit or power in "Hymn to Intellectual Beauty," which Shelley also describes as light and mist and which may "free / This world from its dark slavery."

As if speaking "an accent unwithstood" of freedom, this activist "presence" in "The Mask of Anarchy" empowers the people of England by letting them see how Anarchy's simple figures have chained their minds and political wills. They are being kept down by the iron law of subsistence wages and dehumanized into simple metonymies: "'Loom, and plough, and sword, and spade.'" They are being duped by a figure of finance, paper money, the "'Ghost of Gold'"; they have been in a dream of tyranny's "'dim imagery.'" Freedom, the poem insists, will overcome because it is replete with many actual meanings—not just bread, clothes, fire, and food—but also Justice, Wisdom, Peace, and Love, all in all an "'exceeding loveliness'" or excess of meanings that will absorb the limited figures of Anarchy.

Therefore, the poem enjoins a "'great Assembly'" of self-enfranchising political energies from all different corners, even palaces, of the nation. There the multitude's "'measured words'"—the poetry of real government—will be "keen" and "wide" at once, able to withstand the merely "'fixed'" opposition of the fierce ghostly order. Shelley well knows the cost in blood for such resistance. But his belief is that power's set figures of speech have to be stopped first by the realization of the critical mass of liberty's powerful language: "'Shake your chains to earth like dew / Which in sleep had fallen on you—/ Ye are many—they are few.'"

Murder in "The Mask of Anarchy" wears the face of Castlereagh, the despised Tory leader in the House of Commons. England's government provided many such figures for poetic attention. Himself a member of the House of Lords, Byron typically sympathized with radical causes—as long as that did not mean outright democratic rule. In his maiden speech he advocated alleviating the conditions that pushed the stocking weavers of Nottingham to riot, rather than inflicting punishment on the people. "Lines to a Lady Weeping," which Byron insisted be published with *The Corsair*, sympathizes with Crown Princess Charlotte, the daughter of the Prince Regent, whose father sent her from the room for weeping over "these suffering Isles."

Writing of the death of the Regent's father, George III, in *The Vision of Judgement*, Byron portrays the blind, mad, old king's attempt to get into Heaven. Byron parodies Southey's eulogy for George III, *A Vision of Judgement*, and addresses the prefatory essay in which the "magnamious Laureate" condemned the immoral poetry of what he called the "satanic school," whose members he cited as Byron and Shelley.

In Byron's version George arrives at the Pearly Gates to find a dozing St. Peter who has never heard of him: "*What George? what Third?*" Lucifer follows the king and tries to claim his royal soul. The ensuing debate breaks down when a particularly bad poet—Southey of course—jostles his way onto the scene. One who "Had turn'd his coat—and would have turn'd his skin," Southey offers to produce a nicely bound biography for Satan, demonstrating how he will write on any side of a political issue. He begins to recite, but St. Peter knocks him down, and in the ensuing hullabaloo King George slips into heaven, where he is last seen "practising the hundredth psalm."

In Byron's *Vision* George III is ridiculous rather than evil. Shelley's sonnet "England in 1819" presents a more sinister portrait—"an old, mad, blind, despised, and dying King." The country's rulers are leeches, who suck the blood of people who despise them. The sonnet names the dominant legal, military, and religious forces of oppression. But by delaying the simple main verb "are," until the final couplet, Shelley constructs a syntactic suspension that represents a political reversal—all the apparent entities "Are graves, from which a glorious Phantom may / Burst, to illumine our tempestuous day."

A similar possibility for renewal and resurrection arises in the concluding line of Shelley's "Ode to the West Wind": "If Winter comes, can Spring be far behind?" The wind of this poem is both "Destroyer and Preserver." A world oppressed and numbed by incompetent government, by the Congress of Vienna, by massacres like Peterloo can awaken through the "trumpet of a prophecy," the words of the poet-prophet.

For Shelley action and ontology are one, and the poem is also a statement of poetic possibility. The first three terza rima stanzas of the ode address the "wild West Wind" to describe its presence on earth, air, and sea in autumn, winter, and summer. In the next sections, the speaker seeks a relationship in which he attempts to replace the leaf, cloud, and wave of the preceding stanzas as objects of the wind's force. In a phrase sometimes quoted out of context to support the view of Shelley as Matthew Arnold's "beautiful and ineffectual angel, beating in the void his luminous wings in vain," the speaker cries, "I fall upon the thorns of life! I bleed!" This borrowing of Keats's phrase in "Sleep and Poetry" serves to establish the poet as one who sacrifices in order to triumph. As the speaker realizes, "If Winter comes, can Spring be far behind?" he affirms human possibility and points to Shelley's conclusion in the *Defence*: "Poets are the unacknowledged legislators of the World."

The writing that defines and exposes political systems also speaks in "Ozymandias," a political sonnet on political writing. On the pedestal under his statue Ozymandias (Ramses II) tried to have his monumental will inscribed forever: "'Look on my Works, ye Mighty, and despair!'" That inscription, like the missing trunk and head above it, is part of a wrecked imperial historiography. The sands of time, in the last line's metaphor, level Ozymandias's visage, sneer, name, and works. What he wants us to read about him has been monumentally empty in the "boundless and bare" desert.

What Ozymandias (and his ilk in 1817) refuse to know is that all such inscriptions are writing in the sand—impermanent, not bound by the will of kings. The sestet thus reads the pedestal antithetically, which raises the question of whether this political sonnet is itself monumental, yet another work of words doomed to "stretch far away." But the initial "I" in the poem who listens to the traveler speak of the ruined statue keeps the reader of the poem at a distance from the traveler's set reading of tyranny's "colossal Wreck." Ozymandias's words, the traveler's words, and the speaker's rehearsal of both all make for contingent readings of historical wreckage.

The power of kings and princes is set within and against the power of poetic discourse in the poetry of Shelley, Byron, and Keats. The fortunes of those who govern are also the focus of many of the verse dramas these poets wrote, although works such as Keats's *Otho the Great*, Shelley's *Cenci*, and Byron's Venetian plays have value more for their poetic and philosophical content than for their performance possibilities.

Two of Byron's plays, *Marino Faliero* and *The Two Foscari*, make Italian politics relevant to those of England. In Byron's telling, the personal vendetta of Marino Faliero, a fourteenth-century Venetian doge, becomes a grand plan to set Venice free by destroying the power of "swoln patricians," the senators who limit the power of the prince to bring honor and justice to the state. Marino Faliero typifies the well-intentioned, thinking ruler who becomes involved with the masses of people revolting to find freedom. The struggle corresponds to that of the Carbonari in Italy of 1820, a fight in which Byron was deeply involved, and in which he saw "the very *poetry* of politics." Similarly, in *The Two Foscari* the honor and patriotism of the doge and his son are set against the decrees of the Council of Ten, the "stern oligarchs" who stifle the people and those who care for them. In England, such powerful men joined George IV in his attempts to crush opposition, often those who rallied around his wife Caroline, whom he attempted to divorce and destroy. Another possibility for kingship is shown in *Sardanapalus*, a play in which Byron portrays a ruler whose enforcement of a "live and let live" policy brands him a "slothful" despot who must be eliminated.

The monumental figure of Napoleon evokes conflicting emotions from members of the generation who grew up as he grew to glory but who then witnessed his fall from what they saw as tyranny. Shelley's sonnet "Feelings of a Republican on the Fall of Bonaparte" begins: "I hated thee, fallen tyrant!" Having been seduced by "frail and bloody pomp," Napoleon is the "minister" of "Treason and Slavery, Rapine, Fear, and Lust." The speaker, however, realizes his repugnance has been misdirected: he now recognizes even more destructive forces than Napoleon, a typical Shelleyan trilogy of "old Custom, Legal Crime," and most of all religion—"bloody Faith." In "The Triumph of Life" Napoleon has grown into a "great form," but he is also the great facilitator of evil, the man "Whose grasp had left the giant world so weak / That every pigmy kicked it as it lay—."

Although amused to have acquired by marriage settlement the same initials as the French emperor, Noel Byron realizes the paradoxes of a man who can grasp the world but whose weaknesses destroy it. "Ode to Napoleon Bonaparte" condenses Napoleon's fall into "the Desolator desolate." This fate comes from not knowing when to quit, as did those leaders whom Byron contrasts with Napoleon—Sulla, Washington, and Bolivar. Napoleon's glory derives in part from his very inability to stop, a paradox emphasized in the portrait of Napoleon drawn in Canto III of *Childe Harold's Pilgrimage*. "But quiet to quick bosoms is a hell. . . ." Typically, in Byron's narratives of male power, the very character traits that allow greatness destroy a man: "a fire / And motion of the soul" aspire "beyond the fitting medium of desire." "Quenchless" once "kindled," this fire encompasses all, becoming "fatal to him who bears, to all who ever bore."

The ardor that drove Napoleon to conquer the world inevitably forces him to the island of St. Helena. Byron describes him there in *The Age of Bronze* as an eagle reduced to nibbling at his cage, a man who occupies himself squabbling with his jailers about what he gets to eat. Yet even in ruin, he retains more dignity than the other rulers depicted in the poem. Bound on the rock of St. Helena, Napoleon calls on "earth, air, ocean, all that felt or feel / His power and glory."

This image establishes another association with Napoleon, that of Prometheus. Myths of the Titans, especially of Prometheus, are central to considerations of human history in the poetry of Byron, Shelley, and Keats. In Byron's "Prometheus" the figure becomes representative of man as "part divine, / A troubled stream from a pure source." For Shelley, Prometheus is an "imaginary being" of the most "poetical character," described in the preface to *Prometheus Unbound* as "the type of the highest perfection of moral and intellectual nature, impelled by the purest and the truest motives to the best and noblest ends." Prometheus's gift of fire makes human consciousness possible. His name means "the forethinker," and it is he who knows who will overthrow Jupiter. Prometheus is endurance and wisdom and love.

In *Prometheus Unbound*, Shelley sets out the possibilities for human revolution, regeneration, and renewal that he urged Byron and Keats to take as their poetic material. The lyrical drama takes place over eons, or in one hour, or in an instant—and is set in the mind of Prometheus, in the mind of man, or in the universe. In this revision of Aeschylus's *Prometheus Bound*, Prometheus has cursed Jupiter—the tyrannical, patriarchal authority that men establish to rule and persecute themselves—therefore causing himself to be chained on a rock "eyeless in hate."

When Prometheus "recalls" his curse—remembers it, talks about it, takes it back—he can free himself from Jupiter's tyranny. Prometheus's love allows the earth to get back into its proper position, to turn on its axis, so that the ice of hatred thaws and the springs of affection flow.

Prometheus is reunited with Asia, his wife and counterpart. The closing lines promise the "firm assurance / Which bars the pit over
Destruction's strength" by four great virtues that can dominate human
life—"Gentleness, Virtue, Wisdom and Endurance." The revolution of
Prometheus Unbound may not endure, but the poem promises that it can
always be recalled to grant men "Life, Joy, Empire and Victory."

The antithesis of such victory follows the defeat of endurance in
Shelley's *Cenci*, perhaps the most successful English verse drama written in the nineteenth century. *The Cenci* is a tragedy of perversion.
Beatrice Cenci enters, saying, "Pervert not truth," but her murderous,
incestuous father undoes her sexually and morally. Count Cenci considers himself a "scourge . . . wielded" by God; in denying she is a par-
ricide, Beatrice speaks of "a sword in the right hand of justest God" and
asks, "Wherefore should I have wielded it?" Abused to her very soul,
Beatrice is caught in a deadly repetition. This self-justification or what
the preface terms "anatomizing casuistry" implicates the audience itself,
as it necessarily participates in and responds to "the dramatic character
of what she did and suffered."

Beatrice cannot defend herself. Shelley, however, sees his own age
containing greater possibilities for freedom. In the preface to his lyrical
drama *Hellas* he declares that "a new race has arisen throughout
Europe, nursed in the abhorrence of the opinions which are its chains,
and she will continue to produce fresh generations to accomplish that
destiny which tyrants foresee and dread." *Hellas* draws on Aeschylus's
Persians as a model for celebrating the 1821 revolt of the Greeks against
the Turks who had oppressed them for centuries. The preface sets out
Shelley's intention to "suggest the final triumph of the Greek cause as
a portion of the cause of civilization and social improvement."

In *Hellas* Shelley characterizes this renovation in part as a return to
the rule of Saturn, in Greek thought a golden age—"The world's great
age begins anew, / The golden years return." More typically, the Western world has accepted the myth of progress set out in Virgil's *Aeneid*.
The vegetative, lawless society of the children of Saturn is well replaced
by the military law and order exemplified by Aeneas and the descendants of Jove, the Romans. This view of the shift in mythic cycles—the
why and wherefore of the changes in dominant structures—fascinated
Keats, who took Prometheus and the other Titans as the subject of two
poems about ruling systems and poetic power: *Hyperion: A Fragment*
and "The Fall of Hyperion."

Hyperion: A Fragment tells of the Titans' overthrow by the gods of Olympus. In "The Fall of Hyperion"—written almost two years later—the story of the gods is filtered through the presence of the goddess Moneta or Memory, whose work serves to generate a man's growth from dreamer to poet. The poems show how man's religious and political structures change and evolve as he demands new qualities from those who dominate him. The old gods, the Titans, become aware of why they must be replaced—of why their successors are superior. In *Hyperion: A Fragment* Apollo succeeds Hyperion and is born a god when he can cry, "'Knowledge enormous makes a God of me.'" An awareness of human history—of "'Names, deeds, gray legends, dire events, rebellions, / Majesties, sovran voices, agonies'"—is the basis of his understanding.

Oceanus provides a more general explanation by appealing to "'the eternal law / That first in beauty should be first in might.'" In Keats's "Ode on a Grecian Urn"—in one of English poetry's most discussed assertions—"'Beauty is truth, truth beauty.'" Beauty is not just a pretty face. In "The Fall of Hyperion" the face of Moneta reveals the beauty that is truth, the "high tragedy" that "could give so dread a stress / To her cold lips, and fill with such a light / Her planetary eyes." The man who would be a poet replaces Apollo as he who "dies into life." Only those can approach Moneta's altar "'to whom the miseries of the world / Are misery, and will not let them rest.'" Lovers of mankind or laborers for mortal good or dreamers cannot fathom Moneta's knowledge. The poet has such power, and although he is filled with his own inadequacy, the speaker parts Moneta's veils and tells how he "set myself / Upon an eagle's watch, that I might see."

The position is that of "*Negative Capability*," Keats's phrase in a letter of 1817 defining the poetic character as "capable of being in uncertainties, Mysteries, doubts, without any irritable reaching after fact & reason." Political and religious concerns become part of his generalized statements about the expansion and development of poetic consciousness. "Life," Keats writes in letters of 1818 and 1819, is a "vale of Soulmaking," or a many-chambered mansion through which man progresses. From the "infant" or "thoughtless" chamber he moves to the "chamber of maiden-thought." When that room gradually darkens, he feels the "'burden of the Mystery.'" To explore "those dark Passages" is to fulfill one's poetic genius. The poet of "The Fall of Hyperion" sits poised for such exploration of "truth"—what Keats in a letter of 1817 calls the "holiness of the Heart's affections and the truth of Imagination," for "what the imagination seizes as Beauty must be truth—."

You speak of Lord Byron and me—There is this great difference between us. He describes what he sees—I describe what I imagine—Mine is the hardest task.
   Keats in a letter of 1819 to his brother George and sister-in-law Georgiana

In describing what they see and what they imagine, Keats, Byron, and Shelley narrate the continuity of the individual being over time. Criticism often addresses the construction or energies of self-representation typical of early nineteenth-century literature. In taking the self as a literary subject, these poets write about mind, being, and the apprehending and comprehending of the world as experienced by individual consciousness.

   Keats wrote to his friend John Hamilton Reynolds about the "grand democracy" of mind that allows all men to intersect in a final greeting. In this curved universe of Romantic thought, Keats and Shelley start from different points. Shelley's "Mont Blanc"—a key to much of his poetry—follows Wordsworth's humanist "Tintern Abbey" and Coleridge's religious "Hymn before Sunrise in the Vale of Chamouni" in asking what mind can make of the external world. Shelley's answer seems to be "everything"—a response based on nature's essential inaccessibility to us and imaged by the quiet, snowy top of Mont Blanc: "And what were thou, and earth, and stars, and sea, / If to the human mind's imaginings / Silence and solitude were vacancy?" For Shelley, the imagination finds through interpreting nature the authority people have to repeal all the "large codes of fraud and woe" that suppress human happiness.

   In contrast, Keats, though famous for saying that imagination "seizes" truth, has one of his most transformative experiences in the Lake country in 1818. The material reality of mountains and waterfalls supersedes imagination's desire: "I live in the eye; and my imagination, surpassed, is at rest—." Such rest, however, doesn't last long, as Keats's odes demonstrate. Written with legendary precision in a few months, they are stunning examples of Romantic renovation of received poetic form.

   Even in its modern voices, the serious ode retains its classical purpose as an address to a superior entity. Keats's speakers allegorize and personify common mythical objects. Psyche, the nightingale, the Grecian urn, melancholy, indolence, and autumn all make the eye of the poet's and reader's mind live in the imagination at least until the moment of passing rest occurs. For five of these odes, Keats invented a ten-line stanza—a versatile hybrid from the logic of Shakespeare's and Milton's sonnets as well as from the richness of Spenser's stanza. Keats thereby creates the space and order for an English empirical drama in which questions multiply for feeling intellect to answer without more than the "half knowledge" of negative capability.

As Wordsworth indicated in a note to "Tintern Abbey," Romantic odes turn on transitions, different conjunctions—*if, while, therefore*—positioning the tricky subject at hand. By interrogating a symbolic object, condition, or figure from various perspectives, Keats's odes emphasize knowledge as interpretive activity. The epiphany of beauty is really a focal point of interpretive intention—the silent "working" of the imagination that Keats tells his friend Bailey about in 1817.

As a "Cold Pastoral," the Grecian urn signifies dualities and paradoxes that "tease us out of thought" and deeper into experience. The poem enacts what the urn represents. The urn represents what the poem as process cannot achieve—"eternity" or the closure promised by the last lines: "Beauty is truth, truth beauty,'—that is all / Ye know on earth, and all ye need to know." Similarly, in "Ode to a Nightingale" the nightingale's song initiates the poet's comparison of the "here" of human desire and distress with the bird's "melodious plot" of tenderness and ecstasy. The ode's third and seventh stanzas particularize the historical, material conditions that make the "faery lands forlorn" to the speaker, who, either awake or asleep, has been a conductor for the music he passionately questions.

The vows taken to the mind in the "Ode to Psyche" are done in by the mutability of mind itself in the "Ode on Melancholy." We are had by life's best moments, "hung" among the "cloudy trophies" of melancholy's sovereign power over the fullest experience. Melancholy is a woman in this male allegory, a "she" who "dwells with Beauty . . . that must die," a feminine other who completes the logic of Byron's "she" who "walks in beauty, like the night." Keats gives us many darkening female faces, figures of forced oblivion like Lamia or La Belle Dame or figures of tragic total recall like Moneta.

The beautiful ode "To Autumn" signals an acceptance of poised natural oppositions—"Close bosom-friend of the maturing sun; / Conspiring with him how to load and bless"—before "full-grown lambs" and "gathering swallows" occupy the horizon of "the soft-dying day."

The surpassing of imagination in the odes thus produces moments of rest that signify moments of interpretive work in self-conscious Romantic poetry.

The particular acts of the imagination in Keats's odes serve, he writes in a letter of 1818, "to ease the Burden of the Mystery." He contrasts himself with Byron, who "says, 'Knowledge is Sorrow'"— inverting Byron's Aeschylean "Sorrow is Knowledge" from *Manfred*. Keats goes on "to say that 'Sorrow is Wisdom'—and further for aught we can know for certainty! 'Wisdom is folly.'" Condensing the way the heroes of Byron's poetry know life as certainty, folly, and wisdom, Keats claims for himself the more difficult "task" of describing what he imagines. Byron only "describes what he sees," a distinction to question in reading Byron's representations of male experience in his culture.

In his many manifestations, the Byronic hero contains elements of Aeschylus's Prometheus, Milton's Satan, Shakespeare's Hamlet, Fielding's Tom Jones, Goethe's Faust and Werther. The hero may be an aristocratic outlaw who rebels against injustice and corruption. The object of speculation and gossip, he mesmerizes those with whom he comes into contact. He has a deep secret hidden in his past. Byron's description of Lara includes this summarizing statement: "In him inexplicably mix'd appeared / Much to be loved and hated, sought and feared."

The mix in the various Byronic heroes ranges from the explicable and two-dimensional to the self-reflexive and complex. In the latter vein "So We'll Go No More A-Roving" suspends the sexual will. The lyric's three quatrains try abstinence—"it is now Lent," Byron writes to Moore in enclosing the lines from Venice at Carnival's end—in a light but firm structure of consequence and connection: "So . . . So . . . Though . . . And . . . ." The measured tone about stepping away from desire depends on the rhetorical tension between logical movement and erotic withdrawal; the result is lyrical ease and thematic density.

In 1809 and 1810 Byron shaped events of his own travels in the Levant into the wanderings of Childe Harold, first called "Childe Birun"— a "childe" being a squire of medieval times who is about to become a knight. In Spenserian stanzas Byron draws on Gibbon's ideas about the evolution of empires. He works in a topographical tradition that existed in Roman poetry and that is favored by Samuel Johnson, John Denham, and William Wordsworth. Travels lead to places that generate various sorts of meditation.

Canto I introduces the hero as "a shameless wight / Sore given to revel and ungodly glee." Isolated even in the crowds of revelry, however, the Childe leaves his home feeling: "'My greatest grief is that I leave / No thing that claims a tear.'" Following the Childe to Lisbon, Cintra, Seville, and Cadiz—all significant sites in the Peninsular War (1808–1814), the narrator of the poem begins Canto II meditating on the past glories of Athens. The ruins of the Acropolis serve to link the past and present. The Childe reappears traveling to Albania, where he—like Byron—is received by Ali Pasha.

In his self-imposed exile from England, Byron published Canto III in 1818, taking the Childe—"the wandering outlaw of his own dark mind"—and the narrator, who has not "loved the world, nor the world me," to Waterloo, to the Rhine, and to Lake Leman and the nature of Wordsworth, Rousseau, and Shelley. In a letter of 1819 Keats reports that four thousand copies of Canto IV have been sold even before the work has appeared in print. Standing on the Bridge of Sighs in Venice, the narrator suggests that "states fall, arts fade—but Nature doth not die." Finally, it is the ocean that remains for the pilgrim Childe and for the consciousness that pens the tale: "Time writes no wrinkle on thine azure brow."

To create Childe Harold is to "live / A being more intense." In the figures of the Turkish Tales, Conrad the Corsair, Lara, the Giaour, Selim of *The Bride of Abydos*, Byron shapes beings that embody the intense notion of maleness that so fascinated nineteenth-century readers. *Manfred*, a "dramatic poem" of 1817, seems obsessed with autonomous male power. "Power" and two cognates are spoken over forty times in an insistent debate within and about Manfred's mountainous individualism, as John Martin's watercolor *Manfred on the Jungfrau* (1837) heroically illustrates. In the death scene Manfred faces down infernal spirits that try to claim him for having knowledge they can't comprehend—won "by superior science . . . and skill / In knowledge of our fathers."

Both rumor and Manfred's own search among weird realms for oblivion or forgiveness indicate that he crossed into incest, which killed his sister Astarte. Appearing as raised premonitory phantom, Astarte is the only human female figure in *Manfred*. The tyrannous spirits that harangue Manfred's tortured freedom revert to the devils of morality plays. By 1821 Byron was proclaiming Shakespeare "to be the *worst* of models," but an epigram from *Hamlet* precedes this poem, and its rhetoric slips into that of the Shakespearean stage—"We are the fools of time and terror." Blank verse scenes and rhymed choral insets, how-ever, make Manfred's controlled excess the key to Byron's construction of man's individual will and its wide consequences.

The possibilities for man's exercising of his will in life, love, and war are developed and satirized in the figure of Don Juan. Among the reac-tions of the English friends to whom Byron sent the first canto of *Don Juan* was: "It will not be possible to publish this." Reactions of readers to the cantos of *Don Juan*, which appeared from 1818 through 1821, encompassed the extremes of hostility and admiration. To Douglas Kinnaird—his banker, business advisor, literary agent, friend, and staunch defender—Byron wrote: "As to 'Don Juan,'—confess—con-fess—you dog—and be candid—that it is the sublime of *that there* sort of writing—it may be bawdy—but is it not good English?—it may be profligate—but is it not *life*, is it not *the thing?*"

A treatment of the hero in love and in war, *Don Juan* explores epic, literary, political, sexual, religious and moral codes and pretensions. The narrator—whom Byron characterizes in an unpublished preface as a Spanish gentleman with a jug of malaga and a "segar"—drifts in and out of the poem to tell of Don Juan's exploits after being driven from Seville by an irate husband. A shipwreck washes Juan up on an island, whence he is driven by an irate father, who finds him making love to his daugh-ter. Sold into slavery, Juan arrives in Turkey, participates in the siege of Ismail, and goes to Russia and England. Along the way Juan is besieged with women who find him irresistible: his mother's friend Donna Julia; Haidée, daughter of the pirate Lambro; Gulbeyaz, the Sultana along with her three maids, Lolah, Katinka, and Dudú; Catherine the Great; and three English women—the fierce Duchess of Fitz-Fulke, the inno-cent Aurora Raby, and the knowing Lady Adeline Amundeville.

In 1821 Byron wrote:

To how many cantos this may extend—I know not—nor whether (even if I live) I shall complete it—but this was my notion.—I meant to have made him a Cavalier Servente in Italy and a cause for divorce in England—and a Senti-mental 'Werther-faced man' in Germany—so as to show the different ridicules of the society in each of those countries—and to have displayed him gradual-ly *gâté* and blasé as he grew older—as is natural.—But I had not quite fixed whether to make him end in Hell—or in an unhappy marriage,—not knowing which would be the severest.—The Spanish tradition says Hell—but it is probably only an Allegory of the other state.

Don Juan has proven particularly receptive to contemporary criticism's emphasis on poetry as self-reflexive linguistic production within cultural and political contexts. In assuming the right to talk at length and with ease, Lord Byron has serious fun with English rhymes and puns, with the argots of meditation, seduction, and warfare, and generally with speech of many kinds. In his open-ended epic—in which he wants to "giggle and make giggle" at all forms of moral and literary closure—Byron deploys the eight-line, ottava rima stanza that endlessly builds up and inevitably comes down. *Don Juan* uses the most ample genre—"my poem's epic"—and claims the most room of any Romantic poem. Byron takes a long, laughing view, his sense of possibility and futility in the world ever responding as he writes himself into and around young Juan's readiness for all experience. It is the poem in which Byron succeeds most in renovating the Swiftean, Shandean intersections of reader, writer, and written.

The narrative of Don Juan's experience in the world is perhaps the poem that Shelley "prophecized" for his friend in a letter of 1821: "You *will* write a great and connected poem, which shall bear the same relation to this age as the 'Iliad,' the 'Divina Commedia,' and 'Paradise Lost' did to theirs."

Byron died in a war of national liberation, Shelley in a boat more daring than practical, and Keats in a family plague of tuberculosis. "A Man's life of any worth is a continual allegory," Keats wrote to his brother George in 1819, and went on to deny such allegory to Byron, who "cuts a figure—but he is not figurative."

We tend to disagree with Keats as we make him, Byron, and Shelley figures of writers in the world as well as in literary history. Like Adonais they "beckon" to us from Romantic sureties of will, love, and imagination tempered by comedy, skepticism, and memory.

Susan M. Levin
Robert Ready

Further Reading

Bate, Walter Jackson. *John Keats*. Cambridge: Harvard University Press, 1963.
Bloom, Harold. *The Visionary Company: A Reading of English Romantic Poetry*. New York: Doubleday, 1961.

Butler, Marilyn. *Romantics, Rebels, and Reactionaries: English Literature and Its Background, 1760–1830*. London and New York: Oxford University Press, 1982.

Clark, Timothy. *Embodying Revolution: The Figure of the Poet in Shelley*. London: Oxford University Press, 1989.

Curran, Stuart. *Shelley's Annus Mirabilis*. San Marino, Calif.: Huntington Library, 1975.

Evert, Walter H., and J. W. Rhodes, eds. *Approaches to Teaching Keats's Poetry*. New York: Modern Language Association, 1991.

Joseph, M. K. *Byron the Poet*. London: Gollancz, 1966.

Manning, Peter J. *Reading Romantics: Texts and Contexts*. New York: Oxford University Press, 1990.

Marchand, Leslie. *Byron: A Biography*. 3 vols. New York: Knopf, 1957.

Reiman, Donald H. *Percy Bysshe Shelley*. Rev. ed. Boston: Twayne, 1990.

Vendler, Helen. *The Odes of John Keats*. Cambridge: Harvard University Press, 1983.

Wasserman, Earl. *Shelley: A Critical Reading*. Baltimore: Johns Hopkins University Press, 1971.

Woodring, Carl. *Politics in English Romantic Poetry*. Cambridge: Harvard University Press, 1970.

Wordsworth and Tennyson

TWO of the great seminal poems of the English nineteenth century appeared within weeks of each other in 1850—*The Prelude* and *In Memoriam*—the one a long-awaited landmark of what literary historians have called the Age of Wordsworth, the other an eloquent witness, likewise long in preparation, to the new Age of Tennyson. At the end of that same year, largely on the strength of his elegy, Tennyson was called to succeed Wordsworth as poet laureate, an office he regarded with some misgiving, for he disliked all public ceremony and most verse written for state occasions. Yet recognizing the prestige Wordsworth had given the post, he agreed without much delay to accept "This laurel greener from the brows / Of him that uttered nothing base." He was, in other words, humbly proud to assume the mantle of the Romantic master—and indeed to reify that metaphor, for on his presentation to the queen he wore the same too-small court dress that the great, gaunt Wordsworth had borrowed in 1843 for his own installation as laureate.

The Prelude and *In Memoriam* differ greatly in form and purpose, yet each stands as a public record—a reflection of the essential concerns, hopes, and fears of the society from which it arose. And each is also an intensely personal confession. If *In Memoriam A. H. H.*, as its full title announces, was designed as a tribute to Arthur Henry Hallam, its focus turns quickly to Alfred Tennyson, the depth of his bereavement, and the process by which he recovers assent to life in a world of doubt and denial. *The Prelude* of 1850, clearly labeled "An Autobiographical Poem," is even more directly subjective as it recounts—though with calculated emphases and discreet omissions—the protagonist's development from childhood to early maturity and the influence on him of natural objects—and of Cambridge, London, and the tumultuous course of the French Revolution. Wordsworth was duly sensitive to the magnitude of his self-history, for on completing the 1805 version, he declared amazement at his prolonged subjectivity. It was, he said, "a thing unprecedented in literary history that a man should talk so much about himself."

The implicit sanction for such self-contemplation derives in both poets from a strong commitment to the vocation of poetry, a lifelong dedication, unequalled since the death of Milton (who was to both a high exemplar) and unmatched in later times. To each the "call" seemed a virtual election, carrying with it the charge to bring a quickened sensibility to bear upon the general human condition or on some particular modern instance. The speaker of *In Memoriam* is unmistakably a poet, drawing at will on the traditions of the pastoral elegy, invoking the classical muses, appraising the tenor of the "wild" lyrics he is writing, and even reminding his readers of the difficulty of communicating a mystical vision in the "matter-moulded forms of speech." He is Tennyson in his representative poet's role with a mission, beyond all private grief, to articulate the sentiments of a whole generation—for the "I" of the poem, he claimed, "is not always the author speaking of himself, but the voice of the human race speaking through him."

The "I" of *The Prelude* is more specific in denotation: "A Traveller I am / Whose tale is only of himself." As Wordsworth's subtitle indicates, "the growth of a poet's mind" is the poem's exclusive theme, and the "poet" is distinctly Wordsworth himself, or at least as much of the self as he chooses to reveal or invent. If "the Poet" in context sometimes serves as a general epithet representing heightened awareness, Wordsworth assumes his own typicality and readily aligns himself with his ideal. His dedication to his own vision and work is complete and explicit; in Book IV he describes the "blessedness" he experienced as a young man walking through the fields at dawn:

> My heart was full; I made no vows, but vows
> Were then made for me, bond unknown to me
> Was given, that I should be, else sinning greatly,
> A dedicated Spirit.

Elsewhere Wordsworth claims himself called to a sacred office (in the 1805 version, "the holy life of music and of verse"); "poetic numbers" have come "Spontaneously to clothe in priestly robe / A renovated spirit singled out / . . . for holy services." "The Poet's soul" attends him in the "indolent society" of secular Cambridge, where he responds with something of poetic fervor to the abstractions of geometry, for his is already "a mind beset / With images, and haunted by herself." The "Genius of the Poet" has guided him to the fixed truths of nature beyond all shattering social revolution, has strengthened his faith in his "own peculiar faculty, / Heaven's gift, a sense that fits him to perceive / Objects unseen before," and has virtually given him in his degree a "power like one of Nature's." At the end of his long "protracted Song," he admits some uneasiness about the extent of his self-analysis and celebration, but at the same time he hopes that his mature work will provide sufficient rationale "for having given this story of myself." In any case, he has convinced himself that "the history of a Poet's mind / Is labour not unworthy of regard."

The Prelude was indeed a thing unprecedented in literary history, a personal epic, with poet as hero moving with troubled spirit amid social upheaval and receptively among enduring natural forces. Had it appeared in 1805, the Romantics would have had further evidence of the "egotism" that Hazlitt thought Wordsworth's distinctive attribute or of the "egotistical sublime" that Keats both feared and admired. But the other volumes of verse that Wordsworth published before 1820 provided quite ample proof of a central concern with his poetic persona and the quality of his unique endowment.

The Prelude was intended to introduce a three-part work called *The Recluse*, long planned but never completed—a vast enterprise on an unlikely theme: "the sensations and opinions of a poet living in retirement." The second part, however, appeared as *The Excursion* in 1814, running to some eight thousand lines and consisting of the lucubrations of four characters: the Poet, who is narrator, the Wanderer, who accompanies him on his rambles, the Solitary, whom they interview, and the Pastor, who prescribes fortitude and hope. All four seem patently projections of Wordsworth's own thought and personality. But the most vivid of the group is the Solitary, who confesses to a willful retreat from society, even to a longing for release from life itself, after serious afflictions, loss of loved ones, the dashing of political high hopes (as in the French Revolution), and consequent failures of faith in God and nature.

Although the poem as a whole attempts to establish a final assent to living, there is curiously more poetic conviction in the Solitary's negations than in the positive sentiments of the others. "Despondency" (the actual title of Book III), amounting almost to madness, has become counterpart or shadow to the dedicated blest assurance that dominates *The Prelude*. The melancholia reminds us of the recurrent disaffection of many Romantic and later artists and more specifically of a tragic sense too often denied to the assertive Wordsworth.

Like Tennyson a generation later, the young Wordsworth knew and resisted the attractions of the imagination as escape from painful realities. In *The Prelude* (Book V) he describes his early delight in books as passports to "that delicious world of poesy" where all was "holiday" and "never-ending show." And in his "Elegiac Stanzas Suggested by a Picture of Peele Castle, in a Storm" he confesses that he would once have preferred to depict the castle not—as his friend Sir George Beaumont chose to paint it—shrouded in gloom by a rough sea, but basking in a perpetual summer, suffused with "The light that never was, on sea or land, / The consecration, and the Poet's dream."

Now—the time is 1805—he salutes the "rugged Pile" as fitting image of the endurance of hardship and pain, for his own recent experience of bereavement (the loss of his brother John at sea) has convinced him that the escapist dream cannot satisfy his art when a "deep distress hath humanised [his] Soul."

Yet long before 1805 a sensitivity to the fallible human condition was challenging Wordsworth's "egotism" and his confident poetic commitment. His *Lyrical Ballads* of 1798 reveals an alert sympathy with rural tragedies, loneliness, suffering, and primitive dread—with a mad infanticide, a shepherd bereft of his flock, a destitute old woman pilfering firewood. And for many of these ballads he devised a narrator more naive than the simple characters he describes.

The speaker of "The Thorn," for example, as Wordsworth's own note tells us, is a garrulous and superstitious retired sea captain. The "I" of "The Idiot Boy"—virtually a burlesque of the dedicated poet—intrudes upon his narrative to declare himself apprenticed to the Muses for the past fourteen years, yet still helpless to record half the wonders that befell Johnny on his midnight ride. The "I" of "Simon Lee" awkwardly warns the "gentle reader" not to expect a moral. "We are Seven" involves a speaker pedantically insensitive to a child's sense of ongoing life. And "The Tables Turned" features a cheerful young "William" all too ready to overstate his belief that he may learn more from "one impulse from a vernal wood" than from all the sages of history, and so prepared gleefully to abandon all science and art so that he may respond to the spontaneous lore of nature.

Other poems—also first appearing in the *Lyrical Ballads*—notably "Tintern Abbey" and in the 1800 edition, "Michael," present the dedicated poet-narrator without irony or distortion, a sober reflective voice in a quiet blank verse, quite unlike that heard in the rapid rhythm of the ballad meters. "Michael" is introduced as the first of "those domestic tales" of Cumberland shepherds told to the poet when he was still a boy, "careless of books." The present retelling of the plight of a real shepherd betrayed by his delinquent son—with its subtitle "A Pastoral Poem"— makes it clear that the speaker is now bookish enough to reject the artifice of the pastoral convention in favor of a bare poetic realism. And the purpose of the moving story is explicitly to quicken the sympathy of "a few natural hearts" and, above all, to engage the emotion "Of youthful Poets, who among these hills / Will be my second self when I am gone."

The "I" of "Lines composed a Few Miles above Tintern Abbey" is likewise to be identified with Wordsworth, or at least the persona he adopted in *The Prelude*. Indeed, the poem as self-revelation beautifully forecasts the great autobiography. With none of the intermittent slackness of the latter, it succinctly describes—and even recaptures—the process of vision, the communion with Nature and through it at privileged moments the insight into "the life of things" that Wordsworth deemed the poet's highest function to register. Here, perhaps for the first time in his poetry, appears a self-transcending sublimity behind an apparent egotism:

> And I have felt
> A presence that disturbs me with the joy
> Of elevated thoughts; a sense sublime
> Of something far more deeply interfused,
> Whose dwelling is the light of setting suns,
> And the round ocean and the living air,
> And the blue sky, and in the mind of man:
> A motion and a spirit, that impels
> All thinking things, all objects of all thought,
> And rolls through all things.

Not until Book XII of the 1850 *Prelude* (though sooner in an early draft) does the poet discursively describe such moments of illumination as "spots of time"—the term designating glimpses of some timeless order of being encroaching upon the routine of everyday life. The memorable example there is the impression of a girl with a pitcher on her head, forcing her way painfully against a strong wind—"an ordinary sight," perhaps, but one with extraordinary reverberations, an arrangement of unforgettable aesthetic intensity. But "spots of time"—or psychological epiphanies—animate the poem from the beginning and impel much of its sustained argument. Childhood episodes recalled in Book I, notably the stealing of a boat and the cliff-hung search for birds' eggs, inculcate a sudden but lasting response to the larger than human, all-encompassing presences of Nature. An encounter with a blind beggar in London offers the poet, bewildered and "lost" in the surging crowd, abrupt admonishment, as if "from another world," that we can know but little "of ourselves and of the universe."

Most vividly of all—and most distinctly in the sublime mode—the traveler in the Alps, disappointed that he has unknowingly passed the highest point and "lost" to further simple expectation, is suddenly struck by the magnificence of the Simplon Pass, where the tension of opposites, the static in the dynamic (the "woods decaying, never to be decayed" and the "stationary blasts of waterfalls") evokes the ultimate apocalyptic vision:

> The torrents shooting from the clear blue sky,
> The rocks that muttered close upon our ears,
> Black drizzling crags that spake by the way-side
> As if a voice were in them, the sick sight
> And giddy prospect of the raving stream,
> The unfettered clouds and region of the Heavens,
> Tumult and peace, the darkness and the light—
> Were all like workings of one mind, the features
> Of the same face, blossoms upon one tree;
> Characters of the great Apocalypse,
> The types and symbols of Eternity,
> Of first, and last, and midst, and without end.

The narrative of *The Prelude* moves not by story line but by links often quite prosaic between sharp impressions and poetic epiphanies. A relaxed tension or aimlessness like the "melancholy slackening" of pace that precedes the experience of the Simplon Pass is, even in some of Wordsworth's shorter poems, the precondition of the spot of time or of its recurrence through memory. The first line of the daffodil lyric "I wandered lonely as a cloud" fixes the indifference that the dazzling vision of the golden flowers, symbols of the life force, will displace and redeem; and the last lines recall a state of mind much like the first, a "vacant" or "pensive" mood, which the involuntary recollection of the daffodils will again animate in a sudden "flash" of joy. The great "Ode: Intimations of Immortality" celebrates the child's sense of infinite belonging, which, though apparently lost in the "noisy years" of maturity, may still—in rare spots of time—break through our "listlessness" and "mad endeavour":

> Hence in a season of calm weather
> Though inland far we be,
> Our Souls have sight of that immortal sea
> Which brought us hither,
> Can in a moment travel thither,
> And see the Children sport upon the shore,
> And hear the mighty waters rolling evermore.

Wordsworth's mastery of a style less grandly orchestrated than that of the "Ode," but with similar metaphysical overtones, informs his "Resolution and Independence," a more specific account of poet and epiphany. Here an aged leech-gatherer provides the occasion (like the appearance of the beggar in *The Prelude*) of "apt admonishment" to the vacillating poet-narrator—the poem's real subject—who has begun an early morning walk, well pleased both with himself and with the rain-freshened landscape. But since his mood is self-seeking and unstable, he soon sinks from elation to a "dim sadness" and thence to deeper fears for his own future with its potential "pain of heart, distress and poverty." He ponders the unhappy fate of fellow poets Chatterton and Burns and at once aligns himself with their misfortunes: "We Poets in our youth begin in gladness: / But thereof come in the end despondency and madness."

Then suddenly, as if "by peculiar grace, / A leading from above, a something given," the unexpected sight of the leech-gatherer, as still and elemental as a stone, cuts across his self-pity. A brief exchange of commonplaces intensifies an impression of dignity and stoic courage, until the edges of the image blur, and the old man becomes—as in a dream—an archetype of eternal endurance, pacing "about the moors continually," forever silent and alone. When the spot of time, which is a moment's mute entrancement, recedes, the impact of the experience endures as a source of inspiriting strength, rebuking callow self-indulgence.

With the exception of *The White Doe of Rylstone*, his long historical narrative, Wordsworth's most memorable poetry is subjective in method or reference, relating the projected emotion to the peculiar needs of the narrator, and even the *White Doe* was, by his own testimony, designed less to tell a remote story than to illustrate the workings of a pious and often mystical imagination not unlike his own. But few poems are as self-accusing of the poet-speaker as "Resolution and Independence," and many assign to the recurrent "I" a more recessive or detached role. In "The Solitary Reaper," for example (which actually reflects an image from reading rather than direct experience), the "I" does not signal his presence until the third stanza—and then only with the perplexed question (for the reaper's language is Gaelic), "Will no one tell me what she sings?" But the full melancholy music like something everlasting ("As if her song could have no ending") remains, according to the last lines, as a spot of time to haunt his memory long after he has returned to ordinary life.

In the Lucy lyrics Wordsworth constructs an object of love and loss (for we do not know that a real Lucy ever existed), from which the "I" stands apart in numbed bereavement. In "She Dwelt among the Untrodden Ways" the first person appears only in the understated last line: "But she is in her grave, and, oh, / The difference to me!" In "Three Years She Grew" the "I" lets a quite inhuman Nature speak eloquently of incorporating Lucy into a larger order of being and nonbeing, a eulogy in sharp contrast to the sense of emptiness with which the "I" of the last stanza must go on living. And in "A Slumber Did My Spirit Seal" the poet measures his frail humanity, his lack of "human fears," against the inexorable powers that have deprived Lucy of all motion and force, yet paradoxically have made her a part forever of the moving, insensate earth.

Wordsworth's actual or alleged egotism brought a new psychological dimension to English poetry, but also invited the confessional diffuseness and laxity of form that he himself recognized as defects to be considered in revising *The Prelude*, which was to stand as his masterpiece and most original work. Deliberate self-restraint, on the other hand, led to the understatement and admirable concision of the Lucy lyrics, where his only self-assertion is the quiet but complete control of emotion and medium. The "Ode to Duty" describes the subjective poet's burden of too much "being to myself a guide" and "the weight of chance-desires"; and the sonnet "Nuns Fret Not at Their Convent's

Narrow Room" celebrates the sonnet form itself as an aesthetic release from "too much liberty."

Indeed, with the ideal of disciplined form steadily before him, Wordsworth, at the peak of his strength, emerged as one of the greatest sonneteers in the language, worthy of comparison with Shakespeare and Milton—though much more indebted to the latter, who provided examples of the Italianate form and the moral substance he was consciously to emulate. In the sonnets of 1802–1804 especially he found his own strong social and political voice, the assurance and energy boldly to exercise his personal dedication. The poet-prophet, now with firm resolution, denounces his contemporary England as decadent—guilty of selfishness, glittering materialism, and betrayal of a noble national heritage ("the tongue / That Shakespeare spake," the "faith and morals" of Milton). And in a climactic indictment ("The World Is Too Much with Us")—an attack on the frenetic getting and spending of his time and the consequent loss of reverence and wonder—he combines personal engagement, vehement rhetoric, and superb command of poetic devices (image, cadence, allusion, and assonance) as in the sestet:

> Great God! I'd rather be
> A Pagan suckled in a creed outworn;
> So might I, standing on this pleasant lea,
> Have glimpses that would make me less forlorn;
> Have sight of Proteus rising from the sea:
> Or hear old Triton blow his wreathèd horn.

Although his substantial achievement belongs almost entirely to the one decade following 1797, Wordsworth continued to write and revise for many years thereafter, during which he produced much journeyman work and a few pieces—mostly sonnets—of higher distinction. He survived the second generation of Romantics—Byron, Shelley, and Keats—who had found him a literary presence to be both respected and parodied, and he saw his reputation as a major poet well established by the early-Victorian critics. Yet he rarely recovered in his later verse the visionary gleam of his great spots of time, and his poet's voice retained but little of its past boldness and authority. By the 1830s the new Age of Tennyson was beginning respectfully to question Wordsworth's poetic themes and methods as it defined its own post-Romantic difference.

Declaring Tennyson "decidedly the first of our living poets," Wordsworth confessed himself pleased, despite serious misgivings, to have won Tennyson's praise: "To this I am far from indifferent, though persuaded he is not much in sympathy with what I should most value in my attempts, viz. the spirituality with which I have endeavoured to invest the material universe, and the moral relation under which I have wished to exhibit its most ordinary appearances." Tennyson's suspected reservations, however, were more stylistic than metaphysical. Wordsworth, he admitted privately, was often too prosaic and barren, "too diffuse and didactic for me," and to Wordsworth's simple language he preferred the richer diction of Keats, which exemplified the verbal concentration and intensity he chose to emulate. But his complaints were minor in comparison with his high estimate of Wordsworth's essential power.

Near the end of his own long career Tennyson assured the anthologist Francis Palgrave that he regarded Wordsworth as "the greatest of our poets in this century." And to another friend he explained that when he had his great heroic Lancelot in *Idylls of the King* claim the far surer "greatness" of his liege lord Arthur, "I was thinking of Wordsworth and myself." It was oddly characteristic that in writing of medieval knights, he should have been thinking at all of the relative status of nineteenth-century poets.

Apart from a few verbal echoes, Wordsworth's direct influence on Tennyson is seldom apparent. The Solitary's illusion of "a mighty city" among the mountaintops in *The Excursion* seems to anticipate the vision from the heights in Tennyson's Cambridge-prize poem "Timbuctoo," for in both we have an imagery of "glory," gold and diamonds, "boundless" space, domes, starry battlements, and dazzling canopies— Wordsworth's "wilderness of building" against Tennyson's "wilderness of spires." The un-Wordsworthian debate "The Two Voices" reaches a quite Wordsworthian conclusion:

> And forth into the fields I went,
> And Nature's living motion lent
> The pulse of hope to discontent.
> . . . .
> I wonder'd, while I paced along;
> The woods were fill'd so full with song,
> There seem'd no room for sense of wrong;

And all so variously wrought,
I marvell'd how the mind was brought
To anchor by one gloomy thought.

Here the "living motion" recalls the "motion" in "Tintern Abbey" that impels all living things, and the conquest of "discontent" repeats the pattern of "Resolution and Independence," where also "the birds are singing in the distant woods." On the other hand, Tennyson's "Tears, Idle Tears" (actually written at Tintern Abbey) may have been prompted by his admiration of Wordsworth's "Lines . . .," but it expresses its own sense of the past to quite different effect—with a sad regret rather than a forward-looking satisfaction. Tennyson said he often wished to take up the theme of "Intimations of Immortality" in a poem of his own; but his version, had it ever been attempted, would scarcely have striven for Wordsworth's rhetoric of assertion. At any rate, his "Tithonus," which repudiates the appeal of immortality, has been read as a conscious inversion of the "Ode."

The large differences between the two poets are, of course, more conspicuous than the few parallels. The representative figure in Wordsworth is the solitary (not usually as embittered as that character in *The Excursion*) placed against a bleak wild nature, and the chief value is stoic self-reliance. In Tennyson, conversely, the ideal is human fellowship, whether with the Somersby family circle in early lyrics or within the "reverend walls" of Cambridge in *In Memoriam* or among the Round Table knights of the *Idylls*. Few occasional verses in English can match the Horatian grace of Tennyson's urbane epistles to his many friends. No elegy expresses the dread of aloneness with greater poignancy than *In Memoriam*, and none aspires to a resolution so boldly social:

I will not shut me from my kind,
  And, lest I stiffen into stone,
  I will not eat my heart alone,
Nor feed with sighs a passing wind

—a resolve which should prepare us for the unexpected coda that celebrates the shared ritual of marriage.

Unlike Wordsworth's rugged moors and craggy hills, Tennyson's preferred landscape is a cultivated terrain, "not wholly," as "The Gardener's Daughter" puts it, "in the busy world, nor quite beyond it," within easy reach of good companionship. And the nearby city is not necessarily an intrinsic evil, as it is in "Michael"—though some of Tennyson's late pieces deplore urban squalor and the dismal "warrens of the poor." In the *Idylls* the city represents the brief triumph of Arthur's civilized order, Camelot, "the city . . . built to music"—as opposed to the encompassing wilderness, which is inhuman, brutish, and menacing. More realistically, in *In Memoriam* the city presents both the dark "unlovely street" of the dead Hallam and the same street quickened to new life at early dawn. Elsewhere, most genially, it becomes the setting of the Cock, the chophouse where Will Waterproof shapes his rhymes:

High over roaring Temple-bar,
  And set in heaven's third story,
I look at all things as they are,
  But thro' a kind of glory.

Tennyson's engagement with society extended to the intellectual life of the city and the universities. His personal acquaintance—sometimes close friendship—with Victorian statesmen, liberal theologians, and eminent men of science encouraged wide general reading and a concern with current ideas and the challenges of new knowledge. Tennyson discussed social and political issues on long walks with Carlyle and, in later years, on summer travels with Prime Minister Gladstone. He welcomed the leading Broadchurchmen, Frederick Denison Maurice and Benjamin Jowett, to his home at Farringford. Sir John Herschel stimulated his lifelong interest in astronomy, and Norman Lockyer had him proofread a treatise on cosmology. John Tyndall, the physicist, argued with him the case for materialism. Charles Darwin sent him an advance copy of *The Origin of Species*, and "Darwin's Bulldog," T. H. Huxley, praised him as "having quite the mind of a man of science."

Wordsworth in his 1800 "Preface" had predicted that "if the time should ever come"—the tense and mood were scarcely sanguine—"when what is now called science" should make its theories and abstractions familiar, concrete, and relevant, then the Poet might "lend his divine spirit to aid the transfiguration." But for Tennyson that time was already here; scientific Discovery (personified as early as "Timbuctoo"), both exhilarating and alarming, haunted his imagination all his life.

On its broadest public level *In Memoriam* is a dialogue between science and faith. Nature has now none of the solidity and permanence

Wordsworth assumed, for the rivers and seas, as Lyellian geology teaches, steadily "Draw down Aeonian hills, and sow / The dust of continents to be." Nor is Nature now so much the nurturing mother unwilling to "betray the heart that loved her"—as the predatory force postulated by mid-nineteenth-century evolution, "red in tooth and claw," caring for nothing, but in effect mocking the cherished ideals of a frail humanity:

> And he, shall he,
> Man, her last work, who seem'd so fair,
>   Such splendid purpose in his eyes,
>   Who roll'd the psalm to wintry skies,
> Who built him fanes of fruitless prayer,
> . . . .
> Who loved, who suffer'd countless ills,
>   Who battled for the True, the Just,
>   Be blown about the desert dust,
> Or seal'd within the iron hills?

Moreover, the whole round earth, which, "they say," began "in tracts of fluent heat," is but an infinitesimal part of a universe surveyed by the new astronomers—worlds upon worlds, where "stars their courses blindly run" in a vastness far less reassuring than Wordsworth's most sublime mountain vistas. Such to Tennyson were the real terrors of space and time, negating man's brave illusions and—for the modern poet—denying altogether the classical faith in the immortality of verse and all poetic fame, and presenting instead (in the words of his late "Parnassus") only a grim new inspiration: "These are Astronomy and Geology, terrible Muses!"

Tennyson's cosmic alarms, however, though anticipating the grimmer despair of Thomas Hardy, scarcely lessened the intensity of his personal dedication to poetry, his warm response to craftsmanship, or his care in poem after poem for what he considered the social responsibilities of his calling. "The Poet," for example, affirms his early regard for the poet's privileged insight, mission, and power ideally to shake the world, an assurance shared with fellow members of the "Cambridge Apostles"—the little "band of youthful friends" remembered in *In Memoriam*. And a companion piece, surely with some conscious hyperbole, warns the skeptical rationalist not to dare violate "the poet's mind," for "all the place is holy ground." Many later verses celebrate masters in a venerable tradition—Virgil, Catullus, and Horace, Dante and Milton, Chaucer and the long-neglected author of *Pearl*.

A number of angry squibs, on the other hand, condemn the mistreatment of the "sacred poets" in an age of prose—specifically the insensitivity of "indolent reviewers," the misguided attempt of bibliographers to reprint all that a poet has chosen to suppress, and the irreverence of biographers intent on exposing a poet's private life. The animus here against harsh criticism and undue intrusion is clearly self-serving: Tennyson himself was perpetually defensive against attack, self-conscious, reticent, and eager to protect the privacy of his family circle and intimate friends.

In Memoriam, as T. S. Eliot remarked, reads like "the concentrated diary of a man confessing himself," yet the revelation is discreet in detail and often enigmatic in personal reference. Tennyson's other subjective poetry, apart from lyrics in the vein of the elegy, is characteristically more oblique. Yet with safe distance and indirection he is able to view the foibles of his poet-self in amused perspective. He appears—only at slight remove—as Leonard in "The Golden Year," diffident and bewildered, "a tongue-tied Poet in the feverous days." He mocks himself in "The Epic" as Everard Hall, who belittles his own heroic "Morte d'Arthur," and then with little urging but "with some prelude of disparagement" reads it aloud, "mouthing out his hollow oes and aes, / Deep-chested music." Again he is the vinous Will Waterproof pondering his poet's role in "maudlin-moral" rhymes. In all of these Tennyson disarms invidious criticism of himself and his work by ironic avowals of ineptitude or indifference, just as in *The Princess* he implicitly defends "Tears, Idle Tears" by allowing the chilly Ida to ridicule its warm nostalgia.

Although able to assess his own conduct and performance with becoming good humor, Tennyson nonetheless affirms the serious obligations of both art and artist. An unfinished Cambridge allegory laments the enslavement of the giant Conscience by amoral irresponsible Sense, as a fate which threatens every susceptible poet. "The Vision of Sin," sharpening the argument, passes judgment on a young poet betrayed by his sensuous gift into an abandoned sensuality and eventually a cynical disregard for sustaining values. The weary aesthetes of "The Lotos-Eaters," no longer rough Homeric mariners, are implicitly condemned by their attempt to rationalize a sensuous escapism. The narrator of *Maud* rails at a dissolute age when "The passionate heart of the poet is whirled into folly and vice." The "I" of *In Memoriam* is loath to think of the whole green earth as simply an aesthetic illusion, "Fantastic beauty; such as lurks / In some wild Poet, when he works / Without a conscience or an aim."

The poet's Soul in "The Palace of Art" creates a pleasure dome of rich impressions, where she basks in a "godlike isolation" from humankind until she becomes so miserable in her solitude, "all alone in crime," that she is eager to seek out "a cottage in the vale" (an odd image of social life), where she may purge her "guilt." And *The Princess*, which repeats a similar pattern of retreat into artifice followed by return to reality, depicts the heroine as a "Poet-princess," an austere epic muse as much as an ardent feminist, who must eventually be redeemed by the human emotion she has suppressed.

Behind all these lies a fear of the dangerous seductions of art more intense and persistent than Wordsworth's indictment of a poet's evasion of tragic or merely unpleasant circumstance. For Tennyson's dread of the enticements of poetry testifies in itself to the strength of its contrary, to his perpetual delight in his craft for its own sake and his personal attraction, like that of Keats, to "the life of sensations" and the endless magic of incantatory language, whether it were the deep-chested music of Everard Hall or the horns of elfland echoing through the bugle–song in *The Princess*.

The theme of madness, or dissociation from present reality, also recurs in Tennyson with a greater urgency than Wordsworth brought to it, but again with less apparent self-reference. The Prince who tells the Princess's story suffers "weird seizures" (perhaps representing, as some recent readers suggest, Tennyson's fear of inherited epilepsy), sudden attacks of bedazed confusion during which he cannot distinguish the "shadow" from the "substance." Repeatedly, in Ida's little world of artifice he experiences a "haunting sense of hollow shows" until he sinks into a lingering trance or coma, "quite sunder'd from the moving Universe." The "I" of *In Memoriam* dreads a like schizophrenia, fearful that his grief has destroyed his stability and "all my knowledge of myself," and

> made me that delirious man
> Whose fancy fuses old and new,
> And flashes into false and true,
> And mingles all without a plan.

But the elegist succeeds in identifying, resisting, and so dispelling the threat to his sanity. The hero of *Maud*, on the other hand, succumbs to his own morbid sensibility, which has alienated him from a materialistic world and drives him, after an interlude of more lucid passion, into a certifiable psychosis. Short of such derangement, an intemperate violence of rebellious rhetoric invades both "Locksley Hall" and "Locksley Hall Sixty Years After," but the speaker recovers enough self-control in each to recognize his melodramatic rant—when young, to acknowledge that his "words are wild," and when old, to admit that his "heated" diatribe may signal his dotage.

The quieter, more characteristic melancholy of "Tears, Idle Tears," still irrational (or at least beyond rational accounting), involves Tennyson's "passion of the past," an unmotivated dissatisfaction with things present, a malaise of the heart rising "from the depth of some divine despair," essentially gentle though "wild with all regret." In his masterly appraisal of *In Memoriam* Eliot declared such meditative melancholy Tennyson's true poetic signature, and Tennyson himself "the saddest of all English poets, among the Great in Limbo, the most instinctive rebel against the society in which he was the most perfect conformist."

Sadness, however, is not the single or even dominant note in Tennyson's register, and melancholy often evokes its positive counterpart. In "The Two Voices" the tempter as the first speaker seeks by a cool logical common sense to abet a suicidal impulse, but the stubborn ego with which he must contend finds its best defense in man's irrational will to live, quite beyond the grasp of logic or any empirical demonstration, simply "That heat of inward evidence / By which he doubts against the sense." And the redeeming doubt leads to a more compelling though elusive insight, the conviction of a larger psychic life and an inexplicable déjà vu:

> Moreover, something is or seems,
> That touches me with mystic gleams,
> Like glimpses of forgotten dreams—
>
> Of something felt, like something here;
> Of something done, I know not where;
> Such as no language may declare.

Unlike the Prince's "weird seizures," this mystic intuition is restorative to the brooding ego rather than deranging, normative rather than pathological. Although akin to the Wordsworthian spot of time, it is here more completely inward; it demands no necessary external stimulus, no chasm in the Alps, no daffodil or leech-gatherer. The mystic experience recurs in Tennyson from the early "Armageddon" to the late "Ancient Sage," both of which describe a perplexed contemplation of identity followed by an infinite extension or annihilation of self–consciousness.

Most memorably it appears at the climax of *In Memoriam*, where for once it relates to a specific act, the reading through the night of the lost friend's letters:

So word by word, and line by line,
  The dead man touch'd me from the past,
  And all at once it seem'd at last
The living soul was flash'd on mine,

And mine in this was wound, and whirl'd
  About empyreal heights of thought,
  And came on that which is, and caught
The deep pulsations of the world,

Aeonian music measuring out
  The steps of Time—the shocks of Chance—
  The blows of Death. At length my trance
Was cancell'd, stricken thro' with doubt.

The "doubt" now makes possible a return to the ordinary world but with a stronger selfhood and with the remembered intimation of "that which is" to dispel inevitable future doubt or denial, as one of the final lyrics recalls the vision:

And what I am beheld again
  What is, and no man understands;
  And out of darkness came the hands
That reach thro' nature, moulding men.

In *Idylls of the King* the same mystical insight provides a spiritual sanction for the secular order. Arthur properly rebukes his knights who have abandoned their civic mission to escape into the excitement of a visionary quest for the Holy Grail. He himself meanwhile has remained in Camelot, faithful to the daily rounds of kingship, yet open at the same time to his own involuntary experience of transcendence, his "moments when he feels he cannot die / And knows himself no vision to himself."

The *Idylls* is Tennyson's longest and most objective poem, designed as an oblique commentary on the temper of modern society, rather than a probing self-analysis like *In Memoriam*. In effect, as completed in twelve books, it stands as the epic of a perilously poised imperial culture with the constant threat of "tempest in the distance," a foreboding of some last great "battle in the West," and an almost Spenglerian sense of imminent decline. But it deals less in epic realism than in the matter of romance, allegory, and symbolism. As its epilogue "To the Queen" suggests, it is meant as a tale "New-old, and shadowing Sense at war with Soul." The controlling conflict, then, resembles that of "The Palace of Art," but the resolution now is dark and ominous; Arthur represents Soul, and his ideal Camelot is ultimately destroyed by Sense, or selfish sensuality, which in final fact governs the conduct of his court, including that of the stalwart Lancelot and the beautiful, sad Guinevere. Although given to gnomic utterance, Arthur is not a nineteenth-century poet, surely not Wordsworth (except in Tennyson's calculus of greatness), and the other characters, though more recognizably human than the King, have no clear Victorian referents. Yet their deportment and moral responses apparently engage the poet-narrator's troubled modern judgment, sometimes his latent sympathy with Sense, and often his deepest personal fears.

Early in *In Memoriam* the elegist holds it "half a sin" to declare his inmost grief in words, for words, he believes, "half-reveal / And half-conceal the Soul within." In his many monologues, however, Tennyson welcomed the mediation of ambivalent language as a means of expressing, hiding, and reassigning his private feelings. Some of these pieces, to be sure—like the satiric "St. Simeon Stylites" or the exercises in Northern dialect—seem as objective as Browning's greatest poems, involving, as they do, a sharply drawn individualized protagonist quite unlike the composing poet, a distinct setting, and an implied auditor. But others, especially those on Greek themes, distance and reshape moods which Tennyson will neither admit nor deny as wholly his own.

Each of these is intended as a reading less of character than of emotion—regret or resolve—such as the poet may have felt at the time of composition, but set now in the remote context of ancient legend. "Tiresias" may register Tennyson's political forebodings, and "Demeter and Persephone" his religious aspiration, but an old mythology protectively clothes the sentiments of each, which would hardly, he said, have been so acceptable "in modern garb." "Tithonus" may be taken as a beautiful correlative to Tennyson's sense of the burden of mortality following Hallam's death, concealing the weariness of his youth behind the mask of age and revealing the eternal dawn goddess as a relentlessly antagonistic life force.

"Ulysses," on the other hand, was written to convey Tennyson's "feeling about the need of going forward"—though no one was expected to equate the Victorian poet with the antique warrior. Proclaiming an insatiable appetite for new adventure, Ulysses appeals to men of heroic heart to join him on a final voyage. Yet many recent explicators, trusting neither Tennyson's gloss nor Ulysses' resonant address, detect contradictions in the poem and find a subtext of defeat and death urge, which subverts the affirmed will to live. Tennyson, though often irked by his interpreters, would perhaps have been pleased that his best-known monologue could have achieved such independence of its avowed subjective sources.

When asked to identify the three queens who accompany King Arthur to Avilion, Tennyson complained, "I hate to be tied down to say, '*This* means *that*,' because the thought within the image is much more than any one interpretation." "Poetry," he said, "is like shot-silk with many glancing colours," and each reader must respond "according to his ability." Wordsworth, who also resisted questioning, would scarcely have chosen so aesthetic a simile to describe his medium, for he was less concerned than Tennyson with the artifice of art, less ready to suspect the imprecision and lurking ambiguities of language, and more confident that he could identify and directly affirm the unchanging verities. The young Matthew Arnold found in Wordsworth "the freshness of the early world," sadly lost in the "iron time" of the nineteenth century. But from the beginning, often in spite of himself, he recognized that Tennyson, offering not certitude but simply a relative "faith in honest doubt," addressed—as Wordsworth could not—the temper of Victorian England.

In a review of *Enoch Arden* Walter Bagehot distinguished between the simple style of Wordsworth and the more ornate idiom of Tennyson; and apart from the implied value judgment, the distinction remains useful and suggestive. Wordsworth's effort to approximate—not only in his ballads but later, too, in his lyrics and blank verse—the tenor of real speech has had a continuing appeal to twentieth-century poets as eager as he to avoid a sonorous and remote poetic diction. Yet

Tennyson has many styles, and his ornateness or deliberate contrivance as craftsman springs largely from an essentially modern sense of the elusiveness of words—from his search, foreshadowing that of Yeats and Eliot, for the symbol that would radiate multiple connotations, the many-textured "thought within the image."

But the abiding strength of both Wordsworth and Tennyson transcends any unintended anticipation—verbal or technical—of a later age of literature. It inheres, as *The Prelude* and *In Memoriam* demonstrated in 1850, in the timeless quality of their distinctly individual voices and the intensity and amplitude of their personal vision.

Jerome H. Buckley

Further Reading

WORDSWORTH

Gill, Stephen. *William Wordsworth: A Life*. Oxford: Clarendon, 1989.

Hartman, Geoffrey H. *Wordsworth's Poetry, 1787–1814*. New Haven: Yale University Press, 1965; with "Retrospect," 1971.

Johnston, Kenneth R. *Wordsworth and "The Recluse."* New Haven: Yale University Press, 1984.

Perkins, David. *Wordsworth and the Poetry of Sincerity*. Cambridge: Harvard University Press, 1964.

Woodring, Carl. *Wordsworth*. Corr. ed. Cambridge: Harvard University Press, 1968.

TENNYSON

Buckley, Jerome H. *Tennyson: The Growth of a Poet*. Cambridge: Harvard University Press, 1960.

Eliot, T. S. "In Memoriam." In *Essays Ancient and Modern*. London: Faber, 1936.

Martin, Robert Bernard. *Tennyson, The Unquiet Heart: A Biography*. Oxford: Clarendon, 1980.

Ricks, Christopher. *Tennyson*. London: Macmillan, 1972.

Sinfield, Alan. *The Language of Tennyson's "In Memoriam."* Oxford: Blackwell, 1971.

The Victorian Era

THE Victorian age was a time of extraordinarily rapid change and of often heady confidence in the seemingly inexorable progress of civilization, but also of bewilderment and anxiety as traditional social and religious faiths and structures were displaced. It was also an age of impressive achievements in poetry, even though many Victorians believed that the most striking characteristics of their age rendered it peculiarly unpoetical. As England achieved ever greater wealth and international power, as railroads and telegraph wires crisscrossed England and the Empire spread around the world, and as science and technology produced ever new wonders, few doubted the overall benefits of progress and advanced civilization, but such progress itself seemed antithetical to poetry. At the start of the Victorian period Thomas Babington Macaulay, a poet himself as well as one of the age's most tireless celebrants of material advance, offered the increasingly common argument that "as civilization advances, poetry almost necessarily declines."

Not only did knowledge seem to limit the range of imagination, but as scientific and historical discoveries began to undermine traditional religious faith, knowledge paradoxically produced uncertainty in the form of religious doubt—a "damnèd vacillating state," as Tennyson called it, that was considered utterly incompatible with inherited Romantic notions of the poet as an inspired seer, and as a moral teacher and guide. Religious doubt was in part produced by new scientific discoveries and discourses that incontrovertibly disproved the Biblical account of creation. Discoveries in geology, especially, disproved the

Bible's account of the total time span of the earth's existence and humanity's relatively brief history, and the theory of evolution, speculated upon for decades and conclusively argued in Darwin's 1859 *Origin of Species*, utterly disproved the biblical accounts of God's creation of mankind. In addition, evidences from the "higher criticism" of the Bible were proving more and more emphatically that the Bible was not the direct word of God, but rather a collection of diverse texts from diverse cultures. Further, and very simply, in an increasingly empirical age, fewer people were willing to believe in the supernatural.

Religious uncertainty was one source of seeming intellectual anarchy, of what Matthew Arnold saw as a confused "multitudinousness" in modern intellectual life, which rendered poetry impossible. It was not, however, the only source of multitudinousness, nor the only reason for the perceived necessity of a new unifying discourse. Another was the growth of the multitudes themselves. During the course of the nineteenth century the population of England and Wales quadrupled, from fewer than nine million in 1801 to over forty million in 1901. One of the first problems any poet needed to consider was his or her relation to this burgeoning multitude, and the problem was compounded by the changing character of the population in an increasingly industrialized and urban society. The transition from an agrarian to an industrial society, along with a gradual spread of democratic government, profoundly changed the class structure, as wealth and, eventually, power shifted from the landed aristocracy to the expanding middle classes.

Victorian poetry, for the most part, was very much a middle-class discourse, with not infrequent leanings toward the traditionally conservative values of England's immemorially agrarian traditions. Although poetry's theoretical representation of universal truths by transcendence of such mundane considerations as social position had the effect of marginalizing regional, working-class, and women's poetry, in practice the "teachings" of the major poets inevitably represented their own middle-class culture. Indeed, poetry became, for Arnold and others, a hoped-for means of universalizing middle-class values, and especially of extending them to the lower classes—the majority of the British population, which was becoming increasingly restive and influential with the gradual spread of democracy.

Such hopes for poetry, of course, were doomed to disappointment. As both the population and the literacy rates increased, and as a popular press and commodity culture grew, serious poets became increasingly alienated from the popular culture that developed to serve the literate but unintellectual masses, and the gulf widened between "high" and "low" culture until, by the end of the century, poetry had become a product almost exclusively by and for an intellectual elite.

The conditions that made poetry difficult in the mid-Victorian period also made it seem especially important. In the first place, for those able to retain their Christian faith, religious poetry became an important aid to devotional feeling, and possibly even a means to draw the discordant elements in English society back to the spiritual unity of the Church. Keble's *Christian Year* and innumerable Victorian hymns became extremely popular aids to piety. One of the age's finest religious poets, John Henry Newman, argued that "the poetical mind is one full of the eternal forms of beauty and perfection" so that, inevitably, "Revealed Religion" and "the virtues peculiarly Christian are especially poetical—meekness, gentleness, compassion, contentment, modesty, not to mention the devotional virtues." As Aubrey de Vere made clear, for true Christians the age was not unpoetical at all: "That any age not too late for virtue, too late for religion, and too late for the human affections, should be really too late for poetry we cannot believe,—although it may easily be unpoetical in its outward features." And of course the devotional poetry of Christina Rossetti, Gerard Manley Hopkins, and many others quite clearly shows that religious faith could and did continue to inspire powerful poetry.

But for those troubled by doubt, the call for an authoritative poetry seemed especially urgent when there was seemingly too much to know and apparently no way to integrate and internalize knowledge within a coherent worldview. At mid-century Arnold saw what Keats called the "grand march of intellect" as both an opportunity and a difficulty for the poet: "The poet's matter being *the hitherto experience of the world, and his own*, increases with every century. . . . For me you may often hear my sinews cracking under the effort to unite matter." Arnold felt that the din of competing discourses—and the lack of any one controlling master discourse—had overwhelmed the poetry of Keats, Tennyson, Robert Browning, and Arthur Hugh Clough with a confused "multitudinousness," and ultimately, he came to believe that the lack of a coherent contemporary "Idea of the world" made great poetry impossible in the present age. Although he believed that at some future time poetry might again be possible, he was convinced that his own age of transition was inevitably an age of "unpoetrylessness."

Unlike Macaulay, Arnold did not believe that the unpoetic character of the present age meant that poetry itself was outmoded. On the contrary, he was the most influential spokesman for the view that the high mission of poetry was to provide the kind of intellectual coherence, spiritual solace, and moral guidance that religion had formerly supplied. For Arnold, therefore, "the future of poetry is immense, because in poetry, where it is worthy of its high destinies, our race, as time goes on, will find an ever surer and surer stay." Poetry becomes all the more important precisely because in the present age "there is not a creed which is not shaken, nor an accredited dogma which is not shown to be questionable, not a received tradition which does not threaten to dissolve."

Arnold was one of many Victorians who looked to poetry for a "stay" against the dissolution of all tradition. Francis Palgrave, in his introductory lecture as Oxford Professor of Poetry in 1886, asserted that the "imperial function" of poetry "shines forth as the practical guiding power over a whole nation, leading them to higher, holier, and nobler things." In an otherwise chaotic time it seemed all the more necessary that poets, as Palgrave said, interpret "each country to itself" and so make "the nations alive . . . to their own unity." Reflecting the "unity of the nation" to itself was the object of some ambitious poets, but it was profoundly difficult to reflect the unity of a much-divided nation, and it seemed increasingly difficult to assume the role of bardic prophet and spiritual leader.

Although the early efforts of both Tennyson and Robert Browning were experiments in the high Romantic visionary mode of the prophet-bard, and although a diverse group of poets eventually labeled the "Spasmodic School" (most notably Philip James Bailey, Ebenezer Jones, Alexander Smith, and Sydney Dobell) briefly strutted gargantuan neo-Byronic egos across the Victorian scene, the "egotistical sublime" of Wordsworth discoursing from the mountaintop, the titanic self-revelations of Byron, and the apocalyptic rhapsodies of Shelley gradually came to seem outmoded. The Victorians wrote a great many very long poems, including such astonishingly ambitious epic works as Bailey's *Festus* (1839), Dobell's *Balder* (1853), and E. H. Bickersteth's Christian epic *Yesterday, To-Day, and Forever* (1866), but the age was too diverse to produce anything like a great national epic. Instead, the best long poems of the age reflect multitudinousness by compiling kaleidoscopic perspectives in linked series of shorter poems—the best examples are Tennyson's *In Memoriam* and *Maud*, the sonnet sequences of *Sonnets from the Portuguese* by Elizabeth Barrett Browning, *Modern Love* by George Meredith, *The House of Life* by Dante Gabriel Rossetti, and such experiments in shifting perspectives as Clough's *Amours de Voyage* and Robert Browning's magisterial *The Ring and the Book*.

Palgrave's ideal of a national poet was unrealizable in an age so multitudinous that the Arnoldian injunction to "see life steadily and see it whole" was clearly impossible. Further, to the extent that the individual mind is formed within and as a reflection of the surrounding culture, the instabilities of Victorian culture resulted inevitably in instabilities in the sense of self of individual poets. The poet could hardly represent the national self when he or she could not find or express a fully coherent personal self. Although perhaps best understood as a dramatic portrait, one of Tennyson's early poems suggests a characteristically Tennysonian problem even in its title: "Supposed Confessions of a Second-rate Sensitive Mind not in Unity with Itself."

Similarly, in some of his finest poetry Matthew Arnold lamented the lack of unity both in society and in the self, and noted the lack of a unified outlook in his poetry by remarking "that my poems are fragments—*i.e.* that I am fragments." Fortunately, however, those poets who deeply felt the difficulties of formulating a coherent sense of self in an incoherent age were able to use the difficulties themselves as the complex subject matter of such poems as Tennyson's *Maud*, Elizabeth Barrett Browning's *Aurora Leigh*, Robert Browning's many dramatic monologues, and Clough's *Amours de Voyage*.

The major poets did not abandon either the idea of art as introspective and self-expressive or the commitment to write for the moral edification of their contemporaries, although they struggled to reconcile these somewhat incompatible ambitions. The problem is acutely evident in the early poetry of Tennyson, whose finest early lyrics reflected ambivalence about the role of the poet. "Mariana," "The Lady of Shalott," and "The Palace of Art," for example, evidently allegorize the difficulties of the artistic soul, torn between living in autonomous isolation from the workaday world and the imperative to do one's duty within that world. Further, the representation in these poems of the aesthetic temperament as female suggests a division within the male poet—a sense that artistic cultivation of the feelings is effeminate and escapist and is opposed to a more vigorous (though less attractive) masculine call to duty.

Like Tennyson's, Robert Browning's early works reflect Victorian uncertainties primarily in their concern with the problems faced by a poet who simultaneously wants to serve a Romantic ideal of poetical autonomy and to speak to and for his rapidly changing society. In the first decade of his career Browning attempted a quasi-Shelleyan Romantic "confessional" poem in "Pauline," a Byronic closet drama in *Paracelsus*, a quasi-Shakespearean historical tragedy in *Strafford*, a wholly new form in his earliest dramatic lyrics, a bizarre form of epic narrative in *Sordello*, and an extraordinary medley of conventional drama, closet drama, narrative, and lyric in *Pippa Passes*. In various thematic and formal ways all of these works reflect the uncertainties, the multitudinousness, of the early Victorian age—but as experiments in genre, they particularly reflect Browning's concern to come to terms with the relation of the modern poet to his audience in an increasingly democratic age. They are all concerned with what the speaker of "Pauline" self-mockingly calls "The vaunted influence poets have o'er men!" Although such influence, on the whole, is apparently to be desired, Browning hints that the imperial poetic imagination could be tyrannical in its attempts to "make / All bow enslaved." Similarly, Paracelsus, although he expresses a desire "to serve my race," is characterized by his contempt for the rest of mankind, by a desire for knowledge, which is power.

The thematic concern with poetic authority is paralleled in the experiments in genre. "Pauline," for example, does not merely recapitulate the confessional mode, but calls into question the authority and value of the Romantic egotistical sublime, especially the notion of an autonomous poetic genius "Existing as a centre to all things / Most potent to create and rule." Although the speaker alternately proclaims and repudiates his pride, the desire for knowledge is repeatedly linked with a Faustian desire to usurp the throne of God, to be worshipped.

Browning next attempted to explore the moral issues raised by the quest for authoritative knowledge in *Paracelsus*, a closet drama that enabled him not only to maintain a distance from his central speaker, but also to introduce other speakers and other points of view, to reduce his central speaker to one voice among many. The work was both thematically and formally concerned with the need to share in the making of meaning, not only among the represented characters, but between the poet and his reader: "A work like mine depends more immediately on the intelligence and sympathy of the reader for its success—indeed were my scenes stars it must be his cooperating fancy which, supplying all chasms, shall connect the scattered lights into one constellation—a Lyre or a Crown." *Sordello* seems a still more radical attempt to share the responsiblity for making meaning with the reader, who must actively fill in the gaps left by the speaker: "what I supplied yourselves suggest, / What I leave bare yourselves can now invest." These lines clearly forgo the authoritative, coercive role of the poet, but they state only one of many positions in the poem's bewilderingly conflicted analysis of the poet's role. The choice, or invention, of a genre—a quasi-epic narrative studded with authorial intrusions, questionings, uncertainties, and utterly without epic action—suggests that the real concern of the poem is not its obscure plot, but its meditations on poetic authority. Unfortunately, the audience that was apparently expected to share in the making of meaning in *Sordello* found the task nearly impossible, and Browning's most ambitious attempt to share in the making of meaning led only to an early reputation for impenetrable obscurity.

Browning's other early works were much more traditional in form—dramas intended for the stage. In a series of plays written for the producer/actor Charles Macready, however, Browning achieved only a limited success. Serious theater had fallen on hard times in the nineteenth century, and successful stage production demanded emphatically clear, usually melodramatic plots, and leading characters who could be portrayed in the high histrionic style of Macready and other prominent actors of the day. By any standards—and certainly by these standards—Browning's dramas were deficient in action and clarity. He was far more interested in the subtle and complex motivations of individual characters than in dramatic action, with the result that he overloaded the plays with long soul-searching monologues that obscure more than they clarify the central dramatic conflicts.

As Browning said, his plays were concerned with "the incidents in the development of a soul: little else is worth study." The representation of what he called "Action in Character, rather than Character in Action" was doomed to failure on the conventional stage, but in a different genre it was to become Browning's most distinctive poetic concern. In the remarkably innovative *Pippa Passes* he devised a hybrid genre in which brief dramatic vignettes, interrupted by suddenly overheard lyrics, led to subtle explorations of individual motives, and to sudden revelations—in effect, he constructed a medium in which "incidents in the development of a soul" culminated in abrupt "Action in Character."

Browning achieved these goals still more successfully in the forms he was to make most distinctively his own—variations on the dramatic monologue, dramatic lyric, and soliloquy. In such poems as "Porphyria's Lover," "My Last Duchess," "The Bishop Orders His Tomb at St. Praxed's Church," and many others, he presented dramatized speakers at crucial points in their lives, generally at moments of conscious self-depiction and unconscious self-revelation. The form enabled Browning to explore the psychological depths that had been opened by Romantic poetry, but without the egotism of talking about his own inner depths, or the overarching ambition of formulating universal truths about the relations of the individual mind to the cosmos. Browning cogently described his sense of limitation in a letter to Elizabeth Barrett: "You speak out, *you*,—I only make men and women speak—give you truth broken into prismatic hues, and fear the pure white light."

Browning's remarks call to mind the distinction between what he elsewhere called the "objective" and the "subjective" poet. The "subjective" poet, a thoroughly Romantic ideal, seeks the pure white light: "Not what man sees, but what God sees—the *ideas* of Plato, seeds of creation lying burningly on the Divine Hand . . . and he digs where he stands—preferring to seek them in his own soul as the nearest reflex of that absolute Mind." This kind of poet, Browning acknowledged, must be "the ultimate requirement of every age," but after his early experiments with the "subjective" mode, he found his own distinctive style as an "objective" poet, "one whose endeavour [was] to reproduce things external (whether the phenomena of the scenic universe, or the manifested action of the human heart and brain)" for the better "apprehension of his fellow men."

Something very like Browning's own aesthetic creed is expressed in his dramatic monologue "Fra Lippo Lippi," where the monk enthusiastically describes his true vocation as a painter dedicated to reproducing "the beauty and the wonder and the power" of "God's works—paint any one, and count it crime / To let a truth slip." Yet Browning was far less interested in representing the external beauty of "God's works" than in the generally quirky, always subtle "manifested action of the human heart and brain."

Although he was an "objective" poet by virtue of representing minds other than his own, his real subject was subjectivity, and his dramatic monologues characteristically explore the ways in which individual identity is circumscribed by historical contingency, by prevailing systems of belief, and by emotional needs. Even though Browning himself believed in God and in some ultimate and absolute truth, his historical relativism shows, almost by definition, the limitations of human perception, the impossibility of seeing life steadily and seeing it whole. His works explore the inner workings of a gallery of characters comparable only to Shakespeare's—ranging from the lunacy of "Porphyria's Lover" to the utter lucidity of St. John in "A Death in the Desert," from the bestial growl of the thwarted monk in "Soliloquy of the Spanish Cloister" to the aristocratic eloquence of the Duke in "My Last Duchess," from the subhuman reasonings of "Caliban upon Setebos" to the subtle casuistry of "Bishop Blougram's Apology."

Browning's most ambitious examination of the extreme difficulties involved in finding the truth among the kaleidoscopic perspectives of limited human visions is *The Ring and the Book*, a poem of over twenty thousand lines based on a somewhat lurid and seemingly unpromising Italian account of a murder that occurred in 1698. The poem represents the events in lengthy, intricate monologues from the widely different perspectives of the murderer, the dying victim, the chivalrous priest who attempted to rescue her, various gossiping townspeople, the lawyers involved, and even the Pope, to whom a final appeal has been made. *The Ring and the Book* multiplies the challenge always present in Browning's dramatic monologues—the challenge to read through the distorting subjectivity of any individual speaker to find truth.

Yet although Browning took as his primary subject the difficulties of human subjectivity, his skepticism was limited by the belief that ultimate truths do exist, and can be at least vaguely intuited through a kind of imaginative faith. In fact, Browning offered a cheering faith to readers in his doubting age. In such poems as "A Death in the Desert," "Rabbi Ben Ezra," and many about musicians and painters, he expressed his own conviction that at our best we can intuit a transcendent God, and believe on faith even without empirical evidence.

Indeed, Browning made a virtue of the necessity of doubt—like his Rabbi Ben Ezra, he could "prize the doubt / Low kinds exist without," because doubt is precisely the "spark" that kindles the highest human aspirations. In the words of his Andrea del Sarto (who fails to live up to them), "a man's reach should exceed his grasp, / Or what's a heaven for?" Victorian readers found comfort in Browning's optimistic creed that mortal incompleteness and imperfection only imply an immortal completeness and perfection beyond this life: "On the earth the broken arcs; in the heaven, a perfect round" ("Abt Vogler").

Modern readers, however, far from looking to Browning for an "idea of the world," are more likely to appreciate him as the poet of multitudinousness, of near-anarchic life and energy. His collected works offer not only a multitude of exceedingly diverse characters and voices, but also of exceedingly diverse poetic forms—a seemingly new and different poetic idiom for every speaker. His pages seem as full of grotesquely proliferating life as the leaves of the volume tossed into a stagnant puddle in "Sibrandus Schnafnaburgensis," "tickled and tousled and browsed" by worm, slug, eft, and water beetle: "All that life and fun and romping, / All that frisking and twisting and coupling."

Browning is not likely to have been disturbed by Walter Bagehot's complaint that his "grotesque" art was too "showy" to guide what he regarded as the debased "taste of England." He would, on the other hand, probably have been pleased by G. K. Chesterton's affirmation that *The Ring and the Book* (and Browning's works taken collectively) may be regarded as the epic of a newly democratic age "because it is the expression of the belief . . . that no man ever lived upon this earth without possessing a point of view" and that no one person's point of view, not even the poet's, can adequately represent or even guide all others. For Browning the poetic imagination was no longer "imperial." His departure from traditional forms, his utter break with poetic decorum, his adoption of conversational, idiomatic, occasionally grotesque language enabled him to create a new poetic mode for the modern age. Despite his own belief in the ability of the "subjective poet" to intuit the pure white light of truth, Browning's poetry shows that the myriad prismatic hues of human perception can never be resolved back into whiteness.

Nevertheless, Browning retained enough belief in the expressionistic Romantic aesthetic to praise Elizabeth Barrett in 1845 for being able to "speak out" the "completest expression of [her] being." Browning's praise echoed Barrett's own description of her poetic vocation in her 1844 *Poems*: "Poetry has been as serious a thing to me as life itself; and life has been a very serious thing. . . . I have done my work, so far, as work,—not as mere hand and head work, apart from the personal being,—but as the completest expression of that being to which I could attain." The passage admirably sums up Barrett's poetic aspirations— she conceived of herself within the Romantic tradition of the inspired visionary, and she sought to satisfy the Victorian imperative of social duty by the hard work of leading humanity towards the highest ideals. Such a self-conception would be ambitious for any Victorian poet, but it was quite extraordinary for a woman.

Victorian assumptions about women's role in society made it extremely difficult for a woman to "speak out" at all, let alone to become a prophet-bard. Even Barrett herself believed that "there is a natural inferiority of mind in women . . . the history of art and of genius testifies to this fact openly." According to contemporary science, women's brains were not only small, but were ill-adapted to intellectual pursuits. Even George Eliot thought that women's brains lacked the "voltaic pile" necessary to crystallize ideas. The scientific mumbo-jumbo, of course, merely reinforced the nearly universal assumption that woman's place was in the home—a confined place that felt to many women like a prison.

The cultural limits assigned to women inevitably included women poets, or "poetesses," who were expected to maintain a ladylike submissiveness and humility in their verses, and to confine themselves to relatively "artless" outpourings of approproately womanly emotions—religious devotion, love, loss, and grief. "L. E. L." (Letitia Landon) characterized her role as an early Victorian poetess: "My power is but a woman's power, / Of softness and of sadness made" ("The Golden Violet"). And Mackenzie Bell's comments on Jean Ingelow's range sum up the prevailing view that women's poetry generally should be restricted to a "tender womanliness, a reverent simplicity of religious faith, and a deep touch of sympathy."

Staying within these bounds, Felicia Hemans, Landon, Ingelow, and other women were able to achieve widespread popularity and even considerable (though somewhat condescending) critical praise. But for a poet as ambitious as Barrett, there was no significant female tradition in poetry—there were plenty of "poetesses," but no women poets of real stature. Barrett herself lamented the absence of a tradition to follow: "I look everywhere for grandmothers and see none." Also, within the male poetic tradition, women were represented as the object of the poet's desire or quest or vision—there was no precedent for the woman as the central perceiving or creative subjectivity, and therefore no defined role for the aspirant woman poet. Finally, creativity was defined within the Romantic tradition as a kind of repetition of the creative fiat of God the Father—like priesthood, it was a masculine prerogative.

The normal restrictions on women were actually exaggerated in Barrett's case. Until her marriage to Robert Browning in 1846, the combination of a sternly protective father and her own invalidism kept her almost entirely confined to the home. Struggling to find a poetic role for herself in the mid 1820s, she saw her isolation as a serious handicap: "I am more & more convinced that an unagitated life is not the life for a Poet. His mind should ever & anon be transplanted like a young tree. It should be allowed to shoot its roots in a free soil, & not vegetate in a corner." Significantly, the Poet is gendered male—even in her poetry Barrett consistently represented the poetic character as masculine until the mid-1840s, so that the "completest expression of that being to which [she] could attain" evidently did not include an expression of her being as a woman poet.

In fact, Barrett's early works reflect a resistance to her culturally enforced role and an attempt to find a place for herself within masculine discourse. She studied the traditional masculine subjects, Latin and Greek, and by 1833 had achieved sufficient proficiency to produce a translation of Aeschylus's *Prometheus Bound* and to assert, at the age of thirteen, that "even the female may drive her Pegasus through the realms of Parnassus."

Her first mature volume of original poetry, *The Seraphim and Other Poems* (1838), reveals Barrett's ambivalence about her poetic vocation in several ways. The ambitious title poem, which adopts the form of Greek tragedy to represent the dialogue of two angels watching the crucifixion, significantly avoids the problem of a gendered poetic voice by its dramatic form, and by presenting visionary truths through the ungendered voices of the angels. A human voice only appears in a closing epilogue, and only to deprecate the "counterfeit" of "seraph language." But in her early poems Barrett was ultimately less concerned with the difficulties of singing as a woman than with the difficulties of singing as a Christian—indeed, the most striking feature of these poems is their piety and Christian humility. In several poems where the poet fails to be a priest, *he* is explicitly contrasted with the Christian, especially when he vaingloriously celebrates his own creativity instead of praising God's creation.

Even more frequently, as in "A Song Against Singing," the point is made that fallen human nature can only sing imperfectly—the highest and best utterances should be "prayer in place of singing." Indirectly, of course, gender is probably still an issue here—the humbly submissive stance was especially appropriate to a woman poet. Many of Barrett's difficulties are oddly reflected in the title poem of her 1844 volume, *A Drama of Exile*. Like "The Seraphim," this poem is set squarely in the male tradition—using the form of Greek tragedy to retell the story of Genesis. Again the dramatic form avoids the problem of a gendered poetic voice, but in this poem Barrett began to find poetic opportunities rather than limitations in her gender. She noted that it was written "with a peculiar reference to Eve's allotted grief," which seemed to her "more expressible by a woman than a man." Still, she gave the role of visionary not only to various spirits and to Christ, but also to Adam, who is inspired by "God breathing through my breath." Eve's role is to be "woman, wife, and mother," and her highest good is "worthy endurance of permitted pain."

Characteristically, Barrett's early poems lament the fallen state of humanity and look forward in Christian hope to redemption. "The Island," "The Deserted Garden," "My Doves," "The Lost Bower," "The Romance of the Swan's Nest," and "Hector in the Garden" all express regret for a lost innocence, submission to God's will, and prayerful anticipation of the "Heavenly promise." Like most women's poetry of the day, their dominant tone is melancholy, and despite what contemporary reviewers sometimes referred to as the "virile" appropriation of male forms in some of the most ambitious poems, they both implicitly and explicitly assign a subordinate role to women. The poems that contributed most to Barrett's contemporary popularity were a series of ballad romances about women's tribulations in love—"The Romaunt of Margret," "A Romance of the Ganges," "The Romaunt of the Page," "The Lay of the Brown Rosary," "The Rhyme of the Duchess May," and "Bertha in the Lane." The one ballad that did not represent the woman losing all for love was the extremely popular "Lady Geraldine's Courtship," in which the highborn lady accepts the love of her lowborn suitor—but only because he is a poet, and therefore "noble, certes."

In none of these poems does Barrett seem to "speak out" the full "expression of her being," yet she was certainly not satisfied with the cultural role assigned the mere "poetess," and Robert Browning was right in seeing full self-expression as her ultimate aim. She did "speak out" in "The Cry of the Children," her passionate poem of protest against the exploitation of children in factories and mines. And in a series of sonnets she attempted to sing "the music of my nature," to "utter all myself into the air" ("The Soul's Expression"). In an 1844 letter to Browning she worked toward a female poetics even as she regretted her lack of worldly experience. Her very isolation offered "a compensation to a degree. I have had much of the inner life—& from the habit of selfconsciousness of selfanalysis, I make great guesses at Human Nature in the main." Barrett occasionally compared herself to Tennyson's Mariana in her moated grange—like the feminine subjectivity characterized in Tennyson's early poems, the intensity of her poetically melancholy feelings was a direct result of her loneliness. She was compelled to be the subjective poet described by Browning, to dig where she stood, but she was also, as she recognized, condemned to work within the limited sphere of her isolated experience.

Not surprisingly, her most enduring poetry was written after her elopement and marriage to Robert Browning had freed her from the confinement of her father's home. The poems first published in 1850 show her speaking out with greater confidence, and speaking out explicitly of women's concerns and in a woman's voice. For example, "The Runaway Slave at Pilgrim's Point" was, as she said, a "ferocious" antislavery poem. But the most important new works were the love poems to Robert Browning, thinly disguised under the title *Sonnets from the Portuguese*. Although many modern readers find these poems maudlin, they were popular in their time, and they represented a genuinely impressive innovation. Barrett Browning entirely renovated the conventional uses of the Petrarchan sonnet simply by adapting it to a modern woman's voice and concerns. Christina Rossetti, whose sonnet sequence "Monna Innominata" was one of many Victorian sequences influenced by *Sonnets from the Portuguese*, remarked that Barrett Browning had not adopted the point of view of the conventional beloved in courtly romance because she was "happy" rather than "unhappy" in love, but Barrett Browning was consciously revising the tradition. Her sequence begins with the courtly notion that Rossetti was to use in *Monna Innominata*, that love of God forbids love of man, but it proceeds boldly toward the modern notion that human love is in itself a sufficient end: "I who looked for only God, found *thee*! / I find thee; I am safe, and strong, and glad." Further, *Sonnets from the Portuguese* marks a definitive turning point in Barrett Browning's poetry, a turning away from what she characterized as the "melancholy music" of her confined life, and toward a more vigorous encounter with the world.

The title of her next major poem, *Casa Guidi Windows*, may suggest a still-confined poetic vision, but the vision was now directed outward onto the world instead of inward in Mariana melancholy. The first part of *Casa Guidi Windows*, written in 1848, was inspired by the revolutionary fervor of that year, and by the mass demonstrations that occured in the piazza overlooked by the windows of the Brownings' apartments in Florence. In this rallying cry for Italian independence Barrett Browning called for—and in part tried to embody—a Carlylean hero to lead the Italian masses to freedom. The movement failed, and the second part of the poem, written in 1851, was a scornful, bitter retrospective—but it was also a bold attack on the nations of Europe that were celebrating their new commodities at the Crystal Palace, while offering no help to the victims of society, the poor or the "women sobbing out of sight / Because men made the laws."

Barrett Browning spoke out even more fully in her next major poem, *Aurora Leigh* (1857), which she described as "a sort of novel-poem . . . running into the midst of our conventions, and rushing into drawing rooms and the like 'where angels fear to tread'; and so, meeting face to face and without mask the Humanity of the age, and speaking the truth as I conceive of it out plainly." The poem is a sort of novelized, third-person, female *Prelude*, a story of the growth of the woman poet's mind, but whereas the Wordsworthian poet grew up in harmony with nature, Aurora Leigh grows up within the social restraints imposed upon women, and within the dissonance and perplexities of the modern age. For Barrett Browning, however, the current "age of mere transition" "spends more passion, more heroic heat, / Betwixt the mirrors of its drawing-rooms, / Than Roland with his knights at Roncesvalles." The present state of civilization was, in short, an opportunity not an obstacle for the poet, and especially for the woman poet, whose particular province was the drawing room. Modern critics are divided about the extent to which *Aurora Leigh* is a feminist poem (the heroine ultimately finds her highest vocation in marriage), but there is no doubt that it was courageously outspoken in its day, both in the representation of such social problems as the poverty and squalor of the slums and of prostitution, and in the depiction of a specifically female poet.

Elizabeth Barrett Browning was unquestionably the most celebrated woman poet of her day, but the poetry of a number of other Victorian women deserves more attention than it has usually received. The feminist poet Augusta Webster, for example, has been almost entirely forgotten, although her dramatic monologues skillfully combined the manner and matter of Robert and Elizabeth Barrett Browning in the effort to represent modern life. Other women poets of the time tended to be less outspoken, although their poetry movingly records the inner life that was intensified by socially imposed confinement. The very beautiful poetry of Christina Rossetti, for example, remained for the most part confined to the melancholy and devotional themes expected of women. As she put it, with characteristic self-deprecation, she could not sing out to her "one-stringed lyre. It is not in me, and therefore it will never come out of me, to turn to politics or philanthropy with Mrs. Browning: such many-sidedness I leave to a greater than I."

The sense of confinement, even imprisonment, is even more powerfully present in the poetry of the Brontë sisters, whose childhood in the remote parsonage at Haworth intensified their sense of isolation. Emily Brontë's enigmatic poems, especially, reflect the desolating sense of imprisonment that characterizes much of the women's poetry of the Victorian period. Often Brontë, like Barrett Browning, could see her isolation as a kind of poetic boon, conferring a greater intensity of inward vision: "So hopeless is the world without, / The world within I doubly prize." But as these lines suggest, turning the vision inward increases the isolation of the self, and Brontë's poems often express the anguish of the solitary self brooding upon its own memories. The only escape from the stifling prison of personal identity seems to be into a visionary realm where the ordinary self is dissolved into "only spirit wandering wide / Through infinite immensity." The dissolution of individual identity reflects a Romantic legacy of vaguely mystical aspiration, but it probably also reflects the yearning to escape the constraints of Victorian womanhood.

More often than not, indeed, Brontë's lyrics are spoken in the voices of the men and women who populated the dungeons of Gondal, the melodramatic fantasy kingdom that provided imaginative escape for Emily and her sister Anne. Taken as a whole, Brontë's poems express a profound ambivalence about the enforced inwardness of her life, but the overriding tone of her poems is melancholy—often, in fact, the desire to escape the entrapment of earthly life is expressed simply as a desire for death. At their best, these poems are remarkable for their lyric intensity, but perhaps it is not surprising that the Brontë sisters found wider range for expression in their novels than in their poetry—the novel not only allowed but compelled them to look beyond their own isolated sensibilities, just as the "novel-poem" *Aurora Leigh* helped Barrett Browning to represent the "heroic heat" of the present age.

Certainly George Eliot, whose poetic aspirations included the novel-length narrative *The Spanish Gypsy*, was able to achieve a far suppler, more broad-ranging voice in her novels than in her poems, although her poetry should not be entirely neglected. Unlike Christina Rossetti and Emily Brontë, Eliot's poems are not conspicuous for their lyrical grace, but the closet drama "Armgart" offers interesting insights into the difficulties besetting women as artists, and "A Minor Prophet" presents both an amusing character study and insights into Eliot's own beliefs.

Victorian women had, perhaps, a dubious poetic advantage in their almost enforced need to restrict their poetry to the realm of personal feeling, but in an insistently masculinist, activist age, men could hardly avoid contending with the "many-sidedness" of contemporary life. No one did so more emphatically than Arthur Hugh Clough, who was accused by his friend Matthew Arnold of "plung[ing] and bellow[ing] in the "Time Stream." Yet as Clough's example indicates, "manly" contention with the multitudinousness of modern life could be strangely incapacitating. Although various contemporaries explicitly noted the "manliness" of Clough's works, his ceaseless questioning seemed to epitomize the age's tendency to vacillate in uncertainties. As a writer in *Blackwood's Edinburgh Magazine* put it in 1874, the life and writings of Clough provided the "most striking illustration . . . of the manner in which the poetical faculty may be overridden and paralysed by doubt." From our much later perspective, Clough's questioning spirit and intellectual honesty may better be seen as the sources of his poetic success—and of his continuing modernity.

The star pupil at Thomas Arnold's Rugby School, Clough had been vigorously indoctrinated in the Victorian ideals of earnestness and devotion to duty. As a young man at Rugby and then at Oxford, he was something of a moral and political activist, particularly in the period from 1846 to 1848, when he wrote a series of Carlylean pamphlets on issues ranging from education to political and economic reform. But the decisive single act of this period, the determining act for Clough's future life, was an act of conscience—in 1848 he resigned his comfortable and somewhat influential position at Oxford rather than subscribe to the dogma of the Church of England, and in order to immerse himself in the "actual life," which, he said, "is unknown to an Oxford student." Yet his effectiveness in "actual life" was limited by his deep uncertainties about how best to act. The Carlylean positions he had adopted early in life could only carry him so far—as he said to Emerson in 1848, "Carlyle has led us all out into the desert, and he has left us there." Clough turned the modern problem into the primary subject matter of a poetry characterized by its tough-minded refusal to acquiesce in orthodoxies or to settle prematurely for definitive answers in the intellectual wilderness.

Although Clough's poetry questioned all received dogma, it was not without a kind of faith and hope. In "When Israel Came Out of Egypt," for example, Clough implicitly compared the Victorian age with the Biblical Jews in the wilderness, exiled as it seemed from God. As the Jews had worshipped a false god in the desert, so the Victorians, having lost any true faith, were tempted to worship the mere scientific "truths" that reduce the "heart and mind of human kind" to "a watch-work." But though the poem urged its readers not to worship false gods, it did not offer any alternative worthy of reverence, only the typical Cloughian counsel to "wait in faith" for some future basis for belief. Science may shake traditional faith, it cannot replace it, and as Clough argued in "Epi-Strauss-ium," the same is true of the skeptical higher criticism epitomized by Strauss's *Life of Jesus*. The debunking of the Gospels is, apparently, accepted in the opening lines: "Matthew and Mark and Luke and holy John / Evanished all and gone!"

While Clough denied the literal truth of the Bible, he maintained a faith that it expressed some kind of spiritual truth, and that when the higher criticism had done its utmost, "the place of worship" remained "if less richly, more sincerely bright." And he repeatedly affirmed a faith in ultimate though inapprehensible truth in such poems as "Why should I say I see the things I see not," "Uranus," and the brief untitled poem beginning: "It fortifies my soul to know / That, though I perish, Truth is so." At times, this attenuated faith seemed a sufficient basis for action, for finding a basis to do one's duty, as in "I have seen higher holier things than these": "The Summum Pulchrum rests in heaven above; / Do thou, as best thou may'st, thy duty do." And at times, as in "Qui Laborat, Orat," he adopted the Carlylean and Rugbeian position (the school motto was "Orando Laborando") that work, the fulfillment of duty, was the best approach to spiritual truth.

Yet in such poems as "Hope evermore and believe" it is clear that the poet's most enthusiastic exhortations to action are troubled by the sense that to do one's duty "is good, though there is better than it." Often the failure to find the "better" leads to a sense of the painful futility of existence, as in "To spend uncounted years of pain," which expresses the frustration of forever fearing "the premature result to draw" and so acting on a false basis. Unlike the Romantic poets, Clough certainly did not believe that a true basis could be found within the self, where he doubted his ability to find even "one feeling based on truth" ("How often sit I, poring o'er"). And in "Is it true, ye gods, who treat us" he suggested that poetic inspiration is no more than a "Peculiar confirmation, / Constitution, and condition / Of the brain and of the belly." Not surprisingly, Clough's distrust of poetic inspiration coupled with his sense of the need to leave all questions open made him a deeply ironic, and occasionally satiric poet. Frequently, his satire was a blatant and bitter mockery of contemporary life, as in "In the Great Metropolis," "Duty—that's to say complying," and "The Latest Decalogue," a witty updating of the Ten Commandments that decrees, for example, that "No graven images may be / Worshipped, except the currency."

Although still not as widely read as they deserve to be, Clough's major poetic achievements were his long poems, *The Bothie of Tober-Na-Vuolich*, *Amours de Voyage*, and *Dipsychus*—all of which brilliantly combine his questioning temperament, his analyses of the malaise of contemporary life, his doubts about all things, including the self, and his corrosive irony. Through such characters as the "Tutor, the grave man, nicknamed Adam," Philip Hewson, "the Chartist, the poet, the eloquent speaker," and various other students, *The Bothie*—an account of an Oxford reading party spending the long vacation in Scotland—discusses all manner of contemporary issues, particularly concerning the relations among the social classes and between the sexes. The dialogic structure enabled Clough to take a number of perspectives on the central action—Philip's falling in love with a peasant girl and eventually marrying her. Adam, who has much in common with Clough, is sympathetic, but inclined to fight God's fight in the battles of modern life, while maintaining the distinctions of class: "Let us to Providence trust, and abide and work in our stations." But Hewson, who has still more in common with Clough, doubts the possibility of discerning a providential scheme: "I am sorry to say your Providence puzzles me sadly." For Hewson, as for Clough, the difficulty was to find the battle at all, to identify a cause to fight for: "Neither battle I see, nor arraying, nor King in Israel, / Only infinite jumble and mess and dislocation."

Perhaps Clough's finest poem, *Amours de Voyage* is also his most thorough exploration of the incapacitating skepticism of modern life. The poem consists of a series of letters, mostly written by Claude, a snobby, excessively contemplative self-parody of Clough. Claude falls in love, more or less ("I am in love, you say; I do not think so, exactly"), and the poem chronicles his Prufrockian failure to woo. As Clough's contemporaries frequently noted, Claude is a modern Hamlet, forever deferring commitment, incapacitated by doubting everything, even love, and even the authenticity of his inner self. Like Hamlet, he wonders if he has genuinely loved and suffered, or has merely played a role: "After all, perhaps there was something factitious about it; / I have had pain, it is true: I have wept, and so have the actors." *Amours de Voyage* epitomizes what Matthew Arnold characterized as the peculiarly modern anguish, the unending "dialogue of the mind with itself" that finds no vent in action, but leaves the overcultivated, overthoughtful protagonist trapped within his own consciousness.

The dialogue of the mind with itself is still more overtly the subject of the never-completed *Dipsychus*, a dialogue between a scrupulous protagonist, Dipsychus, and a "Spirit" who represents his tempter—not exactly the devil (though named Mephistopheles) but rather the spirit of worldliness. The structure of the work enabled Clough to satirize modern customs in the worldly speeches of the Spirit, to engage in what the Spirit calls a "sarcastic" or rather "religious bitter" tone in the disillusioned speeches of Dipsychus, and also to parody once again the modern disease of "weakness, indolence, frivolity, / Irresolution."

Like Clough, Dipsychus longs for a basis of action or belief, but always senses the inadequacy of any conception, senses "a More beyond" and so resists the closure of "a completion over-soon assumed, / Of adding up too soon." But without a positive belief, he can resist temptation only for so long before making his compromise with the world, ironically becoming nothing less than Lord Chief Justice. In its complex layering of ironies, *Dipsychus* is one of the age's most thorough—and necessarily most inconclusive—representations of the woes of unanchored earnestness, irresolute sense of duty, and hypercivilized morbidity of conscience.

Modern commentators cite Clough's poetry, along with Arnold's, as representative of the troubled spirit of the Victorian age, although as R. H. Hutton recognized, Clough was representative only of a certain class and temperament in his tendency to look "at all questions of the day from the thinker's point of view, and not from the people's point of view." He undoubtedly mirrored the mind of his age, but only, as William Allingham put it, "the higher mind of cultivated, all-questioning, but still conservative England." Despite his occasionally radical opinions, Clough's poetry epitomized the increasing tendency throughout the nineteenth century for poetry to become a discourse of distinctly high culture, a class discourse. Some of Clough's contemporaries found this unfortunate, but others, such as Walter Bagehot, were perfectly ready to argue on Clough's behalf that "the half-educated and busy crowd, whom we call the public" have no right "to impose their limitations on highly educated and meditative thinkers."

Matthew Arnold's poetry is consistently associated with Clough's, even though Arnold saw Clough's poetry of doubt as the antithesis of the authoritative cultural discourse that poetry should aspire to become. But Arnold's own best poetry, like Clough's, expressed not assured truths, but anguished doubt. In repudiating "the dialogue of the mind with itself," in fact, Arnold was repudiating the poetic representation within his own *Empedocles on Etna* of the "modern problems" evident in the doubts and discouragement "of Hamlet and of Faust." But what John Addington Symonds said in 1868 of Clough's *Amours de Voyage* might also be said of Arnold's *Empedocles*. Their "vindication . . . lies in this: first that it is the poet's function to hold up a mirror to his age, as well as to lead it; and secondly, that we still admire Hamlet and Faust."

For Arnold, however, this clearly was not enough. In his letters to Clough in the late 1840s and early 1850s, he argued that modern poetry was vitiated by a "confused multitudinousness" because poets failed to "understand that they must begin with an Idea of the world in order not to be prevailed over by the world's multitudinousness." His own first publication, *The Strayed Reveller, and Other Poems*, however, was plainly open to the same charge. In poem after poem, Arnold explored the possibilities of an absolutely authoritative voice, but invariably with an anguished honesty that led him back to doubt. The ideal he sought—expressed in a famous phrase from the sonnet "To a Friend"— was to achieve the philosophical serenity of Sophocles, "who saw life steadily, and saw it whole." But other poems in the volume explore the absence of any possible perspective from which to obtain such a view.

In "Mycerinus," for example, the seemingly infallible voice of an oracle is shown to be wholly inconsistent with human ideas of truth and justice. Similarly, "The Sick King in Bokhara" represents the thoroughly unified view of the world represented by Muslim law, but only to suggest that though the laws of God and man provide order, they may be inconsistent with a higher ideal of compassionate justice and with the apparent truths of human feeling. The volume even rejected the Romantic ideal of finding truth in sense of harmony with nature. "In Harmony with Nature" dismisses such Romanticism with contempt and rejects nature in terms consistent with the questioning of the gods and of law in the other poems. Nature is cruel, stubborn, fickle, unforgiving—utterly alien to human compassion and conscience.

Two poems in the volume, "The Strayed Reveller" and "Resignation," explicitly explore ideas about poetic identity and authority, but both seem to raise more problems than they resolve. "The Strayed Reveller" describes two versions of visionary authority—the vision of the gods, who calmly and indifferently view all human life from on high, and vision of "wise bards," who sing authoritatively only at the high cost of sharing the pains of experience. Although the way of the gods seems preferable, it is apparently humanly impossible. And the Reveller, who is often taken to be a poetic surrogate for Arnold, declines the pains of "wise bards"—his own inspiration, such as it is, seems little more than a dehumanizing intoxication. Similar issues are explored in "Resignation," which repeatedly echoes Wordsworth, Arnold's most admired Romantic predecessor, but finally denies the sources of Wordsworthian authority in harmony with nature. "Resignation" offers a version of a unified poetic perspective, but only that of a rather subdued spectator who, like the indifferent gods of "The Strayed Reveller," "looks down" on the folly of human aspiration from "some high station," and who has, in a melancholy resignation, achieved objectivity by an almost inhuman detachment that enables him to "judge vain beforehand human cares."

Despite the less than rhapsodic version of the objective, detached poet as one resigned to "life's uncheer'd ways," Arnold was intent, at least for a time, on becoming just such a poet. His most ambitious poem, *Empedocles on Etna*, was evidently undertaken at first as an attempt to speak from a position of sternly authoritative objectivity. According to a friend, Arnold's initial idea was not so much to write a poem about the historical Empedocles, but rather to use the ancient poet's "name and outward circumstances . . . for the drapery of his own thoughts." His choice of Empedocles as a spokesman would enable him to speak literally from a mountaintop, but would also, as Arnold originally conceived the character, enable him to speak the stark truth because of Empedocles's "refusal of limitation by the religious sentiment." Without the constraints of misguided piety, Empedocles would be able to express a "great and severe truth," the "truth of the truth." But Empedocles's central speech in the finished work, offered as a fundamental lesson in life for his companion Pausanias, indicates that his "truth" consisted only of resigned advice to his friend to "nurse no extravagant hope," to limit his aspirations and expectations.

Unfortunately, although he considers this advice sufficient for Pausanias, Empedocles cannot live with it himself but remains tortured by his unsatisfied longings for a larger, fuller life than mortality affords. The ineffectuality of Empedocles's speech reflected Arnold's increasing sense that rejection of the "religious sentiment" could lead only to the most arid of truths, that "the service of reason is freezing to feeling, chilling to the religious mood. And feeling and the religious mood are eternally the deepest being of man, the ground of all joy and greatness for him." In the end, of course, the joyless Empedocles plunges into the mouth of the volcano.

A third character in the play, the poet Callicles, evidently represents an alternative to Empedocles's despair. His songs, sung from a lower point on the mountain, express a serene classicism and bring some measure of comfort to Empedocles, but Callicles hardly seems to offer an adequate "Idea of the world"—the unified point of view of his songs is the result of an unquestioning acceptance of the "religious sentiment," an acceptance that remains undisturbed by the extraordinary cruelty of the gods described in his songs.

Empedocles on Etna brilliantly represents the dilemma of a mid-Victorian poet attempting to reconcile the new truths of reason with the lingering need for religious faith, but because it offered no resolution, Arnold suppressed it in his 1853 volume of *Poems*, arguing in a preface that the representation of the modern "dialogue of the mind with itself" could only be morbid, painful, and therefore unpoetic. The Preface, in fact, argued consistently against the portrayal of distinctly modern problems in poetry, since poetry reflecting "an age wanting in moral grandeur," "an age of spiritual discomfort," could not be expected to affect its readers "powerfully and delightfully." In an unpoetical age, Arnold somewhat perversely insisted, the best poetry could only be written by the poet who eliminates historically conditioned subjectivity from the work—the poet will be most successful when "he most entirely succeeds in effacing himself, and in enabling a noble action to subsist as it did in nature." Not surprisingly, *Sohrab and Rustum*, *Balder Dead*, and *Merope*, the poems Arnold wrote in a conscious effort to carry out his poetic program, have always struck readers as inert and lifeless.

Almost in spite of himself, it seems, Arnold's best poetry both before and after the Preface of 1853 was, like Clough's, primarily about the "spiritual discomfort" of the individual subject in an age of dizzyingly rapid transition. His beautiful, but rather sad love poems, for example, movingly describe both the great need for human love in an age where all other spiritual solace seems absent—and the great difficulty of love in an age of skeptical self-questioning and spiritual alienation. The lyrics gathered together under the title "Switzerland" chronicle a brief and failed love affair that only reinforced the speaker's sense of intolerable isolation in a world where "we mortal millions live *alone*." "The Buried Life," similarly, depicts a speaker attempting to communicate fully and utterly to his beloved, but finding himself, for the most part, thwarted by the all but insurmountable difficulty of even knowing his own "hidden self," let alone expressing it in language. And in his most famous poem, "Dover Beach," Arnold's speaker pleads for love as the last best hope in a world represented as a "darkling plain" with "neither joy, nor love, nor light, / Nor certitude, nor peace, nor help for pain."

Despite his belief that the greatest poetry must offer joy, Arnold's best and most characteristic poetry expresses the pain of modern life on the darkling plain. "The Scholar-Gipsy," for example, presents a self-consciously mythic alternative to modern life in the legend of a seventeenth-century Oxford scholar who had abandoned modern life to live in pastoral simplicity, and who consequently roamed the countryside still, "exempt from age" because uninfected by the "strange disease of modern life." The legend is beautifully presented in the pastoral descriptions of the first half of the poem, but the most powerful part of the work is the account of the Victorian age, "With its sick hurry, its divided aims, / Its heads o'ertax'd, its palsied hearts." Similarly, in "Thyrsis," his pastoral elegy for Clough, Arnold attempted to find some consolation in the legend of the Scholar-Gipsy and the ideals it embodied, but the power of the poem is far less in its awkward and tentative solace than in the speaker's expression of "hope, once crush'd, less quick to spring again," and in its (somewhat ungracious) representation of Clough beaten down by the raging storms of contention in the modern world.

But perhaps the pathos of Arnold's plight as a poet seeking certainties in a world of doubt is nowhere more evident than in his "Stanzas from the Grande Chartreuse," the poetic account of a visit to a Carthusian monastery. The certainty of Catholic faith is plainly impossible to the speaker who has been educated by the "rigorous teachers" of the nineteenth century, yet even though he regards the faith of the monks as the dead religion of a past age, he attempts to embrace it as preferable to the restless vicissitudes of life in a faithless transitional age, preferable to "Wandering between two worlds, one dead, / The other powerless to be born."

For Arnold the failure of religion in the nineteenth century left unfilled a fundamental human need. As he put it in "Obermann Once More," "now the old is out of date / The new is not yet born," and no apparent way was available to fill the human "need of joy! / Yet joy whose grounds are true." Ultimately, Arnold believed, poetry must fill that void, but such poetry was impossible to write in what he persistently saw as a profoundly unpoetical age. Consequently, it is not surprising that for the last twenty-five years of his life he wrote very little poetry, but devoted himself to the literary and cultural criticism that he hoped might help to usher in a new and more poetical age. And indeed, if judged by Arnold's own announced critical standards in his late essay "The Study of Poetry," his own poetry and that of his contemporaries might well be found wanting. He argued that the "best poetry" would take the place of religion by "forming, sustaining, and delighting us, as nothing else can." This "best poetry" would constitute a secular literary canon, would express the essential and universal truths of human nature, and would therefore transcend merely historical and local concerns. But in our own age the notion of a transcendently authoritative poetry makes little sense, and we are more likely to appreciate poetry on the historical grounds that Arnold dismissed as fallacious. Ironically, Arnold seemed to realize that it was by such an estimate that his own poetry would eventually come to be appreciated. In an 1869 letter to his mother he wrote that although he lacked Tennyson's "poetical sentiment" and Robert Browning's "intellectual vigor and abundance," he would have his day because his "poems represent the main movement of mind of the last quarter of a century."

Arnold was right—his poems have been regarded as an impassioned and powerful expression of the mid-Victorian zeitgeist, particularly in its high moral seriousnessness, its anguished doubt, and its sense of the exalted, even redemptive mission of poetry. But there was, of course, no absoutely unified zeitgeist. Indeed, even during the quarter of a century designated by Arnold, a new generation of poets—notably those loosely designated Pre-Raphaelites—was emerging, and was making quite un-Arnoldian claims for the autonomy of poetry, for the artist's freedom from social responsibility and conventional morality.

To appreciate fully the Victorian age in all the multitudinousness that Arnold deplored, modern readers will turn not only to his works but also to those of Tennyson, the Brownings, Clough, the Pre-Raphaelites, and hosts of others. In fact, a recent anthology of Victorian poetry includes works by well over a hundred poets—peasant poets, working-class poets, feminist poets, conservative and radical poets, religious poets, atheistic poets, regional poets, decadent poets, and nonsense poets. A necessary brevity has allowed little discussion of this vast diversity; emphasis has fallen instead on some of the ways such multitudinousness affected the dominant middle-class poets who contributed most to our sense of the "canonical" literature of the mid-Victorian period.

David G. Riede

Further Reading

Altick, Richard. *Victorian People and Ideas: A Companion for the Modern Reader of Victorian Literature.* New York: Norton, 1973.

Buckley, Jerome Hamilton. *The Victorian Temper: A Study in Literary Culture.* Cambridge: Harvard University Press, 1951.

Christ, Carol. *The Finer Optic: The Aesthetics of Particularity in Victorian Poetry.* New Haven: Yale University Press, 1975.

Culler, A. Dwight. *Imaginative Reason: The Poetry of Matthew Arnold.* New Haven: Yale University Press, 1966.

Greenberger, Evelyn Barish. *Arthur Hugh Clough: The Growth of a Poet's Mind.* Cambridge: Harvard University Press, 1970.

Hickock, Kathleen. *Representations of Women: Nineteenth-Century Women's Poetry.* Westport, Conn.: Greenwood Press, 1984.

Mermin, Dorothy. *The Audience in the Poem: Five Victorian Poets*. New Brunswick, N.J.: Rutgers University Press, 1983.

Mermin, Dorothy. *Elizabeth Barrett Browning: The Origins of a New Poetry*. Chicago: University of Chicago Press, 1989.

Riede, David G. *Matthew Arnold and the Betrayal of Language*. Charlottesville: University Press of Virginia, 1988.

Slinn, E. Warwick. *Browning and the Fictions of Identity*. London: Macmillan, 1982.

Timko, Michael. *Innocent Victorian: The Satiric Poetry of Arthur Hugh Clough*. Athens: Ohio University Press, 1966.

Tucker, Herbert. *Browning's Beginnings*. Minneapolis: University of Minnesota Press, 1980.

Victorian Religious Poetry

W HAT is not religious poetry? Representing the Platonic tradition, Shelley maintained in the *Defence of Poetry* that poetry is itself "something divine." Yet Helen Gardner is surely right to dismiss as meaninglessly broad the position that poetry in which "'man broods upon himself and his history . . . as a spiritual and self-conscious being'" deserves to be called "religious."

Fascinating for the contradictory movements and ideas it harbored, the Victorian era saw both the coining of the term *agnostic* and a proliferation of religious sects or associations, which by 1895 had grown to 293 in number according to *Whitaker's Almanack* (1896). Religious conformity, piety, and fervor were matched by religious doubt, pained questioning, and a sense of loss. Religious ideas and institutions were in turmoil; and those who could no longer believe often sought surrogates for the spiritual dimension they nevertheless could not live without. It is therefore not obvious where to close the circle around Victorian religious poetry. For practical purposes, however, *religious poetry* will here be construed narrowly to mean poetry whose object is a transcendent personal God who is the foundation and final cause of a recognized body of faith.

Even by this narrow definition, the field of Victorian religious poetry is unmanageably vast; for Victorians produced religious poetry in industrial quantities. This was a fertile age for hymnody and other forms of liturgical verse not treated here, in which the quality of the verse mattered less than the quality of the piety. To exclude liturgical poetry from the present account does not however settle the deeper question of the relation between the aesthetic and the religious in religious poetry generally. In a world in which the sacred and the profane no longer overlap, does the secondary or subsidiary relation of religious poetry to its object inevitably work to the detriment of the poem? For religious poetry serves a purpose that is not identical with those of poetry in itself.

Intellectual History

Religious faith suffered a series of blows in the nineteenth century from which it arguably has never recovered. They were dealt mainly by natural science, then still widely referred to as natural history. The change in terminology is significant, marking a shift in emphasis from description to epistemology; but it also reflects a profounder change in the perception of nature itself. Here the names of Charles Lyell and Charles Darwin may stand for the scientific figures whose work dislodged the Bible from its millennial position as a factual document of the creation of the world, thus putting the last nail into the coffin begun by Copernicus and altering the self-understanding of human beings within the sphere of nature. Lyell's *Principles of Geology* (1830–1832) offered persuasive proof against the biblical, cataclysmic view of the creation of the world and for a uniformitarian view that entailed unimaginable stretches of time. Darwin's *Origin of Species* (1859), popularly foreshadowed by Robert Chambers's *Vestiges of the Natural History of Creation* (1844), extended the evolutionary model to animate nature, including implicitly *Homo sapiens*.

Darwin's theory did not merely sweep away everything before it, however. William Thomson, Lord Kelvin, was moved to attempt a refutation of uniformitarianism; and the biologist St. George Jackson Mivart, a convert to Roman Catholicism, tried in a series of works to salvage the human mind from the material processes of evolution, and hence to separate human beings from the rest of nature. (Significantly, Mivart could no longer reconcile his science and his religion towards the end of his life, and he died an excommunicate.)

Finally, the destructive effects of geology and biology were deepened by the results of a new science, philology. German philologists had led the way in applying the systematic methods of "textual criticism"— originally trained on classical and historical texts—to the Scriptures themselves, treating the Word of God as just another text, riddled with

textual corruptions and inconsistencies. The appearance in 1860 of
Essays and Reviews, some contributors to which put these methods into
effect, unleashed a furor.

These developments, and others that have escaped this summary,
affected not only the faith of the pious but their understanding of the
natural world around them. Ruskin heard the clink of the geologist's
hammer at the end of every verse of Scripture. Tennyson's *In Memoriam* contains the greatest and most moving poetic record of the spiritual and intellectual struggle that many believers faced, and much of it can
be read as an agonized debate between the will to believe and the inability to suspend disbelief, a debate that ends inconclusively with the simple assertion of the former.

Social History

Great forces, then, were "making against Christianity," and against traditional religious belief and understanding generally. And yet both religion and religious poetry flourished. The Catholic Emancipation Act
of 1829 largely restored to English Roman Catholics participation in
the life of the nation, from which they had been essentially barred since
the reign of Elizabeth. The repeal one year earlier of the Test Act similarly relieved Protestant "Nonconformists"; and the University Tests
Act in 1871 abolished subscription to the Thirty-nine Articles of the
Church of England as a condition of activity at the universities of
Oxford, Cambridge, and Durham, as well as lifted compulsory chapel
attendance. In 1858–1860 legislation (which had been proposed forty
years earlier) granted full parliamentary privileges to Jews, who had
occupied several public offices since 1835. By the end of the century
Jews sat in Commons and Lords. The spirit of tolerance that inhabits
these historical changes favored diverse religious expression; and poetry remained the form perceived to be by nature suited to this purpose.

The Romantic Legacy

The poetic language and vision most directly available to Victorian religious poets were the legacy of English Romanticism; Wordsworth was
clearly the spiritual (as Coleridge was the intellectual) godfather of
much of the religious poetry of the nineteenth century. Spiritualized
nature was a large part of their patrimony. Wordsworth was in turn the

heir of an idea of nature advanced by eighteenth-century philosophes, of whom Carl Becker once wrote that by deifying nature, they denatured God. Already implicit in Romanticized nature, therefore, was a tension drawing religious poets away from devotion in the narrower sense; and by mid-century, as we have seen, scientific knowledge was undermining even Wordsworthian nature, now "red in tooth and claw."

Yet nature continued to figure centrally in Victorian religious poetry as it had not in the religious poetry of, say, the seventeenth century; and with Romanticism came either an intensely inward human experience of nature or the dialectic of experience advanced by Wordsworth and Coleridge. John Henry Newman lent weight to the latter in *A Grammar of Assent*, arguing that just such a dialectic described religious experience as well. The later Wordsworth, the conservative Wordsworth of the *Ecclesiastical Sonnets* (1822), cast a vague shadow of orthodoxy back over his earlier poems, creating a Victorian view of him that was more influential than any one of his poetic texts. It was to "their" Wordsworth that many Victorian religious poets turned for a voice and a vision adaptable to their ends.

With the exception of Hopkins, Christina Rossetti, and possibly Elizabeth Barrett (Browning) and Coventry Patmore, none of the Victorian religious poets are major poets by any serious standard, although some may be major figures in Victorian religious history. The following account of these secondary and tertiary poets arranges them according to the religious movements to which they adhered. The primary authorities in these sections are H. N. Fairchild's *Religious Trends in English Poetry*, vol. 4, *1830–1880* (for all its self-conscious tendentiousness and acid irony still an indispensable guide) and, for the Tractarians, G. B. Tennyson's *Victorian Devotional Poetry: The Tractarian Mode*.

The Evangelicals

The Evangelical movement, with its roots in reaction against the unenthusiastic, and to many minds lifeless, orthodoxy of the English Church of the eighteenth century, naturally gave rise to a poetry of strong statement and undisguised emotion that was meant to inspire, even in the most obdurate, those passions of awe for Christian mystery and horror of final perdition found lacking in the established Church. The most direct application of these principles was in hymns whose "murky thunderlight," as Lord David Cecil writes, "makes them stirring out of all proportion to their strictly literary merits."

Martin Farquhar Tupper—"the Shakespeare of the Church" according to some Evangelical connoisseurs—was the author of the vastly popular *Proverbial Philosophy*, a collection of moral musings in unrhymed, occasionally rhythmic prose arranged in lines of irregular length. Tupper reflects on, explains, and enjoins his readers to accept humbly God's works, to improve what they have been given, and above all to shun that pride which leads one to imagine oneself autonomous. By the end of the century this work had become the butt of many an easy satire, yet it passed through sixty editions, and by 1881 a million copies had been sold in America alone. Like most of the poetry of the Evangelical movement, it was directed to a largely uncritical public little interested in belles lettres. They responded to the genuine moral and religious feeling in Tupper's poetry rather than to the aesthetics of the verbal artifact that conveyed it. Indeed, the doctrine of the movement clearly discouraged imagination, originality, or brilliance, based as these are on an assertion of individuality, which is the root of pride and hence of evil: "Fruitlessly thou strainest for humility, by darkly diving into self: / Rather look away from innate evil, and gaze upon extraneous good."

Somewhat grander in ambition if not in execution was Robert Pollock's *Course of Time*, a lengthy fulmination in ten books of stock eighteenth-century diction in blank verse upon eternal punishment for inveterate pride and hardened refusal to repent. As recognition of sinfulness was, for the Evangelicals, the precondition of acknowledging salvation in Christ, the drama of this poetry was, for its readers, in the subject rather than the treatment of it. The work became popular as soon as it was published, particularly in Pollock's native Scotland. Similar in tone, Robert Montgomery's *Satan, or Intellect without God* warns of the certain and terrible consequences of intellectual and imaginative independence. For five thousand lines, it was later observed, Satan delivers an unbroken monologue better suited to an Evangelical pastor than to the Archfiend. In Book One he comments sanely on early civilizations and censoriously on the Inquisition in Spain, the Revolution in France, and slavery in the United States; in Book Two he abominates vices and crimes; in Book Three he looks closely at the underside of English society in the age of the industrial revolution. Only in passing does he take in the Creation, the Fall, and the plan of redemption.

Montgomery's *Omnipresence of the Deity* was so remarkably attuned to popular religious sentiment that it went into eight editions in as many months and into twenty more in the next thirty years, despite Macaulay's withering attack in the *Edinburgh Review*.

Less crabbed and grim than the poetry of Pollock or Montgomery, that of Jean Ingelow contains in addition hints of social reform. Whereas Pollock reminds his readers that all will be equal at the Last Judgment and Montgomery storms against slavery and Mammon, Ingelow counsels the poor "to be not humble overmuch," lest they think God to be of the party of the rich. But Ingelow was also, and atypically, troubled by evolution and higher criticism. In "Honours" she addresses those similarly shaken, advising them to "Wait, nor against the half-learned lesson fret, / Nor chide at old belief as if it erred, / Because thou canst not reconcile as yet / The Worker and the Work." Her verse, like Pollock's and Montgomery's, is vitiated by affectation and stiltedness, but unlike them she is able to temper censoriousness with delicacy, sympathy, and simple grace.

Anti-intellectualism, which marks much Evangelical poetry, may also be construed as prudential wariness of intellectual pride; and since for the Evangelicals salvation came by faith alone, there was good reason to set at naught the products of intellect. In addition to Tupper, Pollock, and Montgomery, Horatius Bonar and Charles Tennyson-Turner excoriate in particular intellectual agnostics, rationalists, and proponents of anthropocentric philosophy in any of its forms. To Bonar the Crystal Palace was the cult place of science, "diamond-blazing, / Shrine of her idolatry" (*Hymns of Faith and Hope*). Unappalled by evolutionism and, unlike Bonar, an enthusiast of the spirit of technological advances, Tennyson-Turner (coauthor with Alfred of *Poems by Two Brothers*) nevertheless takes to task those who apply scientific methods to textual analysis of the Bible; in all who burn to see "The Healer's face / . . . Faith shall be born! and, by her natural stress, / Push through these dark philosophies, and live!"

The Tractarians

"On Sunday July 14, 1833, Mr Keble preached the assize sermon in the [Oxford] University pulpit. It was published under the title of *National Apostasy*. I have ever considered and kept the day as the start of the religious movement of 1833." So Cardinal Newman on the act with which the Oxford Movement began. While the immediate occasion of the sermon was the relation between the established Church and the state, the movement soon grew into an effort to revive the flagging principles and practices of the High Church. The intellectual vehicle of this renovation was a series of publications entitled *Tracts for the Times*, which presently gave the Tractarian movement its name. Themselves part of an inchoate but distinct set of developments commonly referred to as the Catholic Revival (comprising both the Roman Catholic restoration in England and catholicizing movements within the Anglican High Church establishment or "Anglo-Catholicism"), the Tractarians sought to revivify in the Church of England all that had grown lifeless and lukewarm since the Reformation, particularly in the eighteenth century.

Six years before the assize sermon, Keble had published anonymously a cycle of poems entitled *The Christian Year, or Thoughts in Verse for the Sundays and Holydays throughout the Year*. By 1872 it had passed through 158 editions and had won the ears and touched the hearts of countless readers in the English-speaking world. Indeed, G. B. Tennyson is able to suggest plausibly that *The Christian Year* "has had a greater impact on the character of English-language Christian worship in the past century and a half than any other single influence." Quite the contrary of the emphatic Evangelicals, the Tractarians adhered to the complementary principles of Reserve and Analogy, principles that find expression in their poetry.

Translated into modern terms, Reserve is that supplement of meaning and presence that always escapes human efforts to grasp God, who can therefore be known only incompletely and by indirection. Analogy, based ultimately on the mechanism of medieval typology, asserts an essential likeness between individual things and creatures on the one hand and their creator on the other. In G. B. Tennyson's words, "Tractarian Analogy means quite simply that the entire universe is a symbol of its creator. . . . Analogy governs the subject matter of [Tractarian] poetry, Reserve the style." Taken together, Analogy and Reserve sacramentalize the world and, a fortiori, nature.

Keble expounded his ideas on poetry in the series of forty lectures that he delivered in Latin as the Professor of Poetry at Oxford between 1831 and 1841 and published under the title *Praelectiones Academicae*. These he dedicated to Wordsworth, "True Philosopher and Inspired Poet *[vati sacro]*, who by the special gift and calling of Almighty God . . . failed not to lift up men's hearts to the holy things . . . [and who] was raised up to be a chief minister, not only of the sweetest poetry but also of high and sacred truth. . . ." Clearly, poetry was, for the Tractarians, the privileged discourse of religion. Insofar as Keble asserts that poetry is sacramental, however, he is at odds with the notion of poetic autonomy underlying Romanticism. What develops from this, in practice more than in theory, is a poetry written primarily not for its own virtues but for those it can incite in its readers. Hence poetry and religion—the aesthetic and the devotional—are not only complementary and mutually enriching; they are essentially homogeneous.

The Christian Year consists of 109 devotional poems that are linked to the *Book of Common Prayer*, in conjunction with which it must be read: for each day of the liturgical year and for all special services in the Prayer Book there is a designated poem. Deeply tinged with a Wordsworthian view of nature, it offers a poetry of simplicity and sincerity, the doctrine of Reserve expressing itself in plainness and lack of emphasis. Conspicuously unoriginal in verbal texture, it seeks to draw no attention to itself but rather to lead the reader beyond the text to its higher subject. The poems are, in a sense, pre-texts to prayer.

If the Tractarian movement began in 1833 with Keble's sermon on national apostasy, it ended in 1845 with Newman's apostasy in favor of Rome. A greater prosaist than a poet, Newman nevertheless contributed the lion's share to a volume of Tractarian verses entitled *Lyra Apostolica* and intended as a proselytizing adjunct to *Tracts for the Times*. On the title page stands a motto from the *Iliad* that announces the volume's militant intent: "Let them learn that I have stayed too long out of the fight." The contributions of R. I. Wilberforce and J. W. Bowden are entirely negligible; those of R. H. Froude occasionally rise to a certain dramatic solemnity (see nos. 36, 133, 139, and 159). Keble, temperamentally unsuited to polemical verse, rarely is able to reach or sustain the rhetorical tension it requires: aside from "The Winter Thrush," the sole nature poem in the volume, only two or three of his poems stand out (see nos. 76, 98, and the Herbertian no. 100). Newman's idea, *Lyra Apostolica* was also Newman's vehicle. The best known of his contributions, called variously "Light in the Darkness," "The Pillar of Cloud," and "Lead, kindly Light" (no. 25), achieves its dramatic effect by a deft alternation of long and short lines and periods. Greek choric meters stiffen the stanzas of "The Elements" (no. 71) and "Judaism" (no. 106) and influence those of

"Rest" and "Knowledge" (nos. 52 and 53). Many of the poems are indeed a call to arms.

Isaac Williams, whose tracts 80 and 87 developed the notions of Reserve and Analogy, went on to produce four volumes of poetry that were widely appreciated—*Thoughts in Past Years*, *The Cathedral*, *The Baptistery*, and *The Altar*. *Thoughts in Past Years* moves from devotional poetry in the manner of Keble to poems on Tractarian topics and reflections on the Church. In *The Cathedral*, *The Baptistery*, and *The Altar*, however, Williams develops the medievalizing strain that was giving rise to the Gothic revival in architecture.

The Cathedral draws its subject matter from the architectural plan of a Gothic church—thus resembling in form the image of Wordsworth's poetic work projected in the preface to *The Excursion*—moving from the exterior through the nave and the choir to the pillars and the windows; before each section are engravings of those architectural elements which organize that section thematically. Each element is then further broken down to provide the themes of the individual poems. G. B. Tennyson observes that Williams is "teaching the nineteenth century how to 'read' a cathedral, much as he and Keble had tried to teach it how to read the book of nature." *The Cathedral* is thus not only a book of poetry but a guide to Gothic church architecture and a devotional vademecum. *The Baptistery* and *The Altar* advance the same procedure, now even more highly organized. Although his poems rarely strike a spark, Williams is remarkable for having pursued radically the integration of poetry with practical worship.

Newman's *Dream of Gerontius*, written long after his conversion and in apprehension of death following a doctor's (mistaken) prognosis, bears the impress of his strong personality, already perceptible in his earlier poetry. Daringly conceived and sustaining a remarkable degree of dramatic intensity, the poem contains the terrified prayer of the dying Gerontius, his death and the parting of his soul from his body, a dialogue between his soul and an angel, and oratorical or choric sections in which figure his soul, angels, demons, angelic choirs, and the voices of souls in Purgatory, where Gerontius's soul has begged to sojourn. In the last line of the poem the angel assures him, "Swiftly shall pass thy night of trial here, / And I will come and wake thee on the morrow." Edward Caswall and Frederic W. Faber, two other noteworthy Tractarian poets, followed Newman into the Roman Catholic Church. At his best, in *Cherwell Water-lily*, Faber often outstrips his spiritual guide.

Other Voices

There were of course many voices of the Catholic revival that were unconnected to the Tractarians. Aubrey Thomas de Vere, who (in the phrase of the time) went over to Rome in 1851, is today somewhat unjustly remembered for his excessively tranquilizing Wordsworthian manner. De Vere's taste for Romantic poetry ran deep, extending to Byron and Shelley, whom he attempts to refute in the light of Christian truth. Robert Stephen Hawker was well known as a poet of Cornwall before publishing a volume of devotional verse entitled *Ecclesia*. Hawker draws successfully on the Romantic discovery of the mystery that dwells in places, a mystery to which he adds holiness. Through such religious genius loci the present touches the past, bridged by sanctity.

Digby Mackworth Dolben is an extraordinary figure by virtue of both his flamboyant personality and his youth. Precocious, Dolben joined the ritualist High Church Puseyites at Eton. He wrote easily and prolifically both imitative verses in the manner of Herbert and the Pre-Raphaelites and poems in which an individual voice is seeking form through experimentation. Both his barely concealed homoeroticism and his equally bold flirtation with Roman Catholicism earned him expulsion. His accidental death at the age of nineteen, before he could pursue his increasingly serious leanings towards Rome, makes the promise of his talent a matter of speculation; but some of what he left behind is worthy to stand with the work of all but a few of the writers so far considered. He is perhaps best remembered for his somewhat equivocal erotico-religious "Homo Factus Est"; but there can be no doubt of the authenticity, if not the maturity, of his religious impulse.

Like Dolben and Hopkins, Richard Watson Dixon owes much of his latter-day currency to the editorial labors of Robert Bridges, his rather dry, scholarly bent being little suited to wide readership; indeed, he is perhaps best known today for his correspondence with Hopkins. A member of the "Birmingham group" at Oxford in the 1850s, Dixon immersed himself on the one side in the middle ages and on the other in Tennyson and Ruskin, drawing from this atmosphere and these readings, and from the Pre-Raphaelite movement in which they merge, an aesthetic medievalism and a rather pallid mystery. The poetry of his first volume of verse, *Christ's Company*, is refined in tone, rhythmically correct, and elaborately decorative, religious themes and moments serving largely as pretexts for a tapestry of poses and images.

Judaism

The series of legal acts and adjustments that began in the mid-1830s resulted in the emancipation of Jews, making possible the emergence of a voice hitherto unheard in the history of English religious poetry. Grace Aguilar is among of the first exponents of this new voice. Born in London in 1816, she moved with her family to Devonshire at the age of twelve and so grew up as the only Jewish child in a rural English village whose tolerance and gentleness appeared to bear no resemblance to the triumphal and aggressive Catholicism of Portugal and Spain of the Inquisition and Expulsions engraved in her family's memory. Cynthia Scheinberg argues that Aguilar nevertheless saw herself as an exiled Jew caught in a Christian culture. Aguilar sought, therefore, to create a literary identity that would permit her to exist and function in both the Christian majority and the Anglo-Jewish minority literary cultures. In a sequence of poems entitled "Sabbath Thoughts," she seeks to establish in literature an identity that is at once Jewish in a Christian world and feminine in a doubly patriarchal world. In one of its aspects, this is a poetry of private spiritual suffering that, since it is inexpressible in language, "God alone should read" (sonnet I). The deepest feeling is unspeakable and is readable only by the unspeakable God.

Aguilar thus so radicalizes the private world of lyric in general and of the devotional lyric in particular that the genre appears to annul itself essentially. It becomes instead a speakable shell enclosing a mute essence. She asks a remote God whether He will ever abandon her, and tenders the mild reproach that "this fair earth has never given / To yearning hearts an answering word" (sonnet III). In keeping with the nonlinguistic character of this essential communication, she asks that God should "breathe" to her his reply. Elsewhere she dwells on the ahistoricity and nonspatiality of prayer, again defining by negation. But if prayer is ahistorical, religious community is profoundly felt in its historical dimension. "Song of the Spanish Jews" and "The Hebrew's Appeal" trace postbiblical Jewish history and by this very gesture implicitly introduce the historicity of her own moment and the extraordinary ambiguities that follow from it: on the one hand, the freedom that makes a cultural flowering again possible, on the other its precariousness.

Unlike most Christian religious writers, Aguilar tends to treat the Bible literally and not typologically. This leads her to reject the Romantic inheritance of the poet as vatic symbolizer for a poetic identity based on parable, as in "A Vision of Jerusalem" and "While Listening to a Beautiful Organ in One of the Gentile Shrines." Landscape, in a poem such as "The Rocks of Elim," consequently functions quite differently than it does in Wordsworth. First, like Keats's vision of the Pacific from a peak in Darien, its origin is in a book—a book not of poetry, however, but of "Letters on the Holy Land." Next, the landscape resonates not with personal history and subjective experience as in "Tintern Abbey" but with biblical history and, as it were, tribal memory. This landscape is also, and significantly, that of the song of Miriam and so a point of departure for women's poetry in the "West." Landscape is not, therefore, a place where the individual finds herself as an individual in communion with God but one where she finds the biblical past whose authority is divine.

Amy Levy deserves mention for her contribution to the lineaments of a contestatory religious position at the heart of Christian religious poetry. Little of Levy's poetry is religious in the sense adopted here; she regards religion as a social phenomenon. The irony implicit in the title of *A Minor Poet and Other Verses* works itself out radically in the dramatic monologue of one of its minor—that is, minority and marginalized—personas, Mary Magdalene. In Scheinberg's view, one of Levy's aims in "Magdalen" is to raise to consciousness the terms of Christian domination of poetic identity. Magdalen speaks to Jesus as to an oppressor, reversing the authorized norm of reverence. Her love of Jesus is physical, and he has betrayed it knowingly; for what Revelation reveals is that the outcome was never in doubt. The whole weight of Christian hermeneutics bears against this representation, and she must deflect its powerful machinery. The conventional image of the rose that she draws on to figure to Jesus her love for him brings with it those of thorns and bleeding flesh—her own. Magdalen is the martyr, and she refuses the sublimation of sexual in divine love. Thus, she will refuse not only Jesus but his status as the Messiah, in this way repeating—but also rejecting—the Jewish betrayal. Levy's intervention at the nodal point of Christian religious drama and discourse represents the position of a quasi-alien voice.

Elizabeth Barrett (Browning)

In 1826, at the age of twenty, Elizabeth Barrett published her second volume of verse, *An Essay on Mind and Other Poems*. Its title work, a long didactic poem in the manner of Pope, she later "repented of"; but among the "other poems" is "The Prayer," which introduces the theme of suffering as an aid to renunciation of the world that underlies much of her early religious poetry. In "The Dream" the pagan world is swept away by the advent of Christ, who replaces Pan as the source of poetry—a theme to which she would later return.

Barrett's mature religious poetry appears mainly in *Poems* (1833), *The Seraphim and Other Poems* (1838), and *Poems* (1844), the two first being marked by conspicuous piety and even preachiness, the last moving towards her later mode, which is more outward-looking and less explicitly religious. She intended *The Seraphim* to transcend "the Titanic 'I can revenge'" of Aeschylus' *Prometheus Unbound* and to attain to "the celestial 'I can forgive'" to which Aeschylus might have turned had he lived in the Christian era. In about a thousand lines, Barrett presents the Crucifixion through the eyes of two seraphim, who struggle to comprehend what they see but whose grasp is limited by the lack of that "humanness" which is the significance of the Incarnation. Yet they acknowledge, before the drama they are witnessing, that "Heaven is dull / . . . to man's earth." The love that human beings will bear for God has no analogue in the purely spiritual realm inhabited by seraphim. The poem, like the volume it heads, received generally favorable treatment by critics, although no second edition was called for. The less ambitious poems in the volume, however, are generally more successful: "The Virgin Mary to the Child Jesus," "Sleep," "The Sea-Mew," "My Doves," "Consolation," and "Cooper's Grave" are worthier of her later work.

Between this volume of poems and the next came the heavy blow of her brother's death by drowning off Torquay, where she had begged him to join her during a long convalescence. Her father blamed her unjustly for the death and grew estranged from her; she accepted the blame and the estrangement. *Poems, by Elizabeth Barrett Barrett* (1844) reflects these trials, and Fairchild observes that her work becomes increasingly evangelical in spirit as her sorrows multiply.

The most ambitious poem in the volume, *A Drama of Exile*, traces the first steps of Adam and Eve in the wilderness, taking up where *Paradise Lost* left off. A vision of Christ lays before them God's plan of redemption; and to a chorus of invisible angels, Adam and Eve "advance into the desert, hand in hand"—"EXILED BUT NOT LOST!" Here Aeschylean form and Miltonic focus converge to rewrite the founding plot of the Judeo-Christian world from the perspective of woman. "Eve's allotted grief," she wrote, had been "imperfectly apprehended hitherto" and was "more expressible by a woman than a man." While allowing that "self-sacrifice belonged to [Eve's] womanhood, and the consciousness of originating the fall to her offense," Barrett quietly advances the parallel in loss between Adam and Satan. A less ambitious but perhaps more perfectly achieved poem in the volume, "The Cry of the Children," suggests a turn away from a theological and towards a political orientation, although still deeply tinged with Christian humanism. The poetry Barrett wrote after her marriage to Browning develops this latter strain.

Coventry Patmore

As a despiser of feminism, democracy, pacifism, the Irish, Jews, and—after his Catholic conversion—Protestants, Coventry Patmore is not likely to win many modern admirers. Popularity he also despised. In the intuitionist mystical fusion of the erotic and the spiritual of his later work and his championing of voluntaristic manly bellicosity and dominance, he comes before us at times like a High Victorian Catholic D. H. Lawrence. And like Lawrence's best fiction, Patmore's best poetry is of a high order and repays study. In the four books that form *The Angel in the House*—*The Betrothal, The Espousals, Faithful Forever,* and *The Victories of Love*—he gives somewhat prolix form to his understanding of ideal Christian marriage and domestic love, a marriage and a love that he possessed with his first wife. The first two books trace the growth in courtship and fruition in marriage of a mutually fulfilling love predicated on the husband's acceptance of dominance, duty, and gallantry and the wife's of submission, guardianship of beauty, and the function of limiting and guiding him. This is indeed not far from a traditional Christian—or at least Pauline—view of marriage, to which Patmore adds a sort of domestic and erotic chivalry: "Her manners, when they call me lord, / Remind me 'tis by courtesy."

Indeed, Patmorean marriage is a continual wooing in which "she's not and never can be mine." Throughout runs an implicit theme that will develop more fully in his later works: "The little germ of nuptial love, / Which springs so simply from the sod, / The root is, as my song shall prove, / Of all our love to man and God." The configuration of marriage as man, woman, and love (sexual and spiritual) will become for Patmore the expression of a divine ordering: "Female and male God made the man; / His image is the whole, not half; / And in our love we dimly scan / The love which is between Himself." *Faithful Forever* and *The Victories of Love*, made up of verse letters and a closing "Wedding Sermon" that carries much of the burden of meaning, trace first the course of disappointed love and then the trials of unequal marriage that, by the unconditional devotion of the wife and the unflagging duty of the husband, transfigures them both in the presence of death.

Shortly after the death of his first wife, Patmore noted in his diary: "The relation of the soul to Christ *as his betrothed wife* is a mine of undiscovered joy and power." In the second book of *The Unknown Eros, and Other Odes* and in his late prose reflections, *The Rod, the Root and the Flower*, he develops the connections between erotic, spiritual, and divine love only hinted at until then. In the former, sexuality is not a metaphor of spiritual and divine love but an instance of them. The mystery at the heart of married love is the same mystery that inhabits, in a finer tone, spiritual and divine perfection; and, conversely, the spiritual, the religious, and the divine both dwell and are uniquely apprehended in the sexuality and happiness of married life.

"Sponsa Dei," "Legem Tuam Dilexi," "To the Body," "Deliciae Sapientiae de Amore," "The Child's Purchase," and the Psyche odes advance the idea that marital sex is a sacrament and the matrimonial bed its altar overtly enough to have discomposed many even among Patmore's sympathetic readers. In *The Rod, the Root and the Flower*, finally, Patmore expresses more directly, though in aphoristic form, the central concerns of his poetry and indeed extends them into congruent regions. "Lovers," he here writes, "are nothing else than Priest and Priestess to each other and of the Divine Manhood and Divine Womanhood which are in God."

Christina Rossetti

Christina Rossetti was esteemed in her own time as its greatest woman poet and by some as the greatest of all English women poets. By the end of her life she had, in Antony Harrison's estimate, written some one thousand poems, about half of them devotional; but as her religiosity was integral to her life, it permeates almost all her work. Both her Victorian and her modern admirers point to the great purity and severe simplicity, even austerity, of her poetic manner and to the welcome contrast it forms with the sentimentality and diffuseness that vitiates much Victorian poetry. Her stylistic concision owes something, no doubt, to the Pre-Raphaelite aesthetics of her brother, just as her restraint reflects her affinities with Tractarianism and the doctrine of Reserve. Concision here means not compression, however, so much as simplicity and directness of utterance, and her weakest poetry has justly been charged with slightness rather than formal shortcomings. On the contrary, Rossetti was notably scrupulous and craftswomanly, submitting poems to Dante Gabriel and others for criticism and perfectly aware when she had achieved the well-made aesthetic object that she insisted on both in her work and in others'.

The fusion of Tractarian and Pre-Raphaelite poetics, Harrison demonstrates, is observable in poems like "'Consider the Lilies of the Field,'" and "'Thou knewest . . . thou oughtest therefore.'" Both poems are marked by a Pre-Raphaelite closeness and intensity of gaze in order to effect an "Analogical reading" of nature à la Keble; but in Rossetti this process culminates in a small and precisely defined religious illumination or an insight into right conduct as an element of Creation. Much of her religious poetry deals with suffering and release; indeed, a world-weary melancholy pervades the poetry, which appears to be written from the point of view of one who has already renounced the world, as in "The Thread of Life," a melancholy that in "'For Thine Own Sake, O My God'" deepens into self-loathing: "Wearied of sinning, wearied of repentance, / . . . Wearied of self, I turn, my God, to Thee; / . . . Wearied I loathe myself, I loathe my sinning, / My stains, my festering sores, my misery. . . ." Fairchild catches in few words the circular negativity of Rossetti's rigorism: "She loved the world, condemned that love as sinful, renounced the world, was made unhappy by that renunciation, condemned that unhappiness as sinful." There is, however, a single ray of light in this bleak outlook: in "'When my heart is vexed I will complain'" she begins with the beauty of the world ("The fields are white to harvest, look and see"), rejects this beauty ("I have no heart for harvest time, / Grow sick with hope deferred from chime to chime"), yet takes heart from Christ, who "can set [her] in the eternal ecstasy / Of his great jubilee."

But the negation of life in this world, or its reduction to a thoroughfare full of woe, seems to be for Rossetti a necessary step towards affirmation of life in the next. This hereafter she images forth in recognizably Pre-Raphaelite terms as an aesthetic paradise, as in "'The Holy

City, New Jerusalem,'"—built of every precious substance, strewn with every delightful flower and fruit, resplendently watered, and ringing with the harps and songs of saints—where "citizens who walk in white / Have nought to do with day or night, / And drink the river of delight." God is the ideal architect and each of his materials bears a moral as well as an aesthetic virtue. But such stock idealizations have little poetic force. At her best, however, which—as in *Monna Innominata: A Sonnet of Sonnets*—is not always in her explicitly religious poetry, Rossetti clearly merits the place among Victorian poets that she has lately won back.

Gerard Manley Hopkins

Alone among Victorian religious poets, Gerard Manley Hopkins may lay claim to greatness. Yet beyond a small circle of readers—in the main, poets today little read—his work was completely unknown in his lifetime and indeed virtually so until well into the twentieth century. When his friend Robert Bridges brought out the first edition of his poems in 1918, Hopkins had been dead for twenty-nine years. Public reaction was mixed, if not bewildered. To most reviewers schooled in Victorian and Edwardian literary decorum, this poetry seemed unfamiliar, odd, even rebarbative; some, however, were able to see deeper than its unsettling surface and to recognize that here novelty, and perhaps even difficulty, might be the price of its beauties. But none could fail to see that the author of this small body of poems—between *The Wreck of the Deutschland* and "To R. B." are scarcely more than fifty finished poems in English, mostly short—had introduced startling innovations in poetic language.

The eldest son in a comfortably well-off High Anglican family, Hopkins won two scholarships (called "Exhibitions") that took him to Balliol College, Oxford, where he obtained a First Class in *Literae Humaniores* or "Greats"—the final examination in classical languages and literatures for the bachelor of arts degree, requiring detailed preparation in linguistic and formal matters. During these years and for some years after, he kept notebooks and journals that reward study. They reveal an intensely curious mind and a taste for precise observation and description that would pass—transformed—into his later poetry. As a student of natural phenomena, he followed the injunctions of John Ruskin; as a student of phenomena of language, he worked in accordance with methods and doctrines of mid-Victorian philology.

While Oxford was no longer the seedbed of religious controversy that it had been in the time of Newman and the Oxford Movement, it harbored opposing religious tendencies and views that were no less firmly held for being quieter in profession. By temperament disposed to religious rigor, Hopkins fell in readily among the ritualist heirs of the movement, led by E. B. Pusey and H. P. Liddon. The poetry that Hopkins wrote at this time is uneven in quality, though at its best (as in "Heaven-Haven" and "The Habit of Perfection") it reveals a delicate poetic talent in the making, one that has learned lessons of Keats and Tennyson. As a foreshadowing of his mature work, however, it is pale.

To appreciate Hopkins's decision to leave the Anglican Church of his family, friends, and spiritual mentors at Oxford, one must bear in mind the profound interpenetrations of ecclesiastical and national identities in England. To enter the Catholic Church was to abandon Canterbury and England for Rome—a step overhung with suspicions of treachery and "perversion," and often causing the rupture of the closest personal bonds. Before entering the Jesuit order, Hopkins symbolically burnt his poems, having taken care to secure the survival of copies of most of them. More significant, however, he resolved to write no more verse, on the grounds that to do so would interfere with his "state and vocation." To this resolution he held firm for over seven years, writing no poetry unless asked by superiors to supply "presentation pieces" on religious occasions.

Even the best of these—"Ad Mariam" and "Rosa Mystica"—scarcely rise above the run of Victorian religious poems and offer no foreshadowing of the poetic language or perceptions that would emerge suddenly with *The Wreck of the Deutschland*. But he continued to keep journals until about ten months before beginning work on the ode, and in these he recorded observations of the natural world in prose of great descriptive exactness and sometimes beauty. Here he makes use of a private terminology that first found its way into his writing in a set of notes towards an essay on Parmenides.

Two of these terms, *inscape* and *instress*, have proved useful enough to merit entries in the 1976 Supplement to the *Oxford English Dictionary*. While his use of them is not always consistent, one may begin to define *inscape* as the essential form dwelling within natural things and within language, especially poetic language, and expressing their uniqueness or specific individuality. "All the world is full of inscape," he wrote in his journal; "it is everywhere near at hand," and if we "had but eyes to see . . . it could be called out everywhere again." Inscapes are not subjective impressions, that is, but objective essential forms that can be recognized if the observer is in sympathy with the object or phenomenon observed. In poetry, individual inscape is what Hopkins will always seek to catch. (The term receives more complex elaborations in his notes on "Poetry and Verse" and in his later reflections "On Personality, Grace and Free Will.") *Instress,* even more difficult to define simply, is not shape but energy, and particularly energy that upholds and communicates inscape to the perceiver across a "bridge" or "stem of stress." The source of this energy is, either immediately or mediately through the individual, God.

For seven of the nine years of his preparation and training for the Jesuit order Hopkins remained faithful to the terms of his self-imposed poetic silence; at St. Beuno's College in Wales, however, where he was sent to study theology, his resolution faltered. He began to study Welsh, attracted by its euphoniousness; and while he never mastered the language, he learned it well enough to hazard a few poetic translations into (flawed) Welsh. More important, however, was his discovery of *cynghanedd,* a technique of Welsh poetic composition that regulates the disposition of assonance and alliteration in a line. One element of the striking musicality of Hopkins's mature poetry is reducible to such sound patterning or "chiming." But the principle is not merely phonetic: in the world, too—in the world of nature, particularly—Hopkins would seek echoes and correspondences, likenesses and variations, that not only form the basis of beauty (as he developed the idea in a dialogue written at Oxford, "On the Origin of Beauty") but bespeak the unifying presence of God behind the manifold world of phenomena (as he would write in "Pied Beauty").

One final technical question and one fastidious scruple remained before Hopkins could end the years of his poetic quiescence. Describing subsequently to another of his small circle of poet-readers the genesis of *The Wreck of the Deutschland,* he referred to the metrical or rhythmic innovations that he had introduced in it and that he calls "sprung rhythm": "I had long had haunting my ear the echo of a new rhythm which I now realised on paper." Although not fully fledged at this point, the rhythmic system that he appears largely to have intuited from the nature of English—as well as from nursery rhymes and jingles, and doubtless from bits of available Old English poetry—is roughly that which underlies early Germanic verse, as in *Beowulf.*

Unlike traditional modern English meter, which is accentual-syllabic, sprung rhythm does not count syllables, only stresses. Provided the number of stresses is regular, the number of syllables is of no account. A foot consists, therefore, of one strong beat and either no weak beats or any (reasonable) number of them. So, for example, the following two lines are metrically equivalent (each having six stresses) even though syllabically they differ as nine to sixteen:

(1) The sóur scýthe crínge, and the bléar sháre cóme
(2) With the búrl of the fóuntains of aír, búck and the flóod of the wáve.

The object of this new rhythm was not simply to satisfy the echo haunting his ear but to restore to English poetry the rhythms of *spoken* English. It is a point Hopkins insists on repeatedly: his poetry is not to be read "slovenly with the eyes but with [the] ears." For Hopkins, poetry is essentially performative and spoken: "*till it is spoken it is not performed*, it does not perform, it is not itself. . . . [P]oetry is emphatically speech, speech purged of dross like gold in the furnace. . . . [S]prung rhythm . . . purges [verse] to an emphasis as much brighter, livelier, more lustrous than the regular but commonplace emphasis of common rhythm as poetry in general is brighter than common speech."

The final scruple to be satisfied before he could again write poetry was the one he had imposed on himself—never to compose unless bidden to do so by a religious superior. In a furious storm and blizzard in early December 1875 the *Deutschland*, a transatlantic steamer under way from Bremen to New York, ran aground on the Kentish Knock, treacherous shoals of sand off the coast of Essex. Among the lost were five Franciscan nuns expelled from Germany in Bismarck's Kulturkampf. The wreck was extensively covered in the English press; Catholic periodicals carried Cardinal Manning's burial sermon; and one of Hopkins's superiors remarked generally that "he wished someone would write a poem on the subject." This remark sufficed to authorize implicitly Hopkins's poetic activity for the remaining thirteen years of his life. When the ode was completed he submitted it for publication in the Jesuit journal *The Month*, which rejected it as too difficult. Hopkins made only two subsequent efforts to publish any of his poetry and, these failing, too, resisted the efforts of others on his behalf. He was certain, however, that he would find an audience in good time.

Hopkins divides the ode into two parts of ten and twenty-five stanzas, respectively. Part the First is at once an invocation of God and an account first of the speaker's own creation, terrified submission, and glad acceptance of Him (stanzas 1–5) and then of the initiatory moment of Christian history and humanity's submission to it and acceptance of it (stanzas 6–10). Implicitly, these spiritual storms and calms prefigure the natural ones to come. Part the Second contains the necessary narrative elements of the drama and its pivotal event, the terror and passionate submission of the tall nun, which climaxes at stanza 24. After a moment of *kairos*, in which language itself appears at first to break down before the enormity of its task and which reveals the meaning of the shipwreck (stanzas 28–30), the poem closes with a powerful prayer both in praise of God and for the conversion of England. That is, the three acts of submission that structure and give meaning to the poem are to be followed, if the prayer is answered, by a fourth.

As an ode, *The Wreck of the Deutschland* owes more to Pindar than to Wordsworth or other English models in the genre, and the difficulty of its linguistic and other innovations has caused more than one reader to incline to Bridges's exaggerated view that it lies at the beginning of Hopkins's mature work "like a great dragon folded in the gate to forbid all entrance." Some of this difficulty is owing to odic writing, which is highly charged and not primarily narrative; some, however, arises from the new poetic language that here erupts into English. In order to achieve the phonetic density and complexity that will yield the design, pattern, or inscape he seeks, Hopkins needs all the lexical and syntactic resources of current English; for "the poetical language of an age shd. be the current language heightened, to any degree heightened and unlike itself, but not . . . an obsolete one."

Consequently, while Hopkins refuses even such archaisms as were commonplace in Victorian verse, he exploits to the full the great word-hoard that was being monumentalized by Victorian philology in the form of the *Oxford English Dictionary* and the *English Dialect Dictionary*. Dialectal words, for example, scorned by Samuel Johnson, are now on an equal footing with literary language. Lexically, Hopkins favors words that stem from or convey the feel of the *formative* elements of English: Anglo-Saxon, Scandinavian, and Norman French. He forms compounds of every grammatical makeup permitted in English (and a few that are not permitted). He plays on the lability of grammatical categories: in English there is usually no mark or inflection to identify a noun, a verb, or an adjective, and Hopkins enjoys imparting to a noun the movement of its homologous verb and to a verb the solidity of its homologous noun. He presses into service any phonological device that causes sounds to accumulate, echo off one another, and thicken into aural shapes directly expressive of what they are conveying—not only the standard devices of end rhyme, assonance, and alliteration but Icelandic *skothending* (the "rhyming" or chiming of final consonants regardless of preceding vowels, e.g., fi*nd* and ba*nd*) and variations on a single vowel (which he calls "vowelling off").

Syntactically, Hopkins again looks for his models and authority to *spoken* English, with its abruptnesses, suppressions (e.g., of relative pronouns), and parataxis. But he goes well beyond spoken syntax in order to achieve the rhythms, both accentual and semantic, that figure his r￼ aning: "Thóu mastering mé / God!" In all, he is drawing or wrenching into the foreground of poetry the very elements—phonetic, lexical, syntactic, and rhythmic—of which it is made. So, in *The Wreck of the Deutschland*, he prunes unneeded verbs ("I steady as a water in a well, to a poise, to a pane"); coins compounds ("I kiss my hand / To the stars, lovely-asunder"); thickens sound patterns (even to excess: "We lash with the best or worst / Word last! How a lush-kept plush-capped sloe / Will, mouthed to flesh-burst, / Gush!—flush the man, the being with it, sour or sweet / Brim, in a flásh, fúll!"); breaches grammatical boundaries ("the hurtle of hell / Behind"); repeats and expands phrases with the breathlessness of panted speech ("where, where was a, where was a place?"); draws on rhetorical devices little favored since the Renaissance (dieremenon, splitting a compound word by another word or phrase: "Brim, in a flásh, fúll"); and combines the simple chiming of internal rhyme with voweling off ("Wíry and white-fíery and whírlwind-swivellèd snów").

These devices and techniques he will continue to develop and refine in his later poetry. But one must not, finally, permit the technical brilliance, verbal energy, and novelty of Hopkins's poetry to obscure the purpose that it always serves. Hopkins's work is a sustained and many-times refined meditation on both words and the Word, and on the world as their sphere of intersection. As a Jesuit reflecting on the "First Principle and Foundation" of Ignatius' *Spiritual Exercises*, he would write, "God's utterance of himself in himself is God the Word, outside himself is this world. This world then is word, expression, news of God. Therefore its end, its purpose, its purport, its meaning, is God and its life or work to name and praise him. Therefore praise [is to be] put before reverence and service."

It is because of this immanent presence in the world and in language—in the form of laws—that Hopkins's work is both unified and charged. And it is therefore little wonder that much of his mature poetry has its initiatory moment in observation of the world, particularly the world of nature—as in "The Windhover": "I caught this mórning morning's mínion, king-/ dom of daylight's dauphin, dapple-dáwn-drawn Falcon in his riding / Of the rólling level úndernéath him steady aír. . . ." But a poem almost never remains at this natural point of departure; almost always it penetrates beyond nature to the presence of a personal God that upholds its beauty. Even, indeed, in his most desperate late sonnets, it is the strain towards Christian transcendence that imparts energy to despair and informs the tension between despair and the consolation so fervently but unsuccessfully sought.

The poems of Hopkins fall, roughly, into five thematic or generic-thematic categories: (1) the two odes, *The Wreck of the Deutschland* and *The Loss of the Eurydice*; (2) poems whose point of departure is the natural world; (3) poems whose point of departure is the human world; (4) poems whose point of departure is the personal world; and (5) poems associated with particular religious occasions. In the 1990 MacKenzie edition, these are (1) nos. 101 and 125; (2) nos. 103, 104, 105, 111, 112, 115, 117, 118, 120, 121, 122, 124, 130, 146, 149, 167, 170, 174; (3) nos. 108, 113, 119, 129, 131, 133, 134, 137, 138, 141, 142, 143, 144, 148, 158, 160, 168; (4) nos. 140, 154, 155, 157, 159, 162, 163, 177, 178, 179; and (5) nos. 102, 126, 139, 151. One may see in this display a trajectory, again rough, of Hopkins's preoccupations, from nature (most poems prior to no. 130, "Binsey Poplars") to human subjects (most poems between nos. 131, "Henry Purcell," and 148, "The Leaden Echo and the Golden Echo") to Hopkins's own spiritual life (most poems from "Not, I'll not, carrion comfort, Despair, not feast on thee" to no. 179, "To R. B.")—the more narrowly religious pieces being interspersed.

To some extent this distribution reflects changes in Hopkins's own life, as he moved from the natural settings of Wales and the environs of Oxford to the places of his pastoral and teaching duties in London, Oxford, Lancashire, Liverpool, and Glasgow, and on to University

College, Dublin—where he was Professor of Greek, where he often felt isolated, impotent, and bleak, and where he composed what are known as the "terrible sonnets" or the "sonnets of desolation." In these last, some of the most harrowing in the English language, Hopkins wrestles with the appalling solitude of God's absence and with the spiritual dryness, desolation, anguish, and self-loathing that are its consequence. Never is God's absence ontological, however; rather, Hopkins's "lament / Is cries countless, cries like dead letters sent / To dearest him who lives alas! away." The chastened language of these late sonnets forfeits none of the intensity of his earlier exuberance over the beauty of a world upheld by God; but the plainer style he once hoped for has been achieved at a terrible cost. Yet even this series of sonnets, written in Dublin, contains moments of hard-won calm, patience, self-irony, and, in "My own heart let me more have pity on," wan cheer.

Formally, Hopkins's favored vehicle is the sonnet; over two-thirds of his finished poems are in this form. In his hands, however, the form underwent some notable transformations, from the ten-and-one-half-line "curtal sonnet" (reduced by arithmetic ratio) to the "caudated sonnet," which—building on a Miltonic model—appends one or more additional tercets (codas, or tails). An example of the former is "Pied Beauty". Of the latter, "That Nature is a Heraclitean Fire and of the comfort of the Resurrection" is the most daring—a triply caudated (twenty-four-line) sonnet in alexandrines enormously swelled by metrically irrelevant slack syllables authorized by sprung rhythm.

Since for Hopkins no aspect of experience was alien to religion, two in particular have appeared to some of his modern readers as worthy of high relief. First, his experience of the appalling conditions of urban life in industrial England led to an assertion to Bridges the enormity of which provoked a hiatus of over three years in their correspondence. Referring to the ideals of the Paris Commune, Hopkins wrote:

I must tell you I am always thinking of a Communist future. . . . Horrible to say, in a manner I am a Communist. Their ideal bating some things is nobler than that professed by any secular statesman I know of. . . . Besides it is just. —I do not mean the means of getting to it are. But it is a dreadful thing for the greatest and most necessary part of a very rich nation to live a hard life without dignity, knowledge, comforts, delights, or hopes in the midst of plenty—which plenty they make.

(This, to the middle-class Englishman was the secular equivalent of defecting to the Roman Catholic Church.) Years later this attitude gave rise to the in-more-than-one-way-radical poem "Tom's Garland: on the Unemployed."

Second, Hopkins recorded in his early notebooks an attraction to male beauty—as indeed to beauty of all kinds—with instructive scrupulosity, alongside notes of nocturnal emissions (whether involuntary or conscious), inattentiveness at chapel, intemperance in food and drink, unkind thoughts, inveterate habits, observations on architecture, shopping lists, lists of dinner guests and of books to read, drafts of verses, and so on. In the later poetry this attraction finds most explicit expression in "Harry Ploughman"; but in his letters, too, he is disarmingly open, albeit not to the point of naming. It is clear that while at Oxford he felt physically drawn to some other young men, attractions he counts among his many "sins." And after reading some of Whitman's poems, he wrote to Bridges: "I always knew in my heart Walt Whitman's mind to be more like my own than any other man's living." But he adds, "As he is a very great scoundrel this is not a pleasant confession." Finally, and typically, his attraction calls forth a vow of renunciation: "And this also makes me the more desirous to read him and the more determined that I will not." The question of the significance of such facts, however, remains psychologically open (see N. H. MacKenzie, *Early Poetic Manuscripts and Note-books*, 21–38).

In the case of someone like Hopkins, whose life, being, and actions were organized around and informed by religious faith, and by a faith that condemned such leanings and behavior unequivocally, the forces and the meaning of control and abnegation must also be weighed in the balance. His poetry offers proof, whatever the case, that religious faith and the life of the senses are not fundamentally at odds.

Cary H. Plotkin

Further Reading

Fairchild, Hoxie Neale. *1830–1880: Christianity and Romanticism in the Victorian Era.* Vol. 4 of *Religious Trends in English Poetry.* New York: Columbia University Press, 1957.

Harrison, Antony H. *Christina Rossetti in Context*. Chapel Hill: University of North Carolina Press, 1988.

MacKenzie, Norman H. *Hopkins*. Edinburgh: Oliver and Boyd, 1968.

MacKenzie, Norman H. *A Reader's Guide to Gerard Manley Hopkins*. Ithaca, N.Y.: Cornell University Press, 1981.

Mermin, Dorothy. *Elizabeth Barrett Browning: The Origins of a New Poetry*. Chicago: University of Chicago Press, 1989.

Plotkin, Cary H. *The Tenth Muse: Victorian Philology and the Genesis of the Poetic Language of Gerard Manley Hopkins*. Carbondale: Southern Illinois University Press, 1989.

Prickett, Stephen. *Romanticism and Religion: The Tradition of Coleridge and Wordsworth in the Victorian Church*. Cambridge: Cambridge University Press, 1976.

Scheinberg, Cynthia. "Miriam's Daughters: Women's Poetry and Religious Identity in Victorian England." Ph.D. diss., Rutgers University, 1992.

Schneider, Elisabeth. *The Dragon in the Gate: Studies in the Poetry of Gerard Manley Hopkins*. Berkeley: University of California Press, 1968.

Tennyson, G. B. "The Sacramental Imagination." In *Nature and the Victorian Imagination*, edited by U. K. Knoepflmacher and G. B. Tennyson. Berkeley: University of California Press, 1977.

Tennyson, G. B. *Victorian Devotional Poetry: The Tractarian Mode*. Cambridge: Harvard University Press, 1981.

Pre-Raphaelite Poetry

ERHAPS no Victorian critical term has been more analyzed and debated in recent years than *Pre-Raphaelite*. Critics have argued that it is an essentially meaningless literary designation, yet have gone on to defend it as necessary—whether as an art-historical concept that offers a convenient way of grouping literary figures (in Cecil Lang's view) or as a signifier of overt Romantics among the Victorians (according to Harold Bloom). In art-historical circles there is more agreement about the meaning of the term, although recent feminist and cultural materialist commentators have sensibily argued that Pre-Raphaelitism, like other tendencies in art, cannot be separated from the society which engendered it or from that society's politics, economics, and history. Moreover, they have suggested that there is none of the monolithic and unifying linkage of style and purpose which generally characterizes a "movement."

But if there are general tendencies that connect a group of Victorian painters ranging from William Holman Hunt and John Everett Millais to Dante Gabriel Rossetti and Edward Coley Burne-Jones, it must be asked what relations these figures and their works bear to Dante Gabriel Rossetti, Christina Rossetti, William Morris, and Algernon Charles Swinburne as poets. Is there something that links these poets to each other, that gives their work a special flavor—one different in kind or degree from that of their contemporaries?

The Victorians, at least, thought they could identify one. For them, the term *Pre-Raphaelite* referred initially to a group of young painters who in 1848, reacting against what they perceived as the dictates of Sir

Joshua Reynold's *Discourses* and the practices of the Royal Academy based on them, attempted to change the nature of English painting. The original Pre-Raphaelite Brotherhood consisted of James Collinson (best known as Christina Rossetti's suitor), Hunt, Millais, Dante Gabriel Rossetti, William Michael Rossetti (the chronicler of the group), Frederic George Stephens (later an art critic), and Thomas Woolner (a sculptor). The brothers had no clear aesthetic manifesto except the all-encompassing generalization that, unlike painters creating brown "slosh" in compositions based on pyramidal structure, they would "follow nature"—paint things as they really are—and return in spirit to the truth of vision held by artists before Raphael. William Michael Rossetti, recreating the movement in 1895, argues that the bond of union among the first brotherhood was (1) "to have genuine ideas to express"; (2) "to study Nature attentively, so as to know how to express them"; (3) "to sympathize with what is direct and serious and heartfelt in previous art, to the exclusion of what is conventional"; and (4) "to produce thoroughly good pictures and statues." This, of course, says little, except that the band was united in knowing what it did *not* want to produce—conventional, superficial genre or history pieces.

The Victorian public immediately identified certain traits in painting as Pre-Raphaelite: preternaturally vivid colors (perhaps in reaction to the fog and smog of Victorian London); subjects often drawn from lesser-known literary sources such as the works of John Keats (whose biography by Monckton Milnes appeared in 1848); compositions filled with incident that took more than the usual care to decipher; static, unidealized, even ugly figures; clear, sharp outlines; and a perspective best described as "peculiar." Perhaps most obviously, Pre-Raphaelitism in painting meant typology and symbolism.

Describing a lady in Charlotte Yonge's novel *Heartsease* (1853), a character sneers: "She is walking prae-raffaelitism herself. Symbols and emblems! . . . Symbolic, suggestive teaching, speaking to the eye. . . ." To those who did not like it, Pre-Raphaelitism was the work of "exceedingly young men of stubborn instincts." Its detractors feared it, on the one hand, as secretly papist or retrograde (it disregarded "modern" principles like perspective and chiaroscuro) or, on the other hand, as excessively democratic, reeking of the mobocracy so threatening in the era of Chartism and the revolutions of 1848.

Some, including Charles Dickens, thought the movement almost immoral in depicting—as Millais did in *The Carpenter's Shop*—a working-class Mary, Joseph, and Jesus. Yet for John Ruskin, defending the brotherhood in "Pre-Raphaelitism," it meant serious, moral art, religious in its truth, and for David Masson, writing in 1852, it was a cross between naturalism or realism and the spiritual and imaginative seen in "things as they really are." For most ordinary folk, it was a matter of complex symbolic detail and brilliant, even garish color.

In literature—and the term was quickly adapted by Victorian literary critics—*Pre-Raphaelitism* signified linguistic archaisms or medievalisms and sharp delineation and specificity in visual detail. Masson defined Pre-Raphaelite verse as created by the same "feeling" as the painting, but as going beyond the simplicity of Wordsworth to the even more archaic simplicity of Dante and his circle. Detractors, like Robert Browning, made it a dysphemism for effeminacy, affectation, and archaizing. In accusing Dante Gabriel Rossetti of engendering "the fleshly school of poetry," in his pamphlet on the subject (1871), Robert Buchanan further defined Pre-Raphaelite poetry, specifically that of D. G. Rossetti, Morris and Swinburne. To him, *Pre-Raphaelite* meant overblown poetry, hysterical in tone and excessive in style; it signaled its unwholesomeness by valuing expression over thought, style over content, sound over sense, and body over soul. To another critic, writing in *Macmillan's Magazine* in 1880, it was equally unsavory—representing "a sick indifference to the things of our own time, and a spurious devotion to whatever is foreign, exotic, archaic or grotesque."

We in the twentieth century have amplified the movement's characteristics. Most critics accept the idea of a widening circle of influence, an accumulation of artistic and literary impulses connected by what T. S. Eliot called "a continuity of admiration." The first brotherhood, lasting from 1848 till 1853, privileged painting over poetry; it believed in truth to nature and truth to imagination as coequal principles. The dominant forces in this formative phase were Holman Hunt, flying the banner of truth to nature—and intricate, deeply felt, Protestant religious typology—and Gabriel Rossetti, with his tendency toward medievalism, Dantesque faith and ideal love, and truth to the inner eye.

Its organ was a famous but short-lived periodical called the *Germ* (1850), which survived for only four issues, yet is an ancestor of today's "little magazines." While the *Germ* was full of thoroughly forgettable verse like Thomas Woolner's "My Beautiful Lady," a pseudomedieval praise of the beloved most noteworthy for Hunt's fine illustrations of it, it also contained significant literary works. Dante Gabriel Rossetti contributed a tale of his vision of art, "Hand and Soul," and seven important poems, including versions of "My Sister's Sleep," and "The Blessed Damozel." Christina Rossetti, age eighteen, contributed seven more, including "Dream Land" and "Repining." The group was clearly a brotherhood—a bonding of close male friends with women excluded; it involved an idea of communality; brothers read aloud their own and others' literary work, edited and revised together, chose subjects in common to paint, and discussed and debated concerns held by all. But by 1853, as Christina Rossetti noted in verse, the brotherhood was "in its decadence."

The second Pre-Raphaelite circle is more amorphous, but still in essence a brotherhood. Lasting from 1856 to about 1865, it was dominated by Dante Gabriel Rossetti and consisted of younger disciples, including William Morris, Edward Burne-Jones, and, by 1857, Algernon Charles Swinburne. Because he once shared rent with two members of the circle, George Meredith has been counted among the Pre-Raphaelites. Yet neither the private, evolutionary religion manifested in poems like "The Woods of Westermain" nor the "modern" guilt and self-examination of "Modern Love" justifies his inclusion. Even before they met Rossetti, Morris, Burne-Jones, and their college friends had created a magazine in imitation of the *Germ*, *The Oxford and Cambridge Magazine* (1856). This journal, originally to be called *The Brotherhood*, celebrated the earlier group both by including in its pages Burne-Jones's laudatory review of the *Germ* and the works by Hunt and D. G. Rossetti in it, and by printing versions of Rossetti's "Blessed Damozel," "Staff and Scrip," and "Burden of Nineveh." The second brotherhood also stressed communal work and spirit, although some of its concerns differed from those of the first group. The differences were not based solely on Rossetti's powerful, if changing, influence but also on the fact that England itself had changed between 1848 and 1856.

The hungry forties, the revolutions on the continent and the Chartists at home, the religious fervor of the Tractarians and the evangelical passion of their opponents, the belief in the imminence of change—all of which had touched the first brotherhood—were over. Talk of revolution had subsided to chat about reform, and the hegemony of the middle class made the possibility of change seem more remote. The second brotherhood's "Crusade and Holy Warfare against the age" took the form of trying to escape its era's materialism and complacency and of attempting to evade or to comment only indirectly on the political and economic problems of the golden 1850s.

By the time of the gradual dissolution of the second group, in the mid-1860s, Pre-Raphaelitism was very much a broad-ranging movement and a broad-ranging term in both painting and literature. What we in the twentieth century now describe as "visual Pre-Raphaelitism" is closely related to what we might define as Pre-Raphaelite in poetry. The traits of the visual compositions are definite contours, brilliant contrasting colors, minute detail (carefully delineated in backgrounds as well as in foregrounds), flatness or two-dimensionality, with texts and subjects designed to bear symbolic meaning, whether that of religious typology or private symbolism. These traits create heavily patterned, compartmentalized works, demanding because they cannot be interpreted in a momentary or single look. The paintings are dense and somewhat mysterious, like multiple point of view in literature, while, like dramatic monologues, they demand that viewers participate in their somewhat ambiguous lives.

Pre-Raphaelite poetry shares with Pre-Raphaelite painting its intensity, its prevailing tones or moods, and much of its subject matter, especially its perpetual gaze at women, its obsession with frustrated and separated love, and its preoccupation with death. Like many of the paintings, the poems utilize dream, providing accounts of actual dreams and using the language, distortion, fragmentation, symbolization, and essential uninterpretability of the dream experience. Through the use of hyperclarity Pre-Raphaelite poets tend to render nature unnatural, whether in creating imaginary landscapes or in examining microscopically what the eye cannot ordinarily see.

These tendencies, as well as the more obvious conventions they develop—the reiterated descriptions of the female form, divine and diabolic, the interchangeability of the imageries of religious and erotic experience, the preference for settings other than the Victorian and the imbuing of them with the realism of a contemporary scene, the use of the preternatural and folkloric, the attempt to fuse the "real" and the visionary—are indeed present in other Victorian poems, but they dominate Pre-Raphaelite poetry. To them the brothers add a special concern for the interaction of poetry and painting—not just a matter of "word-painting" (for that would make Tennyson the true Pre-Raphaelite and remove the later works of the brothers from the canon)—but an attempt to break out of the boundaries of each medium, to emulate in a sonnet, for example, the condition of a painting.

The work of Dante Gabriel Rossetti is a case in point, although it must be remembered that he made his living as a painter, and that he produced only two volumes of original poetry, *Poems* (1870) and *Ballads and Sonnets* (1881). Prior to the volume of 1870, he had earned something of a reputation by translating the poems of the *dolce stil nuovo*, that is, of Dante and his forebears and contemporaries, in *Early Italian Poets* (1861). Here he had demonstrated his Pre-Raphaelitism by reaching back before Petrarch, the Raphael of Italian poetry, to the roots of Italian literary art. Rossetti was most drawn to the *Vita Nuova*; in Dante he found images and conventions fresher and "truer" than those of Petrarchanism, as well as an idealization of love and a paean to its cosmic power. Perhaps Dante also provided him with models for poems full of minute specificity and symbolic atmosphere, poems that suggest the factuality of the mystical.

Within the narratives, ballads, and numerous sonnets that form the corpus of Rossetti's poetry, there are conventionally Pre-Raphaelite works. These are poems—sometimes influenced by Keats or Coleridge—that achieve their effect through accumulations of specific, closely observed detail, foregrounded so that it veils or deflects the poems' central emphasis and produces a static, highly pictorial effect. Among these are the unfinished "Bride's Prelude" (1848–) in which the bride, Alöyse, confesses her fall to her virginal sister, Amelotte, amid remarkable images of heat, sound, and silence. Through most of the poem Alöyse sits statuelike, head turned sideways, while Amelotte kneels in shock at her sister's revelations.

The picture is so carefully particularized that we see the reflections on Amelotte's silver belt and count the pearls that adorn Alöyse's vest. The surreal, dreamlike quality of the poem comes from this technique combined with the evocation of the heat and tension in the room in which the poem is set. The sun is bright enough to etch "the track / Of her [Amelotte's] still shadow sharp and black." The air is so still "that Amelotte / Heard far beneath the plunge and float / Of a hound swimming in the moat." The seemingly irrelevant, naturalistic detail of the dog's swim adds to the sense of heat, airlessness, and pitiless light; the specifics collaborate to create a sense of agoraphobia and claustrophobia analogous to the Bride's account of a passion now turned hellish.

When Gabriel Rossetti wishes to do so, he can particularize with the best, demonstrating in "Jenny" how dawn "creeps in" to the prostitute's room "Past the gauze curtains half drawn-to / And the lamp's doubled shade grows blue," or depicting with the same scientific dispassion the ugliness of a place where

the sea stands spread
As one wall with the flat skies
Where the lean black craft like flies
Seem well nigh stagnated
Soon to drop off dead.

He is a master at presenting seldom-noticed small details of the natural world like "the heart-shaped seal of green / That flecks the snowdrop underneath the snow," or the moment when "the dragon-fly / Hangs like a blue thread loosened from the sky." Yet these details are less common in his poetry than his unique combinations of specific images and personified abstracts, or his substitutions of abstractions for images. Far more prone to create poetic paintings than to write painterly poems, Rossetti is no more a realist in poetry than in painting; in both media he uses the apparatus of realism for symbolic purposes. *The House of Life*, his sequence of 101 sonnets on love, art, change, and death, is filled with these potent yet essentially untranslatable image patterns fusing the sensory and the intangible. "Winged Hours" have "bloodied feathers scattered in the brake." A bright day is "sun-coloured to the imperishable core." A terrifying "something" in the "Monochord" turns the speaker's face "upon the devious coverts of dismay." Critics have carped at the elaborate artifice of this poetic technique, but it is quintessentially Rossettian.

Fundamentally, Gabriel Rossetti is most concerned with the inner life and with the making of art, whether through painting or through "the fundamental brainwork" involved in poetry; he does, however, share the social and political conscience of his first set of compeers. Indeed, most of his overtly political poems date from the late 1840s. Italian politics takes center stage in such sonnets as "On the Refusal of Aid Between Nations" and in his Browningesque dramatic monologue, "A Last Confession." The revolutions of 1848 inspire "At the Sun-Rise in 1848," and memories of the French Revolution empassion another sonnet, "At the Place de la Bastille." "The Burden of Nineveh" is a splendid commentary on England's worship of false gods, especially Mammon, and a poem as much indebted to Carlyle's and Ruskin's warnings to their society as to Layard's archaeological discoveries.

"Jenny," despite all its emphasis on the male poet-hero's self-examination, is a classic Victorian examination of the nature and plight of the fallen woman, more compassionate than most such studies. Indeed, seduced and sexually exploited or abandoned women—often disguised in medieval trappings—are significant in Gabriel Rossetti's poetry; "The Bride's Prelude" raises the question of whether a woman need marry the seducer she no longer respects; "Rose Mary" and "Stratton Water" empower the fallen women they depict. However, Rossetti's interest is not primarily in contemporary problems. His reaction to the Industrial Revolution, for example, is to allude to the bleakness and materialism of a world made unaesthetic, and to emphasize the towns and landscapes of the mind.

Indeed, Rossetti is always more interested in the state of the mind than in the state of the nation. His fascination with mental phenomena results in such lyrics as "Sudden Light," with its recognition of the déjà vu experience, the sense that lover and beloved have met and loved before; his awareness of the traumatic impact of "perfect grief" shapes "The Woodspurge," for the seemingly random observation that "the Woodspurge has a cup of three" is true to the nature of memory during shock. Even in narratives like "Dante in Verona," "A Last Confession," or "Jenny," Rossetti's primary interest is in the presentation and analysis of rapidly shifting emotions or states of mind. Occult speculations, mesmerism, spiritualism, phrenology, all play a role in many of his poems as do the figures, landscapes and occurrences of the preternatural and dream worlds. Folkloric and supernatural elements add power and drama to such ballads as "Sister Helen," "Eden Bower," "Rose Mary," and "The King's Tragedy."

Rossetti defined both his method and the nature of much of his literary art when he wrote: "I shut myself in with my soul / And the shapes come eddying forth." The shapes, engendered by dream and reverie, are not vague in thought or detail; instead, they are preternaturally vivid, condensed, fluid. Dream functions to create imaginary landscapes as well as iconic figures. Not identified with a specific time or place, these landscapes are nonetheless defined and memorable. Rossetti's is a world of thickets, coverts and woods—perhaps an homage to the *selva oscura* of his beloved Dante—and of streams, rivulets and wells that hold or reveal secrets. (See, for example, "The Stream's Secret.") The "Willowwood" sonnets from *The House of Life* typify his approach. In these sonnets of mourning for a lost love (and Christina Rossetti's sonnet of commentary on her brother's poems, "Echoes from Willowwood," suggests that the loss is not caused by death) the speaker stands beside a "woodside well" whose woods are haunted by past memories:

Alas! the bitter banks in Willowwood,
   With tear-spurge wan, with blood-wort burning red:
Alas! if ever such a pillow could
   Steep deep the soul in sleep till she were dead,

the poet laments, yearning for oblivion. In this world of dream, a drama of momentary contact and endless separation occurs. The bitter banks of the place of grief grow their own nightmare flowers, dismal pillows on which the soul is to repose; ordinary woodspurges metamorphose into mythic tear spurges; the common weeds called "worts" both burn with frustrated passion and run with blood. The lover is trapped in a limbo or purgatory of hopeless love. The emphases in sonnets such as this and in such depictions of dream and nightmare worlds as "Love's Nocturne" and "The Orchard Pit" are on inner truths, not those of nature.

The same generalization applies to Rossetti's endless portraits of women, for they, too, are fantasies or icons—images of the women who are the speaker's soul. Recent critical commentary has centered upon his numerous images of Beatrice, Mary, Magdalen, Lilith, Helen, Proserpine, and of the many faces of Venus. Most are described in the language of religion, displaced to explore the varieties of erotic love; many are painted enclosed or "embowered," staring out of their frames at the world, the viewer, or nothing in particular. All are marked by their enthralling hair (usually golden), their prominent lips, and by their eyes. Long before Jacques Lacan, Rossetti is aware of the power of the eye; one of his most frequently used words is "gaze." Interestingly, these iconic female figures, fraught with both desire and anxiety, appear in Rossetti's poetry even before they come to dominate his visual art.

In describing Da Vinci's Madonna in "Our Lady of the Rocks," one of the "Sonnets on Pictures" of 1847, Rossetti depicts an enclosed, inaccessible, female cult figure and describes her gaze—on the Child she holds. In the "Card Dealer" of 1849, another variety of gaze, that of the femme fatale, is fully delineated. "Could you not drink her gaze like wine?" inquires the male narrative voice. But although the awestruck speaker attempts to "search" the dealer's "secret brow," it is her eyes, not his, that "unravel the coiled night / And know the stars at noon," her eyes that control and mesmerize him, threatening to drain his soul.

This potent fatal woman, reminiscent of the Life-in-Death in Coleridge's "Ancient Mariner," is the progenitrix of a number of others. Lilith of "Eden Bower," the Siren of "The Orchard Pit," "Venus Verticordia" feed upon the faces of their male victims, just as masculine gazers, in other Rossetti poems, feed upon those of more passive, conventionally feminine subjects. More threatening to Rossetti than the overt stare of the female who does not perceive herself as object is the icon who refuses to look at the male subject at all, instead commanding him to look at her. In the sonnet "Body's Beauty" from *The House of Life*, for example, Lilith does not look out; she contemplates herself in a mirror, and, in making men stare at her, Medusa-like, she destroys them. The voice of the enigmatic sonnet "A Superscription," also from *The House of Life*, has the same potency and destructive force. Whispering like a deadly femme fatale, the voice orders the poet to "look in my Face," provoking his guilt and remorse. Yet most of Rossetti's female icons are not either the simple, potent nightmare images of anxiety discussed above or the mere objects of the male poet-painter's penetrating, dominating phallic gaze. There are, indeed, many of the latter, especially in *The House of Life*, but this might be expected. For the sonnet sequence is itself grounded in the Dantesque conventions of the power of the eye in engendering love and of the solitary, enclosed, unattainable woman—idealized and worshipped by a lover who dares not approach her.

Thus, the lady of "Her Gifts" and of "Genius in Beauty" is both created and contemplated by her poet-lover; she becomes an object of veneration. In the latter sonnet, the lady's beauty may be a form of genius, but it is the product of the lover who has painted it. The lady of "The Portrait," whose "face is made her shrine," is the most extreme case. She is the landscape the poet-painter is limning, as he depicts "the very sky and sea-line of her soul" and describes the expressive eyes he has created—that "remember and foresee." In an orgy of possession he reveals his sense of power: "They that would look on her must come to me."

The sexual politics of the gaze is shot through Rossetti's poetry (and painting), but it does not always function in binary oppositions; his male personae are not always active in contradistinction to passive females; or male voyeurs to female exhibitionists; or masculine subjects to feminine objects. And Rossetti's female icons are not always passive or masochistic. In "Bridal Birth" from the *House of Life* the Lady stands "at gaze" and smiles, becoming both the mother and creator of Love. In

"Soul's Beauty" the enthroned Lady's gaze strikes awe into her subordinated male viewer, while in "Mid-Rapture" it is the Lady's "summoning eyes" that both "shed dawn" and rule her worshipper's life: "What word can answer to thy word?" he asks,

—what gaze
To thine, which now absorbs within its sphere
My worshipping face, till I am mirrored there
Light-circled in a heaven of deep-drawn rays?

The Lady is empowered by her gaze, if only momentarily, for while her look absorbs her lover, he sees himself mirrored in her eyes. For Rossetti, the perfect moment of love is the moment of reciprocal gaze, and it occurs only rarely. The moment of passion may be commemorated—even monumentalized—in the sonnet, but it cannot be held.

Outside *The House of Life* the gaze of a woman can be even more potent, transcending the role of returning and confirming the glance of a male spectator. The "Blessed Damozel" has such a powerful look that her lover on earth—whose projection it may be—can feel her eye on him. Confined by the golden bar and barrier of heaven, she attempts to pierce the path of time and space visually. She succeeds, for, after having "gazed and listened," her "eyes prayed, and she smil'd." The power of her look is diminished only when, covering her face, she weeps. The power of "Astarte Syriaca"—the larger-than-life Syrian Venus in the sonnet that bears her name—never wanes. Endowed with "absolute eyes," she remains an "amulet, talisman, and oracle." A phallic figure before whom male worshippers can be subjected but content, she is seen, like the Virgin Mary in one of Rossetti's earliest sonnets, as a life force and a "mystery."

Significantly, Christina Rossetti is one of the best analysts of her brother's obsession with these female icons. "One face looks out from all his canvases," she reports in her posthumously published sonnet, "In an Artist's Studio." The one face is really no one's. What the male Rossetti writes about is not, in truth, a woman's face or gaze at all—it is an image of a symbol, "not as she is, but as she fills his dreams."

Yet Christina Rossetti, piercingly perceptive about others, is extraordinarily reticent about herself. Never "Queen of the Pre-Raphaelites," she nonetheless contributed richly to the *Germ* and published the first widely known and well-received Pre-Raphaelite volume, *Goblin Market*, in 1862. In several senses, however, she was a sister among the brothers, although she remained somewhat aloof from them. Framed by her own siblings (one of whom, William Michael, wrote and revised her life, the other of whom, Dante Gabriel, criticized and edited her poems), she still managed to maintain her own independence. Yet her first public appearances were mediated through Gabriel; she appeared not as a poet but as a subject, as the solemn girl Mary in Rossetti's *Girl-hood of Mary Virgin* (1848) and, one year later, as the reluctant Virgin of *Ecce Ancilla Domini*, shrinking from rather than welcoming her Annunciation. These two paintings suggest something of her paradoxical nature; in the first she is the artist, embroidering a lily from life, and keeping her eye firmly on its "truth to nature"; in the second she is the unwilling "chosen one," preferring quiet and obscurity to fame.

Christina Rossetti's own era considered her a Pre-Raphaelite. Swinburne, somewhat hyperbolically, called her the "Jael who led our hosts to victory"; other contemporaries saw her typological imagination, specificity, pictorialism, medievalizing, and intensity, as well as her truth to inner vision, as the essence of Pre-Raphaelitism. Even her religious or "devotional" poetry could be connected to the fervor and sacramental vision of Holman Hunt's paintings or John Ruskin's early prose. Like other Pre-Raphaelites, she is concerned with the religious, the erotic, and the poetic. The themes and subjects that engross her—frustrated love and the desire for death, the pain of loss and mutability, the fallen woman, the dead beloved, the structure of dream, the nature of art—were those shared by others in the movement.

Like her brother, she can create sharply outlined visual images or vivid pictorial effects when she so chooses. The dais of "A Birthday," hung "with vair and purple dyes" and carved in "doves and pomegranates, / And peacocks with a hundred eyes" is as opulent as any throne depicted in Gabriel Rossetti's "women and flower" paintings. Her pictorialism is full-blown and perfectly controlled in such images as the room in "After Death":

> The curtains were half drawn, the floor was swept
> > And strewn with rushes, rosemary and may
> > Lay thick upon the bed on which I lay.

Her skill in decoratively rendering medieval settings is clearly visible in such poems as "A Royal Princess," with its pictures of an ivory throne and an enclosed and "waiting" highborn maiden. The three women who sing of love together in "A Triad" are female icons perfect for a frieze or tapestry. Rossetti's observations of nature, especially of its small things and creatures, like "Shells quaint with curve, or spot, or spike, / Encrusted live things argus-eyed" in "By the Sea," are frequent and accurate. Yet, her primary interests do not lie in this area; her fascination is with worlds within and beyond the realm of nature. Confined, restrained, and private as her life may have been, reticent and passive as she may initially appear, Christina Rossetti has the wildest imagination among the Pre-Raphaelites.

The power and authority of that imagination is revealed in her many poems dealing with preternatural and supernatural events. The best known of these is "Goblin Market," with its fantastic "goblin-men" and its fusion of the folklore motifs of the fairy fair and fairy food and the themes of temptation, sacrifice, and regeneration. Yet her particular fascination is not with goblins but with ghosts—phenomena still within the realm of belief in her era—and is manifested in numerous ballads and narratives. These are of two varieties: ballads derived from Gothic and Romantic sources and those touched with religious or personal conviction. "The Hour and the Ghost," a demon-lover poem, "Moonshine," and "Lord Thomas and the fair Margaret," the ballad of a maiden whose pursuit of the ghost of her murdered lover leads to her own death, are of the first, more traditional order.

Other poems of the supernatural are more purposive, often showing revenants as visitors bringing messages fraught with meaning from the world of death. "The Poor Ghost," for example, rejected in death by the man who ostensibly loved her in life, recognizes the falseness of his mourning and departs content to sleep peacefully until the Second Coming. "The Ghost's Petition," a dialogue between a grieving widow and her newly departed husband, both explores the nature and realm of the dead and teaches the widow to let sleeping ghosts lie. "A Chilly Night" derives its impact not from the fact that ghosts appear to the lonely speaker, but from her failure to communicate with them. Alienated and despairing, she must sorrowfully conclude that "living had failed and dead had failed." Loss and death darken Rossetti's supernatural poems, yet the guise of the supernatural liberates her emotions and empowers her imagination.

Rossetti is not greatly concerned with external events or politics, although she writes a few political poems on events such as the Indian Mutiny and the Franco-Prussian War. Yet she is socially conscious, deeply involved with the condition of fallen women; in various guises, they populate her ballads and monologues. In "The Iniquity of the Fathers upon the Children," a dramatic monologue Gabriel did not wish her to publish, the lament of the illegitimate girl constitutes a challenge to social hypocrisy and Victorian convention. The cast-off women of the ballads "Cousin Kate" and "Maude Clare," the female persona of "An Apple-Gathering," and the stained maiden who seeks "The Convent Threshold" are poignant and memorable figures. Many of them, like Jeanie in "Goblin Market," who ate the fruits of carnal—and other—knowledge, and "who for joys brides hope to have / Fell sick and died" and the unwed mother of "Light Love," are ostensibly "sinners," but they are not morally judged. Rossetti blames "light" or fickle lovers of either sex, not those they seduce and abandon.

More sophisticated than many critics suggest, Christina Rossetti is acutely aware of the power of the gaze and of its relation to desire. Hence, in sonnet VIII of *Monna Innominata*, a sonnet sequence ostensibly composed by one of the unknown beloveds of a *stil nuovisti* male sonneteer, she informs readers that Queen Esther used her beauty to "snare" her royal husband's gaze, and thus to save her threatened people. In "Babylon the Great" she repeatedly cautions the faithful against looking upon the Whore of Babylon. "Gaze not upon her till thou dream her fair," she warns; "Gaze not upon her, lest thou be as she." In Rossetti's poetry it is primarily the evil or the flawed who stare. Even in the playful "Queen of Hearts" the female speaker who has "scanned" Flora with "a scrutinizing gaze" and kept a "lynx-eyed watch" on her rival is revealed as a jealous cheat. Yet, in "Goblin Market," Lizzie must learn to "listen and look," renouncing her blank and cloistered virtue, while Laura's gaze at goblin men is the beginning of her woe.

Moreover, Christina Rossetti dislikes being the object of the gaze and much prefers to see, herself invisible. Nonetheless, although she may wish to be like the woman in "A Portrait," who has "covered up her eyes / Lest they should gaze / On vanity," she is seriously addicted to peeping. In such poems as "At Home" and "After Death" she casts herself in the role of the revenant so that she may return unseen to view the earthly world she has left behind. Only the soul may gaze unblamed, and part of the appeal of death is that beyond its sleep, Rossetti believes, she will finally see "face to face."

With her own gaze turned heavenward—or her eyes averted—Christina Rossetti produces powerful poetry filled with visionary places and imaginary landscapes. Her religious convictions not only lead her to offer readers glimpses of paradise but of the earth below and sod above the grave. Her faith in what Jerome McGann calls "Soul Sleep" and others describe as a belief in an "intermediate abode,"—a mediating state between death and the Last Judgment in which the soul waits, often dreaming, until the final Advent—leads to reiterated descriptions of what the soul perceives in this condition. What the dead are doing underground, what they glimpse in the perpetual twilight of their intermediate abode, is one of her major concerns.

Rossetti typically employs dream visions, derived from medieval traditions, as well as the strategies of actual dreams. While in "Repining" and "A Ballad of Boding" the dream-vision form is used for overtly allegorical purposes, other dream poems are subtler. The dreamscapes of "The Dead City," the wasteland in "The Prince's Progress," the ghostly realm of "A Coast-Nightmare," derive their impact from the displacement, condensation, and symbolism of nightmare. Even Rossetti's ostensibly "natural" landscapes bear the heightened aura of dream; in "An Old-World Thicket," her version of Dante's *selva oscura*, intense visualization guides the poem's narrator to a new resolution and independence. The garden of earthly delights in the great dream poem "From House to Home" is like a Bosch painting in its detail; the dreamlike transformations of time, space, and image the garden undergoes are analogies to the mutability that mars the things of this world, the "house" of the poem.

But Rossetti's unique poetic traits are best revealed in poems such as "Cobwebs" (1855). This posthumously published sonnet about the terrain of an alternative world depicts "a land with neither night nor day, / Nor heat nor cold, nor any wind nor rain / Nor hills nor valleys." In a poem that uses "no," "nor," or "neither" twenty-one times in fourteen lines, readers are given a vivid description of a place by being told what it is *not*. We do not even know who proffers this riddle, for the poem is without an identifiable narrative voice. Yet a powerful nightmare image of a wasteland without life or change, without past or future, hope or fear emerges—as parallel structure, alliteration, and assonance fuse with monosyllabic words and subtle rhythmic variation to create a tour de force of negative description.

Many of Christina Rossetti's famous poems are shaped by negative description. "Life and Death" centers on what the female narrator will *not* feel, hear, or see when she is dead; what she will not experience or share forms the content of "Dream Land" and "Song" ("When I am dead, my dearest"). Part of Rossetti's essential reticence, these negative descriptions are one major element in the impenetrability or silence at the core of her poetry. Her repeated use of grammatically indefinite references is another. The word "it," in the poem "May," for example ("I cannot tell you how it was . . . I cannot tell you what it was") remains undefined; the same is true of the "it" of "Memory," and of several other lyrics. The density, mystery, and deliberate difficulty that her brother achieves through Latinate or polysyllabic language, personified abstracts, elaborate and ambiguous syntax, she achieves by seemingly transparent surfaces that mask a refusal to tell all.

Ultimately, silence joins the veiled look and the postponed desire as a hallmark of Christina Rossetti's poetry. A place marked by the "irresponsive silence of the land," in the first brilliant sonnet of "The Thread of Life," speaks softly but distinctly of the speaker's loneliness. In "Goblin Market" Lizzie triumphs by keeping her mouth shut. The silence of death is a happy "Golden Silence," and the silence of the grave in "Rest" is "more musical than any song." Remarkably, in pared-down sonnets and terse, stripped lyrics Christina Rossetti, eyes averted and lips sealed, creates memorable poetic effects.

To move from Christina Rossetti's poetry to that of William Morris seems, at first, to enter an entirely different world and to test the limits of literary Pre-Raphaelitism. However, closer examination reveals the poets' underlying similarities. Both dwell on frustrated love, on death, on loss and confinement. The blunt utterance and tough, vigorous, often irregular metrics of Morris's early poems veil his detachment and essential reticence; like Christina Rossetti, Morris does not tell his audience all.

Morris's first volume of poems, *The Defence of Guenevere* (1858)— the earliest Pre-Raphaelite volume in print—creates literally a Pre-Raphaelite world by taking its readers back to eras long before Raphael. Initially ignored or dismissed by critics who found it obscure and difficult—especially for those not immersed in Sir Thomas Malory's *Morte D'Arthur* or Jean Froissart's *Chronicle of the Hundred Years War*—it was later admired by a generation of "aesthetic" undergraduates. Significantly, it was dedicated to "Dante Gabriel Rossetti, Painter."

If one volume can be called the quintessence of Pre-Raphaelitism, it is the *Defence*. Filled with details rendered surreally clear, crowded with specific details that serve symbolic functions but often appear irrelevant or peculiarly foregrounded, it creates alternative worlds: those of the

Middle Ages, those of folklore and the supernatural, those of dream. What Dante is to Gabriel Rossetti, Malory and Froissart are to William Morris. Three of the first four and most famous poems in the volume—"The Defence of Guenevere," "King Arthur's Tomb," and "Sir Galahad: A Christmas Mystery"—are attempts at interpreting the texture and spirit of the *Morte D'Arthur*. Poems derived from the *Chronicle*, including "Sir Peter Harpdon's End," "Concerning Geffray Teste Noire," and "The Haystack in the Floods" depict Froissart's Middle Ages, a fifteenth-century epoch of blood, violence, and brutality. A third group of poems, including several that comment on Gabriel Rossetti's watercolors, create medievalized fantasy worlds, grounded in folklore or dream.

Yet the poems, despite their medievalized worlds, are Victorian and Pre-Raphaelite in their concerns: the plight of fallen women, the tensions between romantic passion and the marriage of convenience, political and social injustice, and the attempt to define both heroism and failure. Even the volume's interest in history, its appropriation of the past, is essentially typical of its era. The dramatic monologues and lyrics of Robert Browning, whom Morris then idolized, influence its forms, meters, and moral attitudes.

Honoring both Browning and Gabriel Rossetti, Morris creates painterly details and memorable images. These are often almost metaphysical in their combinations of unexpected elements. Rapunzel, in the poem that bears her name, sees from her tower a knight slain in battle; the blood from his wounds seems "like a line of poppies red / In the golden twilight. . . ." Alice de la Barde, in "Sir Peter Harpdon's End," dreams of sleeping amid the flowers of Avalon: "soft mice and small / Eating and creeping all about my feet." In "Golden Wings" an idyllic castle is so fully described that readers know that green moss grows only on the scarlet brick of its walls, while "yellow lichen [grows] on the stone." Although we are given the precise appearance of the swan-house in the castle moat, we never learn the cause of the castle's destruction or the nature of its destroyers.

Morris's elaborate detail is often symbolic; the mad Norse protagonist of "The Wind" finds, in an orange "with a deep gash cut in the rind," an analogy to the mutilated body of his beloved. Yet often particularity functions as it does in dream or painting—as rich, decorative, evocative, yet essentially untranslatable imagery. The *Defence* is replete with brightly colored pictures, like the rich watercolors Gabriel Rossetti was producing in the 1850s. La belle Marguerite, golden from tip to toe in "The Eve of Crecy," could be a figure in a Rossetti picture, as could the three ladies characterized by the colors they wear and the objects they hold—and posed like models—in "The Sailing of the Sword." "Near Avalon" might be an illumination in a medieval manuscript, a vignette of two small ships, one filled with gold-crowned fair ladies, the second with their sorrowing, lovesick knights. Like the good knight in prison in the poem of the same name, Morris

> paints with knitted brow,
> The flowers and all things one by one,
> From the snail on the wall to the setting sun.

The *Defence* volume is dominated by fallen women, on whom Morris reports without moralizing. If they have fallen because of love, if they are prepared to act and choose, Morris tends to see them as heroic. Fair Ellayne of the ballad "Welland River" is pregnant and careworn, but she wins readers' sympathies and her lover's by her honesty and wit. Guenevere, in "The Defence," repudiates all Victorian values; she considers chastity, responsibility, religious faith, and duty to marriage, country, and social station inferior to the commands of romantic love. Bought "by Arthur's great name and his little love," she will not permit herself to be "stone-cold for ever," because of "a little word [her marriage vow] / Scarce ever meant at all." Morris does not undercut Guenevere's attack on the marriage of convenience and defense of romantic passion; the only direct authorial comment in this long dramatic monologue stresses that the queen "spoke on bravely, glorious lady fair!" Jehane, the tragic protagonist of "The Haystack in the Floods," is clearly Robert's mistress; her moral act is refusing to be Godmar's. Even the whore who spits in Sir Lambert's face, in "Sir Peter Harpdon's End," is proved right; she has simply recognized him as a turncoat and collaborator with the French. Morris's later poems continue the nonjudgmental treatment of fallen women; Helen, in the unfinished "Scenes from the Fall of Troy" is as much victim as victimizer, and the adulterous wife of "The Pilgrims of Hope" (1881) is both sympathetic and heroic.

Blessed damozels, derived from Dante Gabriel Rossetti's, march close behind their fallen sisters. Sir Galahad, a much less mild youth than Tennyson's, is granted a vision of one of them in "The Chapel in Lyonesse." It is he, champion of heavenly love, who sees the reunion of Ozana le cure Hardy, Morris's "Fisher King," and his beloved in an erotic lovers' heaven. Galahad alone witnesses the blissful reunion as Ozana's wasted fingers twine

> Within the tresses of her hair
>   That shineth gloriously
> Thinly outspread in the clear air
>   Against the jasper sea.

The lady of "Summer Dawn" is also heavenly; in this sonnetlike poem praised by Walter Pater in "Aesthetic Poetry," the lady is implored to look *down* at her lover from the sky in which she appears to dwell.

The female figures in this volume are surprisingly assertive. Although there are conventional, beautiful, passive, iconic figures, imprisoned and awaiting rescue as in "Rapunzel" and "The Blue Closet," there are also portraits of active women. Female narrative voices utter a number of poems including "The Defence," "King Arthur's Tomb," and "The Sailing of the Sword." Women are depicted as questers; Jehane du Castel beau of "Golden Wings" dies in her search for her lover, but the lady of the imprisoned knight in "Spell-Bound" may, at least in his fantasy, rescue him. Female figures command the center of Morris's stage. Guenevere, actress and enchantress, uses her "great eyes" (often filled with tears in the course of her "Defence") as a lethal weapon. Utilizing sex, charm, charisma, and threats ("my eyes, / Wept all away to grey, may bring some sword / To drown you in your blood"), she forces her judges to gaze upon her and persuades her readers, if not King Arthur's knights, that her love is more important than her adultery.

In "King Arthur's Tomb," a dramatic dialogue of the last meeting between Lancelot and the queen, Guenevere's loss of power and vitality is signified by the fact that "her eyes did lack / Half her old glory. . . ." The torture of Jehane in "The Haystack in the Floods" is not only her choice between two horrors (becoming the mistress of a man she loathes or sacrificing her own and her lover's life), but in being forced to *see* the results of her refusal to capitulate. Watching her lover slaughtered before her eyes drives her, at least temporarily, insane. We are left with the powerful image of her stunned gaze.

Gabriel Rossetti's sexual politics of gaze is evident in poems by Morris like "Praise of My Lady" (also clearly influenced by Woolner's "My Beautiful Lady" in the *Germ*) in which a worshipping lover kneels before a medievalized cult image of his beloved. As he verbally and visually deconstructs her, he is caught by her "great eyes" which "gaze out very mournfully," but not at him. The Lady's eyes mirror her inaccessibility to her admirer; she remains enshrined and distant. To Morris, as to Gabriel Rossetti, reciprocal gaze marks the occasional moments of union and communication between lovers. (See, for example, the personal lyric "January" in *The Earthly Paradise*.)

Yet in the *Defence* volume Morris's own gaze is intense to the point of scoptophilia. Poem after poem is filled with sharply visualized scenes of sex, blood, and death. Jehane, threatened by the sadistic Godmar with a witchcraft trial, is promised "An end that few men would forget, / that saw it—"; John of Castel Neuf has a gaze so intense that it clothes, reanimates, and causes him to fall in love with the bones of a dead woman. The accounts and sights of violence are heightened by the tone in which they are related; often the narrative voice is cool, factual, unimpassioned. Morris presents horrors in an agressively impersonal way.

As in *Goblin Market*, a sense of mystery, incompleteness, and melancholy broods over the *Defence* volume. Not carelessness (as some critics insist) but a desire to recapture the dramatic quality of the folk ballad leads Morris to withhold information from his audience. Jehane in "Golden Wings" and Margaret in "The Wind" are suddenly and senselessly murdered; readers cannot be certain who has killed them or why. We never learn why the male narrators of "Spell-Bound" and "In Prison" are imprisoned, nor who holds them in bondage. "The Tune of Seven Towers" and "The Blue Closet," the two fantasy poems based on watercolors Morris had purchased from Gabriel Rossetti, carry the element of mystery to its zenith. Each poem is a commentary on, rather than an illustration of, the picture that is its source, and in each case Morris turns Rossetti's visual detail into symbolic narrative. He locates sinister subtexts in Rossetti's brilliantly colored, claustrophobic pictures and creates verbal correlatives to them.

In "The Tune of Seven Towers" a lady seated at a medieval instrument in the watercolor is transformed into a femme fatale, while the towers, depicted on the banner that cuts diagonally across the painting, become the haunted place to which she sends her lover. Readers never learn the lady's motives nor—although the poem hints at death—the final outcome of the lover's quest. In the more complex "Blue Closet" Morris turns a conventional Rossettian composition of four medieval ladies, two singing and two playing instruments, into a supernatural narrative of imprisoned maidens and a demon lover. Locked in a tower, Morris's ladies are trapped by a mysterious "they" who permit them to sing one song on Christmas Eve. The song summons Lady Louise's dead lover; he, too, is imprisoned by a mysterious "she," a mermaid or siren who keeps him under the sea. As a red lily (in the foreground of the painting) shoots up "from the land of the dead," the metamorphosed lover invades the world of the living and leads the ladies to death.

In his 1868 review "Poems by William Morris," reprinted as "Aesthetic Poetry," Walter Pater described the volume as lit by "dreamlight." Eight of the poems contain or allude to dreams, while, in others, dream becomes an important structural device. Connections of time, place, and event are missing; relations between cause and effect are absent; the fragmentation and hyperclarity of dream pervade numerous poems ranging from "Rapunzel," "King Arthur's Tomb," and "The Wind" to minor lyrics like "The Gillyflower of Gold."

Morris never recaptures the intense tone of the *Defence* volume, but Pre-Raphaelite themes and strategies survive in later works. *Love is Enough* (1871), an elaborate medieval morality play, is really "Rapunzel" rewritten and enlarged. *Poems By the Way* (1881) contains numerous poems of fantasy and supernaturalism; here, however, they are translations from or retellings of Scandinavian materials.

In Morris's two long, Chaucerian narratives, *The Life and Death of Jason* (1867) and *The Earthly Paradise* (1868–1869), painting yields to design; the two-dimensional quality of these poems, although loved by the Victorians, has not made them popular in our own time. *Jason*, loosely modeled on the *Argonautica* of Apollonius of Rhodes, is a medievalized, fanciful retelling of the Hellenistic Greek epic of Jason and Medea. *The Earthly Paradise* is an examination of the loss of Eden; it is filled with distant settings, tableaux of figures set in wastelands or gardens, and flat, externally characterized heroes and lovers. The volumes comprise twenty-four tales drawn from Greek and medieval sources. Arranged by a concept of seasonal progression, the tales, like patterns in a carpet, repeat with variations the conventional Pre-Raphaelite themes of love and loss, of heroism and failure, of the fact of mutability and the desire for permanence.

However, embedded in *The Earthly Paradise* are powerful and personal love lyrics, not unlike the sonnets of Gabriel Rossetti's *House of Life*. In a series of poems to the months, a narrator speaks of seasonal and human change, of the decline and death of love, of faint hopes for its rebirth or fulfilment. Melancholy but not static, these lyrics are poignant in their accounts of alienation, of "love left unloved alone." They are Pre-Raphaelite in their carefully observed, specific, and often symbolic images of nature, in their fusion of the concrete and the abstract, in the intensity of their analysis of passion.

When he turned to the Muse of the North in his last major poem, *The Story of Sigurd the Volsung* (1876), Morris left the Pre-Raphaelite fold, though only briefly. Ironically, *Sigurd* rather than *Jason* best represents what Pater saw as Morris's progression from "dreamlight" to "daylight." *Sigurd* contains the "simple elementary passions—anger, desire, regret, pity, and fear and what corresponds to them in the sensuous world—" that Pater found in *Jason*. And there is little reminiscent of either "brotherhood" in this direct, broadly limned epic; instead, Morris's Pre-Raphaelite impulses entered and transformed the long prose romances he began to write in the late 1880s. The energy and intensity of Morris's earlier work passed to an unlikely disciple, the young Algernon Charles Swinburne.

When Swinburne met Gabriel Rossetti, Burne-Jones, and Morris in 1857 and became part of "the Jovial Campaign"—the project to paint murals on Arthurian subjects in the Oxford Union—he also became an immediate if momentary Pre-Raphaelite. He was instantly attracted by Rossetti's contribution to the ill-fated scheme, a fresco on "Sir Launcelot's Vision of the Sanc Grail," and it became the visual source of his unfinished "Lancelot." Later, other Rossetti paintings would directly or obliquely inspire works in Swinburne's *Poems and Ballads*, First Series (1866), including "A Christmas Carol" and "A Ballad of Life."

For poetic inspiration, Swinburne turned to Morris; several of his early poems, including "Lancelot," are highly Morrisian in their meter, matter, and medievalism. Indeed, Swinburne's description of Guenevere, posed against an apple tree, offering Lancelot the fruits of temptation and obscuring his vision of the grail, could well be part of "King Arthur's Tomb." Even the language and form are imitative; we hear the cadence of "The Chapel in Lyonesse":

Lo, between me and the light
Grows a shadow on my sight
A soft shade from left to right,
Branched as a tree.

Furthermore, in his Arthurian "Queen Yseult," Swinburne treats Iseult as if she were Guenevere's sister. Resembling Morris's queen physically, Yseult also shares Guenevere's turbulent, defiant nature. Both she and Queen Blanchefleurs, Tristram's mother, choose love outside of marriage and fidelity to their lovers; Swinburne applauds their moral stance.

Swinburne's closely imitative phase lasted only momentarily; by the time of *Poems and Ballads* he had evolved his own Pre-Raphaelite vision. This also metamorphosed into a poetry different from that of his precursors, although bits of Pre-Raphaelitism remained to flavor his two long quasi-medieval Arthurian poems of later years, *Tristram of Lyonesse* (1882) and "The Tale of Balen" (1896). However, during the late 1850s and early 1860s Swinburne was indeed to be counted among the "fleshly school." While his characteristic form was the roundel rather than Gabriel Rossetti's sonnet or Christina Rossetti's songs or Morris's medievalized dramatic monologues, and while his pulsing meters were sometimes different from theirs, his images, many of his essential themes, and his poetic strategies were, like theirs, Pre-Raphaelite.

Only in his earliest works and in the first series of *Poems and Ballads* does Swinburne highly value specificity. Although perfectly capable of writing formalized, decorative Pre-Raphaelite narratives like "A Lay of Lilies," with its images of "five lilies growing on a hill" and five lilylike maidens "dwelling under it," he tends to intensify or invert the Pre-Raphaelite tendencies he inherits. Nature, for example, is seldom merely natural; few poems contain conventional landscape imagery. Even in "The Sundew," the carefully detailed description of the "little marsh-plant, yellow green, / And pricked at lip with tender red" functions to establish a symbolic register.

For the most part, Swinburne's eye is on the large forces of nature rather than on the three small cups of the Woodspurge. Yet *Poems and Ballads*, dramatic in that most of its poems are uttered by voices other than the poet's own, is filled with vividly pictorial emblematic figures. "Madonna Mia," Swinburne's version of Morris's "Praise of My Lady," is typical:

She has no more to wear
But one white hood of vair
Drawn over eyes and hair,
  Wrought with strange gold. . . .

The three men "garmented with gold" who form the entourage of the Lady of "A Ballad of Life," and the Lady herself, could be figures frozen in the space of a watercolor or tapestry; so, too, could be Queen Venus "with a hood striped gold and black" in "A Ballad of Life." What we have come to perceive as Pre-Raphaelite detail marks the description of the "graven images" of "A Cameo" or the catalogue that enumerates and dismembers Dolores, "Our Lady of Pain," or the features and garb of the mysterious harlot Aholibah, in the poem named after her.

Yet Swinburne's style is already evolving, beginning to stress the ear over the eye and to detach the word from the thing, breaking down accepted syntactical patterns and conventional word associations. Moreover, possibly influenced by Christina Rossetti, Swinburne has begun to use negative description to create powerful images and dreamscapes. "The Garden of Proserpine," for example, vividly depicts the winds that do not blow and the things that do not grow in the realm of death:

> No growth of moor or copice
> No heather-flower or vine,
> . . . .
> Pale beds of blowing rushes
> Where no leaf blooms or blushes.

The poem, reminiscent of "Dream Land," ends with the well-known enumeration of absent sights and sounds that, by their very absence, will create the desired "sleep eternal / In an eternal night."

Swinburne's decision to not merely *épater* but to stun *le bourgeois* with accounts of sadomasochism, necrophilia, bisexuality, and vampirism, makes the entire volume of *Poems and Ballads* political in the broadest sense of the word. In a narrower sense, political verses that look forward to *Songs Before Sunrise* (1871) inhabit the earlier volume. "A Song in Time of Revolution," with its Blakean and Shelleyan assault on priests and kings and its use of biblical rhetoric to discredit the Bible, and "A Song in Time of Order," its companion piece assaulting Napoleon III and the Pope, already evidence Swinburne's passion for Lady Liberty. Swinburne's rebellion against monarchies, pruderies, creeds, and God himself is well underway. Yet *Poems and Ballads* no longer contains verses on the marriage of convenience or on the fallen woman; the very concepts have begun to fade as Swinburne blurs the cultural distinctions between "good" and "evil" women.

Severed and frustrated love, the yearning for death, the preoccupation with failure are writ large in *Poems and Ballads* as are the legions of fatal women—active and passive—linked with these problems. Swinburne is fascinated by powerful matriarchal authority figures, and the numerous narrative voices (some identified, some not) that populate the volume reflect this preoccupation. He had already developed the fantasy of the dominant female figure in his earlier plays, most notably, in Althea, Meleager's mother in *Atalanta in Calydon* (1865). But in *Poems and Ballads* these "daughters of dreams and of stories" become goddesses—powers to be feared and worshipped. Nature is a Great and Terrible Mother, as is Death (in the form of Proserpine), the Sea (in "The Triumph of Time"), and even the force of Creation itself (a concept later developed in "Hertha").

Often described in the language of religion, like the infamous fatal women of "Dolores" and "Faustine," these female icons combine the power of the generatrix with that of the dominatrix of sadomasochistic lore. The role of the male is to prostrate himself before them. In a fascinating inversion of the Pre-Raphaelite tradition, male figures are now depicted as embowered or confined. Tannhauser in "Laus Veneris" is the love object, trapped in the bower of Venus; the scribe in "The Leper" (a poem for which Swinburne invents a medieval French source) is confined with the dead, leprous body of the aristocratic lady he has loved. Swinburne's rather passive male figures abase themselves before female icons so powerful that the men dare look at them only in dream or fantasy or when the ladies are asleep or dead.

Subtle voyeurism pervades the volume, yet, for the most part, eyes are designed for kissing or for weeping rather than for looking. Swinburne's emphasis is on the eyelid rather than the eye. Dolores, the perverse inversion of the Virgin Mother, has "hard eyes that grow soft for an hour," but they are even less accessible to her worshipper than the "Cold eyelids" that hide them. Other cult images: Cleopatra, Lucrezia Borgia, Venus, Aholibah, Faustine, and the twenty-two legendary "fair and foul" queens who appear in "The Masque of Queen Bersabe" seemingly lack eyes and are also not to be looked at; they often bind the eyes of their lovers/victims with their hair. Love is torture; the female beloved does not reciprocate nor does she even look at her adorer, although she may—as with Venus in "A Ballad of Death"—occasionally permit her worshipper to raise his eyes to her.

Gaze, in general, ceases to be significant, and only in "Anactoria," Swinburne's dramatic attempt to replicate the voice and spirit of Sappho, does it retain some of its power. Here the looks that pass between the two women are killing. The enraged, rejected Sappho finds that Anactoria's faithless blue eyes "blind" her; she yearns to make them bright with tears and torture. In a sadistic ecstasy she dreams of devouring them along with the rest of her former beloved. Sappho's own triumph will be that her gaze, the vision of the poet, will survive and become immortal. In a world without reciprocity or communication, ruled by an oppressive Judeo-Christian God and permeated by "the mystery of the cruelty of things," fulfilled love is impossible. The only refuge is in art or dream.

Dream landscapes and interiors—identified as such in the ballads of "Life" and "Death," or more subtly designated as in "The Garden of Proserpine"—permeate the lyrics, dramatic monologues, and narratives of the volume. At times, as in "Hesperia," the absence or vagueness of a specific background highlights the iconic images of the dreamer and the dream. Time is usually dream time—the shortened, extended, or frozen moment of the dream experience as in "A Ballad of Death," and "Laus Veneris"—and the speed of Swinburne's long anapestic and dactylic lines creates a mesmeric dream effect. The poems of *Poems and Ballads* imitate dream structure and language. Settings and figures change, coalesce, and appear and disappear; transitions between stanzas or sections are based on dream logic; logical progression is absent. Fragments of experience are presented but left mysterious (as in "August"); discontinuity becomes a poetic strategy.

Swinburne's style, based on private verbal associations, his use of incantatory repetition, mixed metaphors, modifiers detached from the nouns they ordinarily modify, fusions of concrete and abstract traits, heavy alliteration and assonance, all amplify the dreamlike effect of his poems. As in dream, the reader knows what is being said without being able to analyze the precise words that say it. Less concerned than Gabriel Rossetti and Morris with fidelity to the facts of external nature, less repressed than Christina Rossetti, Swinburne presents things as they appear to the eye and sound to the ear in sleep. Thus he creates works in which the gap between poetry and dream is closed, and the way to symbolism is further opened. Although Swinburne moved away from his Pre-Raphaelite faith toward a poetry of the ear and the indefinite, his Pre-Raphaelite tendencies meshed with those of the two Rossettis and Morris to become part of the lexicon of Victorian poetry.

The widening sphere of Pre-Raphaelite influence can be seen in the concentrated particularity of the poetry of Hopkins. Its effects are clearly visible in the decorated, fairy-haunted early poems of Yeats. Essentially, Pre-Raphaelitism broadened the realm of poetry and freed it from constraints imposed upon its themes and subjects. Moreover, it introduced new conventions of image and association, on which later poets would expand and against which our own era would, ironically, react.

Carole Silver

Further Reading

Bloom, Harold, ed. *The Pre-Raphaelites*. New York: Chelsea, 1986.

Hönnighausen, Lothar. *The Symbolist Tradition in English Literature: A Study of Pre-Raphaelitism and Fin de Siècle*. Translated by Gisela Hönnighausen. Cambridge: Cambridge University Press, 1988.

Hunt, John Dixon. *The Pre-Raphaelite Imagination, 1848–1900*. London: Routledge & Kegan Paul, 1968.

Lang, Cecil Y., ed. *The Pre-Raphaelites and Their Circle*. 2d ed. Boston: Houghton Mifflin, 1975.

McGann, Jerome J. "The Religious Poetry of Christina Rossetti," *Critical Inquiry* 10 (1983): 127–144.

Rees, Joan. *The Poetry of Dante Gabriel Rossetti: Modes of Self-Expression*. New York: Cambridge University Press, 1981.

Riede, David G. *Swinburne: A Study of Romantic Mythmaking*. Charlottesville: University Press of Virginia, 1978.

Rosenblum, Dolores. *Christina Rossetti: The Poetry of Endurance*. Carbondale: Southern Illinois University Press, 1986.

Sambrook, James, ed. *Pre-Raphaelitism: A Collection of Essays*. Chicago: University of Chicago Press, 1974.

Silver, Carole. *The Romance of William Morris*. Athens: Ohio University Press, 1982.

The 1890s

Continuities of Victorianism

ALTHOUGH the 1890s have often been called the "Decadent Nineties," the continuities of Victorianism were predominant in late-nineteenth-century poetry. And although fiction had become more widely read in Victorian households, a poem was still regarded as the noble expression of moral vision, an inspiring and comforting depiction of nature's wonders, and a source of insight into the social, political, and religious preoccupations of the age. The monarch's appointment of the poet laureate was, after all, an acknowledgment of the traditional idea that the poet, as sage and visionary, expressed the conscience and mission of the nation.

Many Victorians had been witness to two of the greatest laureates in the history of British poetry—Wordsworth and Tennyson—whose prominence during the early years of Victoria's reign reinforced earlier Romantic self-exploration as the means of discovering universal truths. Increasingly, however, Victorian social and religious values modified such subjectivity. The evangelistic fervor that permeated the age justified a divinely sanctioned view of Britain's destiny as civilizer of the world. Moreover, scientific discovery and the new, rationalistic approach to biblical study questioned religious dogma, increasingly undermined by doubt and pessimism as the century progressed.

At the threshold of the 1890s, when Tennyson's health became a major concern, William Watson emerged as a formidable contender for the laureateship. A critic at the time who later urged his appointment remarked that Watson was "all for orthodoxy, patriotism, England, home, and duty." Convinced that Milton and Wordsworth were central to England's poetic tradition, Watson had schooled himself in the grand rhetorical style, emphasizing clarity and epigrammatic force. In "The Sovereign Poet" he envisioned himself in the mantle of the poet as prophet who "sits above the clang and dust of Time, / With the world's secret trembling on his lip."

Watson's major poem, "Wordsworth's Grave," laments the decline of late-nineteenth-century poetry, echoing Wordsworth's own sonnet "London 1802" ("Milton! thou shouldst be living at this hour"). Britain, Watson insisted, was in urgent need of spiritual regeneration at a time of cultural decay, as indicated by contemporary poets who "bowed the knee / To misbegotten strange new gods of song"—an allusion to the literary Decadents, both French and domestic. Tennyson had condemned these "strange new gods of song" for their subversion of cultural unity: "Art for Art's sake! Hail, truest Lord of Hell!" Wordsworth, said Watson, provided the "gift of rest" by drawing strength from nature—unlike the self-obsessed Decadents, who celebrated the dark side of human experience, who employed a literary language at variance with common speech, and who rejected the Romantic worship of nature by trumpeting the superiority of artifice:

> No word-mosaic artificer, he sang
>   A lofty song of lowly weal and dole.
> Right from the heart, right to the heart it sprang,
>   Or from the soul leapt instant to the soul.

Such spontaneous, regenerative power as Wordsworth provided—uniting thought with feeling—was rarely found, said Watson, in late-nineteenth-century poetry:

> Where is the singer whose large notes and clear
>   Can heal, and arm, and plenish, and sustain?
> Lo, one with empty music floods the ear,
>   And one, the heart refreshing, tires the brain.

With the death of Tennyson in October 1892 Watson composed "Lacrimae Musarum," an elegy which, in its profusion of *l*s, produces an evocative incantation in mourning the laureate's end:

> Low, like another's, lies the laurelled head:
> The life that seemed a perfect song is o'er:
> Carry the last great bard to his last bed.

Land that he loved, thy noblest voice is mute.
Land that he loved, that loved him!

Deathless eternity is the appropriate resting place for such greatness, for "Him the eternal spring of fadeless fame / Crowns with no mortal flowers."

In identifying Tennyson with the forces of nature, Watson evokes parallels with Tennyson's own tribute to his close friend Arthur Hallam in *In Memoriam* and Milton's similar tribute to his drowned friend Edward King in "Lycidas." Watson's stately iambic pentameter lines provide appropriate rhythms for the profusion of monosyllables, gently invaded and rhythmically enhanced by polysyllables:

Seek him henceforward in the wind and sea,
In earth's and air's emotion or repose,
In every star's august serenity,
And in the rapture of the flaming rose.
And seek him if ye would not seek in vain,
There, in the rhythm and music of the Whole.

In the more than three years during which debates raged over who should be the new poet laureate, the name of Rudyard Kipling emerged as the "Laureate of the Empire," resulting from his depiction of those who served abroad with courage and desperation, if not always with honor. Indeed, to some, Kipling seemed an appropriate choice for the laureateship, since Tennyson had also written poems celebrating England's achievements in building the Empire, which covered approximately one-fourth of the earth's surface—stunning evidence to the social Darwinists that England was indeed the fittest of nations. But the poem that perhaps convinced Victoria's advisors *not* to recommend Kipling for the laureateship was "The Widow at Windsor," which, Robert Graves contended, "had earned Queen Victoria's anger." The speaker in Kipling's poem, a Cockney soldier, queries:

'Ave you 'eard o' the Widow at Windsor
With a hairy gold crown o'er head?
She 'as ships on the foam—she 'as millions at 'ome,
An' she pays us poor beggars in red.

The soldier alludes to "'alf o' Creation [that] she owns" and with splendid ambivalence, consisting of admiration and regret, concludes with two cheers for those who serve (and die for) the queen:

> Then 'ere's to the Sons o' the Widow,
>   Wherever, 'owever they roam.
> 'Ere's all they desire, an' if they require
>   A speedy return to their 'ome.
> (Poor beggars!—they'll never see 'ome!)

With such Cockney speech *Barrack-Room Ballads* (1892), which included "The Widow at Windsor" and which established Kipling's fame, at once celebrated and denigrated the British soldier in strikingly realistic poems. "Danny Deever," among the most notable of Kipling's figures, is "the Regiment's disgrace," who has shot a "comrade sleepin'." In focusing on the reactions by Danny's fellow soldiers to his hanging, the poem presents a narrator interpolating remarks between exchanges of dialogue, as in the opening:

> "What makes you look so white, so white?" said Files-on-Parade.
> "I'm dreadin' what I've got to watch," the Colour-Sergeant said.
>   For they're hangin' Danny Deever, you can hear the Dead March
>   play,
>   The regiment's in 'ollow square—they're hangin' him to-day.

The hanging, undescribed by Kipling, is witnessed by Files-on-Parade, who asks the Colour-Sergeant, "'What's that that whimpers over'ead?'" The response: "'It's Danny's soul that's passin' now.'" The reactions of the Colour-Sergeant and of the "shakin'" young recruits are presented without overt moralizing; rather, such responses mirror the stern but necessary rigors of military life. In "Tommy" the common British soldier learns with bitterness of the hypocrisy evoked by his uniform: "I went into a public-'ouse to get a pint o' beer, / The publican 'e up an' sez, 'We serve no red-coats here.'" Kipling's conviction that such British "'eroes" are merely flawed human beings emerges in Tommy's lines: "if sometimes our conduck isn't all your fancy paints, / Why, single men in barracks don't grow into plaster saints." And "it's 'Saviour of 'is country' when the guns begin to shoot," but "Tommy ain't a bloomin' fool—you bet that Tommy sees!"

The musicality of Kipling's verse has attracted composers to set it to song, as in "Mandalay," once a favorite in the concert halls:

> On the road to Mandalay,
> Where the flyin'-fishes play,
> An' the dawn comes up like thunder outer China 'crost the Bay!

Although the temple-bells urge, "Come you back, you British soldier; come you back to Mandalay!" the image of a Burmese girl "a-wastin' Christian kisses on an 'eathen idol's foot," a "bloomin' idol made o' mud," expresses the ignorance—and, it has often been said, the racist attitudes—of the British soldier in foreign lands. The speaker, however, "sick o' wastin' leather on these gritty pavin'-stones, / An' the blasted Henglish drizzle [that] wakes the fever in my bones," has "a neater, sweeter maiden in a cleaner, greener land! / On the road to Mandalay." There, the Ten Commandments do not exist, he reminds himself: the romantic lure of a more primitive world free of industrialism and puritan morality propels the speaker's desire to return.

In 1897, for Victoria's celebration of her sixtieth year as queen, Kipling composed his famous "Recessional" (following the form of a hymn sung when the clergy and choir retire from the chancel to the vestry after services), which cautions Britons against pride in imperialistic power:

> God of our fathers, known of old,
>   Lord of our far-flung battle-line,
> Beneath whose awful Hand we hold
>   Dominion over palm and pine. . . .

Allusions to Nineveh and Tyre, ancient cities no longer standing, provide a warning that the Empire itself could meet a similar fate, a possibility that haunted late-nineteenth-century Victorians:

> Lo, all our pomp of yesterday
>   Is one with Nineveh and Tyre!
> Judge of the Nations, spare us yet,
> Lest we forget—lest we forget!

The poem's deflation of British complacency in imperialist achievements grows in intensity as four stanzas end with the foreboding refrain "Lest we forget," the final stanza ending: "Thy mercy on Thy People, Lord!"—a curious conclusion to a poem celebrating the queen's Diamond Jubilee.

At the same time, Kipling's vision of empire includes notions of self-imposed responsibility and of noble endeavors that test national character. "The White Man's Burden," written after the American occupation of the Philippines during the Spanish-American War (1898), and whose message soon became a basic premise of Western imperialism, urges the United States to send "forth the best ye breed" and to assume the burden of governing a race unable to govern itself:

> Take up the White Man's burden—
>   The savage wars of peace—
> Fill full the mouth of Famine
>   And bid the sickness cease;
> And when your goal is nearest
>   The end for others sought,
> Watch Sloth and heathen Folly
>   Bring all your hope to nought.

Providing humanitarian aid and enlightenment to the "heathens" despite their possible ingratitude ("The hate of those ye guard") is the true test of the dominant nation's "manhood / Through all the thankless years."

In addition to Kipling, William Ernest Henley, editor of the *Scots Observer: An Imperial Review*, provided a strong voice as journalist and poet in support of British adventures abroad. With his Tory imperialism evoking visions of greatness, Henley sang the glories of muscular achievement and of the indomitable will in his "Invictus," which celebrates the "unconquerable soul." Despite his "bloody but unbowed" head, the speaker declares: "I am the master of my fate: / I am the captain of my soul." Henley's *Song of the Sword* (1892), whose title poem is dedicated to Kipling, invests the sword with symbolic significance in a fusion of religious activism and social Darwinism:

> Sifting the nations,
> The slag from the metal,
> The waste and the weak
> From the fit and the strong
>
> . . . .
> I am the Will of God:
> I am the Sword.

"Pro Rege Nostro," another of Henley's stirring imperialist-oriented poems, affirms England's divine destiny:

> With your glorious eyes austere,
> As the Lord were walking near,
> Whispering terrible things and dear
>   As the Song on your bugles blown, England—
>   Round the world on your bugles blown!

Even the "watchful sun" cannot match the "master-work you've done, / England, my own." With full trust in England's moral probity the speaker affirms his willingness to sacrifice himself for the greater glory of England: "'Take and break us: we are yours, / England, my own!'" Kipling and Henley were by no means the only poets writing such patriotic verse: they were merely the best known. At the time, a critic observed "a tendency among contemporary verse-writers to return to martial and inspiriting themes, and especially the glories of England."

Less concerned with the fortunes of the Empire, Robert Bridges pursued his quest for beauty, convinced that poetry was "non-moral"—that is, "only in so far as we take morals to mean the conventional code of conduct recognised by society." He was convinced, like most Victorian poets, that "pure ethics is man's moral beauty and can no more be dissociated from Art than any other kind of beauty, and, being man's highest beauty, it has the very first claim to recognition." Bridges consequently had no sympathy with the fin-de-siècle Aesthetes and Decadents, who advocated the exclusion from art of political, religious, and philosophical discourse (although he often excluded such elements in his own verse). He maintained a lifelong conviction that the aim of art was to create beauty—which involved the "satisfaction of form, the magic of speech, lying as it seemed to me in the masterly control of the material" beauty being "the highest of all those occult influences / . . . that thru' the sense / wakeneth spiritual emotion in the mind of man."

One of Bridges's best-known poems, "London Snow," combines the Victorian fascination with the city with the Romantic vision of nature—the varying rhythms of its lines move as though in synchrony with the falling snow. For a number of years Bridges had experimented with varied stresses within lines, which he called "stress prosody" (his friend Gerard Manley Hopkins called this metrical device "sprung rhythm," which contains an irregular distribution of stresses per line). Bridges's "London Snow" provides an example of what he regarded as a significant revolution in English metrics, whereas the poem itself presents familiar subject matter and imagery with the precision of objective detail:

> When men were all asleep the snow came flying,
> In large white flakes falling on the city brown,
> Stealthily and perpetually setting and loosely lying,
>   Hushing the latest traffic of the drowsy town;
> Deadening, muffling, stifling its murmurs failing. . . .

The schoolboys, "peering up from under the white-mossed wonder," exclaim: "'O look at the trees!'. . .'O look at the trees!'"—nature's spectral presence in the midst of the snow-covered city.

Bridges's "Nightingales"—its subject recalling Keats's singing bird—is another example of "stress prosody." The speaker asks where the "starry woods" are in which these birds learn their song: "O might I wander there, / Among the flowers, which in that heavenly air / Bloom the year long!" The nightingales, however, do not come from beautiful mountains and fruitful valleys but pour their "dark nocturnal secret" of desire into the "raptured ear of men" amid barren mountains and spent streams—the intimate relationship between man and nature affirming Romantic/Victorian continuities.

Like Bridges (and indeed most artists), Oscar Wilde was also preoccupied with beauty, but he preferred it divorced from overt moralizing. Although he welcomed fame as the leading fin-de-siècle Aesthete, his early poetry—dating from the 1870s—was filled with political and religious preoccupations commonplace in Victorian verse. Progressively, however, he attempted (although without complete success) to purge such discourse from his work in order to stress art's autonomy. Written after his release from prison, however, Wilde's *Ballad of Reading Gaol* expresses a renewed reformist zeal, although he insisted that the poem contained more than mere social protest.

Employing a modified form of the traditional ballad, Wilde portrays the inhuman conditions of Reading Prison and the indifference of those charged with the prisoners' care ("The Doctor said that Death was but / a scientific fact: / And twice a day the Chaplain called, / And left a little tract"). Although Wilde focuses on the reactions of the inmates to the hanging of a murderer, the personal allusions in the poem are obvious—"For each man kills the thing he loves" alludes not only to the guardsman's slaying of his wife but also to Wilde's reckless destruction of his own life and career. Indeed, at one point, he identifies himself as the narrator by punning on his own name and alluding to his double life: that of the acclaimed married writer violating the law against homosexuality:

And the wild regrets, and the bloody sweats,
    None knew so well as I:
For he who lives more lives than one
    More deaths than one must die.

Although Wilde conceded that his ballad suffered from "a divided aim in style"—"some is realistic, some is romantic: some poetry, some propaganda"—it remains his most powerfully didactic poem.

With the outbreak of the Boer War (1899–1902) poets produced a considerable body of patriotic poetry reminiscent of Tennyson's poetic effusions in previous British conflicts. The day following the initial attack by the Boers on October 12, 1899, Swinburne published his overwrought poem "The Transvaal," which calls the Boers "dogs, agape with jaws afoam" and urges, "Strike, England, and strike home!" Alfred Austin—the poet laureate who had succeeded Tennyson—published "Inflexible as Fate" as a reminder that the Roman Empire had also been attacked by barbarians: "Not less resolved than Rome, now England stands, / Facing foul fortune with unfaltering hands." When the Boers achieved dramatic victories in the first few months, Henley published "Remonstrance," raising the question: "Where is our ancient pride of heart?" Urging, "Rise, England, rise!" he borrows Swinburne's line from "The Transvaal": "Strike, England, and strike home!"

Although such mediocre patriotic verse no doubt aroused the appropriate responses from Britons disheartened over the progress of the war, a body of poems also appeared that discreetly focused on the war's consequences without overtly condemning Britain's moral position. Perhaps the most notable of these was Thomas Hardy's "Drummer Hodge" (originally entitled "The Dead Drummer"). A young farm boy, whose body was thrown "to rest / Uncoffined—just as found," never understood why he was sent to South Africa. On that "unknown plain / Will Hodge forever be," the poem concludes, "And strange-eyed constellations reign / His stars eternally."

Like Hardy's tribute to a senseless death, Austin Dobson's "Rank and File" celebrates those whose identity and sacrifice remain unknown:

> for you
> I mourn—I weep,
> O Undistinguished Dead!
> None knows your name.

In "Midnight—31st of December, 1900" Stephen Phillips depicts the Lord pronouncing judgment on the past century, the poet's method of condemning jingoist patriotism that had led to war: "I will make of your warfare a terrible thing, / A thing impossible, vain. . . ." In the final

months of the war Kipling's "Islanders" attacked British sloth and pleasure seeking at home while soldiers from the Empire were being sacrificed in South Africa: "Ye set your leisure before their toil and your lusts
above their need." Public reaction to the poem overwhelmingly
endorsed Kipling's view, one that continued to trouble the Edwardians.
Nevertheless, when the seemingly interminable conflict with the Boers
ended, Robert Bridges published "Peace Ode: On Conclusion of the
Boer War, June, 1902," a poem eminently appropriate for the future
poet laureate:

> Now joy in all hearts with happy auguries,
> And praise on all lips: for sunny June cometh
>   Chasing the thick warcloud, that outspread
>   Sulfurious and sullen over England.

The Roman Catholic Revival

The Romanticism of much Victorian verse was often associated with
the revival of Roman Catholicism (its symbolism and iconography
employed, for example, in the verse and painting of the Pre-Raphaelite
Dante Gabriel Rossetti). The widespread number of conversions, particularly among intellectuals and artists, owed some of its energy to the
Oxford Movement of the 1830s and 1840s, when those in the Anglican
church (notably John Henry Newman, who converted in 1845) reacted
to the liberalism among clerics by advocating the adoption of elaborate
ritualism and of theological views consistent with those of Roman
Catholicism. In addition, the impact of scientific discovery and the biblical higher criticism from the Continent had disturbed many who
sought the ancient authority of the orthodox church as a bulwark
against doubt and despair. The belief that the apostolic succession provided reliable authority to Catholic dogma convinced converts that liberal Anglicanism lacked conviction. Progressively, Catholic poets followed the lead of the Tractarians in the Oxford Movement, who
believed that poetry—particularly Romantic poetry—was essentially
religious in its intense yearning for God. In their own verse, poets such
as the convert Gerard Manley Hopkins employed the language and
imagery of sacramental ritualism as well as ancient hymns and prayers.
By embracing the "old faith" that England had abandoned, Catholic
poets acquired an enriched symbology for their art and a new spiritual
challenge for the soul.

Like other converts, Alice Meynell remarked that she, too, "returned to the hard old common path of submission and self-discipline which soon brought [her] to the gates of the Catholic Church." In "The Young Neophyte" she wonders: "Who knows what days I answer for to-day?" Nevertheless, she bends her "feeble knees" and prays: "I light the tapers at my head and feet, / And lay the crucifix on this silent heart." Despite such submission she questions God's dispensation in "Veni Creator," her reaction to the death of her five-month-old son:

> For we endure the tender pain of pardon:
> One with another we forbear. Give heed,
> Look at the mournful world Thou hast decreed.
> The time has come. . . .
>   Lord of Heaven,
> Come to our ignorant hearts and be forgiven.

The irony is implicit: the Lord must be forgiven by "ignorant hearts," which do not reject faith but which require confirmation of God's goodness. In "Christ in the Universe," however, the ultimate significance of Jesus' sacrifice is concisely presented within the ambiguous framework of earthly existence:

> With this ambiguous earth
> His dealings have been told us. These abide:
> The signal to a maid, the human birth,
> The lesson, and the young Man crucified.

Such simplicity of diction implies the clarity and directness of God's intent despite human ignorance: "None knows the secret, cherished, perilous, / The terrible, shamefast, frightened, whispered, sweet, / Heart-shattering secret of His way with us." In "The Crucifixion" Meynell contrasts mere human suffering—"Oh, man's capacity for spiritual sorrow"—with the divine drama involving the incarnated Son of God: "Man's human Lord / Touched the extreme."

Without the aid of Alice Meynell (and her journalist husband, Wilfrid) Francis Thompson, an opium addict who lived the life of a derelict on the London streets, might have perished from his addiction in the 1880s before writing his major poem, "The Hound of Heaven." Having been raised by parents who converted to Roman Catholicism and having planned to become a priest, Thompson dramatizes in "The Hound of Heaven" the spiritual terror with which the believer reacts to God's pursuit of his soul. Among the major influences on the poem are St. Augustine's *Confessions*, which depicts the flight from God as a central trope, and the poems of Richard Crashaw, among other seventeenth-century Metaphysical poets. Thompson's startling conceit—involving the pursuing hound as metaphor for God—suggests the speaker's irrational flight from the very source of his salvation:

> I fled Him, down the nights and down the days;
>   I fled Him, down the arches of the years;
> I fled Him, down the labyrinthine ways
>   Of my own mind; and in the mist of tears
> I hid from Him, and under running laughter.

In a parenthetic aside the speaker reveals his paradoxical spiritual state: "(For, though I knew His love Who followed, / Yet was I sore adread / Lest, having Him, I must have naught beside)." This "tremendous Lover" is too overwhelming for the speaker's spiritual frailty. His flight from divinity becomes a quest for a less-demanding reality, the constant shifts in meter, from the five iambic stresses to three, suggesting the speaker's spiritual turmoil. Only when he is overtaken by the Hound does he acknowledge that he is "of all man's clotted clay the dingiest clot." Then Heaven's voice is heard: "Rise, clasp My hand, and come." But the hand is not grasped by the speaker, whose gloom implies doubt of achieving salvation. The impatient, loving voice concludes the poem but not without final ironies: "Ah, fondest, blindest, weakest, / I am He Whom thou seekest! / Thou dravest love from thee, who dravest Me." The poet, critic, and Catholic convert Coventry Patmore has written that, by such a poem as "The Hound of Heaven," Thompson placed himself "in the front rank of the [Catholic] movement, which, if it be not checked as in the history of the world it has once or twice been checked before . . . , must end in creating a 'new heaven and a new earth.'"

The movement also touched two poets whom Thompson met at a meeting of the Rhymers' Club, Lionel Johnson and Ernest Dowson—both converts in 1891—whose verse, in part, also reflects the desire for a new heaven and earth. To suggest his ecclesiastical preoccupations, Johnson gave Latin titles to a number of his poems. "Te Martyrdum Candidatus," a rousing poem on the Church Militant, depicts "the fair chivalry," the "companions of Christ! / White Horsemen, who ride on white horses, the Knights of God!" And characteristic of Catholic Revival verse, the poem's focus is on the ritual of crucifixion: "They saw with their eyes the Eyes of the Crucified," who inspires the White Horsemen—"with Christ their Captain"—to endure martyrdom and achieve triumph within the communion of saints. Like Hopkins, who perceives nature as a mirror of divinity (the Romantic inheritance that informs Tractarian verse), Johnson in "Pax Christi" celebrates the paradox of the world that "fails," for the "glory of the rose" is a manifestation of divine beauty: "I / Know, that from mortal to immortal goes / Beauty: in triumph can the whole world die."

Two of Johnson's best-known poems express his spiritual despair and yearning for deliverance: "Mystic and Cavalier" ("Priests of a fearful sacrament! I come, / To make with you mine home") and "The Dark Angel," which allegorizes his struggle with forbidden desire (critics intimate Johnson's homoeroticism): "Dark Angel, with thine aching lust / To rid the world of penitence." The "dark Paraclete" (a transformation of the Holy Spirit as advocate into a destructive demon) turns the "gracious Muses" to Furies: "And all the things of beauty burn / With flames of evil ecstasy." Resistance to such tempting evil ("I fight thee, in the Holy Name!") concludes the poem:

> Do what thou wilt, thou shalt not so,
> Dark Angel! triumph over me:
> *Lonely, unto the Lone I go;*
> *Divine, to the Divinity.*

Ernest Dowson, who converted at Johnson's urging, gradually drifted from the Church as his family life deteriorated (both parents committed suicide in 1894). In his quest for solace in a fallen world he envisions the nuns, in "Nuns of the Perpetual Adoration," as isolated "behind high convent walls":

> They heed not time; their nights and days they make
>   Into a long, returning rosary,
> Whereon their lives are threaded for Christ's sake;
>   Meekness and vigilance and chastity.

The world outside is "wild and passionate; / Man's weary laughter and his sick despair / Entreat at their impenetrable gate," but "Mary's sweet Star dispels for them the night," for "beside the altar, there, is rest." The turmoil of Dowson's life, complicated by alcoholism, depression, and the need for spiritual retreat, provides the subtext for this conventional vision of the nuns' existence.

In "Extreme Unction," dedicated to Lionel Johnson, Dowson depicts the ritual of the "atoning oil" and its "renewal of lost innocence." The "Vials of mercy! Sacring oil!" provide confirmation of hope as death nears, for as the "walls of flesh grow weak. . . . / Through mist and darkness, light will break, / And each anointed sense will see." Yet in "Song of the XIXth Century" (probably written after his parents' death but unpublished in his lifetime) Dowson expresses the doubt common among Victorians: "O give us faith—/ In God, Man, anything to rise and break / The mists of doubt."

Aside from the publication of *Silverpoints* (1893)—a volume noted for its Decadent motifs and "imitations" of French Symbolist verse—the convert John Gray, who met Johnson and Dowson at meetings of the Rhymers' Club, also wrote religious poems in the 1890s, most notably those in *Spiritual Poems* (1896). In poems to the Blessed Virgin, St. Thomas Aquinas, and St. John of the Cross, Gray (the homoerotic poet, soon-to-be chaste priest) concludes with "Paul Verlaine" (Gray had imitated Verlaine's "Parsifal" in *Silverpoints*). The recently deceased Symbolist/Decadent French poet had turned to the Catholicism of his youth when he wrote religious verse while imprisoned for shooting Arthur Rimbaud during a turbulent homosexual relationship. Gray's elegy for Verlaine is in effect a prayer (inspired by the phrase "Agnus Dei"—"Lamb of God"—intoned during the Mass), in which the cursed poet is the symbolic parallel of Christ—martyred outcast and sacrificial lamb: "God's Lamb, thou Saviour of us / God's Lamb, who tell'st us passing to our pen; / God's Lamb, have pity of us that we are but men."

Versions of Pastoral Pessimism

Much melancholy poetry in the 1890s expressed a yearning for a past age (historical or mythical) superior to the industrialized nineteenth century, or lamented the brevity of life (the resulting anguish associated with the loss of religious faith or the death of a loved one). Some poets, like Dowson, turned to Old French forms of verse, such as the villanelle (originally, a pastoral genre), in order to suggest a less complex world. The classical scholar A. E. Housman drew inspiration from the ancient form of the pastoral elegy and from the traditional

English ballad (in Housman, often consisting of a stanza of two rhyming couplets). In *A Shropshire Lad* (1896), his only volume of verse published in the nineties, Housman depicts what B. J. Leggett, in *Housman's Land of Lost Content*, has called the "uncomplicated country life, the longing for a return to the simple in the face of the increasing complexity of the problems of life and death." The elegiac tone of many of the poems, half of which have contemporary pastoral settings and half of which are set in London, reveals Housman's acute sense of transient existence, although often accompanied by the poet's ironic voice.

In "To an Athlete Dying Young" (no. XIX) Housman expresses his recurrent theme that an early death in one's prime—that moment of victory: "The Time you won your town the race / We chaired you through the market-place"—may be preferable to the loss of one's powers and the eclipse of one's achievement ("Eyes the shady night has shut / Cannot see the record cut"):

> Smart lad, to slip betimes away
> From fields where glory does not stay
> And early though the laurel grows
> It withers quicker than the rose.

As a major theme in the volume—the illusion of permanence in a world subject to change—the enduring image of the athlete dying young provides an ironic contrast to the withering laurel. A variation of this theme occurs in poem XVI (untitled), in which the permanence of death and the brief span of life are the poem's entire burden. Here, the nettle's symbolic dance of life—"It nods and curtseys and recovers / When the wind blows above"—occurs on the "graves of lovers / That hanged themselves for love." In the following stanza the man in the grave "does not move," in contrast to the recovering nettle. Nevertheless, the "lover of the grave" has achieved a state of permanent deliverance from the ravages of time.

In "Bredon Hill" (no. XXI) the progression of the seasons from summer to winter parallels the progression of youthful love to early death. When the lovers, lying on Bredon Hill, ignore the church bells calling them to prayer, the speaker interprets the ringing bells as an expression of their love:

> I would turn and answer
>   Among the springing thyme,

'Oh, peal upon our wedding,
  And we will hear the chime.'

But the chimes ironically become funeral bells for the lad summoned to
his death. The tone of the pastoral elegy is also prominent in poem
LIV, in which the speaker laments his loss:

With rue my heart is laden
  For golden friends I had,
For many a rose-lipt maiden
  And many a lightfoot lad.

In the following stanza Housman again envisions the grave as the permanent refuge from the impermanent world: the "lightfoot boys" and
the "rose-lipt girls" are sleeping while "roses fade." Indeed, the poem
itself—as artifact and illusion—preserves the enduring image of the
"golden friends."

Terence, the central persona of *A Shropshire Lad* (identified in no.
LXII), loses his innocence when he discovers that death threatens his
relationship with nature (nowhere in Housman is there a suggestion of
reassuring spiritual presences in nature, as in Wordsworth's "Ode: Intimations of Immortality"). Leggett suggests that "a gradual disintegration of [Terence's] initial harmony with the world around him . . . ends
finally in complete alienation"—the Modernist note in Housman. Terence's departure for London does not, however, end his elegiac yearning for lost innocence, associated with Shropshire:

And if my foot returns no more
To Teme nor Corve nor Severn shore,
Luck, my lads, be with you still
By falling stream and standing hill,
By chiming tower and whistering tree,
Men that made a man of me.
                    (no. XXXVII)

The recurrent symbolic wind in Housman (perhaps drawn from
Shelley's "Ode to the West Wind," where the wind is both preserver
and destroyer) suggests in poem XL the effect of the irretrievable past
on the Shropshire lad, who is resigned to his exile in London:

Into my heart an air that kills
  From yon far country blows

What are those blue remembered hills,
  What spires, what farms are those?

That is the land of lost content,
  I see it shining plain,
The happy highways where I went
  And cannot come again.

Unlike Housman, whose pastoral verse does not follow classical models in depicting shepherds and shepherdesses at leisure, Dowson employs a title from Virgil's tenth eclogue to suggest the source of his inspiration in "Soli cantare periti Arcades" ("Arcadians, alone gifted to sing"). The familiar landscape includes a vision of rustics "piping a frolic measure" and delineates the traditional contrast of town and country—"For the town is black and weary, / And I hate the London street." The speaker "will live in a dairy, / And its Colin I will be." Many of Dowson's pastoral poems, however, depict autumn, the approaching winter heralding the inevitability of oblivion. In "Autumnal" the love relationship is envisioned as "a twilight of the heart" briefly eluding time, but then the speaker muses: "Are we not better and at home / In dreamful Autumn, we who deem / No harvest joy is worth a dream?" Winter and night lie beyond the "pearled horizons," providing only a brief respite "Until love turn from us and die / Beneath the drear November trees." In "Amor Profanus" the speaker, invoking the traditional carpe diem theme, urges: "while life is ours, / Hoard not thy beauty rose and white, / But pluck the pretty, fleeting flowers." Far too soon, he laments, "we twain shall tread / The bitter pastures of the dead."

The Revolt of Aestheticism

In his 1862 review of Baudelaire's *Les Fleurs du mal* Swinburne argued that "a poet's business is presumably to write good verse, and by no means to redeem the age and remould society"—in short, he echoed what Théophile Gautier had publicized in his preface to *Mademoiselle de Maupin* (1835) as *l'art pour l'art* (art for art's sake). In *William Blake* (1866) Swinburne developed this view of poetry, suggestions of which had been voiced by Keats and Coleridge: "Handmaid of religion, exponent of duty, servant of fact, pioneer of morality, she cannot in any way become. . . . Her business is not to do good on other grounds, but to be

good on her own. . . . Art for art's sake first of all, and afterwards we
may suppose all the rest shall be added to her" (Swinburne here suggests
that any subject matter is suitable so long as it does not transform the
poem into an instrument of instruction or propaganda). This challenge
to the conventional Victorian aesthetic that art should provide moral
indoctrination was increasingly ridiculed in the 1870s and 1880s as an
effeminate devotion to beauty—by *Punch*'s satirical cartoons and skits,
by Gilbert and Sullivan's *Patience*, by Wilde's aesthetic costume pressed
into service on his lecture tour of America, and by Kipling's poem
"Mary Gloster," in which the dying shipowner, Sir Anthony Gloster,
says to his aesthetically inclined son: "For you muddled with books and
pictures, an' china an' etchin's an' fans, / And your rooms at college were
beastly—more like a whore's than a man's."

However, the serious Aesthetes, including Wilde, insisted that art
must be resuscitated from its fallen state as the handmaid of Victorian
pieties—whether religious, political, or social—and its outworn
rhetoric abandoned. In addition, they rejected the materialism and utilitarianism of those who congratulated themselves on the extraordinary
achievements of the British Empire. In the 1870s James Abbott
McNeill Whistler, who championed art's autonomy—although he
rejected any implication that he was an Aesthete—introduced a new
visionary style of painting in a series of works using "nocturne,"
"arrangement," and "symphony" in their titles. Such a focus on the
transposition of the arts as well as the elimination of anecdotes with
moral implications had been suggested by Gautier in his "Symphony in
White Major." (Walter Pater, a major influence on the fin-de-siècle
Aesthetes, proposed in his *Studies in the History of the Renaissance*, 1873:
"All art constantly aspires toward the condition of music"—that is, toward
the elimination of any distinction between the "matter" and the "form"
of art.) Wrote Whistler: "Art should be independent of all clap-trap—
should stand alone, and appeal to the artistic sense of eye or ear, without confounding this with emotions entirely foreign to it, as devotion,
pity, love, patriotism, and the like. . . ."

Whistler's flair for public exposure in the service of an autonomous
art deeply influenced many poets, among them Wilde, whose "Impression du Matin" suggests Whistlerian impressionism in the opening
lines, which borrow one of Whistler's titles and eliminate the poet's
presence: "The Thames nocturne of blue and gold / Changed to a Harmony in gray." Yet Wilde introduces the moralizing that Whistler had

avoided—a prostitute, a "pale woman all alone," loiters beneath the "gas-lamp's flare, / With lips of flame, and heart of stone." In the more successful "Symphony in Yellow" Wilde foreshadows later Imagism in clearly defined (perhaps un-Whistlerian) images and the absence of discourse, with a final image of the Thames: "And at my feet the pale green Thames / Lies like a rod of rippled jade."

Henley, generally scornful of the Aesthetes, was an admirer of Whistler, even naming four sections of *London Voluntaries* (1893) with musical terms and envisioning London as though a Whistler painting: "At night this City of Trees / Turns to a tryst of vague and strange / And monstrous Majesties." Arthur Symons also wrote three Whistler-inspired poems, entitled "Pastel," "Impression," and "Nocturne," the last evoking "The long Embankment with its lights / The pavement glittering with fallen rain / The magic and mystery that is night's." Likewise, Richard Le Gallienne's "Sunset in the City" captures similar magic: "Within the town the streets grow strange and haunted, / And, dark against the western lakes of green, / The buildings change to temples."

Following contemporary fashion, John Davidson—who, T. S. Eliot later said, "impressed me deeply in my formative years between the ages of sixteen and twenty"—wrote "Nocturne" and "Fog," the latter suggesting that "Doomsday somewhere dawns among / The systems and the galaxies" while we are "simply swallowed up / In London fog for evermore." In "Railway Stations: London Bridge" Davidson depicts a "human tide" flowing across the bridge "As callous as the glaciers that glide / A foot a day, but as a torrent swift." Such visions of London led the way to Modernist depictions of the modern world's spiritual deadness, as in T. S. Eliot's *Waste Land*: "Unreal City. . . . / A crowd flowed over London Bridge, so many, I had not thought death had . . . undone so many."

The use of the dance as trope was another method of eliminating intellectual discourse from art. In "The World as Ballet" Symons remarks of the dance: "Nothing is stated"; the dancer is "all pure symbol . . . and her rhythm reveals to you the soul of her imagined being." Frank Kermode has called the dance "the most perfect emblem" of the "Romantic Image," which fuses movement with stillness, form with content, body with soul "in a higher order of existence, largely independent of intention, and of any form of ethical utility." Such Symons poems as "La Mélinite: Moulin Rouge"—"Before the mirror's dance of shadows / She dances in a dream"—which Yeats called "one of the most perfect lyrics of our time," stimulated the use of the image in the nineties and, like the transposition of the arts, prepared the way for modernism, Yeats making brilliant use of the dance in his verse plays and poems, particularly later in "Among School Children."

Decadence and the Fin du Monde

In the preface to *The Picture of Dorian Gray* (1891) Wilde declares a central concept of nineteenth-century Aestheticism: "All art is quite useless," an antiutilitarian view of autonomous art also central to literary Decadence. In the novel, Wilde depicts Dorian's jaded sensibility as one that yearns for the end of the world, *fin du monde*: "Life is such a great disappointment"—the Decadent pose of *taedium vitae* that repudiates Victorian activism but later functions as the motive for Dorian's self-destruction. His wish to experience the beauty of evil, which underscores the homoerotic subtext of the novel, also convinced reviewers, despite Dorian's death at the end, that Wilde's work was decadent (its lowercase denoting, at the time, decline or degeneration; but capitalized, a new mode of expression and a precursor of modernism).

In *Silverpoints* John Gray's daring poem "The Barber" reveals the darker impulses and startling images associated with such Decadence. The speaker, dreaming that he is a barber—indeed, a Decadent artist—employs artifice in order to transcend nature by painting the eyebrows of "many a pleasant girl" and by placing gems on their thighs. Anticipating twentieth-century Surrealism, he experiences striking synesthetic effects: "My fingers bled / With wonder as I touched their awful limbs"—the result of his sexual exploration: "I moulded with my hands / The mobile breasts, the valley." In the final lines, however, nature achieves its supremacy over artifice, albeit farcically, as the barber discovers his own impotence ("the blood of me stood cold"): "The breasts rose up and offered each a mouth. / And on the belly pallid blushes crept, / That maddened me, until I laughed and wept."

While Aubrey Beardsley's reputation as a Decadent artist rests on his drawings of a bizarre imaginative world, he was also the author of "The Ballad of a Barber," undoubtedly influenced by Gray's poem. Beardsley's barber, like Gray's, is an artist in artifice, employing "powders, paints, and subtle dyes" as though following Baudelaire's essay "Praise of Cosmetics." The epicene barber typifies what nineties critics regarded as a characteristically decadent preference for ambiguous gender and sexuality: "nobody had seen him show / A preference for either sex." In attempting to curl the young Princess's hair, he undergoes a sudden loss of control: "His fingers lost their cunning quite, / His ivory combs obeyed no more." With a broken bottle he cuts her throat and leaves on "pointed feet; / Smiling that things had gone so well." To be sure, the barber's death by hanging satisfies Victorian moral sensibilities. As Jerome H. Buckley remarks in *The Victorian Temper*, Beardsley's poem was "surely intended to convey a complete allegory of Decadence itself through the tale of the artist-barber . . . whose amoral art for art's sake crumbled forever on the intrusion of insane desire."

The introduction of French Decadence into English poetry prompted Richard Le Gallienne—like William Watson before him—to launch a minor campaign against such foreign intrusions. Although, with his flowing hair and knee breeches, Le Gallienne looked like an Aesthete from Gilbert and Sullivan's *Patience*, he regarded Decadence as a Gallic threat to British culture. In his introductory poem to *English Poems* (1892) he charges that the sound of the English nightingale ("that for six hundred years / Sang to the world") has been usurped by the "new voice" (associated with the symbol of Decadence, the artificial green carnation, which Wilde and his friends wore on occasion to the theater and which was allegedly an emblem of homosexuality in Paris): "not of thee [the English nightingale] these strange green flowers that spring / From daisy roots and seem to bear a sting." The volume also contains his satire "The Decadent to His Soul," in which the Decadent asks his soul:

Poor useless thing, he said,
Why did God burden me with such as thou?
. . . .
His face grew strangely sweet—
As when a toad smiles.
He dreamed of a new sin:
An incest 'twixt the body and the soul.

Responding to Le Gallienne's condemnation with a brilliant transvaluation of values, Arthur Symons's essay "The Decadent Movement in Literature" declares that "this representative literature of to-day, interesting, beautiful, novel as it is, is really a new and beautiful disease. Healthy we cannot call it, and healthy it does not wish to be considered." Decadence expressed, Symons said, "a spiritual and moral perversity." In

Symons's *London Nights* (1895)—called his most Decadent work, although it also includes Wordsworthian nature poems—harlotry and flesh are celebrated, as in "To One in Alienation" (modeled loosely after Baudelaire's poem in *Les Fleurs du mal* (Une nuit que j'étais près d'une affreuse Juive"—"One night as I lay near a frightful Jewess"): ". . . I lay on the stranger's bed, / And clasped the stranger-woman I had hired."

However, the work that outraged many reviewers was "Stella Maris," for its title alludes to the Virgin Mary, while the poem depicts a chance meeting with a prostitute, "the Juliet of a night." The daring Swinburnian imagery, as in the following lines, provoked in the critics, said Symons, a "singular unanimity of abuse": "I feel your breast that heaves and dips, / Desiring my desirous lips." The reviewer in the *Pall Mall Gazette* (September 2, 1895), for example, ranted: "Mr. Arthur Symons is a dirty-minded man, and his mind is reflected in the puddle of his bad verses. . . . By his own showing, his life's more like a pig-sty, and one dull below the ordinary at that."

Offensive to most reviewers at the time, the Decadent icon of the prostitute achieved notorious expression in Ernest Dowson's "Non Sum Qualis Eram Bonae Sub Regno Cynarae" (the title taken from Horace's *Odes*: "I am not what once I was in Cynara's day"). The speaker, addressing Cynara, his true love, recalls: "Last night, ah, yesternight, betwixt her lips and mine / There fell thy shadow, Cynara!" Though he is "desolate and sick of an old passion," he protests: "I have been faithful to thee, Cynara! in my fashion." The prostitute's kisses from her "bought red mouth were sweet," and though he "cried for madder music and for stronger wine," he insists on his faithfulness to Cynara in the refrain at the end of each stanza. Symons called this poem "one of the greatest lyrical poems of our time," and T. S. Eliot later wrote that, "by a slight shift in rhythm," Dowson liberated himself from current poetic convention.

In "The Harlot's House" Wilde depicts prostitutes as unliving things by using images perhaps inspired by Baudelaire's "Danse Macabre" in *Les Fleurs du mal*. The setting, dominated by moral vision, again indicates Wilde's difficulty in adhering to his own insistence on art for art's sake:

> Like wire-pulled automatons,
> Slim silhouetted skeletons,
> Went sidling through the slow quadrille.
> . . . .

Sometimes a horrible Marionette
Came out and smoked its cigarette
Upon the steps like a live thing.

When the speaker says to his love, "The dead are dancing with the dead," she leaves the speaker's side: "Love passed into the house of Lust." If this allegorical trope, after the vivid scene preceding it, is weak, Wilde weakens the poem further with the final simile: "And down the long and silent street, / The dawn with silver-sandalled feet, / Crept like a frightened girl."

In a graceful lyric that Yeats admired, "Villanelle of Sunset," Dowson expresses the weariness associated with the Decadent pose of languor (an affront to Victorian activism) in the highly artificial form of the villanelle (consisting of only two rhymes throughout): "Come hither, child! and rest: / This is the end of day, / Behold the weary West!" Managing the rhythms with such great skill that the fixed form of the poem is not intrusive, Dowson concludes: "Tired flower! upon my breast, / I would wear thee, alway" (the imagery probably influenced by Wilde's remark in "The Decay of Lying" concerning the "Tired Hedonists," who—as the "elect"—wear faded roses).

Although the disturbed Lionel Johnson, whose chronic alcoholism intensified by the mid-1890s, wrote religiously inspired poems and parodied Decadence, he was nevertheless touched deeply by the fantasy of self-annihilation. In "Nihilism" the vision of "Man's life, my life" under the Heavens and upon the Earth leads to the confessional: "of life I am afraid." The speaker welcomes the figure of Death, who will confer "calm" upon him: "the eternal tomb / Brings me peace, which life has never brought." The lyric ends with the "hollow music of a bell, / That times the slow approach of perfect death." Only twenty-one when this was written, Johnson had already immersed himself in the Decadent motif of the *fin du monde*.

The Symbolists and Occultists

The effects of nineteenth-century science, industrialism, positivism, and the higher criticism of the Bible on many fin-de-siècle poets resulted, as we have seen, in a variety of artistic strategies that reasserted the primacy of the imagination in the service of the human spirit. (Earlier, the Pre-Raphaelite painter Edward Burne-Jones had announced: "The more materialistic Science becomes, the more angels shall I paint.") In

one of his characteristic early poems, "The Song of the Happy Shepherd," Yeats rejects scientific "truth" as inferior to subjective vision:

> There is no truth,
> Saving in thine own heart. Seek, then,
> No learning from the starry men,
> Who follow with the optic glass
> The whirling ways of stars that pass.

In the final two decades of the century, as artists and intellectuals
sought escape from the materialism of their time, a new interest in the
occult arose that promised confirmation of an eternal realm beyond that
of the senses. Access to such a world lay in the study of correspondences
between earthly and transcendental realities, magic rituals, and arcane
symbols—knowledge of which had been accumulated and codified over
the centuries. Occult doctrine offered poets new sources of aesthetic
theory, subject matter, and images revealing cosmic unity—as Yeats
said, "Unity of Being"—a fusion of physical and spiritual worlds as well
as of past and present. In the mid-1880s Yeats and the visionary poet-
painter George Russell (using the pseudonym of "AE") were among the
founders of the Dublin Hermetic Society (the first of several such
groups that Yeats joined), its members devoted to the quest for occult
knowledge, which Yeats called his "secret fanaticism." The close connection between the "ancient doctrine" and symbolism is suggested by
AE in his poem "Symbolism": "Now when the spirit in us wakes and
broods, / Filled with home yearnings, drowsily there rise / From its
deep heart high dreams and mystic moods." The speaker concludes:
"We rise but by the symbol charioted."

Yeats asserted that the poet's imagination—able to fuse sound,
rhythm, and image into a magical structure—can evoke symbols from
the cosmic "Great Memory." Such a transcendent reality, he said, was
not merely in the "other world" but discernible in this world to one
adept at vision (a significant influence on the Symbolists was Baudelaire's "Correspondances" in *Les Fleurs du mal*, which envisioned the
world as a "forest of symbols" awaiting interpretation). Moreover, Yeats
believed, dreams were repositories of eternal truths—in "Wisdom and
Dreams," he writes: "Wisdom and dreams are one." But when in "Fergus and the Druid," Fergus craves of the semimythical Druid "the
dreaming wisdom that is yours," he laments when he receives it: "But
now I have grown nothing, knowing all. / Ah! Druid, Druid, how great

webs of sorrow / Lay hidden in the small slate-coloured thing!" Richard Ellmann remarks in *The Identity of Yeats* that instead of "yielding to another world of the spirit," Yeats, possessed of an imagination that dramatized opposition to itself, "is always demonstrating that we had better cling to this one."

Acknowledging the influence of William Blake, who revealed the means by which myth and symbol could be forged to express private vision, Yeats called him "the first great *symboliste* of modern times, and the first of any time to preach the indissoluble marriage of all great art with symbol." In Yeats's first long narrative poem, "The Wanderings of Oisin," Celtic myth and elaborate Theosophical correspondences are employed in the quest for a unified reality—that of self, matter, and spirit as well as the Celtic heroic age and the modern world.

The traditional Christian symbol of the rose—used by Pre-Raphaelite artists and poets—acquired occult significance in Yeats's rose poems, such as "To the Rose upon the Rood of Time," which employs the Rosicrucian image of the mystical rose of love blossoming from the sacrificial cross, here associated with the heroes of Irish mythology:

Red Rose, proud Rose, sad Rose of all my days!
Come near me, while I sing the ancient ways:
Cuchulain battling with the bitter tide;
The Druid, grey, wood-nurtured, quiet-eyed,
Who cast round Fergus dreams, and ruin untold.

In "The Rose of the World," Yeats associates Helen of Troy with the Irish actress Maud Gonne (though unnamed) and the mythic Deirdre, suggesting that beauty, in its various forms and occult meanings, has transformed these figures into spiritual emanations uniting past and present.

The widespread use of the traditional rose symbol—associated with occult and Symbolist vision—attracted other poets, such as the Scotsman William Sharp, who published under the pseudonym of "Fiona Macleod." Like Yeats, he, too, immersed himself in the Celtic Twilight in search of an ancient reality, as his poem "The Rose of Flame" reveals: "Oh, fair immaculate rose of the world, rose of my dream, my Rose! / Beyond the ultimate gates of dream I have heard thy mystical call." John Davidson, Yeats's associate in the Rhymers' Club, envisions a spiritual rose in "The Last Rose" ("The wonderful vast rose / That filled all the world") blossoming miraculously as the "traitor" winter, representing the figure of Death, claims not only the century but the world itself.

Arthur Symons, Yeats's closest friend in the late 1890s, was so touched by occult possibilities for poetry that he wrote "Rosa Mundi" (the original title of Yeats's "The Rose of the World"). In Symons's poem an "angel of pale desire" urges the speaker to "live / In ease, in indolent mirth" and choose "a delicate Lust" in the rose garden, but the speaker has a vision of "the mystical rose" and rejects its earthly counterpart. (Yeats, however, emphasized unity, not rejection). In "The Loom of Dreams" Symons demonstrates the Symbolist conviction that the poet, like the magus, has occult powers: "I am master of earth and sea, / And the planets come to me. . . . / And the only world is the world of my dreams."

While Symons was writing *The Symbolist Movement in Literature* (1900)—on such French Symbolists as Mallarmé, Verlaine, Laforgue, and Rimbaud—he acquainted Yeats with their work, which confirmed occult belief that the poet could summon "other worlds" and that, by means of symbol and imagination, could bring about cosmic unity. In his dedication Symons calls Yeats "the chief representative of [the Symbolist] movement in our country" and the Irish Literary Renaissance as "one of its expressions."

Yeats, however, differed from the French Symbolists in his use of traditional symbols, such as the rose and the island, which he infused with personal meaning. In Yeats's "The Lake Isle of Innisfree," for example, biblical and Thoreauvian echoes are prominent ("I will arise and go now, and go to Innisfree, / And a small cabin build there"), the rhythms suitable for chanting, a device that increasingly interested Yeats. The isolated and secluded "lake isle" acquires symbolic meaning from the speaker's need to return to the source of his spiritual being as he stands on London's "pavements gray" (like Housman's Shropshire lad in exile) and hears the lake water in his "deep heart's core"—suggesting correspondences between matter and spirit.

In the first version of "A Man Who Dreamed of Fairyland" Yeats draws closer to ancient Celtic realities when the dreamer hears fish sing "how day a Druid twilight sheds / Upon a dim, green, well-beloved isle." Other intimations of a transcendent world occur when a lugworm sings of "a gay, exulting, gentle race" and of "blessed skies," finally of "how God leans His hands out of the sky, / To bless that isle with honey in His tones." Yet the man who dreams of fairyland can find no peace (even in the grave) because, throughout his life, the world of spirit has beckoned him from the world of matter—Yeats's warning to himself.

Yeats's final volume of verse in the nineties, *The Wind among the Reeds* (1899), contains much of the best Symbolist verse of the 1890s, such as

"The Song of Wandering Aengus," "The Cap and Bells," "He Wishes for the Cloths of Heaven," and "The Secret Rose." Although the French Symbolist movement had a direct influence on relatively few British poets of the nineties, possibly because of its close relationship with Decadence and because of its tendency to obscurity, Symbolist theory and practice—like that of Aestheticism and Decadence—nevertheless became part of the mainstream of twentieth-century modernism.

Karl Beckson

Further Reading

Beckson, Karl. *Arthur Symons: A Life*. New York: Oxford University Press, 1987.

Beckson, Karl. *London in the 1890s: A Cultural History*. New York: Norton, 1993.

Buckley, Jerome Hamilton. *The Victorian Temper: A Study in Literary Culture*. Cambridge: Harvard University Press, 1951; New York: Random House, 1964.

Buckley, Jerome Hamilton. *William Ernest Henley: A Study in the "Counter-Decadence" of the 'Nineties*. Princeton: Princeton University Press, 1945; New York: Octagon, 1971.

Dobrée, Bonamy. *Rudyard Kipling: Realist and Fabulist*. London: Oxford University Press, 1967.

Ellmann, Richard. *The Identity of Yeats*. 2d ed. New York: Oxford University Press, 1967.

Hönnighausen, Lothar. *The Symbolist Tradition in English Literature: A Study of Pre-Raphaelitism and Fin de Siècle*. Translated by Gisela Hönnighausen. Cambridge: Cambridge University Press, 1988.

Kermode, Frank. *Romantic Image*. London: Routledge, 1957; New York: Vintage, 1957.

Leggett, B. J. *Housman's Land of Lost Content: A Critical Study of A Shropshire Lad*. Knoxville: University of Tennessee Press, 1970.

Longaker, Mark. *Ernest Dowson*. 3d ed. Philadelphia: University of Pennyslvania Press, 1967.

McCormack, Jerusha Hull. *John Gray: Dandy, Poet, and Priest*. Hanover, N.H.: University Press of New England, 1991.

Munro, John M. *The Decadent Poetry of the Eighteen Nineties*. Beirut: American University of Beirut, 1970.

Nelson, James G. *Sir William Watson*. New York: Twayne, 1966.

Smith, M. Van Wyk. *Drummer Hodge: The Poetry of the Anglo-Boer War, 1899–1902*. Oxford: Clarendon, 1978.

Temple, Ruth Z. *The Critic's Alchemy: A Study of the Introduction of French Symbolism into England*. New York: Twayne, 1953.

1898–1945: Hardy to Auden

"My mother had a Tennyson; her present parallel would not possess Eliot or Auden."   Sir Frederic J. Osborn

The canon of English poetry since the Renaissance, as established by the High Victorian Francis Palgrave in his selections for *The Golden Treasury* (1861), had "a certain unity"; he divided his anthology "Of the Best Songs and Lyrical Poems in the English Language" into "Books of Shakespeare, Milton, Gray, and Wordsworth." If Palgrave had continued his canon into his own time, he would most certainly have added a "Book of Tennyson"—the friend to whom his collection was dedicated. Palgrave's mid-nineteenth-century assumptions remained explicitly turn-of-the-century Romantic—tradition defined as "natural growth," and canon understood on the basis of Shelley's Neoplatonic ideal of "'that great Poem which all poets, like the cooperating thoughts of one great mind, have built up since the beginning of the world.'" A hundred years later—by the time Palgrave's nineteenth-century selection had been supplemented by Philip Larkins's twentieth-century one in *The Oxford Book of Twentieth-Century Verse* (1973)—another book had been added to the English canon that could be called the "Book of Hardy."

For the generation of poets like Larkin who came of age after World War II, it was Thomas Hardy, and not W. B. Yeats, T. S. Eliot, or Ezra Pound, who seemed central—again—to the English canon. Between the world wars, the figures of the international Modernist movement, particularly Eliot through his essays, aggressively attempted to displace Hardy and the English tradition from the literary mainstream (a displacement that still continues in the anthologies presented to students by scholars with a Modernist bias), but Larkin, who declared Hardy's *Collected Poems* "the best body of poetic work this century has to show," allotted the most poems in his Oxford anthology to Hardy and acknowledged how the model for his own poetry had shifted to him from Yeats: "Hardy taught me to feel rather than to write—of course one has to use one's own language and one's own jargon and one's own situations and he taught one as well to have confidence in what one felt." Donald Davie, speaking for the poets of this postwar generation—seen by the mid-1950s to be "the Movement"—thought that "in British poetry of the last fifty years (as not in American) the most far-reaching influence, for good or ill, has not been Yeats, still less Eliot and Pound, not Lawrence, but *Hardy*."

The revival of Hardy's reputation by Larkin and "the Movement" was a reaffirmation of a tradition of interrelated insular and Romantic attitudes quintessentially *English*: observation over participation, self-absorption over reaching out, withdrawal over involvement, nature over art, simplicity over complexity, the old-fashioned over the modern, naïveté over sophistication—most of all, the personal voice of a Wordsworth over the impersonal one of an Eliot. During the first two decades of the century these qualities continued to be expressed in work by a group of poets known as the "Georgians," whose models came from Palgrave's English canon; these poets regularly published in popular anthologies entitled *Georgian Poetry* and edited by Edward Marsh. D. H. Lawrence, reviewing the first volume of 1911–1912, found it to be a healthy antidote to the nightmare world of early Modernism: "This collection is like a big breath taken when we are waking up after a night of oppressive dreams. The nihilists, the intellectual, hopeless people—Ibsen, Flaubert, Hardy—represent the dreams we are waking from. It was a dream of demolition."

To include Hardy among the founders of the movement of intellectual pessimism that stirred in Europe at the turn of the century and continued between the world wars is to acknowledge the disturbing, dark anxiety about the state of civilization that underlies and shapes the best poetry of the twentieth century, both traditional and Modernist. Indeed, expression of a sense of crisis in modern history had begun with Wordsworth's "Preface" to *Lyrical Ballads* (1800). Fearing that his own violent Age of Revolution, in which "the multitude of causes, unknown in former times . . . now acting with a combined force to blunt the discriminating powers of the mind," might overwhelm poetic creativity, he argued for stylistic clarity, for "a selection of language really used by men," and for the retention of rhyme and meter as a kind of formal frame "in tempering the painful feeling which will always be found intermingled with powerful descriptions of the deeper passions." While in the twentieth century the Moderns expressed this anxiety about the state of civilization in a style that became increasingly difficult and obscure, the poets of the English tradition coped with and consciously expressed the same anxiety by retaining Romantic strategies.

Because of the propaganda of the Modernists, the Georgians constitute a lost generation in the history of twentieth-century English poetry. Yet, along with Hardy, the Georgians liberated English poetry from the stultifying conventions of flowery, archaic diction and constant moralizing of the late Victorians; as post-Darwinians, they could engage poetically with the bloody violence and fateful brutality of nature. Edmund Gosse, in reviewing Marsh's 1911–1912 collection of Georgian poetry, acknowledged this engagement by finding that these poets "exchange the romantic, the sentimental, the fictive conception of literature, for an ingenuousness, sometimes a violence, almost a rawness in the approach to life itself." Hence, the poetic world of W. H. Davies has the pessimism of Blake's *Songs of Experience* in which the imagery of innocence becomes twisted by predatory violence. In "The Villain" description of a delightful pastoral evening closes with this disturbing image:

> I turned my head and saw the wind
>   Not far from where I stood,
> Dragging the corn by her golden hair,
>   Into a dark and lonely wood.

The emaciated corpse of a four month old baby haunts the coroner at "The Inquest" with the refrain,

> And I could see that child's one eye
>   Which seemed to laugh, and say with glee:
> 'What caused my death you'll never know—
>   Perhaps my mother murdered me';

and from the point of view of "The Rat" an old woman, abandoned at home while her husband drinks, her daughter flirts, and her son taunts a lame cobbler, is a victim ready for sacrifice:

'Now with these teeth that powder stones,
I'll pick at one of her cheek-bones:
When husband, son and daughter come,
They'll soon see who was left at home.'

Innocence lost to survival of the fittest is chronicled in "A Woman's History," in which Mary Price at five years old loses her pet bird and "called her friends to pray to God, / And sing sad hymns for hours"; at fifteen loses her virginity and marries "With no more love-light in her eyes / Than in the glass eyes of her doll"; at thirty-five mourns her dead husband while "neighbors winked to see the tears / Fall on a lover's neck"; and

Now, Mary Price is seventy-five
    And skinning eels alive:
She, active, strong, and full of breath,
    Has caught the cat that stole an eel,
And beaten it to death.

Another Georgian, Edmund Blunden, captures the decay and violence of a world of survival in his naturalistic "Malefactors." The observer in the poem addresses the remains of two predators, a kite and a stoat, nailed to the boards of an old, abandoned mill; he speculates on how they were killed by the miller for their intrusion, and then meditates on Time's "revenge"—"the wheel at tether, / The miller gone, the white planks rotten, / The very name of the mill forgotten"—and on the criminality of a fallen world that links man and beast in their mortality. The observer asks, can "There lurk some crime in man, / In man you executioner, / Whom here Fate's cudgel battered down?" Thus, the Georgians in their tragic renderings of natural and human life imagine a cynicism and harshness about the nature of reality that the suffering and death of the First World War confirmed.

Indeed, the poets who went to war in 1914 were Georgians, and the death of one of the founders of the movement, Rupert Brooke, became the defining tragedy of the literary generation. Brooke became famous before the war for poems like "The Old Vicarage, Grantchester (Cafe des Westens, Berlin, 1912)," which in celebrating the speaker's longing to escape decadent Europe and recover the purity of home, seems to express the very provincialism that the Modernists abhorred in Georgian poetry: "Here I am sweating, sick, and hot, / And there the shadowed waters fresh / Lean to embrace the naked flesh." Yet, there is a

Byronic tone of self-mockery about the English and their heritage in Brooke's poem that would have been more obvious if it had retained its original title, "The Sentimental Exile." This irony, reinforced by the forced rhyming of couplets, is evident in Brooke's catalogue of his literary ancestors, starting with Byron:

> Still in the dawnlit waters cool
> His ghostly Lordship swims his pool,
> And tries the strokes, essays the tricks,
> Long learnt on Hellespont, or Styx.
> Dan Chaucer hears his river still
> Chatter beneath a phantom mill.
> Tennyson notes, with studious eye,
> How Cambridge waters hurry by

and in his sardonic treatment of the virtues of village life:

> In Grantchester their skins are white;
> They bathe by day, they bathe by night;
> The women there do all they ought;
> The men observe the Rules of Thought.
> They love the Good; they worship Truth;
> They laugh uproariously in youth;
> (And when they get to feeling old,
> They up and shoot themselves, I'm told).

But the war took Brooke a long way from Grantchester and turned his mood from playfulness to patriotism; as a result, he is commemorated as a soldier-poet of war sonnets. In the sestet of one of his most famous, "The Soldier," the speaker contemplates death:

> And think, this heart, all evil shed away,
>   A pulse in the eternal mind, no less
>   Gives somewhere back the thoughts by England given;
> Her sights and sounds; dreams happy as her day;
>   And laughter, learnt of friends; and gentleness,
>   In hearts at peace, under an English heaven.

When Brooke died in 1915 of disease on a troopship bound for Gallipoli, Winston Churchill wrote of him in *The Times*: "The thoughts to which he gave expression . . . will be shared by many thousands of young men moving resolutely and blithely forward into this, the hardest, the cruellest, and the least-rewarded of all the wars that men have fought. They are a whole history and revelation of Rupert Brooke himself." Receiving recognition of this kind, Brooke took a place among the legendary poets who have died in their prime—Chatterton for the Romantics, Keats for the Victorians, Brooke for the Georgians.

Other Georgian poets approached the horror and violence of world war either with Darwinian cynicism about sacrifice and death or a Coleridgean sense of the nightmare wrought from mankind's violation of the order and beauty of nature. For Edward Thomas, whose poetic career began at the time of the war and who died on the western front, war presented seasons of despair:

> The cherry trees bend over and are shedding
> On the old road where all that passed are dead,
> Their petals, strewing the grass as for a wedding
> This early May morn when there is none to wed.
> ("The Cherry Trees")

> It is enough
> To smell, to crumble the dark earth,
> While the robin sings over again
> Sad songs of Autumn mirth.
> ("Digging")

Far more bitter, twice-wounded Siegfried Sassoon wrote wartime poems on the model of Blake's *Songs of Experience*, attacking the authorities and their patriotic and sentimental clichés. "The General" greets his troops with smiling "good-mornings" before sending them to destruction with "his plan of attack." "They" presents a Blakean dialogue between a Bishop's naive and abstract pieties about "the boys" who fight "the last attack on Anti-Christ" and who will "not be the same" spiritually and the realistic and specific voices of "the boys" themselves:

> "We're none of us the same!" the boys reply.
> For George lost both his legs; and Bill's stone blind;
> Poor Jim's shot through the lungs and like to die;
> And Bert's gone syphilitic: you'll not find
> A chap who's served that hasn't found *some* change."
> And the Bishop said: "The ways of God are strange!"

One of those killed in the trenches, Isaac Rosenberg, wrote vividly and honestly of the surreal experiences of soldiers on the western front: the "queer sardonic rat" amid the poppies at "Break of Day in the Trenches," naked soldiers, "Nudes—stark and glistening, / Yelling in lurid glee," engaged in "Louse Hunting," the wheels of caissons crunching bones and faces of the newly killed in "Dead Man's Dump." For Wilfred Owen, who met Sassoon while being treated for shell shock, the hell of the war is essentially emotional and psychological rather than physical. The real horror, he writes in "Apologia Pro Poemate Meo," comes from thought and understanding of one's condition in war, "Where death becomes absurd and life absurder." "Insensibility" speaks of the loss of not only feeling and compassion but imagination and mind in battle. And terror at the loss of mind is summed up in the plight of poor Jim told in dialect in "The Chances":

> 'e's livin' an' 'e's not;
> 'E reckoned 'e'd five chances, an' 'e 'ad;
> 'E's wounded, killed, and pris'ner, all the lot,
> The bloody lot all rolled in one. Jim's mad.

For the "Disabled" confined to a wheelchair in a hospital and awaiting an attendant to remember to put him to bed, the final hardship is the terrible indifference of fellow human beings that his condition brings, the loss of beauty and the possibility of warm affection; for the "blind, and three parts shell" who speaks in "A Terre (Being the Philosophy of Many Soldiers)," it would be better to be dead and buried, "Pushing up daisies," as he recalls soldiers saying, than to live disabled, "dead-old," "a dug-out rat": "Friend, be very sure / I shall be better off with plants that share / More peaceably the meadow and the shower." Owen himself escaped both disability and madness; he was killed in action a week before the armistice.

Some poets who survived continued to cope with their experiences long after the armistice. Ivor Gurney was wounded and gassed and was eventually confined for mental problems for the rest of his life. His were poems recounting times of quiet terror for the soldiers, moments of anticipation within the action when troops on the march notice the "sweet air" and experience "homethoughts soft coming," as they anticipate the barbwire and "ditches of heart-sick men" they will soon join at the front ("Towards Lillers"), or in "The Silent One," when a soldier quietly refuses to advance the line in the face of certain death:

"Do you think you might crawl through there: there's a hole."
"I'm afraid not, Sir." There was no hole no way to be seen.
Darkness, shot at: I smiled, as politely replied—
Nothing but chance of death, after tearing of clothes.

David Jones published in 1937 a retrospective epic on the war, combining poetry with prose to describe the experiences of an infantry unit
from their arrival in France in December 1915 to their tragic discovery—bogged down a few months later at the western front in the
Somme offensive—that the legendary role of the amateur soldier had
been transformed by trench warfare of the twentieth century. As Jones
writes in his preface: "July 1916 . . . roughly marks a change in the character of our lives in the Infantry on the West Front. From then onward
things hardened into a more relentless, mechanical affair, took on a
more sinister aspect. The wholesale slaughter of the later years, the conscripted levies filling the gaps in every file of four, knocked the bottom
out of the continuing, intimate, domestic life of small contingents of
men. . . ." Only one (wounded) soldier of the English and Welsh unit
survives at the end of Jones's epic, testimony to the terrible suffering
and loss of a war in which 780,000 British troops were killed. Published
in 1937 and entitled "In Parenthesis"—"I don't know between quite
what," as Jones said—this epic effort commemorated the past war and
anticipated the frightening, unknown violence of a second world war
about to begin.

Laurence Binyon, a Red Cross orderly too old for soldiering, predicted accurately in his poem "For the Fallen": "They shall grow not
old, as we that are left grow old: / Age shall not weary them, nor the
years condemn." Keeper of Prints and Drawings in the British Museum with special interests and competence in Oriental art (and in
Blake), Binyon, like his friend T. Sturge Moore, dedicated his life to
art, a Romantic vein of poetry, and poetic drama. After an almost continuous flow of lyrics on the sweetness of love in London and life
abroad, he survived to ask, "Where lost we then, this peace?" Moore,
looking to classical subjects and resorting often to awkwardly classical
diction, only occasionally achieved the creative tension central to the
aesthetics of his *Armour for Aphrodite*.

In spite both of the involvement of many of the Georgians in the war
and their poems expressing post-Darwinian naturalism, the movement
became denounced as a "bloodless school" of pallid Romanticism.

While some poets who published in *Georgian Poetry*, like Lawrence and Robert Graves, remained influential and became associated with the Modernists, the Georgian movement could be declared "dead" (as it later was, by Laura Riding and Graves) for producing many poems that were too derivative and conventional to be memorable; the Romantic qualities could be easily mocked, as one wag did by asking,

Have you even been on a walking tour?
Do you make friends easily with dogs, poultry etc.?
Are you easily exalted by natural objects?

For Eliot and the Modernists, it was the Anglo-American movement of Imagism, rather than the Georgian movement, that afforded a stylistic transition away from the effusive late Victorians. English Imagists like T. E. Hulme, F. S. Flint, Ford Madox Ford, and Richard Aldington, along with their expatriate American colleagues, Amy Lowell, H. D. (Hilda Doolittle), Pound, and Eliot, were fostering a movement contemporary with the Georgians but asserting classical restraint, clarity, and simplicity—usually in spare lyric poems and haiku that avoided ideas and narrative while expressing "momentary phases in the poet's mind" (according to Hulme) or "an intellectual and emotional complex in an instant of time" (Pound). Along with vigorous debate of their movement in essays published in the "little magazines" of the mid-teens, anthologies entitled *Some Imagist Poets* were published in 1915, 1916, and 1917. Ironically, then, while it was the so-called bloodless Georgians who engaged poetically—and personally—in the "bloody" tragedy of the time, the Imagists stylistically evaded issues of death and suffering, offering instead their superficial glances at the surfaces of things; Pound published his influential example of Imagism, "In a Station at the Metro"—"The apparition of these faces in the crowd; / Petals on a wet, black bough"—in 1916, as the tragic Somme offensive unfolded.

Nevertheless, in essays published just after the First World War, Eliot, in the wake of Imagism and in an effort to make way for his own, Modernist style of verse, tried to bury—and did quite effectively smother for a while—the Georgian movement with its early nineteenth-century English roots: "England puts her Greater Writers away securely in a Safe Deposit Vault, and curls to sleep like Father. There they go rotten; . . . Keats, Shelley, and Wordsworth (poets of assured though modest merit) . . . punish us from their grave with the annual scourge of the Georgian Anthology." Pound and Wyndham Lewis declared emphatically that democracy had brought decay of language. Eliot wanted to replace the Romantics—and especially Wordsworth ("To remain with Wordsworth is equivalent to ignoring the whole of science subsequent to Erasmus Darwin")—with the Metaphysical Poets and the French *symbolistes*, as a source and model for poetry. He directly attacked Wordsworth's definitions of poetry and poetic diction (in the "Preface" to *Lyrical Ballads*): "Poetry is not a turning loose of emotion, but an escape from emotion; it is not the expression of personality, but an escape from personality." Against Wordsworth's emphasis on clear and natural poetry, Eliot asserted the syntactical complexity and "artificiality" of his own style of poetry: "Poets in our civilization, as it exists at present, must be *difficult*. . . . The poet must become more and more comprehensive, more allusive, more indirect, in order to force, to dislocate if necessary, language into his meaning. . . ." Eliot prescribed "town" poetry for a cosmopolitan elite in place of the accessible, familiar "country" poetry of the popular "Georgians."

In his campaign against the established Georgians and their anthologies Eliot even praised the first volume of *Wheels*, edited by Edith Sitwell in 1916. Eliot called it "a more serious book" than the current volume of Marsh's *Georgian Poetry*, one that, like his own work, looked outside the English canon—to classical and European poetry, especially the French, for its sources: "Instead of rainbows, cuckoos, daffodils, and timid hares, they give us garden-gods, guitars and mandolins . . . they have extracted the juice from Verlaine and Laforgue." However, Eliot damned the Georgians with faint praise for the poets in *Wheels*, saying that "the book as a whole has a dilettante effect" and adding, in another review, "The poets who consider themselves most opposed to Georgianism, and who know a little French, are mostly such as could imagine the Last Judgement only as a lavish display of Bengal lights, Roman candles, catherine-wheels, and inflammable fire-balloons."

Certainly poetic extravagance and personal flamboyance identify the work of Sitwell, who, along with her brothers, Osbert and Sacheverell, published six volumes of *Wheels* between 1916 and 1921. In 1923, when she and Osbert introduced the poems in the volume *Façade* with a public performance in London, the two spoke through megaphones from behind masks on a curtain, accompanied by music composed by William Walton. One of the poems from *Façade*, "Hornpipe," begins,

Sailors come
To the drum
Out of Babylon;
　Hobby-horses
Foam, the dumb
Sky rhinoceros-glum

Such a style of free associations, mixed metaphors, and metrical experiments—rather than meditation and thought—mark Sitwell's work; Judgement Day is evoked in "The Shadow of Cain" through passages like this:

There were great emerald thunders in the air
In the violent Spring, the thunders of the sap and the blood in the heart
—The Spiritual Light, the physical Revelation.

In the streets of the City of Cain there were great Rainbows
Of emeralds: the young people, crossing and meeting.

Focusing on Sitwell's effort to shake up the established Georgians, Eliot may have associated her work with that of the Modernists, but in introducing her *Collected Poems* (1957), Sitwell traces her wit and rebellion against literary custom to sources well within the English canon—to the energetic satire of poets like Christopher Smart and Blake. Moreover, when she proclaims her poems to be "hymns of praise to the glory of life," she is certainly fulfilling the ambition of a Romantic rather than a Modernist. Nevertheless, like most avant-garde art that startles the expectations of the audience, Sitwell's work continues to be considered evocative rather than significant.

Hardy responds to harsh criticism like Eliot's—and Lawrence's—by defending his tradition, and implicitly, that of the Georgians, in an ironically entitled "Apology" for his *Collected Poems* (1922). He invokes the precedent of Wordsworth's "Preface" (itself an answer to critics) to speculate on causes for "the precarious prospects of English verse at the present day": "Whether owing to the barbarizing of taste in the younger minds by the dark madness of the late war, the unabashed cultivation of selfishness in all classes, the plethoric growth of knowledge simultaneously with the stunting of wisdom, 'a degrading thirst after outrageous stimulation' (to quote Wordsworth again), or from any other cause, we seem threatened with a new Dark Age." Hardy sums up this cultural malaise as the rise of a new form of superstition in sharp contrast to his own scientific Darwinian philosophy; referring to his "obstinate questionings" and "blank misgivings" (phrases borrowed from Wordsworth's *Immortality Ode*), he defends as philosophical the pessimism for which he had been criticized: "the visible signs of mental and emotional life, must like all other things keep moving, becoming; even though at present, when belief in the witches of Endor is displacing the Darwinian theory and 'the truth that shall make you free', men's minds appear . . . to be moving backwards rather than on." This seems to be a sweeping— although in light of the German aggression of the First World War allusive—rebuke to the Modernist zeitgeist of Nietzschean pessimism and disbelief and of fascination with the darker forces of the Freudian unconscious. Donald Davie associates it with Hardy's dismay as a "scientific humanist" at the ignorance of Modernists substituting their own mythologies for philosophy or religious belief. Hardy's explicit Darwinian response to the issue of the loss of faith made him seem "Victorian" and old-fashioned, easy to dismiss by the advocates of "make it new" on their own terms, but his work would be returned to fashion in view of a century's appalling work by reactionary "witches."

Molly Holden's poem "T. H." looks at Hardy's intermixture of peasant simplicity and keen irony, comparing him to a sly dog fox:

I see now how much alike these Wessex creatures,
fox and man, in their wariness were; for the latter also,
despite his downcast eyes, saw everything he needed
about his fellow-men and the world, marking it all
upon the full-mapped country of his mind and memory.

In form, Hardy remains a poet of Romantic pastoral modes, of the ballad and lyric in the tradition of Wordsworth, of the elegy in the tradition of Coleridge, and of the music of dialect in the tradition of Burns; but in philosophy his Darwinian sense of chance and fate mitigates the Romantics' confidence in the design of nature as an expression of the Creator. The skepticism of his more scientific-minded antecedents, Blake, Coleridge, and Keats, has been honed through the dismay at an indifferent universe expressed by a believing Tennyson and an unbelieving Arnold into Hardy's "pessimism" in the face of an arbitrary and often tragic world. After all, Hardy chose to abandon fiction and to publish poems for the first time in 1898—the very moment of awakening awareness of the imperial "heart of darkness" when the Victorian sense of confidence in civilization was being challenged by violence in the Sudan and South Africa; he continued to write poetry through the horrible conflict of the European colonial powers in the First World War. In that sense, Hardy's 1898 volume, *Wessex Poems*, could be said to mark the beginning of the modern period in poetry. Yet Hardy's poems often focus on and convey—even celebrate in a Romantic's way—a sense of attachment to local place (the title of his first volume evoked the fictional name of the world of Dorset and southwest England of his novels). His poems express the desire to hold on to this sense of place amid fear of the displacing and trying destiny identified by personifications like "Crass Causality" or "Immanent Will" or "Sinister Spirit" that disrupt and destroy human lives. As a result, the landscape of Hardy's poetry is not that of Wordsworth's spring and summer lyrics but that of the winter cruelty of Coleridge's "Dejection: An Ode" and Keats's "Drear Nighted December" and "Upon Visiting the Tomb of Burns," a wasteland of "the God-cursed sun, and a tree, / And a pond edged with greyish leaves" ("Neutral Tones"), where even April hints of being a cruel month—"Say, on the noon when the half-sunny hours told that April was nigh, / And I upgathered and cast forth the snow from the crocus-border" ("In Tenebris" III). In such a place, the personal concern of the poet is to survive in a season of death—"Birds faint in dread: / I shall not lose old strength / In the lone frost's black length" ("In Tenebris" I).

The irony that defines Hardy's poetry is that of Blake's innocence and experience; many poems are tales or personal anecdotes "showing contrary states of the human soul." This tragic human condition is expressed in the story of "Drummer Hodge," whose fate is to die in the Boer War and be buried "uncoffined" in Africa, in a place so alien to his native land that he could not even understand the place-names:

> Young Hodge the Drummer never knew—
>   Fresh from his Wessex home—
> The meaning of the broad Karoo,
>   The Bush, the dusty loam,
> And why uprose to nightly view
>   Strange stars amid the gloam.

The poet's persona in most of Hardy's poems is still innocent enough to be in awe of the evidence of a terrible cosmic indifference and silence to human needs, even though he must accept this fate—it is a persona created out of the elegiac voices of a Romantic who has lost faith in the renewing possibilities of nature (Coleridge in "Dejection: An Ode") and of a Victorian who is desperately reaching for love (Matthew Arnold in his "Marguerite" poems). These voices can be heard in the complaint of the octave of "Hap"—"If but some vengeful god would call to me / From up the sky" before causing loss and suffering—or the confusion of hearing the joyful voice of "The Darkling Thrush" in the midwinter of New Year's 1900, that marks for Hardy the turn of the century:

> So little cause for carolings
>   Of such ecstatic sound
> Was written on terrestrial things
>   Afar or nigh around,
> That I could think there trembled through
>   His happy good-night air
> Some blessed Hope, whereof he knew
>   And I was unaware.

This is also the voice of sheer horror expressed in "The Convergence of the Twain" at the oblivious nature that buries the *Titanic* and the "vain-gloriousness" of the civilization the ship represents:

> Over the mirrors meant
>   To glass the opulent
> The sea-worm crawls—grotesque, slimed, dumb, indifferent.

In "Channel Firing," the sounds of war threaten the very idea of civilization, and Hardy relates his fear for his own world to that of other high moments of English civilization that have passed into legend:

> Again the guns disturbed the hour,
> Roaring their readiness to avenge,
> As far inland as Stourton Tower,
> And Camelot, and starlit Stonehenge.

In such a dangerous and evolving universe, Hardy finds philosophical consolation when the hills of home provide the momentary solace of a Wordsworthian landscape. He walks "Wessex Heights," for instance, to escape the "ghosts" of his haunting memories of personal loss:

> So I am found on Ingpen Beacon, or on Wylls-Neck to the west,
> Or else on homely Bulbarrow, or little Pilsdon Crest,

> Where men have never cared to haunt, nor women have walked
>   with me,
> And ghosts then keep their distance; and I know some liberty.

Only in such fleeting moments in high, familiar places can Hardy join the Wordsworth of "Lines Written a Few Miles Above Tintern Abbey" in a close companionship within nature defined by a keen sense of place and a fleeting sense of serenity in knowledge of the self.

Under the same cultural pressures, D. H. Lawrence's poetic treatment of nature narrowed from Hardy's panoramic sense of landscape in a Darwinian universe to a focus on vital, living details. Inevitably, Lawrence's early model was Hardy, but, as the titles for later collections suggest—*Birds, Beasts and Flowers* (1923) and *Pansies* (1929)—his Romantic antecedents became the *Immortality Ode* (not "Tintern Abbey") of later Wordsworth and the odes of Keats and Shelley, lyrics in which natural details like a pansy (Wordsworth's "meanest flower that grows") or a nightingale (Keats's "light-winged Dryad of the trees") or a wind (Shelley's "Wild Spirit, which art moving everywhere") inspire meditation and philosophy. For Lawrence after the First World War—as for the Wordsworth after the rise of Napoleon—the focus of poetry must be these intense, immediate experiences of nature, as he explains in his introduction to *New Poems* (1918): "There is another kind of poetry: the poetry of that which is at hand: the immediate present. In the immediate present there is no perfection, no consummation, nothing finished. . . . There is no static perfection, none of that finality which we find so satisfying because we are so frightened."

In form, Lawrence affected a compromise with the English tradition using the style of the American Walt Whitman, discovering in "free verse" a clarity of diction combined with the expressive exuberance that allowed "the insurgent naked throb of the instant moment." The result is a poem like "Medlars and Sorb-Apples," in which sucking the decaying fruit evokes a sense of loss and loneliness of the fallen world, a literal tasting of "the flux of autumn," and, through references to the mythology of the Underworld of Dionysus and Orpheus, a sense—like Keats's—of eternal leave-taking: "Orphic farewell, and farewell, and farewell." The apples falling in "The Ship of Death" trigger brooding on the need to prepare for death—"A little ship, with oars and food / And little dishes, and all accoutrements / fitting and ready for the departed soul," for a journey that will lead to "no port, there is nowhere to go"—yet the poem provides a kind of consolation by becoming the means to be "renewed with peace," even in contemplating that a "voyage of oblivion awaits you." Nevertheless, Lawrence's universe is one of frightening supernatural portents: bats replace swallows at nightfall to give an "uneasy creeping in one's scalp," and a snake that the poet attacks out of fear is found to be, like the infamous "albatross" of Coleridge's Ancient Mariner, an inviolable sign of the potential for nightmare in the world of nature: "For he seemed to me again like a king, / Like a king in exile, uncrowned in the underworld, / Now due to be crowned again." Lawrence's sense of the world seems finally still as much postlapsarian as post-Darwinian as he poetically explores myth, both classical and literary, as a means to understand the ambiguous dark forces of his age.

For Robert Graves, another poet whose career began in the company of the Georgians, poetry was also to offer a healing vision in the face of the nightmare of modern history that he had personally experienced in the First World War. His stated goal was "to help the recovery of public health of mind as well as my own by writing of 'therapeutic poems'"; initially he worked within the English tradition to present his healing topic, eros and love. These love poems range in topic from the playful phallicism of "Down, wanton, down!,"

> Will many-gifted Beauty come
> Bowing to your bald rule of thumb
> Or love swear loyalty to your crown?

to the frustration of courtship of "Not at Home,"

> And yet I felt, when I turned slowly away,
> Her eyes boring my back, as it might be posted
> Behind a curtain slit, and still in love,

to the grizzled veteran's desire for the female ideal in "The Face in the Mirror,"

> I pause with razor poised, scowling derision
> At the mirrored man whose beard needs my attention,
> And once more ask him why
> He still stands ready, with a boy's presumption,
> To court the queen in her high silk pavilion.

Over time, Graves evolves a poet's mythology of hope and salvation centered around the celebration of an imagined female deity who rivals the terrible, dark "witches" of the neoclassical Modernists. His poem, "The White Goddess," begins by describing his search for this elusive and obscure female figure, whose erotic power threatens prevailing cultural values:

> All saints revile her, and all sober men
> Ruled by the God Apollo's golden mean—
> In scorn of which we sail to find her
> In distant regions likeliest to hold her
> Whom we desired above all things to know,
> Sister of the mirage and echo.

Eventually, Graves's literary quest for renewing vision during the course of history in the first half of the twentieth century culminates not in poetry but in a grand prose work of mythology called *The White Goddess*.

The White Goddess is a work like the "Preface" to *Lyrical Ballads* that Wordsworth wrote after the French Revolution and like the "Apology" that Hardy wrote after the First World War; Graves's narrative critiques the assumptions of modern culture and suggests a new understanding of the civilized for the era. His inspiration is the writer's compelling need under duress of the history of his times to explain what has brought the disaster represented by World War II to civilization and to express, spontaneously and haphazardly, a radical new view to replace the old, dishonored one. Graves's creation of what he subtitled "a historical grammar of poetic myth" was an outpouring of syncretic mythologizing (he wrote the first version in a frenzy in six weeks); as such, it was part of the neo-Romantic movement that arose in the arts of the 1940s in reaction against the legacy of Modernism. Graves modestly claims his intention is only to recover the mythology necessary to reinspire poetry in his time: "My task in writing *The White Goddess* was to provide a grammar of poetic myth of poets, not to plan witches' Sabbaths, compose litanies and design vestments for a new orgiastic set, nor yet to preach matriarchy over a radio network." Like Yeats in *A Vision* (1925), he is a poet merely needing to find and define metaphors for poetry, particularly his own, yet in the effort there is clearly higher aspiration.

While not proclaiming a new religion, Graves, like Lawrence in his fiction, is affirming the Romantic desire to reclaim for civilization humane—and perhaps, humanizing—experiences of powerful feelings to confront the dominant, patriarchal rationalism of the modern age:

The function of poetry is religious invocation of the Muse; its use is the experience of mixed exaltation and horror that her presence excites. But "nowadays"? it is now a reminder that he [man] has disregarded the warning, turned the house upside down by capricious experiments in philosophy, science and industry, and brought ruin on himself and his family. "Nowadays" is a civilization in which the prime emblems of poetry are dishonored. In which serpent, lion and eagle belong to the circus-tent; ox, salmon and boar to the cannery; race horse and grey-hound to the betting ring; and the sacred grove to sawmill. In which the Moon is despised as a burned-out satellite of the Earth and woman reckoned as "auxiliary State personnel."

Like Wordsworth's "Preface" to *Lyrical Ballads*, which finds in old pastoral themes of the importance of nature and the simple life a basis for the renewal of the human spirit, Graves's "grammar" finds in old themes of the battle of the sexes, feminism and the relations of women and men, a new civilized beginning; it offers a vision of an ideal, the "golden age" of a matriarchal society, past and future, for which human beings should aspire. Wordsworth after long argument in his "Preface" states, "The Poet writes under one restriction only, namely, the necessity of giving immediate pleasure to a human Being possessed of that information which may be expected from him, not as a lawyer, a physician, a mariner, an astronomer, or a natural philosopher, but as a Man." In a similar vein Graves writes, "Certainly, I hold that critical notice should be taken of the Goddess, if only because poetry which deeply affects readers—pierces them to the heart, sends shivers down their spine, and makes their scalp crawl—cannot be written by Apollo's rhetoricians or scientists." Like Wordsworth, Graves is defending passion and ecstasy to a world dedicated to the cult of reason and death. He affirms the creative necessity of the female principle in society by asserting the mythology of the Goddess in response to what he perceives to be a dominant tradition of effete, masculine rationality. And he concludes: "The main theme of poetry is, properly, the relations of man and woman, rather than those of man and man, as the Apollonian Classicists would have it." If Graves's vision of culture were to prevail, art would be restored to its proper role and civilization would be revived by the love of man and woman.

Graves's concern, saving civilization, was the context for poetry of the English tradition between the world wars, and especially once the

Great Depression began. John Masefield had known and reported hard times from the beginning of the century. An admirer of Hardy and of the Romantics, Masefield had made his own way in book-length narratives of the last age of the sea under sail and of country life when individual character still seemed to determine events. Renewal of the once enormous popularity of such pungent narratives as *Dauber* and *The Widow in the Bye Street* has never quite come off, although he left, for after times as well as for his own, "Sea Fever" in *Salt-Water Ballads* (1902)—"I must down to the seas again, to the lonely sea and the sky"—and "Cargoes," a succinct history of shipping, in *Ballads and Poems* (1910). In an introduction to *Poems* (1925), he declared for "a school of life" instead of the "school of artifice" that had made disciples of Tennyson speak only to "a small comfortable class." With Binyon, Sturge Moore, and Gordon Bottomley, he strove against the grain of realism in the theater to revive poetic drama. They won respect, but not the later commercial success of Eliot and Christopher Fry. Masefield declined, as Byron would say, into Poet Laureate in 1930, and holder of the Order of Merit in 1935.

In Scotland a poet still more independent, and probably greater, wrote for a smaller audience than the Georgians and Masefield enjoyed. Hugh MacDiarmid (Christopher Murray Grieve) brought into brief being a phase of writing poetry in Scots to replace the revival by Ramsay, Fergusson, and Burns, and with it an intenser nationalism expressed in Gaelic verse. In several volumes of the 1920s MacDiarmid harnessed fervor and skill to counteract the romantic influence of Burns, with greatest success in the organic collection of poems *A Drunk Man Looks at the Thistle* (1926). In the 1930s, declaring allegiance to Lenin as the best program for achieving the full development of the individual, and needing a scientific terminology lacking in Scots, he began to compose poems in English. With a sharp focus from the beginning on particulars, he now described in "The Kind of Poetry I Want" (in *Lucky Poet*, 1943) a poetry of fact: "A poetry full of erudition, expertize, and ecstasy / —The acrobatics and the fly-like vision,"— "'wide-angle' poems, / Taking in the whole which explains the poet." David Daiches analyzed an earlier poem, "Ex Vermibus," on a worm conspiring with the bird that eats it to produce superior song—"Gape, gape, gorlin', / For I ha'e a worm / That'll gi'e ye a slee and sliggy sang"—to illustrate the thesis that MacDiarmid possessed at all stages "a rock-like apprehension of the sheer stubbornness of life."

Meanwhile, W. H. Auden and the other "pylon poets" in his circle brandished aerodromes, speedways, power stations, Freud, and Marx as economic, social, and political emblems and cures for "a low dishonest decade." At Oxford or soon after, Auden gathered into this circle—briefly but with proclamations and redounding tributes—Stephen Spender, C. Day Lewis, Louis MacNeice, and in Berlin the novelist Cristopher Isherwood. Adept as a schoolboy in diction and prosody, he accumulated devices from Old English, Skelton, Hopkins, music halls, Hardy (rejections of Tennysonian melody), Wilfrid Owen (half-rhyme and near rhyme), and inevitably from Eliot. In his poems of the 1930s words of moral implication, pointed toward contemporary objects, speak obliquely of crises in British and European culture. Auden made the particular universal by mere omission of article: "Where solitary man sat weeping on a bench"; in nearly every poem, the shrewdly contrived understatement: "As for ourselves there is . . . a reasonable chance of retaining \ Our faculties to the last."

Colloquial in diction but chock-full of theories, Auden became, in C. H. Sisson's words, "the pedagogue or doctor advising others what truth is." He was to write with assurance in 1956: "My first Master was Thomas Hardy, and I think I was very lucky in my choice. He was a good poet, perhaps a great one, but not *too* good." Admired by academics and intellectuals who abhorred Hitler and welcomed a poetry of public commitment, Auden departed for the United States in January 1939 and announced, in "In Memory of W. B. Yeats (D. Jan. 1939)," that a poet's and poem's meaning is whatever diverse readers make of it, "modified in the guts of the living." He was to say, a little further on, that poets and poems make nothing happen. He renounced one of his best-known poems, "September 1, 1939," because it had come to seem dishonest in a Christian to strive for the honesty or improvement of society. And in transition from near-Marxist to Christian, he composed one of his finest poems, "Musée des Beaux Arts," generalizing from several Brueghels—particularly the "Icarus" seen in Brussels—that art can elevate above the untidy banalities of life, where "the torturer's horse" scratches "its innocent behind on a tree."

Spender and Day Lewis had less to exhibit, although Day Lewis in the 1930s expressed in poetry and action views much more revolutionary than Auden's. Auden in America remained a poet and librettist. Day Lewis wrote detective fiction, served on committees of the Establishment, and issued poems as Professor of Poetry at Oxford

(1951–1956) and Poet Laureate (1968). As a poet of Auden's school, Spender was notably personal, variable, and recessive, in Sisson's phrase, "disarming and disarmed"; in Francis Scarfe's, with the "hesitation and recoil" of a "sensitive"; in Spender's own words,

> What I had not foreseen
> Was the gradual day
> Weakening the will
> Leaking the brightness away.

When he chose to honor, there was no "not *too* good," no "perhaps." After decades of disparagement, respect and praise for Spender's poetry of dilemma has revived, as in Samuel Hynes's *The Auden Generation* and in Michael O'Neill and Gareth Reeves, *Auden, MacNeice, Spender: The Thirties Poetry* (1992). Accepting what has been often said, that Spender was to Auden as Shelley was to Byron, and aware of Shelley's intellectual subtlety, O'Neill and Reeves describe Spender's rare failures of fluency as deliberate.

The political, social, and psychological poetry of the Auden circle made mandatory poems about war from 1939 to 1945, but could not afford it competitive advantage. Poetry of the First World War had survived the pacifist years preceding the rise of Hitler and the Great Depression; poems both of patriotism and of outrage remained too well known for emulation. No certainties inflated hopes; with grim determination the conflict had to be engaged. Perhaps most inhibiting of all for soldiers at the front, destruction and deprivation struck unceasingly at home. Where could heroic or complaining rhymes find lodging? No poet in Britain could avoid the subject except in total silence, but those identified as poets of World War II are three who were killed in uniform—Sidney Keyes, Alun Lewis, and Keith Douglas. Poets somehow independent of Sassoon and Brooke they had to be; Linda Shires identifies Rilke as the single major influence. Both Keyes and Lewis emphasized boredom, rain, resentment that the subject needed to be combat, talk of girls. The subject came more acceptably to Douglas; angry, political, he had chosen a military role and honed his language to greet conscripted comrades with scorn. As if to acknowledge the supremacy of irony, the poem that spoke most poignantly for the besieged and for the era came from Laurence Binyon, in "The Burning of the Leaves" (1942), regarding things past with "Rootless hope and fruitless desire":

Now is the time for the burning of the leaves
. . . .
Let them go to the fire, with never a look behind.
The world that was ours is a world that is ours no more.

George H. Gilpin

Further Reading

Davie, Donald. *Thomas Hardy and British Poetry*. Oxford: Oxford University Press, 1973.

Hynes, Samuel. *The Auden Generation: Literature and Politics in England in the 1930s*. New York: Viking, 1977.

Hynes, Samuel. *A War Imagined: The First World War and English Culture*. London: Macmillan, 1990.

Paulin, Tom. *Thomas Hardy: The Poetry of Perception*. London: Macmillan, 1975.

Perkins, David. *A History of Modern Poetry*. 2 vols. Cambridge: Harvard University Press, 1976–1987.

Press, John. *A Map of Modern English Verse*. London: Oxford University Press, 1969.

Ross, Robert H. *The Georgian Revolt, 1910–1922: Rise and Fall of a Poetic Ideal*. Carbondale: Southern Illinois University Press, 1965.

Shires, Linda M. *British Poetry of the Second World War*. London: Macmillan, 1985.

Silkin, Jon. *Out of Battle: The Poetry of the Great War*. London: Oxford University Press, 1972.

Sisson, C. H.. *English Poetry, 1900–1950: An Assessment*. London: Hart-Davis, 1971.

Yeats, Lawrence, Eliot

"Everything mattered—except everything."
—G. K. Chesterton (1905)

Chesterton's summation of Victorian metaphysical claustrophobia is as succinct as it is accurate. Nineteenth-century positivism pinched spirituality like a cop. The genius of the Religion of Humanity, as of utilitarianism, was ethical. But, in the 1910s,
along came writers for whom religion was, and had to be, once again
divine in essence—that is, inhuman, an experience of what is so deeply
inside that it is also out there, so endless that it is everything. Several of
the English-language modernists rediscovered the sacred as unlimited
continuity, hence as immediacy, intimacy—a clear violation of the paltry pocket of socially convenient ideas and practical habits called the
"human." D. H. Lawrence summoned back an old name: Pan. W. B.
Yeats used newer old names: Plato's Sphere, Plotinus's There. T. S.
Eliot spoke of the Absolute. These three, together with Ezra Pound,
whose traffic with the sacred was more sporadic, were chief among the
English-language modernist poets who reopened negotiations with the
divine.

For the most part, English-language modernism was (and is) the
wrestling back into human experience (imagined human experience, to
be sure) of the sublime, what Longinus called the "too much" (too
much for a steady heart rate or clear thought). The Great War (the title
itself invokes sublimity) seemed to show, in a flare light, that the human
cause was already lost. Which left the inhuman, something that the
semicolonial poet Yeats, shying away from English humanism as from

a lifted boot, anyway preferred. The inhuman other is elsewhere, even when it is violently here. It gives the lie, the laugh, to worldly powers. How could it not appeal to those sickened by their human country, their human blood?

Yeats

"The Dolls" and "The Magi," which appeared side by side in *Responsibilities* (1914), were Yeats's first modernist poems. Clean as a whistle of spiritual alarm, they implied that an acceptance of our alienated animality was long overdue. In the first poem, the human ego is a failed doll—an anxious, self-exhausting refusal of biological life. How aloof sit the dolls on their shelf of self-sufficiency! But their fear of death, hence of change and accident, persists beneath their planned perfection: they are alarmed, shrilly repulsed, when the doll maker's wife brings among them her newborn baby—"A noisy and filthy thing." Yeats intuits that this is the condition of prewar life: this mean opposition to death, this hollowing out of the body in the interest of a doll self—the static thing in us that says no to the flesh.

The human as dissatisfied doll is the burden, also, of "The Magi"; but, in contrast to the dolls, the magi, appearing and disappearing "in the blue depth of the sky," cannot bear their divorce from animality. They have identified themselves with the good, have practiced renunciation, to the point of becoming like stone—religious statues. In preferring the holy (the divine as purified of everything malefic) to the sacred (the animal, spontaneous mixture of benign and malefic qualities), they have lost everything, even their souls. For the soul is erotic, psychosensual; its true religion is the sacred. This is the view not merely of Yeats (if only at times), but of D. H. Lawrence, Seamus Heaney, and Ted Hughes (as, also, in muted ways, of Virginia Woolf and James Joyce)—the view of the neopagan branch of literary modernism.

Whether in the experience of the holy or the sacred, the divine consists of continuity. But the sacred fosters the continuity of all that we are with everything that exists; the painfully persistent and finite flesh is not excluded. What the magi seek is a renewal of the "uncontrollable mystery on the bestial floor," the sacred as manifested in ritual blood sacrifice (for instance, "Calvary's turbulence"). The blood victim is the surrogate of a pain-induced intimacy with the divine, which the profane order prevents the unsacrificed from experiencing directly. But the turbulence dies out, the "bestial" becomes exorcized, the flesh stiffens. In "The Magi," it is time for sacred spasms to afflict such unliving flesh.

The partial inversion of the human into the animal (the rediscovery of life as power) is figured in the sacred "rough beast" of Yeats's next major religious poem, "The Second Coming" (1919). This god-stuff of a new historical dispensation, this "shape with lion body and the head of a man," combines pitiless intellect with ponderously sensual thighs. Yeats, then, is not prepared to abdicate mind: it is a great weapon in the midst of enemies, and the sacred monumentalist in the poet had many at the time he wrote "The Second Coming"—especially Marxists ("the worst," full "of passionate intensity"), who he feared would divert Irish nationalism from its native spiritual strain (whatever that was; Yeats seems to have invented it) by their murderous ways and grubbing materialism. All the same, he delights to juxtapose "power" and "knowledge," the sensual and the lucid, in the same being: it makes a kit for sacred admixtures—explosions. The "rough beast" that "Slouches towards Bethlehem to be born," its "hour come round at last" (the impatience is the poet's, not the beast's), is rank with the malefic components of the sacred, and thus a veritable anti-Christ. Christianity has had its crack at evoking the sacred; the inspiration fails; the ethical (e.g., Marxism) predominates; and so an uncontrollable mystery *must* return.

"The Second Coming" is hard-edged, impersonal, emotionally stark. Its resonance is bone-deep; it is enormously grave. Little else in the language can compare with it. The asymmetrical form—eight lines followed by fourteen—registers the unequal powers of the present and of what is to come. The rhyme—often even less than slant, as in the four consecutive lines that end "everywhere," "drowned," "worst," and "intensity" (an *a b b a* rhyme, if you will, that consists in syllable count alone)—is far more comfortless, less established, than in any of Yeats's other poems. Even though the poem is in "form"—Yeats said he would fall to pieces in free verse—it stands frighteningly close up to what it says. For Yeats, form was not evasion.

His next great poem in this prophetic and pro-prophetic series was "Leda and the Swan." ("Easter, 1916" is in it, too, but there the sacred has only nationalist bearings; more on this later.) But, despite Jean-François Lyotard's argument that modernism is limited by its nostalgia for good form, for communal ritual—hence not sublime, as achronic "postmodernity" always is—"Leda and the Swan" sets the teeth of the sonnet form on edge through sheer dramatic power of content, beginning with its syntax-violating opening: "A sudden blow: the great wings beating still / above the staggering girl. . . ." No, the community for which Yeats is nostalgic here is precisely the sublime union he imagines between Leda and the bird-god—a confrontation that is at once harrowing and exalting for the human subject, the entity (if it is one) that Leda represents. She does not represent either woman or the Greeks, exactly, still less "the colonized everywhere," as Edward Said puts it in *After Strange Skies: Palestinian Lives*. (Yeats would glorify neither men nor imperialism the way he idealizes the swan.) The swan itself is, in part, our own animal heritage (sex and aggression): the main ingredients of our turbulent history (the eggs Leda lays, Yeats said, hold Love and War). He is our animal history in its sacred aspect—as "caught up" in a mysterious, uncontrollable totality. (Even the swan lacks free will: it must mate with Leda, must determine the Greek history to come).

As the conscious human subject, Leda would be independent of everything blind, accidental, disorderly. But an assault "from above" (and only from there, Yeats said, could a new movement start, one that would reverse the effects of Hobbes, the Encyclopedists, and the French Revolution) throws her into the sort of turbulence craved by the magi (the human subject in petrified form). She is shattered, uplifted, penetrated, then dropped by all that she would (but perhaps finally would not) exclude. Such vulnerability, Yeats implies, is our tragedy and our hope. For if we are the controlled and not the controlling, can we not at least "put on" not only the "power" but the knowledge of what somehow needs us, wants us so brutally? (The locution comes from Paul's First Epistle to the Corinthians [15:23], where what is to be put on is immortality.) If sex and aggression are our ways of putting on its power, its knowledge could only be put on through a startlement of mind that opens it up to something previously hidden. (The poet questions whether Leda is so privileged; he doesn't dare conclude that she is.) The sacred, says Georges Bataille in *The History of Eroticism* (volume II of *The Accursed Share*), "is a leap into the unknown, with animality as its impetus." Such is Leda's leap, such her impetus. Bataille speaks, further, of "the poverty of a desire not enhanced by any horror." This is Yeats's view exactly.

Yeats had small tolerance for profane life except in its aristocratic form, where the beautiful is an end in itself, thus marked enough to be a substitute for the sublime—and where the ethical life is exalted as nobility: heroism and largesse. The vapidity of democracy, science, rationality, economics, *things*—everything far removed from the sacred—is what the swan must jostle Leda free of, if she is to represent the too-passive present of 1923, the date appended to the poem, and its possibility of renewal through terror. George Moore had asked Yeats for a poem on the contemporary state of things for his magazine, *The Irish Statesman*, but the sonnet ends forlornly in a glance back over three thousand years of history. The poet himself has been dropped, like Leda, from the visionary intensity of the octave, has fallen into the history books, has lost the prophetic note. So the poem comes off as an elegy for sacred experience.

To go back to "Easter, 1916": here the sacred is a magical element of hope, but in relation to Ireland's renewal alone. The only constant line of the two-line refrain, "A terrible beauty is born," names the fusion of the appalling and the moving, shared by tragedy, the sublime, and the sacred. Something has entered and transformed Irish nationalism, something with a self-perpetuating life (hence "is born," not "was"). Out of sacrifice has come new life and a new intimacy and continuity, Irish to Irish. This is how the sentiment of the sacred announces itself, this opening of a customary "me" into a sense of community that is endless to feeling.

Yeats doesn't narrate any of the incidents of the Easter Rebellion; he even hides the act of rebellion itself by speaking only of the rebels' dreams: "We know their dream; enough / To know they dreamed and are dead." Only the adjective "terrible" acknowledges their sacrifice. But the poet's knees bend to the "terrible beauty" in a way that cannot be doubted. He does the rebellion the greatest homage in his refrain. But in the rest of the poem, he chafes, scolds, lectures.

There was so much about the rebellion for Yeats to disapprove of. For one thing, its emotional inspiration came from a Catholic, Patrick Pearse, and Yeats had long since counted himself a sort of adopted son of the Protestant aristocracy. Another leader, James Connolly, was a Marxist. There was one aristocrat among the leaders, Constance Markievicz, but she is presented as a traitor to her class: descending from her former heights ("young and beautiful, / She rode to harriers"), she became a leftist hag ("That woman's days spent / In ignorant goodwill, / Her nights in argument / Until her voice grew shrill"). Besides, as Yeats stated in a later poem, "The Man and the Echo," he feared that the rebels' rashness could perhaps be traced to his play *The Countess Cathleen*. So, on the one hand, he might have grieved that the rebellion was not his, and, on the other, felt that it rested on his conscience with unbearable weight. In any case, he himself had been trying to pull away from politics, because poetry exists, he said, in our quarrel with ourselves, not with others.

Certainly in "Easter, 1916" Yeats quarrels with himself. His heart is like a mobile with three hangings, each dipping and swinging to gain preeminence, none content with the presence of the others. First, there is the surprise and gratitude of his own Irishness, which the rebels' sacrifice of life (the British were so unwise as to execute sixteen leaders) has made terribly beautiful, that is, sacred. Then there are two reasoned objections to the uprising (among the several that remain concealed). One is nothing less than a worldview that leads to the poet's wind-brisk celebration of the profane earth in stanza three. It is to this world, he implies, that we naturally belong, a world in which things—clouds, birds, streams, horses and their riders—change minute by minute, in contrast to the rebels, all of whom changed "utterly," were sublimely "transformed."

From the same atmosphere of thought that inspired Bergson; from Yeats's own aristocratic values (the world he paints in the third stanza is like an aristocratic parkland, and its horserider recalls Con Markievicz in her youth); and from his profound love of natural mobility—equal, almost, to his counterlove of historical monumentality—Yeats conjures up a "living stream" that a fanatical heart, however "Irish," can only "trouble" like "a stone." (Maud Gonne's fervid patriotism similarly troubled Yeats himself, kept her from calling to him as, in the words of stanza three, "hens to moor-cocks call.") So the rebels violated the very principle of existence. (Yeats never acknowledges that only thus could they have brought about that miraculous renewal and universality of Irish sentiment.)

The other objection to the rebels is grounded in the related ethic of moderate behavior (this from the poet of "The Second Coming"!). Perhaps England will "keep faith," make good on the parliamentary promise of Home Rule (checked by the outbreak of the Great War)—perhaps, then, the rebellion was "needless death." Yeats even patronizes the rebels as childlike, unable to curb their native wildness (a view uncomfortably close to that of the colonizers):

To murmur name upon name,
As a mother names her child
When sleep at last has come
On limbs that had run wild.

Again: "And what if excess of love / Bewildered them till they died?"

So Yeats the sublime poet converts himself into Yeats the voice of reason, the proponent of the most gradual, the gentlest, change, in order to keep his heart from melting and pouring into the shock-sentiment of the aftermath of the rebellion—as if afraid that it would never to be recovered, never to be his very own again. This is the effect of sacred sacrifice: to transfer the responsibility for continuity and intimacy onto the survivors. The rebels have conscripted all the Irish to continue what they started. Yeats resists—then, again, cannot.

What keeps the poem ever living is precisely its honest (if not perfectly honest) division of heart. It is not one of those political poems that dies with its ideological moment. "The Statues," which came over twenty years later but is in effect a sequel, is less successful, but is saved by its status as a classical meditation on the interaction between abstraction and eroticism, or the provocatively underspecified ideal and the detail-adding imagination. Precisely because Greek statuary "lacked character," and especially when midnight obscured whatever features its careful measures allowed, "boys and girls pale from the imagined love / Of solitary beds . . . pressed at midnight in some public place / Live lips upon a plummet-measured face."

Likewise, the ethnic imagination of the Irish has been quickened by the gloriously indefinite movement that began when Pearse "summoned Cuchulain to his side," by a nationalism itself somehow marked by "intellect" and "measurement" (a reference, perhaps, to certain eighteenth-century Irish intellectuals, Yeats's favorite minds). With seeming contradiction the poet casts this movement (after asking, "What stalked through the Post Office?") in the form of a stationary statue— a sort of colossus of Irishness. Because this last is deep in shadow, in the "proper dark" of an intuitive rather than explicit sense of what is Irish, it incites movement: "We Irish . . . / Climb to our proper dark, that we may trace / The lineaments of a plummet-measured face." Here Yeats recovers the substance and momentum of the Easter Rebellion for a more nearly Protestant "sect." The note of sacred intimacy dies down into a whisper (as of a colossal mother's encouraging love), but is still present in the image of a tactile intimacy.

"News for the Delphic Oracle" (1939) is Yeats's last great poem on sacred animality. Its three boldly divided sections offer a changing topography of joys: those of mind, soul, and body. The news Yeats has for the Delphic Oracle is that Paradise is the home of all three. If he is nonetheless ironic toward the first two, however, it may be partly because they have had their champions for over two thousand years, and at the expense of the flesh, of sacred eros. In any case, the third section—the most powerfully and beautifully written—supplies what is missing in the first two: youth, erotic love, and Dionysian ecstasy.

Here Peleus, a mortal, and Thetis, a sea goddess, represent amorous idealization, and the accompanying nymphs and satyrs the exorbitance native to lust. What is netted in the named lovers—out of respect for the human subject in the other—is unleashed in thrashing fury in the beings who are far more proximate to animal immediacy. In fact, Peleus is but a trembling boy (Yeats based the stanza on a Poussin painting of Acis and Galatea in the National Gallery of Ireland, when it was still mislabeled *Peleus and Thetis*; unlike the virile Peleus, Acis was a lad pursued by the older river nymph, Galatea). Peleus wants Thetis to look upon him with a mother's tender absorption; her limbs are even said to be "delicate as an eyelid." But the impersonal, animal destiny of reproduction already has her in thrall: her "belly listens" to Pan's "Intolerable music." ("Belly" is deliberately jarring after the sweet lines on Peleus.) And how alarmingly proximate Peleus is to what might serve as an illustration of the ferocious parents of the primal scene, castrative in relation not only to their as-yet unconceived child but even to each other, indeed apparently dismembering:

> Foul goat-head, brutal arm appear,
> Belly, shoulder, bum,
> Flash fishlike; nymphs and satyrs
> Copulate in the foam.

Yeats does not disguise the repugnance of such "animality"—in fact, there are no foul goat heads in Poussin's painting, nor is there anything flashing "fishlike." Such horror of animality is precisely the baseline of our humanness, as of the valorization of the holy order over a sacred disorder. But to rejoin the all, one must overcome the fear of abjection, and orgasm is the very type of ceasing to be outside, of an animality at the brink of the totality of being. So the nymphs and satyrs fascinate as well as repel. Yeats's presentation of Peleus's idealization of Thetis may be free of irony and extraordinarily delicate, but it is less than a protective seal: the poet deliberately places the Peleus in himself next to the satyrs, as if out of a dare to expose him to Dionysian disinhibitions. His writing insists on the awesome bestiality of the scene—an immolative bestiality that is itself an uncontrollable mystery, the rites of the sacred god eros.

Yeats, then, displays a religious courage of a kind long absent from English literature. It is Romantic in its embrace of nonhuman forces, but its hunger for a ferocious turbulence surpasses that of the English Romantics (Emily Brontë comes nearest to it). It is offered as the harshest of cures to a humanity gone rigid from adherence to principles, rather than freed for a disorderly immediacy. It is also the rediscovery of the divine as a terrifying power—the burden of Rudolph Otto's book of 1917, *Das Heilige*. By the second decade of the century it was apparently time "at last" for the sacred to re-present itself to, if not altogether to win over, the Western psyche.

Lawrence

A more consistent and explicit radical of life than Yeats was, Lawrence, too, opposed "an assertive newspaper-parcel of ego," social dolls that squeak "when you squeeze them." He respected only what he called "the true self," one not held "according to a picture" but, instead, like a bird that, "as it sings, sings itself" yet "has no idea of itself." This "original individuality" has many enemies: Socrates, Christ, love, democracy, Bolshevism . . .

Lawrence dreamed the return of the human to the verge of a "royal" animality. Connected and in the flow: that, for him, was "life." Desire itself is purity—"a pure thing, like sunshine, or fire, or rain. It is desire that makes the whole world living to me, keeps me in the flow connected . . . not shut outside of the natural paradise." "The element of wonder," he said when noting the power of "rather banal Nonconformist hymns" to penetrate his childhood, is "fundamental to life":

Plant consciousness, insect consciousness, fish consciousness, all are related by one permanent element, which we may call the religious element inherent in all life, even in a flea: the sense of wonder. That is our sixth sense. And it is the natural religious sense.

Religion is the capacity to be open—the Pan spirit. Pan is the All in every sentient thing.

Lawrence, too, wants wonder's burn, its utter transformations. Yet, like Yeats, he's ambivalent; the practical advantages of being human check his devotion to the sacred. In fact, far more than Yeats, Lawrence looked closely at objects, studied them like a naturalist, even if one whose bifocals are half rainbow of metaphor. Usually he was pagan on the Apollonian, not the Dionysian, side.

Lawrence's contribution to English poetry lay in his religious redirection of vision and sympathy toward actual things and in devising a form of flow and connection—he was the first English poet to catch off of Whitman a bright limberness of voice. He even sought, as Whitman did, the rapport of the colloquial and the sacred, Sunday skirts held at the hip by a safety pin.

As a young man, Lawrence wrote a lot of young man's poetry in conscientious rhyme and meter. He was still down beside his mother's "small, poised feet," as in his poem "Piano," still "A child sitting under the piano, in the boom of the tingling strings" at Sunday hymn-singing time in the parlor. In contrast to Yeats's distant-seeming mother, who fostered in him the crypto-nothing that his apocalyptic fervor tests, pursues, loves, hates, Lydia Lawrence supersaturated her son David's wick; she was both origin and end. With her by his side, what need for the world? The early poems are, in partial consequence, overfelt and underobserved. Even after Mrs. Lawrence died, her son's sense of her closeness muffles the poems like perfumed cotton. Studied, self-conscious, the rhymes fold the damp mood in on itself.

Lawrence became modern when he learned to make each stanza like the skip of a flat rock across water. To be modern, a poem must have attack. It must not emote, it must leap and lead the reader on. Speed is essential to it, a gappy movement. That Lawrence would discover a direct speaking voice for such poetry is no small part of his distinction.

In the first poem of his transition volume, *Look! We Have Come Through!* (1918), "Bei Hennef," Lawrence is almost there. But even this charmingly lyrical, arresting poem is secretly mother-scotched as well as slightly slick (verbal and emotional soapstone). As for the volume itself, it is oddly pied between familiar "verse" and lines new to the art. Some of the first is enchanting (as, occasionally, it was earlier, not least in the lovable "Piano"). Conversely, some of the free verse in the book is as facile as some of the rhymes. But already the new beauty Lawrence was to bring into English poetry is testing itself. For instance, a section of "She Said as Well to Me" presses toward the rapt, prodigal detail of *Birds, Beasts and Flowers* (1923):

Don't touch me and appreciate me.
It is an infamy.
You would think twice before you touched a weasel on a fence
as it lifts its straight white throat.
. . . .
Nor the adder we saw asleep with her head on her shoulder
curled up in the sunshine like a princess;
when she lifted her head in delicate, startled wonder
you did not stretch forward to caress her . . .

This is part clean embodiment of a "natural religious sense," part phal-
lus-guarding "attitude" (Lawrence would later do "attitude" less viper-
ishly). The future-salient poem in the book is "Song of a Man Who
Has Come Through." The opening line, "Not I, not I, but the wind
that blows through me!" is irresistible, a bugle call. Modern in its
urgency, its air-stream phrases, the poem is informed by an earthly
future-wonder:

If only I am sensitive, subtle, oh, delicate, a winged gift!
. . . .
If only I am keen and hard like the sheer tip of a wedge
Driven by invisible blows,
The rock will split, we shall come at the wonder, we shall
    find the Hesperides.

Lawrence's mother has finally released him to the adventure of other
wonders, at least of displaced ones (the Hesperides, the apple grove of
the West, belonged to a mother goddess, Hera.)

The poems in *Birds, Beasts and Flowers* fuse prophetic ardor with
winningly relaxed, lavish, and precise observations of real things.
Lawrence's genius has stopped rocking, mother-sick, and sings forward
on a deep keel. The obsessions have opened like an ark and taken on
board the world. Seldom have acts of attention seemed so creative and
lively, so electric with voice, so generous of sight and prolific of figure
(metaphor as both the flash point of perception and fusional bliss).

A few poems are exceptions, works (so to say) of prophetic nostalgia.
"Grapes," for instance, addresses the white Western anemia implicated
in Yeats's "The Magi." Startlingly, Prohibition in the United States is
taken as a sign of an irresistible need for intoxication: "It is like the agonized perverseness of a child heavy with sleep, yet fighting, fighting to
keep awake." The lost children of a dark-skinned Bacchus, "we are on

the brink of re-remembrance." Too much unfolding, too little deep secretiveness. We see too much, touch too little. We must "Take the fern-seed on our lips, / Close the eyes, and go / Down the tendrilled avenues of wine and the otherworld." This is renewed Romanticism, this reinjection of mystery into the overclarified veins of being. What is modernist in it is the radical sensualization of mystery, the elixir of the sacred.

"Southern Night," that slender but brilliant straggler from the auto-biographical cache out of which *Look! We Have Come Through!* was drawn, is, in this sense, Romantic-modernist. This unofficial epilogue to Lawrence's vastly visionary novel *Women in Love* may lack the vigorous lyricism and crowding perceptual plenitude of the other poems in the volume, but it serves as their empowering satyr cry. It is one of the first poems in which Lawrence is, as artist, hard and arrogant throughout—modern. Here is the final part:

Call it moonrise
This red anathema?

Rise, thou red thing,
Unfold slowly upwards, blood-dark;
Burst the night's membrane of tranquil stars
Finally.

Maculate
The red Macula.

This is as brutal as Picasso; gaudily assertive, its colors burn. Not an easel painting of a poem, it breathes and moves. It alters poetic structure in the direction of instant thought flashes, feeling burns. Through the star-speckled holy paper screen of Platonic and Christian idealism, which had seemed to seal the whole Western night, it heaves a blood-red challenge.

A series of slipknots, each tied on the spot, or of rungs up which the poet climbs to greet the "red thing," the poem abolishes the human order in favor of sacred animal sexuality. Like "The Second Coming," it staggers from the force of an ambivalent wonder, a pro-orgasmic violence. The biblical and hymnal "thou" may link this sexual bloodying of white consciousness with the hymn-playing mother, but what the poem defies is just the good, tranquil dead point that she constitutes in the poet's passionate being. "The first evidence of the basic connection between [the human] and the denial of . . . sensual animality," Bataille remarks, is "incest." Lawrence's eroticism erects itself on this prohibition. And so the mother, on whom the moon drops a cold sexual white in *Sons and Lovers*, is here less the moon (even if this last is as good as drenched in menstrual blood, terror of primitive prohibitions) than Mother Night herself; and the speaker would be her consort and son, the womb-invasive moon, sacrificially surrendered to sex and death, no Christ who drops the tomb like a soiled garment.

Can the tough membrane of the "human" be ruptured "Finally"? Must the animal in us remain always apologetic? Lawrence will not apologize. Using the language of anathema against itself, he converts it, in a familiar radical strategy, into praise. "Southern Night" marks Lawrence's sexual acceptance of death—of life as its own blood sacrifice. Nothing could more completely subvert Western culture, which is based on denial. Elsewhere Lawrence says, "The breath of life is in the sharp winds of change / mingled with the breath of destruction." Along with Robert Graves and Ted Hughes, Lawrence is the most moon-maddened of the modern English writers, the most earnest in trying to face civilization toward its roots in the senses' sacred and furious seriousness.

Lawrence's most bravely beautiful poem of what Nietzsche called "affirmative pathos," of a Yes to sex and death, is "Pomegranate":

> And, if you dare, the fissure!
>
> Do you mean to tell me you will see no fissure?
> Do you prefer to look on the plain side?
>
> For all that, the setting suns are open.
> The end cracks open with the beginning:
> Rosy, tender, glittering within the fissure.

The poet adds: "For my part, I prefer my heart to be broken. / It is so lovely, dawn-kaleidoscopic within the crack." (Here the rhythms and vowels are themselves kaleidoscopic.) Yeats had his own version: "Man is in love and loves what vanishes." Eros, as Bataille says, is "the tragic god."

"Pomegranate" parries two opposed ways to refuse a broken heart. First, Dionysian rendings of the finite, so as to pluck out and devour the hidden infinite:

> In Syracuse, rock left bare by the viciousness of Greek women,
> No doubt you have forgotten the pomegranate-trees in flower,
> Oh so red, and such a lot of them.

This glances at sadistic impatience with slow growth, at an intoxicated obliviousness to the beauty made possible only by change. The other refusal of the Apollonian and organic is the Christian anticipation of immortality: in Venice, "Abhorrent, green, slippery city," the pomegranates are hidden in back gardens, significantly unripe and barbed—"crown of spiked green metal."

Lawrence, then, is in his own way complex; though almost entirely free of attraction to the holy, he vacillates between the organically profane and the burstingly sacred—is often at points in between. His interest in Pan, as an All consonant with organic individuality, is thus understandable. He sidles, rather than dashes, toward the sacred. He holds back from Yeatsian crisis and violence; he wants the sacred as coals, not fire—or as limited fire, as when, referring to peasants resting from labor at "dark" noon in "Andraitx—Pomegranate Flowers," he says that "from out of the foliage of the secret loins / red flamelets here and there reveal / a man, a woman."

"Southern Night" and "Pomegranate" are examples of what for Lawrence is a new kind of poem—indeed, new for everyone except his mentor, Whitman. The items in these poems marshal themselves in bunches. They proceed in spasms of concentration and purpose. Attack, and again attack. In all, they combine successive proddings and insouciant poise. Structurally, they trust more profoundly than Yeats's poems do (with a few exceptions) in the spontaneous, the here-in-the-moment—which is to say that they are more accepting of death. A species of action writing, they respond unpredictably but (as it were) naturally to some immediate provocation.

To put *Birds, Beasts and Flowers* beside Lawrence's earlier poems is to see that his work's ruling principle of growth is the movement from constriction to "the free motion of life." The formal logic of the later poems is a cinematic flow and cut, a sidestepping of the static within the limits of occasional steps back. These last not only imprint matters more deeply but toe the poem over on itself, in a self-acknowledging unity.

The new formal procedure has everything to do with the discovery of time as the "insurgent now," as also with the love and advocacy of kaleidoscopic heterogeneity, the febrile desire of metaphor, the paradox of boundless animacy, the sense of life as a gorgeous, inexhaustible resource. It is an attempt to pull alongside a surging chaos, to photograph it so that it appears almost still—now at this moment, now at the next—but really to be in transit, to write on the go. The poet, Lawrence thought, must have less "terror of chaos" than other people. Enemies of convention, poets make slits in the cosmos umbrella ("the chaos which we have got used to we call a cosmos"), "and lo! the glimpse of chaos is a vision, a window to the sun." In any given poem, Lawrence's slit is made in a suspenseful series of little rips, all along the same line of discovery.

"Fish" goes further than the other poems in being the mimesis of the sentiment of the mother as (now) mercifully everywhere ("cast abroad," in a phrase from the end of *Sons and Lovers*). For Lawrence, poetry, wherever it turns, touches a Great Being, but never in the same place twice (or it ceases to be poetry). "Who is it ejects his sperm to the naked flood? / In the wave-mother? / Who swims enwombed?": the question carries friendly envy as well as wonder. The poem's structure emulates such unrestricted fish-bellied immediacy with the source. "The rhizome," Deleuze and Guattari point out in *A Thousand Plateaus*, "operates by variation, expansion, conquest, capture, offshoots"; it is a "short-term memory." Rhizomatic poetry is situated in various points of contact, as against contracting into "the dismal unity of an object declared lost," as did Lawrence's early verse. Such poetry carries the logic of lyricism into structure itself, beyond local wording and rhythm. Poetry becomes a body art of empathy with its creaturely subject. The model is not the syllogism, a square balanced on a rolling loss, but, instead, response-stirred physiological rufflings and rerufflings ("Turkey-Cock," incidentally, is another instance of the free-based poem). In a late work, *Apocalypse*, Lawrence says: "To appreciate the pagan manner of thought we have to drop our own manner of on-and-on-and-on, from a start to a finish, and allow the mind to move in cycles, or to flit here and there over a cluster of images."

Many of Lawrence's subsequent poems pulled back from the generosity of a maternally sanctioned mimesis. Lawrence felt drawn away from creatures to "the unknowable reality which causes us to rise into being." With a few exceptions—notably "Bavarian Gentians"—his later poems are either more harshly wiry or, at the other extreme, more mushily yearning than the best pieces of *Birds, Beasts and Flowers*. They poke and rail (sometimes effectively) or else fall (never effectively) into religious consolation: "Lift up your heads, O ye Gates! / for the silence of the last great thundrous laugh / screens us purely, and we can slip through." Lawrence's language fell, at its worst, into imaginative dullness. It lost the lust for the refreshments of chaos.

At his greatest, Lawrence was a poet of love (though not of human relationships: his gift for portraying *them* was largely restricted to his fiction). Yeats, too, honored vital flow in such poems as "To a Squirrel at Kyle-na-no," "Stream and Sun at Glendalough," and "The Cat and the Moon," among others. But Yeats is strongest as a poet of high demands, of dissatisfaction, not love. And Eliot—Eliot's love smokes off immediately into Love. It disdains the accidents of creatures.

Eliot

Crafted to have the broken form of a confused will, Eliot's first masterpiece, "The Love Song of J. Alfred Prufrock" (1912), is already cinematic: image plus juxtaposition. Prufrock is, however belatedly, one of Nietzsche's nineteenth-century young men, his moral and religious spine broken by the say-so weight of history. Wriggling miserably between God and woman, the there and the here, Prufrock would like to be heroic, if that didn't require standing out, and to be a lover, if that didn't require putting it in. Something nags him to get beyond the toast and marmalade, the smoke and fog—beyond death. But what is beyond wants all, and that is not what Prufrock means to give, not it at all.

Prufrock was Eliot's first self-portrait in a distorting mirror. If the invisible alone matters, the poet's quandary was only in part how to tolerate a weak but spasmodic sensuality. The rest was his diffusion in what Wittgenstein called "feeling space," which "has nothing to do with position in visual space." How either find or lose himself there? Eliot was space-dispersed. In each of his masterpieces the *here* shifts, it is not to be mapped. He was already atomized toward genesis or terminus, but at the intersection of time and eternity the particles halted, drifted, waited.

For Eliot, the sacred, as distinct from the holy, had too much gravity, too much blood. This is his great difference from Yeats and Lawrence. He may have thrilled to Stravinsky's *Le Sacre du Printemps* (threatening a noisy member of the London audience with his umbrella); but he was not about to stir his hands in steaming bowels to find the *other*. For him, deity is ultimate refinement, and only this refinement has reality. Something finer, even, than light: the heart of light. Finer, even, than silences: the silence.

By modernist standards, Eliot was an anachronism, a poet not of the sacred but of the holy. If he could not accept the body, the reason is that it accepted him. Perhaps his marriage in 1915 to the disastrously volatile English woman Vivienne Haigh-Wood was either a sudden gamble at making it acceptable or a way. But it only doubled his unacceptability with hers. The marriage trailed sin like snail slime. It forced Eliot away from women toward a God already volatilized beyond staining.

Shocking the Prufrock in himself past inquisition ("Gerontion") into the beauty of terror (*The Waste Land*), the poet declared women the enemies of the Absolute, along with time and society (which, anyway, is women's stuff until *Four Quartets*). He thus prepared himself for the terror of—the capital is daunting—"Love."

Prufrock himself is unable to love either a woman or Love. His narcissism is a plastic suit in which he malingers, sweating a dull paranoia. Nothing touches him, and he will not touch anything except the imaginary fog lying like a cat beside his chair. The sea-girls by whom he says he lingers in the chambers of the sea (*by*, not *with*) are signs of death, wreathed as they are in "seaweed red and brown." Prufrock stews in his own incest dread. But his sense that he ought to squeeze the universe into a ball and roll it toward some overwhelming question (if such athletic spirituality were still the fashion) betrays the bad conscience of a would-be saint. For, like the young Eliot, Prufrock has had (according to a rejected passage) fantasies of conducting vigils. To leave the senses behind like the dust they are once the moistened mother-matter is removed, to get away from acid and sloppy particles ("Do I dare to eat a peach?"), would ensure that the mermaids will not sing to him again. But, really, he has no vocation for austerity.

"I would meet you upon this honestly," says the hero of Eliot's next masterpiece, "Gerontion" (1919). Yet this geronion (little old man) hardly gets beyond Prufrock's cowardly amends to mother and God. Here Eliot's smarting salve is to imagine himself aged and shrunken past matings of any kind. The almost mock-grand woman "about to reach her journey's end" in "Portrait of a Lady" is succeeded in this poem by the woman who "keeps the kitchen, makes tea, / Sneezes at evening, poking the peevish gutter": the phallic mother as decrepit servant! This speaker is even more distant from the genius of mimesis and memory—the mother's body—than the one in "Rhapsody of a Windy Night" (another early poem), who wants midnight to shake the memory only "as a madman shakes a dead geranium." The geronion is matter long since dried of the mother and her legacy (what in "Preludes" Eliot calls "some infinitely gentle . . . thing").

"After such knowledge, what forgiveness?"—after the knowledge that worldly caresses "Weave the wind." Something else, some love, or Love, has been neglected. Whose heart was the gerontion once "near . . . removed therefrom / To lose beauty in terror, terror in inquisition"? Was it male or female? Still in the mother's force field, in the wrath world of matter, the gerontion imagines the dead as "fractured atoms" "whirled / Beyond the circuit of the shuddering Bear." As for Christ, his energy seems fiercely material ("Christ the tiger"). What is still missing from Eliot's spiritual exploration is an utterly incorporeal Other, a mother-free "you."

In his greatest poem, *The Waste Land*, the poet finds this Other in the Eastern indifference to incarnation. The poem dedicates itself to the Om, the Eternal Silence, of the Upanishads, but chiefly by bitter negation, by portraying the human world as a tower of Babel. This required many voices—voices too much, or too little, satisfied with themselves. It required (in both senses) a *rendering* of incoherence. The poem tips the reader off to its method: "Why then Ile fit you. Hieronymo's mad againe." To "fit," as Thomas Kyd's Hieronymo does, is to devise a deluding language farrago in which sinners, at first unknowing, will be trapped and killed. Eliot thus pointed to the poem's deep coherent purpose. Relatively few readers have seen this. Many speak of the poet's mere grouse against life (quoting Hieronymo Eliot on this score), not recognizing how Eliot invites their hearts to beat obedient to controlling hands, including his own.

Here is the fullest development of his patch-and-jump cinematic method. From the first this poet, who composed in fragments, practiced an evasion of any "whole" that, like a nursing breast or beat, would ease him into being here. His instinct—protective, brilliant—was to touch and abandon. Superficially, the movement of "Prufrock" and "Gerontion" resembles that of, say, Lawrence's "Fish," but the meaning has been reversed—disjunction is brokenness, mimesis handles only wormy apples. This world is something to have done with.

To address a few of the reasons that *The Waste Land* is a great poem: one is the way Eliot's typical touch-and-go movement expands here to take in a variety of countries, cityscapes, landscapes, personalities, classes, idioms, periods, texts, moods, perspectives, and levels of intensity. Nothing like this perplexed and perplexing heterogeneity had ever appeared in English. (*Ulysses*, published in the same year, 1922, is perplexing but not perplexed.) *The Waste Land* is the great poem of the age of the novel, sharing the latter's penchant for raw contemporaneity, mixed styles, dialogic movement. But its compression rebuffs the jabbering world, even so. Missing is Joyce's epic appetite for earthly life's seriocomic losses and gains.

Also worth stressing is the absolute modernity of the diction. In fact, this up-to-dateness, which was initially for Yeats and Lawrence a struggle, is already perfected in "Prufrock." No dry bits then or now to snip from the plant. In addition, like "Prufrock" and "Gerontion," *The Waste Land* has authoritative new rhythms. There is none of that faded literariness that mars two earlier poems, "Portrait of a Lady" and "Rhapsody on a Windy Night." The smartness of "Half-past three, / The lamp sputtered / The lamp muttered in the dark. / The lamp hummed," from "Rhapsody," is like Virginia Woolf at her most self-conscious (which may well mean Woolf remembering "Rhapsody"). Although "Rhapsody" shows Eliot's horror of attachment to this world, bidding us see the cat devouring "a morsel of rancid butter," the child pocketing "a toy that was running along the quay," "An old crab with barnacles on his back" that "Gripped the end of a stick which I held him," the poem itself is conspicuously attached to the conventional idea of verse, and brings out the relative—the serious—austerity of *The Waste Land*.

Not least, this last is great in being religious beyond the channels cut out by the currents of sensibility in the West—religious in the way Eliot continued to approve, as "an act of the imagination." As "act," *The Waste Land* frees Eliot from the crab claws that consist of being a mother's son, a creature. To what can we surrender and "By this, and this only, . . . have existed"? Not human love, as most interpreters—sentimental Westerners—have supposed: except for the rare moment of casual secular grace, say, "Where fishmen lounge at noon," the human in this poem is unreal, it is death. Rather, to that superhuman Grace to which the heart responds "Gaily, when invited." Gaily? The first invitation in the poem had seemed a sudden blow of light and silence. For Eliot, too, made the modern rediscovery of religion as terror. Find a decayed hole in the heart's mountains and wait.

But Eliot could not long hold to the Eastern Absolute-without-distinctions (to so radical, devastating, and exalting a continuity). Perhaps he needed, after all, to incorporate the feminine in his religion, the more so because his youthful near-sweetheart, the American Emily Hale, had reentered his life as spiritual companion. Perhaps he needed neighborly and pacifying church ritual, as Vivienne deteriorated first before his eyes, then as he hid them from her, hid himself, his address—everything except his conscience. Then, too, as a follower of the French hierarchist, Maurras, Eliot adopted Christianity, considering it the necessary discipline of the West. (He even said that "*the* Christian world-order is ultimately the only one which, from any point of view, will work.")

However that may be, "Ash-Wednesday" (1930) is addressed to a female figure—token, phantom, idol—who hovers between the sacred and the holy, who is now all but transparently Emily Hale, now the Virgin, now the Deity, as her panels are moved this way and that by a speaker at once starved for female care and committed to starvation as the rectification of hunger. Is Eliot sure of his ground here? In *The Waste Land* he acts (as the working title has it, "he do the police in different voices"); here, he alternately poses, his speech wadded with high-sounding phrases,

> (Why should the agèd eagle stretch its wings?)
> Why should I mourn
> The vanished power of the usual reign?

and sings:

> The single Rose
> Is now the Garden
> . . . .
> Grace to the Mother
> For the Garden
> Where all love ends.

Is it the presence of the feminine in high places that makes Eliot write with a slight insincerity, and as if before sympathetic, admiring eyes?

In this poem, the poet half turns the primal mother fantasy against itself; he plucks out its gentle element and lets the rest go. The forbidden but not forbidding Lady of the poem teaches the love that is denial—the denial of the appetite and desire that lead, for Eliot, only to "an old man's mouth drivelling, / beyond repair." Not hers the sweet "Blown hair . . . , brown hair over the mouth blown"—and yet, if not hers, no one's. She walks in "White light folded."

Thus reconciled to the feminine, having etherealized it, Eliot would now "Redeem / The time." Or he would and would not. He is not altogether ready to forgo primal nostalgia: "And *after this* our exile" (emphasis added). But he would avoid this world's pregnancies ("a slotted window bellied like the fig's fruit"). What arrests him is "unheard, unspoken." Is he, then, reattached to the maternal principle or, on the contrary, does he seek to transcend it? His ambivalence is somehow at once persistent and mild.

Much the same ambivalence separates "The Journey of the Magi" from "Marina" (both part of *Ariel Poems*). The first perhaps rejoices more in "a temperate valley, / Wet, below the snow line, smelling of vegetation," than in Christ's birth, "this Birth . . . / Hard and bitter agony for us, like Death, our death." But "Marina" (as an *Ariel* poem) is ethereal. Although the speaker enumerates (like one stuck to the stuff of this world) seas, shores, rocks, islands, "scent of pine and the woodthrush singing through the fog," he calls these "images"—they are filmy things stripped of matter and floating about in memory. They constitute a place in which "grace" is "dissolved." Eliot's poem hovers at the point of total etherealization. It is the beautiful as the sublime, a contradictory condition:

> What is this face, less clear and clearer
> The pulse in the arm, less strong and stronger—
> Given or lent? more distant than stars and nearer than the eye

Drawn like spiritual air from Shakespeare's more solid Pericles, the speaker recovers his daughter, Marina, who is herself less flesh than a metaphor of the marine and feminine essence of memory and continuity. She is thus both near (inexplicably intimate and familiar) and distant (inexpressible). She allegorizes the speaker's more-than-Periclean hope for new life after this our exile, one that will recover something inestimably precious (hence the suitability, here, of the New World landscape along which Eliot sailed as a youth):

> This form, this face, this life
> Living to live in a world of time beyond me; let me
> Resign my life for this life, my speech for that unspoken
> The awakened, lips parted, the hope, the new ships.

This poetry of the noun is Eliot's stylistic approximation to impersonal grace. Even as it articulates a hope blessed by the feminine, the language denies itself a feminine texture.

Eliot's last masterwork, or series of them, *Four Quartets* (1943), prods the possibility of a Death that is Birth, but favors—or falls down on—the desiccated approach of "The Journey of the Magi," not the exquisite aeration of "Marina." Nonetheless, the first *Quartet*, "Burnt Norton," begins with this last: Eliot was with Emily Hale at the abandoned estate of Burnt Norton when a dry pool "was filled with water out of sunlight" and "The surface glittered out of heart of light." Unlike the hyacinth girl in *The Waste Land*, demanding that she be heaped with signs of fertility and devotion, the new female companion is the sidelong muse of a "reality" beyond human affections. But many of the following passages in the *Quartets* cultivate, as hinted, a humbling desolation that is acridly, then odorlessly, male. Eliot chooses redemption from love over a redeeming love.

Again, not for Eliot "The backward look behind the assurance / Of recorded history, the backward half-look / Over the shoulder, towards the primitive terror." He could not join Yeats and Lawrence in a renewing atavism (the originally pagan fertility myth of the Fisher King in *The Waste Land* is just a feint, a foldable structure). The "moments of happiness" are "not the sense of well-being, / Fruition, fulfilment, security or affection . . . but the sudden illumination" for which "agony" prepares. The "time of death is every moment"; death is the frontier. "Fare forward, travellers!" ("The Dry Salvages"). Eliot pressed the human to inhuman limits on the ethereal, not the material, side.

Instead of the mimesis of a dissolving grace, as in "Marina," what predominates here is a fallen *arrangement*, the more conspicuous for being repeated four times in its larger outline. The grand design of the *Quartets* has significance chiefly as the frame, occasion, and support of meditations that, although it is much to say that they are richly varied, are also frequently compelling and beautiful, if occasionally too much the exercise, a performance, or too prosy ("I have said before / That the past experience revived in the meaning / Is not the experience of one life only / But of many generations," etc.) This marks a great difference from *The Waste Land*, which is at once a seeming Brownian motion and a total action. *Four Quartets* recalls Eliot's announcement in "Ash-Wednesday" that he must "construct something / Upon which to rejoice." The lack of an engaged and complex dramatic movement leaves the poem open to a connoisseur's pick-and-choose operations. And it allows the poet's diction to skitter, skirt the donnish. Eliot is immeasurably more self-conscious in the *Quartets* than in *The Waste Land*.

Like Yeats and Lawrence, Eliot was great not least in allowing his imagination to go to the limits of conceiving a deity that, given his private torments and the want of a fertilizing intensity in the age, he thought it was of the utmost importance to summon. All three poets drew themselves up to full height to oppose the godless secularism inherited from the nineteenth century, and whatever corpses of Christianity it bore in its current. All three were explorers, pioneers of continuity. But Eliot—largely because he repudiated as unregenerate the "whole personality" favored by Yeats and Lawrence—had no single style, was not at home in a living man's speech. Speech hurt him into poetry. He ventriloquized (*The Waste Land*); he litanized ("Ash-Wednesday"); he stripped the language down ("Marina"). Finally, like a John Ashbery—without, as yet, the historical provocation to be edgily flippant, almost cheerfully deprived of the great beliefs—he practiced in *Four Quartets* a heterogeneity of verse manner and forms that, unlike those in *The Waste Land*, are not so much reinvented or deconstructed as quoted—donned and discarded. It was late in Eliot's career, late in modernism, late for new faith that could move poetry in new ways.

Calvin Bedient

Further Reading

Donoghue, Denis, ed. *The Integrity of Yeats*. Cork: Mercier, 1964. Reprinted Folcroft, Penn.: Folcroft, 1971.

Donoghue, Denis. *William Butler Yeats*. New York, Ecco Press, 1989.

Gilbert, Sandra. *Acts of Attention: The Poems of D. H. Lawrence*. 2d ed. Carbondale: Southern Illinois University Press, 1990.

Gordon, Lyndall. *Eliot's Early Years*. Oxford: Oxford University Press, 1977.

Gordon, Lyndall. *Eliot's New Life*. Oxford: Oxford University Press, 1988.

MacNeice, Louis. *The Poetry of W. B. Yeats*. London: Oxford University Press, 1941.

Marshall, Tom. *The Psychic Mariner: A Reading of the Poems of D. H. Lawrence*. New York: Viking, 1970.

Moody, Anthony David. *Thomas Stearns Eliot, Poet*. Cambridge: Cambridge University Press, 1979.

North, Michael. *The Political Aesthetic of Yeats, Eliot, and Pound*. Cambridge: Cambridge University Press, 1991.

Stead, Christian Karlson. *Pound, Yeats, Eliot, and the Modernist Movement*. New Brunswick, N.J.: Rutgers University Press, 1985.

Whitaker, Thomas R. *Swan and Shadow: Yeats's Dialogue with History*. Chapel Hill: University of North Carolina Press, 1964.

Poetry in England, 1945–1990

THE anonymous leading article in the *Spectator* of October 1, 1954, "In the Movement," hailed the emergence of a new group of writers, a generation whose sensibility was "*bored* by the despair of the Forties, *not much interested* in suffering, and extremely *impatient* of poetic sensibility. . . . The Movement, as well as being *anti*-phoney, is *anti*-wet; *sceptical*, robust, *ironic*. . . ." This is a Movement manqué, it seems, for the reviewer defines its energy entirely by negatives. Again, in the polemical introduction to the first English anthology of Movement verse, *New Lines* (1956), Robert Conquest groups his poets under "a negative determination to avoid bad principles." And in a poem that now reads as a thesis piece for the movement, Philip Larkin's "I remember, I remember," the speaker lists the high moments in the life of the conventional poet as nonexperiences: remembering where his "childhood was unspent," including the garden where he "did not invent / Blinding theologies of flowers and fruits," he recalls how his uninspired juvenilia "was not set up in blunt ten-point, nor read," and drifts (hardly drives) toward the proverbial wisdom that "'nothing, like something, happens anywhere.'"

While this sensibility appears (it is hard to think of it "flourishing") in the mid-1950s, its cartoonlike simplifications have prolonged its life among critics of postwar English poetry, especially American commentators. They can use it to label the imaginative project of a subsiding world power, whose poets, formally conservative and reactionary, battle the (putative) excesses of an energy they do not own, in particular the experimental and convention-dismaying verve of American

modernists and postmodernists. The credibility of this caricature will
be questioned, but the tendency to regard English poetry as behind the
times derives from the reality of circumstances in postwar Britain. By
1946 it was clear that the chain of poetic generations had been broken—the departure of W. H. Auden for America in 1939 was followed
by the deaths of the best war poets (Keith Douglas, Alun Lewis, Sidney Keyes)—and this disruption of continuity helped to create the
impression that English poets would never catch up. The war itself represented a hiatus in English cultural life, when intellectuals became
people who sent messages to captive Europe.

Yet the duress that slowed the initial renaissance of English verse
might also remain as a potent imaginative memory, a resource that supplies poetry with a sense of the reality of history and the truths of
tragedy. The best English poets of the postwar period—Larkin, Donald Davie, Geoffrey Hill, Ted Hughes, and Charles Tomlinson, in the
first generation—engage those awarenesses, among other things, in
ways that certainly challenge a critical stereotyping of their diminished
force. The negativism of the movement writers, first of all, represents
more than a justification of inertia: it is a response, sometimes pre-
dictable but in other ways searching and intelligent, to the intellectual
and political culture of the recent war. In this context their poetry
recovers some of its original strength and complexity.

Movement writers aimed their rebukes at the excesses of the major
school of the preceding decade. The New Romantics or Apocalyptics,
seeking to reach an emotionally and sensually charged awareness equal
to that of war, had exaggerated the mannerisms of Romantics such as
Dylan Thomas, and their extravagant surrealism was countered by the
dour probity of the 1950s. More subtle and interesting are the connections the movement poets drew between those literary excesses and the
calamities of history. Kingsley Amis, writing a Fabian tract on Romanticism, linked the ideological extremism of the war with the emotional
and imaginative excesses of Romanticism, which leads one, he argued,
to believe in causes which are not one's own, not subject to the approval
of the individual's reason.

While the movement poets feared ideological commitment and the
verbal inflation attending it, they had also gone through adolescence in
the 1930s, a decade in which English verse had ostensibly regained its
social commitment. Their sense of lost purpose emerges in a play whose
energies are often likened to theirs, John Osborne's *Look Back in Anger*

(1956); the problems of its disaffected protagonist—the "angry young man" Jimmy Porter—turn around the fact that there are "no great causes left." An understanding of this moment in literary history is properly thickened, then, in Donald Davie's 1955 poem, "Remembering the Thirties," which reads at once like a rejection of heroic intellectual causes and a lament for their passing: "A neutral tone is nowadays preferred," he notes, but then concedes, "it may be better, if we must, / To praise a stance impressive and absurd / Than not to see the hero for the dust."

Another point of provocation for movement poets was the vatic posturing of the New Romantics—the quasi-prophetic intensities of apocalyptic poets such as G. S. Fraser. On one hand the incomprehensibility of that verse allowed it to stand as the most recent example—a kind of terminus ad quem—of the whole cult of difficulty in literary modernism. The phenomenon in the 1920s and 1930s of coterie literature proved synonymous, a number of commentators agreed, with the destruction of meaning, the global nihilism of recent history. More specifically, Donald Davie linked the mysterious, irreducible images of Pound (and other Imagists) with the hieratic powers of fascism, claiming that the line of descent from aesthetics to politics was direct. Thus Davie's *Purity of Diction in English Verse* (1952) and *Articulate Energy: An Enquiry into the Syntax of English Poetry* (1955) attempted to raise the standards of intelligent lucidity and rational statement in verse to replace the coercive unintelligibility of the postsymbolists, modernists, and New Romantics.

The oracular difficulty of this verse fractured the old contract between writer and reader, complained Philip Larkin, who joined others in blaming it for the "decline" in contemporary English culture and society. The very dire nature of postwar circumstances, on the other hand, placed the poet in the role of a reformer, who may assume the mantle of moral authority, the character-in-voice of the social prophet. Thus their *rappel à l'ordre* comprises but exceeds the orderly surfaces of neo-Augustan verse, calling upon the latent strengths of the visionary. Davie's poem on the 1930s, for example, moves its grammar of discursive statements toward final images no less elemental, no more readily convertible into easy prose meaning, than the hierophantic figures of Isaiah:

> For courage is the vegetable king,
> The sprig of all ontologies, the weed
> That beards the slag heap with his hectoring,
> Whose green adventure is to run to seed.

"Run to seed": degenerated, or passed on to the next generation? The phrase catches up divided attitudes to the social causes of the 1930s poets and, more crucially, to the value of prose clarity that its oracular ambivalence defies.

That the movement was nonprogrammatic but eclectic or even dialectical is suggested most forcibly by its youngest member, Thom Gunn, who combined its severe punctilio of prosodic form with the stagy machismo of the Angry Young Man. As in "Lines for a Book":

> I think of all the toughs through history
> And thank heaven they lived, continually.
> I praise the overdogs from Alexander
> To those who would not play with Stephen Spender.

Filtering his fantasies of sexual dominance through the traditions of poetic wit and the Renaissance school of magnificence, measuring the excitements of motorcycle gangs and rock-and-roll music to the decorous cadences of the heroic couplet, Gunn seemed to allow the elements of verbal and metrical control to hypostatize as themes. Thus he validated, unwittingly it now seems, the coarsest of masteries, producing a verse of fiercely intelligent brutality. His self-awareness in this regard coincided with his move to the United States later in the 1950s, where the influence of Yvor Winters both extended and modified his earlier formalism, and where his poetry developed in response to pressures different from those affecting his English contemporaries. Yet he remains the most visible register of the tensions and countercurrents at work in the popular and literary culture of the decade.

These conflicts enriched the more important poetry Larkin wrote through the 1950s. He overtly rejected by 1946 the hieratically Yeatsian manner of his earlier verse, but later (mostly unpublished) pieces witness its more than residual force. His most productive challenge lay in its accommodation to the plain-speech ethic of Thomas Hardy (the "neutral tones" Davie hears in the 1950s acknowledge a model in Hardy's poem of that title). Little accommodation occurs in "Church Going," however, one of Larkin's best known poems. Here the typically wry and sardonic English wit, the poet-clerk, asserts a poetics of common sense against the portentous absurdity of the poet-prophet:

> Mounting the lectern, I peruse a few
> Hectoring large-scale verses, and pronounce
> 'Here endeth' much more loudly than I'd meant.
> The echoes snigger briefly . . .

Despite a strategic concession to the value of "seriousness" that religion reinforces, the poem is really an opportunistic deflation of sacral majesties. It differs from the more complex engagements of "Next, Please," whose character-in-voice is waiting in a ration queue. Speaking in lines politely filed, waiting for his proverbial ship to come in, he hears the call of the title, but notes drolly:

> Only one ship is seeking us, a black-
> Sailed unfamiliar, towing at her back
> A huge and birdless silence. In her wake
> No waters breed or break.

Unlike "Church Going," which opposes its blandly reasonable speaker to the mysteries, "Next, Please" allows its title idiom—the whole order of civil normality that it invokes—to tap into the dark backward and abysm of fate.

Such interactions between the vatic and prosaic were prepared for in a number of poems Larkin tried unsuccessfully to publish in the later 1940s (gathered in the book-length manuscript *In the Grip of Light*). In "Many Famous Feet Have Trod," for example, the gnomic, incantatory voice is moderated by a plonky pentameter, a homey decasyllabic that does not neutralize it, but rather grounds it in a kind of proverbial wisdom. Those "famous feet" have trod

> Sublunary paths, and famous hands have weighed
> The strength they have against the strength they need;
> And famous lips interrogated God
> Concerning franchise in eternity . . .

Behind this measure lies a force of critical intelligence articulated in Davie's 1957 poem, "Rejoinder to a Critic." Just as the prophetic intensity of the apocalyptics partakes of the riot of recent history, emotional excess risks the catastrophes of the last war. "'Alas, alas, who's injured by my love?'" he quotes Donne to query, "And recent history answers: Half Japan!" At this moment of political and literary history, then, the one thing needful is a controlling of the time, a simple metrical regularity, and Davie offers this as the tonic measure: "Appear concerned only to make it scan!"

Davie's new metrical contract opens a middle way between social normality and imaginative intensity and so defines an area of common ground for poets normally regarded as antithetical talents. Geoffrey Hill, usually heard as a poet thriving in solitary defiance of his times, enters into the same compromises that characterized the work of Larkin and Davie. The fiction of "Holy Thursday" (1952), for example, leads the poet toward "the wolf's lair," emblematic of the dangerous precincts of apocalyptic poetry (Hill's title identifies a sacred location), while the taming of the beast in the final lines relies for its poetic credibility on the normalizing cadence, more interestingly varied but no less stabilizing than Larkin's or Davie's:

> 'I have been touched with that fire,
> And have fronted the she-wolf's lair.
> Lo, she lies gentle and innocent of desire
> Who was my constant myth and terror.'

Similarly, in "The Bidden Guest" (1953), a regular iambic octosyllabic parcels out the blessings of the pentecostal inspiration, scanning and counterstressing the vatic inrush:

> The starched unbending candles stir
> As though a wind had caught their hair,
> As though the surging of a host
> Had charged the air of Pentecost.

With the movement poets Hill also shares a central, ramifying wariness about the morality of poetic engagement with the horrors of history. In "Eight Years After" Davie speaks for the conscience of his contemporaries—we might "have no stomach for atrocities," he concedes, but "we brook them better once they have been named." "To name," as Davie continues, "is to acknowledge," ultimately to make reasonable and acceptable, and so the one responsible strategy for engaging the unspeakable is to leave it unnamed, to evoke it in an art of extreme obliquity. These needs help to explain the broad appeal in the 1950s of the New Criticism, which allowed paradox and irony, those hallmarks of movement tone, to stand in place of the violent conflicts of history and nature.

If poetic appeasement is the one phobia of the decade, however, movement poets often avoid its dangers to a fault, settling for the most attenuated presentation of the world's torn body; more frequently, they choose not to engage at all, not to risk the accommodation. It is Hill who turns the anxiety of the age into the lasting art of the period, at once forcing the problem to critical mass and breaking through to unique solutions. In "Two Formal Elegies: For the Jews in Europe"

(1955–1956) he echoes Davie, to begin with, noting how the "long death" of the last war, in being "documented," will be sanitized, made verbally "safe." In his radical definition, however, the problem goes to the roots of poetry, which "deceives with sweetness harshness," traducing the matter of sordid fact into the consonance of aesthetic form, thus making it not only acceptable but attractive.

The task is to find a music that replicates the brutality of history without abandoning a sense of the superior order of poetry, a tonic possibility that gives nothing away to the realist. These ambitions generate the distinctive textures of the poems he begins to write in 1955. Witness the studied ineloquence of the abrupt overture to "Requiem for the Plantagenet Kings":

> For whom the possessed sea littered, on both shores,
> Ruinous arms; being fired, and for good,
> To sound the constitution of just wars,
> Men, in their eloquent fashion, understood.

A parallel extension of New Critical principles informs the early work of Ted Hughes, who is usually (and wrongly) seen as a poet wild and whirling as the moors of his native Yorkshire. The challenge and value of that critical sensibility—to densify the world's body in the physical body of language and thus subject it to the formal order of art—inspires Hughes's imaginative vision as well as his technical practice in *The Hawk in the Rain* (1957). The title poem, for example, uses heavy alliteration to thicken the verbal texture and consolidate the material reality of words, while its fiction shows the poet straining toward the hawk's steady flight—a point of supernal perfection, an overmastering formal control:

> I drown in the drumming ploughland, I drag up
> Hell after heel from the swallowing of the earth's mouth,
> From clay that clutches my each step to the ankle
> With the habit of the dogged grave, but the hawk
>
> Effortlessly at height hangs his still eye.
> His wings hold all creation in a weightless quiet . . .

The vantage of the hawk is associated more specifically with the advantage of art in other poems, as in "A Modest Proposal." Here two lovers, likened to two frenzied wolves in the wood, are recomposed and calmed at the sight of the great huntsman, depicted here in the lineaments of aesthetic concord. As "His embroidered / Cloak floats" by, the lovers may follow the model of "the two great-eyed greyhounds," who "leap like one, making delighted sounds."

Like Hill and, before him, Allen Tate, Hughes utters "the 'formal pledge of art against aimless power.'" These principles are pushed to visionary extreme in "The Martyrdom of Bishop Farrar," which includes the (reputed) last words of the title figure in the epigraph: "'If I flinch from the pain of the burning, believe not the doctrine that I have preached.'" Like this witness's body, Hughes's own artifice attests to the powers of a transcendent art by containing the pain of history, subduing its primary violence to the higher order of art—a poetry lined by the silence of its own constraint.

The skill and nerve needed to hold this New Critical balance are too often lost in *Hawk in the Rain*, which lapses frequently into sheer verbal sensationalism. The textured tensility of its best poems proves the norm rather than the exception in Hughes's second book, *Lupercal* (1960). His achievement finds precept and example in "To Paint a Water Lily," which develops a contrast between the exquisite flower— precious as the verbal surfaces of his best verse—and the submarine horrors, the elemental forces that Hughes both replicates and contains in the well-behaved body of his poetic language. Here the trim couplets convey a sense of immanent force—as a barrel of water charged with a million volts might show only the faintest rippling on the surface:

Now paint the long-necked lily-flower

Which, deep in both worlds, can be still
As a painting, trembling hardly at all

Though the dragonfly alight,
Whatever horror nudge her root.

The successes of *Lupercal* turn on acts of verbal restraint that suggest a psychological complex and interest of their own. The first two poems frame it. "Things Present" develops a comparison between a tramp's shelter, fabricated out of materials at hand, and the make-shift constructions of the poet, whose "hands" use words to "embody a now, erect a here"—a homey version of the New Critic's verbal icon. But the lowly circumstances of the tramp's abode generate a compensatory fantasy— "My sires had towers and great names, / . . . dreams / The tramp in the

sodden ditch"—and a similar fiction informs the second poem, "Everyman's Odyssey." Here Telemachus awaits his own noble forebear, who
"arrives out of the bottom of the world" to avenge himself on "the beggars that brawl on my porch"; they will be "flung through the doors,"
the poet's diction promises exultantly, "with their bellies full of arrows."
The parallel situations of the two poems suggest that the energies being
repressed in Hughes's best art may well return to be revenged. The New
Critical compact is being observed in *Lupercal* in a fashion equally
charged and precarious.

No such doubts attend the technical masteries of Charles Tomlinson, who returns the New Critical emphasis on craft to its formative
energies in Anglo-American modernism. If the movement poets
shared at least partially in the spirit of early modernism, echoing the
anti-Romantic exertions of T. E. Hulme, these affinities were realized
only in the face of similar enemies. Despite Davie's (rejected) suggestion that Tomlinson be included in *New Lines*, this poet was alone from
the start. On his own he discovered and drew upon the eclectic verve of
radical modernism; painter as well as poet, he projected the possibility
of a synthetic art, like the vorticists'. Its debts are acknowledged and its
dividends promised already in "Poem" (1951):

> Wakening with the window over fields
> To the coin-clear harness-jingle as a float
> Clips by, and each succeeding hoof fall, now remote,
> Breaks clean and frost-sharp on the unstopped ear.

The allusion to Odysseus' stopping of his mariners' ears against the
Sirens' song recalls Pound's evocation of the same myth in *Hugh Selwyn
Mauberley*. That dangerous music is made safe here, for its sensuous
acoustic has been rinsed and wrung clean by a visual stringency:

> The hooves describe an arabesque on space,
> A dotted line in sound that falls and rises
> . . . .
> And space vibrates, enlarges with the sound;
> Though space is soundless, yet creates
> From very soundlessness a ground
> To counterstress the lilting hoof fall as it breaks.

Tomlinson directs his attentions to the dynamics and subtleties of sense
perception. For him, the aesthetic object offers the sacramental occa-

sion for sense activity, and its quasi-sacred quality accounts for the visual puritanism here.

To make verse a kind of painterly music is the ambition that accounts for a major body of work in Tomlinson's poems of the 1950s. Much of *The Necklace* (1955) extends the synthetic principle of "Poem," using the silence of the painter's space to edge a valid poetic speech, parsing and sharpening verbal music with the divisions and definitions special to the eye, as enacted by short plastic lines and radical enjambments:

Facts have no eyes. One must
Surprise them, as one surprises a tree
By regarding its (shall I say?)
Facets of copiousness.

By the early 1960s it was easy to see Tomlinson's turn to American modernism as a symptom and warning of the depletion of English poetic resources. The image of *The Stagnant Society* (the title for Michael Shanks's 1964 study first instanced the phrase) depicted the mood in the early years of that tumultuous decade. The 1950s had succeeded in stabilizing Britain, producing the limited triumphs of consensus politics—the "middle way" of democratic socialism testified to the broad center of English political life, which witnessed the practical reconciliation of Tory and Labour interests. Its most notable achievements were the (by and large) peaceful contraction of the old empire and the establishment of programs in the new welfare state. These two developments were cited in Anthony Hartley's *A State of England* (1963), however, as an explanation for the current malaise: the waning of global power and the expenses of the domestic agenda conspired to produce a feeling of shrinkage—financial, intellectual, spiritual—in English national life.

This sense of enervation generated two poetic responses. On one hand there was the rejuvenation of art by mass culture, whose energies had been stimulated by the democratic programs of the 1950s and whose voices were heard most memorably in the pop poetry of "the Liverpool scene." The prospect of a huge audience for poetry certainly affected the work of the major poets, but they did not participate in that culture so much as respond to the whole social upheaval it seemed to symbolize; their reactions may best be assessed later, from the vantage of the end of the decade. The other response to stagnancy, integral to the ongoing work of these poets in the 1960s, was set out by A. Alvarez, in his now well known 1962 essay "The New Poetry, or Beyond the Gentility Principle." Identifying the misguided faith of the English in normality (the principle of good manners), Alvarez asked contemporary poets to open themselves to the awarenesses of modern history, both political and intellectual. "The forcible recognition of a mass evil outside us," he stated, "has developed precisely parallel with psychoanalysis; that is, with the recognition of the way in which the same forces are at work within us." Alvarez called for a poetry written in the elemental clarity of these basic facts. These issues inform some of the most important English verse to be written in the 1960s, although not all poets resolve the problems in his terms.

The most interesting poems of Larkin's *The Whitsun Weddings* (1964) elude the blandishments of gentility and engage the crisis Alvarez defined—for Larkin a critical point at which poetry always finds itself. "At this unique distance from isolation," Larkin writes in an Auden-like discourse on the poet's social contingency, "It becomes still more difficult to find / Words at once true and kind, / Or not untrue and not unkind." The Old English style of litotes (negating the contrary) is a form of understatement, which here both concedes and defies the awful truth, affirming the humanist wish to resist it through the antithetical powers of poetry. These powers translate the subject of "MCMXIV," Larkin's poem on the outbreak of the Great War, into the unpronounceable silence of the Roman numerals in its title.

Unspeakable, these archaic letters provide a powerful coadjutor to the atrocity of mass war, and they promise an oppositional force in the English language of the verse that follows. How forceful is this opposition? "Never such innocence, / Never before or since," Larkin concludes, as he envisions that last moment, the climacteric of the premodern, with

> the men
> Leaving the gardens tidy,
> The thousands of marriages
> Lasting a while longer:
> Never such innocence again.

The very resistance of human language to the fury and mire of human veins causes the poem, in the actual fabric of its images, to lose touch with the dire reality, and, in its imaginative attention, to lapse into the single vision of golden age nostalgia.

The limitations of Larkin's engagements appear as nothing less than dangerous delusions to Geoffrey Hill, much of whose work in *King Log* (1968) sounds a vital challenge to the humanist compromise. "September Song," responding to a Jewish child "deported" from the Reich, holds the art of *not* saying to a fierce rebuke. The negative constructions in its opening lines show the susceptibilities of poetic avoidance:

> Undesirable you may have been, untouchable
> you were not. Not forgotten
> or passed over at the proper time.

"Not forgotten" reads here as an obscene euphemism for the all too powerful memory of the Nazi state, whose seizure (the Passover failing) of the child assumes the normality of a bureaucratic timetable—"at the proper time." The humanist tendency to mark the atrocity as alien, thus to push it to the fringes of language and celebrate the normal, amounts to nothing less than appeasement. Atrocity is accepted (in the rhetorical fiction of the poem) in the pastoral elegy of the final lines, which assimilate the child's death to the beneficent cycles of the seasons:

> September fattens on vines. Roses
> flake from the wall. The smoke
> of harmless fires drifts to my eyes.
> This is plenty. This is more than enough.

Far from countering the horror, Hill suggests, such poetry enters into passive complicity with it, as revealed in the (strategically failed) apologia of "Ovid in the Third Reich," a poet who remained silent under Hitler. "I love my work and my children," this caricature of the poet-clerk protests, but "God / Is distant, difficult." And "Things happen."

Hill's own poetry of historical engagement appears at its finest in "Funeral Music," a sequence of eight sonnets that move freely through the political and intellectual circumstances of the Wars of the Roses, commemorating the deaths of three prominent aristocrats in particular. The nascent Neoplatonism of the period gives all three a touch of *contemptus mundi*, a diffidence that intersects oddly but engagingly with the momentum of worldly power they assumed with their birthrights. This contradiction goes to a formative paradox in the sequence. The sonnets combine a severe punctilio with a riot of sensations, a fastidious observation of rules with the densely sensuous sounds of history—

a counterpoint Hill characterizes as "an ornate and heartless music punctuated by mutterings, blasphemies, and cries for help." As in the third sonnet:

> They bespoke doomsday and they meant it by
> God, their curved metal rimming the low ridge.

Here the need to maintain the decasyllabic line of the blank-verse pentameter causes the exclamation to be broken at the formal division, heightening the force of the expletive. The aesthetic form applies an ascetic edge that serves to echo and amplify the primary violence of history, not to deny it. The same paradox generates the complex verbal textures of "History as Poetry," Hill's dramatic declaration on the subject. Its quatrains are rigidly syllabic, featuring nine counts per line, but the very strain of observing this ascetic form—syllabic measure goes against the stress rhythms natural to the physical body of the English language—fractures the language into phrasal fragments, orchestrating a music as abrasive as history:

> Poetry as salutation; taste
> Of Pentecost's ashen feast. Blue wounds.
> The tongues's atrocities. Poetry
> Unearths . . .

It is Hill's studied effort to handle language as verbal plastic, reshaping it as a material no less thickly resistant than the history to which the contemporary muse has called poets. The corporeal word is also the mark of Ted Hughes's achievement in *Wodwo* (1967). These poems witness a remarkable combination of acoustic density and representative immediacy, an effect that depends on the substantiality of the words themselves. Not onomatopoeia but a more individual and intricate art shows in Hughes's practice of loading his line with two sound patterns: an outcrop stone is "*wart*ed with *quartz* pe*bb*les from the sea's wom*b*." The repetition gives weight to the language, while the double pattern injects variety, a sense of suppleness, effecting all in all a kind of elastic substantiality. The poetic line moves like a muscle flexing, exerting a force equally compelling and disturbing when it is exercised on the subjects of recent history—as in "Out," on the two wars of the century.

It is the nerve and sinew of the world's body that Hughes is seeking to capture in words. In doing so, however, he is testing the limits of the (now old) New Critical compact. A sign of his opportunistic compliance with its rules appears in a now dominant stylistic mannerism. He frequently allows the title of a poem to run into its first line: "Her Husband (Comes home dull with coal-dust . . .")"; "Boom (And faces at the glutted shop window . . .")"; "Bowled Over (By kiss of death, bullet on brow . . . ")"; "The Howling of Wolves (Is without world . . .")"; "You Drive in a Circle (Slowly a hundred miles through the powerful rain . . .")". According to convention, the title works like the frame on a painting, both composing the verbal icon and providing distance on it. Hughes obliterates the distance he has invoked; the vantage is titillating in being precarious—it exerts the excitement of a foothold being washed from under us. The old sense of absolute separation on which the artifact relies for its status as re-presentation now seems to be valued mainly for the sensation it conveys in being violated.

These tricks signal an exhaustion of the resources Hughes drew upon in his early career. Between 1963 and 1966, in fact, he wrote almost no poetry. This inactivity is not surprising, in light of Sylvia Plath's suicide in 1963, but it also attests to Hughes's need for new points of poetic growth. His productivity revives strikingly in 1966, when he begins (with Daniel Weissbort) to edit *Modern Poetry in Translation*, and discovers the work of Eastern Europeans such as Miroslav Holub and Vasco Popa. Having grown up in the midst of World War II, these poets showed Hughes an imagination fired and hardened by the worst history had to offer. Thrown back on their primitive wits, negotiating grimly but jauntily with the void, their language sounds equally banal and hieratic, clichéd and secretly wise, displaying the same kind of heroism in minimal conditions that characterizes the best theatrical art of the absurd. Their compatibility with Hughes seemed natural, given his characteristic concerns, but it is fair to say that the English poet seems to be mimicking a sensibility too hard won to be imitated successfully. Their gallows humor, testifying to their own unkillable humanity, never quite assumes for Hughes the grace of the gratuity it represents in their world. In fear of rubbing away the horror in "Karma"—"When the world-quaking tears were dropped / At Dresden at Buchenwald"—he tends to rub it in: "Earth spewed up the bones of the Irish." He fails the chance for redemptive laughter that Holub or Popa would seize with suitably somber gusto.

While Hughes's cultivation of this foreign influence betrays a stance alien to theirs, it is a mark of Tomlinson's major achievement that he appropriates the pyrotechnics of American modernism for the sake of praising and preserving a specifically British tradition. The challenge emerges in "Return to Hinton, Written on the author's return to Hinton Blewett from the United States" (1963), the first poem he composed in the three-step line of William Carlos Williams. How can that rhythm, reputedly shaped to the cadences of Williams's own regional speech, work to the advantage of the English tradition, as typified in the poem by the King James Bible lying open on the parlor table?

The American technique offers the English poet an externality of perspective, promoting a higher than usual self-consciousness in his presentation of British material and a speech rooted in that culture. This motive appears clear in light of "History," where Tomlinson depicts a provincial Englishman, entirely tied to his locale, as "the guardian / Of a continuity he cannot see." Tomlinson's is a characteristically modernist enterprise, for it turns on the central crisis of the modern—the perception that present and past are not continuous; that tradition, far from living on its own, must be consciously maintained and restored.

In technique as well as in spirit Tomlinson follows the lead of the modernists Pound and Williams, Olson and Creeley. The line is his focus of critical attention and poetic experiment. Returning in "Lines" to the original image (and etymological meaning) of verse (*versere*, to turn) as lines ploughed in a field, he attends specially to the moment of the turn, the hiatus between consecutive lines, "when, one furrow / more lies done with / and the tractor hesitates." The pause at the end of a line provides a point of heightened awareness, a kind of high ground from which we can see language as language, as the content as well as the means of artistic representation. Similar aims had been instanced in the work of Stevie Smith (b. 1902), who could present her own character-in-voice—a rich compound of generic idiom and individual inflection—as the center of verbal attention. And while Tomlinson's initiative also aligns him with the poetics of avant-garde movements such as Dadaists and the language school, it works to essentially conservative purposes for him.

Displaying the language as well as speaking it expressively, Tomlinson can exhibit styles otherwise archaic or outdated. He recovers forms of traditional eloquence—regaining an Augustan decorousness and symmetry in isochronous lines, or reviving a Renaissance splendor in diction. In "The Picture of J. T. in a Prospect of Stone," for

example, the irregularly enjambing line disrupts the Marvellian period, making its grandiloquence seem equally self-conscious and
assured:

> but let her play
> her innocence away
>   emerging
>   as she does
> between
>   her doom (unknown),
>   her unmown green.

Renewed by experiment and invention, Tomlinson's traditionalism
stands opposed to developments in contemporary literary culture,
above all the pop-poetry and mass-reading scene of the later 1960s.
Sharing the stage with crowd-pleasing poets in "A Dream, or the worst
of both worlds" (1969), he feels no connection to their newly expanded audience. A nearly ascetic revulsion drives him back "to the sobriety of a dawn-cold bed, to own / my pariah's privilege, my three-inch
spaces, / the reader's rest and editor's colophon." Asserting the strin-
gencies of print-based literacy against the casual orality of the public
muse, he is reacting to forces that have produced changes greater than
a shift in poetic media. The freedoms of the new poetry were synonymous with the license of the new "permissive society." Poetry drew a
demotic brio from its expanded base, but its alignment with the idiom
and sensationalism of rock music signaled a coalition aimed at ends
more drastic and far-reaching than a removal of verse from the hands
of an aging poetic clerisy. To numerous commentators the new per-
missiveness announced nothing less than the end of the old civic culture that had made Britain great. Old certainties undone, a sense of
living at the end of history: these conditions inform much of the poetry written in the later 1960s and early 1970s. The most durable, like
Tomlinson's, seems to have been conceived in opposition to mainstream developments, but these reactions vary in their quality and
credibility.

The title of Donald Davie's "Or, Solitude" (1969) promises an obvious alternative to the mass compulsions of the 1960s. "A farm boy lost
in the snow," who "is called 'alone,'" leads Davie to proclaim:

The metaphysicality
Of poetry, how I need it!

And yet it was for years
What I refused to credit.

Trading the movement poet's skeptical empiricism for transcendent principles and fixed assumptions, Davie's reaction to the convention-dismaying decade now ending seems complete but simplistic.

A more complex engagement sustains the book-length sequences of Ted Hughes's *Crow* (1970) and Geoffrey Hill's *Mercian Hymns* (1971), which proceed according to needs and aims similar to those explained, simultaneously but independently, in a set of lectures by George Steiner, published in 1971 as *In Bluebeard's Castle: Some Notes Towards the Redefinition of Culture*. Echoing Eliot in his subtitle but addressing other redefinitions of culture in the 1960s, Steiner places Eliot's idea of a centered, unified tradition in crisis. Drastic uncertainty in the present returns him to the roots of cultural identity: a story of origins. He directs attention to "the myth of the nineteenth century" and its "imagined garden of liberal culture"—a secular, post-Enlightenment version of the Eden tale. Identifying the now widespread need to (re)claim the primary values of human civilization, Steiner provides context and rationale for the essential imaginative action of Hughes's and Hill's sequences, which return, variously, to myths of the beginning.

The title figure of Hughes's *Crow* belongs to the "trickster" type in primitive and folk literature. He engages in a game of wits with the creator, ostensibly attempting to improve nature and make it suitable for human habitation. No idealistic messiah, the trickster is usually greedy, oversexed, and perverse, but his actions spring out of a kind of unkillable biological optimism, seeking to ameliorate the first conditions of existence. This project brings Crow to the scenes of biblical Genesis. In "A Childish Prank," for example, God's work has left Adam and Eve in somatic stupor, which Crow attempts to cure by inventing human sexuality:

He bit the Worm, God's only son,
Into two writhing halves.

He stuffed into man the tail half
With the wounded end hanging out.

He stuffed the head half headfirst into woman.

The change hardly marks an improvement, however. "Neither knew what had happened" as "Man awoke being dragged across the grass" and "Woman awoke to see him coming." Failing to alter creation for the better (the high jinks generate no redemptive laughter), the sequence revisits the Eden topos constantly, expressing the protagonist's indefatigable energy but inscribing no new design worth changing the world into. Mired in the old Paradise, tied to scenes of contested beginnings, *Crow* has taken on the challenge Steiner defined, but it seems to have failed the task of rewriting the myth of origins credibly, satisfactorily.

This judgment should not miss another level of meaning in the poem, however, one which shows it participating in the conflicts of its own historical moment. While Hughes is responding to Steiner's perception that contemporary mass culture has disrupted traditional certainties, and is thus returning to the site of origins for the sake of clarifying first principles, the poem relies for its literary manner on the very stuff of the popular culture it is reacting against. The farcical logic of the absurd, Crow's miraculous comeback from spectacular deaths, and Hughes's denial of cause-and-effect sequence in the progression between episodes: these features align Crow with the durable comic-strip character, the rubbery cartoon hero of popular culture. Building a poem up to a final punch line, concentrating its effect on the sudden "Bang!" or reversal of expectation, Hughes shows a crowd-exciting touch that testifies as well to the compulsions of the new mass audience. And so Crow's attempt to restart the world out of the ruins of the old witnesses his historical contingency, revealing Hughes's own imprisonment in the circumstances he is straining so powerfully to counter.

While Hughes fails to rewrite a myth of cultural beginnings, he manages to inscribe a legend of the self, one which he generates out of his evident connection to the protagonist. Like Crow, Hughes is a survivor—of the death of Plath, of the various holocausts that provide the sequence with its vocabulary of historical reference. Yet this self-enlargement also marks another reaction syndrome. Hughes is protesting the anti-individualist premise of contemporary history, specifically, the leveling tendency of commodity culture, swollen in the 1960s to previously untold proportions: the fate of art and artist in the age of mechanical reproduction is to have uniqueness annulled. Anticipating this reaction in the early 1960s, Hartley's *A State of England* proleptically denied the power of popular masses to generate culture and offered a fervent apologia for the primacy of the single, creative individual. A decade later, Hughes's defensive myth of the self—a fabulous figure pumped up to gigantistic proportions—records, in its very distortions, the assaults the private individual has suffered.

The same enterprise of mythologizing the self informs Geoffrey Hill's sequence of thirty prose poems (or versets) *Mercian Hymns*, which turns on a single dramatic conceit. Hill presents his own character as a child in Worcestershire, in his own native Mercia, in the likeness of its first king, the eighth-century Offa. The self-aggrandizement implicit in this scheme does not issue into the egotistical indulgence of *Crow*, however. Hill grounds the sequence in provincial history and local geography; he subjects his sometimes airy fantasy of the self to those elementary facts, a limitation that produces a tone of complex, modulating ironies:

> Exile or pilgrim set me once more upon that ground:
> my rich and desolate childhood. Dreamy, smug-faced, sick on
> outings—I who was taken to be a king of some kind, a prodigy,
> a maimed one.

Hill's identification of king and child also allows him to transform the order of the political state into the rules of a child's game. In this way he follows the motive and plot of trickster literature: he revisits the origins of human society (Offa's is the *first* Mercian kingdom) and reorganizes it according to the paradigms of desire; of child's games. He follows the psychology of play in Johan Huizinga's *Homo Ludens*, which presents it as equally anarchic and regulated, spontaneous and disciplined, and Hill uses this vision in his redefinition of the original character of human society. In Hymn VII, for example, he balances the child's antic and disruptive behavior, his regal caprice, with the formal order of his imaginative domain, and he matches this complex in the tonality, which assimilates the child's violence to the decorous repetitions of ritual:

> After school he lured Ceolred, who was sniggering
> with fright, down to the old quarries, and flayed him. Then,
> leaving Ceolred, he journeyed for hours, calm and alone, in
> his private derelict sandlorry named *Albion*.

The ceremonial demeanor of *Mercian Hymns* extends from these local moments to its containing form, which ritualizes beginning and end. It opens with an invocation of the medieval king in the cadenced heroic catalogue of the Old English *scop*, and it concludes with a protracted liturgy for Offa's death. Formal closure and integral structure appear as well in the model sequences of English poetic modernism— *The Anathemata* of David Jones (b. 1895) and the autobiographical *Briggflatts* of Basil Bunting (b. 1900)—and these features tend to distinguish English examples of the genre from their modern American counterparts. Following the polycentric design of Pound's *Cantos*, contemporary American sequences seem to proceed in the fear that a rigid structure will choke the spontaneity and intensity of the lyric moment; they tend to leave their energies open-ended, pursuing a sense of form that is purely potentialist. The English poet who most notably varies and enriches this convention is Roy Fisher, who adds to the literature of the open-form sequence in *City* (1961) and *A Furnace* (1986).

City assembles poems and prose in a discontinuous montage, which imitates the fluctuating intensities of urban perceptual life (in his native Birmingham) and its rhythms of mental fragmentation. Antidiscursive and antinarrative as his strategy may be, it adheres at least to a quasi-musical presentation, returning to motifs as figures in a composition. Evocative but dense and impenetrable images—"the bell in the river, / the loaf half-eaten, / the coat of the sky"—prove perplexing until they recur, when each appears, like a musical note or chord, as a moment of untranslatable, sensuous feeling. Drawing on his work as a jazz musician, Fisher combines a directness of emotional or imaginative experience with a sense of fluid artifice. He seeks not only to reach an intensity of lyric feeling but to stylize it, thus achieving the "mannerism of intensity" that he regards as the special virtue of jazz. Thus he can create a sequence that is "rigidly composed" but free, in his own nomenclature, of "an authoritarian centre," that is, "a rule or mandate somewhere in its middle which the work will unfold and reach."

Fisher's resistance to this "authoritarian centre" expresses values equally political and aesthetic. More than a shift in structural tactic is occurring twenty-five years later, in *A Furnace* (Birmingham is again the site), which uses a single image as manifest center for the sequence: the double spiral, a whirlpool or vortex. Now, the avant-garde energies of the original vorticists (Pound and Wyndham Lewis, among others) led them to see artistic form as a vortex, a mere trace left by a force, and Fisher uses this figure to record the movements, alternately centripetal and centrifugal, in the history of a city. Yet the same shape suggested to Pound a model form and endorsement of authoritarian government (he linked that "form-sense 1914" to Lewis's own later "discovery" of Hitler's Reich).

It is this possibility that Fisher realizes sardonically in the fourth section of *A Furnace*, where he complements that central position with a dramatic—symptomatic, not expressive—articulation of the totalitarian principle immanent in the design:

> We're carving the double spiral
> into this stone; don't
> complicate or deflect us.
> We know what we're at
> . . . .
> Write sky-laws into the rocks. . . .

The static, programmatic form of the spiral, here appropriately cut into stone, inscribes an inflexible political order, its "sky-laws" imposed from above. This picture of formal authority and central power clearly warns that such developments are the susceptibility of any society like the one whose geography Fisher maps in this sequence. Yet he is responding as well to a development in British political history of the 1970s and 1980s, one which allowed his own socialist humanism to wane under the imperial standards of Thatcherite conservatism.

The currents that carried Thatcher into office were clearly gathering momentum in the early 1970s, when the Labour government had already outlived the energies of its mid-1960s initiatives. A growing disaffection with the idea of social welfare, an antagonism to Keynesian economics and the sense of government responsibility, emerged in her turn toward privatization and her emphasis on entrepreneurialism and technology. Asserting that "there is no such thing as society, only individuals and families," Thatcher not only denied the Tory-Labour consensus of the preceding decades. She departed sharply from one source of moral authority and value in traditional conservatism, the communitarian spirit in the old Toryism of the shires. By the mid-1970s these developments are already generating a poetic response from Hughes and Hill, whose increasing conservatism is sometimes misleadingly conceived as a collateral development to Thatcherism. Their main effort lies instead in a return to those lost locales of conservative value.

Season Songs (1975) and *Moortown* (1979) present a Virgilian or practical-moral pastoral new to Hughes, a development which traces a parabolic return to the topography of an older, local, rooted Toryism. The political significance of Hill's *Tenebrae* (1978) appears both more obvious and complex. His sequence of thirteen sonnets "An Apology for the Revival of Christian Architecture in England" takes its epigraph from Disraeli's *Coningsby* (1844), a devoted apologia for the orderly echelons of Old England: altar, throne, country house, cottage. Like William Morris and Richard Oastler, Disraeli admired the hierarchy of feudal society as a community of reciprocal interests and shared responsibilities—a kind of vertical socialism—and Hill gives this archaic political ideal an appropriately complicated formulation. No less attractive than it is problematic, its values (seen in retrospect) do not mitigate its severities. Ultimately, the sequence reads like an elegy to a forgone order; its poignancy is sharpened, its images edged more clearly with resentment, in view of its immediate and local context—the bogus conservatism (for Hill it conserved nothing) that had risen since the early 1970s:

> it is an enclave of perpetual vows
> broken in time. Its truth shows disrepair,
> disfigured shrines, their stones of gossamer,
> Old Moore's astrology, all hallows,
>
> the squires's effigy bewigged with frost.

Nostalgia also enters the poetry of Tony Harrison, but from another angle: his background in the urban working class of industrial Leeds accounts for sensitivities strikingly different to those of Hughes or Hill. By 1970 his poems are witnessing a crisis of belief in the values that had defined the cohesive center of national postwar politics—liberal social welfare. The bind of Progress, the irony of advancement: the material circumstances of working-class life have been improved but—in his elegiac presentation—the grainy strength of its soul has been lost. Harrison is not simply writing pastoral backwards, however; at his best, he avoids an inverted nostalgia for the starkly chastening force of poverty. He confronts a paradox, one which he focuses constantly, if obsessively, on the impoverishing benefits of literacy. His poems give literate speech to an underclass, and present a dramatic, searching analysis of the conditions of language and class in England.

The poems in *The Loiners* (1970; a "Loiner" is a citizen of Leeds) display a studied coarseness, a kind of street-ballad brio that Harrison stylizes sufficiently to suggest its claim on literature:

In Leeds it was never *Who* or *When* but *Where*.
The bridges of the slimy River Aire,
Where Jabez Tunnicliffe, for love of God,
Founded the *Band of Hope* in eighteen odd

The hurdy gurdy rhythms and rigmarole music show the end rhyme exerting inordinate control over the language, whose subjection is otherwise witnessed in an excessive reliance on cliché. Predetermined, this is the speech of a class whose accent still determines its imprisonment.

This symptomatology is balanced by Harrison's ability to tap the expressive potential of class dialect, as in the final lines of "Allotments," where the Loiner, greeting the end of World War II from the privations it has enforced,

                                                   cried
For the family still pent up in my balls,
For my corned beef sandwich, and for genocide.

Relying on Harrison's considerable metrical skill, these lines express the speaker's feeling of frustrated potential, at the crucial point, through those monosyllables' fiercely compacted energy. Yet this effect becomes credible mainly through the working-class character's perspective-in-voice, where a corned beef sandwich and genocide vie for primacy of attention.

The ambitious task of Harrison's *Continuous* (1981), a sequence of fifty sonnets written in the sixteen-line form devised by George Meredith for *Modern Love*, is announced through an allusion in its first poem to the local Leeds lore of class strife. Like the "Enoch of Leeds," the iron sledgehammer used by Luddites to smash the oppressive frames made by its namesake, Enoch of Marsden, Harrison writes his sonnet against itself, clanging "a *forged* music on the frame of Art, / the looms of owned language smashed apart!" Harrison may have faked the conventional sonnet by writing it in dialect, thus destroying the privilege an ownership of literary language has traditionally sanctioned, but he has also forged a new and durable product of his own. He reclaims the Luddites's share of a common language and gives their speech the dignity and gravity of literature.

This project accounts for the major importance of *Continuous*, but the strenuousness of the enterprise should not excuse Harrison's tendency to lapse from it. Not only does he quit the struggle, falling into

facile contrasts between languages raw and cooked (his father's awkwardly genuine usage is constantly opposed to his own deviously polished Latinisms); he tends to idealize inarticulateness. That first sonnet, "On Not Being Milton," already raises "three cheers for mute
ingloriousness." To praise this silence actively is to endorse, if passively, the same economic and political conditions that have strangled
Harrison's people into speechlessness. As though to correct that error,
V. (1985) recounts Harrison's experience of finding his parent's graves
defaced by the local hooligans. He presents their language—rank,
clannish, densely vulgar—as a speech steeped in the culture of deprivation.

The title *V.* stands for "versus" and puns on "verses." Yet the poem
studiously denies itself the New Critical satisfaction of assimilating historical conflicts into forms of aesthetic concord. Unattenuated, the
miners' strike of 1984–1985 provides both a containing context for *V.*
and a primary example of unresolved struggle. "Standing up to the
unions," the Thatcher government ultimately forced the miners back to
work, and this result could be taken to signal, finally and uncompro-
misingly, the reversal of the whole postwar tradition of social welfare.
In this light the indignity of the graffiti scrawled on Harrison's parents'
tomb reads as no merely local, motiveless malignancy. It is the sign of
lost values, the signature of those fallen, not only through the social
safety net, but through the web of human culture. These are the lost
people, who include (but are not limited to) the growing homeless population of Britain in the 1980s.

To this historical reality Peter Reading's poems give urgent, terse,
and disturbing witness. *Diplopic* (1983), *C* (1984), and *Ukelele Music*
(1985) present a panorama of urban violence and hopelessness. Representative scenes—an infant sliced with glass by thugs stealing the
mother's wedding ring; an octogenarian ritually and gratuitously murdered—seem to make his the poetic voice of the 1980s. But his timeliness lies in his manner of presentation: a postmodern diffidence, a
deadpan coolness of observation that redeems the mannerisms of that
contemporary style with his own greater complexity.

Reading's strategy follows the formula announced in the title of
Diplopic, whose double vision contrasts an empathic response with a
nearly insane scientific detachment, as in "Telecommunication," where
news of a grandmother's death, at first making the boy feel "scared,
excited, numb. Sad / memories of—," issues into a parent's instruction-

al response: "'Yes, Grandma's bones *might* fossilize, of course, / like those in your *First Book of Dinosaurs*.'" Stimulating compassion, then disrupting it, he makes the reader question that habituated response—sympathy more than horror is his subject. Earlier Stevie Smith's experiments with idiom hardened the language into a poetic material, leaving it unmoved by the (not always comic) horrors she reported, but Reading's verse moves a turn further, perhaps in response to the currents of his own time. Provoking and denying the consolations of fellow feeling, he forces the reader back to ask the questions that the ideal society of consensus socialism had answered, and whose solutions were being undone through the decade.

Such diffidence also presents a response to the culture of verbal excess—to the coercive appeals of commodity sentiment on television; to the vacuous overstatements, equally compelled and compelling, of mass media politics. Silences locate the main points of attention in the social poetry of James Fenton. Sometimes Fenton presents this reticence symptomatically, as in *A German Requiem* (1981), where survivors of the war steer monologues of careful avoidance. At other times his clipped, brisk, abstemious report seems the only tonic response, as in "Dead Soldiers," which recounts an absurdly elegant lunch on a Cambodian battlefield (Fenton attended it).

This manner reveals its center of moral gravity and political conscience in a poem from his 1989 collection *Manilla Envelope* (mailed in a "manilla" envelope to English readers from the Philippines, where Fenton had moved to finance and sustain a local fishing industry). "Jerusalem" overheats the language of contemporary political divisions, allowing its rhythms to run away with the speaker and push him into the intense inane of factional fanaticisms—a mania dramatized still more remarkably for being attached seamlessly, in the final lines here, to a voice of self-awareness and self-indictment:

> I'm an Armenian. I am a Copt.
>   This is Utopia.
>   I came here from Ethiopia
> ·
>   Have you ever met an Arab?
>   Yes, I am a scarab.
> I am a worm. I am a thing of scorn.
>   I cry Impure from street to street
> And see my degradation in the eyes I meet.

The circumstances that force Reading and Fenton to court silence in their political verse may explain, conversely, the appeal of personal lyric, but the same historical moment makes it more difficult to legitimate a song of subjective experience. The lyric voice of Craig Raine is individualized but highly stylized; the zones of perception are idiosyncratic without being private. Strange metaphors—the oddness of outlook belongs to the alien or "Martian," the label given to a gathering of like-minded poets in the early 1980s—offer their exotic likenesses as the stuff of sensuous music. Yet Raine's usual unwillingness to consolidate a person at the core of these perceptions seems to deprive the pyrotechnic of a necessary fiction, an intensity of presence.

Such intensity appears as aim and effect in the poems of Alan Jenkins, whose early lyrics assume a persona at once fictional and true, imaginatively heightened and historically informed. Picaresque lover, the main speaker of *In the Hot House* (1988) is driven through scenes of the post-1960s milieu. This is a story of eros furens—of a sexual liberation now jaded and sung in a language of disappointed excitements. Jenkins proceeds to poems of greater personal directness and emotional complexity in *Greenheart* (1990). A lyric elegy to his father, for example, "Keep-Net," alternates his sense of present loss—focused in a fishing rod lost overboard—with the memory of experiences shared with his father, balancing that immediacy of lived affection in a unique and beautiful counterrhythm with memory's sharp melancholy:

> The float bobs, I want him
> to catch one too, more than I want to catch them all
> myself, I who have caught the past, which is made of him,
> maroon or silver flashes in a grey-brown river, into which I dive,
> as my rod, in slow motion, disappears, as the spools
> of our reels click and whirr, click and whirr,
> the Imperial Bruyere has fallen into my lap
> as I wake, a book for keep-net, and mouth *My father*.

The energies of poets coming to maturity in the 1970s and 1980s have not been organized by single critical anthologies like Conquest's in the 1950s, Alvarez's in the 1960s. Literary culture has become decentered—or multicentered. The old hegemony of London-based houses like Faber has been challenged from Manchester, for example, by Carcanet Press, which publishes talents as various as C. H. Sisson and Michael Hamburger and Jeremy Hooker, or from Newcastle-upon-

Tyne, where Bloodaxe Books maintains a commitment to northern poets like Ken Smith and to a political sensibility similar to Harrison's. The increasing democratization of education has simply dissolved the old London-Cambridge-Oxford triangle into the new polygon of provincial universities and local writing groups, and it becomes increasingly difficult to legislate an *ars poetica* for a generation. (The center of gravity in English poetry might be said to have shifted, around 1975, to Northern Ireland, where the political situation served both to unify poets and to challenge the "English" character of their verse.)

The voices of Harrison, Reading, Fenton, Raine, and Jenkins are various and particular; they share common historical ground but, for now, no recognizably common purpose. The groupings of poets from previous decades seem fixed, but the permanence of individual achievements is still uncertain. Of these Larkin and Hughes have proved to be the most popular, addressing their technical skills to subjects at the antipodes of central human experience. The large if diverse audience they share also suggests their equal appeal to current attitudes, their joint mastery over the contemporary, that is, the conventional.

"Tradition" posits a frame of reference and standard of judgment at once more elusive and demanding. Eliot's claim that the "existing monuments form an ideal order among themselves, which is modified by the introduction of the new (the really new) among them" has of course suffered the postmodern challenge to the canonical—tradition proves impermanent, its values arbitrary. Yet these awarenesses replicate those made in the early century by modernists. They also sensed a break between past and present and took these circumstances as the impetus for radical invention, at once delighting in technical experiment for its own sake and using it to revive materials no longer expected to live on their own.

This project continues in poems that orchestrate the mutterings and blasphemies of history into the sweet ceremony of sonnet form; in versets that adjust the rhythms of an Old English psalter to the pace and psyche of contemporary speech; in lines that reconcile the projective energy of American postmodernism to an Augustan diction of civil latinity or the stately cadences of Elizabethan verse. The really new poems, perhaps the most lasting, have come from Geoffrey Hill and Charles Tomlinson.

Vincent Sherry

Further Reading

Astley, Neil, ed. *Tony Harrison*. Newcastle-upon-Tyne: Bloodaxe, 1991.

Bedient, Calvin. *Eight Contemporary Poets*. London: Oxford University Press, 1974.

Brown, Merle E. *Double Lyric: Divisiveness and Communal Creativity in Recent English Poetry*. London: Routledge, 1980.

Davie, Donald. *Under Briggflatts: A History of Poetry in Great Britain, 1960–1988*. Chicago: University of Chicago Press, 1989.

Homberger, Eric. *The Art of the Real: Poetry in England and America since 1939*. London: Dent, 1977.

Sagar, Keith. *The Art of Ted Hughes*. Cambridge: Cambridge University Press, 1975.

Sagar, Keith, ed. *The Achievement of Ted Hughes*. Manchester: Manchester University Press, 1983.

Schmidt, Michael, and Peter Jones, eds. *British Poetry since 1970: A Critical Survey*. Manchester: Carcanet Press, 1980.

Schmidt, Michael, and Grevel Lindop, eds. *British Poetry since 1960: A Critical Survey*. Manchester: Carcanet Press, 1972.

Sherry, Vincent. *The Uncommon Tongue: The Poetry and Criticism of Geoffrey Hill*. Ann Arbor: University of Michigan Press, 1987.

Sherry, Vincent, ed. *Dictionary of Literary Biography: Poets of Great Britain and Ireland, 1945–1960*. Detroit: Gale Research, 1984.

Sherry, Vincent, ed. *Poets of Great Britain and Ireland since 1960*. Detroit: Gale Research, 1985.

Poetry in Ireland, Scotland, and Wales, 1930–1990

THIS survey does not pretend to be comprehensive. The first three sections, which are thematic and historical, discuss poems and ideas about poetry, mainly in relation to Edwin Muir, Hugh MacDiarmid (Christopher Murray Grieve), Patrick Kavanagh, Louis MacNeice, John Hewitt, R. S. Thomas, and Dylan Thomas. Several younger poets are also featured. The last section explores a specific case history: Northern Irish poetry, 1962–1992. Let the following epigraphs set the scene:

I owe my soul to Shakespeare, to Spenser and to Blake, perhaps to William Morris, and to the English language in which I think, speak and write . . . my hatred tortures me with love, my love with hate.   W. B. Yeats

Ulster was British, but with no rights on
  The English lyric.
            Seamus Heaney

My function in Scotland during the last twenty to thirty years has been that of the catfish that vitalizes the other torpid denizens of the aquarium.
            Hugh MacDiarmid

Regarded in England as a Welshman (and a waterer of England's milk) and in Wales as an Englishman, I am too unnational to be here at all. I should be living in a small private leper-house in Hereford or Shropshire, one foot in Wales and my vowels in England.
            Dylan Thomas (talking to Scottish writers in Edinburgh)

"Problems and Cleavages"

The English lyric no longer belongs to England, and its migrations—
especially to places near at hand—have taken on new significance in the
late twentieth century. In *Devolving English Literature* (1992), a study
written from a Scottish viewpoint, Robert Crawford notices "a widespread wish in recent poetry to be seen as in some manner barbarian, as
operating outside the boundaries of standard English and outside the
identity that is seen as going with it. Such a wish unites . . . the post-
colonial and the provincial." However, as the epigraphs suggest, Crawford simplifies the dynamics of poetic devolution if he presumes that
nonmetropolitan literary identities are given, unproblematic, and united against the notional center. Solidarity in the United States among
those whom Seamus Heaney calls "poets from the outskirts," like
Derek Walcott and Heaney himself, may obscure the complexity of
receding local ties.

Nor does Crawford resolve the perennial ambiguity as to whether
distinctive identities afford a support system for poetry (and vice versa),
or whether they are constituted and reconstituted by poems themselves.
Such a process might be most subtly at work in poetry with its mind on
other matters and with other claims on our attention. Even in political
terms Crawford's Australian and Caribbean instances hardly derive
from identical "post-colonial" situations. Similarly, the Celtic bits of the
British Isles differ among and within themselves—politically, religiously, culturally, aesthetically—besides pursuing their several quarrels with
London. And, as Crawford indeed points out, regional, class, and ethnic factors in England itself (including immigration from the Celtic
countries) affect the literary issue. Poetry by first or second generation
"Irish in Britain," as well as by the Caribbeans in Britain, can show distinctive qualities. Ian Duhig, whose first collection of poems *The Brad-
ford Count* was published in 1991, is a talented example.

Nonetheless, contemporary poetry from Ireland, Scotland, and
Wales often bears the marks of cultural, if not always political, revolt
against the nineteenth-century construction of "Britain." We still
await the "Break-up of Britain," anticipated by the Scottish socialist
thinker Tom Nairn as coda to the breakup of empire. But if Scotland
still wobbles on the brink, the slow civil war in Northern Ireland has
caused enormous tremors since 1969. Signs of literary revolt in the
British Isles include efforts to rescue discrete literary histories from

what Crawford terms "a crude unitary view of English literature." Yet, while English and American undergraduates are depressingly liable to lack contexts for W. B. Yeats, Hugh MacDiarmid, and Dylan Thomas, neither cultural nor literary hegemony is a straightforward matter where the British Isles are concerned. The historian Keith Robbins, in *Nineteenth-Century Britain: England, Scotland, and Wales: The Making of a Nation* (1989), denies that "anglicisation in nineteenth-century Britain [was] a simple and uniform process: a matter of assimilation, under some degree of duress, into what is believed to be *the* dominant English mode. . . . Scotland and Wales were not 'absorbed' by England in any simple fashion." Contrariwise, Ireland was not to be so easily disgorged by the United Kingdom. Perhaps British Isles literary history might do worse than adopt the model proposed by Hugh Kearney, in *The British Isles: A History of Four Nations* (1989), for British Isles history in general:

My own efforts to deal with the problems raised by "national" histories have led me to see what I have called the "Britannic melting pot" in terms of a complex of interacting cultures. . . . Cultures change over time, are influenced by other cultures, cross national boundaries and often contain sub-cultures within themselves.

Northern Ireland, or—to use a politically neutral term—the North of Ireland, epitomizes Kearney's point. It can be seen as a Britannic melting pot within a Britannic melting pot—a set of cultural interactions to which Irish, Scottish, and English traditions contribute. These interactions have produced mutations and hybrids—and ultimately, poems. Ulster had already undergone extensive immigration from Scotland before parts of it were "planted" with Scottish and English Protestant settlers in the early seventeenth century. Nevertheless, cultural interaction cannot be divorced from political antagonism. Melting pots usually contain unassimilated lumps. According to Cairns Craig, Scotland, let alone Northern Ireland, is "riven by internal divisions," including "the great unspeakable divide, the religious divide."

In Northern Ireland the divide between Protestant and Catholic speaks loud and clear. Long before the current polarization John Hewitt's seminal essay, "The Bitter Gourd: Some Problems of the Ulster Writer" (1945), recognized that "Ulster's position in this island involves [the writer] in problems and cleavages for which we can find no counterpart elsewhere in the British archipelago." Contemporary

Northern Irish poetry is widely seen as the most important poetic movement in the British Isles during the last quarter-century. Its vitality seems inseparable from the area's diverse cultural elements and from the political subtexts that have accrued to word and image.

But if Northern Irish poetry represents the molten core of a melting pot within a melting pot, literary traditions are pitched in there, too. Coming from a deeply traditional as well as a deeply fractured society, the poetry casts wider light on the workings of English-language poetic traditions in the twentieth century. T. S. Eliot, an authoritarian arch-metropolitan who fled American heterogencity and had a bee in his bonnet about a "powerful literature with a powerful capital," published an essay called "Was There a Scottish Literature?" (1919). Eliot also managed to ignore Yeats and the Irish literary revival in "Tradition and the Individual Talent," when he pronounced: "In English writing we seldom speak of tradition" (Yeats spoke of little else). So much for traditions and the individual country. It was through regional specificity rather than through Dante that Yeats made contact with the mind of Europe. The supposed margins can surprise the metropolis not only by their "barbarian" energies but by their conservative instincts: their adherence to traditional structures, their maintenance of what the center cannot hold. But the center—Belfast, Dublin, London, Boston?—is itself as much in question for Northern Irish poetry as for Northern Irish politics. This poetry destabilizes British Isles canons—and the Anglo-American axis—in more than one direction.

Place, Nation, Region, Parish, Religion

In Irish history, we are often told, the stable element is the land. The same might be said of twentieth-century poetry from Ireland, Scotland, and Wales. The Romantic attraction to Nature and place included a generally spurious "Celtic" dimension, but at least this led Yeats in the 1890s to appreciate how "Irish legends move among known woods and seas." Nationalist critics are unconvincing when they claim (as does Ned Thomas in his introduction to R. S. Thomas's *Selected Prose*, 1986) a total divorce between English Romantic traditions—Wordsworth or the "late Romanticism of the far horizon that was so often projected onto the Celtic west"—and "a new and fresh Romanticism, grounded in *this* place."

Yeats's peculiar and influential nexus of legend and locality was not wholly alien to longer-earthed literary traditions: *dinnseanchas* (the Gaelic lore of place names in Ireland and Scotland); the vernacular verse of Scots and Ulster Scots townland bards—the Robert Burns tradition; and what excited the young Edward Thomas in Welsh poetry—"it is entirely Welsh; it refers constantly to Welsh men, traditions, places, by name, and is proud of all, whereas English poetry has no such character—except Wordsworth, perhaps." (Later he would discover Clare and Hardy). In the early twentieth century Thomas also found the Irish literary revival a stimulus to his quest for an English poetics, based upon an inner-directed Englishness, that might replace "the word Imperialism." Reviewing an anthology of Irish poetry in 1910, he said: "They sing of Ireland herself with an intimate reality often missing from English patriotic poetry, where Britannia is a frigid personification." Thomas's influence (and that of his American poetic ally, Robert Frost) on the local precisions of Northern Irish poetry shows an aesthetic of "intimate reality" moving around these islands and beyond.

At the same time, Thomas's antithesis—intimate reality versus frigid personification—implies an inescapable friction between cultural and political versions of national affiliation. Nationalists would argue that cultural topographies, although often helpful to the cause, merely conceal an absence of territorial power. For example, the kitsch "kailyard" (cabbage patch) streak in Scottish writing, a cosy idealization of small-town life, can be seen as a compensatory kilt to cover the fact that, according to Edwin Muir, "there's no Scotland," i.e., since the Union with England in 1707. R. S. Thomas's Welsh Nationalist poem "Reservoirs" (from *Not That He Brought Flowers*, 1968) questions an aesthetic of place built upon "the putrefying of a dead / Nation":

> There are places in Wales I don't go:
> Reservoirs that are the subconscious
> Of a people, troubled far down
> . . . .
> The serenity of their expression
> . . . is a pose
> For strangers . . .
> . . . instead of the poem's
> Harsher conditions . . .

If Irish, Scottish, and Welsh landscapes are less populated, less modernized and urbanized, more imaginatively susceptible than their English counterparts, this is not only a function of romantically rugged terrain or cultural choice, but of economic and political history. The Great Famine and continuing emigration underlie the emptiness of the West of Ireland, a landscape much inscribed with visionary and utopian prospects since Yeats first veiled its contours in twilight. And it was the enclosing landlords who made the Scottish Highlands, in Cairns Craig's words, "one of Europe's most sparsely populated areas." Iain Crichton Smith's poem "The Clearances" (from *The Law and the Grace*, 1965) strikes the same antipastoral note as "Reservoirs": "The thistles climb the thatch. Forever / this sharp scale in our poems / as also the waste music of the sea."

Yet the representation of waste and loss, however harshly or sharply phrased, can return poetry to "the backward look" of Celtic stereotype. Industrialism, following upon Acts of Union, has compounded problems of cultural and literary accommodation. Yeats's myth and idiom just about held out against the incursions of technology. Edwin Muir, twenty-two years younger, said that to be born in the Orkney islands was to be "born before the Industrial Revolution." Muir never quite resolved the historical and psychic distance between his Orkney origins and Glasgow (where his family moved in 1901). Another Orcadian poet, George Mackay Brown, is currently making a last-ditch—or last-island—stand. Brown's most recent collection, *The Wreck of the Archangel* (1989) still confines its social vocabulary to traditional rural labor set within a mythic and seasonal framework—as in "Building the Croft House": "Flashing scythes, falling corn. / The doorstep set. / We drank ale from a stone jar."

In his 1940s essays (reprinted in *Selected Prose*) R. S. Thomas wanted Welsh poetry "to show some difference from the essentially urban-minded English poets who write for the most part in a highly sophisticated manner and with a consistently town outlook." Thomas's Nationalism "epitomizes" Wales as "the bright hill under the black cloud" and balks at urban, industrial Wales: "towns are not characteristic of Wales; they are evidence of foreign influence. . . ." In *The Rough Field* (1972) the Northern Irish poet John Montague couples the defeat of Gaelic Ireland with the impact of new farming methods and new roads on his native Tyrone, but accepts historical necessity: "Our finally lost dream of man at home / In a rural setting!"

A younger Northern Irish poet, Derek Mahon, took a brisker attitude when he complained in 1970 that the Belfast shipyards and housing estates were anathema to the westward-pointing compass of much
Irish poetry. Similarly, Douglas Dunn seems to question the antiurban
reflex when he observes in his preface to *The Faber Book of Twentieth-
Century Scottish Poetry* (1992):

Scottish literature has not always been the city's friend. . . . Until well into the
twentieth century, Scottish cities were depicted as stone wildernesses into
which rural Lowlanders, displaced Highlanders and immigrant Irish families
drifted in search of a livelihood, becoming industrial fodder.

According to Dunn, the tension between rural Scotland (itself diverse)
and "slums, squalor and urban hardships" is "part of the drama of modern Scottish literature." Even Hugh MacDiarmid's fusion of Nationalism and Marxism could not stomach Glasgow. More recently, a self-
consciously "Glasgow" school of poets (Tom Leonard, Liz Lochhead)
and novelists (Alasdair Gray, James Kelman) has imaginatively inhabited the city—warts, beauty spots, accents, and all.

A similar phenomenon now centers on Dublin, which has swollen
immensely since the 1960s—the so-called Finglas writers, named after
a deprived working-class suburb. These writers, who include the novelist Roddy Doyle (author of *The Commitments*) and poet-novelist Der-
mot Bolger, insist on the differences between their own gritty Dublin
and Joyce's city. Yet there can be urban as well as rural pastoral, and
structures of Scottish and Irish local attachment may have been transformed rather than abandoned.

Clearly, the city has been subject to uneven poetic development in
the British Isles. Urban realism (and urban fantasy) associated with
left-wing politics took hold earlier in England, for obvious reasons, and
earlier in fiction than in poetry—always the conservative medium. As
Raymond Williams says in *The Country and the City*, "the English
experience is especially significant, in that one of the decisive transformations, in the relations between country and city, occurred there very
early and with a thoroughness which is still in some ways unap-
proached." Williams criticizes postindustrial literary sublimations,
including the invention of pastoral "Old England"—the English kailyard. Yet while he shows how sanitized rural heritage not only functions
as opium for the urban masses but masks the exploitation of rural laborers, Williams's Welshness still draws him to "knowable communities."

Thus "the country and the city" in British Isles literature is partly a question of relations between England and the rest.

Williams's movement from rural Welsh village to the English city parallels, in historical and ideological contours, the transitions of Louis MacNeice. Brought up in the small town of Carrickfergus near Belfast but schooled at Marlborough and Oxford, MacNeice was the poet from the Celtic countries who most centrally shared in and shaped English "thirties" poetry, with its stress on assimilating the city. Whereas, for Auden, the city symbolizes civilization, the forum of rational discourse and "new styles of architecture," MacNeice gives it sensory and social presence in poems such as "Birmingham":

> the streets run away between the proud glass of shops,
> Cubical scent bottles artificial legs arctic foxes and electric mops,
> But beyond this centre the slumward vista thins like a diagram:
> There, unvisited, are Vulcan's forges who doesn't care a tinker's damn.

Derek Mahon has said that "the pre-war urban England of rainy tram-lines, Corner Houses, Bisto Kids and Guinness is Good for You could probably be roughly simulated from a reading of [Graham] Greene and MacNeice." But although *Autumn Journal* (1939), a summation of the 1930s in the context of Munich, is inter alia a great "London" poem, MacNeice's response to the city goes beyond reportage or social criticism. Urban images and speech patterns are internal to his poetic structures. At the same time, less aligned than Auden with metropolitan or national authority, MacNeice holds in tension the knowable community and "Vulcan's forges." In "Western Landscape" (1945) he terms himself "a bastard / Out of the West by urban civilization." His poem "The Hebrides" makes these Scottish islands the locus of wider conflict between the utopian and dystopian elements in traditional culture, and between such culture and destructive flux. On the one hand, "the art of being a stranger with your neighbor / Has still to be imported"; on the other, "many live on the dole or on old-age pensions / And many waste with consumption and some are drowned. . . ." This is also a dialectic about imaginative focus and literary coordinates. In *Autumn Journal* XVI MacNeice represents a larger island, Ireland, as at once archaically insular ("Let the round tower stand aloof / In a world of bursting mortar!") and enticingly "small enough / To be still thought of with a family feeling." Thus the knowable community translates into a poem's cognitive horizons—the aesthetic island facing the historical flux.

How knowable a community, how firm a horizon, is the nation? How does it affect the context within which poetry is conceived and received? MacNeice's criticism of the Irish Free State for opting out of European crisis contravenes not only Nationalist isolationism, but the literary boundaries set by Yeats. Yeats's construction of an Irish national literature, although contested by later Irish canon makers, has been paradigmatic for writers elsewhere who dispute the hegemony of Eliot's "powerful capital." Edwin Muir wrote in 1934:

There is now . . . an increasing public prepared to give a special welcome to Scottish work, and that is quite a new state of things, and provides for the first time for a century the possible conditions of a literary revival. But this is probably the most that can be said: there is a great deal of literary activity in Scotland; there is no Scottish literary movement to compare with the Irish movement whose chief figure was Mr. W. B. Yeats.

The argument between Muir and MacDiarmid over the strength and continuity of Scottish literary traditions is paradigmatic, too. But it should be prefaced by a reminder of Yeats's own difficulties with Nationalism, as opposed to nationality. His literary and cultural Nationalism was stimulated but (aesthetically) repelled, by the patriotic ballads of the nineteenth-century political movement, Young Ireland. The Irish literary revival came under fire from sterner Republicans than Yeats; from proponents of the Irish language; and from the Catholic Church. And after the 1916 Rising, which ultimately led to the foundation of the Free State, Yeats wrote to Lady Gregory:

At the moment I feel that all the work of years has been overturned, all the bringing together of classes, all the freeing of Irish literature and criticism from politics.

From the mid-1920s, when Hugh MacDiarmid began "writing in Scots and conducting my anti-English propaganda," as he puts it in *Lucky Poet* (1943), he was determined to attach Scottish literature and criticism to the politics of Scottish Nationalism. Muir greatly admired MacDiarmid's Scots poetry, he loathed both the kailyard and Scottish writers who processed Scotland for an English audience (two sides of the same coin), and he was no less anxious than MacDiarmid for a Scottish literary revival. But Muir could not believe in the reality of a more general project to reconnect contemporary poetry with Dunbar and the makars.

For MacDiarmid, the Reformation as much as the Union was a foreign imposition to be thrown off by the nascent Scottish literary spirit, which would prove itself unbroken. For Muir, Calvinism was a self-mutilating theology embraced by a self-mutilating people who had connived in their own destruction, their poetry-crushing philistinism. The Scottish literary tradition could not help but be sporadic, since John Knox had "robbed Scotland of all the benefits of the Renaissance":

> We with such courage and the bitter wit
> To fill the ancient oak of loyalty
> And strip the peopled hill and the altar bare
> And crush the poet with an iron text,
> How could we read our souls and learn to be?
> ("Scotland 1941")

Muir's tone here seems self-mutilating, too. It echoes the touch of Calvinist determinism or masochism in the thinking behind his controversial *Scott and Scotland* (1936), published after a disappointing return home:

Scottish literature as such will disappear, and London will become quite literally the capital of the British Isles . . . "Hugh MacDiarmid" will become a figure like Burns—an exceptional case, that is to say—an arbitrary apparition of the national genius, robbed of his legitimate effect because there will be no literary tradition to perpetuate it.

MacDiarmid read *Scott and Scotland* as craven surrender to the quisling hegemony of Anglo-Scots. The rift between the poets was never healed.

In fact the same bleak diagnosis, the same sense of national absence, impelled Muir and MacDiarmid towards different, Calvinistic extremes—literary extinction, and literary millennium. Andrew Noble, in his excellent introduction to Muir's *Uncollected Scottish Prose* (1982) calls the two poets "opposites who did not attract." As negations rather than contraries, they forwent the dialectic that Muir himself saw as essential to Scottish intellectual progress. There was little creative, tradition-building interaction between their positions. As it is, their poetry runs out of cultural and formal frameworks, structures that mediate between the self and the universe. At its worst, MacDiarmid's poetry becomes all self, a solipsistic aggrandizement; Muir's becomes all universe. These strictures do not apply to MacDiarmid's great achievements: his long, fantastic, anguished meditation in the persona of *A Drunk Man Looks at the Thistle* (1926) and the concentrated Scots lyrics that he produced between 1922 and 1933. Here the rural or island settings conjured by the vernacular serve a cosmology at once vibrant and visionary—as in the Shetland poem "With the Herring Fishers":

"I see herrin'." I hear the glad cry
And 'gainst the noon see ilka blue jowl
In turn as the fishermen haul on the nets
And sing: "Come, shove in your heids and growl"
. . . .
For this is the way that God sees life
. . . .
—It's his happy cries I'm hearin'.

But MacDiarmid was to sacrifice his lyrical rhythms to ideological rant, even glorying in the destruction:

Fools regret my poetic change—from my "enchanting early lyrics"—
But I have found in Marxism all that I need—
(from "The Kind of Poetry I Want," in *Lucky Poet*)

Robert Crawford and others have sought to validate the structural chaos of MacDiarmid's later poetry as a postmodernist "multiplicity of linguistic possibilities." Comparing MacDiarmid with Ezra Pound, Crawford urges "the forcefully provincial nature of Modernism." But it is equally possible to see both poets as dominies or "village explainers," disabled more than enabled by unselfcritical logorrhea and the avoidance of genuine formal challenges. Andrew Noble has pointed out the contradictions between MacDiarmid's own view of Scottish provincialism as "morbidly Anglicized" and Crawford's definition of it as "the source of original, seminal, eclectic and heteroglot writing."

Edwin Muir's poetry comes to life when it attacks Scottish matters with the cutting edge of his critical prose, or when his fables are imbued with historical urgency. He is best known for postwar parables such as "The Combat" and "The Horses"—and "The Labyrinth," which begins:

Since I emerged that day from the labyrinth
Dazed with the tall and echoing passages,
The swift recoils, so many I almost feared
I'd meet myself returning at some smooth corner

In "The Impact of Translation" (*The Government of the Tongue*, 1988) Seamus Heaney argues that Muir, "the poet who translated Kafka in the 1920s and who witnessed the Communist takeover in Czechoslovakia after the war [was] the one poet from the British island with an eschatological if somewhat somnambulistic address to the historical moment in postwar Europe." Heaney had, himself, imitated Eastern European parabolists (like Zbigniew Herbert) in *The Haw Lantern* (1987). However, the attempt to package Muir as an Eastern European poet in translation seems little more plausible than the attempt to package MacDiarmid as a postmodernist. Both arguments dress disabilities as deliberate art. The hiatus in Muir's sense of Scotland, "One foot in Eden" and the other nowhere, empties his poetry of local habitation. Nor do most of Muir's allegorical beasts contain enough actual blood for existential terror. MacNeice, whose poetry was more concretely in touch with the postwar, as with the prewar, moment, says in *Varieties of Parable* (a set of lectures given shortly before his death in 1963): "[Muir's] metaphysico-mystical writing is so unadulterated either by topical or documentary elements or by primarily aesthetic ones, such as images used for their own sake, that I find reading many of his poems on end is like walking through a gallery of abstract paintings."

Nonetheless, "the possible conditions for a literary revival" in Scotland made waves around the archipelago. For instance, R. S. Thomas declared his enthusiasm, especially for MacDiarmid, in "Some Contemporary Scottish Writing" (1946). Yet although he shared MacDiarmid's anglophobia and contempt for fellow Celts "whose sole criterion of success is appointment to some post under the English Government," Thomas noted: "The poet's chief problem is, how in virtue of his mind and vision can he best save his country—directly through political action, or indirectly through his creative work?" Later, in fact, growing "rather tired of the themes about nationalism and the decay of the rural structure in Wales," Thomas was to separate his political activism from his poetry.

John Hewitt, in Northern Ireland, faced still more testing questions. A friend of Muir's, he was a poet, socialist, and atheist from a Protestant (Methodist) family. On cultural as well as political grounds Hewitt opposed a Unionist establishment that had its own reasons for promoting the kind of Anglicization so resented by Scottish and Welsh Nationalist literati. However, he also disliked what he saw as the atavistic, antiprogressive, and theocratic character of Irish Nationalism. Accordingly, literary "regionalism" seemed a way of negotiating the "problems and cleavages" produced by Unionism and Nationalism. His essay "The Bitter Gourd" takes heart from Scotland and Wales. But a movement in the West of England has been less successful, Hewitt writes:

Perhaps a warning for us. Wales and Scotland are, after all, well-defined geographical and national entities. . . . Where then does Ulster stand? After all, we have a frontier. What then of Donegal?

For fifteen years, from the early 1940s to the mid-1950s, Hewitt preached and promoted a cross-sectarian regionalist consciousness in literature and the arts. His activities (which took their cue from Yeats as well as MacDiarmid) included the recuperation of Ulster's literary and cultural resources—for example, the "Rhyming Weavers," who wrote in the Ulster Scots vernacular while working at their preindustrial looms. Denied an influential job at the Ulster Museum by Unionist intrigue, Hewitt left Northern Ireland in 1957. He returned in 1972, after retiring as director of the Coventry Art Gallery, and found himself the grand old man of a new literary scene, with regionalist residues. Hewitt criticized his earlier regionalism as being predicated too much on the counties of Down and Antrim—on Protestant east Ulster. His preferred regional model, New England, carried less cultural justification in the Catholic areas of western Ulster. Hewitt's regionalism was primarily an attempt to articulate Ulster Protestant identity in terms more complex and indigenous than Unionism allowed, and simultaneously to create a distinctive aesthetic for himself. His well-known poem "Once Alien Here" (1945) sums up these aspirations. On the one hand, the poem reproduces a binary (not to say stereotypical) view of national poetic traditions: "graver English, lyric Irish tongue." On the other, it represents relations between landscape, language, history, and poetry in such a way as to open up fundamental questions about "a native mode" in a divided society and within the archipelago's "complex of interacting cultures."

A particular place usually lies at the heart of national or regional allegiance, and may even be its real object: for Yeats, Sligo; for Hewitt, the Glens of Antrim; for Muir, a lost Orcadian Eden—distinct from Scotland as well as from Glasgow. In her essay "Region and Nation: R. S. Thomas and Dylan Thomas" (*The Literature of Region and Nation*, ed.

R. P. Draper, 1989), Barbara Hardy distinguishes between R. S. Thomas's occasionally strained relation to Wales and Dylan Thomas's relaxation into "a deep sense of region." Certainly a bitter nuance in R. S. Thomas's poetry represents Welsh nonconformist culture as materialistic, hypocritical, and puritanical.

There is a mismatch between his "prototypical" hill farmer Iago Prytherch ("something frightening in the vacancy of his mind"), and the "bright hill" that symbolizes the nation. This may be both the prejudice of an Anglican priest and the disappointed romanticism of a newcomer to rural Wales. Dylan Thomas, on the other hand, was happy to call himself "a border case," and his deepest imaginative topography roots him in Anglo-Welsh Swansea: an "ugly lovely" sea town, English-speaking but close to the Welsh language and to the countryside (Ann Jones's farm at Fernhill). His poetry is also rooted in the nonconformism that R. S. Thomas views from an Anglican distance. Dylan Thomas's highly wrought rhetoric mediates the Bible through the *hwyl* and hellfire of evangelical preaching, for instance in "The Crucifixion":

> This was the crucifixion on the mountain,
> Time's nerve in vinegar, the gallow grave
> As tarred with blood as the bright thorns I wept:
> The world's my wound, God's Mary in her grief,
> Bent like three trees and bird-papped in her shift,
> With pins for tear-drops is the long wound's woman.

Thomas's poetry is itself crucified by dualisms of life and death, body and soul, sex and sin, world and wound. Insofar as these dualisms are intrinsic to Thomas's Welsh religious identity, they complicate his relations to Wales and to cultural borders. His unease abroad, cloaked by excessive alcohol and excessive eloquence, partook of unease at home.

Karl Shapiro in *In Defense of Ignorance* (1955) argues that "Like D. H. Lawrence [Thomas] is always hurling himself back into childhood and the childhood of the world." Thus his more truly "relaxed" Welsh poems are Edenic reconstructions—"Fern Hill," "Poem in October"— written in the mid-1940s. These poems wonderfully but wistfully restore a primal universe in which human beings, animals, birds, plants, "the trees and the stones and the fish in the tide"—locality and cosmos, then and now, male and female, word and thing, word and word—have not undergone separation and differentiation:

And I saw in the turning so clearly a child's
Forgotten mornings when he walked with his mother
   Through the parables
    Of sun light
. . . .
   And the twice-told fields of infancy
That his tears burned my cheeks and his heart moved in mine.
("Poem in October")

Throughout Thomas's poetry, prolonged noun phrases suspend time and history.

Shapiro's remark that Thomas "said everything he had to say: it had little to do with wars and cities and art galleries" parallels the conclusion of Patrick Kavanagh's "Innocence" (1951):

I do not know what age I am,
I am no mortal age;
I know nothing of women,
Nothing of cities,
I cannot die
Unless I walk outside these whitethorn hedges.

Once again what Kavanagh called "that childhood country" is counterposed to an urban, historical, fluid world beyond some defensive psychic perimeter. (By now this seems virtually a collective Celtic narrative, testifying to more than merely personal experience.) While Kavanagh's poetry does not resolve various dualisms encountered elsewhere, it dramatizes them in terms that generate fresh aesthetic possibilities. Kavanagh was that rare thing in this century—a poet with very little secondary education. He worked the "stony grey soil" of Inniskeen in County Monaghan until he left for Dublin in 1939, "the worst mistake of my life." Kavanagh began as a naive poet, a believer in the poet as visionary, able to see farming tasks in the light of his poetic vocation, overimpressed by stale Romantic diction. The early poem "Ploughman" ends:

I find a star-lovely art
In a dark sod.
Joy that is timeless! O heart
That knows God.

Then, in 1942, Kavanagh published one of the most remarkable long poems of the twentieth century, *The Great Hunger*—a poem that savages the pastoral idioms propagated by English Romanticism, the Irish literary revival, the Irish Free State (which idealized a blend of piety and agriculture), and even his own early poetry:

> *There* is the source from which all cultures rise,
> And all religions.
> *There* is the pool in which the poet dips
> And the musician.
> Without the peasant base civilisation must die,
> Unless the clay is in the mouth the singer's singing is useless.

A strong influence on R. S. Thomas's Prytherch poems, *The Great Hunger* anatomizes the sexual and spiritual inhibitions of Patrick Maguire, paralyzed by "Religion, the fields and the fear of the Lord." The Irish Catholic version of puritanism produces a structural irony whereby Maguire's life stands still from cradle to grave, while the seasons, the natural world, and the cycle of the farming year wheel on: "The cows and horses breed, / And the potato seed," but Maguire can only open "his trousers wide over the ashes / And [dream] himself to lewd sleepiness." That Maguire is tied by "the wind-toughened navel-cord" to farm, family, and community makes the poem an extraordinary cross between documentary and psychodrama, reportage and symbol, lyric and epic:

> Life dried in the veins of these women and men:
> The grey and grief and unlove,
> The bones in the backs of their hands,
> And the chapel pressing its low ceiling over them.

Kavanagh's great antipastoral outcry—"The hungry fiend / Screams the apocalypse of clay / In every corner of this land"—has both literary and political resonance. His motif of clay in the mouth, "a speechless muse," implies how the poem itself speaks not only for unarticulated rural experience but for deep repressions in Irish culture: the poet-narrator and the silent Maguire divide up a split psyche. *The Great Hunger* was censored by the state, ostensibly because it mentions masturbation, but perhaps also because of the contradictions it exposes in Catholic theology and Nationalist ideology.

Kavanagh disliked the brand of Irishness enshrined in revival literature, and considered that Yeats's Protestantism made him "a doubtful Irishman"; but he also objected to the totalizing Nationalist myth of Ireland. In "Nationalism and Literature" (reprinted in *Collected Pruse,*

1967) he maintains that "nationalism is seldom based on those sinceri-
ties which give any true spiritual force its power. Good work cannot survive in an angry atmosphere." He even distinguishes English literature
from "the often scoundrelly nation." For Kavanagh, "love of the land and
landscape is of course a different kettle of potatoes altogether. Constable, Wordsworth, Clare, most of them were great patriots in that sense."

Kavanagh's celebrated essay "The Parish and the Universe" suggests
how a "parochial" poetry might bypass both the Nation and the
metropolis:

The provincial has no mind of his own; he does not trust what his eyes see until
he has heard what the metropolis . . . has to say on any subject. . . . The
parochial mentality on the other hand is never in any doubt about the social
and artistic validity of his parish.

Kavanagh's poetic parochialism took the form of a more self-conscious relation to Inniskeen and to the phenomenal world. This self-
consciousness extends to language:—his sonnet "The Hospital"
affirms: "Naming these things is the love-act and its pledge." Another
sonnet, ironically entitled "Epic," relishes a local boundary dispute: "the
Duffys shouting 'Damn your soul' / And old McCabe stripped to the
waist." The sonnet ends:

> That was the year of the Munich bother. Which
> Was more important? I inclined
> To lose my faith in Ballyrush and Gortin
> Till Homer's ghost came whispering to my mind.
> He said: I made the Iliad from such
> A local row. Gods make their own importance.

The discrepancy between *The Great Hunger* and his poems of return
to Inniskeen, such as "Epic" or "Innocence," indicates that Kavanagh,
too, could not make up time lags between country and city. His disaffection from Dublin, an internal exile, was aggravated by his North-
ernness: coming from one of the three Ulster counties outside Northern Ireland, he was doubly displaced from his cultural hinterland. In
this way, Kavanagh's trajectory parallels that of Louis MacNeice, even
if MacNeice's displacements overshoot rather than undershoot national boundaries. It may seem an irony that *Autumn Journal*'s twenty-four
cantos pivot on "the Munich bother," whereas "Epic" marginalizes it in
a phrase. Nonetheless, the emphases are complementary. And *Autumn*

Journal, the other defining poem of the Irish mid-century, is as angry as
The Great Hunger about Ireland's "purblind manifestoes"—Unionist as
well as Nationalist:

> And one read black where the other read white, his hope
>   The other man's damnation:
> Up the rebels, To Hell with the Pope
>   And God Save—as you prefer—the King or Ireland.
> The land of scholars and saints:
>   Scholars and saints my eye . . .

At the same time, Kavanagh's "A Christmas Childhood" (1940) and
MacNeice's "Carrickfergus" (1937) differ significantly in their nexus of
place and autobiography. Less elaborately than Dylan Thomas,
Kavanagh invokes a unified primal vision: "Cassiopeia was over / Cas-
sidy's hanging hill." The assonance between Greek and Irish names
suggests once again that language shares in a cosmic harmony. Similarly, parish, universe, and poetry chime when the "child-poet's" mother
"makes the music of milking." Carrickfergus, too, has imprinted a
poet's imagination and verbal textures, but there the resemblance stops:

> The little boats beneath the Norman castle,
>   The pier shining with lumps of crystal salt;
> The Scotch Quarter was a line of residential homes
>   But the Irish Quarter was a slum for the blind and halt.

The difference is not only between rural and urban scenarios, or
between Inniskeen's homogeneity and the sectarian North. "Carrickfergus," which begins with the advent of the Normans in Ireland and
ends with the Great War, is informed—like all MacNeice's poetry—by
a historical consciousness generally lacking in Kavanagh. The poem's
most pervasive images are of barriers, fissures, mutilations, and continuing war in Europe—its last phrase, "the soldiers with their guns," is
not really a closure. There is also religious difference. Different religious backgrounds also have shaped the cosmologies of these poems. A
British perspective indicates that "Spilt religion" has poured more pro-
fusely and continuously into poetry beyond secular England. Muir,
MacDiarmid, Dylan Thomas, MacNeice, and Kavanagh may wrestle
with various forms of life-denying, sex-denying, art-denying puritanism, but their poetry still inclines to the metaphysical or visionary
and to quests for cosmic pattern.

R. S. Thomas is primarily a religious poet: "It was I, said God, / Who formed the roses / In the delicate flesh / And the tooth that bruises" ("Pisces"). Two of Kavanagh's successors in the Republic, Brendan Kennelly (b. 1937) and Paul Durcan (b. 1944), notably combine critiques of the institutional Catholic Church with their own version of the poet as parish priest. Kennelly's massively long sequence *The Book of Judas* (1991) is an idiosyncratic sermon on a motif that links Christianity and Irish history. Durcan's oeuvre abounds in titles like "Priest Accused of Not Wearing Condom" and "Archbishop of Kerry to Have Abortion." Nevertheless, his poetry is dedicated to an intense anarcho-pacifist-feminist-spiritual mission and it follows Kavanagh in believing in poetry itself: "I have not 'met' God, I have not 'read' / David Gascoyne, James Joyce, or Patrick Kavanagh: / I believe in them" ("They Say the Butterfly is the Hardest Stroke").

The dialectic between faith and doubt is as fundamental to poetry as the dialectic between country and city, or Eden and history. MacNeice's poetry encompasses all three dialectics. His well-known poem "Snow" zestfully surrenders to relativistic flux: "World is crazier and more of it than we think, / Incorrigibly plural." But, saturated in Bible and prayer book, he also conducts an implied dialogue with the clergyman-father who had originally given him "a box of truisms / Shaped like a coffin" ("The Truisms"). MacNeice tired of thirties reportage, and (partly a result of his friendship with Dylan Thomas) his poetry became increasingly "in need of myth" ("The Blasphemies").

MacNeice's last two collections, *Solstices* (1961) and *The Burning Perch* (1963), contain more varieties of parable than Edwin Muir could produce. These exemplify his Beckett-like view that "the nearest one gets to an answer is in the sheer phrasing of the question." Transcendence receives a bad press today, as does Celtic mysticism, yet Yeats originally needed his mysteries because Darwin and Huxley had "robbed" him of his childhood religion. Symbol and myth are part of that Yeatsian legacy to later poets. For good and ill, religion remains a major cultural force in certain parts of the British Isles. Like the sense of place, it has helped keep poetry alive there.

Language, Canon

Celtic languages shadow the English lyric in the British Isles: the Irish language; Scots Gaelic, which is close to Ulster Irish; and the Welsh language. There is also the lowland Scots variety of English, pressed back into dialect and called, by its poetic champion Hugh MacDiarmid, "Doric" or "Lallans" or "the Vernacular." English hegemony in the archipelago cannot be divorced from the English language; hence the role of language in separatist ideologies. Independently of nationalism, the very existence or influence of another language promotes linguistic literacy. The locally diverse effects of Gaelic (or Scots) on spoken English in Ireland set up a double consciousness, a deviation from the standard that need not be construed only in political terms. Kavanagh tested English and Irish pastoral against his Monaghan car: "I heard the Duffys shouting 'Damn your soul!'" Vice versa, Philip Larkin during his years in Belfast (1950–1955) was stimulated by "the salt rebuff of speech, / Insisting so on difference."

The Irish revival had two linguistic modes fruitfully linked by translation. However, the Gaelic League became politicized and attacked Yeats's movement as an alien (and Protestant) imposition. From a linguistic viewpoint, English won the "battle of two civilizations" in that Irish, although currently enjoying a small revival, will never be other than a minority language. Meanwhile Hiberno-English—in the wake of Yeats, Synge, and Joyce—has had remarkable literary success. R. S. Thomas, writing in "Words and the Poet" (1964), is ambivalent about the transaction whereby "frequent transfusions of Celtic blood" invigorate "the worn out veins of English." But English has been the "native" language of Irish people, apart from small enclaves on the west coast, for a long time.

Perhaps the greater tenacity of Welsh makes it harder for Anglo-Welsh poets not to feel monolingualism as guilt and bilingualism as compromise. Dylan Thomas felt no guilt, and some contemporary Welsh poets would do well to remember Louis MacNeice's question in "An Alphabet of Literary Prejudices" (1948): "When will well-known Irish writers who publish nothing but English stop preaching nothing but Gaelic?" (MacNeice may have had Austin Clarke in mind.) Today influence cuts both ways, and relations between English and Gaelic poetry from Ireland have eased considerably. Witness the bilingual poet Michael Hartnett or *Pharaoh's Daughter* (1990), in which well-known English-language poets translate the leading Gaelic poet Nuala Ní Dhomhnaill. Formerly banned as betrayal, collections in translation are reaching new audiences.

In fact, poetry in Wales has suffered from a cultural protectionism that embraces both Welsh and Anglo-Welsh poetry. As for Scotland, Douglas Dunn's *Faber Book of Contemporary Scottish Poetry* announces a kind of linguistic peace treaty: "Scottish poetry has moved gradually into its liberty . . . it is more and more the poetry in three languages of one nationality." But if this begs the National question—and overrides the regional fractures noticed by Cairns Craig—it also suggests zones of influence rather than keen mutual stimulus. More broadly, fine Scottish poets such as Norman MacCaig (b. 1910) and Iain Crichton Smith (b. 1928) tend to establish one style and stick to it. MacCaig's charming, occasional aperçus, as in "Blue Tit on a String of Peanuts" (from *The Equal Skies*, 1980), depend on images rather than on surprising verbal liaisons: "Your hair-thin legs / (one north-east, one due west) support / a scrap of volcano."

Edwin Muir may be rationalizing the inertness of his own English idiom (the "tall and echoing passages" of "The Labyrinth") when he argues that Scotland has lost one language and not found—or not found itself in—another. Yet Scotland has done less than Ireland to reinvent the English lyric (supposing that to be an objective). If Welsh poets seem too close together, Scottish poets often seem too far apart—and linguistic difference becomes an alibi.

Both Muir's and MacDiarmid's difficulties with English stem from their origins as dialect-speakers in Orkney and Dumfriesshire. Muir, indeed, associated the vernacular with "regression to childhood," saying in *Scott and Scotland* that "dialect is to a homogeneous language what the babbling of children is to the speech of grown men and women." MacDiarmid, who briefly made a homogeneous poetic language by grafting dictionary words onto the green shoots of his childhood speech, could not agree. In "English Ascendancy in British Literature" (1931), reprinted in *Selected Prose*, ed. Alan Riach (1992), he had argued that the repression of "Gaelic and Scots dialect poets" was, in European terms, "a sort of self-infliction of an extensive spiritual and psychological blindness."

For MacDiarmid as for R. S. Thomas, language precipitates loss of meaning on all fronts. His writings advance two models whereby the darkness might lift. The first is Joyce's "multi-linguistic" example, followed in MacDiarmid's Poundian poems, and endorsed by his postmodernist admirers. The second model, interlingual rather than multilingual, seems predicated on MacDiarmid's genuine poetic breakthrough—English literature should be "broad-basing itself on all the diverse cultural elements and the splendid variety of languages and dialects, in the British Isles."

This splendid variety affects poetry in equally various ways. Tom Paulin's *Faber Book of Vernacular Verse* (1990) relishes variety to the extent of herding quite heterogeneous effects into the vernacular fold: folk traditions, English regional poetry, Scots poetry, poetry with marked Hiberno-English features, phonetic poetry, discursive or conversational poetry, and much poetry—by Dickinson, Yeats, Edward Thomas—not usually considered "vernacular" that simply bears some relation to the language "really used" by men or women. However, there is a political dimension to Paulin's project. Aside from Scots or regional variants of English, accent and idiom are the areas on which a politics of English poetic language most often impinges; for instance, in West Indian "rap" poetry, although its rhythms in performance are significant, too.

Tom Leonard's poems, whose orthography reproduces Glaswegian phonetics, satirically exploit the reading difficulties of outsiders (see *Intimate Voices: Selected Works 1965-1983*). "Good Style" begins: "helluva hard tay read theez init," and "Paroakial" adds political bite to Kavanagh's aesthetic by sending up a speaker who commands: "goahty learna new langwij / sumhm ihnturnashnl / Noah Glasgow hangup." Leonard anticipates his critics in "Fathers and Sons": "'Don't you find / the use of phonetic urban dialect / rather constrictive?' / Asks a member of the audience. . . ." Yet it can be constrictive in the work of Leonard and his imitators—whether read aloud or on the page, phonetic poetry tends to foreclose other verbal possibilities. So does poetry that fetishizes diction.

Paulin's anthology, as Robert Crawford recognizes, is designed "to support his own poetic endeavours." His Northern Irish Protestant background attracts him to the Scots words that color Ulster speech (as do words of Gaelic origin), although true Ulster Scots vernacular verse, like its Scottish counterpart, died out during the nineteenth century. In *Liberty Tree* (1983) Paulin highlights a particular consonantal range of words—"glubbed," "choggy," "chug," "screggy"—to self-consciously barbaric effect. (This differs from the role of dialect words in the homogeneous language of Seamus Heaney.) *Liberty Tree* also attempts to conceive a linguistic basis for an idealized form of Republicanism.

Crawford approves of Paulin as a "sophisticated barbarian" (which seems to be having it both ways) and notes that Paulin's "dialect usages and his nationalist stance can be paralleled by the sprinkling of such Scots words as 'dailygone,' 'brose' and 'jorum-jirger' through *St. Kilda's Parliament*, the 1981 collection by his friend Douglas Dunn." Dunn's earlier collection, *Barbarians* (1979), also invokes a politics of language. In "The Student" he adopts the persona of a disaffected worker who might have taken part in "the Scottish insurrection" of 1820: "*Difficult Latin sticks in my throat / And the scarecrow wears my coat.*" This refrain parallels, as do Paulin's barbarisms, the strategies of Tony Harrison toward region and class in England. Yet political-linguistic will should not be taken, in all cases, for poetic deed. Dunn's most concentrated and moving collection is *Elegies* (1985), which commemorates his wife ("It is very lonely on the green settee").

There are less obvious forms of Celtic blood transfusion. Generally speaking, the survival of oral traditions—strongest in Ireland— has kept the rhythms, the corpuscles, moving. Forms of verbal display are still valued: recitation, story telling, contests of wit. Even Presbyterianism and Welsh Baptism have their preachers. Just as Dylan Thomas's poetry remembers his evangelical grandfather, so is the style of Northern Irish poet W. R. Rodgers (b. 1909), who spent ten years as a Presbyterian minister, shaped by the "old sea-roar and surge / Of rhetoric and Holy Writ." Whatever the cultural reasons, Paul Durcan and Liz Lochhead—like Dylan Thomas before them— are as celebrated as rap poets for reading their work. Durcan invests with priestly intensity poems whose structures draw on a range of contemporary media and the recitative of Bob Dylan. "The Kilfenora Teaboy" recasts the Irish patriotic ballad in a plangent sixties mode:

> I'm the Kilfenora teaboy
> And I'm not so very young,
> But though the land is going to pieces
> I will not take up the gun . . .
> *Oh but it's the small piece of furze between two farms*
> *Is what makes the Kilfenora teaboy really run.*

For Lochhead as for Durcan, what goes into the reading goes into the writing. Her edged, colloquial dramatic monologues incorporate the twentieth-century consumerist flux, including the built-in obsolescence of words themselves. "The Grim Sisters" (1981) harks back to the prefeminist fifties:

In those big mantrap handbags
they snapped shut at any hint of *that*
were hedgehog hairbrushes
cottonwool mice and barbed combs to tease.
Their heels spiked bubblegum, dead leaves.

The title of Lochhead's *Bagpipe Muzak* (1991) pays tribute to Louis MacNeice's poem of 1937. In "Bagpipe Music" MacNeice's rhythms and vocabulary dramatize—at the level of language—the culture clash between modernity and tradition: "Their knickers are made of crepe-de-chine, their shoes are made of python." MacNeice's central role in releasing everyday words into poetry has been acknowledged by Philip Larkin as well as by Derek Mahon, yet he also absorbed classical syntax and the impact of Christianity on the English language. Perhaps MacNeice's zest in mixing lexical and grammatical registers was influenced by his generational duel with Yeats, and by his Irish/English double consciousness. In the preface to *Modern Poetry* (1938) MacNeice defies Yeatsian precepts: "This is a plea for *impure* poetry, that is, for poetry conditioned by the poet's life and the world around him."

When it comes to canon making, however, aesthetic pleas often seem of less account than the politics of language and nation. To take the Irish case, anthologies of Irish poetry have recently engaged in a complex quarrel about traditions, which has thrown into question understandings of Irish literary history since 1921. Hence Thomas Kinsella's reactionary *New Oxford Book of Irish Verse* (1986). Kinsella pronounces the muse of Irish poetry to be "a past heavy with loss," yet contradictorily insists on a Platonic unity that transcends linguistic and historical difference.

Yeats has always caused problems for proponents of a unified Irish tradition. And as we have seen in the case of Kavanagh, "anxiety of influence" can be compounded by cultural and sectarian factors. As it turns out, Kavanagh's parochial strengths liberated him from Yeats. MacNeice, who shared Yeats's middle-class Irish Protestant background, engaged more profoundly with Yeatsian practice and theory than did any other Irish or English poet of his generation. He wrote the first major critical study of Yeats (*The Poetry of W. B. Yeats*, 1941), which concluded that Yeats's message to his successors was: "*Go thou and do otherwise.*"

For Austin Clarke (b. 1896), this was easier said—or desired—than done. Clarke's most achieved poems are to be found in *Pilgrimage and Other Poems* (1929), which mythologizes the medieval "Celtic Romanesque" period and blends the vowel assonances of Gaelic meter with English sound patterns. "The Lost Heifer" begins: "When the black herds of the rain were grazing / In the gap of the pure cold wind / And the watery hazes of the hazel / Brought her into my mind . . ." Clarke's subsequent metrical experimentation was less successful, and his anticlerical satires (although of historical interest) lack the punch of Paul Durcan's.

The uncertainties of Clarke's oeuvre exemplify wider confusions, ever since the 1920s, as to how—or whether—Irish poetry in English should declare its independence, too. (The really independent moves by Kavanagh and MacNeice were not on any ideological agenda.) One obvious option seemed to be Gaelicism; another, modernism. But Irish prose modernism, thanks to Joyce, has been infinitely more significant than Irish poetic modernism.

Denis Devlin (b. 1908) and Brian Coffey (b. 1905)—and in one view Thomas Kinsella (b. 1928)—opt for feeble imitations of T. S. Eliot rather than feeble imitations of Yeats. The real free-verse achievement of that period is *The Great Hunger*, a poem that had digested *The Waste Land* but "did otherwise" in indigenous terms—as did MacDiarmid's *A Drunk Man Looks at the Thistle*. And the strategic position of Mac-Neice vis à vis the English thirties generation enabled him to synthesize the disparate influences of Yeats and Eliot in a context after ideologies were tested by the politics of the period. This was to prove important for Northern Irish poetry later on.

MacNeice's place in the canon and the term *Northern Irish poetry* tend to be—somewhat shakily—interdependent. There are still taboos on partitioning Irish poetry, even for analytical purposes. Yet canonical bids have been made from the North: Frank Ormsby's diplomatically entitled *Poets from the North of Ireland* appeared in 1979 and was updated in 1990. Paul Muldoon's *Faber Book of Contemporary Irish Poetry* (1986) placed Kavanagh and MacNeice at the head of a select group of living poets, chiefly from the North. This bid has been countered by *The Penguin Book of Contemporary Irish Poetry* (1990), whose editors, Peter Fallon and Derek Mahon, firmly pull the poetic center back from Belfast to Dublin and—like Kinsella—assert a unitary Irish poetry: "as ever, poets from the North contribute to a national body of work which, in its turn, belongs to a global community." Blotting out the island of Britain, Fallon and Mahon emphasize European links and a "transatlantic neighbourhood" with the United States.

This battle of the anthologies began with *The Penguin Book of Contemporary British Poetry* (1982), which includes six Northern Irish poets (Seamus Heaney, Michael Longley, Medbh McGuckian, Derek Mahon, Paul Muldoon, and Tom Paulin). In a verse *Open Letter* Seamus Heaney objected to his inclusion under "British"—since "My passport's green." Here political and literary or cultural vocabularies clash. How does this affect the influence of Wordsworth or Ted Hughes on Heaney's poetry? In practice, Heaney's poems remain in the *Penguin British*; the presence of the Northern poets in the *Penguin Irish*, as well, accurately suggests a degree of condominium and provides for reader reception in different contexts. At the same time, the glaring literary-historical deficiencies in the conception and execution of both these anthologies confirm that, during the last seventy years, little thought has gone into Irish-British poetic relations.

Heaney's *Open Letter* was written for the Field Day Theatre Company, a group of writers and academics who have done much to politicize Irish literary criticism since 1980. Its apotheosis is the three-volume *Field Day Anthology of Irish Writing* (1991)—a massive canonical and hegemonic bid on many fronts. The anthology has been criticized on two main grounds: for underrepresenting women and for overrepresenting Nationalist politics. (Its general stress on "political speeches and writings" makes the neglect of women's utterance all the more surprising.)

Indeed, a strongly negative aspect of Celtic traditionalism is its patriarchal character, reinforced through all the churches. As elsewhere, Irish women have made their mark in fiction rather than in poetry, and only Medbh McGuckian and, in Irish, Nuala Ní Dhomhnaill have reinvented language and form. However, Eavan Boland (b. 1944) instituted a greater self-consciousness on the part of Irish women poets when she published her pamphlet *A Kind of Scar: The Woman Poet in a National Tradition* (1989). Boland criticizes the literary-political invention of that blighting, silencing figure "Dark Rosaleen. Cathleen ni Houlihan. The nation as woman: the woman as national muse." But although her poems bring a new slant to suburban motherhood, some of Boland's work rather too deliberately inverts Irish male poetic premises. The impact of feminist theory on poetry by Irish women has been double-edged—as yet insufficiently acclimatized, it tends to pre-empt or usurp creative practice. But the numbers of women now writing poetry belong to the great surge of sociopolitical confidence that made Mary Robinson President of the Irish Republic, and more good poems will surely follow.

The "Contemporary Irish Poetry" section of the *Field Day Anthology* is another example of literary-historical and critical inadequacy. The anthology as a whole uses literature and theory to challenge so-called revisionist history, i.e., the way in which most Irish historians, for several decades now, have complicated the Nationalist narrative represented at its simplest by Kinsella's "past heavy with loss." Thus Field Day also rules out poetic partitionism, obscures distinctive developments in the North and South, and shows a significant hostility towards Paul Durcan, printing none of his political poems and calling his work "loose to the point of garrulity."

If Durcan is sometimes vulnerable to the charge of journalism, his real sin seems to be that his critique of Church and state, of hierarchy and patriarchy, of political violence from all quarters, manifests a revisionist tendency. But Durcan's poetry embodies and prophetically imagines cultural change at a deeper level than either historians or journalists can reach. Its popularity in the Irish Republic, together with that of Brendan Kennelly and Nuala Ní Dhomhnaill, indicates that a communal psychodrama—a communal psychotherapy—is taking place, which has to do with growing up. Childhood countries have recurred in this discussion—Durcan's *Daddy, Daddy* (1990) enacts a psychological and political rite of passage in relation to his dead father, a pillar of the state who once put his poet-son into a mental home. This suggests that arguments about poetry are not purely academic in Ireland.

Northern Irish Poetry, 1962–1992: A Formal History

The issues raised so far—place, history, nation, religion, language, canon—are deeply implicated in the dialectics that Northern Irish poets conduct with one another and with themselves. Here the theoretical term *intertextuality* applies in a living, social sense. Relations between poems can help to interpret a society—in MacNeice's words—"small enough / To be still thought of with a family feeling," yet simultaneously engaged in a bloody family feud. Since the cultural mix that produces the conflict also conditions the poetry, it is well placed both to empathize and to criticize.

Poetic intertextuality improves on the black-and-white "readings" encapsulated in *Autumn Journal*, and passes the Northern Irish problem through finer meshes than those available to political science. Indeed, John Whyte's useful survey of twenty years' scholarly research, *Interpreting Northern Ireland* (1991), comes to a conclusion that the poetry might have anticipated: "Areas only a few miles from each other can differ enormously—in religious mix, in economic circumstances, in the level of violence, in political attitudes. . . ."

In Northern Irish poetry parochial variables are of the essence. They cover the spectrum between "A Christmas Childhood" and "Carrickfergus," between our need to construct parishes and history's need to dissolve them. This is a matrix for poetry itself. If at one level poetic intertextuality interprets a civil war, at another it represents literary traditions at work. Because Northern Irish poetry reads the historical English lyric from a peculiar angle on the British Isles, it has reinvented lyrical categories—not only war poetry—and reopened the debate about form that took place earlier in this century.

It was in the late 1960s that Northern Irish poetry became a recognized phenomenon. Seamus Heaney, still Northern Ireland's most internationally known poet, published his first collection, *Death of a Naturalist*, in 1966. Derek Mahon followed with *Night Crossing* (1968), and Michael Longley with *No Continuing City* (1969). The first reciprocity between these poets occurred at Trinity College Dublin, where Longley (b. 1939) and Mahon (b. 1941) met, although they had earlier attended the same Protestant grammar school in Belfast. A second phase began when young writers from Queen's University Belfast, including Heaney (b. 1939), originally from rural County Derry, joined the literary "Group" run by Philip Hobsbaum, a poet and critic from England. Longley also joined the Group, and met Heaney there, when he returned to Belfast in 1964. Mahon only attended the Group once and said he "didn't like it. Too Leavisite and too contentious, intolerant" (interview in *Poetry Review*, summer 1991). Since the Group is sometimes credited with being the only begetter of Northern Irish poetry, the Trinity College Dublin connection should not be forgotten. From the early 1950s Trinity possessed a flourishing magazine, *Icarus*, which was the literary nursery of Brendan Kennelly as well as of Mahon and Longley.

All three Northern poets were stimulated by exemplars outside Ireland and the British Isles. To take the United States alone: Mahon looked to Crane and Lowell, Heaney to Frost, and Longley to Stevens and Wilbur. They also looked back: Heaney to Wordsworth and Hopkins, Longley to the Classics and Metaphysical poetry, and Mahon to Baudelaire and Rimbaud. But three literary contexts were more immediate in uniting cultural and aesthetic significance for the poets: first, the Anglo-Irish poetic tradition (Yeats and Robert Graves mediated by MacNeice), in which Trinity College Dublin still had a particular stake; second, the impact of Philip Larkin and Ted Hughes, whose own cross-currents involved differing relations to such "Celtic" poets as Yeats and Dylan Thomas; and third, Kavanagh's Ulster parochialism and Hewitt's Ulster regionalism. The poets' varying relation to these varied influences produced strikingly diverse results.

What *Night Crossing*, *Death of a Naturalist*, and *No Continuing City* do have in common is a formal concentration only matched at that period by Philip Larkin. Virtually all the poems in *Night Crossing* and *No Continuing City* are stanzaic and rhymed—in almost every stanza length between two and ten lines. Heaney's *Death of a Naturalist* generally prefers the quatrain (as does his later poetry), but also includes richly textured blank verse in the tradition of Edward Thomas and Ted Hughes. Differences in approach to the stanza can be seen if we compare Heaney's "Personal Helicon," Mahon's "An Unborn Child" and Longley's "Freeze-Up." "Personal Helicon," a poem at the center of Heaney's early poetic parish, is both springy (like Hopkins) and weighted (like Hughes):

> As a child, they could not keep me from wells
> And old pumps with buckets and windlasses.
> I loved the dark drop, the trapped sky, the smells
> Of waterweed, fungus and dank moss.

This quatrain alternates between strongly consonantal monosyllables and the contrasting stresses that fall on the disyllabic and trisyllabic words, which seem counterpoised at the end of the second and beginning of the fourth lines. Yet, overall, the single line counts for more than the stanza. The rhythmical force is centripetal, turning on "dark drop."

In Mahon's "An Unborn Child" individual lines may have their own rhythmic verve, but they also participate in a freer version of Yeats's "exact coincidence between period and stanza":

I must compose myself in the nerve-centre
Of the metropolis and not fidget—
Although sometimes at night, when the city
Has gone to sleep, I keep in touch with it
Listening to the warm red water
Racing in the sewers of my mother's body—
Or the moths, soft as eyelids, or the rain
Wiping its wet wings on the window-pane.

Here alliteration and assonance are not primarily geared to sensuous meditation. They accentuate the beat (which in this case suggests the rhythms of life itself) and punctuate a declarative, dramatic momentum. The six-line stanza of Michael Longley's "Freeze-Up" hovers between mimesis and declaration. Double rhymes and internal assonances prolong the line, while shifting sentence lengths also help to construct the relations between flux and stasis on which the poem pivots:

The freeze-up annexes the sea even,
Putting out over the waves its platform.
Let skies fall, the fox's belly cave in—
This catastrophic shortlived reform
Directs to our homes the birds of heaven.
They come on farfetched winds to keep us warm.

Critics who disparage the "well-made poem" forget that its compression, its semantic layers—the interplay between rhythm, syntax, and sound—set up the conditions for metaphorical or symbolic intensity. In "An Unborn Child" language makes the vital connections between the womb and the world—the pun on "nerve-centre," the interchange between moths, eyelids, and rain. In "Personal Helicon" the fact that words are also objects of sensory relish helps to release the Jungian echoes that become the poem's subject: "I rhyme / To see myself, to set the darkness echoing." The drama of "Freeze-Up" is partly a drama of diction. Longley sets Latin or Greek etymologies or compound adjectives alongside "the fox's belly" in a way that stresses the massing of impersonal forces against the animate and homely.

It is no accident that these poems are partly about form itself, which figures as a container for the unconscious, an organic microcosm, and a problematic "Freeze-Up" of flux: "The bittern whom this different weather / Cupboarded in ice like a specimen." All three poets place art and the artist firmly in the thematic foreground. In *Night Crossing*

Mahon's generally dark vision favors doomed, self-destructive artists—
"Dowson and Company," Marilyn Monroe, De Quincey—scapegoats
for the bourgeois condition. Like Edwin Muir, Mahon perceives
Calvinism (which had similar effects in Protestant Ulster) as the enemy
of art. But he negotiates this blockage by endowing the artist with an
equally extreme sense of mission. "Van Gogh among the Miners" unites
the evangelical and the aesthetic: "Setting fierce fire to the eyes / Of
sun-flowers and fishing boats."

   Death of a Naturalist and Heaney's second volume, *Door into the Dark*
(1969), celebrate the blacksmith "beating real iron out" and the thatcher's "Midas touch." Longley's heroes and heroines tend to be virtuosi,
perfectionists (Fats Waller, Emily Dickinson) who yet must risk chaos
and suffer loss of control. Dr. Johnson on the Hebrides "construes himself again." "To Bix Beiderbecke" salutes "The havoc there, and the
manoeuvrings!"

   Artistic maneuvrings were soon put to the test by political havoc and
the dogs of war. A "local row" turned deadly serious. In his poem "Rage
for Order" (an ironical allusion to Wallace Stevens's "Idea of Order at
Key West") Mahon represents the poet as marginalized by history and
poetry as reduced to "An eddy of semantic scruple / In an unstruc-
turable sea." Heaney's *Wintering Out* (1972), Mahon's *Lives* (1972), and
Longley's *An Exploded View* (1973) register the "stereophonic nightmare" that began with Unionist repression of the civil rights movement
in Northern Ireland. This led to the arrival of the British army, the
campaigns by the IRA and Protestant paramilitaries, direct rule from
London, and many deaths. The poets responded according to their differing backgrounds and their different aesthetics.

   Frank Ormsby's anthology *The Rage for Order: Poetry of the Northern
Ireland Troubles* (1992) proves that there is no single model for the
"troubles" poem. Heaney in *Wintering Out* plumbs a more collective
unconscious, bringing to light unarticulated aspects of Northern
Catholic experience by (as he puts it) "politicizing the terrain" of his
earlier poetry. As Heaney's parochial helicon discloses its territorial
imperatives, language and place-names turn out to be marked and fis-
sured by history. For example, "A New Song" opposes the Gaelic names
Derrygarve and Moyola to the planter names Castledawson and
Upperlands. However, perhaps revising the "native mode" adumbrated
in John Hewitt's "Once Alien Here," Heaney offers poetry as the
ground where languages might meet: "our river tongues must rise . . . /

To flood, with vowelling embrace, / Demesnes staked out in consonants."

Yet ambiguities ("problems and cleavages") are not entirely resolved by this conceit—itself a political allegory. Heaney also seeks "befitting emblems of adversity" (a phrase of Yeats's) through the mythopoeic, iconic, and ritualistic procedures of his collection *North* (1975). *North* is founded on the haunting images in P. V. Glob's *Bog People*, which earlier inspired Heaney's fine poem "The Tollund Man."

Mahon and Longley also look to their hinterlands—with more dismay. Mahon's poetry continues its critique of the repressions in Protestant culture that generate violence rather than art: "this is your / country, close one eye and be king" ("Ecclesiastes"). "Courtyards in Delft," from *The Hunt by Night* (1982), uses de Hooch's genre paintings to probe what the Protestant housework ethic omits (and thereby permits): "We miss the dirty dog, the fiery gin." Yet this culture secretes "A strange child with a taste for verse / While my hard-nosed companions dream of war."

Mahon's poetry transposes the Protestant housing estates of his childhood into a strange "parish," where the mundane ("gardens and washing-lines") may disintegrate into the apocalyptic: "In a tiny stone church / On a desolate headland / A lost tribe is singing 'Abide with me'" ("Nostalgias"). Images of apocalypse internalize the guilts that Mahon associates with his own background. Influenced by Beckett as well as by MacNeice (all three conditioned by Irish Protestantism), Mahon takes upon his poetry the original sin of having been born into history—the human stain. His celebrated poem "A Disused Shed in Co. Wexford," from *The Snow Party* (1975), tries to conceive some kind of recovery, beginning: "Even now there are places where a thought might grow . . ." Through the bizarre symbol of mushrooms left "in a foetor of / Vegetable sweat since civil war days," Mahon encompasses a great sweep of historical disaster that cries out for redemption: "Lost people of Treblinka and Pompeii!"

It is characteristic of Northern Irish poetry to use other wars and cataclysms as direction finders. Longley's poem "Wounds" juxtaposes images from World War I—"two pictures from my father's head"—with the even more futile casualties of civil war: "Three teenage soldiers, bellies full of / Bullets and Irish beer . . . the Sacred Heart of Jesus / Paralyzed as heavy guns put out / The night-light in a nursery forever." A later poem, "Bog Cotton" from *The Echo Gate* (1979), perceives the Ulster impasse through Keith Douglas in World War II remembering Isaac Rosenberg in World War I: "You saw that beyond the thirstier desert flowers / There fell hundreds of thousands of poppy petals."

Longley's particular historical emphasis implies that all Northern Irish poetry can be seen as war poetry, still caught up in the aftermath of European and Irish wars from 1914 to 1945. This perspective, which partly derives from his English parentage, also brings literary and cultural relations between the islands into a focus different from either Hewitt's or Heaney's. Wilfred Owen is relevant to the protest elegies in the sequence "Wreaths"; Edward Thomas to Longley's West of Ireland poems, where the ecological strand in English nature poetry meets the Yeatsian visionary tradition.

Part of MacNeice's legacy—part of modernism and modernity—is Heraclitean flux. A younger generation of Northern Irish poets, Paul Muldoon, Medbh McGuckian, and Ciaran Carson (all from Catholic backgrounds) carry flux further into language and form. Concentrated artistic construction has been followed by equally concentrated—and equally various—deconstruction. Paul Muldoon (b. 1951) was the first of these poets to be discussed in deconstructionist or postmodernist terms. However, his poetry lends itself to such readings not so much because it has absorbed international trends, as because it responds both to the absolutism in Northern Irish mentalities, and to the poetry of his seniors.

Muldoon's first two collections, *New Weather* (1973) and *Mules* (1977), involve a bleaker version of rural terrain and rural community than is to be found in early Heaney. Heaney deals with sexual awakening, but not with themes of infidelity, mutual destructiveness between the generations or sexes, and confusion of gender roles. For instance, whereas the father in Heaney's poetry personifies continuity and stability, in Muldoon's the father becomes a fictive point of reference denoting the history, traditions, ties, and authority that the poetry questions. Thus the title poem of *Mules* is a parable of hybridization between the Northern Irish communities:

> We had loosed them into one field
> I watched Sam Parsons and my quick father
> Tense for the punch below their belts,
> For what was neither one thing or the other.

The "field" where this problematic birth occurs suggests the contraction and expansion to which Muldoon subjects the poetic parish. He reinvents his native Moy in County Armagh as a fabulous locale where "anything wild or wonderful" might happen. Interviewed by John Haffenden, Muldoon said of "the Moy": "I'm very interested in the way in which a small place, a parish, can come to stand for the world."

Although all first-person lyrics should be understood as dramatic structures, Muldoon goes further and introduces a phantasmagoria of emblematic figures: "Sam Parsons," the signs of the Zodiac, "an Oglala/Sioux." Individual poems also contribute to a hall of mirrors, a multifaceted dialectic, in which one parable or story catches light from another. This has led Muldoon to an idiosyncratic kind of narrative poetry, and to greater formal experiment. "Immram," in *Why Brownlee Left* (1980), is a blackly comic farrago that crosses Raymond Chandler with the Irish medieval "voyage-tale" and the Byron of *Don Juan*. *Quoof* (1983) and *Meeting the British* (1987) are variations on a deconstructed sonnet sequence—varying line lengths, outrageous rhyme, tangential linking motifs, the sonnet sometimes functioning as a stanza, sometimes standing free. The Muldoonian mutability—well-made poetry that pretends not to be—is bound up with the question of language. Like the later MacNeice, he exposes the disturbing assumptions and implications hidden in everyday phrases or clichés. Thus "neither one thing or the other" questions the desire for fixed identity.

Muldoon's critique of language in general, and of Ulster's political clichés in particular, undermines cultural determinism—together with Heaney's presumption that "right names" exist. Muldoon suspects etymology, like other fixed histories, and embraces "incorrigibly plural" verbal associations. A sequence of rhymes in the poem "Sushi" (from *Meeting the British*) runs: "arrogance," "arcane," "oregano," "orgone," "organs," "Arigna," "Arragon." When Muldoon deals more directly with violence he, too, uses scenarios from other wars—World War I again, Korea, the genocide of American Indians. "Truce" recreates Christmas 1914 to suggest the necessity and difficulty of peacemaking: "It begins with one or two soldiers / And one or two following . . ." "Gathering Mushrooms" questions armed struggle in a different way— by representing its ideology as its real prison: "Come back to us . . . / Beyond this concrete wall is a wall of concrete / and barbed wire." Muldoon's poetry picks the locks of word prisons.

It seems a comment on Irish patriarchies that Medbh McGuckian's aesthetic should stand so far back from the structures of her male contemporaries. Beside McGuckian (b. 1950) even Muldoon looks logo-centric. While her poems appear to make statements and observe syntactical norms, their logic is one of relations between images. "The Orchid House," from *The Flower Master* (1982), begins:

A flower's fragrance is a woman's virtue;
So I tell them underground in pairs;
Or in their fleshy white sleeves, how
Desirable their shapes, how one
Was lost for sixty years, with all
Its arching spikes, its honeyed tessellations . . .

These exfoliating images, however, are neither impressionistic nor primarily sensuous. Flowers (and clothes) recur in McGuckian's poetry as counters in an interior drama about sexuality, gender, marriage, motherhood, and poetry. Here, orchids' complex reproductive system enables her to play around with androgynous and autoerotic zones: "virtue" faces the testicular implications of "underground in pairs," the "lost" orchid possesses "spikes" and "tessellations."

McGuckian's distinctive concern with houses, gardens, and deeply conflicting images of women may involve a dialogue with Catholicism, which places mother or virgin on the only available pedestals. This aligns authority with procreation and thus further complicates women's creativity. McGuckian, like her male peers, is obsessed with poetry itself. Some of her poems encode responses to theirs or turn the tables on a male muse. "The Sitting," in *Venus and the Rain* (1984), is one of the many poems about paintings or painting in which McGuckian explores the politics of representation. The positions of artist-subject and sitter-object appear equally uncomfortable: "she questions my brisk / Brushwork, the note of positive red / In the kissed mouth I have given her." "Harem Trousers," in *On Ballycastle Beach* (1988), develops this theme in relation to an androgynous garment: "A poem dreams of being written / Without the pronoun 'I.'" Ultimately, McGuckian writes a kind of metapoetry, like Wallace Stevens, whose images belong more to words than to the phenomenal world. Yet her slippery language outmaneuvers the egotistical sublime.

It is as if Muldoon, McGuckian and Carson have reconceived the English (or Northern Irish) lyric not only by making it so linguistically self-conscious, but by pushing particular structural aspects to extremes. Muldoon emphasizes narrative and verbal accumulation;

McGuckian image and symbol, while Ciaran Carson (b. 1948) emphasizes narration. Over ten years after a rather conventional first collection, *The New Estate* (1976), Carson produced two much more radical
volumes: *The Irish for No* (1987) and *Belfast Confetti* (1989). The latter
title alludes to a wry local euphemism for nuts and bolts dropped on
Catholics in the Belfast shipyards, which becomes a metaphor for war
poetry's "fount of broken type." Carson's formal radicalism consists in
his long line—another deviation from the stanzaic shapes laid down by
Heaney, Longley, and Mahon. This line functions less smoothly than
that of the American poet C. K. Williams (an influence on Carson),
being interrupted by sudden breaks, twists and turns. Carson's syntax
imitates the digressions of story telling and conversation. The unpred-
icatable relation between line and syntax reproduces a fractured communal narrative:

> Maybe you can figure it, why The Crown and Shamrock and The
>   Rose and Crown
> Are at opposite ends of the town. Politics? The odds change. The
>   borders move.
> Or they're asked to. A nod's as good as a wink . . .

This self-consciousness has referential origins and referential point.
Carson has said that his poems are not "about" but "of" "the Troubles."
If one poetic role model is the Irish traditional storyteller (*seanachie*),
another is a crazy with a notebook: "Squiggles, dashes, question-marks,
dense as the Rosetta stone." Language seems unable to pin down a city
mutating under the stresses of urban renewal and cultural change as well
as civil war. Symptomatically, the members of "The Exiles' Club" in
Wollongong "just about keep up with the news of bombings and demolition" and try to hold on to old maps and obsolete names in their heads.

In one aspect, Carson's poetry is about culture shock—it genuinely
engages with the disjunctions between tradition and modernity, country
and city. His audacious poem "Hamlet" rewrites both the parish and
Shakespeare as an evening in a Belfast neighborhood pub, which takes in
(but never resolves) such topics as a soldier being killed in 1922, a Guinness stain on a ten-pound note, the Armada, lost streets, fictions, truth,
and language. We are told the etymology of the (Catholic) Falls Road—
from "hedge," "*frontier*," "*boundary*." But "Hamlet" dissolves Kavanagh's
parish into the talk—the poem—that keeps it going: "time / Is conversation: it is the hedge that flits incessantly into the present . . ."

Part of the generational dialectic in Northern Irish poetry (although older poets have moved on, too) is a fresh encounter between traditional forms and modernism. Why this should happen with reference to Northern Ireland might seem mysterious, until we remember that the dialectic between Yeats and Joyce continues in Ireland, and that it has both a political and a theological element. Perhaps the metaphysical differences set in motion by the Irish religious antinomy are among the most significant determinants of poetic vitality.

Four recent collections keep all the arguments in play: Muldoon's *Madoc* (1990), Heaney's *Seeing Things* (1991), McGuckian's *Marconi's Cottage* (1991), and Longley's *Gorse Fires* (1991). Heaney's book is visionary, transcendental, and traditionalist; McGuckian continues her teasing strategies; Longley condenses dark images from the Holocaust and the *Odyssey*; and Muldoon throws in a neo-Joycean literary-critical-political satire. *Madoc*, subtitled "A Mystery," imagines that Coleridge and Southey, the poet-pantisocrats, really did found their utopian community on the banks of the Susquehanna. Through Muldoon's veil of puns and allusions we can see that it all ends in colonialism, violence, literary rows, and tears. Since the pantisocrats are heading for the village of "Ulster," it may be presumed that Muldoon also has his eye on politics and poetics nearer home. His irony extends poetic intertextuality over centuries as well as continents. But, despite the irony, *Madoc* itself belongs to a new frontier for the English lyric in the British Isles.

Edna Longley

Further Reading

Andrews, Elmer, ed. *Contemporary Irish Poetry: A Collection of Critical Essays*. London: Macmillan, 1992.

Andrews, Elmer, ed. *Seamus Heaney: A Collection of Critical Essays*. London: Macmillan, 1992.

Corcoran, Neil, ed. *The Chosen Ground: Essays on the Contemporary Poetry of Northern Ireland*. Bridgend: Seren, 1992.

Crawford, Robert. *Devolving English Literature*. Oxford: Clarendon, 1992.

Davies, Walford. *Dylan Thomas*. Milton Keynes: Open University Press, 1986.

Deane, Seamus. *Celtic Revivals*. London: Faber, 1985.

Heaney, Seamus. *Preoccupations: Selected Prose, 1968–1978*. London: Faber; New York: Farrar, Straus and Giroux, 1980.

Johnston, Dillon. *Irish Poetry after Joyce.* Notre Dame, Ind.: Notre Dame University Press, 1985.

Longley, Edna. *Louis MacNeice: A Study.* London: Faber, 1988.

Longley, Edna. *Poetry in the Wars.* Newcastle-upon-Tyne: Bloodaxe; Newark: University of Delaware Press, 1991.

McDonald, Peter. *Louis MacNeice: The Poet in His Contexts.* Oxford: Oxford University Press.

Quinn, Antoinette. *Patrick Kavanagh: Born-Again Romantic.* Dublin: Gill and Macmillan, 1991.

Robinson, Alan. *Instabilities in Contemporary British Poetry.* London: Macmillan, 1988.

Brief Biographies of the Poets

Mark Akenside (1721–1770)
Born at Newcastle, the son of a butcher, Akenside studied theology but abandoned it for medicine, practicing as a physician at Northampton and London. He contributed verses to *Gentleman's Magazine*, and wrote *Pleasures of Imagination* (1744, 1757), *Hymn to the Naiads*, and *An Epistle to Curio*.

Matthew Arnold (1822–1888)
Arnold was born in Middlesex and educated at Oxford. He served as secretary to Lord Lansdowne (1847) and inspector of schools (1851–1886). Arnold's first two volumes of poetry, *The Strayed Reveller* (1849) and *Empedocles on Etna* (1852), were followed by two volumes of *Poems* (1853, 1855) and by *Merope* (1858). Appointed Professor of Poetry at Oxford (1857–1867), he turned his attention to literary, theological, and educational criticism after 1861.

W. H. Auden (1907–1973)
Born in Yorkshire, Wystan Hugh Auden attended Oxford (1925–1928), served as schoolmaster in Scotland and England (1930–1935), and traveled to Spain to support the loyalists (1936). After marrying Erika Mann (1935) to provide her with a British passport, he emigrated to the United States (1939) and became an American citizen (1946). In England again, he was appointed Professor of Poetry at Oxford (1956–1961). Auden's lifelong companion was Chester Kallman, with whom he collaborated on opera libretti. *Poems* (1930) and three further volumes established Auden's reputation. He wrote plays with Christopher Isherwood, including *The Dog Beneath the Skin* (1935). Five volumes written in the United States reflect his growing commitment to Anglicanism.

Anna Letitia Barbauld (1743–1825)
Born in Kibworth-Harcourt, Barbauld wrote *Poems* (1773), and established a boy's school at Palgrave, Suffolk, which she closed (1785) due to her husband's mental decline; he died insane (1808). The couple adopted a nephew (1777), for whom she wrote *Hymns in Prose for Children* (1781). After traveling abroad (1785), Barbauld wrote an epistle to Wilberforce on the slave trade, and an apocalyptic poem, "Eighteen Hundred and Eleven." Her essays defending public worship (1792) and attacking war (1793) prefigure the novel of social reform. Barbauld's literary criticism appears in editions of poets (1794 and 1797), essayists (1804), Samuel Richardson's correspondence (6 vols., 1804), and a fifty-volume anthology, *The British Novelists* (1810).

John Barbour (1320?–1395
Appointed archdeacon of Aberdeen (1357), Barbour studied at Oxford (1357) and helped ransom King David II, prisoner in England after his capture in the Battle of Nevelle's Cross (1346). Barbour probably studied in Paris, was appointed Clerk of Audit and Auditor of the Exchequer to Robert II (1372), and received a life pension (1388). *The Bruce* (1376), a Scottish national epic, charts the history of the Scottish struggle for independence.

Sir John Betjeman (1906–1984)
Born in Highgate and educated at Oxford, Betjemen worked as a schoolmaster, wrote for the *Architectural Review* (1931), and served as press attaché in Dublin during World War II. *Mount Zion* (1931) and *Continual Dew* (1937) were his first publications; *Collected Poems* (1958) has sold close to a million copies. Appointed poet laureate (1972), Betjeman wrote satires of middle-class life that exhibit his religious perspective.

Laurence Binyon (1869–1943)
Born at Lancaster and educated at Oxford, Binyon worked in the printed-books department of the British Museum (1893–1933), and was Norton Professor of Poetry at Harvard (1933–1934). He wrote dramas, such as *Arthur* (1923) with music by Elgar, and several volumes of verse, including *Collected Poems* (1931) and *The Burning of the Leaves* (1944).

William Blake (1757–1827)
Born in London, Blake was apprenticed to an engraver (1772) and entered the Royal Academy (1779). Married to Catherine Boucher (1782), who assisted him in his publications, Blake became friendly with the radical bookseller, Joseph Johnson. After his brother Robert's death (1787), he began engraving texts with illustrations and published most of his work, including *Songs of Innocen*ce (1789), in this way. In 1793 he moved to Lambeth, wrote the

"Prophetic books," including *The Book of Urizen* (1794); designed engravings; and drafted an epic, *Vala*. While living with William Hayley at Sussex (1800–1803), Blake was briefly arrested on trumped-up charges of sedition, and his final epics, *Milton* (1804–1808) and *Jerusalem* (1804–1820), reflect this experience.

Edmund Blunden (1896–1974)
Born in London and educated at Oxford, Edmund Charles Blunden fought in the trenches during World War I and was the M. C. Professor of English Literature at Tokyo (1924–1927) and Hong Kong (1953). Blunden was a fellow of Merton College, Oxford (1931), joined *The Times Literary Supplement* (1943), and became Professor of Poetry at Oxford (1966). He wrote nature poetry, including *Pastorals* (1916), and a prose work, *Undertones of War* (1928). He edited John Clare, Shelley, and Collins; wrote a life of Leigh Hunt (1930) and a study of Hardy (1941).

Emily Brontë (1818–1848)
Born in Yorkshire, Emily Brontë attended Cowan Bridge with her sister, Charlotte (1824–1825), and was then largely self-educated. She attended Roe Head (1835), but suffered from homesickness. Far more than her other sisters, she was attached to the moorland scenery of Haworth, which *Wuthering Heights* (1847) evokes. Governess at Law Hill, near Halifax (1837), Emily went to Brussels with Charlotte to study languages, but returned on her aunt's death that same year. Emily's poems were "discovered" by Charlotte (1845) and their work was published together, along with Anne's, in *Poems, by Currer, Ellis and Acton Bell* (1846).

Elizabeth Barrett Browning (1806–1861)
Born in Herefordshire, Browning was largely self-educated and wrote *The Seraphim* (1838) and *Poems* (1844), which gained her critical and public attention. Forbidden to marry, she eloped secretly with Robert Browning (1846) to Florence, Italy, where she lived for the rest of her life. Her support for Italian unity found expression in such poems as *Casa Guidi Windows* (1851) and *Poems Before Congress* (1860). Her other volumes include *Sonnets from the Portuguese* (1850) and *Aurora Leigh* (1857).

Robert Browning (1812–1829)
Born in London, Browning attended London University, but was largely self-educated. After visiting Russia (1834), he wrote *Paracelsus* (1835); two further collections of poems, *Sordello* (1840) and *Bells and Pomegranates* (1841–1846), were less favorably received. After a second trip to Italy (1838, 1844), Browning married Elizabeth Barrett (1846) and settled in Florence, where they had

a son (1849). Publication of three further collections, including *The Ring and the Book* (1868–1869), revived Browning's reputation. After Elizabeth died, he lived with his sister in London.

Robert Burns (1759–1796)

Born at Alloway and self-educated, Burns worked as a farmer at Mossgiel (1784–1788) and as a government exciseman (1789–1796). He fell in love with Jean Armour (1785), but when her father prevented their marriage, he had affairs with Alison Begbie ("Mary Morison") and Mary Campbell ("To Mary in Heaven"). Beset by financial problems, he considered emigrating to Jamaica, but the success of *Poems, Chiefly in the Scottish Dialect* (1786) made this unnecessary. Lionized in Edinburgh (1787), Burns wrote many songs, including "Auld Lang Syne." He returned to farming in Dumfriesshire, where he married Armour (1788), had four children, and wrote "Tam o' Shanter" (1791).

George Gordon, Lord Byron (1788–1824)

Born in London with a club foot, Byron attended Cambridge, wrote *Hours of Idleness* (1807), and toured Europe and the Levant (1809–1811), which inspired *Childe Harold* (I, II; 1812) and a series of oriental tales. After a brief parliamentary career (1812–1813), he married Annabella Milbanke (1815), but was separated from her shortly after the birth of their first child, Ada (1816). In Geneva, he fathered Claire Clairmont's child, read Wordsworth at Shelley's prompting, and continued *Childe Harold* (III, 1816; IV, in Rome, 1817). Byron wrote *Don Juan* in Italy, where he also met Teresa Guiccioli (1820) and completed four closet dramas. He fought for Italian (1821) and Greek independence (1823), dying of fever in Missolonghi.

Thomas Carew (1594/5–1640)

Born at West Wickham and educated at Oxford, Carew studied law at the Inner Temple (1612), and served as secretary to Sir Dudley Carleton at Venice and the Hague. In London again (1616), he was employed by Sir Edward Herbert, ambassador to France; became friendly with Charles I; and received an estate. A noted Cavalier poet, Carew wrote an elegy for Donne (1633), a masque, *Coelum Britannicum* (1634), and *Poems* (1640).

Lewis Carroll (1832–1898)

Born in Cheshire, Charles Lutwidge Dodgson was educated at Christ Church, Oxford, where he lectured in mathematics (1855); he was ordained in 1861. The work that began as *Alice's Adventures Underground* (1864) originated in a boat trip with the daughters of H. G. Liddell and was followed by *Through the Looking Glass* (1871), and a long nonsense poem, *The Hunting of the Snark* (1876).

Elizabeth Carter (1717–1806)
Born in Kent and a master of nine languages, Carter refused a post as royal governess and toured the Continent with Elizabeth Montagu (1763, 1782). Her published verse includes *Poems upon Particular Occasions* (1738) and *Poems on Several Occasions* (1762); "Ode to Wisdom" appears in Richardson's *Clarissa*. Friendly with Johnson, she contributed to his *Rambler*, wrote *Remarks on the Athanasian Creed* (1752), and translated Epictetus (1752) and Algarotti's "Sir Isaac Newton's Philosophy Explain'd for the use of the Ladies."

George Chapman (1559?–1634)
Born near Hertfordshire and educated at Oxford, Chapman took no degree, worked for Sir Ralph Sadler (1585), and is believed to have traveled to the Low Countries (1585). His verse includes *The Shadow of Night* (1594) and *Ovid's Banquet of Sense* (1595). He translated the *Iliad* and *Odyssey* (1598–1614), which inspired a sonnet by Keats (1815), and many other works. Associated with the Admiral's Men (1595–1596), he wrote seven comedies, including *Eastward Hoe* with Jonson and Marston, tragedies such as *Bussy D'Ambois* (1604?), and a masque (1613) celebrating the marriage of Princess Elizabeth.

Geoffrey Chaucer (1343–1400)
Educated at St. Paul's Cathedral School and the Inner Temple, Chaucer served the Countess of Ulster (1357) and entered Edward III's army (1359). He married Philippa Pan (1366), was appointed a court official (1367), and wrote *Book of the Duchess* (1369 or 1370). In the next decade Chaucer traveled on diplomatic missions, was appointed comptroller of the customs, and completed *House of Fame* (1372–1380). *Parlement of Foules*, *Boece*, and *Troilus and Criseyde* were completed between 1380–1390. During the 1390s, Chaucer remained on close terms with the future Henry IV and wrote *The Canterbury Tales* (1387–1392).

Arthur Hugh Clough (1819–1861)
Born in Liverpool and educated at Rugby and Oxford (1837), Clough was a tutor of Oriel College (1842–1848) until he resigned to become principal of a student hostel and an examiner in the Education Office (1853). Clough's religious doubts found expression in *The Bothie of Tober-na-Vuolich* (1848), *Amours de Voyage* (1858), and *Dipsychus* (1865).

Samuel Taylor Coleridge (1772–1834)
Born in Devon, Coleridge left Cambridge (1792–1794) to enlist in the 15th Light Dragoons. He developed plans for a commune with Robert Southey (Pantisocracy), collaborated on *The Fall of Robespierre* (1794), and married

Sarah Fricker. After writing *Poems on Various Subjects* (1796) and collaborating with Wordsworth for *Lyrical Ballads* (1798), he visited Goslar, Germany (1797–1798), studied German philosophy, and served as secretary to the governor of wartime Malta (1804–1806). In 1807–1808 he returned to England, lectured on Shakespeare (1808–1810), and published *Christabel* with "Kubla Khan" (1816) and *Biographia Literaria* (1817). He lived with the surgeon James Gillman for the remainder of his life.

William Collins (1721–1759)

Born in Chichester and educated at Oxford, Collins traveled to London (1744) to begin a literary career. Penniless, he accepted an advance from a London bookseller for a translation of Aristotle's *Poetics*. When he inherited two thousand pounds (1749), he repaid the advance. Collins suffered a mental collapse after a journey in France (1750) and died insane at his sister's house in Chichester. He wrote *Persian Eclogues* (1742), *Odes on Several Descriptive and Allegoric Subjects* (1746), and is best remembered for "Ode to Evening," and "Ode on the Popular Superstitions of the Highlands."

Abraham Cowley (1618–1667)

Born in Devon and educated at Westminster, Cowley left Cambridge for Oxford, where he wrote the *Puritan and the Papist* (1643) and *The Civil War* (1679), which express his support for the royalist cause. Secretary to Queen Henrietta Maria (1644) in France, he was imprisoned as a royalist spy upon his return (1655). His other verse includes *Poetical Blossomes* (1633), *The Mistress* (1647), a biblical epic, and several imitations of Donne and Pindar.

Hannah Cowley (1743–1809)

Born in Devon, Hannah Parkhouse married Captain Cowley of the East Indian Company (1768). She wrote two tragedies, and several comedies of manners, including *The Runaway* (1776), *The Belle's Stratagem* (1780), and *A Bold Stroke for a Husband* (1783). Cowley is the author of nondramatic work, including sentimental romances. Her poetic correspondence with Robert Merry was satirized by Gifford in *The Baviad* (1794).

William Cowper (1731–1800)

Born in Hertfordshire and educated at Westminster, Cowper graduated from the Inner Temple (1754), but never practiced law. Suffering from severe depression, intensified by a thwarted love, he attempted suicide when confronted with an examination for a clerkship (1763). A patient in Dr. Cottin's Collegium Insanorum, he was then cared for by Rev. Morley Unwin and adopted Evangelical beliefs. After Unwin's death, Cowper collaborated with the curate, John Newton, on *Olney Hymns* (1779), and wrote *The Task* (1785) at Lady Austen's suggestion. His other poems include "Yardley Oak" (1791) and "Castaway" (1796).

George Crabbe (1754–1832).

Born in Suffolk, Crabbe was apprenticed to a doctor, studied botany and surgery, and married Sarah Elmy (1783). A curate at Aldeburgh (1781), he was appointed chaplain to the duke of Rutland at Belvoir (1782–1785), and vicar of Trowbridge (1814). The poems *Inebriety* (1775) and *The Village* (1783) established his reputation.

Richard Crashaw (1612/3–1649)

Born in London, Crashaw attended Cambridge (1634), where he was a fellow (1635–1643). He converted to Catholicism (1645) and fled to Paris (1642–1651). Attendant to Cardinal Palotta, he then held a minor post at the Cathedral of Loreto. Influenced by continental baroque poets, Crashaw wrote *Steps to the Temple* (1646). *Carmen Deo Nostro*, a more complete collection, was published posthumously (1652).

Samuel Daniel (1562–1619)

Born near Taunton, Daniel attended Oxford (1579), visited Italy, and worked as a tutor. Favored by Queen Anne for his masques, he licensed all entertainments played by the Children of the Queen's Revels (1604), but resigned the post when his second tragedy, *Philotas* (1605), was viewed as sympathetic to the earl of Essex's rebellion. Remembered especially for *Delia* (1592), a sequence of sonnets, Daniel also wrote *Civil Wars* (1595), *The Complaint of Rosamond* (1592), and several court masques.

Donald Davie (1922–)

Born in Yorkshire, Davie joined the navy (1941–1943), received a doctorate from Cambridge (1951), and lectured at Trinity College, Dublin (1950–1957), Cambridge (1958–1964), and Essex (1964–1968). He emigrated to the United States to teach at Stanford and Vanderbilt. *Purity of Diction in English Verse* (1952) led "the Movement"'s break with Imagism. His verse includes *Brides of Reason* (1955), *Essex Poems* (1969), and two volumes of collected poems (1972, 1983).

Sir John Davies (1569–1626)

Born in Wilshire, Davies was educated at Winchester and Oxford (1585); he pursued his legal studies at New Inn and Middle Temple (1588) and then worked as a barrister (1595). Disbarred for assaulting a friend (1598), he was reappointed (1601) and served as M.P. (1601, 1614, 1621) and attorney general for Ireland (1606–1619). Shortly before his death, he was appointed chief justice for legal services to Charles I. His works include *Orchestra* (1596), *Nosce Teipsum* (1599), and *Hymnes of Astraea* (1599).

John Donne (1572–1631)

Born in London, Donne was educated at Oxford, and possibly at Cambridge. He may have toured the Continent (1589–1591) before becoming a law student at Lincoln's Inn (1592). Donne renounced his Catholicism shortly after his brother's death (1593), sailed with Essex to sack Cadiz (1596), and with Ralegh against Spanish treasure ships (1597). Secretary to Sir Thomas Egerton and M.P. for Brackley, Northants (1601), Donne was dismissed by Egerton and briefly imprisoned after secretly marrying Lady Egerton's niece (1601). His patrons included Sir Walter Chute, with whom Donne went to the Continent (1605–1606), and Sir Robert Ker, whom Donne assisted in the Essex divorce case. At James I's urging, Donne took holy orders (1615). His poems include *Satires and Elegies* (1790s), "The Progress of the Soul" (1601), and *Holy Sonnets* (1610–1611).

Gavin Douglas (1476?–1522)

Douglas studied at St. Andrews (M.A., 1494) and perhaps at Paris; he was provost of St. Giles, Edinburgh (1501), abbot of Aberbrothock, and archbishop of St. Andrews. Nominated by Queen Margaret (1515), Douglas became bishop of Dunkeld (1516–1520); in the interim, he was imprisoned by the duke of Albany for receiving bulls from the pope. Douglas accompanied Albany to France (1517), but was deprived of his bishopric and accused of high treason by the Scottish Lords of Council (1522) for seeking Henry VIII's support. Douglas wrote allegorical poems, including *The Palice of Honour* (1501) and possibly *King Hart*, as well as a translation of the *Aeneid* (1513).

Ernest Dowson (1867–1900)

Born in Kent and educated at Oxford, Ernest Christopher Dowson left without taking his degree, and worked in his father's docking business. In 1891 he met the twelve-year-old Adelaide Foltinowicz, who became a symbol of innocence in his poetry. After his parents committed suicide (1895), he traveled between France, Ireland, and London, writing *Poems* (1896), *Decorations* (1899), and a one-act verse play, *The Pierrot of the Minute* (1897).

Michael Drayton (1563–1631)

Born in Warwickshire, Drayton served Sir Henry Goodere, whose daughter Anne inspired *Idea: The Shepherds' Garland* (1593) and *Idea's Mirror* (1594). He wrote poems on legendary and historical figures, as well as *Poems Lyric and Pastoral* (1606), *Poly-Olbion* (1612–1622), and wrote plays for the public theater.

John Dryden (1631–1700)
Born in Northamptonshire and educated at Cambridge (1650–1654), Dryden wrote verse that reflects his shifts in politics and religion. He praised the Puritan Cromwell (*Heroic Stanzas*, 1658), but also celebrated the Stuart King Charles II (*Astraea Redux*, 1660). He defended Anglicanism (*Religio Laici*, 1683), and then Catholicism when he became Catholic (*The Hind and the Panther*, 1687). He wrote comedies (*Marriage à la Mode*, 1672), satires (*Absalom and Achitophel*, 1681), tragedies (*All for Love*, 1677), and Pindaric odes such as *A Song for St. Cecilia's Day* (1687). In 1688 he lost both of his court offices and wrote for the theater. *Fables Ancient and Modern* (1700) includes his work as a critic and translator.

William Dunbar (1460?–1513?)
A Franciscan novice and Scottish Chaucerian, Dunbar graduated from St. Andrews (M.A., 1479) before traveling abroad (1479–1500) and receiving a pension from James IV (1500). He assisted in negotiating James I's marriage to Queen Margaret Tudor (1503), and commemorated that event in "The Thrissill and the Rois." This was followed by "The Flyting of Dunbar and Kennedie," a work of poetic abuse, as well as satires such as "The Dance of the Sevin Deidly Synnes" (1509). He is believed to have died in the Battle of Flodden (1513).

T. S. Eliot (1888–1965)
Born in St. Louis, Missouri, Thomas Stearns Eliot was educated at Harvard, the Sorbonne, and Oxford. He emigrated to England in 1914 and taught at the Highgate School (1916); served as a bank clerk in Lloyd's Bank, London (1917); and as director of Faber & Faber (1925–1965). In 1927 Eliot became a British subject and a member of the Anglican Church. *Prufrock and Other Observations* (1917) was followed by *Poems* (1919), *The Waste Land* (1922), and *Four Quartets* (1943), for which he was awarded the Nobel prize (1948). Eliot wrote several plays, of which *The Cocktail Party* (1950) was perhaps the most successful. His numerous critical volumes include *The Sacred Wood* (1920); he founded and edited *The Criterion* (1922–1939).

James Fenton (1949–)
Born in Lincoln, Fenton won the Newdigate prize at Oxford for *Our Western Furniture* (1968). After graduating from Oxford (1970), he worked as a journalist and wrote several collections of poems, including *A German Requiem* (1981). His experiences as a correspondent in Vietnam and Cambodia inspired *The Memory of War* (1982), which was followed by *Children in Exile: Poems 1968–1984.*

Robert Fergusson (1750–1774)
Born in Edinburgh, Fergusson attended St. Andrews University and worked as a copier in the Commissary Clerk's office. He contributed poems to Ruddiman's *Weekly Magazine* (1771) but manic-depression, religious guilt, and a head injury incurred by a fall led to forced confinement (1773) and premature death. A leading reviver of Scottish vernacular writing, Fergusson wrote "Leith Races" and "The Farmer's Ingle," which influenced Burns, as well as "The Daft Days" and "Auld Reikie."

Roy Fisher (1930–)
Born in Birmingham, Fisher graduated from Birmingham University (M.A., 1970), and taught at Bordesley College of Education (1963–1971) and the University of Keele (1971–1982). He has worked as a free-lance writer and jazz musician since 1982. Fisher's first book, *City* (1961), was followed by *Collected Poems, 1968* (1969), and *Poems, 1955–1980.*

George Gascoigne (1534?–1577)
Born at Cardington, Gascoigne attended Cambridge, studied law at Gray's Inn (1555–1565), and was an M.P. for Bedford (1557–1559). His marriage to Elizabeth Boyes led to legal disputes, which ended in his imprisonment for debt (1570). Gascoigne served with English troops in the Netherlands (1572–1574), and spent four months as a prisoner of the Spanish. His poetry includes *A Hundreth Sundrie Flowres* (1573) and an augmented edition entitled *The Posies of Georgie Gascoigne* (1575); *The Steel Glas: A Satyre* (1576), and *The Grief of Joy*. He wrote two plays: *Supposes* (1566), based on Ariosto, and *Jocasta* (1566), a Greek tragedy.

Oliver Goldsmith (1730?–1774)
Born in Ireland and educated at Trinity College, Dublin (1749), Goldsmith was rejected for ordination and studied medicine in Edinburgh and Leyden. His first important poem was *The Traveller* (1764), followed by *The Deserted Village* (1770), *Retaliation* (1774), and *The Haunch of Venison* (1776), published posthumously. Author of *The Vicar of Wakefield* (1766), Goldsmith is also known for his collection of essays, *The Citizen of the World* (1762), and plays such as *She Stoops to Conquer* (1773).

John Gower (1330?–1408)
A court official who was friendly with Richard II and Henry IV, Gower married Agnes Groundoff (1398), and went blind around 1400. He wrote poetry in French (*Mirour de l'omme*, 1376–1379), Latin (*Vox Clamantis*, 1379–1382), and English (*In Praise of Peace*); his best-known work is the *Confessio Amantis* (1386–1390), a collection of exemplary tales of love.

Robert Graves (1895–1985)
Born in Wimbledon and educated at Charterhouse, Graves joined the army (1914) and was severely wounded (1916). His first poems reflect his wartime experiences and include *Fairies and Fusiliers* (1917). After a brief marriage to Nancy Nicholson, he read English at Oxford and met Laura Riding, an American poet who accompanied him to Egypt, Britanny, Majorca, and the United States (1929–1939). Graves spent World War II in England, returned to Majorca (1946), and married Beryl Hodge. He wrote verse influenced by nursery rhymes (*Poems, 1914–26*), love poetry (*Poems, 1938–45*), and theories of poetic inspiration (*Collected Poems*, 1975). His popular autobiography, *Goodbye to All That* (1929), was followed by several works of literary criticism, historical novels (*I, Claudius*, 1934), and numerous translations. Graves was elected Professor of Poetry at Oxford (1961–1966).

John Gray (1866–1934)
Born in Woolwich as a Nonconformist, Gray became a Roman Catholic (1901) and rector of St. Peter's Church in Edinburgh. Encouraged by Wilde, Gray published *Silverpoints* (1893), which included translations from Verlaine and Mallarmé. His best long poem, "The Flying Fish," appeared in *The Dial* (1896).

Thomas Gray (1716–1771)
Gray was born in London and educated at Cambridge. He toured the Continent with Horace Walpole (1739–1741), and wrote "Ode on a Distant Prospect of Eton College" (1742) and "Elegy wrote in a Country Church Yard" (1751) after returning to England. He became a resident at Peterhouse (1742–1756), and then at Pembroke, Cambridge. After composing his Pindaric odes (1754, 1757), Gray studied Old Norse and Welsh poetry; his imitations were included in *Poems* (1768). Later that year, he became Regius Professor of Modern History at Cambridge.

Thom Gunn (1929–)
Thomson Gunn was born in Gravesend, attended Cambridge, and then Stanford University on a creative writing fellowship. He has published several volumes of poetry, including *Fighting Terms* (1954), *Moly* (1971), and *The Passage of Joy* (1982). Gunn has written studies of Fulke Greville (1968) and Ben Jonson (1974).

Thomas Hardy (1840–1928)
Born at Upper Bockhampton, Hardy was an apprentice to the architects John Hicks (1856–1861) and Sir Arthur Blomfield (1862–1867). In 1871 he published *Desperate Remedies*, the first of ten novels. The success of *Far from the Madding Crowd* (1874) enabled him to abandon architecture and marry Emma

Gifford (1874). When *Tess of the D'Urbervilles* (1891) and *Jude the Obscure* (1895) were negatively reviewed, Hardy turned to poetry and published eight volumes, including *Wessex Poems* (1898) and *Poems of the Past and Present* (1902). Many of his most moving poems in *Satires of Circumstance* (1914) were inspired by the death of his wife (1912); in 1914 he married Florence Dugdale. He assembled the *Life* published posthumously as her work.

Seamus Heaney (1939–)
Born in Northern Ireland, Heaney attended Queen's University, Belfast, worked as an English teacher in Belfast, a lecturer at Queen's University (1966–1972), a guest lecturer at the University of California, Berkeley (1970–1971), and later as a professor at Harvard. *Death of a Naturalist* (1966) was followed by *Field Work* (1979), *Selected Poems, 1965–75* (1980), and *Station Island* (1984).

Felicia Hemans (1793–1835)
Born in Liverpool and educated by her mother, Felicia Browne was the most popular woman poet of the nineteenth century. Her early verse includes *Poems* (1807) and *The Domestic Affections* (1812). An acknowledged beauty, she married Capt. Alfred Hemans (1812), who left for Rome (1818) and never returned. She then wrote two plays and twenty-four volumes of poetry to support her five sons, including *The Forest Sanctuary* (1825), *Records of Women* (1828), and *Songs of the Affections* (1830). She lived briefly in Liverpool (1828) and Dublin (1831), where she wrote *National Lyrics and Songs for Music* (1834) and *Scenes and Hymns of Life* (1834).

Robert Henryson (1430?–1504?)
An original member of Glasgow University (1462), Henryson was probably a clerical schoolmaster at Dunfermline Abbey. Henryson wrote *The Testament of Cresseid*, which provides a tragic ending to Chaucer's *Troilus and Criseyde*; *The Morall Fabillis of Esope*, a version of thirteen fables based on John Lydgate and William Caxton; *Orpheus and Eurydice*, based on Boethius; and *Robene and Makyne*.

George Herbert (1593–1633)
Born in Montgomery to a prominent family, Herbert was educated at Cambridge, where he was a fellow and Public Orator (1619–1627). He served as M.P. for Montgomery (1624–1625), became a deacon (1626), and married Jane Danvers (1629). In 1630 Herbert worked as a rector of Bemerton and was subsequently ordained. *The Temple* (1634), a collection of his verse, appeared in thirteen editions; *A Priest to the Temple* (1652) offers advice to members of the clergy.

Robert Herrick (1591–1674)
Apprenticed to his uncle, a goldsmith (1607), Herrick graduated from Cambridge (M.A., 1620) before being ordained (1623). He was friendly with Ben Jonson and court society and served as chaplain to the duke of Buckingham on a disastrous military expedition (1627). Presented (1629) and then deprived (1647) of the living of Dean Prior because of his royalist connections, he published *Hesperides* (1648), which includes a body of devotional verse entitled *Noble Numbers*.

Geoffrey Hill (1932–)
Hill was born in Bromsgrove, attended Oxford, and has lectured at the University of Leeds and at Cambridge. His published verse includes *For the Unfallen* (1959), *Tenebrae* (1978), and *The Mystery of the Charity of Charles Peguy* (1983).

Thomas Hoccleve (1368?–1437?)
Born in London, Hoccleve trained at the Inns of Court and became a clerk in the Office of the Privy Seal (1387–1388; 1399–1422). Hoccleve opposed the Lollards, a religious group that demanded a reduction in the power of the Church. After failing to become a priest, he married (1410–1411), suffered from mental illness (1416–1421), and was granted a minor benefice at Southwick priory (1424), where he remained until his death. *La Male Règle* (1406) describes a bachelor's evening, and *L'Epistre au Dieu D'amours* (1402) is an alternative ending to Chaucer's *Troilus and Criseyde*.

Gerard Manley Hopkins (1844–1889)
Born in Essex, Hopkins attended Oxford (1863), where he published "Winter with the Gulf Stream" and converted to Catholicism (1866). In 1868 he joined the Jesuits and burned his youthful verses; his subsequent poetry was not published until 1918. Hopkins studied theology at St. Bueno's College in North Wales (1874), learned Welsh, and composed "The Wreck of the *Deutschland*" (1875). At this time, Hopkins articulated his theories of instress, inscape, and sprung rhythm. Ordained to the priesthood (1877), Hopkins was appointed professor of Greek and Latin at University College, Dublin (1884), where he composed a series of sonnets, beginning with "Carrion Comfort."

A. E. Housman (1859–1936)
Born near Bromsgrove, Alfred Edward Housman was educated at Oxford, worked as a clerk in the Patent Office in London, and became a Professor of Latin at London University (1892). A disappointed attachment to Moses Jackson inspired verse published in *Last Poems* (1922) and *Collected Poems* (1939). At London University he wrote *A Shropshire Lad* (1896), balladlike

poems published at his own expense. Appointed Professor of Latin at Cambridge (1911), Housman is also known for *The Name and Nature of Poetry* (1933) and *Praefanda* (1931).

Ted Hughes (1930–)

Born in Yorkshire and educated at Cambridge, Edward James Hughes married Sylvia Plath (1956) and published *Hawk in the Rain* the same year he visited America (1957). His early works such as *Lupercal* (1960) and *Crow* (1970) emphasize the cunning and savagery of animal life and make use of the dialect of Hughes's native West Riding. Appointed poet laureate (1984), Hughes completed *Remains of Elmet* (1979), *River* (1983), and several plays for children.

Lionel Johnson (1867–1902)

Born in Kent, Johnson attended Oxford (1886) and joined the Roman Catholic Church (1891). A close friend of Yeats, whose early work he influenced, Johnson edited *The Irish Home Reading Magazine* (1894) and was a member of the Irish Literary Society in London. He wrote *Poems* (1895), *Ireland with Other Poems* (1897), and *Complete Poems* (1953), as well as a study of Thomas Hardy (1894). His alcoholism, confessed in "Mystic and Cavalier," is depicted along with his vivid personality in Yeats's *Autobiographies* (1955).

Samuel Johnson (1709–1784)

Born in London, Johnson was afflicted with scrofula, which affected his sight. He attended Oxford (1728–1729) and suffered as under-master at Market Bosworth, before moving to Birmingham, marrying a widow (1735), and starting a school. He wrote for *The Gentleman's Magazine*, began *The Rambler* (1750–1752), and received the honorary doctorate the same year he published his *Dictionary* (1755). His poetry includes *London* (1738) and *The Vanity of Human Wishes* (1749). *Rasselas* (1759) and *The Lives of the English Poets* (1779–1781) are among his more popular prose works.

David Jones (1895–1974)

Born in Brockley, Kent, David Michael Jones attended Westminster Art School (1919–1921). His engravings for the Chester Cycle play, "The Deluge," and for Coleridge's "The Ancient Mariner" (1924–1929), were followed by water color paintings displayed in Venice (1934) and the National Gallery (1940–1942). His writings include *In Parenthesis* (1937), which reflects his experiences as a soldier in World War II; *The Anathemata* (1952), which draws upon his conversion to Catholicism (1921), and *The Tribune's Visitation* (1969).

Ben Jonson (1572/3–1637)

Born in Westminster and educated at Westminster School, Jonson worked as a bricklayer and served in the military in Flanders. Imprisoned for contributing to *The Isle of Dogs* (1597), Jonson converted to Roman Catholicism temporarily and killed an actor in a duel upon his release (1598). Jonson tutored Ralegh's son (1612–1613) and received a pension from James I (1616). A playwright and regarded as the first poet laureate, Jonson wrote nondramatic verse including *Epigrams* (1616), *The Forest* (1616), and *Underwoods* (1640). Jonson suffered a stroke (1628) and was probably bedridden until his death.

John Keats (1795–1821)

Born in London, Keats entered Guy's Hospital (1815), received his license as an apothecary (1816), and published *Poems* (1817) to harsh reviews. In 1817–1818 he finished a draft of *Endymion* and met Wordsworth and Hazlitt. Touring the Lake District with Charles Brown, Keats visited Scotland and Northern Ireland; nursed his brother Tom until his death (1818); and moved into Brown's house in Hampstead. There he met Fanny Brawne, whom he loved in illness and despair. During this time he began *Hyperion*, completed "Lamia," and wrote his famous odes (1819). Too ill to continue writing, he traveled to Rome where he died of tuberculosis, nursed by his friend Joseph Severn.

Rudyard Kipling (1865–1936)

Born in Bombay, Kipling was separated from his parents and sent to Southsea, England (1871), which inspired a short story (1888) and a novel, *The Light That Failed* (1890). Kipling joined the United Services College, Westward Ho! (1878), an experience recorded in *Stalkey and Co.* (1899). In 1882 he returned to India, worked as a journalist, and published stories and poems gathered in such volumes as *Departmental Ditties* (1886). In 1889 he moved to London, married Caroline Balestier, and published *Barrack Room Ballads* (1892). The Kiplings lived in Vermont (1892–1896) and various parts of England before settling in Sussex (1902). In 1909 he became the first English author to receive the Nobel prize.

Letitia Elizabeth Landon (1802–1838)

Landon published her first poem, "Rome," in William Jerdan's *Literary Gazette*. Her published verse includes *The Fate of Adelaide* (1821), *The Improvisatrice* (1824), *The Troubadour* (1825), *The Golden Violet* (1826–1829), and *The Venetian Bracelet* (1828). Motivated by the financial need of her family, she wrote for, and edited, periodicals. Landon's engagement to biographer John Forster was broken off. She secretly married George MacLean, governor of Cape Coast Castle, and sailed with him for Africa. She was found dead in her room, probably from an overdose of prussic acid.

William Langland (1330?–1386?)
Author of *Piers Plowman*, a religious allegory in alliterative verse, Langland has been the subject of much speculative biography. He may have lived in Malvern Hills and attended Trinity College, Dublin. Scholars assume he was a cleric in minor orders who was influenced by the asceticism of St. Bernard of Clairvaux.

Philip Larkin (1922–1985)
Born in Coventry and educated at Oxford (1943), Larkin worked as a librarian at Wellington in Shropshire, as well as at universities in Leicester, Belfast, and Hull (1955). He wrote a column on jazz records for *The Daily Telegraph* (1961–1971), and two novels, *Jill* (1946), and *A Girl in Winter* (1947). *The Less Deceived* (1955) established his reputation as a poet and was followed by *Whitsun Weddings* (1964) and *High Windows* (1974). His prose is collected in *Required Writing* (1983).

D. H. Lawrence (1885–1930)
David Herbert Lawrence was born in Nottinghamshire and attended University College, Nottingham, before working as a junior clerk in a surgical appliance factory (1904), and as a pupil-teacher (1907). He married Frieda Weekley, a German aristocrat (1914), and traveled with her to Ceylon, Australia, New Mexico, and Mexico (1922), before dying of tuberculosis in France. He published numerous short stories, novels, travel books, and collections of verse, including *Love Poems* (1913), *Look! We have Come Through!* (1917) and *Pansies* (1929).

Mary Leapor (1722–1746)
Born in Northamptonshire, Leapor worked as a kitchen maid in a gentleman's family. As a child, she read Dryden and Pope, whose verse she imitated in an "Essay on Friendship" and "An Essay on Hope." Her "Poems On Several Occasions," edited by Isaac Hawkins Browne, appeared in two separately published volumes (1748, 1751). Admired by Cowper, she wrote an "Essay on Women" and a blank verse tragedy, "The Unhappy Father." She satirized the patronage system and upper-class marriage, and commented upon the moral dangers of enforced obedience for young girls.

Matthew Gregory Lewis (1775–1818)
Born in London and educated at Oxford and Weimar, Lewis entered the diplomatic service and held a seat in the House of Commons (1796–1802). After his father's death (1812), he twice visited the sugar plantations in Jamaica that were the source of his wealth. His best-known work, *The Monk* (1796), includes poems that captivated Walter Scott, among others. Coleridge

accurately described "The Isle of Devils: A Metrical Tale," published with Lewis's *Journal of a West Indian Proprietor* (1834), as "a fever dream, horrible."

Sir David Lindsay (1486?–1555)
Lindsay was Lyon King of Arms, equerry in the royal service, and attendant to the future James V (1512–1522). Dismissed from court when James V was influenced by the Douglas faction, he returned (1528) to represent the king on diplomatic missions to Charles V (1531), Henry VIII (1544), and other European monarchs. His works include a morality play (*Ane Satyre of the Thrie Estaitis*, 1540), a verse allegory (*The Dreme*, 1528), and a celebration of the king's escape from the Douglas faction (*The Testament and Complaynt of Our Soverane Lordis Papyngo*, 1530). He also wrote a work of poetic abuse ("flyting") (1536) and a satire of court life from the perspective of a dog (1536?).

Michael Longley (1939–)
Born in Belfast and educated at Trinity College, Dublin, Longley was a schoolteacher and then Combined Arts Director of the Northern Ireland Arts Council. Praised for his lyric poetry, Longley wrote *No Continuing City* (1969), *Selected Poems* (1981), and *Poems, 1963–1983* (1985).

Richard Lovelace (1618–1657/8)
Heir to estates in Kent, Lovelace received his M.A. from Oxford (1636), and fought for Charles I during the Bishops' Wars (1639–1640). Imprisoned for presenting a royalist petition to a hostile House of Commons (1642), Lovelace wrote "To Althea, from Prison" and passed much of the next four years abroad. He was wounded fighting for the French against the Spaniards at Dunkerque (1646). Imprisoned again (1648) for ten months upon his return to England, he prepared *Lucasta* (1649) for publication.

John Lydgate (1370?–1449)
Born in Suffolk, Lydgate was ordained a priest (1377), joined the monastery of Bury, St. Edmunds (1385), and visited Paris (1426). He served as abbot of Hatfield Broadoak in Essex (1421–1432). In the century following his death he was considered the equal of Chaucer and Gower. His early verse includes *The Complaint of the Black Knight*, *The Temple of Glas*, *The Floure of Curtesy*, and the allegorical *Reason and Sensuality* (1408). He translated works such as *The Troy Book* (1412–1421) from French and Latin, as well as Boccaccio's *The Fall of Princes* (1431–1438).

Louis MacNeice (1907–1963)
Born in Carrickfergus and educated at Oxford (1930), MacNeice lectured at the University of Birmingham (1930–1936) and the Bedford College for

Women, London (1936–1940). From 1941 he wrote and produced radio plays for the BBC, including *The Dark Tower* (1947), and translated Goethe's *Faust*. His first book of poetry, *Blind Fireworks* (1929), was followed by several volumes, including *Letters from Iceland* with Auden (1937), and *Collected Poems, 1925–48* (1949).

Christopher Marlowe (1564–1593)

Born in Kent, Marlowe received his M.A. from Cambridge (1587) and may have served in Elizabeth I's secret service. Marlowe was killed in a tavern brawl in 1593. Known for his atheism, Marlowe translated Ovid and Lucan and wrote several plays, including *Tamburlaine*, *Dr. Faustus*, and *The Jew of Malta*. Marlowe's narrative poem, *Hero and Leander*, was "completed" by George Chapman.

Andrew Marvell (1621–1678)

Born in Yorkshire and educated at Cambridge (1639), Marvell visited the Continent (1643–1647), possibly to avoid the civil war. He wrote verses for Lovelace's *Lucasta* (1649), an elegy on Lord Hastings (1649), and "An Horatian Ode upon Cromwell's Return from Ireland" (1650). Marvell composed "Upon Appleton House" while serving as tutor to Lord Fairfax's daughter (1650); he was also tutor to William Dutton, a ward of Cromwell's (1653–1656), and a Latin Secretary to the Council of State (1657–1661). Elected M.P. for Hull (1659–1661), Marvell traveled to Holland (1662–1663) and, as secretary to the earl of Carlisle, visited Russia, Sweden, and Denmark (1663–1665). His satires include "The Last Instructions to a Painter" (1667) and *The Rehearsal Transpros'd* (1672–1673).

John Masefield (1878–1967)

John Edward Masefield was born at Ledbury and educated at King's School, Warwick; he trained for the merchant navy. After voyages to Chile, and across the Atlantic (1895), he deserted ship and lived in New York (1895–1897). In England again, he joined *The Manchester Guardian* (1907). Appointed poet laureate (1930), Masefield wrote *Salt-Water Ballads* (1902), long narrative poems such as *The Everlasting Mercy* (1911), as well as novels, plays, and numerous volumes of verse.

George Meredith (1828–1909)

Born in Portsmouth, Meredith worked for a London solicitor (1845). At Chapman and Hall publishers, he encouraged Thomas Hardy and George Gissing. Meredith's poetic works include *Poems* (1851), *Modern Love* (1862), and *Poems and Lyrics of the Joy of Earth* (1883). Described by Wilde as "a prose Browning," Meredith wrote over ten novels including *The Egoist* (1879).

John Milton (1608–1674)
Born in London, Milton graduated from Cambridge (M.A., 1632), and studied privately at his father's house. He moved to Buckinghamshire (1635), composed *Lycidas* (1638), and met Grotius in Paris and Galileo in Italy (1638). Returning to London (1639), he became tutor to his nephews. During the second Bishops' War (1641) he wrote five pamphlets against episcopacy. He married Mary Powell (1642), whose desertion inspired Milton's four pamphlets arguing for the legitimacy of divorce (1643–1645). *Areopagitica* (1644) and "L'Allegro" and "Il Pensoroso" (1645) were also composed during this period. Reconciled with his wife (1645), who was to die after the birth of their third daughter (1652), Milton became totally blind (1652), later marrying Katherine Woodcock (1656) and then Elizabeth Minshull (1663). He completed *Paradise Lost* (1663), *Paradise Regained* (1671), and *Samson Agonistes* (1671).

Alexander Montgomerie (1550?–1598)
Born near Beith, Montgomerie held office under the Scottish regent Morton and then under James VI, and was awarded a pension (1583). He traveled on the Continent (1586) and was implicated in a pro-Catholic plot (1597). His principal work is *The Cherrie and the Slae* (1597), an allegorical poem; he also wrote *Flyting betwixt Montgomery and Polwart*, sonnets, psalms, and songs and is considered one of the last of the makars.

Thomas Sturge Moore (1870–1944)
Born in Sussex and brother of G. E. Moore, Thomas produced four studies of artists, including *Correggio* (1906), and designed the covers for several volumes by Yeats. His published poetry includes, besides several verse dramas, *The Vinedresser* (1899) and *Judas* (1923).

William Morris (1834–1896)
Born in Essex, Morris attended Oxford and worked for the architect G. E. Street. He translated Greek and Icelandic sagas (1868–1875), moved to Oxfordshire, and wrote several tales in prose. Morris conducted a manufacturing and decorating firm (Morris & Co.) and founded the Socialist League (1884). He wrote collections of verse, *The Defense of Guenevere* (1858) and *Poems by the Way* (1891), and longer poems such as *The Earthly Paradise* (1868–1870). Morris founded the Kelmscott Press (1890), which published much of his later work.

Edwin Muir (1887–1959)
Born in Orkney, Scotland, Muir moved to Glasgow, married Willa Anderson (1919), and contributed to Orage's *New Age*. In 1921 the Muirs went to Prague, where they collaborated on the translations of Kafka (1930–1949) that

established Kafka's reputation in England and inspired Muir's poetry, including *Chorus of the Newly Dead* (1926). His other verse includes *The Labyrinth* (1949), and *Collected Poems* (1952, 1960).

Wilfred Owen (1893–1918)
Born in Oswestry and educated at Shrewsbury Technical College, Owen taught English in Bordeaux (1913), and joined the army (1915). After trench fever on the Somme (1917), Owen entered Craiglockhurt Hospital, Edinburgh, where he edited *Hydra* (May 1917), met Siegfried Sassoon (August 1917), and was discharged (October 1917). He won the Military Cross (October 1918), and was killed near the Sambre Canal in France. "Dulce et Decorum Est" is his best-known poem.

Katherine Philips (1631–1664)
Known as the "Matchless Orinda," Katherine Fowler was born in London. She organized a circle which included Vaughan, Cowley, and Jeremy Taylor. In 1648 she married James Philips and published her first poetry in a prefix to Henry Vaughan's *Poems* (1651). She translated Corneille's *Pompée* (1663), Horace (1668), and wrote *Collected Poems* (1667).

Alexander Pope (1688–1744)
Born in London, Pope was largely self-educated and could not attend university because he was Catholic; his posture and health were adversely affected by tuberculosis (1700). By 1713 he abandoned Addison's anti-Catholic Whigs for the Tories headed by Swift, and joined the Scriblerus Club. His attachment to Lady Mary Wortley Montagu ended in frustration (1717), but he developed a lifelong friendship with Martha Blount. In 1719 he moved to Twickenham and became fascinated by landscape gardening. His verse includes his *Essay on Criticism* (1711), *The Rape of the Lock* (1712, revised 1714), *Windsor Forest* (1713), *An Epistle to Dr. Arbuthnot* (1727, revised 1735), *The Dunciad* (1728–1743), and *An Essay on Man* (1733–1734). Pope's translations of Homer's *Iliad* (1715–1720) and *Odyssey* (1725–1726) rendered him financially independent. His later years were spent editing and amending his "Literary Correspondence" (1735).

Sir Walter Ralegh (1554?–1618)
Born in South Devon, Ralegh attended Oxford (1566–1569), joined the Huguenot forces in France, and participated in battles at Montcontour (1569), Smerwick, and Cadiz Harbor (1596). Imprisoned for marrying Elizabeth Throckmorton (1592), he then journeyed to Guiana (1595) and the Orinoco (1617) in search of gold. Tried for treason upon his return, he was imprisoned in the Tower (1603–1616) and, eventually, executed. Ralegh's poetry includes his "Epitaph of Sir Philip Sidney," and a prefatory sonnet to *The Faerie Queene*. The authorship of other poems often attributed to him is

in dispute. He wrote numerous prose works, including *The History of the World* (1614).

Allan Ramsay (1686–1758)
Born in Lanarkshire, Ramsay was an apprentice wigmaker (1701) who helped found a Jacobite literary society (The Easy Club), a circulating library (1728), and a playhouse (1736). He became a bookseller (1718), editing and often altering works in *Christis Kirk on the Green* (1718), *The Tea Table Miscellany* (1724–1737), *The Ever Green* (1724), and *A Collection of Scots Proverbs* (1736). His pastoral comedy, *The Gentle Shepherd* (1725), includes Scots songs. He introduced Henryson and Dunbar to the public and helped revive Scottish verse.

Peter Reading (1946–)
Born in Liverpool, Reading attended Liverpool College of Art (1967), where he lectured in art history (1968–1970). He worked at an animal feed compounding mill in Shropshire, England (1970–1981), and taught writing at Sunderland Polytechnic (1981–1982). His verse includes *Water and Waste* (1970), *Diplopic* (1983), and *C* (1984).

Christina Rossetti (1830–1894)
Born in London and self-educated, Christina Rossetti was a devout High Anglican, who ended her engagement with the Pre-Raphaelite painter, James Collinson, when he rejoined the Roman Catholic Church (1850). Rossetti contributed poems to *The Germ* (1850) and to *Macmillan's Magazine* (1861); her published collections include *Goblin Market* (1862), *A Pageant* (1881), and *Time Flies, A Reading Diary* (1885). Marked by technical virtuosity, her poems include lyrics, sonnets, and ballads and treat the themes of frustrated love and premature resignation.

Dante Gabriel Rossetti (1828–1882)
Born in London, Rossetti was educated at King's College School, London and helped found the Pre-Raphaelite Brotherhood (1848). The suicide of Rossetti's wife two years after their marriage led him to enclose the manuscripts of his poems in her coffin; they were later retrieved and published as *Poems* (1870). Criticized as a member of "the fleshly school of poetry" (1871), Rossetti is perhaps best known for "The Blessed Damozel," the ballad "Sister Helen," and "The House of Life," although his translations from Villon and from early Italian poets (1861) were also influential.

Alexander Scott (1525?–1585?)
Scott is believed to have lived near Edinburgh and Dalkeith, Midlothian. His love lyrics, burlesques ("The Justing and Debait up at the Drum"), and a cere-

monial poem ("Ane New Year Gift to Quene Mary, quhen scho come first Hume, 1562") reflect the culture of early Reformation Scotland.

Sir Walter Scott (1771–1832)

Born in Edinburgh and educated at Edinburgh University, Scott became a lawyer (1792), married (1797), and was deputy sheriff of Selkirk (1799). He edited *Minstrelsy of the Scottish Border* (1802–1803), and wrote *The Lay of the Last Minstrel* (1805). A partner in J. Ballantyne's printing firm, he was twice rescued from bankruptcy (1811, 1826) by his prolific pen. His long poems include *Marmion* (1808), *The Lady of the Lake* (1810), and *Rokeby* (1813), while *Waverley* (1814), *Rob Roy* (1817), and *The Heart of Midlothian* (1818) are among his numerous novels. Scott was an especially popular narrative poet until Byron's *Childe Harold* captured his readers.

William Shakespeare (1564–1616)

Born in Stratford-on-Avon, Shakespeare married Anne Hathaway (1582), by whom he had three children. His narrative poems, *Venus and Adonis* (1593) and *The Rape of Lucrece* (1594), were followed by his sonnets (1593–1598), published in 1609. Actor, shareholder, and playwright in the Lord Chamberlain's Men (1594), which grew prosperous, occupying the Globe Theatre (1599), becoming the King's Men on James I's accession (1603), and taking over Blackfriars (1608). The First Folio of his *Works* was published in 1623.

Percy Bysshe Shelley (1792–1822)

Born in Sussex and expelled from Oxford (March 1811), Shelley married Harriet Westbrook (1811), before eloping with (1814), and then marrying, Mary Godwin (December 1816). In early 1816 he and Mary Godwin joined Byron on Lake Geneva. Denied custody of his first two children, Shelley emigrated to Italy (1818), where his other children, Clara and William, died (1819); he registered an adopted or illegitimate child in Naples, and in 1820 his youngest son was born. Shelley had a platonic love affair with Emilia Viviani (1821); he drowned during a storm in the Bay of Spezia. His verse includes *Queen Mab* (1813), *Alastor* (1816), *Prometheus Unbound* (1820), *Adonais* (1821), *Epipsychidion* (1821), and *Hellas* (1822). He wrote many prose works (*Defence of Poetry*, 1821), a verse drama (*The Cenci*, 1819), and numerous translations.

Sir Philip Sidney (1554–1586)

Born in Kent and educated at Oxford, Sidney traveled on the Continent (1572–1575) and witnessed the St. Bartholomew's Day Massacre. Knighted (1582) and appointed governor of Flushing (1585), he married Frances Walsingham (1583). The "Stella" named in his sonnet sequence is Penelope Devereux, whose father had wished her to marry Sidney. Sidney's greatest military success was a surprise attack on the town of Axel (1586). That same year, he attacked a Spanish convoy, was wounded in the thigh, and died of an infection. Remembered as the perfect Renaissance courtier, he wrote *Arcadia* (1590), and *Defence of Poesie*.

Edith Sitwell (1887–1964)
Born in Scarborough, Sitwell was largely self-educated and published poems in *The Mother* (1915) and later volumes. She is best known for editing *Wheels* (1916–1921), which repudiated Georgian verse, and *Façade* (1922), which was accompanied by William Walton's music. The first poet to be made Dame of the British Empire (1954), Sitwell wrote *The Sleeping Beauty* (1924), *Gold Coast Customs* (1929), and verse inspired by World War II; she converted to Roman Catholicism in 1955.

John Skelton (1460?–1529)
Educated at Cambridge, Skelton was court poet to Henry VII (1489) and tutor (1496–1501) to Prince Henry (Henry VIII). Ordained (1498), he became rector of Diss in Norfolk (1503) and Orator Regius (1512). Skelton satirized Henry VII's court in *The Bowge of Courte*, and wrote *The Garland of Laurel* and *Philip Sparrow* (1505). *Magnificence* (1516), the first secular morality play in English, was followed by three satirical attacks on Cardinal Wolsey (1521–1522), including *Speak Parrot* and *Colin Clout*.

Charlotte Smith (1749–1806)
Born in Sussex, Charlotte Turner attended boarding schools, married Benjamin Smith, a young merchant (1765), and lived on the Hunts-Sussex border (1774–1783). After the collapse of her husband's business (1782), she went to debtor's prison with her husband (1784) and published *Elegiac Sonnets and Other Essays* (1784, 1797). Smith's novels include *Emmeline* (1788) and *The Old Manor House* (1793).

Robert Southey (1774–1843)
Southey was born at Bristol and educated at Oxford. He collaborated with Coleridge, and they married sisters. Byron made notorious Southey's shift from radical to Tory. Southey's verse includes *The Curse of Kehama* (1810), *Roderick: The Last of the Goths* (1814), and *A Vision of Judgment* (1821), which produced Byron's famous rejoinder. Appointed poet laureate (1813), he wrote lives of *Nelson* (1813) and *Wesley* (1820) and several histories.

Edmund Spenser (1552–1599)
Born in London, Spenser graduated from Cambridge (M.A., 1576). Secretary to the bishop of Rochester (1578), he entered Leicester's service (1579), where

he met Sidney, to whom he dedicated his *Shepheardes Calender* (1579). He married Maccabeus Chylde (1579), had two children, and became secretary to Lord Grey de Wilton, Lord Deputy of Ireland. In Ireland from 1580 until his return to London (1598), he served as an "undertaker" for the settlement of Munster (1588), acquired Kilcolman Castle in Cork, and wrote "Astrophel" on Sidney, and *The Faerie Queene* (I–III, 1590; IV–VI, 1596). In 1594 Spenser had a son by Elizabeth Boyle and may have celebrated their marriage in *Amoretti* and *Epithalamion* (1595). In 1598 his castle at Kilcolman was burned and he fled to Cork with his wife and children; he died in London.

Sir John Suckling (1609–1642)

Suckling was educated at Cambridge, entered Gray's Inn (1627), and was knighted (1630). A member of Sir Henry Vane's embassy to Gustavus Adolphus (1631), he returned to London (1632) and became gentleman of the privy chamber to Charles I. A leader of the royalist party, Suckling fled to France after unsuccessfully rescuing the earl of Strafford from the Tower (1641). An alleged suicide, Suckling wrote four plays, including a tragedy, *Aglaura* (1637), and a romantic comedy, *The Goblins* (1638); his poems are collected in *Fragmenta Aurea* (1646).

Henry Howard, Earl of Surrey (1517?–1547)

Surrey married the earl of Oxford's daughter, Frances Vere (1532), at Anne Boleyn's suggestion. When Jane Seymour accused Surrey of favoring the Catholics in the rebellion of 1530, he was imprisoned at Windsor (1537–1539). Surrey served in the campaign of Scotland (1542), joined the army in France and Flanders (1543–1546), and was wounded, imprisoned, and executed on frivolous charges. He translated *The Aeneid* (II, IV), introduced blank verse into English poetry, and adapted the Italian sonnet to English.

Jonathan Swift (1667–1745)

Born in Dublin, Swift attended Trinity College, Dublin (1682), and was secretary to Sir William Temple at Moor Park (1684–1694; 1696–1699). He composed Pindaric odes and acted as tutor to Esther Johnson (the future Stella), whom he may have secretly married (1716). Ordained the year he returned to Ireland (1695), he wrote *The Battle of the Books*, which was published with *A Tale of a Tub* (1704), and began his career as a satirist (*Gulliver's Travels*, 1726), political journalist, and churchman. His verse includes "A Description of the Morning" (1709), "Cadenus and Vanessa" (1726), and "Verses on the Death of Dr. Swift" (1739).

Algernon Charles Swinburne (1837–1909)

Born in London and educated at Eton and Oxford, Swinburne wrote *Atalanta in Calydon* (1865), a drama in the Greek form, that made him famous.

Swinburne's morality was questioned with the publication of *Poems and Ballads* (1866). *A Song of Italy* (1867) and *Songs Before Sunrise* (1871), demonstrating his support for Mazzini and Italian independence, were followed by the more temperate *Poems and Ballads: Second Series* (1878). In 1879, he moved to Putney, where Theodore Watts-Dunton helped Swinburne curtail his heavy drinking. He subsequently published three volumes of poems, dramas, and influential works of literary criticism.

Arthur Symons (1865–1945)
Born in Pembrokeshire, Symons contributed to *The Yellow Book* and edited *The Savoy* (1896), where he published Beardsley, Conrad, Dowson, and others. A leading member of the Decadent movement (1890s), he introduced French Symbolism to England with *The Symbolist Movement in Literature* (1899); wrote studies of Blake, Baudelaire, Pater, and Wilde; and published his own poetry, including *Days and Nights* (1889) and *Images of Good and Evil* (1899). In 1908–1909 he suffered a nervous collapse, recorded, with his recovery, in *Confessions* (1930).

Jane Taylor (1783–1824)
Born in London, the daughter of a dissenting minister, Taylor lived in Suffolk (1786–1795), Colchester (1796–1810), and Ongar (1811), writing stories, plays, and verse from an early age. She worked as an engraver and, with her sister Ann, wrote *Original Poems for Infant Minds* (1804) and *Rhymes for the Nursery* (1806). Her novel, *Display* (1815), was followed by essays for *Youth's Magazine* (1816–1822); *Essays in Rhyme* (1816), and collections of poems and fiction.

Alfred Tennyson, First Baron (1809–1892)
Born in Lincolnshire to a psychically unstable family, Tennyson was educated at Cambridge. He joined the Apostles, befriended Arthur Hallam, and traveled with him to the Continent. *Poems, Chiefly Lyrical* (1830) was followed by *Poems* (1833), which was reviewed harshly. A ten years' silence followed, during which Tennyson wrote brief elegies on Hallam, who had died abroad (1833). He published *Poems* (1842), followed by *In Memoriam* (1850), and *Maud* (1855). Appointed poet laureate (1850), Tennyson married Emily Sellwood that same year, establishing his fame with "The Charge of the Light Brigade" (1854) and several volumes, including *Idylls of the King* (1859).

Dylan Thomas (1914–1953)
Born in Swansea, Thomas worked as a journalist before moving to London (1934) and marrying Caitlin Macnamara (1937). He worked as a script writer and broadcaster for the BBC during World War II. *18 Poems* (1934) and *Twenty-Five Poems* (1936) attracted the attention of Edith Sitwell, while *New Poems*

(1943) established his reputation. Thomas undertook three reading tours of the United States for financial reasons, and died of alcoholic poisoning on the fourth. His *Adventures in the Skin Trade* (1955) is one of several collections of stories, and *Under Milk Wood*, a "play for voices," is his most famous work.

Francis Thompson (1859–1907)
Born in Lancashire, Thompson attended Ushaw College and studied medicine at Owens College. Rescued by Alice Meynell and her husband from a life of poverty in London, Thomson is best known for "The Hound of Heaven," which describes the pursuit of the human soul by God. He also wrote *Poems* (1893), *Sister Songs* (1895), and *New Poems* (1897). Intermittent opium addiction, combined with tuberculosis, contributed to his early death.

James Thomson (1700–1748)
Born at Ednam and educated at Edinburgh University (1715), Thomson arrived in London (1725) and wrote *The Seasons* (1726–1730), which contributed to the vogue for the picturesque. The first of his several patrons introduced him to Arbuthnot, Pope, and Gay. He wrote tragedies, including *Sophonisba* (1730), a masque; *Alfred* (1740), containing "Rule, Britannia"; and *The Castle of Indolence* (1748).

Charles Tomlinson (1927–)
Born in Stoke-on-Trent and educated at Cambridge and London University, Alfred Charles Tomlinson has taught at the University of Bristol (1968–1982), the University of New Mexico (1962–1963), and Colgate University (1967). His verse includes *Relations and Contraries* (1951), *Seeing is Believing* (1958), and *American Scenes* (1966). He collaborated with Octavio Paz on a sonnet sequence, *Air Born/Hijos del Aire* (1979), and translated Paz and Antonio Machado in *Translations* (1983). *In Black and White* (1975) is a collection of his graphic work.

Thomas Traherne (1637–1674)
Traherne was born in Hereford and attended Oxford (M.A., 1661; B.D., 1669). Appointed rector of Credenhill (1657) and ordained (1660), he became chaplain to Sir Orlando Bridgeman, the Lord Keeper of the Great Seal (1667). He published *Roman Forgeries* (1673) and *Christian Ethics* (1675); his poems and autobiography, published as *Centuries of Meditations* (1908), were discovered after 1900.

Henry Vaughan (1621–1695)
Born in Wales, Vaughan attended Oxford but did not finish his degree. He studied law in London (1640), probably fought on the royalist side during the

civil war, and returned to London to work as a physician. His twin brother, Thomas, was a disciple of Cornelius Agrippa and published treaties on alchemy and magic; Henry's own verse exhibits his fascination with hermeticism and mysticism. *Poems, with the Tenth Satire of Juvenal Englished* (1646) was followed by *Olor Iscanus* (1647), *Silex Scintillans* (1650), and *Thalia Rediviva* (1678). His prose works include *The Mount of Olives* (1652).

Oscar [Fingal O'Flahertie Wills] Wilde (1854–1900)

Born in Dublin and educated at Trinity College there and at Oxford, Wilde won the Newdigate prize for "Ravenna" (1878) and published *Poems* (1881). He lectured in the United States (1882–1883), married (1884), and wrote children's stories (*The Happy Prince*, 1888), a novel (*The Picture of Dorian Gray*, 1890), and several plays (*The Importance of Being Earnest*, 1895). *The Soul of Man Under Socialism* (1891), a response to G. B. Shaw, argues for individual freedom. In 1895 Wilde was imprisoned for homosexual offenses, declared bankrupt, and wrote *De Profundis*. *The Ballad of Reading Gaol* (1898), written in France, was inspired by his prison experience.

William Wordsworth (1770–1850)

Born in Cockermouth, Wordsworth graduated from Cambridge. In 1791–1792 he visited France, had a daughter by Annette Vallon, and was encouraged in his early enthusiasm for the French Revolution by Michel Beaupuy. In England again, Wordsworth received a legacy from Raisley Calvert (1795) and a sinecure as Distributor of Stamps (1813). He collaborated with Coleridge on *Lyrical Ballads* (1798, 1800), visited Goslar, Germany (1798), and wrote sections of *The Prelude* (1850). Wordsworth began "The Recluse" in 1799, and married Mary Hutchinson (1802). He succeeded Robert Southey as poet laureate (1843). His published verse includes *Poems in Two Volumes* (1807), *The Excursion* (1814), *The White Doe of Rylstone* (1815), two volumes of *Miscellaneous Poems* (1815), and *Peter Bell* (1819).

Lady Mary Sidney Wroth (1587?–1651?)

Born into a literary family, Mary Sidney married Sir Robert Wroth (1604), whose death (1613) left her in considerable debt after the birth of their only child. Protected from creditors (1623), she had two illegitimate children by her cousin, William Herbert, third earl of Pembroke. A patroness of contemporary literature, Wroth acted in Ben Jonson's "Masque of Blackness," and received dedications from Jonson, Chapman, and others. *The Countess of Montgomerie's Urania* (1621), a close imitation of her uncle Sidney's *Arcadia*, is her only published work and satirizes James I's courtiers; it was withdrawn six months after printing because of objections. She also wrote *Loves Victorie* (1853), a pastoral verse play.

Sir Thomas Wyatt (1503–1542)
Educated at Cambridge, Wyatt married Elizabeth Brooke (1520–1526). He served Henry VIII on missions to the Papal court (1527), as High Marshal of Calais (1528–1532), and as ambassador to Charles V (1537–1539). Wyatt was imprisoned in the Tower on suspicions of adultery with Anne Boleyn (1536), but pardoned and knighted (1537). After embassies in France and Holland, he was charged with treason, but acquitted (1541). His poetry introduced into English the Italian sonnet, terza rima form, and the rondeau, and includes *Certayne Psalmes* (1549), three satires, and *Songes and Sonettes* (1557).

William Butler Yeats (1865–1939)
Born in Dublin, Yeats studied at the School of Art in Dublin (1883–1886) and helped found an Irish Literary Society in London (1891) and Dublin (1892). He began his project of an Irish national theater with an 1899 performance of *The Countess Cathleen* (1892); *Cathleen Ni Houlihan* (1902) was his most successful play. Yeats wrote on Irish legends in *The Celtic Twilight* (1893). Maude Gonne (1889) inspired poems in *The Land of Heart's Desire* (1894) and other volumes. Lady Gregory's estate, Coole Park, provided the emotional landscape for *The Wild Swans at Coole* (1919). He married Georgie Hyde-Lees (1917), whose system of symbolism—described in *A Vision* (1925)—affected his subsequent work. A senator of the Irish Free State (1922–1928), Yeats received the Nobel prize in 1923.

Edward Young (1683–1765)
Born at Upham rectory, Young attended Oxford, where he became a fellow of All Souls (1708). His early dramas, such as *Busiris* (1719) and *The Revenge* (1721), were successfully produced at Drury Lane. In 1730 Young became rector at Welwyn, married Elizabeth Lee, daughter of the earl of Lichfield (1731), and published a patriotic ode, *The Foreign Address* (1735). The deaths of his stepdaughter (1736) and his wife (1740) provided the impetus for *Night-Thoughts* (1742–1746), which placed Young in the company of 'graveyard' poets.

Jonathan Gross

Editions

Arnold, Matthew. *Poems*. 2d ed., edited by Kenneth and Mariam Allott. London and New York: Longman, 1979.

Audelay, John. *Poems*. Edited by E. K. Whiting. Oxford: Oxford University Press, 1931; reprinted 1971. Early English Text Society 184.

Auden, W. H. *Collected Poetry*. New York: Random House, 1945.

Auden, W. H. *Collected Shorter Poems, 1930–1944*. London: Faber, 1950.

Auden, W. H. *Collected Shorter Poems, 1927–1957*. New York: Random House, 1967.

Auden, W. H. *Complete Works*. Princeton: Princeton University Press, 1988–.

Barbauld, Anna Letitia. *Works*. 2 vols. London: Longmans, 1825.

Barbour, John. *Early Scottish Poetry: Thomas the Rhymer, John Barbour, Andrew of Wyntoun, Henry the Minstrel*. Westport, Conn.: Greenwood, 1971.

Beddoes, Thomas Lovell. *Works*. Edited by H. W. Bonner. London: Oxford University Press, 1935; reprinted 1978.

Betjeman, John. *Collected Poems*. 4th ed., edited by the Earl of Birkenhead. London: Murray, 1979.

Binyon, Laurence. *Collected Poems*. 2 vols. London: Macmillan, 1931.

Blake, William. *Complete Poetry and Prose*. Edited by David V. Erdman. Rev. ed. New York: Doubleday, 1988.

Brontë, Emily Jane. *Complete Poems*. Edited by C. W. Hatfield. New York: Columbia University Press, 1941.

Browning, Elizabeth Barrett. *Complete Works*. Edited by Charlotte Porter and Helen A. Clarke. 6 vols. New York: Crowell, 1900.

Browning, Robert. *The Poems*. Edited by John Pettigrew and Thomas J. Collins. 2 vols. New Haven: Yale University Press, 1981.

Browning, Robert. *The Ring and the Book*. Edited by Richard D. Altick. New Haven: Yale University Press, 1971.

Burns, Robert. *Poems and Songs*. Edited by James Kinsley. 3 vols. Oxford: Clarendon, 1968.

Byron, George Gordon, Lord. *Complete Poetical Works.* Edited by Jerome J. McGann. 7 vols. Oxford: Clarendon, 1980–1992.

Campbell, Thomas. *Complete Poetical Works.* Edited by J. Logie Robertson. Oxford: Oxford University Press, 1907.

Carew, Thomas. *Poems, with . . . Coelum Britannicum.* Edited by Rhodes Dunlap. Oxford: Clarendon, 1949.

Carroll, Lewis. *Complete Illustrated Works.* Edited by Edward Guiliano. New York: Avenel, 1982.

Carter, Elizabeth. *Memoirs of Mrs. Elizabeth Carter, with a New Edition of Her Poems.* Edited by Montagu Pennington. London: Rivington, 1808.

Chapman, George. *Poems and Translations.* In *Works*, 3 vols. London: Chatto & Windus, 1874–1875.

Chatterton, Thomas. *Complete Works.* Edited by Donald S. Taylor and B. B. Hoover. 2 vols. Oxford: Clarendon, 1971.

Chaucer, Geoffrey. *The Riverside Chaucer.* Edited by Larry D. Benson. 3d ed. Boston: Houghton Mifflin, 1987.

Chaucer, Geoffrey. *A Variorum Edition of the Works of Geoffrey Chaucer.* Edited by Paul G. Ruggiers and Daniel J. Ranson. Norman: University of Oklahoma Press, 1979–. In progress.

Clough, Arthur Hugh. *The Poems.* Edited by F. L. Mulhauser. Oxford: Clarendon, 1974.

Coleridge, Samuel Taylor. *Complete Poetical Works.* Edited by E. H. Coleridge. 2 vols. London: Oxford University Press, 1912.

Coleridge, Samuel Taylor. Editions in progress by Fran Carlock Stephens for Oxford University Press and by J. C. C. Mays for the *Collected Coleridge.*

Collins, William. *Works.* Edited by Richard Wendorf and Charles Ryskamp. New York: Oxford University Press, 1979.

The Court of Sapience. Edited by E. Ruth Harvey. Toronto: Toronto University Press, 1984.

Cowley, Abraham. *Complete Works in Verse and Prose.* Edited by Alexander B. Grosart. 2 vols. Edinburgh: Constable, 1881; New York: AMS, 1967.

Cowley, Hannah. *Works.* 3 vols. London: Wilkie & Robinson, 1813.

Cowper, William. *Poems.* Edited by John D. Baird and Charles Ryskamp. New York: Oxford University Press, 1980– .

Crabbe, George. *New Poems.* Edited by Arthur Pollard. Liverpool: Liverpool University Press, 1960.

Crabbe, George. *Poetical Works.* Edited by A. J. and R. M. Carlyle. Oxford: Oxford University Press, 1914.

Crashaw, Richard. *Complete Poetry.* Edited by George Walton Williams. Garden City, N.Y.: Anchor, 1970.

Daniel, Samuel. *Poems and a Defence of Ryme.* Edited by Arthur Colby Sprague. Cambridge: Harvard University Press, 1930; Chicago: University of Chicago Press, 1965.

Davie, Donald. *Collected Poems, 1950–1970.* New York: Oxford University Press, 1972.

Davie, Donald. *Collected Poems, 1971–1983.* Manchester: Carcanet, 1984.

Davies, Sir John. *Poems*. Edited by Robert Krueger. Oxford: Clarendon, 1975.

Death and Liffe. Edited by Joseph M. P. Donatelli. Cambridge, Mass.: Medieval Academy of America, 1989. Speculum Anniversary Monographs 15.

Donne, John. *The Elegies and Songs and Sonnets*. Edited by Helen Gardner. Oxford: Clarendon, 1965.

Donne, John. *Poetry and Prose*. Edited by H. W. Garrod. Oxford: Clarendon, 1946; New York: AMS Press, 1976.

Douglas, Gavin. *Poetical Works*. Edited by John Small. Edinburgh: Patterson, 1874.

Dowson, Ernest. *Poetry*. Edited by Desmond Flower. Rutherford: Fairleigh Dickinson University Press, 1970.

Drayton, Michael. *Works*. Edited by William Hebel, Kathleen Tillotson and Bernard Newdigate. 5 vols. Oxford: Clarendon, 1931–1941.

Dryden, John. *Poems*. Edited by James Kinsley. 4 vols. Oxford: Clarendon, 1958. Oxford English Texts.

Dryden, John. *Poems and Fables*. Edited by James Kinsley. London: Oxford University Press, 1962.

Dryden, John. *Works*. Edited by Edward Niles Hooker, H. T. Swedenborg, et al. Berkeley: University of California Press, 1955–.

Dunbar, William. *Poems*. Edited by James Kinsley. Oxford: Clarendon, 1979.

Eliot, T. S. *Complete Poems and Plays*. London: Faber, 1969, 1973.

Eliot, T. S. *Collected Poems, 1909–1962*. London: Faber; New York: Harcourt Brace, 1963.

Fenton, James. *Children in Exile: Poems, 1968–1984*. New York: Vintage, 1984.

Fergusson, Robert. *Poems by Allan Ramsay and Robert Fergusson*. Edited A. M. Kinghorn and Alexander Law. Edinburgh: Scottish Academic Press, 1974.

Fisher, Roy. *Collected Poems, 1955–1980*. Oxford: Oxford University Press, 1980.

Gascoigne, George. *Complete Works*. Edited by J. W. Cunliffe. 2 vols. Cambridge: Cambridge University Press, 1907–1910.

Gay, John. *Poetry and Prose*. Edited by Vinton A. Dearing with Charles E. Beckwith. 2 vols. Oxford: Clarendon, 1974.

Goldsmith, Oliver. *Works*. Edited by J. W. M. Gibbs. 4 vols. London: Bell, 1901–1908.

Gower, John. *Complete Works*. Edited by G. C. Macaulay. 4 vols. Oxford: Clarendon, 1899–1902; reprinted 1957. Early English Text Society, Extra Series 81, 82.

Gray, John. *Poems*. Edited by Ian Fletcher. Greensboro, N.C.: ELT Press, 1988.

Gray, Thomas. *Complete Poems, English, Latin, and Greek*. Edited by H. W. Starr and J. R. Hendrickson. Oxford: Clarendon, 1966. Oxford English Texts.

Gunn, Thom. *Selected Poems, 1950–1975*. London: Faber, 1979.

Hardy, Thomas. *Complete Poems*. Edited by James Gibson. London: Macmillan, 1976.

Hardy, Thomas. *Complete Poetical Works*. Edited by Samuel Hynes. Oxford: Clarendon, 1982–.

Hawes, Stephen. *The Minor Poems*. Edited by F. Gluck and A. Morgan. Oxford: Oxford University Press, 1974. Early English Text Society 271.

Hawes, Stephen. *The Pastime of Pleasure*. Edited by W. Mead. Oxford: Oxford University Press, 1928; reprinted 1971. Early English Text Society 173.

Heaney, Seamus. *Poems, 1965–1975*. New York: Farrar Strauss, Giroux, 1980.

Hemans, Felicia. *Poetical Works*. Edited by W. M. Rossetti. London: Collins, 1879.

Henryson, Robert. *Poems*. Edited by Denton Fox. Oxford: Clarendon, 1981.

Herbert, George. *Works*. Edited by F. E. Hutchinson. Oxford: Clarendon, 1941.

Herrick, Robert. *Complete Poetry*. Edited by J. Max Patrick. Garden City, N.Y.: Anchor, 1963.

Herrick, Robert. *Poems*. Edited by L. C. Martin. London: Oxford University Press, 1965.

Hill, Geoffrey. *Collected Poems*. London: Andre Deutsch, 1986; New York: Oxford University Press, 1986.

Hoccleve, Thomas. *Regiment of Princes*. Edited by F. J. Furnivall. Oxford: Early English Text Society, 1897; reprinted 1988. Extra Series 72.

Hoccleve, Thomas. *Hoccleve's Works: The Minor Poemsa*. Edited by F. J. Furnivall and I. Gollancz. Oxford: Early English Text Society, 1892, 1897; reprinted (as one volume) 1970. Extra Series 61, 73.

Hoccleve, Thomas. *Selections from Hoccleve*. Edited by M. C. Seymour. Oxford: Clarendon, 1981.

Hopkins, Gerard Manley. *Poetical Works*. Edited by Norman H. MacKenzie. Oxford: Clarendon Press, 1990.

Housman, A. E. *Collected Poems*. Edited by John Carter. Cambridge: Cambridge University Press, 1939; New York: Holt, 1965.

Hughes, Ted. *Selected Poems, 1957–1981*. London: Faber, 1982. Republished as *New Selected Poems*. New York: Harper, 1983.

Hunt, James Henry Leigh. *Poetical Works of Leigh Hunt*. Edited by H. S. Milford. London: Oxford, 1923.

Jenkins, Elizabeth. *Collected Poems, 1953–1985*. Manchester: Carcanet, 1986.

Johnson, Lionel. *Complete Poems*. Edited by Ian Fletcher. London: Unicorn, 1953.

Johnson, Samuel. *Poems*. Edited by David Nichol Smith and E. L. McAdam. Revised by J. D. Fleeman. Oxford: Clarendon, 1974.

Jones, David Michael. *The Anathemata*. New York: Chilmark, 1963.

Jones, David Michael. *In Parenthesis*. New York: Chilmark, 1961.

Jonson, Benjamin. *Ben Jonson*. Edited by Ian Donaldson. Oxford: Oxford University Press, 1985.

Jonson, Benjamin. *The Yale Ben Jonson*, various hands. New Haven:Yale University Press, 1974–.

Keats, John. *Poems*. Edited by Jack Stillinger. Cambridge: Harvard University Press, 1978.

Kipling, Rudyard. *Rudyard Kipling's Verse: Inclusive Edition, 1885–1926*. London: Hodder & Stoughton, 1931.

Landon, Letitia Elizabeth. *Poetical Works of Mary Howitt, Eliza Cook, and L. E. L.* Boston: Phillips, 1856.

Landor, Walter Savage. *Poetical Works*. Edited by Stephen Wheeler. 3 vols. Oxford: Clarendon, 1937.

Langland, William. *Piers Plowman, C-text*. Edited by Derek Pearsall. Berkeley: University of California Press, 1979.

Langland, William. *The Vision of Piers Plowman, B-text*. Edited by A. V. C. Schmidt. Everyman's University Library. London: Dent, 1978.

Larkin, Philip. *Collected Poems*. Edited by Anthony Thwaite. London: Marvell Press and Faber, 1988; New York: Farrar Strauss Giroux, 1989.

Lawrence, D. H. *The Complete Poems of D. H. Lawrence*. Edited by Vivian de Sola Pinto and F. Warren Roberts. New York: Viking, 1964.

Leapor, Mary. *Poems upon Several Occasions*. London: Roberts, 1748.

Lindsay, Sir David. *Ane Satyre of the Thrie Estaitis*. Edited by Roderick Lyall. Edinburgh: Canongate Press, 1989.

Longley, Michael. *The Echo Gate: Poems, 1975–1979*. London: Secker & Warburg, 1979.

Longley, Michael. *An Exploded View: Poems, 1968–1972*. London: Gollancz, 1973.

Lord, George deF., et al., eds. *Poems on Affairs of State, 1660–1714*. 7 vols. New Haven: Yale University Press, 1963–1970.

Lovelace, Richard. *Poems*. Edited by C. H. Wilkinson. Oxford: Clarendon, 1963.

Lydgate, John. *The Fall of Princes*. Edited by Henry Bergen. Oxford: Oxford University Press, 1924–1927; reprinted 1967. Early English Text Society, Extra Series 121–124.

Lydgate, John. *The Troy Book*. Edited by Henry Bergen. Oxford: Early English Text Society, 1906–1935; reprinted 1973. Extra Series, 103, 106, 126.

MacDiarmid, Hugh. *Complete Poems 1920-1976*. Edited by Michael Grieve and W. R. Aitken. 2 vols. London: Brian and O'Keefe, 1978.

MacNeice, Louis. *Collected Poems*. Edited by E. R. Dodds. New York: Oxford University Press, 1967.

Marlowe, Christopher. *Complete Works*. 2d ed., edited by Fredson Bowers. 2 vols. Cambridge: Cambridge University Press, 1981.

Marvell, Andrew. *The Poems and Letters*. 2d ed., edited by H. M. Margoliouth. 2 vols. Oxford: Clarendon, 1952.

Masefield, John. *Poems*. London and New York: Macmillan, 1930.

Masefield, John. *Poems*. Selected by Henry Seidel Canby et al. New York: Macmillan, 1945.

Meredith, George. *Poems.*. Edited by Phyllis B. Bartlett. 2 vols. New Haven: Yale University Press, 1978.

Milton, John. *Complete Poems and Major Prose*. Edited by Merritt Y. Hughes. New York: Odyssey, 1957.

Milton, John. *John Milton*. The Oxford Authors. Edited by Stephen Orgel and Jonathan Goldberg. New York: Oxford University Press, 1991.

Montgomerie, Alexander. *Alexander Montgomerie*. Edited by R. D. S. Jack. Edinburgh: Scottish Academic Press, 1974.

Moore, Thomas. *Poetical Works*. Edited by A. D. Godley. London: Oxford, 1910.

Moore, Thomas Sturge. *Poems*. 4 vols. London: Macmillan, 1931–1933.

Morris, William. *Collected Works*. Edited by May Morris. 24 vols. London: Longmans, 1910–1915. Reprinted, New York: Russell & Russell, 1966.

Muir, Edwin. *Collected Poems*. 2d ed. New York: Oxford University Press, 1965.

Owen, Wilfred. *Collected Poems*. Edited by C. Day Lewis. London: 1963, 1971.

Owen, Wilfred. *Poems*. Edited by Jon Stallworthy. New York: Norton, 1986.

The Parlement of the Thre Ages. Edited by M. Y. Offord. Oxford: Oxford University Press, 1959; reprinted 1967. Early English Text Society 246.

Philips, Katherine Fowler. *Poems*. London: Tonson, 1710.

The Poems of the Pearl Manuscript. Edited by Malcolm Andrew and Ronald Waldron. Berkeley: University of California Press, 1982.

Pope, Alexander. *The Twickenham Edition of the Poems of Alexander Pope*. Edited by John Butt et al. 11 vols. London: Methuen; New Haven: Yale University Press, 1967–1970.

Pope, Alexander. *Poetry and Prose*. Edited by Aubrey Williams. Boston: Houghton Mifflin, 1969. Riverside Editions.

Raine, Kathleen. *Collected Poems, 1931–1980*. London, 1981.

Ralegh, Sir Walter. *Poems*. Edited by Agnes M. C. Latham. London: Athlone, 1965.

Ramsay, Allan. *Poems by Allan Ramsay and Robert Fergusson*. Edited by A. M. Kinghorn and Alexander Law. Edinburgh: Scottish Academic Press, 1974.

Reading, Peter. *Diplopic*. London: Secker & Warburg, 1983.

Rossetti, Christina. *The Complete Poems of Christina Rossetti: A Variorum Edition*. Edited by R. W. Crump. 3 vols. Baton Rouge: Louisiana State University Press, 1979–1990.

Rossetti, Dante Gabriel. *The Works of Dante Gabriel Rossetti*. Edited by William M. Rossetti. Rev. ed. London: Ellis, 1911.

Scott, Alexander. *Poems*. Edinburgh: Oliver and Boyd, 1952.

Scott, Sir Walter. *Complete Poetical Works*. Edited by Andrew Lang. 6 vols. Boston: Estes, 1902.

Shakespeare, William. *Poems*. Edited by John Roe. Cambridge: Cambridge University Press, 1992.

Shakespeare, William. *Shakespeare's Sonnets*. Edited by Stephen Booth. New Haven: Yale University Press, 1971.

Shakespeare, William. *The Riverside Shakespeare*. Edited by G. Blakemore Evans. Boston: Houghton Mifflin, 1974.

Shelley, Percy Bysshe. *Complete Works*. Edited by Roger Ingpen and Walter E. Peck. 10 vols. London: Benn, 1926–1930. Reprinted New York: Gordian, 1965.

Shelley, Percy Bysshe. *Shelley's Poetry and Prose: Authoritative Texts, Criticism*. Edited by Donald H. Reiman and Sharon B. Powers. New York: Norton, 1977.

Sidney, Sir Philip. *Poems*. Edited by William A. Ringler, Jr. Oxford: Clarendon, 1962.

Sir Philip Sidney. Edited by Katherine Duncan-Jones. Oxford: Oxford University Press, 1989.

Sitwell, Edith. *Collected Poems*. New York: Vanguard, 1968.

Skelton, John. *The Complete English Poems*. Edited by John Scattergood. Hammondsworth: Penguin, 1983.

Smith, Charlotte. *Elegiac Sonnets, and Other Essays*. 2d ed. London: Dodsley, 1784.

Smith, Stevie. *Collected Poems*. Edited by James MacGibbon. London: Allen Lane, 1975.

Southey, Robert. *Poetical Works*. 10 vols. London: Longmans, 1853–1854. Reprinted (as 5 vols.) New York: AMS Press, 1977.

Spenser, Edmund. *Poetical Works*. Edited by J. C. Smith and E. de Selincourt. Oxford: Oxford University Press, 1912.

Spenser, Edmund. *Works*. Edited by Edwin Greenlaw et al. 11 vols. Baltimore: Johns Hopkins Press, 1932–1957.

Spenser, Edmund. *The Yale Edition of the Shorter Poems of Edmund Spenser*. Edited by William A. Oram et al. New Haven: Yale University Press, 1989.

Surrey. *Poems of Henry Howard, Earl of Surrey*. Edited by Emrys Jones. Oxford: Clarendon, 1964.

Swift, Jonathan. *Poems*. Edited by Harold Williams. 3 vols. Oxford: Clarendon, 1958.

Swinburne, Algernon Charles. *Complete Works*. Edited by Sir Edmund Gosse and Thomas James Wise. 20 vols. London: Heinemann, 1925–1927.

Symons, Arthur. *Poems*. 2 vols. London: Heinemann, 1901; reprinted 1924.

Taylor, Jane. *Prose and Poetry*. Edited by F. V. Barry. London: Oxford University Press, 1925.

Tennyson, Alfred. *The Poems*. Edited by Christopher Ricks. 3 vols. London: Longmans, 1987.

Thomas, Dylan. *The Poems*. Edited by Daniel Jones. New York: New Directions, 1971.

Thomson, James. *Complete Poetical Works*. Edited by J. Logie Robertson. Oxford, 1908. Oxford Standard Authors.

Tomlinson, Charles. *Collected Poems*. Oxford: Oxford University Press, 1987.

Traherne, Thomas. *Centuries, Poems, and Thanksgiving*. Edited by H. M. Margoliouth. 2 vols. Oxford: Clarendon, 1958.

Vaughan, Henry. *Complete Poetry*. Edited by French Fogle. New York: New York University Press, 1965.

Henry Vaughan: The Complete Poems. Edited by Alan Rudrum. New Haven: Yale University Press, 1981.

Waller, Edmund. *Poems*. Edited by G. Thorn Drury. New York: Scribners, 1893. Reprinted New York: Greenwood, 1968.

Wilde, Oscar. *Complete Works*. Edited by Vyvyan Holland. London: Collins, 1966.

Wordsworth, William. *The Poems*. Edited by John O. Hayden. 2 vols. New Haven: Yale University Press, 1977.

Wordsworth, William. *Poetical Works*. Edited by Ernest de Selincourt and Helen Darbishire. 5 vols. 2d ed. Oxford: Clarendon, 1940–1954.

Wordsworth, William. *The Prelude, 1799, 1805, 1850*. Edited by Jonathan Wordsworth, M. H. Abrams, and Stephen Gill. New York: Norton, 1979.

Wroth, Mary. *The Poems of Lady Mary Wroth*. Edited by Josephine A. Roberts. Baton Rouge: Louisiana State University Press, 1983.

Wyatt, Sir Thomas. *Complete Works*. Edited by Ronald A. Rebholz. Harmondsworth: Penguin, 1978; New Haven: Yale University Press, 1981.

Wynnere and Wastoure. Edited by Stephanie Trigg. Oxford: Oxford University Press, 1990. Early English Text Society 297.

Yeats, William Butler. *Poems*. Edited by Richard J. Finneran. Rev. ed. New York: Macmillan, 1983.

Young, Edward. *Poetical Works*. 2 vols. London: Bell, 1896.

Notes on Contributors

Paul Alpers is Professor of English and Comparative Literature at the University of California at Berkeley. He is the author of *The Poetry of "The Faerie Queene"* (1967), *The Singer of the Eclogues: A Study of Virgilian Pastoral* (1979), and the forthcoming *What Is Pastoral?*

Karl Beckson is Professor of English at Brooklyn College, City University of New York, and the author or editor of nine books on such figures of the 1890s as Oscar Wilde, Max Beerbohm, and Arthur Symons. Among his recent publications are *Arthur Symons: A Life* (1987) and *London in the 1890s: A Cultural History* (Norton, 1993).

Calvin Bedient, Professor in the English Department, University of California, Los Angeles, is the author of several books, including *Eight Contemporary Poets* (1974), *In the Heart's Last Kingdom: Robert Penn Warren's Major Poetry* (1984), and *He Do the Police in Different Voices: The Waste Land and its Protagonist* (1986). He is completing a book on W. B. Yeats.

Jerome H. Buckley is Gurney Professor Emeritus of English Literature at Harvard University. He is author of a number of nineteenth-century studies, including *The Victorian Temper*, *Tennyson: The Growth of a Poet*, *Season of Youth: The Triumph of Time*, and *The Turning Key* (concerned with the subjective impulse since 1800 and the influence of Wordsworth).

David Daiches, C.B.E., has taught at universities on both sides of the Atlantic, including Edinburgh, Cambridge, Sussex, Chicago, and Cornell. His latest position (1980–1986) was Director of the Institute for Advanced Studies in the Humanities at Edinburgh. He holds honorary doctorates from Edinburgh, Glasgow, Stirling, Sussex, Brown, Guelph, the Sorbonne, and Bologna. Among his many books are *The Novel and the Modern World*, *A Critical History of English Literature*, *Robert Burns*, *The Paradox of Scottish Culture*, and *God and the Poets*.

Elizabeth Story Donno is Senior Research Associate in the Huntington Library. She has edited a number of Renaissance texts, both poetry and prose, including *Elizabethan Minor Epics*; *The Diary of Richard Madox, Fellow of All Souls, 1582*; *The Complete Poetry of Andrew Marvell*; and most recently, *Three Renaissance Pastorals*.

Margaret Anne Doody is Andrew W. Mellon Professor of Humanities and Professor of English, and presently Director of the Comparative Literature Program, at Vanderbilt University. Her publications include *A Natural Passion* (on the novels of Richardson); *The Daring Muse* (on Augustan poetry); *Frances Burney*; five volumes as editor or coeditor, two novels (*Aristotle Detective* and *The Alchemists*), and numerous essays in such journals as *Genre* and *London Review of Books*.

George D. Economou is the author of many articles and several books on medieval literature, including *The Goddess Natura in Medieval Literature* and *Geoffrey Chaucer: A Collection of Original Articles*. He has published eight books of poetry and translations. He is Professor of English at the University of Oklahoma.

Martin Elsky is Professor of English at Brooklyn College and the Graduate School of the City University of New York. He is the author of *Authorizing Words: Speech, Writing, and Print in the English Renaissance*, and has published numerous articles on George Herbert, John Donne, Francis Bacon, and Ben Jonson. He is currently writing a book on Jonson's country-house poems in relation to local identity and family history.

Richard Feingold is Professor of English at the University of California at Berkeley. His publications include *Nature and Society: Later Eighteenth-Century Uses of the Pastoral and Georgic* (1978) and *Moralized Song: The Character of Augustan Lyricism* (1989).

Roberta Frank, Professor in the Department of English and the Centre for Medieval Studies at the University of Toronto, is the author of *Old Norse Court Poetry* and of numerous articles on Old English and Old Norse literature. She is the General Editor of the Publications of the *Dictionary of Old English* and of the Toronto Old English Series.

George H. Gilpin, Professor of English and Provost at the University of Tulsa, is author of *The Art of Contemporary English Culture*. He is now writing a sequel to that volume. His essays on Romantic and contemporary literature include "In Wordsworth's English Gardens" in his edition of *Critical Essays on William Wordsworth*.

Jonathan Gross is Assistant Professor in the English Department of DePaul University. He recently completed a dissertation at Columbia University on Byron's politics.

E. Ruth Harvey, who completed her formal education in the Warburg Institute of the University of London, is a Professor in the English Department and the Centre of Medieval Studies at the University of Toronto. Author of *The Inward Wits: Psycholog-*

ical Theory in the Middle Ages and the Renaissance, she has edited *The Court of Sapience* in the Toronto Medieval Texts and Translations Series.

Susan M. Levin is Professor of English and Comparative Literature at the Stevens Institute of Technology, author of *Dorothy Wordsworth and Romanticism*, and performer of Songs by Women Composers, 1650–1950.

Edna Longley, a professor of English at the Queen's University of Belfast, is the author of *Poetry in the Wars*, *Louis MacNeice: A Study*, and many essays on the poetry, culture, and politics of Ireland. She has edited the poetry and prose of Edward Thomas, and the selected poems of Dorothy Hewett, Paul Durcan, and James Simmons. Her most recent book is *The Living Stream: Historical Revisionism and Irish Literature* (1993).

Richard C. McCoy, Professor of English at the Graduate Center and Queens College of the City University of New York, is author of *Sir Philip Sidney: Rebellion in Arcadia* (1979) and *The Rites of Knighthood: The Literature and Politics of Elizabethan Chivalry* (1989).

Jerome McGann is Commonwealth Professor of English at the University of Virginia. Among his works are the Oxford English Texts edition of *Lord Byron. The Complete Poetical Works* (in seven volumes) and *The New Oxford Book of Verse of the Romantic Period*. Two of his general studies of Romanticism are *The Romantic Ideology* (1983) and *The Beauty of Inflections: Literary Investigations in Historical Method and Theory* (1988).

David McKitterick is Fellow and Librarian of Trinity College, University of Cambridge. His publications include *A History of the Nonesuch Press* (written with John Dreyfus, 1981), *Cambridge University Library: A History—The Eighteenth and Nineteenth Centuries* (1986), *Andrew Perne: Quatercentenary Studies* (1991), and *Printing and the Book Trade in Cambridge, 1534–1698* (1993). His edition of Stanley Morison's *Selected Essays on the History of Letter Forms in Manuscript and Print* was published in 1981. His Engelhard lecture at the Library of Congress was printed in *The History of Books and Libraries: Two Views* (1986).

Morton D. Paley is Professor of English at the University of California at Berkeley. Among his studies of Romantic literature and art are *Energy and the Imagination*, *The Continuing City*, and *The Apocalyptic Sublime*. He edited the William Blake Trust edition of *Jerusalem* (Tate Gallery Publications, 1991); and he is coeditor of *Blake: An Illustrated Quarterly*.and (with T. J. Fulford) of a volume of new essays on Coleridge, *Coleridge's Visionary Languages* (Boydell and Brewer, 1993).

Cary H. Plotkin is Assistant Professor of English at Barnard College, Columbia University. He is the author of *The Tenth Muse: Victorian Philology and the Genesis of the Poetic Language of Gerard Manley Hopkins* and of an essay on Hopkins's theodic language in *Gerard Manley Hopkins and Critical Discourse*.

Robert Ready, Professor of English at Drew University, is the author of *Hazlitt at Table* (1981) and of various essays on English Romantic authors.

David G. Riede is Professor of English at the Ohio State University. He is the author of *Swinburne: A Study of Romantic Mythmaking* (1978), *Dante Gabriel Rossetti and the Limits of Victorian Vision* (1983), *Matthew Arnold and the Betrayal of Language* (1988), *Oracle and Hierophants: Constructions of Romantic Authority* (1991), and numerous articles on Romantic and Victorian literature.

James Shapiro is Associate Professor of English and Comparative Literature at Columbia University. He is the author of *Rival Playwrights: Marlowe, Jonson, Shakespeare* (1991), and is currently completing a book entitled *Shakespeare and the Jews.*

Vincent Sherry teaches at Villanova University. *His James Joyce: Ulysses* will be published in 1994 by the Cambridge University Press. His studies of modern and contemporary poetry include E*zra Pound, Wyndham Lewis, and Radical Modernism* (1992), *The Uncommon Tongue: The Poetry and Criticism of Geoffrey Hill* (1987), essays and reviews in major quarterlies and such periodicals as the *Times Literary Supplement*. He has edited the *Dictionary of Literary Biography* volumes on *Poets of Great Britain and Ireland, 1945–1960* (1984) and *Poets of Great Britain and Ireland since 1960* (1985).

Carole Silver, Professor of English at Stern College, Yeshiva University, and Chairperson of the university's Division of Humanities, has written widely on the Pre-Raphaelites. Author of *The Romance of William Morris*, editor of several volumes on Morris's work, most recently S*ocialism and the Literary Artistry of William Morris* (with Florence Boos), she is also coauthor of *Kind Words: A Thesaurus of Euphemisms* (revised, 1990). With a book in progress on the Victorian fascination with the fairies, she has prepared an exhibition and catalogue on the Morris Circle in Canada.

Richard Strier is Professor of English and the Humanities at the University of Chicago. His publications include *Love Known: Theology and Experience in George Herbert's Poetry*, essays and reviews on Renaissance poetry and on critical theory, and, edited with Heather Dubrow, *The Historical Renaissance: New Essays on Tudor and Stuart Literature and Culture.*

Carl Woodring is George Edward Woodberry Professor of Literature, Emeritus, of Columbia University. His several books include *Nature into Art, Politics in English Romantic Poetry, Wordsworth, Virginia Woolf,* and two volumes of *Table Talk* in *The Collected Works of Samuel Taylor Coleridge.*

Index

138, 414–416, 421–422; "Lady of Shalott, The," 429; "Locksley Hall," 420; "Locksley Hall Sixty Years After," 420; "Lotos-Eaters, The," 416; "Mariana," 429; *Maud*, 152, 419–420, 429; *In Memoriam A. H. H.*, 138, 378, 405–406, 415–417, 419–422, 424, 429, 454; "Palace of Art, The" 377, 419, 422, 429; "Parnassus," 417; *Poems by Two Brothers*, 457; "Poet, The," 417; *Princess, The*, 418–419; "St. Simon Stylites," 422; "Supposed Confession of a Second-rate Sensitive Mind not in Unity with Itself," 429; "Tears, Idle Tears," 415, 418, 420; "Timbuctoo," 414, 416; "Tiresias," 422; "Tithonus," 415, 422–423; "Two Voices," 414–415, 420; "Ulysses," 378, 423; "Vision of Sin, The," 418

Tennyson-Turner, Charles (1808–1879), 457

Work: *Poems by Two Brothers*, 457

Tenth Muse, The, 250

Terza rima; in "Ode to the West Wind," 393; in *Tottel's Miscellany*, 184

Teseida, 64

Testament and Complaynt of Our Soverane Lordis Papyngo, The, 92

Testament of Cresseid, The, 86–87, 654

"That Nature Is a Heraclitean Fire and of the comfort of the Resurrection," 475

"They," 537

"They Are All Gone into the World of Light," 248

"They Say the Butterfly is the Hardest Stroke," 623

"Things Present," 584–585

"This Lime-Tree Bower My Prison," 347

Thomas Aquinas, Saint, 28–29

Thomas, Dylan Marlais (1914–1953), 578, 606–607, 618–619, 623–624, 627, 633, 667–668

Works: "Crucifixion, The," 618; "Fern Hill," 619; "Poem in October," 619

Thomas, (Philip) Edward (1878–1917), 537, 609, 626, 633, 637

Works: "Cherry Tree, The," 537; "Digging," 537

Thomas, Ronald Stuart (1913–), 609–611, 616–618, 620, 623–624

Works: *Not That He Brought Flowers*, 609; "Pisces," 623; "Resevoirs," 609–610; *Selected Prose*, 609–611; "Some Contemporary Scottish Writing," 616; "Words and the Poet," 624

Thompson, Francis (1859–1907), 515–516, 668

Work: "Hound of Heaven, The," 515–516

Thomson, James (1700–1748), 303–305, 310, 312–313, 668

Works: "Spring," 304; "Summer," 303

Thomson, James (B. V.) (1834–1882), 127

Work: "City of Dreadful Night, The," 127

"Thorn, The," 408

Thoughts in Past Years, 460

"Thread of Life, The," 467, 493

Three Sunsets, 123

"Three Years She Grew," 412

Thrissil and the Rose, The, 88

Through the Looking Glass, 122

Timber, 207

"Timbuctoo," 414, 416

"Tintern Abbey." *See* "Lines Composed a Few Miles above Tintern Abbey"

"Tiresias," 422

"Tithonus," 415, 422–423

"To a Child of Quality," 114–115

"To a Friend," 445

"To a Friend for Her Naked Breasts," 250

"To a Mouse," 85, 105

"To an Athlete Dying Young," 519

"To a Sky-Lark," 383

"To a Squirrel at Kyle-na-no," 569

"To Autumn," 381, 400

"To a Young Lady with a Poem on the French Revolution," 342

"To Bix Beiderbecke," 635

"To His Coy Mistress," 252

"To Jane," 383

"To Lucy, Countess of Bedford, with Mr. Donne's Satires," 225

Abbey," 363–364, 398–399, 409, 415; "London 1802," 506; "Lucy Gray," 355; *Lyrical Ballads*, 110, 113, 141, 343, 346–347, 357, 368, 408, 416, 533–534, 542–543; "Michael," 358; 409, 416; "Nuns Fret Not at Their Convent's Narrow Room, 412–413; Ode to Duty," 412; "Ode: Intimations of Immortality," 347–348, 411, 520, 543, 546; "*Pre-lude, The*, 348, 353, 359, 366, 371, 377, 405–408, 410–412, 423; "Reso-lution and Independence," 359, 411–412, 415; "She Dwelt among the Untrodden Ways," 412; "Simon Lee," 408; "Slumber Did My Spirit Seal, A," 412; "Solitary Reaper, The," 358, 378, 412; "Tables Turned, The," 408; "Thorn, The," 408; "Three Years She Grew," 412; "We Are Seven," 408; *White Doe of Rylstone, The*, 412; "William," 408; "World Is Too Much with Us," 413
"Wordsworth's Grave," 506
Works of Benjamin Jonson, The, 144, 224, 237
"Work without Hope," 350
"World, The," 248
"World as Ballet, The," 523
"World Is Too Much with Us," 413
"Wounds," 637
"Wreaths, 637
Wreck of the Deutschland, The, 468–474
"Written on the Day That Mr. Leigh Hunt Left Prison," 386
Wroth, Lady Mary Sidney (1587?–1651?), 200–201, 249–250, 669
  Work: *Pamphilia to Amphilanthus*, 200–201, 250
Wulf and Eadwacer, 19
Wyatt, Sir Thomas (1503–1542), 179, 181–185, 191, 193, 670
  Works: "Blame Not My Lute," 179; epigram 70, 182; "In Mourning Wise," 182; Psalms (translation), 184; "Spending Hand, A," 184; "If Waker Care," 182; "What word is that changeth not," 182; "Who list

his wealth and ease retain," 182; "Whoso list to hunt," 182
Wyntoun, Andrew (1350?–1424?), 83
  Work: *Orygynale Cronykil of Scotland*, 83

"Yarn of the Nancy Bell, The," 126
Yeats, William Butler (1865–1939), 527–531, 554–562, 670; aristocractic views of, 557–559; assessment of, 562; and William Blake, 151, 529; and book design, 141–142; concerns of, 527–531, 554–562, 569; early work of, 527–528; imagery of, 524; influence of, 580, 628–629, 633; influences on, 504, 530, 605; and Irish literature, 607–610, 613, 626; and Irish politics, 613; and mod-ernism, 554–555; mysticism of, 527–531, 623–624; poetic forms of, 556; on poetry, 523–524, 527; rhyme and meter of, 530, 556; on Edmund Spenser, 214, 216; Symbolism of, 529–531, 557–558, 561; and the Symbolists, 530–531
  Works: "Among School Children," 524; "Cap and Bells, The," 530; "Cat and the Moon, The," 569; *Countess Cath-leen, The*, 558; "Dolls, The," 555; "Easter 1916," 556, 558–560; "Fergus and the Druid," 528; "Lake Isle of Innisfree, The," 530; "Leda and the Swan," 556–558; "Magi, The," 555–556; "Man and the Echo, The," 558; "Man Who Dreamed of Fairy-land, A," 530; "News for the Delphic Oracle," 560–562; *Poems*, 141–142; *Responsibilities*, 555; "Rose of the World, The," 529–530; "Second Coming, The," 529–530; "Song of the Happy Shepherd, The," 527–528; "Song of the Wandering Aengus," 530; "Statues, The," 560; "Stream and Sun at Glendalough," 569; "To a Squirrel at Kyle-na-no," 569; "To the Rose upon the Rood of Time," 529; "Wanderings of Oisin, The," 529; *Wind among the Reeds, The*, 530; "Wisdom and Dreams," 528